Your Classroom Learning experience is just one part of the **New Horizons** learning solution; an enriching, dynamic and valuable experience that includes Web-based resources during and after class.

The **New Horizons** learning solution includes online resources such as assessments, eCourseware and self-study tutorials, making it the finest and most robust learning environment available.

A full electronic version of the user manual - eCourseware - is available for reference and use post-class. Updates to the content within the eCourseware manual are automatic, providing you with access to the latest version of the course material at all times.

To access eCourseware and other online resources for this class, visit **www.newhorizons.com** and select **Student Resources**. **New Horizons Learning Port** a hosted, Web-based platform supports the delivery and management of your post-class resources. For more information about other available learning options, contact your local **New Horizons Computer Learning Center**.

Access Key: 6920-LPCLASS-8532

(Note: Access keys are case-sensitive and must be entered exactly as displayed.)

AF700442

To access your online resources:

1. Go to the **New Horizons** homepage at **www.newhorizons.com**.
2. Click the **Student Resources** link on the lower left side of the **New Horizons** homepage.
3. Click on the **Learning Port** link to log in to the site.
4. Log in to the **Learning Port** using one of the options below:

Option 1: Returning User -- if you have an existing classroom **Learning Port** account, enter your Username and Password in the Registered Student area and click **Login**.

a) Once you are successfully logged in to **Learning Port**, the homepage will display.
b) Enter the **Access Key** box and click on **Send**.
c) Your online learning resources will be added to your **Catalog**.

-OR-

Option 2: New User -- if you are a new classroom **Learning Port** user, you will need to complete the **Personal Information** form.

a) Begin by clicking on the Enroll button. The **Access Key** box will display.
b) Enter the **Access Key** in the **Access Key** box and click on **Send**.
c) The **Personal Information** form will display. Enter your information and click on **Submit**. (Note: Remember to write down your Username and Password for future reference. This login will be used to access post class resources for current and future classes.)
d) The student login page will display. Enter the Username and Password you created in your new student profile and click **Login**.
e) Your online learning resources will be added to your **Catalog**.

Username: ______________________________

Password: ______________________________

This login provides access to class resources only. When creating your "Username" enter something unique such as adding the letters ILT (Instructor Led Training) to the end of the name. This will set it apart from logins that you may use for other types of online training.

Network+® Certification: Fourth Edition — A CompTIA Certification

Part Number: NH85821 (CWEE)
Course Edition: 2.0

ACKNOWLEDGMENTS

Project Team

Instructional Designers: Nancy Curtis, Network+ Certified Professional, and Pamela J. Taylor, i-Net+ Certified Professional • **Development Assistance:** Gail Sandler, Judith A. Kling, Andrew LaPage, Timothy J. Poulsen, David Dahrsnin and David Pesce • **Content Manager:** Susan B. SanFilippo • **Graphic Designers:** Tracie Drake, Yen-Miao Lin and Alex Tong • **Project Coordinator:** Carrianne Hughes and David Fazio • **Content Editors:** Peter Bauer and Cory Brown • **Material Editor:** Frank Wosnick • **Business Matter Expert:** Chuck Swanson • **Technical Reviewer:** Chuck Swanson • **Project Technical Support:** Mike Toscano

NOTICES

The logo of the CompTIA Authorized Curriculum Program and the status of this or other training material as "Authorized" under the CompTIA Authorized Curriculum Program signifies that, in CompTIA's opinion, such training material covers the content of CompTIA's related certification exam. CompTIA has not reviewed or approved the accuracy of the contents of this training material and specifically disclaims any warranties of merchantability or fitness for a particular purpose. CompTIA makes no guarantee concerning the success of persons using any such "Authorized" or other training material in order to prepare for any CompTIA certification exam. The contents of this training material were created for the CompTIA Network+ exam covering CompTIA certification exam objectives that were current as of 2005.

How to Become CompTIA Certified: This training material can help you prepare for and pass a related CompTIA certification exam or exams. In order to achieve CompTIA certification, you must register for and pass a CompTIA certification exam or exams. In order to become CompTIA certified, you must:

1. Select a certification exam provider. For more information, please visit **www.comptia.org/certification/general_information/test_locations.asp**.
2. Register for and schedule a time to take the CompTIA certification exam(s) at a convenient location.
3. Read and sign the Candidate Agreement, which will be presented at the time of the exam(s). The text of the Candidate Agreement can be found at **www.comptia.org/certification/general_information/candidate_agreement.asp**.

NETWORK+® CERTIFICATION: FOURTH EDITION — A COMPTIA CERTIFICATION

LESSON 1: NETWORK THEORY

Contents

LESSON 3: NETWORK DATA DELIVERY

Contents

Lesson 4: Network Media and Hardware

Contents

Lesson 7: TCP/IP Services

LESSON 8: OTHER NETWORK PROTOCOLS

Contents

Lesson 12: Remote Networking

LESSON 13: DISASTER RECOVERY

LESSON 14: NETWORK DATA STORAGE

Contents

Lesson 16: Network Troubleshooting

ABOUT THIS COURSE

The *CompTIA Network+ Certification* course builds on your existing user-level knowledge and experience with personal computer operating systems and networks to present fundamental skills and concepts that you will use on the job in any type of networking career. If you are pursuing a CompTIA technical certification path, the CompTIA A+ certification is an excellent first step to take before preparing for the CompTIA Network+ certification.

The *CompTIA Network+ Certification* course can benefit you in two ways. If your job duties include network troubleshooting, installation, or maintenance, or if you are preparing for any type of network-related career, it provides the background knowledge and skills you will require to be successful. Or, it can assist you if you are preparing to take the CompTIA Network+ certification examination, 2005 objectives (exam number N10-003).

Course Description

Target Student

This course is intended for entry-level computer support professionals with basic knowledge of computer hardware, software, and operating systems, who wish to increase their knowledge and understanding of networking concepts and skills to prepare for a career in network support or administration, or to prepare for the CompTIA Network+ certification, 2005 objectives (exam number N10-003). A typical student in the CompTIA Network+ Certification course should have nine months or more of professional computer support experience as a PC technician or help desk technician. Network experience is helpful but not required; A+ certification or the equivalent skills and knowledge is helpful but not required.

Course Prerequisites

An introductory course in a Windows operating system, or equivalent skills and knowledge, is required. Students can take any one of the following Element K courses: *Windows 98: Introduction*, *Windows Millennium Edition: Introduction*, *Windows 2000: Introduction,* or *Windows XP: Introduction.*

CompTIA A+ certification, or the equivalent skills and knowledge, is helpful but not required. Students may wish to take both of the following Element K courses: *A+™ Certification: Core Hardware Third Edition - A CompTIA Certification* and *A+™ Certification: Operating Systems Third Edition - A CompTIA Certification.*

How to Use This Book

As a Learning Guide

Each lesson covers one broad topic or set of related topics. Lessons are arranged in order of increasing proficiency with *CompTIA Network+ certification*; skills you acquire in one lesson may be used and developed in subsequent lessons. For this reason, you should work through the lessons in sequence.

We organized each lesson into results-oriented topics. Topics include all the relevant and supporting information you need to master *CompTIA Network+ certification*, and activities allow you to apply this information to practical hands-on examples.

In some cases, you get to try out a new skill on a specially prepared sample file. This saves you typing time and allows you to concentrate on the skill at hand. Through the use of sample files, hands-on activities, illustrations that give you feedback at crucial steps, and supporting background information, this book provides you with the foundation and structure to learn *CompTIA Network+ certification* quickly and easily.

As a Review Tool

Any method of instruction is only as effective as the time and effort you are willing to invest in it. In addition, some of the information that you learn in class may not be important to you immediately, but it may become important later on. For this reason, we encourage you to spend some time reviewing the topics and activities after the course. For additional challenge when reviewing activities, try the "What You Do" column before looking at the "How You Do It" column.

As a Reference

The organization and layout of the book make it easy to use as a learning tool and as an after-class reference. You can use this book as a first source for definitions of terms, background information on given topics, and summaries of procedures.

Course Objectives

In this course, you will identify and describe all the major networking technologies, systems, skills, and tools in use in modern PC-based computer networks, and learn information and skills that will be helpful as you prepare for the CompTIA Network+ certification examination, 2005 objectives (exam number N10-003).

You will:

- identify the basic components of network theory.
- identify the major network communications methods.
- identify network data delivery methods.
- list and describe network media and hardware components.
- identify the major types of network implementations.
- identify the components of a TCP/IP network implementation.
- identify the major services deployed on TCP/IP networks.

- identify characteristics of a variety of network protocols.
- identify the components of a LAN implementation.
- identify the components of a WAN implementation.
- identify major issues and technologies in network security.
- identify the components of a remote network implementation.
- identify major issues and technologies in disaster recovery.
- identify major data storage technologies and implementations.
- identify the primary network operating systems.
- identify major issues, models, tools, and techniques in network troubleshooting.
- practice working with IP addressing and subnetting.

Course Requirements

Hardware

This course requires one computer for each student, one computer for the instructor, and one computer to function as a classroom server. Each computer will need:

- At least 256 MB of RAM.
- A Pentium III 133 MHz (or greater) processor.
- An SVGA (or better) video card and monitor.
- At least 5 GB of free hard disk space.
- A mouse or other pointing device.
- A 12X (or faster) CD-ROM drive.
- Network adapters and media.
- The instructor's computer requires a projection system.
- Internet access is optional.
- To support the activities in Lesson 4, the instructor should provide as many physical examples of different types of network media and connectors as possible.
- For the data backup activity in Lesson 13, the instructor needs to provide a blank floppy disk for each student, or use an alternative backup location (such as a removable jump drive or a folder on the hard disk).
- To support the activities in Lesson 16, the instructor should provide as many physical examples of hardware tools as possible.
- For the optional cable assembly activity in Lesson 16, the instructor will need to provide students with raw cable, the appropriate connectors, the appropriate crimping tool, a cable tester, and an optional eye loupe.

Software

The setup instructions and the classroom activities were designed and tested for systems running Windows Server 2003 (Standard or Enterprise Edition). It is very possible that the activities will work properly or with little alteration if the classroom systems are running Windows Server 2000 instead, but Element K has not tested this configuration.

- The instructor should have at least one copy of the Windows Server 2003 installation CD-ROM available in the classroom. It might be needed during the administrative tools installation activity in Lesson 15.

Class Setup

For the Classroom Server

1. Run Windows Server 2003 Setup from the installation CD-ROM or a network setup location. (Note: The exact order of the setup steps can vary depending on the method you use to launch the installation.)
   a. Accept the license agreement.
   b. Delete any existing partitions.
   c. Create a new 5 GB C partition (or larger if you have available disk space) and set up Windows in the new partition.
   d. Format the new partition with the NTFS file system. (Quick format is acceptable.)
   e. Configure the regional and language options as appropriate for your locale.
   f. Complete the Name and Organization fields as appropriate for your organization. If you are unsure, you can use "Software Manager" as the name and "Classnet" as the organization.
   g. Enter the product key.
   h. Enter the appropriate number of per-server licenses for your classroom. The training organization is responsible for obtaining the necessary software licenses.
   i. Enter DC as the computer name.
   j. Enter and confirm !Pass1234 as the Administrator password.
   k. Configure the appropriate date and time settings for your locale.
   l. On the Networking Settings page, select Custom Settings.
   m. Configure the properties of the TCP/IP protocol.
      — Configure 192.168.1.200 as the IP address, with a subnet mask of 255.255.255.0.
      — Configure 192.168.1.200 as the DNS server address.
      — Configure a default gateway as appropriate for your network environment; it is not a classroom requirement.
   n. Accept the default workgroup membership.
   o. After installation is complete and the computer has restarted, log on as Administrator with a password of !Pass1234.
2. Screen resolution should be set to at least 800 x 600 pixels. If you are prompted to adjust the display settings, click the Display Settings balloon and click Yes in the Display Settings message box. Click Yes again to confirm the new settings.
3. The training organization is responsible for meeting Microsoft's licensing and activation requirements, and providing the necessary activation information. If your Windows Server 2003 software requires activation, double-click the Activate Windows icon in the notification area of the Windows taskbar. Use the Activate Windows wizard to complete the activation process.

4. Add the Active Directory, DNS, and DHCP services.
    a. The Manage Your Server wizard should run automatically. In the Manage Your Server wizard, click Add Or Remove A Role.
    b. On the Preliminary Steps page, click Next.
    c. Select Typical Configuration For A First Server and click Next.
    d. In the Active Directory Domain Name text box, type classnet.class and click Next.
    e. On the NetBIOS Name page, verify that the NetBIOS name is CLASSNET and click Next.
    f. On the Forwarding DNS Queries page, select the option that is appropriate for your environment if you intend to provide Internet access. If you are not providing Internet access, or if you are unsure, select No, Do Not Forward Queries. Click Next.
    g. View the summary of services and click Next.
    h. In the Configure Your Server message box, click OK.
    i. After the computer restarts, log on as Administrator with a password of !Pass1234.
    j. In the Configure Your Server Wizard, when server configuration is complete, click Next and then click Finish.
5. Verify the DNS configuration.
    a. In the Manage Your Server window, click Manage This DNS Server.
    b. In the Dnsmgmt console window, expand the DC server object and expand Forward Lookup Zones.
    c. Select the Classnet.class zone and verify that seven folders and the NS, SOA, and two A records appear in the right pane.
    d. Right-click Classnet.class and choose Properties.
    e. Verify that the Type is Active Directory–Integrated, and that Dynamic Updates is set to Secure Only. Click OK.
6. Add a reverse-lookup DNS zone.
    a. Expand Reverse Lookup Zones.
    b. Right-click Reverse Lookup Zones and choose New Zone.
    c. Use the New Zone Wizard to configure a zone with a network ID of 192.168.1. Accept all other defaults in the New Zone Wizard.
    d. Click Start and choose Command Prompt.
    e. Enter `ipconfig /registerdns` to force the server to reregister its DNS host and pointer records.
    f. Close the command prompt window.
    g. In Dnsmgmt, press F5 to refresh the view and verify that the pointer record for dc.classnet.class appears in the reverse-lookup zone.
    h. Close the Dnsmgmt console window.
7. Configure DHCP.
    a. In the Manage Your Server window, click Manage This DHCP Server.
    b. In the DHCP console window, expand the dc.classnet.class server object and expand the Scope object.
    c. Right-click Scope and choose Properties.
    d. On the General page, in the Scope Name text box, enter Classnet Scope.

e. In the Start IP Address box, type 192.168.1.50.
f. In the End IP Address box, type 192.168.1.75.
g. Click OK.
h. Click the Scope Options folder. Verify that the 006 DNS Servers scope option appears in the right pane, and that the Value is 192.168.1.200.
i. Right-click Scope Options and choose Configure Options.
j. Check 003 Router.
k. In the IP Address text box, type 192.168.1.200, click Add, and then click OK.
l. Close the DHCP console window.

8. Create administrative user accounts in Active Directory.
    a. In the Manage Your Server window, click Manage Users And Computers In Active Directory.
    b. In Active Directory Users And Computers, expand the Classnet.class domain and select the Users folder.
    c. Right-click the Users folder and choose New→User.
    d. For the instructor's logon account, in the First Name and User Logon Name text boxes, type User100. Click Next.
    e. In the Password and Confirm Password text boxes, type !Pass1234.
    f. Uncheck User Must Change Password At Next Logon.
    g. Click Next and then click Finish.
    h. For the student logon accounts, create user accounts named User##, where ## is a two-digit number unique to the classroom. Start with User01 and continue through User16 (or however many students you have). Assign passwords of !Pass1234.
    i. Select all the new user accounts. (If the accounts are not still selected, click the first account, then press Shift and click the last account).
    j. Right-click the selected accounts and choose Add To A Group.
    k. In the Enter The Object Name To Select text box, type Domain Admins and then click Check Names.
    l. Click OK, and then click OK in the Active Directory message box.
9. Create non-administrative user accounts.
    a. For the instructor, create a user account named Test100. Assign a password of !Pass1234.
    b. For the student logon accounts, create user accounts named Test##, where ## is a two-digit number unique to the classroom. Start with Test01 and continue through Test16 (or however many students you have). Assign passwords of !Pass1234. Uncheck User Must Change Password At Next Logon.
    c. Close Active Directory Users And Computers.
10. To install the course data files from the interactive CD-ROM, click the Data Files button on the main menu. Click Yes, and then click Unzip. This will install a folder named Data on your C drive. This folder contains all the data files that you will use to complete this course. Remove the Read-Only attribute on the folder, and verify that the Administrators group has the Full Control NTFS permission.

11. There are also simulated versions of certain course activities provided on the CD-ROM. These simulations can be run on any Windows computer to review the activities after class, or as an alternative to performing the activities as a group in class. The activity simulations can be launched either directly from the CD-ROM by clicking the Interactives link and navigating to the appropriate one, or from the installed data file location by opening the C:\Data\Simulations\Lesson#\Activity# folder and double-clicking the executable (.exe) file.
12. Install Internet Information Services.
    a. In the Manage Your Server window, click Add Or Remove A Role and click Next.
    b. Click Application Server (IIS, ASP.NET) and click Next three times.
    c. When the installation is complete, click Finish.
13. Configure and test a classroom website.
    a. Copy the C:\Data\Default.htm file to the C:\Inetpub\wwwroot folder.
    b. In the Manage Your Server window, click Manage This Application Server.
    c. In the left pane, expand Internet Information Services (IIS) Manager.
    d. Expand DC (Local Computer) and expand Web Sites.
    e. Select the Default Web Site and verify that the Default.htm file is listed in the right pane.
    f. Open Internet Explorer.
    g. In the Internet Explorer message box, check In The Future, Do Not Show This Message and click OK.
    h. In the Address bar, enter http://dc.classnet.class to load the default page for the default website.
    i. Close Internet Explorer.
14. Configure a classroom FTP site.
    a. Choose Start→Control Panel→Add Or Remove Programs.
    b. Click Add/Remove Windows Components.
    c. Select Application Server but do not uncheck the check box.
    d. Click Details.
    e. Select Internet Information Services (IIS) but do not uncheck the check box.
    f. Click Details.
    g. Check File Transfer Protocol (FTP) Service and click OK twice.
    h. Click Next.
    i. When the installation is complete, click Finish.
    j. Close Add Or Remove Programs.
    k. Copy the C:\Data\FTP_Sample.txt file to the C:\Inetpub\ftproot folder.
    l. In the Application Server window, select DC (Local Computer), choose Action→ Refresh, and verify that an FTP Sites folder appears under DC (Local Computer).
    m. Expand FTP Sites and verify that the Default FTP Site appears.
    n. Close Application Server.
15. Close the Manage Your Server window.
16. Create an installation source folder.

a. Place the Windows Server 2003 installation CD-ROM in the CD-ROM drive, or copy the \I386 folder and its contents from the CD-ROM to a folder on the server.

b. Share the \I386 folder as *2003install* with the default share permissions.

For the Instructor and Student Computers

1. Run Windows Server 2003 Setup from the installation CD-ROM or a network setup location. (Note: The exact order of the setup steps can vary depending on the method you use to launch the installation.)
   a. Accept the license agreement.
   b. Delete any existing partitions.
   c. Create a new 5 GB C partition (or larger if you have available disk space) and set up Windows in the new partition.
   d. Format the new partition with the NTFS file system. (Quick format is acceptable.)
   e. Configure the regional and language options as appropriate for your locale.
   f. Complete the Name and Organization fields as appropriate for your organization. If you are unsure, you can use "Software Manager" as the name and "Classnet" as the organization.
   g. Enter the product key.
   h. Enter the appropriate number of per-server licenses for your classroom. The training organization is responsible for ensuring that you obtain the necessary software licenses.
   i. Enter the computer name.
      — On the instructor's computer, enter Computer100.
      — On the student computers, enter Computer##, where ## is a two-digit number that is unique to the classroom. Start with Computer01 and continue through Computer16 (or however many computers you have).
   j. Enter and confirm !Pass1234 as the Administrator password.
   k. Configure the appropriate date and time settings for your locale.
   l. On the Networking Settings page, accept the Typical settings.
   m. Configure the computer as a member of the Classnet domain. Use Administrator and !Pass1234 as the credentials for joining the domain.
   n. After installation is complete and the computer has restarted, log on to the Classnet.class domain.
      — In the Log On To Windows dialog box, click Options and select Classnet from the Log On To drop-down list.
      — Log on to the instructor computer (Computer100) as User100, with a password of !Pass1234.
      — Log on to Computer01 through Computer16 as User01 through User16, where the user number matches the computer number. Use a password of !Pass1234.
2. Close the Manage Your Server window.
3. Screen resolution should be set to at least 800 x 600 pixels. If you are prompted to adjust the display settings, click the Display Settings balloon and click Yes in the Display Settings message box. Click Yes again to confirm the new settings.

4. The training organization is responsible for meeting Microsoft's licensing and activation requirements, and providing the necessary activation information. If your Windows Server 2003 software requires activation, double-click the Activate Windows icon in the notification area of the Windows taskbar. Use the Activate Windows wizard to complete the activation process.
5. To install the course data files from the interactive CD-ROM, click the Data Files button on the main menu. Click Yes, and then click Unzip. This will install a folder named Data on your C drive. This folder contains all the data files that you will use to complete this course. Remove the Read-Only attribute on the folder, and verify that the Administrators group has the Full Control NTFS permission.
6. There are also simulated versions of certain course activities provided on the CD-ROM. These simulations can be run on any Windows computer to review the activities after class, or as an alternative to performing the activities as a group in class. The activity simulations can be launched either directly from the CD-ROM by clicking the Interactives link and navigating to the appropriate one, or from the installed data file location by opening the C:\Data\Simulations\Lesson#\Activity# folder and double-clicking the executable (.exe) file.
7. Log off.

List of Additional Files

Printed with each activity is a list of files students open to complete that activity. Many activities also require additional files that students do not open, but are needed to support the file(s) students are working with. These supporting files are included with the student data files on the course CD-ROM or data disk. Do not delete these files.

NOTES

LESSON 1

Network Theory

Lesson Time
2 hour(s)

Lesson Objectives:

In this lesson, you will identify the basic components of network theory.

You will:

- Define common terms used in computer networking.
- Identify the primary building blocks used to construct networks.
- List the standard networking models.
- List the primary network topologies.
- List the primary categories of networks.

Lesson 1

Introduction

CompTIA Network+® certification information requires a wide range of knowledge and skills that can pertain to all types of different networking job roles. You can begin your study by learning a common set of networking concepts. In this lesson, you will identify the basic components of current networking theory.

With a background in CompTIA Network+ information and skills, your networking career can lead in many directions. But whether you become a network support technician, a network installer, or a network administrator, you'll always draw on the same basic set of concepts and information. A good grasp of fundamental networking theory will help you succeed in any network-related job role.

This lesson covers the following CompTIA Network+ (2005) certification objectives:

- Topic A:
  - Objective 3.2: Identify the basic capabilities needed for client workstations to connect to and use network resources (for example, media, network protocols, and peer and server services).
  - Objective 3.7: Given a connectivity scenario, determine the impact on network functionality of a particular security implementation (for example, port blocking/filtering, authentication, and encryption).
- Topic B:
  - Objective 2.7: Identify the purpose of subnetting.
- Topic D:
  - Objective 1.1: Recognize the following logical or physical network topologies, given a diagram, schematic, or description: star, bus, mesh, and ring.
  - Objective 4.7: Given a troubleshooting scenario involving a network with a particular physical topology (for example, bus, star, mesh, or ring) and including a network diagram, identify the network area affected and the cause of the stated failure.
- Topic E:
  - Objective 3.9: Identify the main characteristics and purpose of extranets and intranets.

TOPIC A

Networking Terminology

This lesson introduces the primary elements of network theory. In the computer industry, there is a set of common terminology used to discuss network theory. In this topic, you will define common terms used in computer networking.

The business of networking is like any other technical discipline; it has a language of its own. Part of the task of mastering the technology is to master the language used to describe that technology. While the terms used in PC networking may be confusing at first, the information and definitions in this topic will help them become second nature to you.

Networks

Definition:

A *computer network* is a group of computers that are connected together to communicate and share resources such as files, printers, and email. Networks include network media, such as a cable, to carry network data; network adapter hardware to translate the data between the computer and the network media; a network operating system to enable the computer to recognize the network; and a network protocol to control the network communications.

Example:

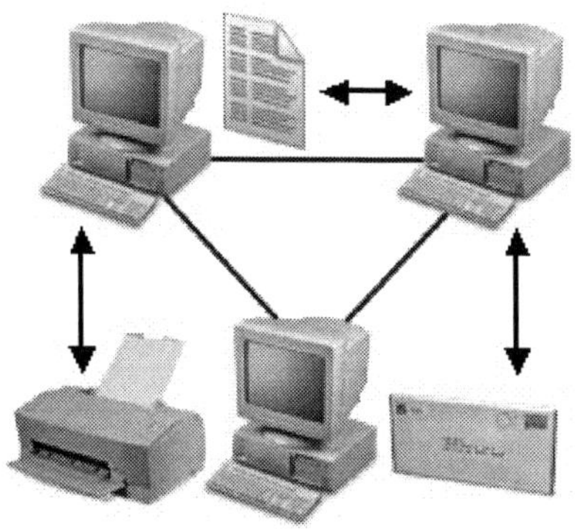

Figure 1-1: *A computer network.*

Servers

Definition:

A *server* is a network computer that shares resources with and responds to requests from other network computers, including other servers. Servers provide centralized access and storage for resources that can include applications, files, printers or other hardware, and specialized services such as email. A server can be optimized and dedicated to one specific function, or it can serve general needs. Multiple servers of various types can exist on a single network.

Example:

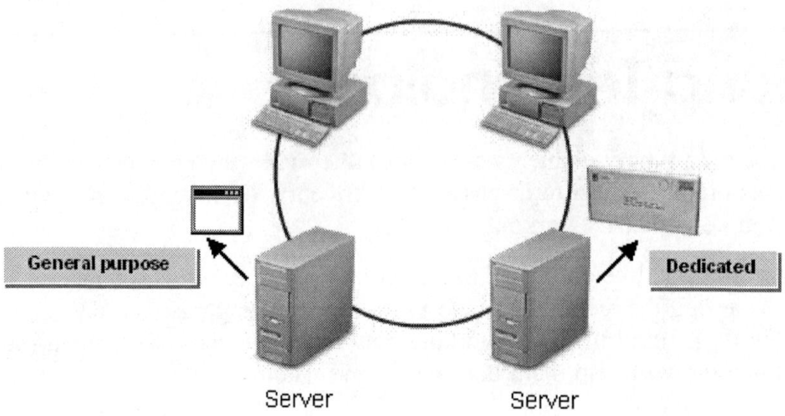

Figure 1-2: *Network servers.*

Clients

Definition:

A *client* is a network computer that utilizes the resources of other network computers, including other clients. The client computer has its own processor, memory, and storage, and can maintain some of its own resources and perform its own tasks and processing. Any type of computer on a network can function as a client of another computer from time to time.

While any computer on the network can function as a client when it uses other computers' resources, such as a windows Server 2003 computer accessing resources on another server, the term "client" most often refers to the workstation or desktop computers employed by end users.

Example:

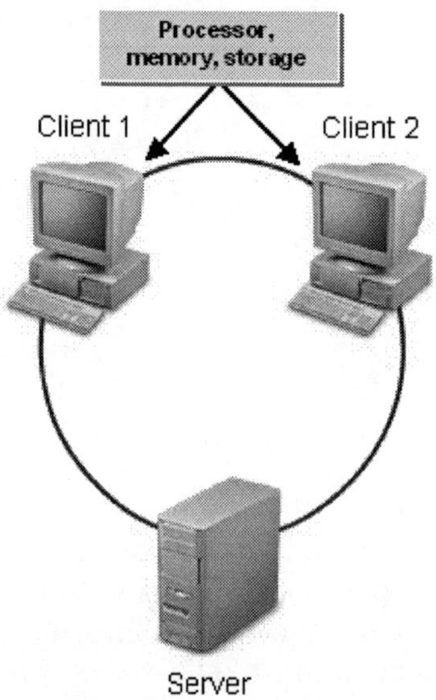

Figure 1-3: *Client computers.*

Peers

Definition:

A *peer* is a self-sufficient computer that acts as both a server and a client to other similar computers on the network. Peer computing is most often used in smaller networks with no dedicated central server, but both clients and servers in other types of networks can also share resources with their peer computers.

Example:

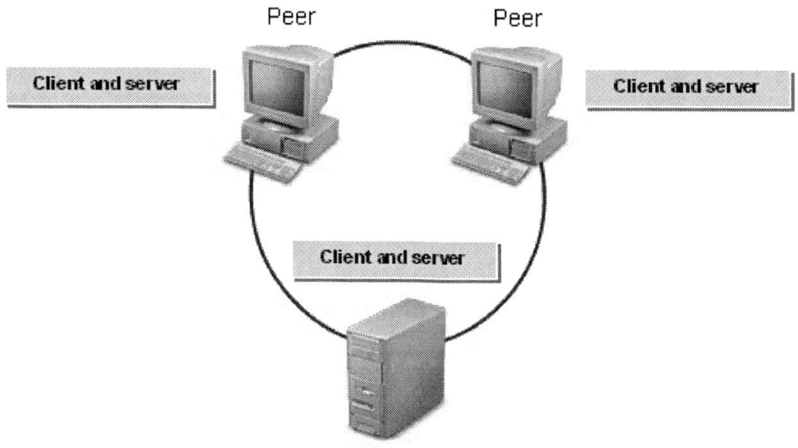

Figure 1-4: *Peer computers.*

Host Computers

Definition:

A *host computer* is a powerful, centralized computer system, such as a mainframe computer, that performs data storage and processing tasks on behalf of clients and other network devices. On a host-based network, the host computer does all the computing tasks and returns the resultant data to the end user's computer.

TCP/IP Hosts

In the early days of computer networking, all computers were host computers that controlled the activities of network terminal devices. The hosts were joined together to communicate in the early research networks that laid the foundation for the Internet. As the TCP/IP protocol was adopted and became ubiquitous, and as personal computers joined the networks, the term *host* was generalized and is now used to refer to virtually any independent system on a TCP/IP network.

Example:

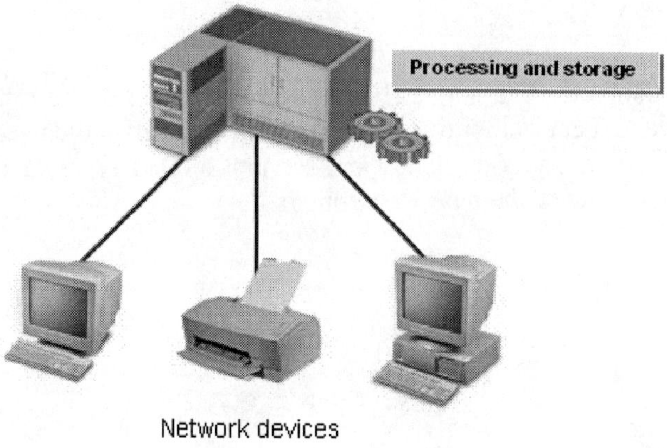

Figure 1-5: *A host computer.*

Terminals

Definition:

A *terminal* is a specialized network device on a host-based network that transmits the data entered by the user to the host for processing and displays the results. Terminals are often called "dumb" because they have no processor or memory of their own. True terminals consist of little more than a keyboard and a monitor. Standard client computers that need to interact with host computers can run software called a *terminal emulator* so that they appear to the host as dedicated terminals.

Example:

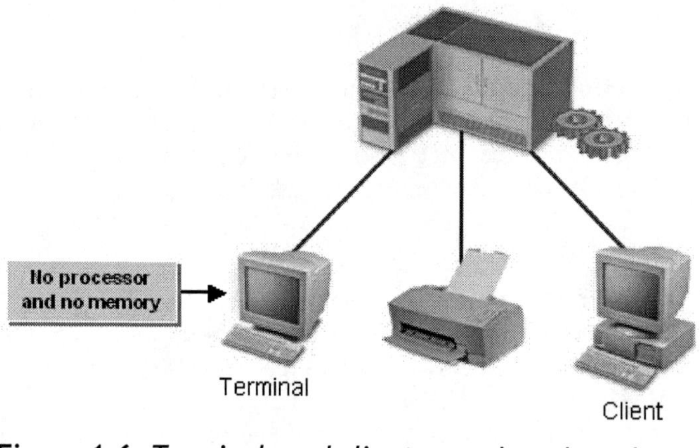

Figure 1-6: *Terminals and clients on a host-based network.*

Authentication

Definition:

Authentication is a network security measure in which a computer user or some other network component proves its identity in order to gain access to network resources. There are many possible authentication methods, with the most common being a combination of user name and password.

User Name and Password Authentication

In user name and password authentication, the user name is considered *public* information; that is, user names are generally available and there may be little effort to keep them secure or secret. The password is *private* information, which should be carefully protected and known only to the individual users and to the network authentication database. Even network administrators do not know individual users' passwords.

Example:

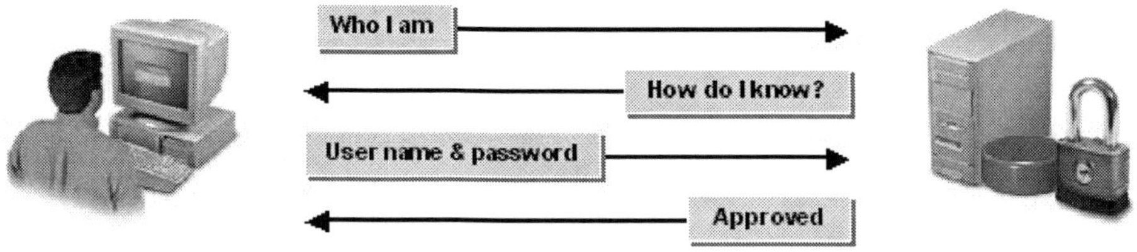

Figure 1-7: *Authentication.*

ACTIVITY 1-1

Logging On to Windows Server 2003

Conditions:

Your computer is running Windows Server 2003 and is turned on. Your computer name is Computer*##*, where ## is a two-digit number (for example, Computer01). Your user name is User*##*, where ## matches your computer number (for example, User01). Your password is !Pass1234. The classroom network is named CLASSNET.

Scenario:

In this activity, you will use your authentication credentials to log on to your Windows Server 2003 computer on the classroom network.

What You Do	How You Do It
1. **Log on to Windows Server 2003.**	a. **Press Ctrl+Alt+Del** to open the Log On To Windows dialog box.
	b. If necessary, in the User Name text box, **type your user name.** For example, if you are User01, type User01.
	c. In the Password text box, **type *!Pass1234***
	d. In the Log On To list, **verify that CLASSNET appears.**
	e. **Click OK.**
	f. In the Manage Your Server window, **check Don't Display This Page At Logon.**
	g. **Close the Manage Your Server window.**

2. **Verify your logon identity.**

a. **Click Start.** Your user name appears at the top of the Start menu.

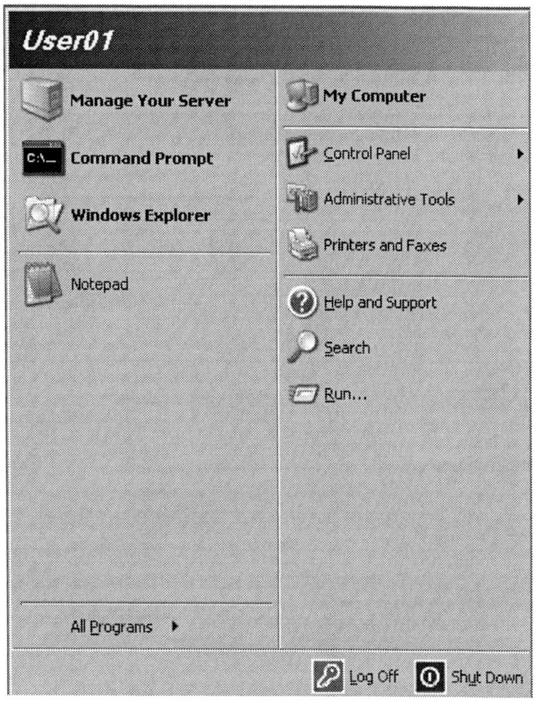

b. **Press Ctrl+Alt+Del** to open the Windows Security dialog box.

c. **Verify that your logon information is correct.**

d. **Click Cancel** to return to Windows.

Encryption

Definition:

Encryption is a network security measure in which information is encoded or scrambled prior to transmission so that it cannot be read unless the recipient knows the decoding mechanism, or *key*. Encryption is used in some form on almost every network, often to protect passwords during authentication, but also to protect the data inside network messages.

Example:

Figure 1-8: *Encryption.*

Network Directories

Definition:

A network *directory* is a centralized, hierarchical database that stores and organizes data about network users and network resources. Each piece of data is an object and each object has a set of attributes associated with it. Objects stored in a directory such as Novell's eDirectory, Microsoft's Active Directory, or Unix's Directory Services include users, groups, passwords, shared folders, computers, and servers, among others.

The directory may be stored on one server or it may be replicated among several servers on the network. Network directories provide central administration and centralized authentication, which offer administrators greater control over network resources.

Common Directories

There are many directory services available from different network vendors. Common directories include Microsoft's Active Directory and Novell's Novell Directory Services (NDS).

Example:

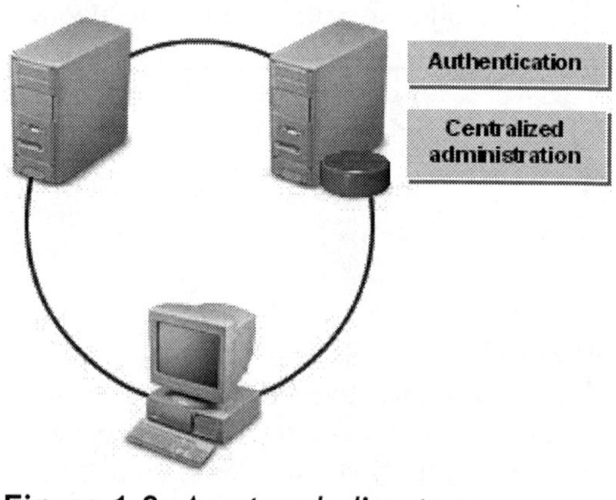

Figure 1-9: *A network directory.*

Network Media

Every network utilizes some type of network media to carry signals between and among computers. Basically, there are two types of media used in networks: cable-based, such as twisted pair and fiber optic, and wireless networking, which transports signals via radio waves.

Protocols

A network protocol is a formal set of rules that governs how computers and other networked devices communicate to exchange data over a network. Think of a network protocol as a "language" that one network device uses to communicate with another. Both devices must use the same "language" or protocol(s) in order for communication to take place.

Networking Standards

Definition:

A *networking standard* is a set of specifications, guidelines, or characteristics applied to network components to ensure interoperability and consistency between them. Networking standards determine everything from the size, shape, and type of connectors on network cables to the number of computers than can attach to a network.

Formalization of Standards

Standards can be *de facto*, meaning that they have been widely adopted through use, or *de jure*, meaning that they are mandated by law or have been approved by a recognized body of experts, such as the International Organization for Standardization.

To help recall which is which, you can think of words like jury and jurisdiction, which are words related to the legal system. These words, and the term *de jure*, come from the same Latin root.

Many familiar standards exist in everyday life, outside the network arena. In North America, it is a standard to drive on the right side of the road. Standards ensure that electrical plugs fit into electrical outlets. Specifications for children's car seats are *de jure* standards. Setting a table with the fork on the left is a *de facto* standard.

Example:

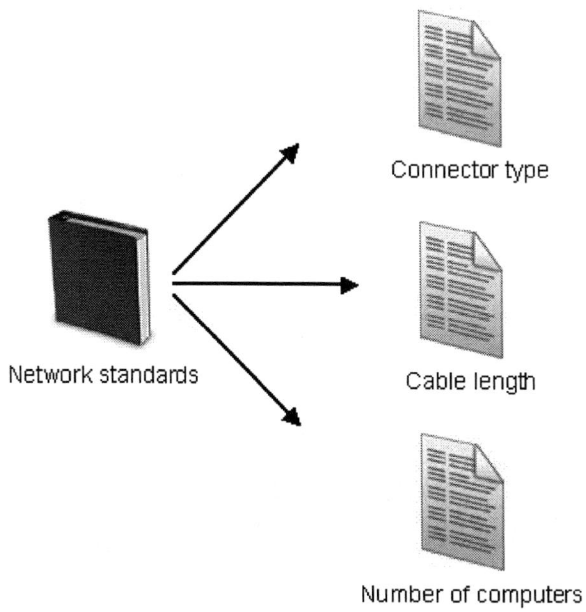

Figure 1-10: *Networking standards.*

Standards Organizations

There are a number of standards bodies that issue standards that are important in the field of computer networking.

Standards Organization	Description
International Organization for Standardization (ISO)	The largest standards-development body in the world, comprising the national standards institutes of 148 countries. It is a nongovernmental organization issuing voluntary standards in dozens of fields from agriculture to textiles. Of most significance for networking, in 1984, the ISO developed a reference model called the Open Systems Interconnection (OSI) model. The OSI model is a seven-layered framework of standards and specifications for communication in networks. The short name ISO is not an abbreviation for the name of the organization in any particular language, but was derived from the Greek word *isos*, meaning *equal*. Source: **www.iso.org**
Institute of Electrical and Electronics Engineers (IEEE)	The IEEE is an organization dedicated to advancing theory and technology in the electrical sciences. The standards wing of IEEE issues standards in areas such as electronic communications, circuitry, computer engineering, electromagnetics, and nuclear science. Source: **www.ieee.org**
American National Standards Institute (ANSI)	ANSI is the national standards institute of the United States, and facilitates the formation of a variety of national standards, as well as promoting those standards internationally. Individually accredited standards bodies perform the standards development under ANSI's guidance. The best-known ANSI standard in the computer world is a method for representing keyboard characters by standard four-digit numeric codes. Source: **www.ansi.org**
Telecommunications Industry Association (TIA) and Electronic Industries Alliance (EIA)	These two trade associations are accredited by ANSI to develop and jointly issue TIA/EIA standards for telecommunications and electronics. Sources: **www.tiaonline.org** and **www.eia.org**
Internet Engineering Task Force (IETF)	The IETF is one of a loosely organized set of boards, working groups, committees, and commercial organizations that together develop and maintain Internet standards and contribute to the evolution and smooth operation of the Internet. All published Internet standards documents, known as Requests for Comments (RFCs), are available through the IETF. Source: **www.ietf.org**

ACTIVITY 1-2

Defining Networking Terminology

Scenario:

In this activity, you will define the common terms used in computer networking.

---

1. **A network computer that shares resources with and responds to requests from other computers is known as a:**
   a) Client
   b) Server
   c) Terminal
   d) Key

---

2. **A network computer that utilizes the resources of other network computers is known as a:**
   a) Server
   b) Host computer
   c) Client
   d) Media

---

3. **A group of computers connected together to communicate and share resources is known as:**
   a) A computer network
   b) A server
   c) A client
   d) Authentication

---

4. **A self-sufficient computer that acts as both a server and a client is known as a:**
   a) Host computer
   b) Client
   c) Server
   d) Peer

---

5. **True or False? A host computer transmits data to another computer for processing and displaying the result to the user.**
   __ True
   __ False

---

6. **A powerful, centralized computer system that performs data storage and processing tasks on behalf of clients and other network devices is known as a:**

   a) Client

   b) Host computer

   c) Terminal

   d) Network

7. **Match the term with the definition.**

	Term		Definition
___	Authentication	a.	A network security measure in which information is encoded or scrambled prior to transmission so that it cannot be read unless the recipient knows the decoding mechanism.
___	Encryption	b.	A network security measure in which a computer user or some other network component proves its identity in order to gain access to network resources.
___	Key	c.	In an encryption scheme, the piece of information required to encode or decode the encrypted data.

8. **Match the standards organization to its description.**

	Organization		Description
___	ISO	a.	An organization dedicated to advancing theory and technology in the electrical sciences.
___	IEEE	b.	A United States standards institute that facilitates the formation of a variety of national standards, as well as promoting those standards internationally.
___	ANSI	c.	A nongovernmental organization issuing voluntary standards in fields ranging from agriculture to textiles.
___	TIA/EIA	d.	An organization that develops and maintains Internet standards and contributes to the evolution and smooth operation of the Internet.
___	IEFT	e.	An organization that develops and issues standards for telecommunications and electronics.

9. **True or False? A network directory is a centralized database of user names and passwords that the network server uses as a reference to authenticate network clients.**

   __ True

   __ False

TOPIC B

Network Building Blocks

The previous topic introduced basic networking terms. Now that you know the terms, you can use them to discuss the basic components used to build networks. In this topic, you will identify the building blocks used to construct networks.

All networks employ server and client systems, but they can group those systems together in a variety of ways. The way the network is divided and how the components are connected can have a big impact on network performance and troubleshooting. As a network professional, you should understand the basic physical and logical building blocks used in all PC networks.

Nodes

Definition:

A *node* is any network device that can connect to the network and can generate, process, or transfer network data. Every node has at least one unique network address. Some nodes can have multiple addresses.

Example:

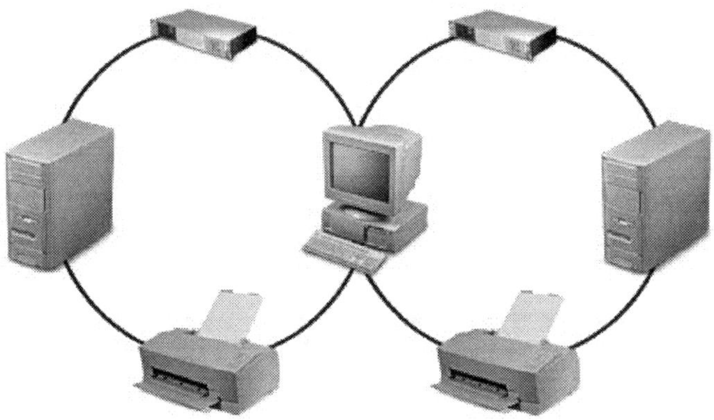

Figure 1-11: *Network nodes.*

Endpoints and Redistribution Points

Network nodes are either endpoints or redistribution points. *Endpoints* are nodes that function as the source or the destination of data. *Redistribution points* are devices used to transfer data, such as a network hub or router.

The Network Backbone

Definition:

The network *backbone* is the highest-speed transmission path that carries the majority of the network data. It can connect small networks together into a larger structure, or connect server nodes to the networks where the majority of the client computers are attached. The technology used on the backbone network can often be totally different than the client network sections.

Example:

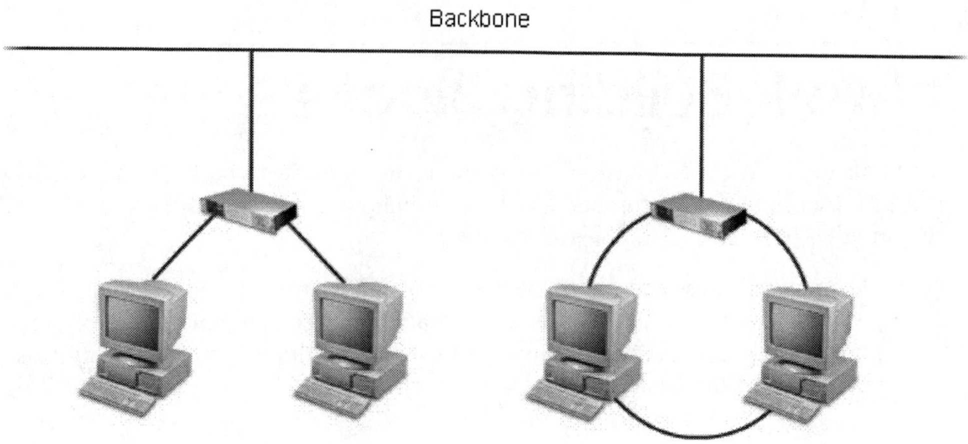

Figure 1-12: *The network backbone.*

Segments

Definition:

A *segment* is any discrete physical subdivision of a network. A segment is bounded by physical internetworking devices such as hubs, switches, and routers. All nodes attached to the same segment have common access to that portion of the network. The segment can link a number of devices, or serve as a connection between two specific nodes.

Segmenting for Performance

Dividing a network into segments can make network performance more efficient. With segments, traffic is confined to a portion of the network containing nodes that communicate with each other most often. However, performance can suffer if nodes must regularly communicate to devices on other segments, as the devices that link segments can be slower than communications within a segment.

Example:

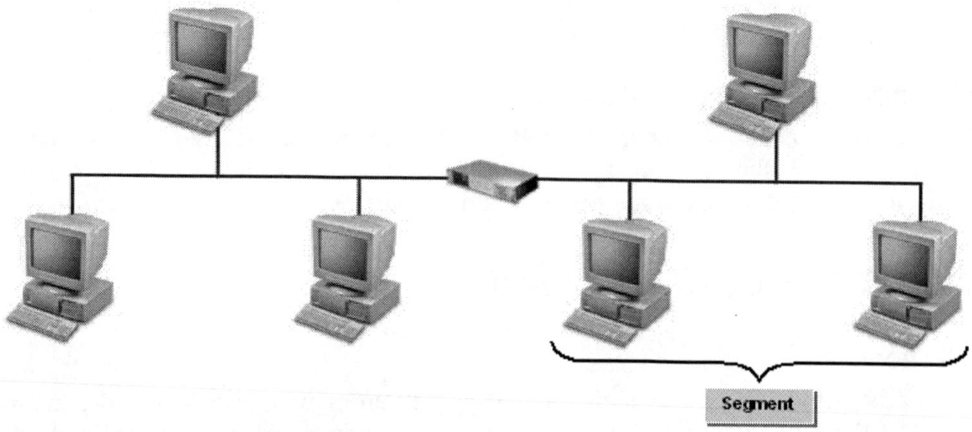

Figure 1-13: *Network segments.*

Subnets

Definition:

A *subnet*, which is short for subnetwork, refers to how a network administrator subdivides a large network into smaller, logical networks. The network administrator configures each node with a network address (called an IP address) and a subnet address in order to segment a network into subnetworks and to create a routing structure. By creating logical groupings of network devices based on an addressing scheme, an administrator can better manage data flow on large networks. The subnet can be on a separate physical segment, or it can share segments with other logical subnets.

Example:

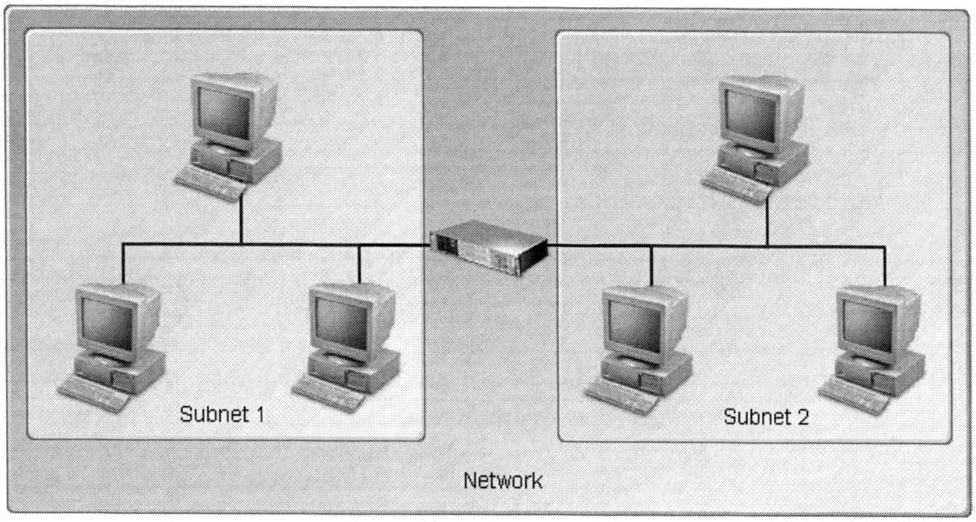

Figure 1-14: *Network subnets.*

ACTIVITY 1-3

Defining Network Building Block Terms

Scenario:

In this activity, you will identify the primary building blocks used to construct networks.

1. **Any network device that can connect to the network and can generate, process, or transfer network data is:**
   - a) An endpoint
   - b) A segment
   - c) A node
   - d) A redistribution point

2. **Match the term with the definition.**

	Term		Definition
___	Backbone	a.	Any portion of a network that has been assigned a unique logical address within the addressing scheme of the larger network.
___	Segment	b.	A discrete physical subdivision of a network.
___	Subnet	c.	A network node that is the source or destination of network data.
___	Endpoint	d.	The highest-speed transmission path that carries the majority of the network data.

3. **True or False? A network node that is used to transfer data is a redistribution point.**

   __ True

   __ False

TOPIC C

Standard Network Models

Previously, you learned definitions for the terms used to describe the basic building blocks of networks. Those basic components can be connected together according to various different models of networking. In this topic, you will identify the standard networking models currently in use.

As a networking professional, you might work in a variety of network environments that use all types of technologies, designs, and models. Although some of these technologies might be more prevalent than others, you need to be ready to understand the systems that are in place in any network environment you might encounter.

Network Models

Definition:

A *network model* is a design specification for how the nodes on a network interact and communicate. The network model determines the degree to which communications and processing are centralized or distributed. There are three primary network models: centralized or hierarchical, client/server, and peer-to-peer. Some networks can exhibit a mixture of characteristics.

Example:

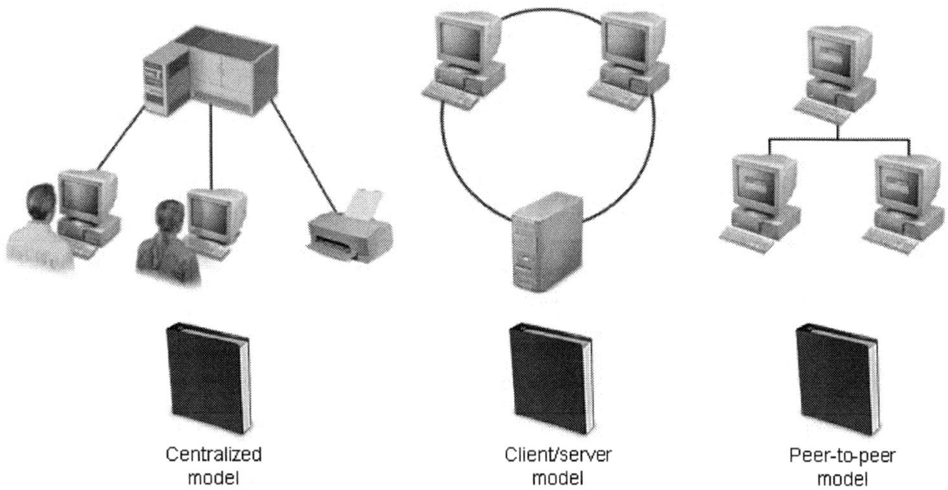

Figure 1-15: *Network models.*

Centralized Computing Networks

Definition:

A *centralized network* is a network in which a central host computer controls all network communication and performs data processing and storage on behalf of clients. Users connect to the host via dedicated terminals or terminal emulators. Centralized networks provide high performance and centralized management, but they are also expensive to implement.

The terms "hierarchical network" and "host-based network" can also be used to describe centralized networks.

Host computers are often a powerful mainframe running a customized operating system or some form of PC or workstation running the UNIX operating system or one of its variants.

Example:

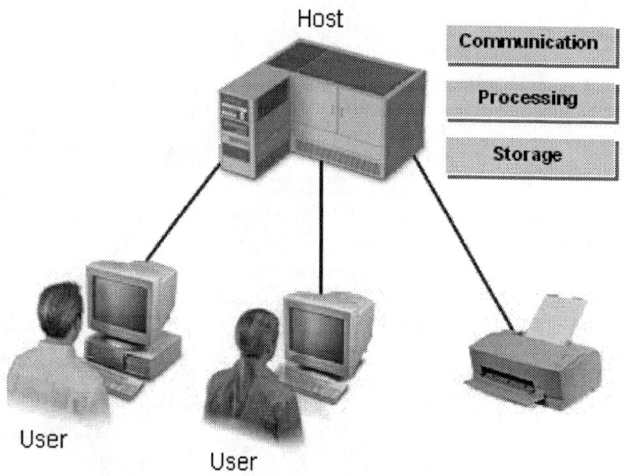

Figure 1-16: *A centralized network.*

Client/Server Networks

Definition:

A *client/server network* is a network in which servers provide services to clients. Typically, there is at least one server providing central authentication services. Servers also provide access to shared files, printers, hardware, and applications. In client/server networks, processing power, management services, and administrative functions can be concentrated where needed, while clients can still perform many basic end-user tasks on their own.

Example:

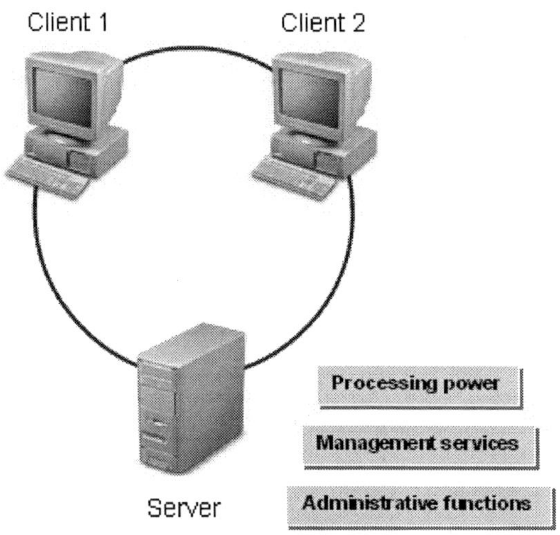

Figure 1-17: *A client/server network.*

Peer-to-Peer Networks

Definition:

A *peer-to-peer network* is a network in which resource sharing, processing, and communications control are completely decentralized. All clients on the network are equal in terms of providing and using resources, and users are authenticated by each individual workstation. Peer-to-peer networks are easy and inexpensive to implement. However, they are only practical in very small organizations, due to the lack of central data storage and administration.

A peer-to-peer network is often referred to as a *workgroup*.

In a peer-to-peer network, user accounts must be duplicated on every workstation from which a user accesses resources. Such distribution of user information makes maintaining peer-to-peer networks difficult, especially as the network grows.

Example:

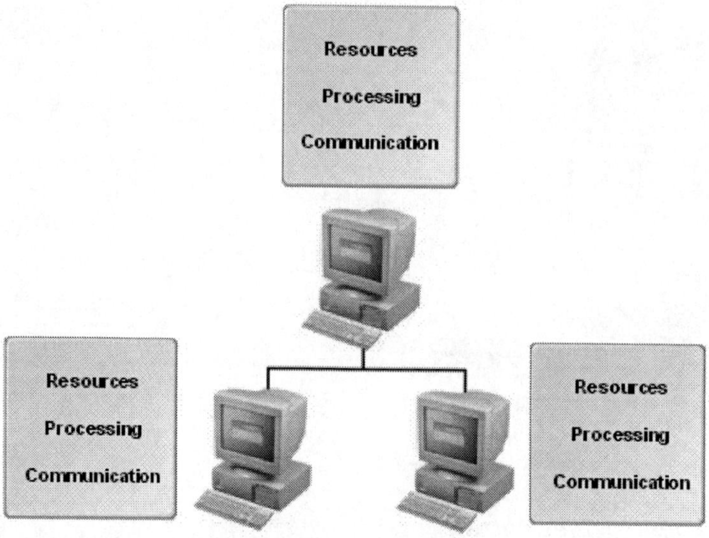

Figure 1-18: *A peer-to-peer network.*

Mixed Mode Networks

Definition:

A *mixed mode network* is a network that incorporates elements from more than one of the three standard network models.

Mixed Mode Networks Uses

One common example of a mixed mode network is a workgroup created to share local resources within a client/server network. For example, you might share one client's local printer with just a few other users. The client sharing the printer on the network does not use the client/server network's directory structure to authenticate and authorize access to the printer.

Another example of a mixed mode network might include a client/server network combined with a centralized mainframe. An end user's workstation functions as a client to the network directory server, and employs terminal emulation software to authenticate to the host system.

Example:

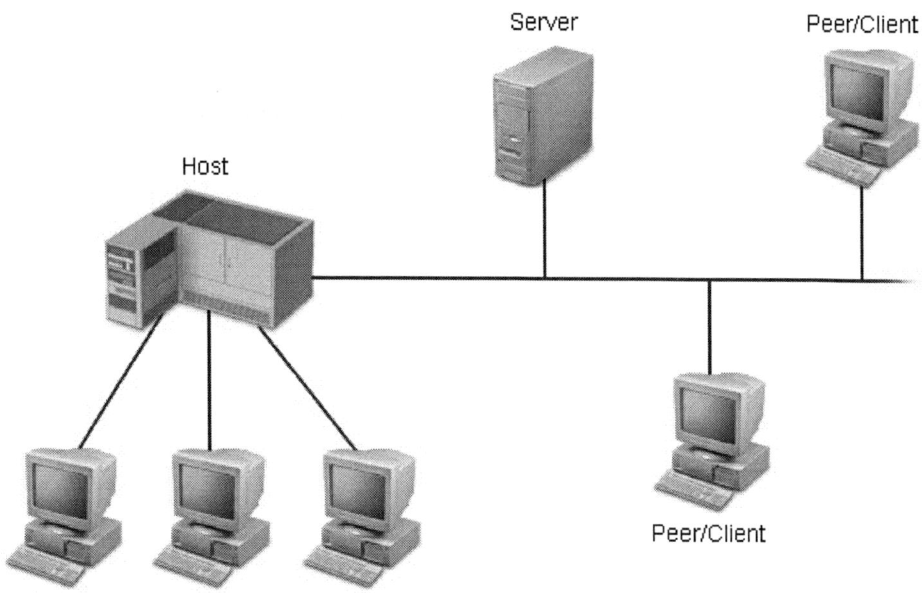

Figure 1-19: *A mixed mode network.*

ACTIVITY 1-4

Identifying Standard Network Models

Scenario:

In this activity, you will identify the standard network models.

---

1. **Which of the following terms describes how the nodes on a network interact and share control of the network communications?**

    a) Network directory

    b) Network model

    c) Network theory

    d) Network structure

---

2. **On your network, users share files stored on their Windows XP computers between themselves directly. Additionally, they access shared storage, and printing and fax resources, which are connected to a department-wide server. Your network uses which network model?**

    a) Peer-to-peer

    b) Client/server

    c) Centralized

    d) Mixed mode

---

3. **Match the network model with its description.**

___	Centralized network	a.	A network in which some nodes act as servers to provide special services on behalf of other nodes.
___	Client/server network	b.	A network in which resource sharing, processing, and communications control are completely decentralized.
___	Peer-to-peer network	c.	A network in which a central host computer controls all network communication and performs the data processing and storage on behalf of network clients.
___	Mixed mode network	d.	A network that displays characteristics of more than one of the three standard network models.

TOPIC D

Network Topologies

In the previous topics, you identified a number of general network concepts and components. Now you are ready to see how these components can combine together to create large structural units called network topologies. In this topic, you will identify the primary network topologies.

Just as you might encounter a variety of network models in your career as a network professional, you might also encounter a number of different physical and logical network topologies. No matter what your professional role, you'll need to understand the characteristics of the network topology you're working with, and identify how the topology affects network performance and network troubleshooting.

Topology

Definition:

A *topology* is a network specification that determines the network's overall layout and the network's signaling and data flow patterns. A topology comprises the *physical topology,* which describes the network's physical wiring layout or shape, and the *logical topology,* which describes the paths through which the data moves. The physical and logical topologies do not have to be the same. Common topologies include a star pattern, ring pattern, and bus or straight-line pattern.

Example:

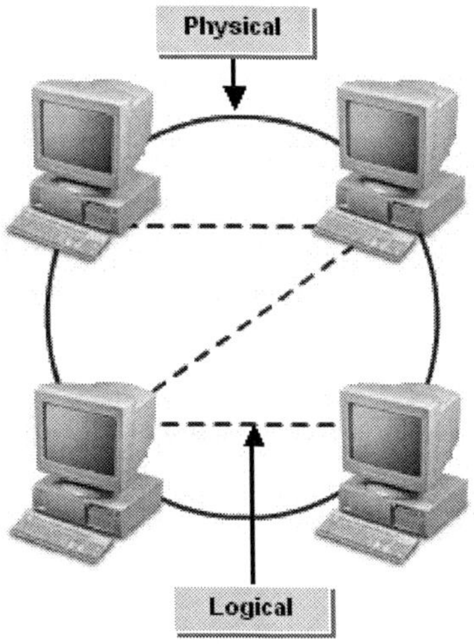

Figure 1-20: *Network topologies.*

Physical Bus Topology

Definition:

A *physical bus topology* is a physical topology in which network nodes are arranged in a linear format, with each node connected directly to the network cable with a T-connector or tap. The data signal passes by the node, not through the node. A bus network is easy to implement but can be unreliable, because the entire bus fails if there is a break in the wire. Signals can reflect off the ends of the wire, so you must install terminators at both ends of the bus. Attaching a terminator at both ends of the signal wire impedes or absorbs signals so they cannot reflect onto the wire.

Example:

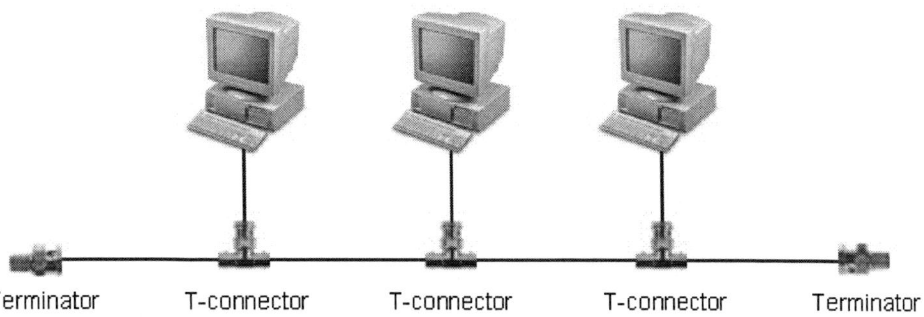

Figure 1-21: *A physical bus topology.*

Physical Star Topology

Definition:

A *physical star topology* is a network topology that uses a central connectivity device, with separate physical connections to each node. The individual nodes send data to the connectivity device and the device will then either forward the data to the appropriate destination node or simply pass it through to all attached nodes. Because a single failed node does not bring down the whole network, star topologies are reliable and easy to maintain.

Although star topologies are extremely common in client/server networks, a host-based computing system is a classic example of a physical star topology. Each node has a connection to the host computer and is not even aware of other nodes on the network.

Example:

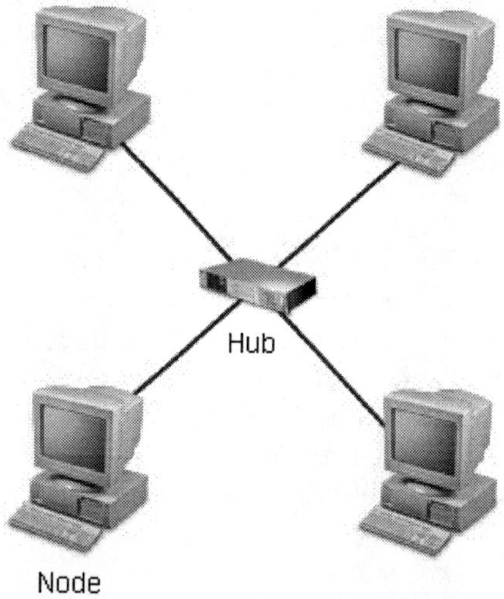

Figure 1-22: *A physical star topology.*

Physical Ring Topology

Definition:

A *physical ring topology* is a network topology in which all network nodes are connected in a continuous circle. Each node in turn reads the network signal from its upstream neighbor and then retransmits it to its downstream neighbor, so signal quality is high. Because the failure of a single node can bring down the whole network, ring topologies are potentially unreliable.

Example:

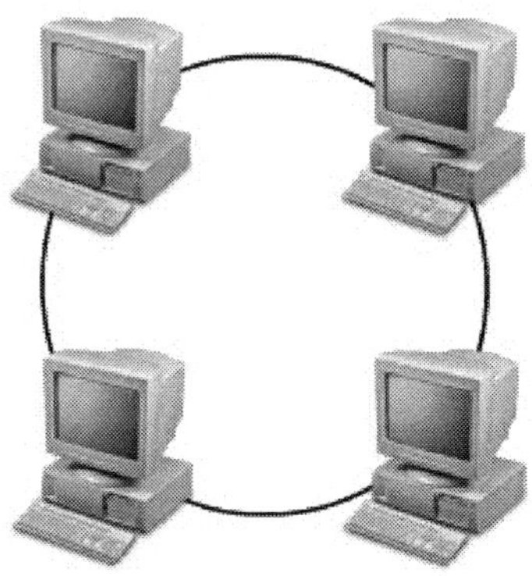

Figure 1-23: *A physical ring topology.*

Physical Mesh Topology

Definition:

A *physical mesh topology* is a network topology in which each node has a direct connection to every other node. This topology is extremely reliable, because no node can ever be isolated from the network. It is also extraordinarily difficult to implement and maintain because the number of connections increases exponentially with the number of nodes. Mesh topologies are typically used to provide reliable connections between separate independent networks.

The connections between major divisions of the Internet use a mesh topology.

Example:

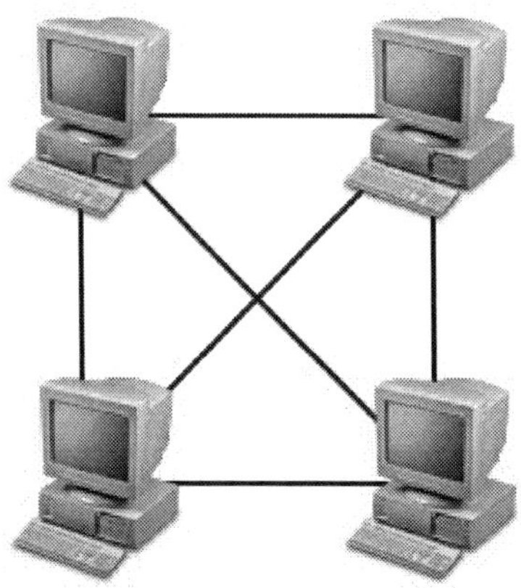

Figure 1-24: *A physical mesh topology.*

Hybrid Topology

Definition:

A *hybrid topology* is any topology that exhibits characteristics of more than one standard physical topology. Each section of the network follows the rules of its own topology. They can be complex to maintain because they incorporate a wide range of technologies.

Hybrid topologies are not typically built on purpose. Instead, they arise when administrators connect existing networks that were implemented independently using different topologies.

Example:

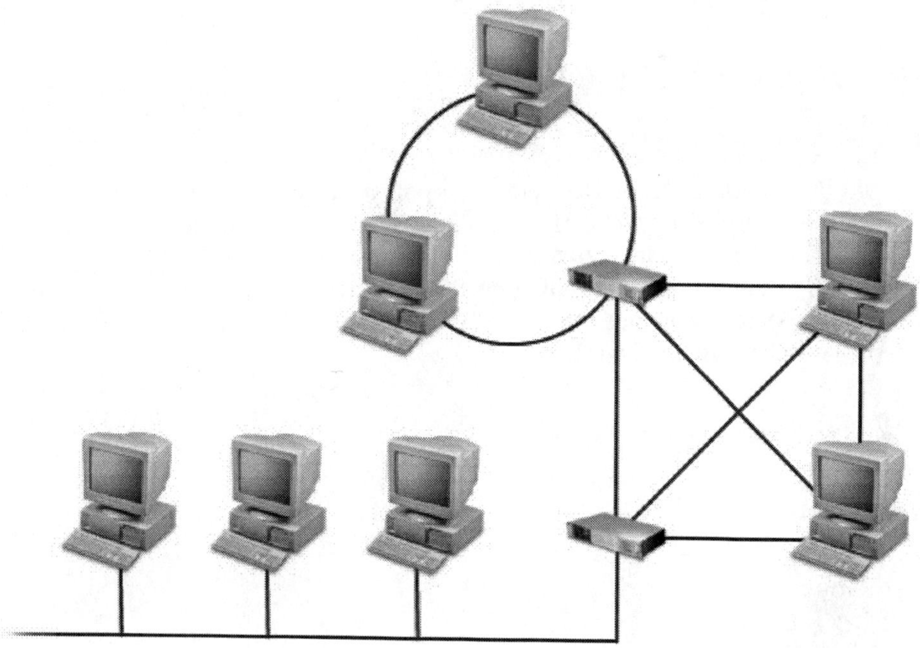

Figure 1-25: *A hybrid topology.*

Logical Bus Topology

Definition:

A *logical bus topology* is a network topology in which all nodes see the network signal at the same time, regardless of the physical wiring layout of the network. Even though the nodes might be connected to a central hub and resemble a star, the data flow appears to move in a single, continuous stream.

Example:

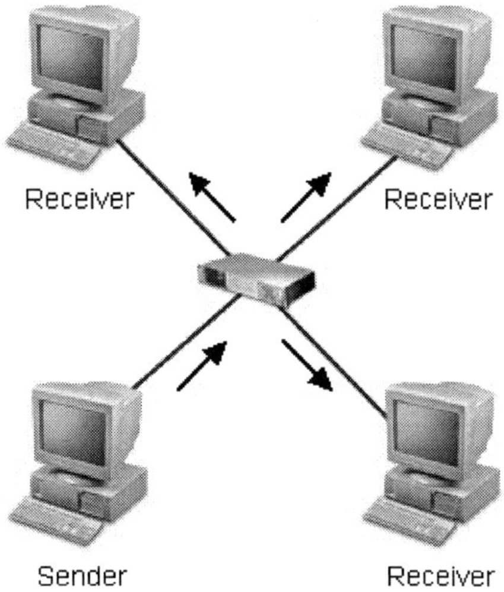

Figure 1-26: *A logical bus topology.*

Logical Ring Topology

Definition:

A *logical ring topology* is a network topology in which each node receives data only from its upstream neighbor and retransmits it only to its downstream neighbor, regardless of the physical layout of the network. Although the nodes might be connected to a central device in a star layout, the data moves through the network in a continuous circle.

Example:

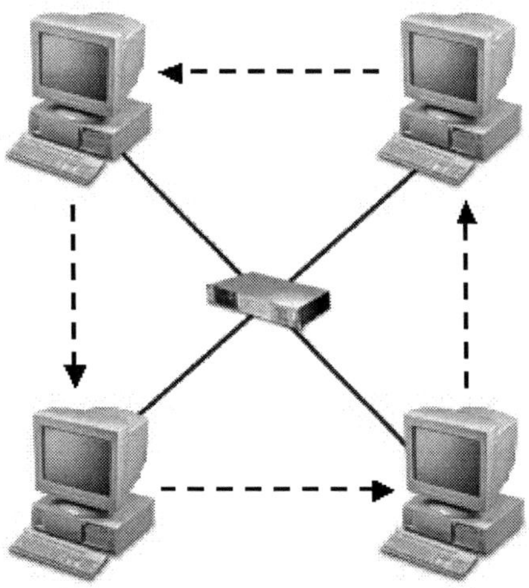

Figure 1-27: *A logical ring topology.*

Logical Star Topology

A *logical star topology* is implemented less commonly than a logical ring or a logical bus. In a logical star topology, all nodes might be wired onto the same bus cable, but a central device polls each node to see if it needs to transmit, and then controls the amount of access the node has to the cable. A multiplexer (mux) device manages the separate signals and enables them to share the media.

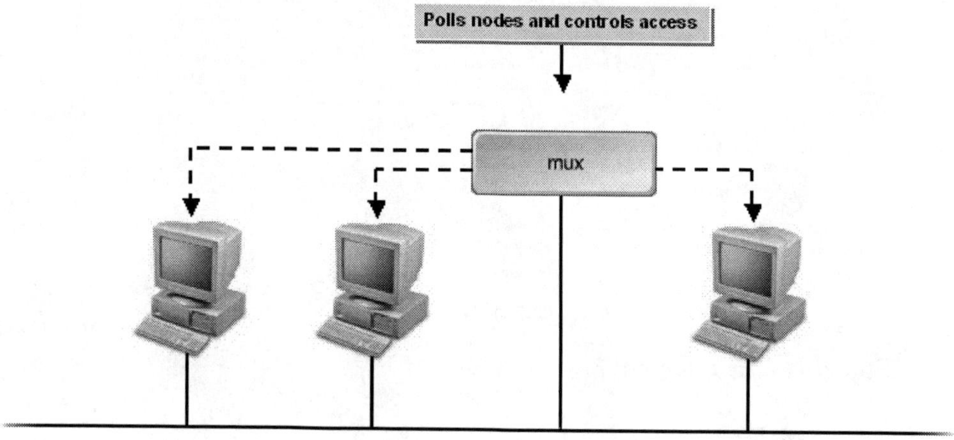

Figure 1-28: *A logical star topology.*

ACTIVITY 1-5

Identifying Network Topologies

Scenario:

In this activity, you will identify and describe network topologies.

---

1. **True or False? Physical topology is the topology that describes data flow patterns in the network.**

   __ True

   __ False

---

2. **Match the physical topology with its description.**

___	Physical bus	a.	Exhibits the characteristics of more than one standard topology.
___	Physical star	b.	Network nodes are connected in a continuous circle.
___	Physical ring	c.	Network nodes are arranged in linear format.
___	Physical mesh	d.	Network nodes all have a direct connection to every other node.
___	Hybrid	e.	Network nodes are connected by a central connectivity device that provides separate connections to each device.

3. **The network topology in which all nodes see the network signal at the same time, regardless of the physical wiring of the network, is a:**
    a) Logical bus topology
    b) Physical bus topology
    c) Logical ring topology
    d) Physical ring topology

TOPIC E

Network Categories

Throughout this lesson, you've learned about various specific network components and how they are assembled into different network structures. Now you can examine how those basic network structures are categorized on a larger scale. In this topic, you will identify the primary categories that describe a network's size and extent.

Companies can deploy different categories of networks depending on the company's size and communications needs. You might find yourself working with a network of any possible size or type. Whether it's a LAN or a WAN, the Internet or an intranet, as a network professional, you'll need to recognize and understand the terms that describe these network categories.

Local Area Networks (LAN)

Definition:

A *local area network (LAN)* is a self-contained network that spans a small area, such as a single building, floor, or room. In a LAN, all nodes and segments are directly connected with cables or short-range wireless technologies.

Example:

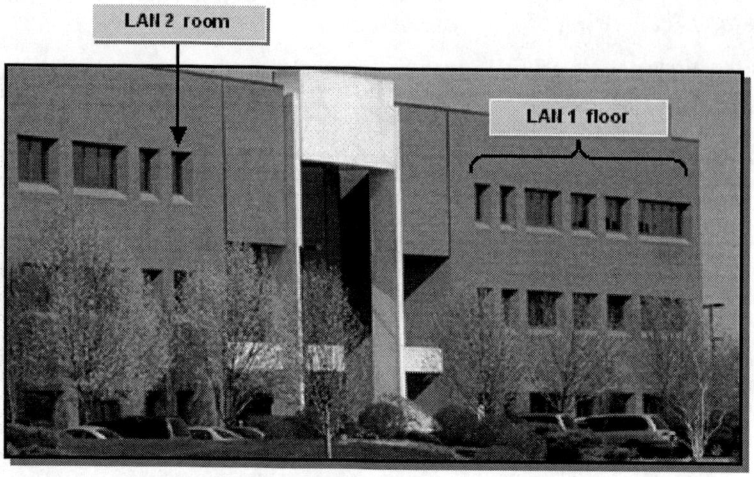

Figure 1-29: *LANs within a building.*

LAN Administrator Duties

LAN administrators are specifically charged with managing and maintaining the local network. The administrator's responsibilities include maintaining not only machines and cabling but also network software. LAN administrators might also perform installation and deployment, upgrades, and troubleshooting for applications. LAN administrators are typically versatile and adaptable with a broad range of skills and knowledge.

Wide Area Networks (WAN)

Definition:

A *wide area network (WAN)* is a network that spans multiple geographic locations. WANs typically connect multiple LANs using long-range transmission media.

Example:

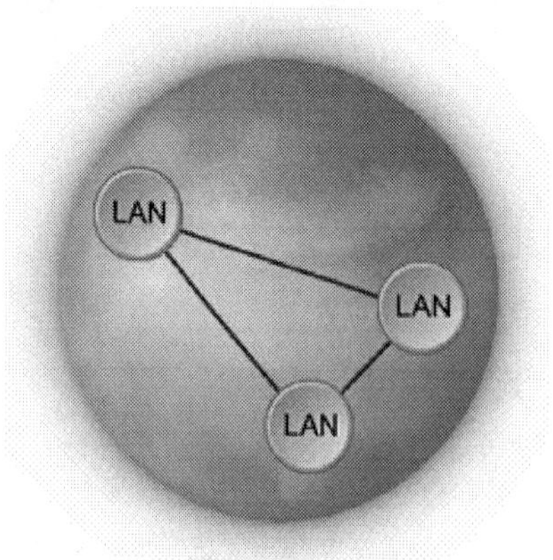

Figure 1-30: *A WAN.*

WAN Administrator Duties

WAN administrators typically work with more complex technical issues than LAN administrators and focus more on network issues than user issues. A WAN administrator designs and maintains the connection scheme between remote offices and may also develop and troubleshoot routing structures, work with voice and data systems, develop scripts to automate complex administrative tasks, as well as plan, test, and implement hardware and software upgrades.

Metropolitan, Campus, and Other Network Coverage Areas

There are several loosely defined network categories, named according to the geographic area they cover. These include:

- A *metropolitan area network (MAN)*, which covers an area equivalent to a city or other municipality.
- A *campus area network (CAN)*, which covers an area equivalent to an academic campus or business park. A CAN is typically owned or used exclusively by one company, school, or organization.
- A *global area network (GAN)*, which is any worldwide network.
- A *wireless personal area network (WPAN)*, which connects devices in very close proximity to exchange data and resources directly, but not through a wireless access point.

The Internet

The Internet is the single largest global WAN, linking virtually every country, continent, and organization in the world. No single person, country, or entity owns or controls the Internet. Instead, Internet standards and practices are overseen by an international consortium that is coordinated by the Internet Society (ISOC).

You can get more information on ISOC at its website, **www.isoc.org**

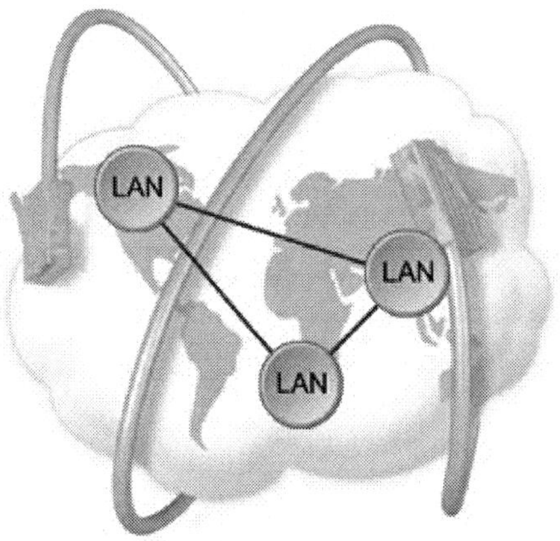

Figure 1-31: *The Internet.*

Intranets

Definition:

An *intranet* is a private network that uses Internet protocols and services to share a company's information with its employees. As with the Internet, employees access an intranet via a web browser and navigate a company's web pages.

Example:

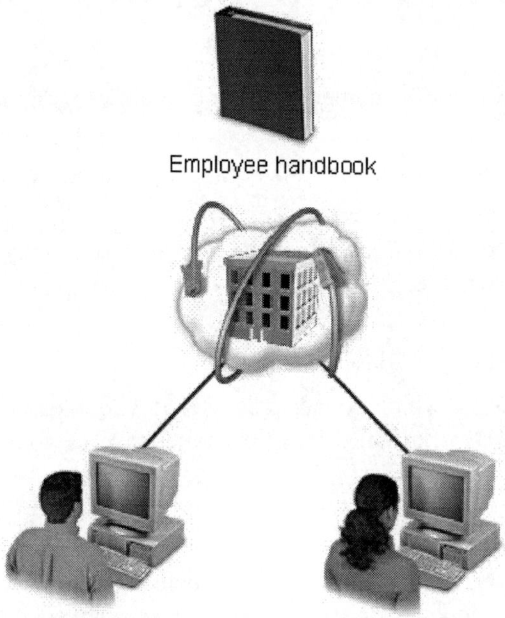

Figure 1-32: *An intranet.*

Extranets

Definition:

An *extranet* is a private network that uses Internet protocols and network connectivity to provide access to company web pages via a web browser. An extranet enables an organization to store and share specific information or operations with vendors, partners, customers, and other businesses. One of the companies that participates in the extranet might own, build, maintain, and control it, and then share access with specific partners. Or, extranet partners might all share responsibility for developing the network.

Example:

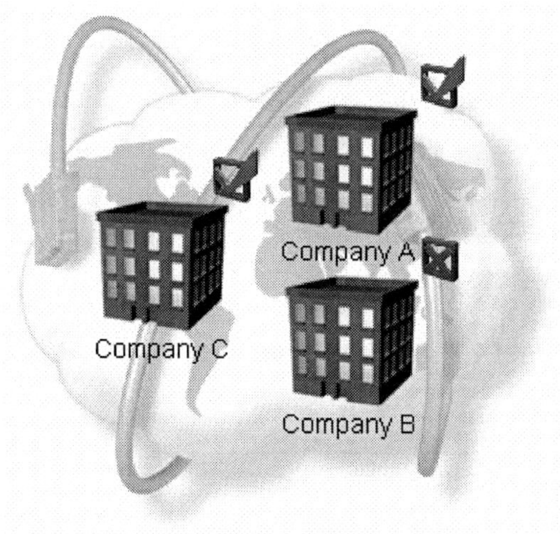

Figure 1-33: *An extranet.*

Enterprise Networks

Definition:

An *enterprise network* is a network that encompasses all the separate network components employed by a particular organization. An enterprise network can be of any size required by the organization and can employ any number of networking technologies.

Example:

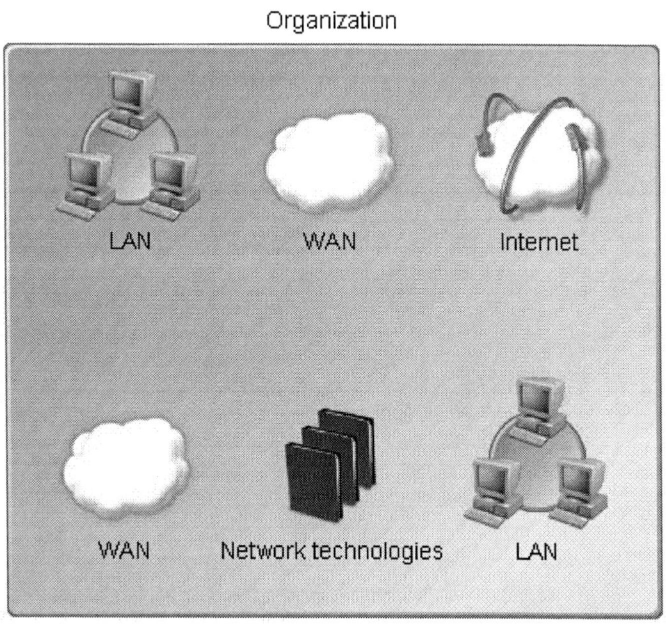

Figure 1-34: *An enterprise network.*

ACTIVITY 1-6

Identifying Network Categories

Scenario:

In this activity, you will identify the primary categories of networks.

1. State University maintains a network that connects all residences, academic buildings, and administrative facilities. All the locations share a common data center in the Computing Services building. This network fits the category of a:

    a) WAN

    b) LAN

    c) CAN

2. The company Chester Unlimited has a remote office that must have access to its corporate office with relatively high bandwidth. This network fits the category of a:

    a) LAN

    b) WAN

    c) CAN

    Williams Ltd. occupies four floors in the East building of the River View Business Complex. Their network would fit the category of a:

    a) LAN

    b) WAN

    c) CAN

3. **Select the portions of the network in the figure that are LANs.**

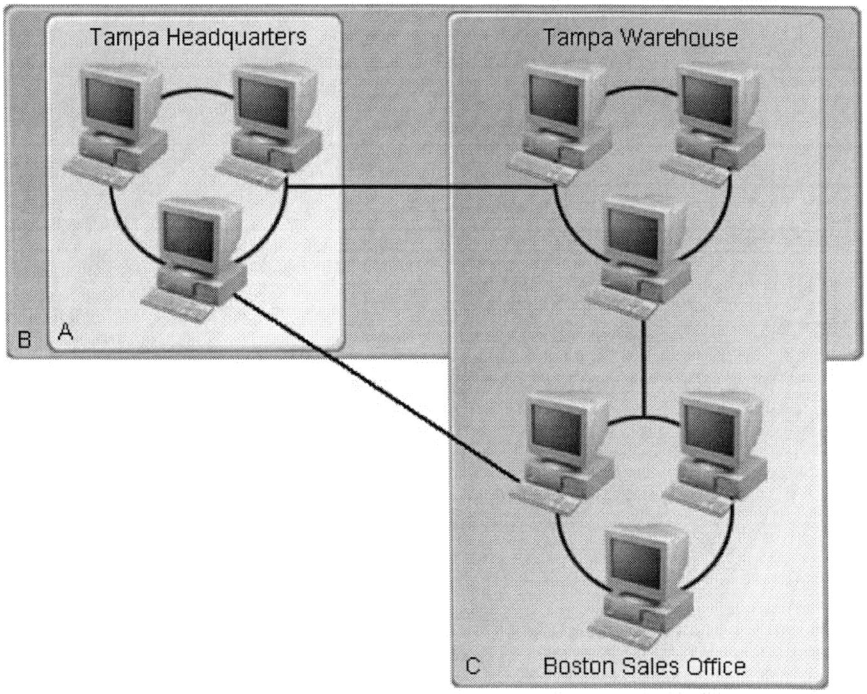

a) Section A—Tampa Headquarters

b) Section B—Tampa Headquarters and Tampa Warehouse

c) Section C—Tampa Warehouse and Boston Sales Office

4. **Select the portion of the network in the figure that is a WAN.**

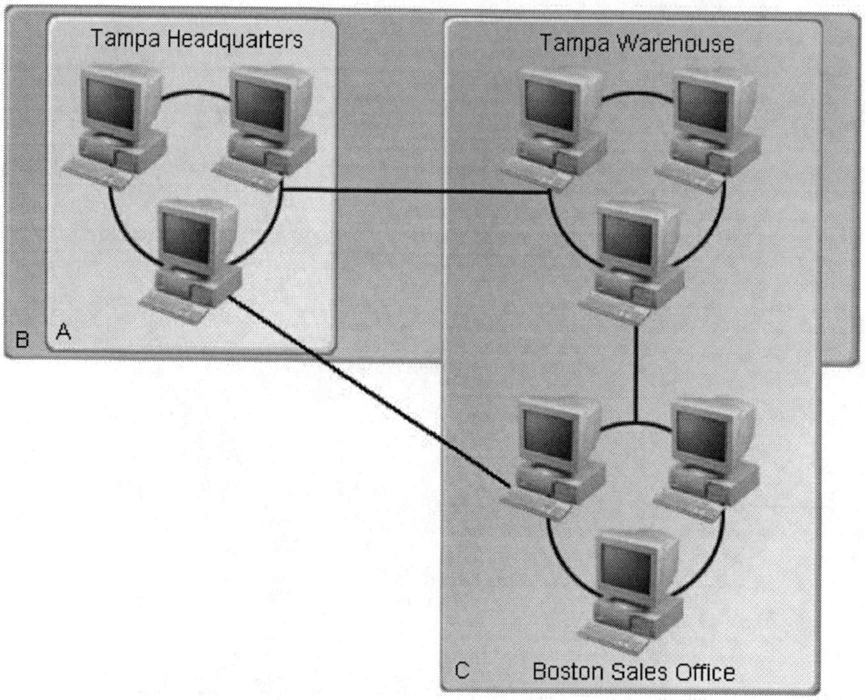

a) Section A—Tampa Headquarters

b) Section B—Tampa Headquarters and Tampa Warehouse

c) Section C—Tampa Warehouse and Boston Sales Office

5. **Match the type of network with its corresponding section in the figure.**

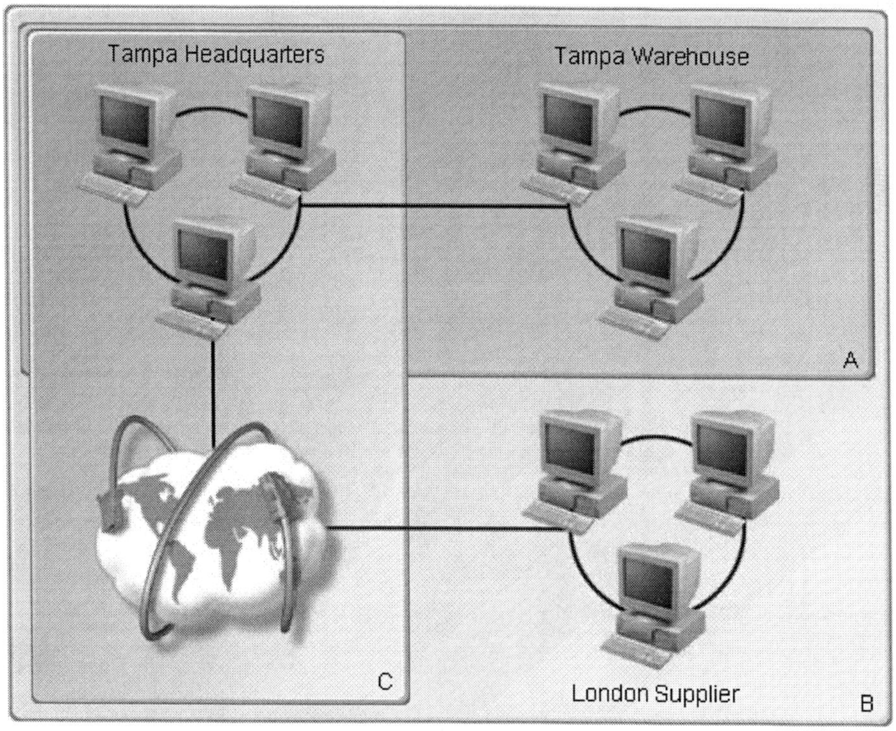

___	Section A—Tampa Headquarters and Tampa Warehouse	a.	Internet
___	Section B—Tampa Headquarters, Tampa Warehouse, London Supplier, and Internet	b.	Intranet
___	Section C—Tampa Headquarters and Internet	c.	Extranet

Lesson 1 Follow-up

In this lesson, you identified the basic components of current networking theory. Because any network you encounter will utilize at least some of these basic components and concepts, you need a good understanding of these fundamentals in order to succeed in your professional networking career.

1. **List some of the advantages and disadvantages you think various network topologies might have. Which topology do you think you might implement, and why?**

2. **Describe any background experience you have working with LANs, WANs, or other types of networks.**

NOTES

LESSON 2

Network Communications Methods

Lesson Time
1 hour(s), 30 minutes

Lesson Objectives:

In this lesson, you will identify the major network communications methods.

You will:

- Identify the primary network transmission methods.
- Identify the main types of media access methods.
- Identify the major network signaling methods.

Introduction

In the previous lesson, you learned about a number of different basic network components and layouts. All these network types employ a set of communications methods to transmit data. In this lesson, you will identify the primary transmission, media access, and signaling methods that networks use to communicate.

The essence of networking is communication—sending data from node to node, to be shared between users and systems. So, the methods networks use to communicate are vital to the proper functioning of the network. And, your understanding of those communications methods will be critical to your success as a networking professional.

This lesson covers the following CompTIA Network+ (2005) certification objectives:

- Topic B:
  - Objective 1.2: Specify the main features of 802.2 (Logical Link Control), 802.3 (Ethernet), 802.5 (Token Ring), 802.11 (wireless), and FDDI (Fiber Distributed Data Interface) networking technologies, including access methods, such as CSMA/CA (Carrier Sense Multiple Access/Collision Avoidance) and CSMA/CD (Carrier Sense Multiple Access/Collision Detection).
- Topic C:
  - Objective 1.6: Identify the purposes, features, and functions of modems.

TOPIC A

Transmission Methods

This lesson discusses three different categories of communications methods: transmission, media access, and signaling. In this topic, you will identify the primary transmission methods.

As a network professional, you'll probably be expected to monitor network performance and response time. The manner in which data is transferred between one or more nodes on the network can have a big impact on network traffic and performance. You'll need to understand the characteristics and potential effects of the transmission mechanisms—unicast, broadcast, or multicast—that are implemented on the networks you support.

Unicast Transmission

Definition:

Unicast transmission is a transmission method in which data is transferred from a specific source address to a specific destination address. Network nodes not involved in the transfer ignore the transmission.

CompTIA Network+ Exam Objectives

An Appendix is available to assist you in mapping CompTIA Network+ exam objectives to the course content. You can download the Appendix at the end of this lesson.

Example:

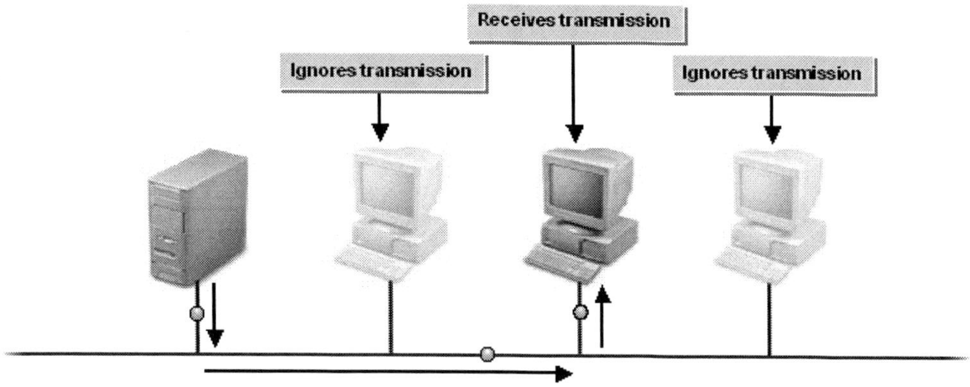

Figure 2-1: *Unicast transmission.*

Broadcast Transmission

Definition:

Broadcast transmission is a transmission method in which data goes from a source node to all other nodes on a network. Each one receives the data and acts on it. Network services that rely on broadcast transmissions can generate a great deal of network traffic.

Nodes sometimes use broadcast transmissions to discover if there is a particular service running on the network. The nodes broadcast a request for the service, and if a server is present, it responds. Conversely, some servers periodically advertise their presence to the entire network by means of broadcasts.

Example:

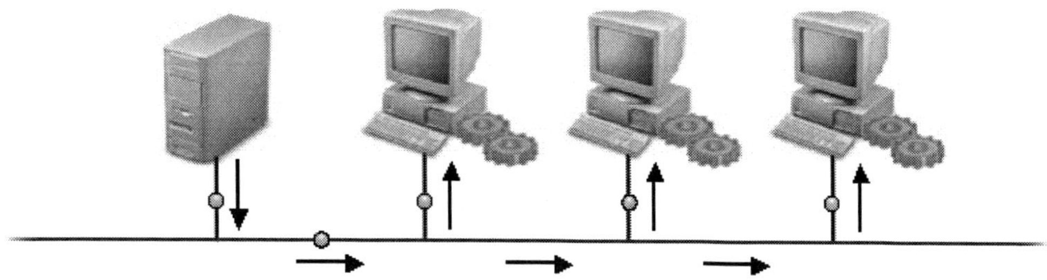

Figure 2-2: *Broadcast transmission.*

Multicast Transmission

Definition:

Multicast transmission is a transmission method in which data is sent from a server to specific nodes that are defined as members of a multicast group. Network nodes not in the group ignore the data.

Communication with nodes outside of a multicast group must be done through unicast or broadcast transmissions.

Example:

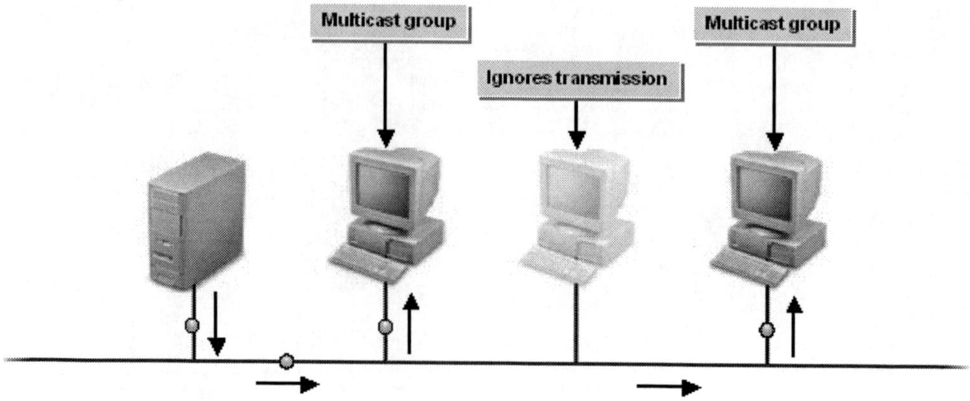

Figure 2-3: *Multicast transmission.*

ACTIVITY 2-1

Identifying Transmission Methods

Scenario:

In this activity, you will identify the primary network transmission methods.

1. **Identify the transmission method depicted in the graphic.**

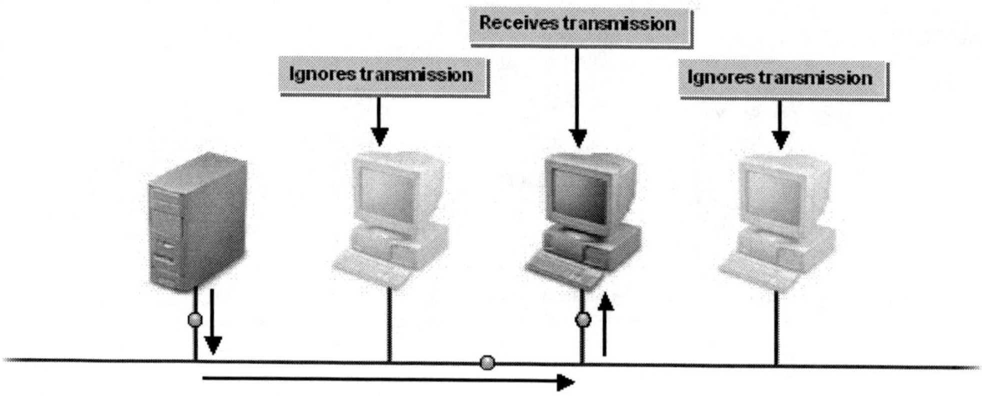

a) Unicast

b) Broadcast

c) Multicast

2. **True or False? Multicasting can be a more efficient use of the network media than unicast transmissions when many clients need to receive a communication from the server.**

    __ True

    __ False

---

3. **Match the transmission method to its description.**

___	Unicast	a.	Transmission of data to all nodes.
___	Broadcast	b.	Transmission of data directly to the intended receiving device.
___	Multicast	c.	Transmission of data to a subset of nodes.

TOPIC B

Media Access Methods

Communication method categories include transmission, media access, and signaling. In this topic, you will identify the most common media access methods.

Human communications follow unwritten rules that help everyone involved hear and be heard. Computers on a network must also follow rules so that every node has a fair chance to communicate. As a network technician, you need to understand these media access methods so that you can make sure that every node on your network follows the same set of rules.

Media Access Methods

Only one node can transmit at a time. The *media access method* determines whether or not a particular node can place data on the network at a given time. Media access methods fall into one of two categories. With *contention-based* or *competitive* media access, the nodes themselves negotiate for media access time. With *controlled* or *deterministic* media access, some centralized device or system controls when and for how long each node can transmit.

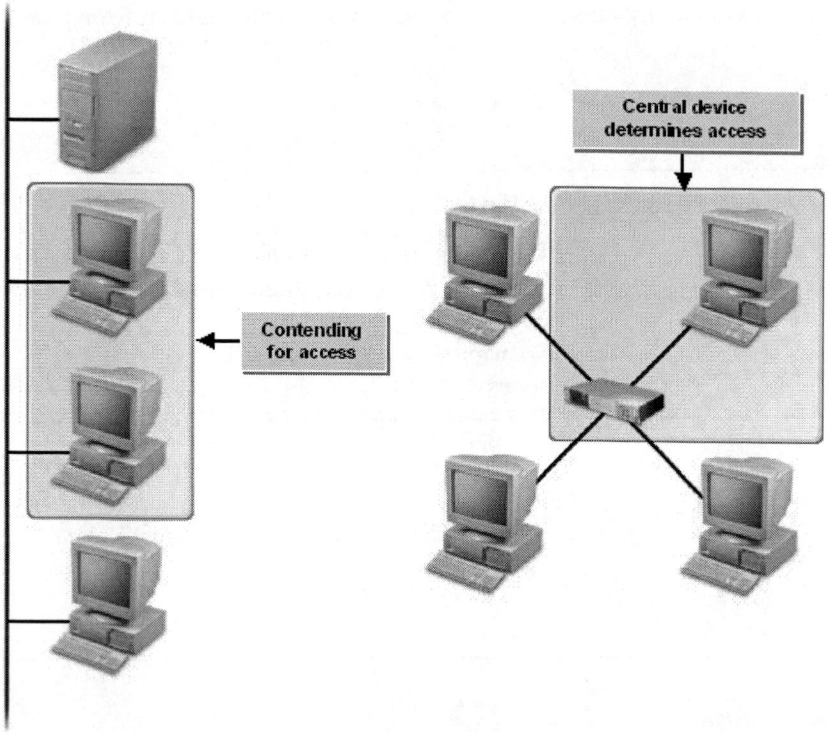

Figure 2-4: *Media access methods.*

Comparing Media Access Methods

Deterministic access methods are beneficial when network access is time critical. For example, in an industrial setting, key pieces of control and safety equipment, such as flow-shutoff sensors in chemical storage facilities, must be guaranteed transmission time. Deterministic systems ensure that a single node can't saturate the media; all nodes get a chance to send data. However, they require additional hardware and administrative time to configure and maintain. Contention-based systems are much simpler to set up and administer, but timely media access is not guaranteed to any node.

Multiplexed Media Access

Definition:

Multiplexing is a controlled media access method in which a central device combines the signals from multiple nodes and transmits the combined signal across the medium. Signals can be muliplexed using time-division multiplexing (TDM) or frequency-division multiplexing (FDM). Both rely on a central device, called a multiplexer, or *mux*, to manage the process.

TDM

With TDM, each sender is given exclusive access to the medium for a specific period of time. Nodes have exclusive access to the connection between themselves and the mux. The mux combines each node's signal in turn, sending the resulting combined signal over the primary network medium.

FDM

With FDM, data from multiple nodes is sent over multiple frequencies, or channels, over the network medium. Nodes have exclusive access to the connection between themselves and the mux. The mux puts each node's signal onto its own channel, sending the resulting combined signal over the primary network medium.

Example:

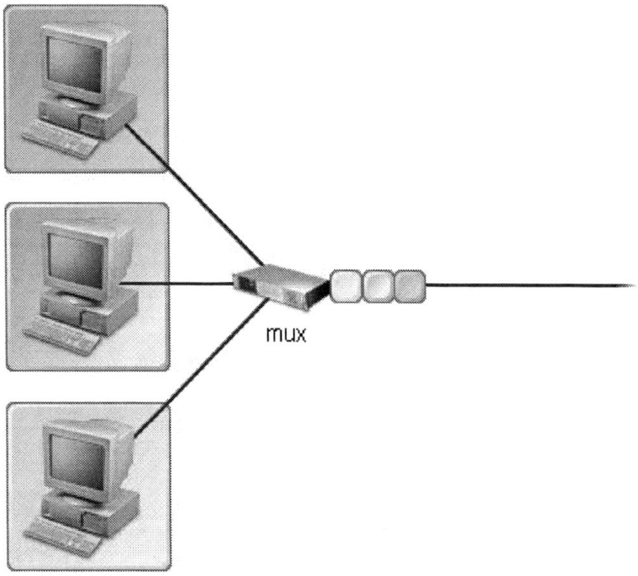

Figure 2-5: *Multiplexing.*

Polling

Definition:

Polling is a controlled media access method in which a central device contacts each node in turn to see whether it has data to transmit. Each node is guaranteed access to the media, but network time can be wasted polling nodes that have no data.

The IEEE has not standardized polling itself. However, the 802.12 standard defines 100VG-AnyLAN, which uses a polling technique called demand priority to control media access.

Demand Priority

Demand priority is a polling technique in which nodes signal their state—either ready to transmit or idle—to a hub. The hub polls the state of each node and grants permission to transmit in turn. Additionally, a node can signal that not only does it need to transmit, but also that its data is high priority. The hub will favor high-priority transmission requests. Safeguards in the protocol prevent nodes from assigning their every transmission request as high priority.

Example:

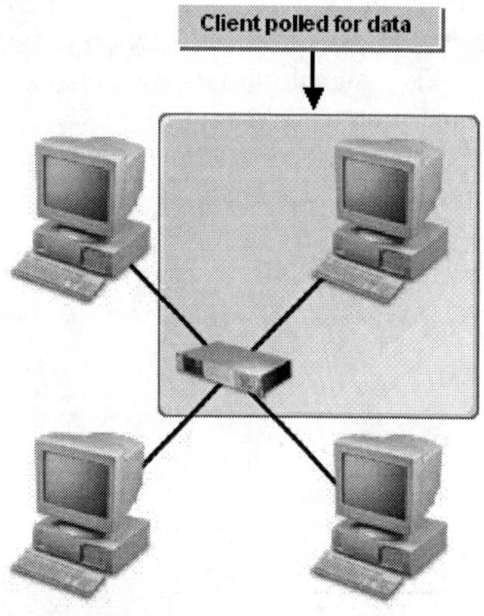

Figure 2-6: *Polling.*

Token-Based Media Access

Definition:

Token-based media access is a media access method in which computers pass a special sequence of bits called a *token* between them. Only the node holding this token can transmit on the network. After transmitting its data, or if it has no data to transmit, a node passes the token to the next computer on the network. Standards dictate how long a node can possess the token and what to do if the token is damaged or lost.

The IEEE has formalized token-based media access in the 802.5 and 802.4 standards; 802.5 defines the more-popular Token Ring network model used extensively by IBM, while 802.4 formalizes the token bus system used by ARCNET.

Advantages and Disadvantages

Token-based media access is said to be deterministic because each computer is guaranteed access to the media. This is ideal for networks in which timing is critical. Furthermore, even when traffic is very high, every station still has the same opportunity to transmit its data. However, token passing is inefficient when traffic is low because a station may have to wait while many other nodes hold the token and pass it on without transmitting data. Also, each node requires complex software to manage the token passing process and may need reconfiguring whenever you add or remove a node from the network.

Example:

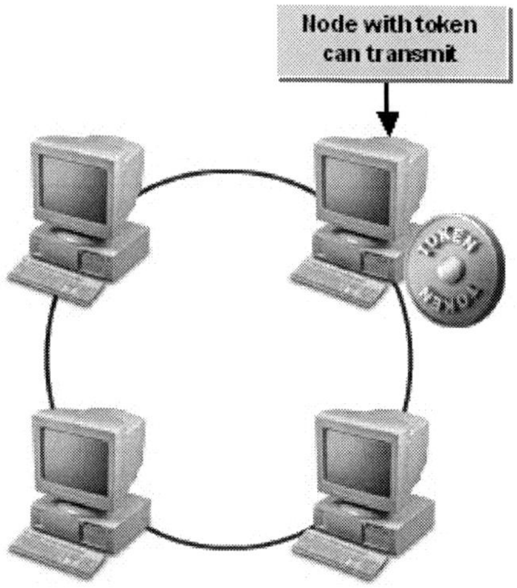

Figure 2-7: *Token-based media access.*

Carrier Sense Multiple Access/Collision Detection (CSMA/CD)

Definition:

Carrier Sense Multiple Access/Collision Detection (CSMA/CD) is a contention-based media access method in which nodes can transmit whenever they have data to send. However, they must detect and manage the inevitable collisions that occur when multiple nodes transmit at once.

In CSMA/CD:

1. A node has data to transmit.
2. The node determines if the media is available.
3. If so, the node transmits its data.
4. The node determines if a collision occurred by detecting the fragmented data that results from the collision.
5. If a collision occurred, the node waits a random *backoff* period measured in *milliseconds*, then repeats the process until successful.

The IEEE has formalized CSMA/CD in the 802.3 standard. This standard is implemented by the popular Ethernet networking standard.

Example:

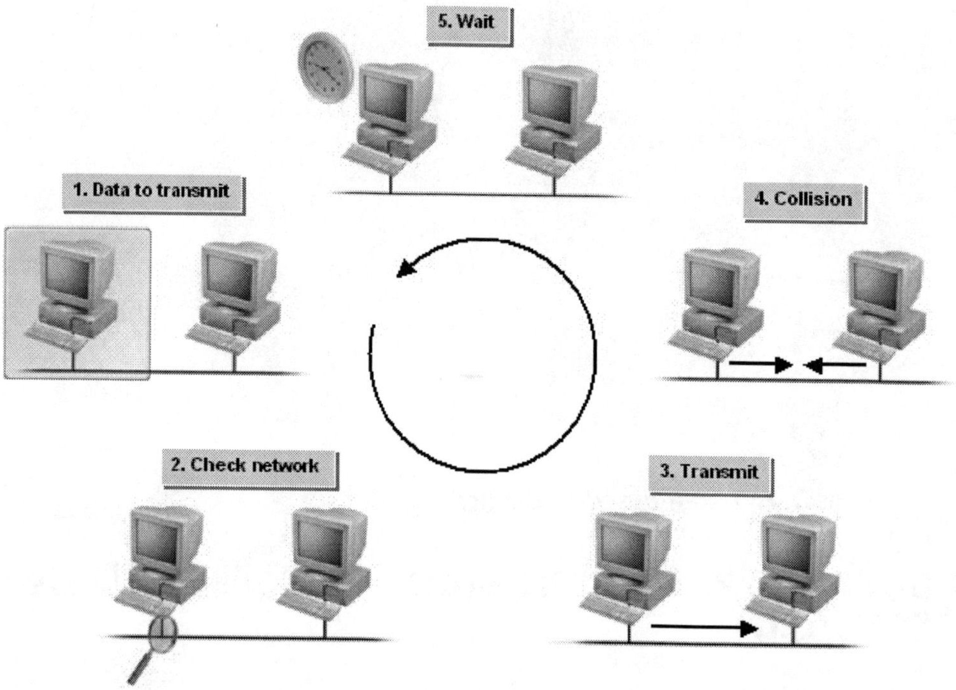

Figure 2-8: *CSMA/CD.*

Carrier Sense Multiple Access/Collision Avoidance (CSMA/CA)

Definition:

Carrier Sense Multiple Access/Collision Avoidance (CSMA/CA) is a contention-based media access method in which nodes can transmit whenever they have data to send. However, they take steps before they transmit to ensure that the media is unused.

In CSMA/CA:

1. A node has data to transmit.
2. The node determines if the media is available.
3. If so, the node transmits a jam signal, which advertises its intent to transmit data.
4. The node waits until all nodes should have had time to receive the jam signal.
5. The node transmits its data.
6. While transmitting, the node monitors the media for a jam signal from another node. If received, it stops transmitting and retries after a random delay.

Example:

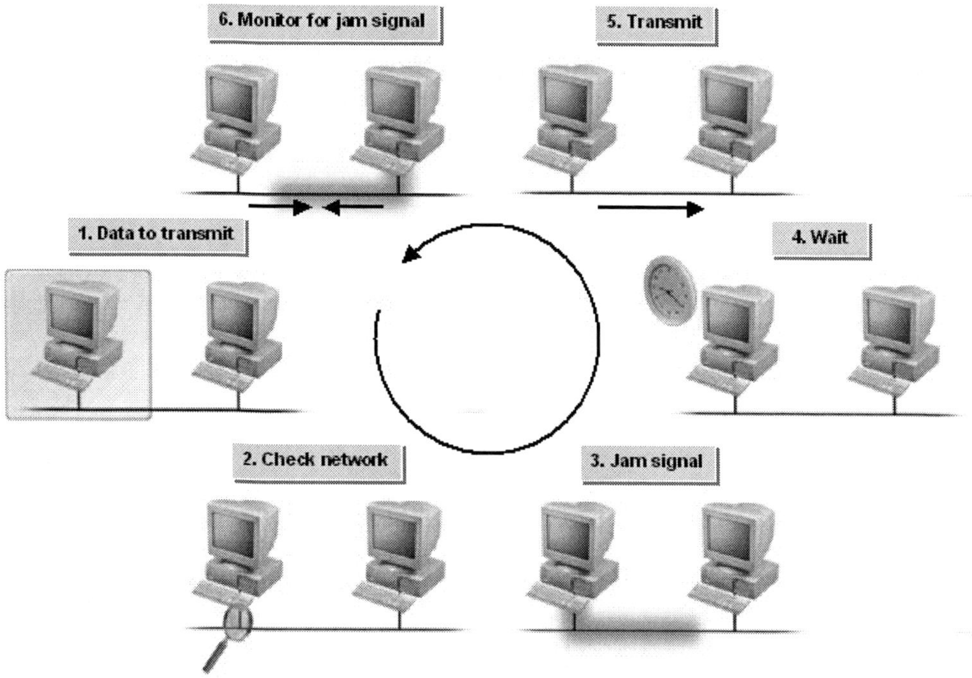

Figure 2-9: *CSMA/CA.*

Contention Domains

Definition:

A *contention domain*, also called a *collision domain*, is a group of nodes on a contention-based network that compete with each other for access to the media. Dividing a large network of many nodes into smaller contention domains reduces collisions and, therefore, improves network speed.

Example:

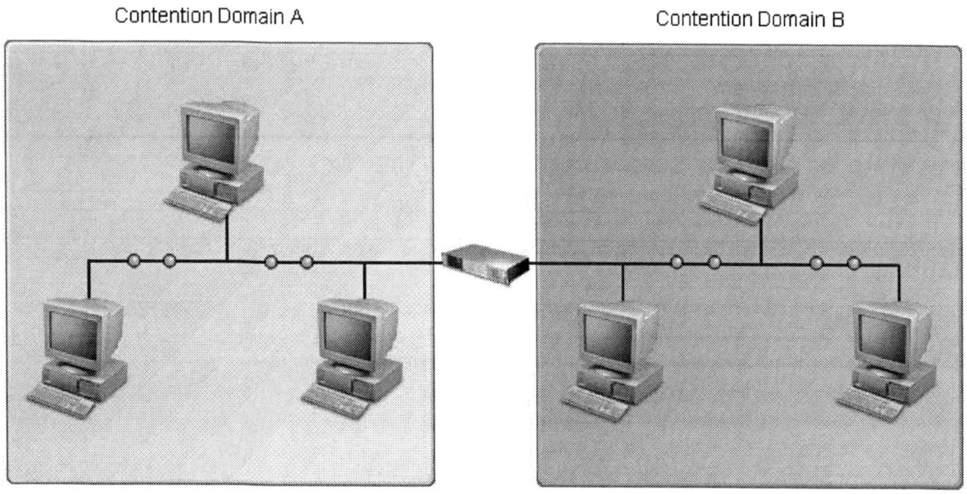

Figure 2-10: *A network divided into contention domains.*

ACTIVITY 2-2

Identifying Media Access Methods

Scenario:

In this activity, you will identify the main types of media access methods.

1. **From the following choices, select the statements that describe deterministic media access.**
   a) Controls when the node can place data on the network.
   b) Competes for network access.
   c) Is the most popular method and easiest to implement.
   d) Is used when the node must access the network in a predictable manner.

2. **From the following choices, select the statements that describe contention-based media access.**
   a) Controls when the node can place data on the network.
   b) Competes for network access.
   c) Is the most popular method and easiest to implement.
   d) Is used when the node must access the network in a predictable manner.

3. **True or False? Polling uses the bandwidth of the network medium more efficiently than CSMA/CD.**
   __ True
   __ False

4. **Which statement describes the purpose of a contention domain?**
   a) Defines the group of computers that will be polled by the hub.
   b) Logically groups CSMA/CD devices so that they can be more easily managed.
   c) Improves network performance by reducing the number of devices that contend for media access.

TOPIC C

Signaling Methods

In this topic, you will examine the ways in which electronic signals are put onto the communication media of your networks. You will investigate analog and digital, serial and parallel, and baseband and broadband transmission methods.

Trying to connect devices that use different signaling techniques is like trying to cram a square peg in a round hole. You need to be able to identify the signaling methods used by various networking devices so that you can install compatible devices and get them communicating.

Analog Signals

Definition:

An *analog signal* is one that oscillates over time between maximum and minimum values and can take on any value between those limits. The size, shape, and other characteristics of that *waveform* describe the analog signal and the information it carries.

Analog Signal Characteristics

The shape and characteristics of an analog signal are given specific terms, by which you can describe or categorize the signal. These terms are listed in the following table.

Term	Definition
Amplitude	The height (or depth) of a wave from the midpoint between the top and bottom of the waveform. Put another way, the amplitude is one half of the overall distance from the peak of the wave to the valley.
Cycle	One complete oscillation of an analog signal.
Frequency	The number of complete cycles per second in the wave, measured in *hertz*. One cycle per second equals one hertz. The frequency is also called the period of the wave.
Phase	A description of where a wave's cycle begins in relation to another wave. Thus, two waves of the same frequency that begin at the same time are said to be in phase. Those that either start at an offset from each other or have different frequencies are out of phase.
Wavelength	The distance between two successive peaks in a waveform.

Oscilloscope

An oscilloscope is a device that plots the amplitude of a signal as a function of time. Typically, it displays its output on a small CRT screen, letting you view the shape of the signal in real time. If you used an oscilloscope to view an analog signal, you would see a generally sine wave–shaped plot.

Sine Waves

A sine wave is a smoothly oscillating curve that is the result of calculating the sine of the angles between zero and 360 and plotting the results. A sine wave can vary in amplitude, phase, or frequency. A wave that follows a sine curve is said to be sinusoidal.

Example:

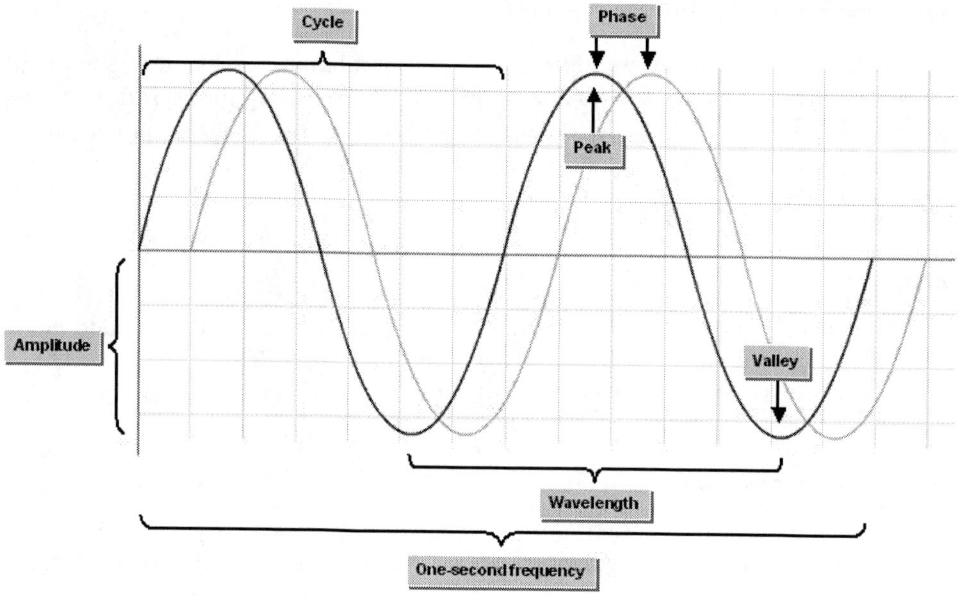

Figure 2-11: *The characteristics of an analog signal.*

Digital Signals

Definition:

A *digital signal* is an electrical signal that holds just two values—ones and zeroes. These values represent an on and off state, respectively. Digital data, which is a sequence of ones and zeroes, can be translated into a digital waveform. In computer systems and other digital devices, a waveform switches between two voltage levels representing zero at the ground or a zero voltage state and one at either a positive or negative voltage level.

Binary Data and Digital Signals

Because digital signals can hold just two values, they are well suited for encoding digital data, which is simply a sequence of ones and zeros. Data can be translated into a digital waveform by assigning zero to the ground, or zero voltage, state and one to either a positive or negative voltage level.

Units of Binary Data

Units of digital data are given specific names, as described in this table.

Unit	Description
Bit	A single 1 or 0

Unit	Description
Crumb	Two bits
Nibble	Four bits
Byte	Eight bits
Word	Depends on the processor. For a 32-bit processor, a word is 32 bits. For a 16-bit processor, a word is 16 bits.

Example:

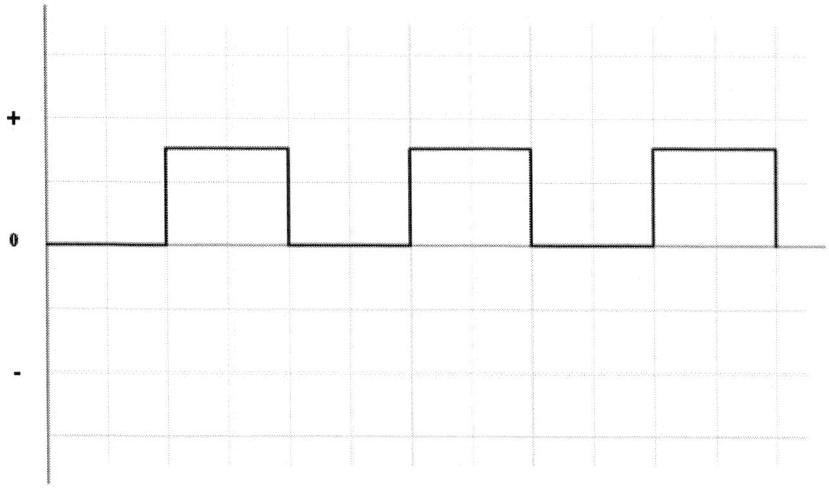

Figure 2-12: *A digital signal.*

Modulation and Demodulation

With analog transmissions, a high frequency oscillating signal is used as a base, or carrier, for the information. The lower frequency data signal is superimposed over the carrier's waveform in a process called *modulation*. The receiver decodes the signal, removing the data from the carrier, in a process called *demodulation*.

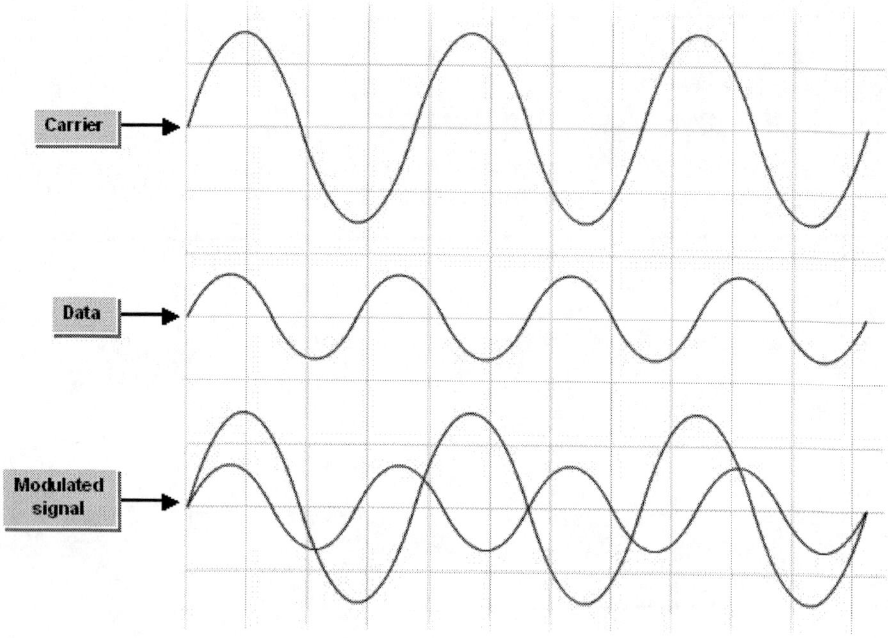

Figure 2-13: *Modulation.*

Advantages

High frequency waves transmit well over long distances. In contrast, low frequency signals degrade quickly with distance. By combining the low frequency data signal with a high frequency carrier signal, data can be sent over long distances with less degradation.

Modem

A *modem* is a device that modulates and demodulates data over an analog signal sent via a common telephone line. Its name is a blending of *mo*dulate and *dem*odulate.

Signal Reference Methods

To demodulate a signal, you must have a reference to determine the condition of the data signal. There are two ways to do this. With the first method, called differential, the signal on two halves of the transmission medium are compared to each other. The output difference becomes the resulting data. With the second method, called single-ended, the signal on one line is compared to ground. The difference from ground becomes the output data.

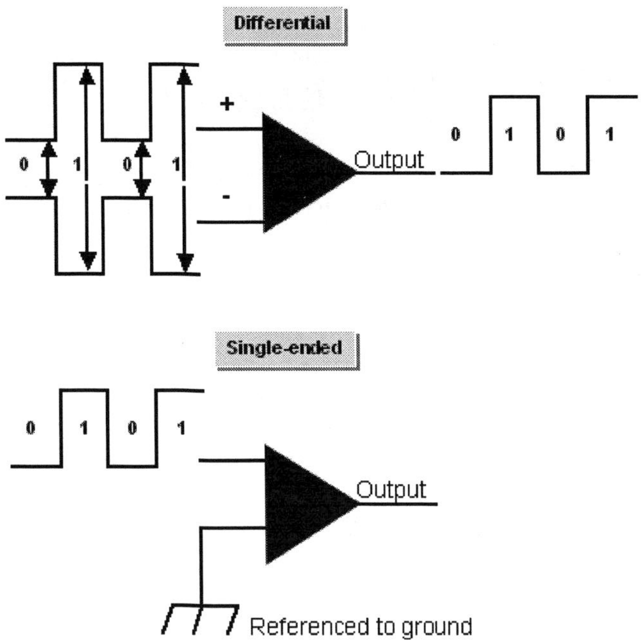

Figure 2-14: *Differential and single-ended demodulation.*

Codecs and DACs/ADCs

A *codec* is software or hardware that codes and decodes data to and from analog format. A modem is a type of codec. The specific chips that perform the digital-to-analog and analog-to-digital conversion are called DACs and ADCs, respectively.

Synchronous vs. Asynchronous

The receiver of an analog signal must have a way of delineating between bytes in a stream of data. It can do so using either asynchronous or synchronous techniques.

With asynchronous communications, special start and stop bit patterns are inserted between each byte of data. By watching for these bit patterns, the receiver can distinguish between the bytes in the data.

With synchronous communications, a byte is sent in a standardized time interval. The receiver assumes that one byte is transmitted every interval. However, the two devices must start and stop their reckoning of these intervals at precisely the same time.

Synchronous devices include a clock chip. A special bit pattern is inserted at specific intervals in the data stream, enabling the receiving device to synchronize its clock with the sender. With clocks synchronized, the receiver can use the predetermined time interval as the means to distinguish between bytes in the data stream.

Digital Data Transmission

Digital transmissions use voltage differences to directly represent the 1s and 0s that make up the data and are not modulated over a carrier. Data is converted into a digital waveform using on-off keying, Manchester encoding, or another scheme. Each bit takes a predefined time to transmit, and the sender and receiver synchronize their clocks using either a transmitted bit pattern or by monitoring for the reception of 1s bits.

On-Off Keying

On-off keying is a digital transmission encoding scheme in which a change in voltage from one state to another within a predetermined interval is symbolized by a 1. No voltage transition is symbolized by a 0. The receiver must synchronize its clock with the sender, which it can do by watching for 1s.

Variations of this scheme are called Non-Return to Zero (NRZ) and Non-Return to Zero Inverted (NRZI) encoding. On-off keying is used over serial ports and other relatively low-speed digital data connections.

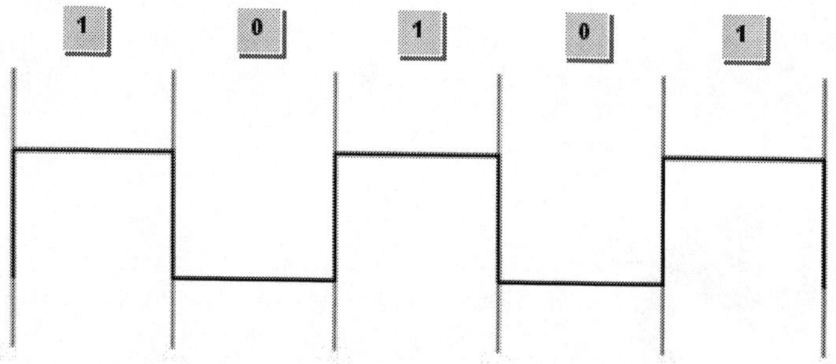

Figure 2-15: *On-off keying of the value 10101.*

Because the receiver synchronizes its clock by watching for 1s, problems can arise when long sequences of 1s or 0s must be sent. The receiver may not be able to synchronize its clock for a long interval. With its clock out of sync, the receiver could incorrectly decipher how many 1s or 0s have been transmitted, leading to corrupted data.

Manchester Encoding

Manchester encoding was developed as a way to overcome the limits of on-off keying. It represents the transition from positive to ground with a 0 and the transition from ground to positive with a 1. Thus, every bit involves a voltage transition and the problem of transmitting a long string of 1s or 0s is eliminated.

Manchester encoding is used over Ethernet and other high-speed digital data connections.

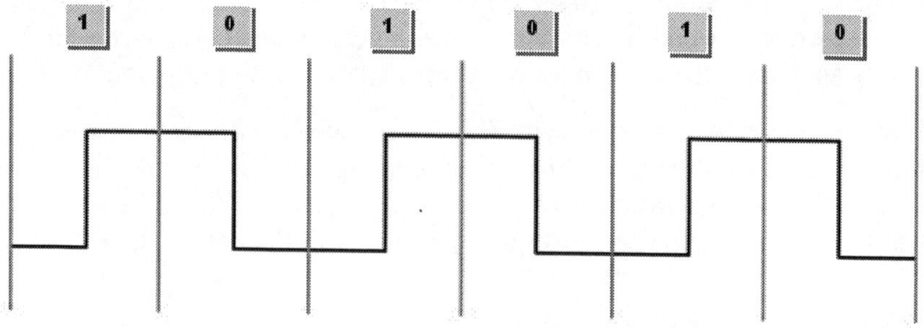

Figure 2-16: *Manchester encoding of the value 101010.*

Serial Data Transmission

With serial data transmission, bits are transmitted, one per clock cycle, across a single transmission medium. Synchronization, start/stop, and error correction bits are transmitted in line with data bits, limiting the overall throughput of data. Serial transmissions can delineate bytes by using either synchronous or asynchronous techniques.

Many common networking systems, such as Ethernet, use serial data transmission. Keyboard, mouse, modems, and other devices can connect to your PC over a serial transmission port.

Parallel Data Transmission

With parallel data transmission, multiple bits are transmitted across multiple transmission lines. Many bits—even multiple bytes—are transferred per clock cycle. Synchronization, start/stop, and error correction bits can be transmitted in line with data bits. More often, they are sent over additional transmission lines, improving overall throughput of data.

An obvious use of parallel transmission is the parallel port on your computer, to which you can connect printers or scanners. Other uses include the system bus inside your PC, the SCSI data bus, and the PC Card bus.

Baseband Transmissions

In *baseband* transmissions, digital signaling is used to send data over a single transmission medium using the entire bandwidth of that medium. Signals are sent in pulses of electrical energy or light. Devices can send and receive over the same baseband medium, but they cannot simultaneously send and receive. Multiple baseband signals can be combined and sent over a single medium by using time-division multiplexing.

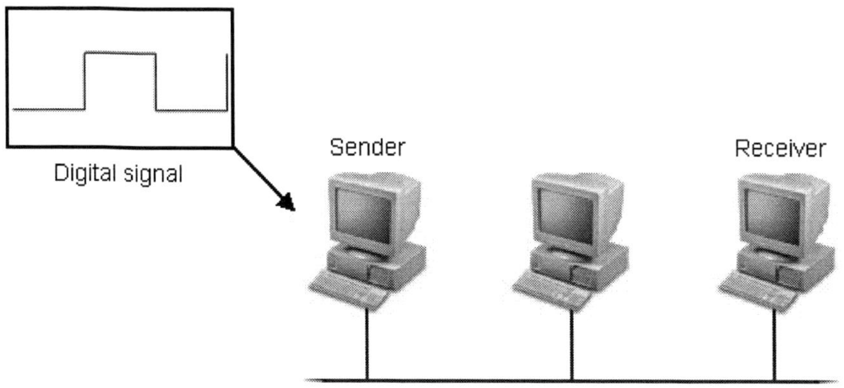

Figure 2-17: *Baseband transmission.*

Broadband Transmissions

In *broadband* transmissions, analog signaling is used to send data over a transmission medium using a portion of the bandwidth of that medium. Signals are sent as waves of electromagnetic or optical energy. Devices cannot send and receive over the same broadband channel. However, multiple broadband signals can be combined and sent over a single medium by using frequency-division multiplexing.

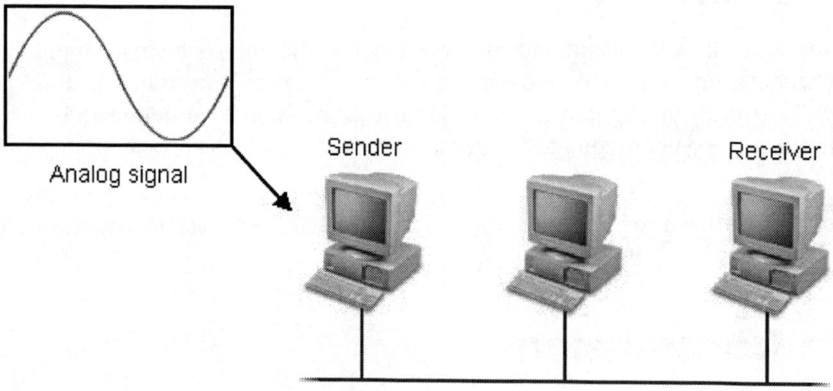

Figure 2-18: *Broadband transmission.*

ACTIVITY 2-3

Identifying Signaling Method Terminology

Scenario:

In this activity, you will identify the major network signaling methods.

---

1. **Match the signal characteristic with its description.**

___	Frequency	a.	The distance a wave varies from the starting value.
___	Amplitude	b.	The period of the wave, measured in hertz.
___	Wavelength	c.	The distance between peaks or crests in a wave.

---

2. **Constantly varying electrical signals that change in a smooth, rounded pattern are:**

   a) Analog

   b) Digital

   c) Discrete

   d) Demodulated

---

3. **True or False? Binary bits are used to create digital signals.**

   __ True

   __ False

4. **Place these units of binary data in order from smallest to largest.**

   Crumb

   Word

   Byte

   Bit

   Nibble

---

5. **The modulation/demodulation process:**

   a) Enables transmission of data signals over long distances.

   b) Occurs only on the sending end of the transmission.

   c) Places the data signal on top of and removes it from a high frequency analog carrier.

   d) Sends the data as a digital signal.

---

6. **Digital signals are built around the _____ number system.**

   a) Hexadecimal

   b) Binary

   c) Decimal

   d) Alphanumeric

---

7. **Serial digital data:**

   a) Is synchronized by a clock signal.

   b) Uses multiple lines to send data a byte at a time.

   c) Is the data signaling method typically used within a computer system.

   d) Can be synchronous or asynchronous.

---

8. **The transmission method that allows multiple signals to be carried separately on the same media at the same time is:**

   a) Baseband.

   b) Broadband.

   c) Modulated.

   d) Multicast.

Lesson 2 Follow-up

As you saw in this topic, understanding the methods networking devices use to communicate is vital to being able to ensure the proper functioning of your network. Having investigated the ways nodes send data to each other, you are well positioned to be a successful networking professional.

1. **How will you use unicast, broadcast, and multicast transmissions in your networking environment?**

2. **In your opinion, which media access method is best and why?**

3. **Which is better for your networking needs, devices that use analog or digital signaling methods? Why?**

LESSON 3
Network Data Delivery

Lesson Time
1 hour(s), 30 minutes

Lesson Objectives:

In this lesson, you will identify network data delivery methods.

You will:

- Identify the elements of the data addressing and delivery process.
- Identify common network connection mechanisms.
- Identify techniques for ensuring reliable network data delivery.

Introduction

In the previous lesson, you examined the transmission and signaling methods used on various types of networks. However, just sending data out onto the wire isn't enough. The data must arrive at its intended destination reliably and unaltered. In this lesson, you will learn how data is delivered to its destination by examining data addressing, connection mechanisms, and the techniques that ensure the reliable delivery of data.

When users make a request for a network service or send data across your network, they assume that their request or the data arrives at its destination in a timely manner. However, network requests or data can be misdirected, intercepted, or altered as they travel to their destination. By understanding how networks deliver data, you can ensure that requests for services and data travel reliably through your network.

This lesson covers the following CompTIA Network+ (2005) certification objective:

- Topic A:
  - Objective 2.1: Identify a MAC (Media Access Control) address and its parts.

TOPIC A

Data Addressing and Delivery

One of the first things that must happen to ensure that a network request arrives at its intended destination is data addressing. Getting data packaged for delivery so it can be routed to its correct destination is the root of networking. In this topic, you will examine how data is packaged and addressed so that it can be accurately delivered to its intended destination.

When users make network requests, they expect that the requests arrive at their destination so they can be processed. If the data is being packaged or addressed incorrectly for your network, users will experience symptoms of network communication problems. If you understand how data is packaged by the client and then addressed to travel to its destination on your network, you can use this information to identify causes of network communication problems.

MAC Address

Definition:

A *MAC address*, also called a physical address, is a unique, hardware-level address assigned to every networking device by its manufacturer. MAC addresses are six bytes long. The first three bytes uniquely identify the manufacturer and are referred to as the Organizationally Unique Identifier (OUI). The remaining three bytes identify the device itself and are known as the Universal LAN MAC address.

Example:

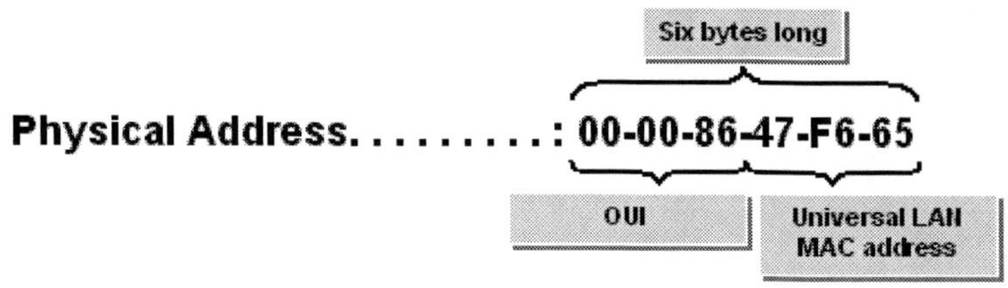

Figure 3-1: *A typical MAC address.*

Determining the MAC Address

Depending on your operating system and version, you can use the following techniques to determine the MAC address of the network adapter in your computer.

Operating System	Method to Determine MAC Address
Windows 9x	Choose Start→Run, type winipcfg, and press Enter.
Windows NT, Windows 2000, Windows Server 2003, and Windows XP	At a command prompt, enter `ipconfig /all`
Windows Server 2003 and Windows XP	Right-click the connection, choose Status, select the Support tab, and click Details.
Linux	At a command prompt, enter `ipconfig -a`
Novell NetWare	At a console prompt, enter `config`
Cisco IOS	Enter `sh int` *`interface_name`*

ACTIVITY 3-1

Identifying the Local MAC Address

There is a simulated version of this activity available on the CD-ROM that shipped with this course. You can run this simulation on any Windows computer to review the activity after class, or as an alternative to performing the activity as a group in class. The activity simulation can be launched either directly from the CD-ROM by clicking the Interactives link and navigating to the appropriate one, or from the installed data file location by opening the C:\Data\Simulations\Lesson#\Activity# folder and double-clicking the executable (.exe) file.

Setup:

You are logged on as your User## account. Your password is !Pass1234.

Scenario:

In this activity, you will identify your computer's MAC address.

What You Do	How You Do It
1. If necessary, **unlock your computer.**	a. If the Computer Locked dialog box appears on your screen, **press Ctrl+Alt+Del** to open the Unlock Computer dialog box.
	b. In the Password text box, **type *!Pass1234* and click OK.**
2. **Open the Status dialog box for your Local Area Connection.**	a. **Choose Start→Control Panel→Network Connections.**
	b. **Right-click Local Area Connection and choose Status.**
3. **Identify your MAC address.**	a. **Select the Support tab.**
	b. **Click Details.**
	c. To determine the MAC address, **identify the Physical Address value.**

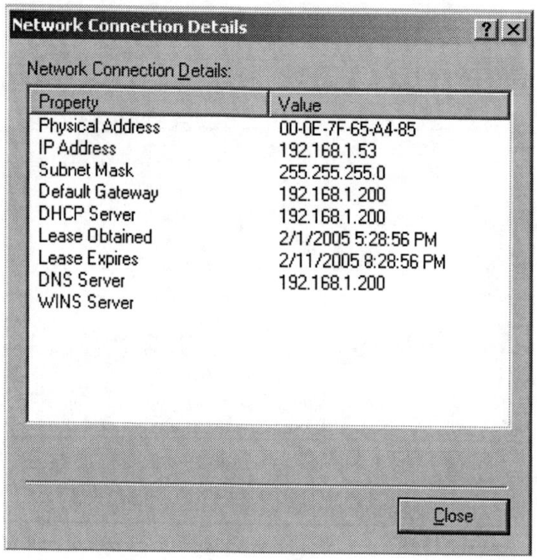

d. **Click Close twice.**

Network Address

Definition:

A *network address* is a protocol-specific identifier assigned to a node. A network address typically includes two parts: one that identifies the network and another that identifies the node. A network address is typically a number and is mapped to the MAC address by software running on the nodes.

Example:

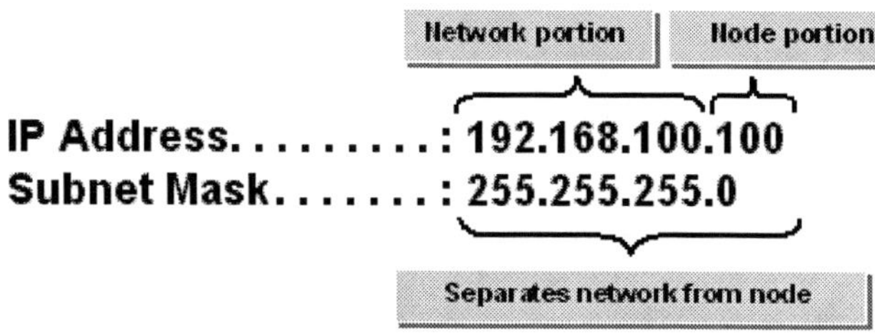

Figure 3-2: *A TCP/IP network address.*

ACTIVITY 3-2

Identifying the Local Network Address

There is a simulated version of this activity available on the CD-ROM that shipped with this course. You can run this simulation on any Windows computer to review the activity after class, or as an alternative to performing the activity as a group in class. The activity simulation can be launched either directly from the CD-ROM by clicking the Interactives link and navigating to the appropriate one, or from the installed data file location by opening the C:\Data\Simulations\Lesson#Activity# folder and double-clicking the executable (.exe) file.

Scenario:

In this activity, you will identify your computer's network address.

What You Do	How You Do It
1. **Open the Status dialog box for the Local Area Connection.**	a. **Choose Start→Control Panel→Network Connections.**
	b. **Right-click Local Area Connection and choose Status.**
2. **Identify the network address.**	a. **Select the Support tab.**

b. To determine the network address, **identify the IP Address value.**

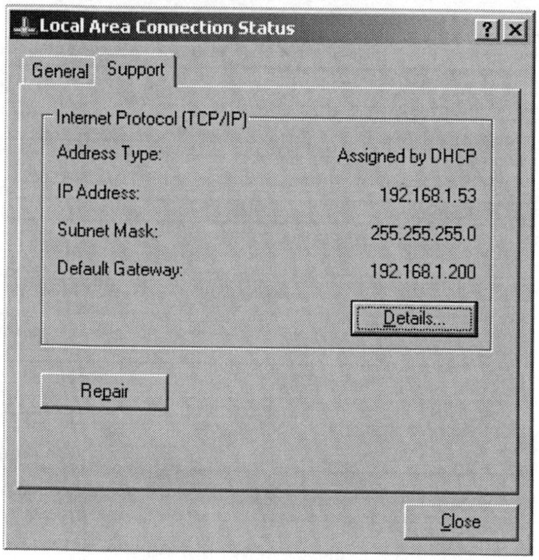

c. **Click Close.**

Network Names

Definition:

A *network name* is a word or phrase assigned to a node to help users and technicians more easily recognize the device. A naming service, enabled by software running on one or more nodes, maps a network name to a network address or MAC address.

Example:

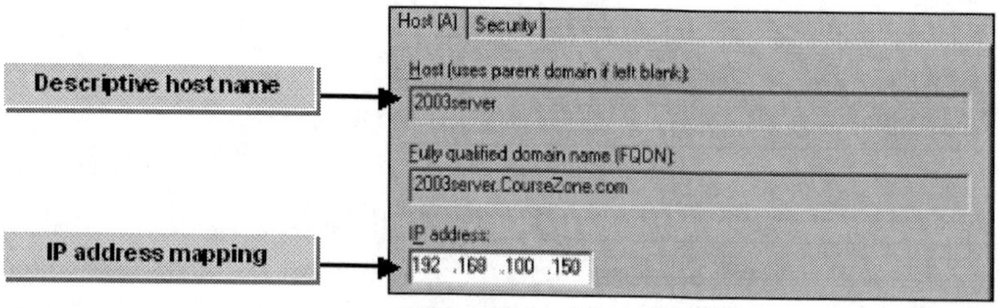

Figure 3-3: *A DNS network name.*

Naming Services

Naming services map network names to network addresses. There are many naming services in use, a few of which are listed in the following table.

Naming Service	Description
DNS (Domain Name Service)	The naming service used on the Internet and many TCP/IP-based networks. For example, the IP address 209.85.165.99 might map to **www.google.com**.
NetBIOS	A simple, broadcast-based naming service.
WINS (Windows Internet Naming Service)	An older type of naming service used on Windows-based networks.

ACTIVITY 3-3

Identifying the Local Computer Name

There is a simulated version of this activity available on the CD-ROM that shipped with this course. You can run this simulation on any Windows computer to review the activity after class, or as an alternative to performing the activity as a group in class. The activity simulation can be launched either directly from the CD-ROM by clicking the Interactives link and navigating to the appropriate one, or from the installed data file location by opening the C:\Data\Simulations\Lesson#\Activity# folder and double-clicking the executable (.exe) file.

Scenario:

In this activity, you will identify your computer's network name.

What You Do	How You Do It
1. **Open the System Properties dialog box.**	a. **Click Start.**
	b. **Right-click My Computer and choose Properties.**

2. **Identify your computer's network name.**

    a. **Select the Computer Name tab.**

    b. **Identify the Full Computer Name value.**

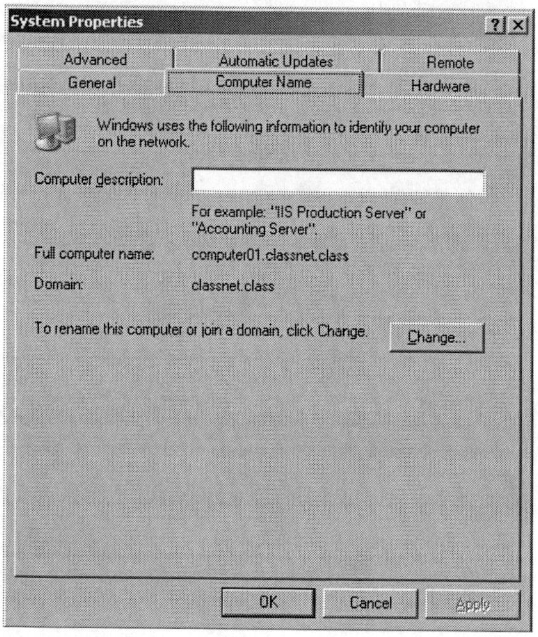

    c. **Click Cancel.**

Packets

Definition:

A *packet*, also called a *datagram*, is a unit of data sent across the network. In general, all packets contain three parts: a header, the data itself, plus a trailer or footer. In the simplest case, a sender transmits one packet and then waits for an acknowledgement from the recipient, an "ACK" signal. If the recipient is busy, the sender sits idle until it receives the ACK, after which it sends the next packet. Throughput could be increased if data could be sent in larger packages, with the recipient sending fewer acknowledgements. The contents of a packet depend on the network protocol in use.

Table 3-1: *Packet Contents*

Packet Component	Description
Header	Made up of a preamble, and destination and source addresses, the header describes the source and target of the packet.
Data	The data being transmitted.
Trailer or footer	An error detection code (EDC).

Example:

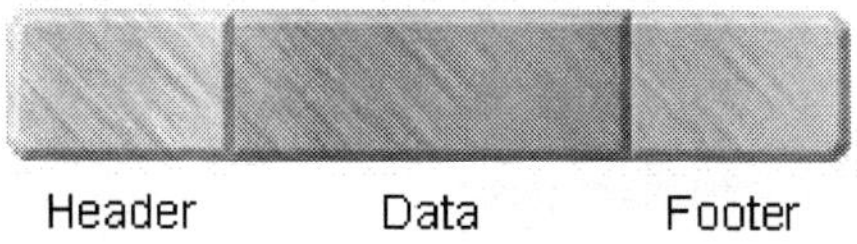

Figure 3-4: *A packet.*

Ethernet Packet Header Contents

An Ethernet packet's header begins with an 8-byte preamble. The preamble is a standardized pattern of bits that the receiving node uses to synchronize timing so that it can properly read the rest of the packet.

Following the preamble, the header contains the destination node's 6-byte MAC address. Following that is the sending node's 6-byte MAC address. These addresses help nodes and other networking devices deliver the packet to its destination and provide the necessary information for replies.

The header may contain other data, such as bytes identifying the type of data contained in the packet.

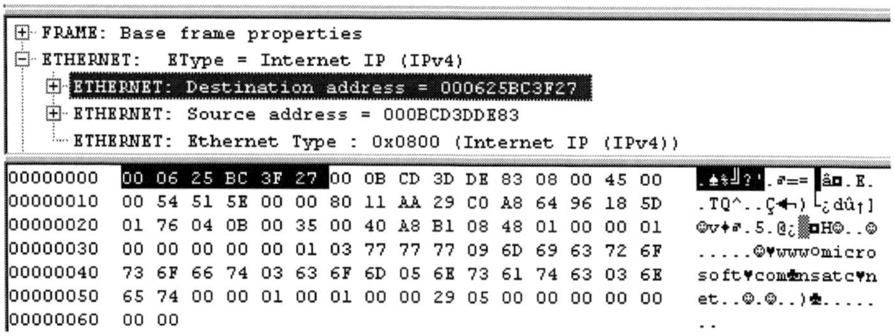

Figure 3-5: *An Ethernet header showing the destination address.*

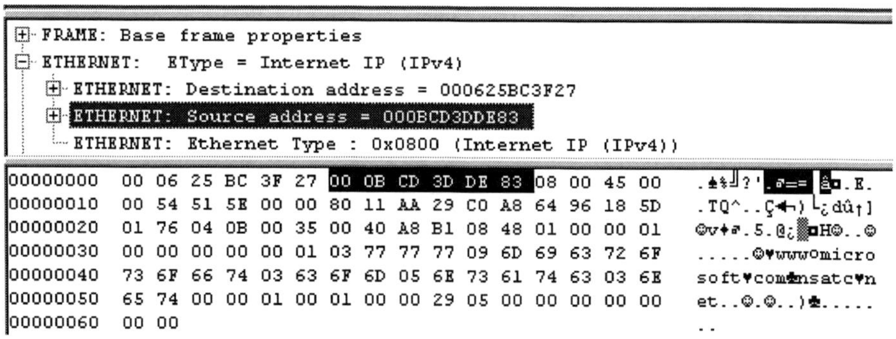

Figure 3-6: *An Ethernet header showing the source address.*

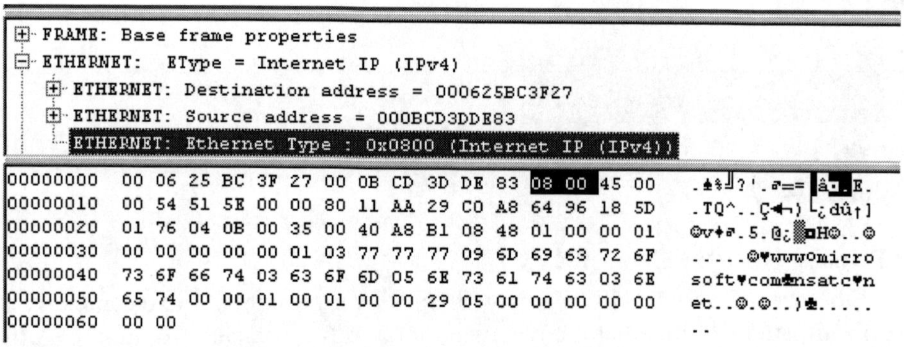

Figure 3-7: *An Ethernet header showing the protocol.*

Ethernet Packet Footer Contents

An Ethernet packet's footer contains the results of a mathematical operation performed on the data. The sending node computes an error checking value for the data to be sent. The receiving node performs the same calculation and compares its error checking value with the one sent with the data. If its results match those contained in the packet's footer, then the packet is assumed to have arrived undamaged.

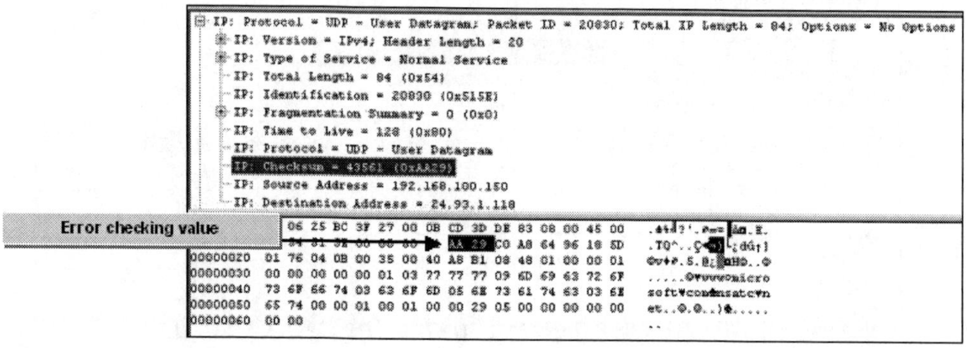

Figure 3-8: *The error checking value in the packet's footer.*

ACTIVITY 3-4

Identifying Components of Packet Addressing and Delivery

Scenario:

In this activity, you will identify components of packet addressing and delivery.

1. **Select the example of a MAC address.**
   a) webserver1
   b) 201.183.100.2
   c) 00-08-02-D4-F6-4C
   d) M123-X7-FG-128

2. **Select the example of a network address.**
   a) webserver1
   b) 201.183.100.2
   c) 00-08-02-D4-F6-4C
   d) M123-X7-FG-128

3. **Select the example of a network name.**
   a) webserver1
   b) 201.183.100.2
   c) 00-08-02-D4-F6-4C
   d) M123-X7-FG-128

4. **Match the packet component with its definition.**

___	Header	a.	Includes an error checking code.
___	Data	b.	Includes the destination address and source address.
___	Footer	c.	Includes the data to be transmitted.

TOPIC B

Network Connection Mechanisms

You have looked at how data is packaged and addressed for delivery. Before they can exchange packets, however, the two nodes involved must connect to each other. In this topic, you will examine the network connection mechanisms.

When a node has data to send to another node in the network, it must establish a connection to the other node. This connection will be used to send the packet. If a connection cannot be established, the packet can't be sent. Knowing the ways that devices on a network are supposed to connect will help you identify the symptoms that occur when those devices don't link up.

Simplex Mode

Simplex mode communication is the one-way transmission of information. There is no return path. Because the transmission operates in only one direction, simplex mode can use the full bandwidth of the medium for transmission.

Radio and television broadcasts and public address (PA) systems operate in simplex mode. However, this mode is not used in networking.

Some of the very first serial connections between computers were simplex mode connections.

Figure 3-9: *Simplex transmissions occur in one direction only.*

Half Duplex Mode

Half duplex mode communications permit two-way communications, but in only one direction at a time. When one device sends, the other must receive; then they can switch roles to transfer information in the other direction. Half duplex mode can use the full bandwidth of the medium because the transmission occurs in only one direction at a time.

Some networking devices use this transmission mode, as do devices such as walkie-talkies and citizen band (CB) radios.

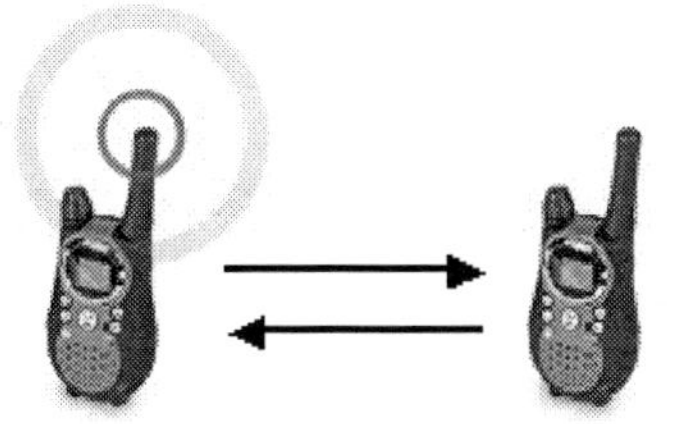

Figure 3-10: *Half duplex communications are two way.*

Full Duplex Mode

Full duplex mode communications permit simultaneous two-way communications. A device can both send and receive at the same time. Sending and receiving could occur over different channels or on the same channel. Generally, neither the sender nor the receiver can use the full bandwidth for their individual transmission because transmissions are allowed in both directions simultaneously.

Telephone systems are full duplex devices—all persons involved can talk simultaneously. Many modern networking cards support full duplex mode.

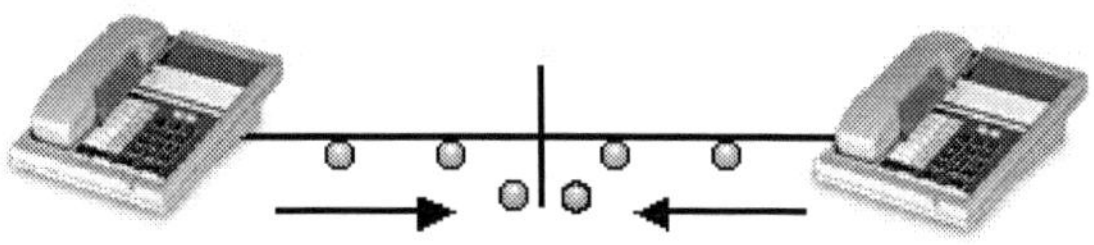

Figure 3-11: *Full duplex permits simultaneous two-way communications.*

Point-to-Point Connections

A point-to-point connection is a direct connection between two nodes. Data transmitted by one node goes directly to the other. Dial-up modem connections are point-to-point connections.

A terminal connected to a host is another example of a point-to-point connection.

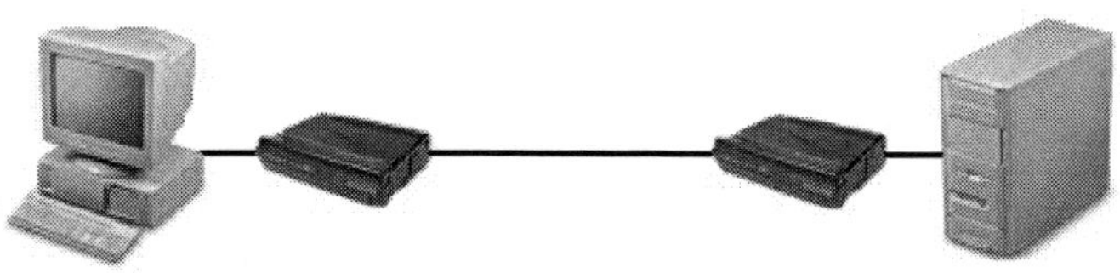

Figure 3-12: *A point-to-point connection.*

Multipoint Connections

Multipoint connections are connections between many nodes. Each multipoint connection has more than two endpoints. A signal transmitted by any device on the medium is not private. All devices that share the medium can detect the signal but do not receive it.

Multipoint connections are the most common way to physically connect a network. Physical bus and star networks are examples of multipoint connections.

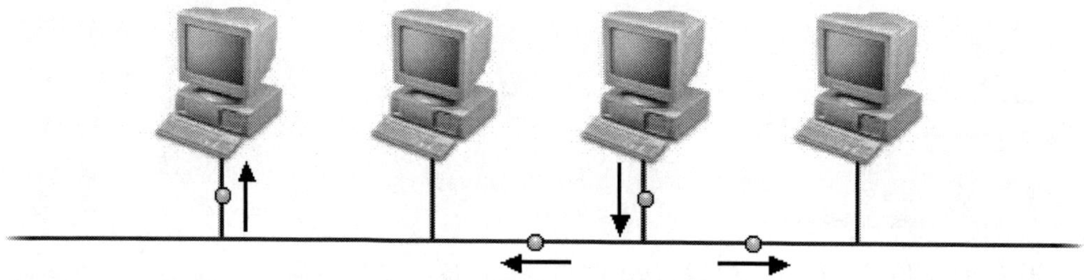

Figure 3-13: *A multipoint connection.*

Radiated Connections

A radiated, or broadcast, connection is a wireless point-to-point or multipoint connection between devices. Wireless LAN, infrared, and WiFi networks are all radiated connections.

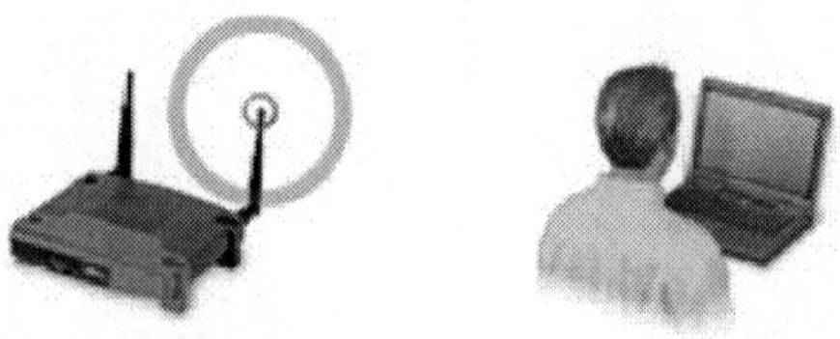

Figure 3-14: *A radiated connection.*

Connection Services

Connection services ensure reliable delivery by detecting and attempting to correct transmission problems.

Connection Service	Description
Unacknowledged connectionless	This service provides no acknowledgement of successfully transmitted data. The application must provide its own reliability checks. Simplex communications use this type of service.
Acknowledged connectionless	Nodes do not establish a virtual connection. However, they do acknowledge the successful receipt of packets. Web (HTTP) communications use this type of connection service.
Connection-oriented	Nodes establish a virtual connection for the duration of the session. Nodes negotiate communication parameters and typically share security information to establish a connection. This connection service provides the means for flow control, packet sequencing, and error recovery functions. Traditional, non-web-based networking applications often use connection-oriented services.

Connection Service Types Compared to Everyday Communication Methods

When trying to understand and remember the different connection service types, it may help to compare each type to other communications in your everyday life:

- Unacknowledged connectionless service can be compared to regular USPS mail. You drop a letter in the mailbox and get no notification if it's delivered.
- Acknowledged connectionless service can be compared to requesting a return-receipt for your letter from the post office. In this instance, you get acknowledgement that your letter was delivered.
- Connection-oriented service is similar to a phone connection. You get a virtual private channel between you and the person you call.

ACTIVITY 3-5

Examining Network Connection Methods

Scenario:

In this activity, you will examine network connection methods.

1. **Match the form of transmission with its description.**

___	Simplex	a.	Two-way transmission of data, but only in one direction at a time.
___	Half duplex	b.	One-way transmission of data.
___	Full duplex	c.	Two-way transmission of data, in both directions simultaneously.

2. **Which transmission methods enable the sender to use the full bandwidth of the medium?**

   a) Simplex

   b) Half duplex

   c) Full duplex

   d) Full simplex

3. **Match the connection service with its description**

___	Unacknowledged connectionless	a.	With this connection service, nodes acknowledge the successful receipt of packets. However, they do not establish a virtual connection.
___	Acknowledged connectionless	b.	With this connection service, applications provide their own reliability checks. No acknowledgement of successfully transmitted data is provided by the service.
___	Connection-oriented	c.	With this connection service, nodes negotiate communication parameters and share security information to establish a virtual connection for the duration of the session. Additionally, this connection service provides the means for flow control, packet sequencing, and error recovery functions.

TOPIC C

Reliable Delivery Techniques

In terms of network data delivery, you have identified two pieces of the puzzle—data addressing and network connection mechanisms. Once you have the data properly packaged and addressed, and a functional network connection established between the source and destination computers, you are ready to transmit data across the network. In this topic, you will examine the techniques that make sure that data is transmitted completely and accurately across the network.

Data that is sent through a network can encounter several variables that can delay or even change the data before it is received. The challenge for network administrators is to implement delivery techniques within the network to ensure that data is transmitted correctly and accurately across the network. When implemented, these delivery techniques can detect errors in data transmissions and recover from the errors.

Error Detection

Networking devices should detect when errors have been introduced into transmitted data and recover gracefully. Senders should transmit enough data, but not too much, so that the recipient neither sits idle nor is overwhelmed by data. Electronic interference, loose connections, substandard equipment, and other factors can cause signals to be changed while data is in transit. Networking devices ensure reliable delivery by using error detection and flow control.

Error detection is the process of determining if transmitted data has been received correctly and completely. Typically, the sender attaches extra bits in the form of an error detection code (EDC) to the transmitted data to indicate its original contents. The receiver checks that EDC to determine if the data has been altered en route.

- If the EDCs match, the data is processed by the receiver.
- If the receiver finds an error, it requests that the data be retransmitted.
- Error detection can also include a correction component, *error detection and correction (EDAC)*, where if an error is found in the data, it can be rebuilt by the receiver.

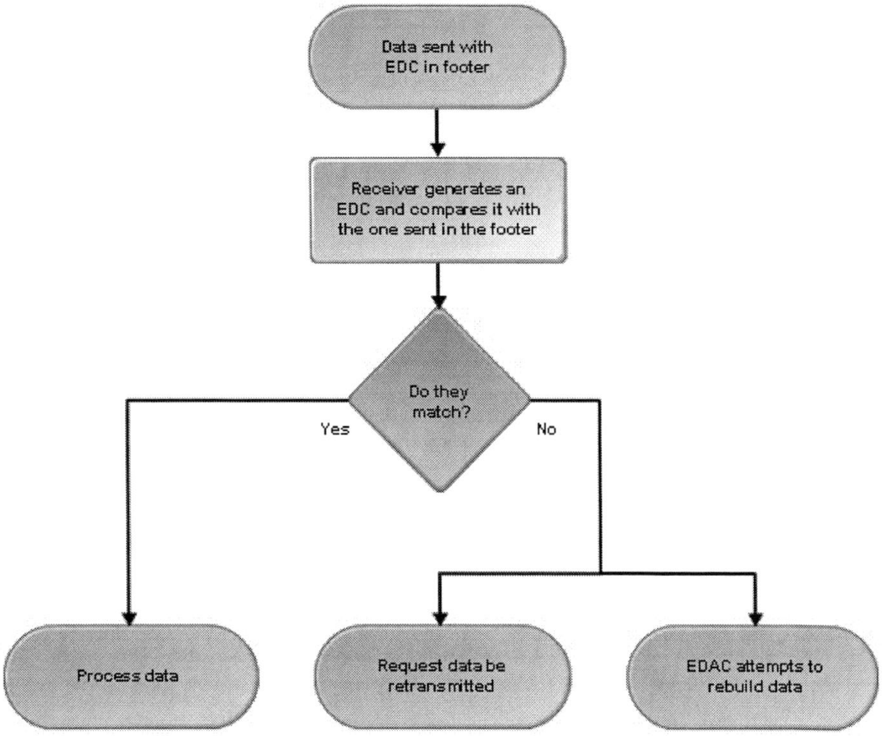

Figure 3-15: *The error detection process.*

Parity

Parity operates on a word-by-word basis. The sender adds one bit to each word of the data and then transmits to the receiver. The receiver compares the number of ones within a transmitted byte to those received. If the count matches, the data is assumed to be valid. If a word is determined to be corrupt, the receiver requests that the data be retransmitted.

Parity checking operates on a word-by-word basis and can only reliably determine if a single bit has been changed.

One bit is added to each word, adding 12.5 percent overhead to transmitted data.

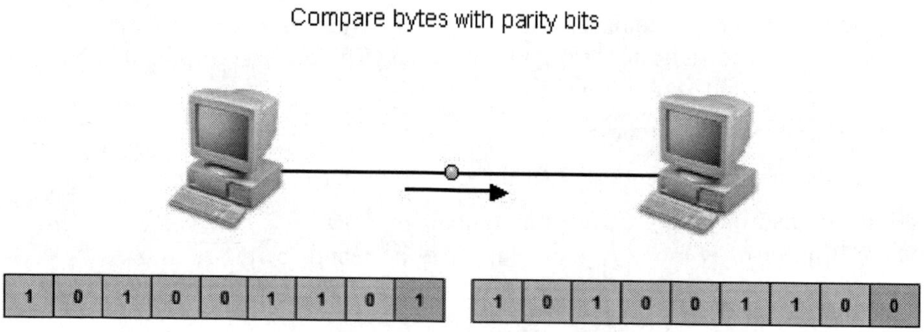

Figure 3-16: *Parity checking is an error detection method.*

Even and Odd Parity

The receiver must be configured to use the same type of parity checking as the sender. Parity checking can be implemented as either even or odd parity. With even parity, the sender counts the ones in a word of data and appends a 1 or 0 to the word to make the count even. With odd parity, the sender appends the bit as needed to make the count of ones odd.

Internal Computer Parity Checking

Parity checking is sometimes used internally within a computer. For example, memory chips can use parity bits so that the processor can determine if data in memory has been altered during storage.

Cyclic Redundancy Check

A *cyclic redundancy check (CRC)* uses a predefined mathematical operation to calculate a CRC code. It attaches the CRC to a block of data and transmits it to the receiver. The receiving node calculates its own CRC value for the data block and compares it to the transmitted CRC. If the values match, the receiver assumes the data was unaltered during transmission.

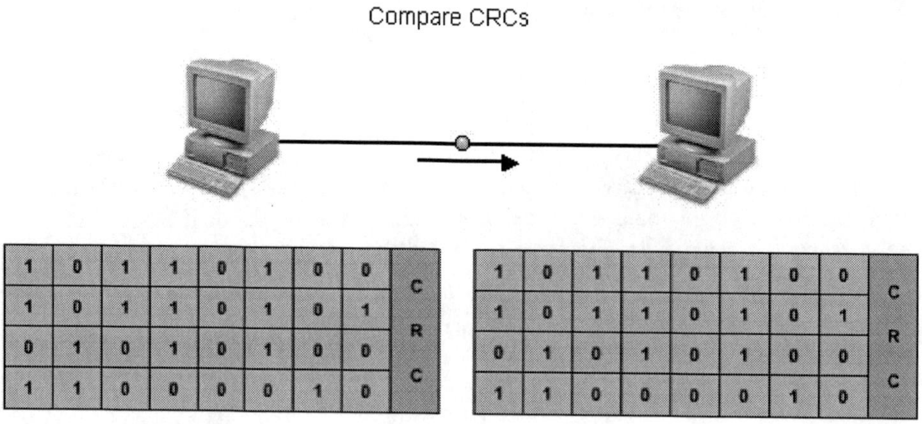

Figure 3-17: *Comparing CRC values can tell the receiver if data is valid.*

CRC Considerations

Typically, CRC checks are applied to large blocks of data, such as the entire data sent in a packet. Thus, fewer error detection bits must be transmitted with the data in a packet. However, if a CRC check fails, the entire block must be retransmitted. In general, though, CRC checking uses less network bandwidth than parity checking.

Flow Control

Definition:

Flow control is a class of techniques for optimizing the exchange of data between systems. If too much data is sent at once, the receiving node can become overwhelmed, dropping packets that arrive too quickly to process. If too little data is sent, the receiver sits idle waiting for more data to arrive. Buffering and data windows are two flow control techniques commonly used in computer networking.

Example: Buffering

Buffering is a flow control technique in which received data is stored in a temporary high speed memory location, called a *buffer*, until the main system components are ready to work with the data. In a networking situation, the network card itself handles buffering so that the system CPU does not have to become involved. Buffering is also used when reading information from disk or RAM, in which case the buffer is more often called a *cache*. A cache controller, a specialized processor chip, manages caching so that the CPU doesn't have to.

Even with a high-speed buffer, data can sometimes arrive too quickly to be handled. This situation is called *flooding*. To avoid flooding, receiving devices typically send a squelch signal to the sender when the buffer is approximately 75 percent full. Upon receiving a squelch signal, the sender will slow or halt further data transmissions until the receiver has caught up.

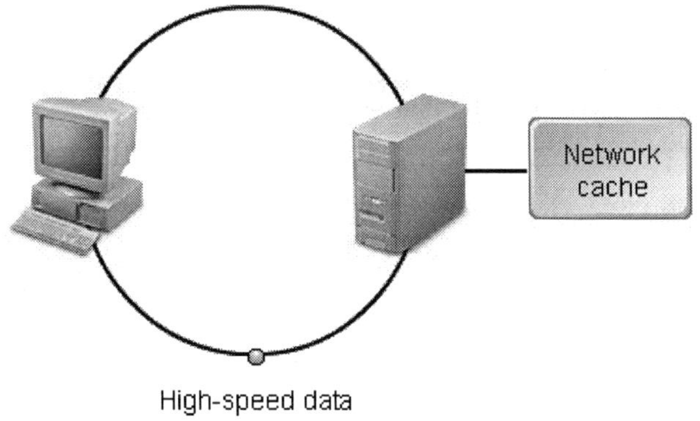

Figure 3-18: *Buffering network data.*

Example: Data Windows

In the simplest case, a sender transmits one packet and then waits for an acknowledgement from the recipient, an "ACK" signal. If the recipient is busy, the sender sits idle until it receives the ACK, after which it sends the next packet. Throughput could be increased if data could be sent in larger packages, with the recipient sending fewer acknowledgements.

Data windows provide just such a flow control technique. Multiple packets are sent as a unit called a block or window. The recipient acknowledges each window rather than each packet, resulting in higher throughput.

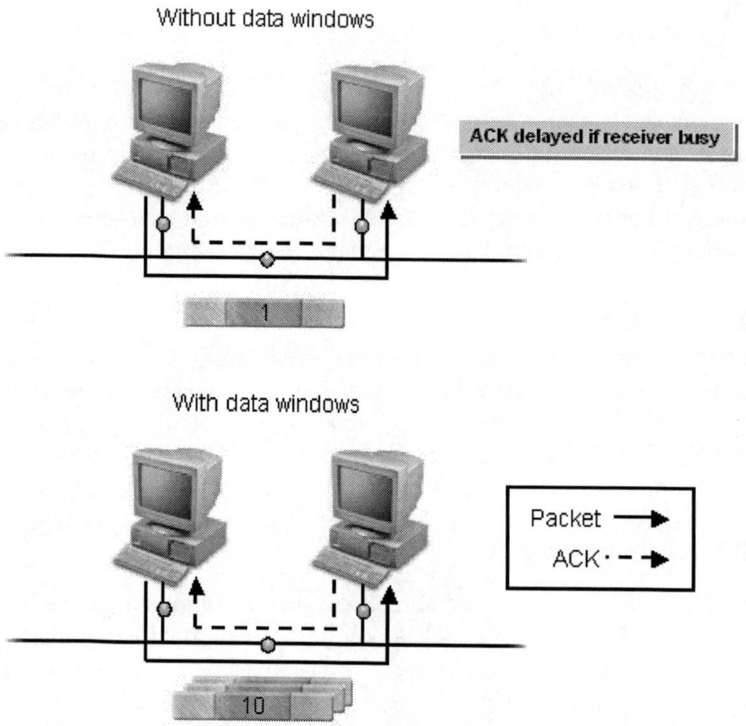

Figure 3-19: *Data windows.*

Data window size can be fixed or variable. With *fixed length windows*, every block contains the same number of packets. To avoid flooding the buffers of some devices, fixed length windows are typically small. So, while fixed length windows are more efficient than sending individual packets, they are less efficient than sliding windows.

Sliding windows use variable block sizes. The first block sent contains a small number of packets. Each subsequent block is a bit larger, until the sender floods the buffers of the recipient. Upon receiving the squelch signal, the sender reduces the window size and resumes transmission. The window size is continually re-evaluated during transmission, with the sender always attempting to send the largest window it can to speed throughput.

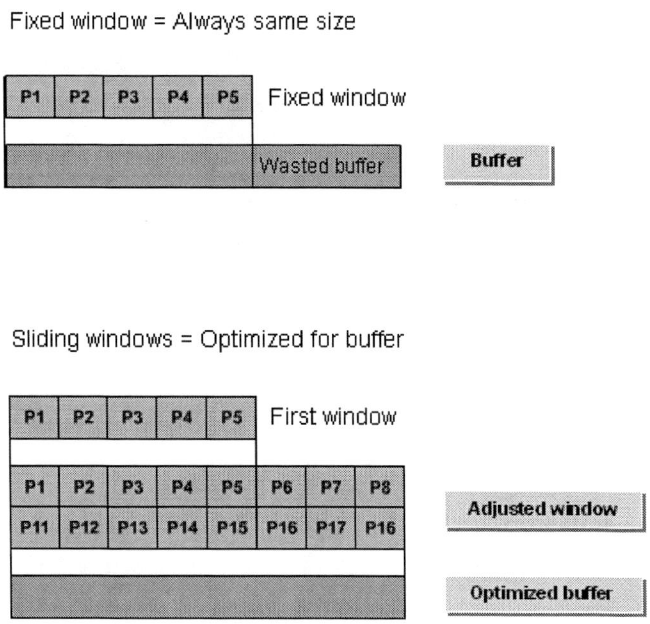

Figure 3-20: *Fixed length and sliding windows improve throughput.*

ACTIVITY 3-6

Exploring Reliable Data Delivery Techniques

Scenario:

In this activity, you will identify the characteristics of reliable data delivery techniques.

---

1. **Which are examples of error detection?**

   a) Sliding windows

   b) Parity checking

   c) CRC

   d) EDAC

   e) Buffering

---

2. **True or False? Parity checking adds overhead to network transmissions while ensuring that data is error free.**

   __ True

   __ False

---

3. **Which statement best distinguishes sliding windows from fixed length windows?**

   a) Sliding windows are groups of packets selected at random from transmitted data, whereas fixed length windows always include the same sequence of packets.

   b) Fixed length windows always contain the same number of packets, while sliding windows contain either 8, 16, or 32 packets.

   c) Sliding windows contain a variable number of packets in a block, while fixed length windows always contain the same number.

   d) Fixed length windows contain a variable number of packets in a block, while sliding windows always contain the same number.

4. **Buffer flooding is:**

   a) Overfilling the buffers in the sender.

   b) Corrupting the buffers in the receiver.

   c) Filling the buffer of the receiver with padding (empty) packets.

   d) Overfilling the buffers in the receiver.

Lesson 3 Follow-up

In this lesson, you learned how data is delivered to its intended destination reliably and unaltered by examining data addressing, connection mechanisms, and the techniques that ensure the reliable delivery of data. Using this knowledge, you can ensure that when users make a request for a network service or send data across your network, their request or data arrives at its destination in a timely manner. It won't be misdirected, intercepted, or altered as it travels to its destination.

1. **Which connection modes do you expect to work with most often: Simplex, half duplex, or full duplex? Point-to-point, multipoint, or radiated?**

2. **Which reliable delivery techniques will be used most often between the networking devices you will work with?**

LESSON 4

Network Media and Hardware

Lesson Time
2 hour(s), 15 minutes

Lesson Objectives:

In this lesson, you will list and describe network media and hardware components.

You will:

- Identify the major types of bounded network media.
- List the major types of unbounded network media.
- Identify methods for noise control.
- Identify the primary types of network connectivity devices.

LESSON 4

Introduction

In the previous lesson, you examined reliable network data delivery. One of the components that needs to be functioning without interruption for network data to reliably travel across the network is the network media and hardware that carry data communication packets from one computer to another. In this lesson, you will examine the different types of media over which network data can be transmitted, as well as the networking devices that help transmit your data.

Networking media is like the highways and subways of a city. Without roads and rails, people cannot move through a city to work or home. Without networking media and the networking devices that support them, data cannot move from one computer to another.

For data to successfully travel across your network from one computer to another, you must verify that the network media and network devices are compatible with one another and set up correctly for your particular network implementation.

This lesson covers the following CompTIA Network+ (2005) certification objectives:

- Topic A:
    - Objective 1.4: Recognize the following media connectors and describe their uses: RJ-11 (Registered Jack); RJ-45 (Registered Jack); F-Type; ST (Straight Tip); SC (Subscriber Connector or Standard Connector); IEEE 1394 (FireWire); Fiber LC (Local Connector); and MT-RJ (Mechanical Transfer Registered Jack).
    - Objective 1.5: Recognize the following media types and describe their uses: Category 3, 5, 5e, and 6; UTP (unshielded twisted pair); STP (shielded twisted pair); coaxial cable; SMF (single-mode fiber) optic cable; and MMF (multimode fiber) optic cable.
    - Objective 4.8: Given a network troubleshooting scenario involving an infrastructure (wired or wireless) problem, identify the cause of the stated problem (for example, bad media, interference, network hardware, or environment).
- Topic B:
    - Objective 1.7: Specify the general characteristics (for example, carrier speed, frequency, transmission type, and topology) of the following wireless technologies: 802.11 (frequency hopping spread spectrum), 802.11x (direct sequence spread spectrum), and infrared.
    - Objective 4.8: Given a network troubleshooting scenario involving an infrastructure (wired or wireless) problem, identify the cause of the stated problem (for example, bad media, interference, network hardware, or environment).
- Topic C:
    - Objective 4.8: Given a network troubleshooting scenario involving an infrastructure (wired or wireless) problem, identify the cause of the stated problem (for example, bad media, interference, network hardware, or environment).
- Topic D:
    - Objective 1.6: Identify the purposes, features, and functions of the following network components: hubs, switches, bridges, routers, gateways, NICs (network interface cards), WAPs (wireless access points), and transceivers (media converters).
    - Objective 4.7: Given a troubleshooting scenario involving a network with a particular physical topology (for example, bus, star, mesh, or ring) and including a network diagram, identify the network area affected and the cause of the stated failure.
    - Objective 4.8: Given a network troubleshooting scenario involving an infrastructure (wired or wireless) problem, identify the cause of the stated problem (for example, bad media, interference, network hardware, or environment).

TOPIC A

Bounded Network Media

The network media that carries the data across your network can be bounded or unbounded. In this topic, you will begin your exploration of network media and hardware by examining the most common network media—bounded.

Bounded media is the most common networking medium. You will likely work with it on a daily basis as part of your duties as a network professional. Understanding the characteristics of this form of media will enable you to properly install and service your networks.

Media Types

Network media, the conduit through which networking communications flow, can be either bounded or unbounded. *Bounded media* use a physical conductor. This conductor can be a metal wire though which electricity flows or a glass or plastic strand through which pulses of light flow. *Unbounded media* use electromagnetic signals that are transmitted through the air with radio, microwave, or infrared radiation.

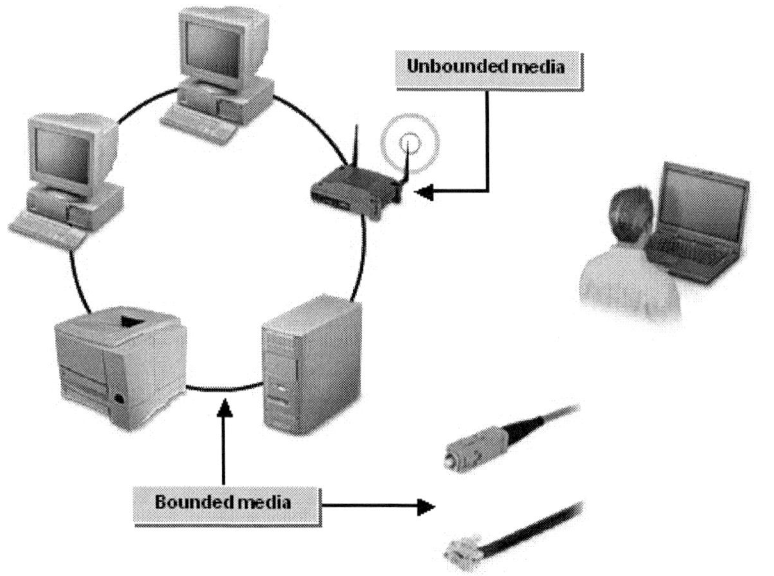

Figure 4-1: *Network media can be bounded or unbounded.*

Signals, Noise, and Attenuation

Signal is the electromagnetic communications you want to be transmitted across a network medium. *Noise* is electromagnetic interference that disrupts the signal. The ratio of signal to noise typically goes down—that is, gets poorer—as distance increases. *Attenuation* is the degradation of a signal as it travels across a network medium, usually caused by the accumulation of noise or fading strength of the signal. Different media types are more or less susceptible to noise and attenuation.

Copper Media

Definition:

Copper cable is a type of bounded media that uses one or more copper conductors surrounded by a non-conductive insulated coating. The conductors can be made of a solid wire or built from braided strands of wire. Sometimes shielding, in the form of braided wire or foil, is wrapped around one or more of the conductors to reduce signal interference from nearby electromagnetic radiation.

Example: Coaxial Cable

Coaxial cable, or *coax*, is a type of copper cable that features a central conductor surrounded by braided or foil shielding. A *dialectric* insulator separates the conductor and shield and the entire package is wrapped in an insulating layer called a jacket. The data signal is transmitted over the central conductor. The outer shielding serves to reduce electromagnetic interference.

Coaxial cable is so named because the conductor and shield share the same axis, or center. They share a COmmon AXis or are "co-axial." This arrangement helps prevent electromagnetic interference from reaching the conductor.

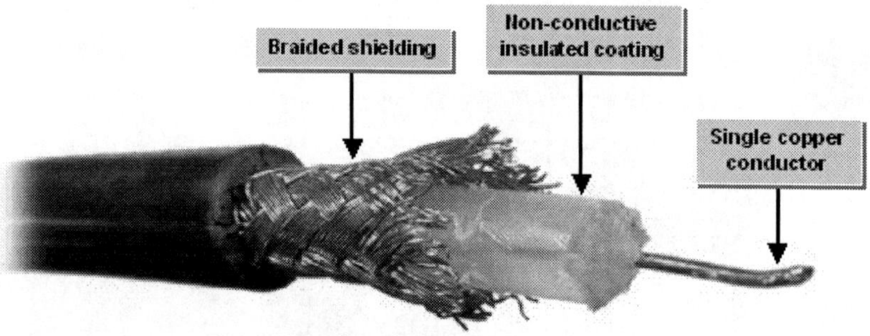

Figure 4-2: *Coaxial cable.*

Coaxial Cable and Connector Types

Coax cable comes in many varieties, not all of which are used for computer networking.

Coax cables are assigned a combination alphanumeric identification that identifies the size and electronic characteristics of that type of cable.

Cable Type	Characteristics
RG58/U (Radio Guide 58/Universal)	A 5 mm (0.25 inch) coax cable with a solid core and 50 ohms impedance. RG58/U is used for Ethernet networking.
RG58A/U	A 5 mm (0.25 inch) coax cable with a stranded core and 50 ohms impedance. RG58A/U is used for Ethernet networking.
RG8	A 10 mm (0.5 inch) coax cable with a solid core and 50 ohms impedance. RG8 is used for Ethernet networking.

Cable Type	Characteristics
RG9	A 5 mm (0.25 inch) coax cable with a stranded core and 75 ohm impedance. RG9 is used for cable television transmissions and cable modems.
RG62	A 5 mm (0.25 inch) coax cable with a solid core and 93 ohms impedance. RG62 was used for ARCNET networking.

The RG specification codes come from their page numbers in the Radio Guide manual, the original military specification (Mil-Spec) for coax cable, which is no longer in use. For example, the RG8 specification appeared on page 8.

Impedance

Impedance is the force that opposes the flow of electricity in an alternating current (AC) circuit. Impedance is measured in ohms (Ω).

Ohms

An *ohm* is a unit of electrical resistance. One ohm is the value of resistance through which one volt will maintain a current of one ampere.

Termination

Coax network segments typically must be *terminated* to prevent signal reflections off the end of the cable. Cables are terminated by installing a resistor of an appropriate rating, typically 50 ohms, on the end of the cable.

ThinNet

ThinNet is the name given to Ethernet networking over RG58/U or RG58A/U cabling. ThinNet is wired in a bus configuration in which segments can be up to 185 meters (or 607 feet) long. ThinNet connections are made with a twist-lock connector called a BNC connector. Devices connect to the network with T-connectors and each end of the cable must be terminated with a 50-ohm resistor.

ThickNet

ThickNet is the name given to Ethernet networking over RG8 cabling. ThickNet is not commonly used today, but was popular as a network backbone because ThickNet segments can be up to 500 meters (or 1640 feet) long.

Networking devices are not directly connected to ThickNet cable. Instead, transceivers are connected to the cable with *vampire taps*, which pierce the cable to make contact with its conductors. Transceivers can be installed as needed at intervals of 2.5 meters along the length of the cable. The networking device connects to the transceiver via a 15-pin *AUI connector* and a short section of cable called a drop cable. An AUI connector is also known as a DIX connector, which gets its name from the three companies that invented it: Digital Electronics Corporation (DEC), Intel, and Xerox.

Connections between ThickNet segments are made with a screw-type connector called an N-connector. ThickNet segments must be terminated with a 50-ohm resistor.

F-Type Connectors

Another coax connector type is the F-type connector, which is used with 75-ohm cable to connect cable TV and FM antenna cables. It comes in a secure screw-on form or as a non-threaded slip-on connector.

Twisted Pair Cable

Definition:

Twisted pair is a type of cable in which multiple insulated conductors are twisted around each other and clad in a protective and insulating outer jacket. Typically, two conductors are twisted around each other. These pairs may be twisted together with other pairs depending on the type and size of cabling. Shielding can be added around the bundle of twisted pairs to reduce electronic interference.

Color Schemes

The conductors in older twisted pair cables use a solid color scheme. Old telephone cable, for example, uses black, green, red, and yellow wires. The current color scheme uses striped colors.

A pair of wires shares a base color and white. Consider the blue pair of wires: one wire will be mostly blue with white stripes. It will be identified on wiring diagrams as the blue/white wire. The corresponding wire in the pair will be mostly white with blue stripes, and be identified as the white/blue wire.

Wire colors are standardized and are used for specific functions. The first four standard color pairs are listed in the following table.

Primary Wire	Secondary Wire
White/blue	Blue/white
White/orange	Orange/white
White/green	Green/white
White/brown	Brown/white

In the solid color scheme, red corresponds to blue/white, green to white/blue, yellow to orange/white, and black to white/orange.

Example:

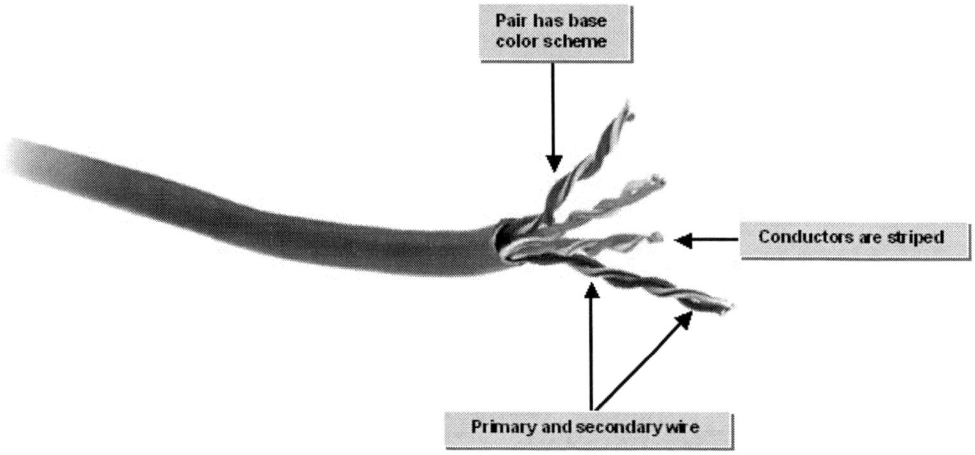

Figure 4-3: *Twisted pair cable.*

UTP vs. STP Cable

Twisted pair cable can be *unshielded twisted pair (UTP)* or *shielded twisted pair (STP).*

Cable Type	Description
UTP	Does not include shielding around its conductors. Typically contains four pairs of stranded or solid conductors. Inexpensive and reliable. Supports distances of up to 100 meters (328 feet). Supports data transfer rates up to 1 Gbps.
STP	Includes shielding, typically a foil wrapper, around its conductors to improve the cable's resistance to interference and noise. Typically contains four pairs of stranded or solid conductors. Supports distances up to 100 meters (328 feet). More expensive than UTP. Most commonly used in Token Ring networking.

UTP is the most popular type of twisted pair cabling because it is inexpensive, reliable, and supports data transfer rates up to 1 Gbps.

STP cable is sometimes referred to as IBM-type cable because of its use with Token Ring networks.

Twisted Pair Cable Categories

Twisted pair cable comes in different grades, called categories, which support different network speeds and technologies. These categories are summarized in the following table.

Category	Network Type and Maximum Speed
1	Voice grade; not suitable for networking. Maximum speed: n/a
2	Digital telephone and low-speed networks. Maximum speed: 4 Mbps

Category	Network Type and Maximum Speed
3	Ethernet. Maximum speed: 10 Mbps
4	IBM Token Ring. Maximum speed: 16 Mbps
5 and 5e	Category 5: Fast Ethernet. Maximum speed: 100 Mbps Category 5e: Gigabit Ethernet. Maximum speed: 350 Mbps
6	Gigabit Ethernet. Maximum speed: 1 Gbps
7	Gigabit Ethernet. Maximum speed: 1 Gbps+

A cable's category is typically printed on the cable itself, making identification easy.

Twisted Pair Connectors

The RJ-45 connector is used on the twisted pair cable. RJ-45 is an eight-pin connector used with networking connections other than LocalTalk. All four pairs of wires in the twisted pair cable are used with this connector.

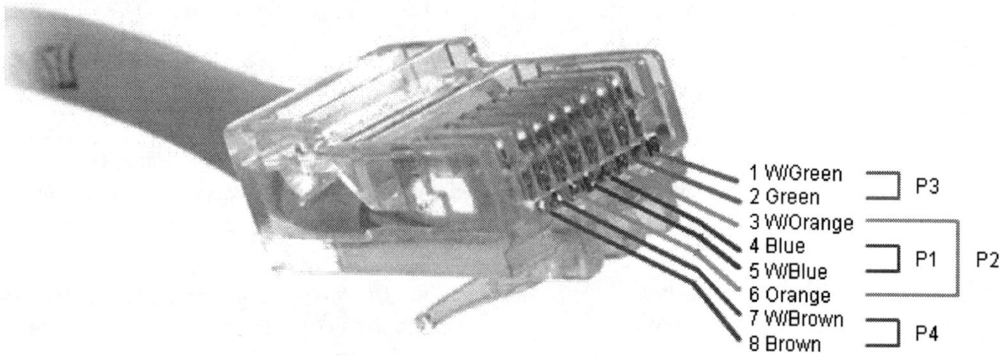

Figure 4-4: *An RJ-45 connector.*

The RJ in RJ-11 or RJ-45 is an abbreviation for "registered jack."

RJ-45 Wiring Schemes

There are two standard wiring schemes for RJ-45: EIA/TIA 568A and 568B. It is important that you use the wiring scheme that matches the devices on your network and that all cables are the same.

Pin	EIA/TIA 568A	EIA/TIA 568B
1	White/green	White/orange
2	Green/white	Orange/white
3	White/orange	White/green
4	Blue/white	Blue/white
5	White/blue	White/blue
6	Orange/white	Green/white
7	White/brown	White/brown

Pin	EIA/TIA 568A	EIA/TIA 568B
8	Brown/white	Brown/white

The RJ-11 Connector

The RJ-11 connector is used with Category 1 cable in telephone system connections and is not suitable for network connectivity. However, because the RJ-11 connector is similar in appearance to the RJ-45 connector, they are sometimes confused. RJ-11 connectors are smaller than RJ-45 connectors, and have either four or six pins.

Fiber Optic Cable

Definition:

Fiber optic cable is a type of network cable in which the core is one or more glass or plastic strands. The core is between 5 and 100 microns thick and is surrounded by silica cladding, which adds strength and protection for the fragile glass or plastic core. An outer jacket, sometimes called armor, wraps and protects the whole assembly. Light pulses from a laser or high intensity LED are passed through the core to carry the signal. The cladding reflects the light back into the core, increasing the distance the signal can travel without being regenerated.

Example:

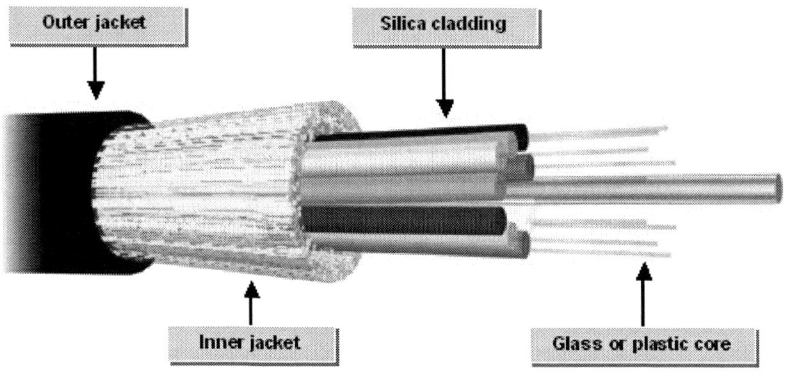

Figure 4-5: *A fiber optic cable.*

Fiber optic cables are the least sensitive of any cable type to electromagnetic interference.

WARNING! You should not look into the end of any operating fiber. In particular, the intensity of light leaving the end of a single-mode fiber is strong enough to cause temporary or permanent eye damage.

Fiber Optic Cable Mode Types

Fiber optic cables can be single-mode or multimode fiber.

Mode Type	Description
Single-mode fiber	Carries a single optical signal. Has a small core, which allows only a single beam of light to pass. A laser, usually operating in the infrared portion of the spectrum, is modulated in amplitude (intensity) to transmit the signal through the fiber.
Step index multimode fiber	Permits multiple optical signals. Core is typically 50 or more microns, which allows multiple beams of light to pass. Light is sent at angles to the fiber so that it reflects off the sides of the strand along its length. Less expensive than graded index multimode fiber.
Graded index multimode fiber	Permits multiple optical signals. Core is typically 50 or more microns, which allows multiple beams of light to pass. Light is sent down each of the multiple layers inside the core to carry an individual signal, allowing multiple signals to be sent down a single strand. Has a longer maximum transmission distance than step index multimode fiber, but is more expensive.

Fiber Connectors

Various connectors are used with fiber optic cable.

It often takes a specially trained and certified technician, plus specialized equipment, to install these connectors.

Connector	Description
ST	Used to connect multimode fiber, ST (Straight Tip) connectors look like BNC connectors. They have a straight, ceramic center bin and bayonet lug lockdown. They are often used in network patch panels. ST connectors are perhaps the most popular type of fiber connector. 
SC	Box-shaped connectors that snap into a receptacle. SC (Subscriber Connector or Standard Connector) connectors are often used in a duplex configuration where two fibers are terminated into two SC connectors that are molded together. SC is used with single-mode fiber. 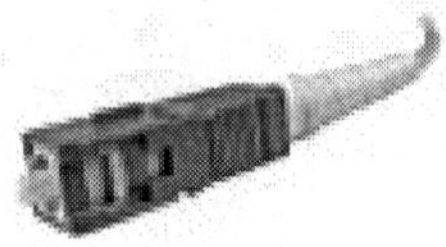

Connector	Description
FC	Similar to SMA connectors, FC (Face Contact) connectors use a heavy duty ferrule in the center for more mechanical stability than SMA or ST connectors. These connectors are more popular in industrial settings where greater strength is required. 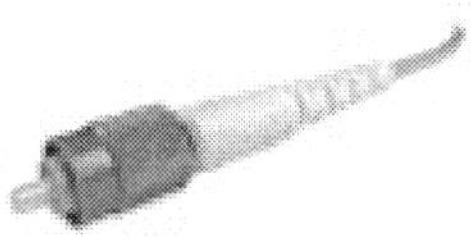
FDDI	The FDDI (Fiber Distributed Data Interface) connector is a push/pull-type, two-channel snap-fit connector used for multimode fiber optic cable. Also called a MIC (Media Interface Connector). 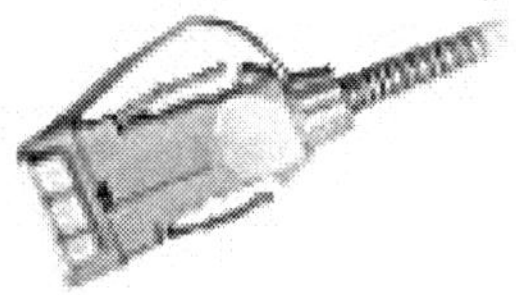
Mini-BNC	A bayonet-style connector using the traditional BNC connection method. 
Biconic	The biconic connector is a screw-on type connector with a tapered sleeve that is fixed against guided rings and screws onto the threaded sleeve to secure the connection. When the connector is inserted into the receptacle, the tapered end of the connector locates the fiber optic cable into the proper position. The biconic connector is one of the earliest connector types and is, for most part, no longer in use. 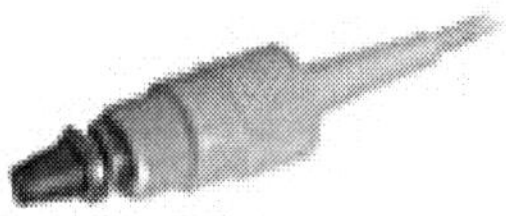
LC	The LC (Local Connector) is a small form factor ceramic ferrule connector for both single-mode and multimode fiber. It is about half the size of the SC or ST. The LC uses an RJ-45-type latching and can be used to transition installations from twisted pair copper cabling to fiber. 

Connector	Description
SMA	Similar to ST connectors, SMA (Sub Multi Assembly or Sub Miniature type A) connectors use a threaded ferrule on the outside to lock the connector in place. These are typically used where water or other environmental factors necessitate a waterproof connection, which wouldn't be possible with a bayonet-style connector. 
MT-RJ	The MT-RJ (Mechanical Transfer Registered Jack) connector, sometimes called a Fiber Jack connector, is a compact snap-to-lock connector used with multimode fiber. The MT-RJ is easy to use and similar in size to the RJ-45 connector. Two strands of fiber are attached with one connector. 

IEEE 1394

While not as common as other bounded network media, IEEE 1394, better known as FireWire, can be used to connect up to 63 devices to form a small local network. FireWire cables use a shielded cable similar to STP with either four or six conductors. Connections to devices are made with either a six- or four-pin connector.

IEEE 1394 is most often called FireWire, a name given to the standard by Apple Computer, Inc. Sony names the same standard i.Link™, which is often written iLink.

Figure 4-6: *FireWire uses either four- or six-pin connectors.*

Plenum and PVC Cables

Plenum cable is a network cable that is jacketed tightly around the conductors so that fire cannot travel within the cable. The jacket of the plenum cable does not give off noxious or poisonous gases when it burns. Fire codes require that you install this special grade cabling in the plenum—between the structural ceiling and any suspended ceiling, and under raised floors, as well as in firebreak walls.

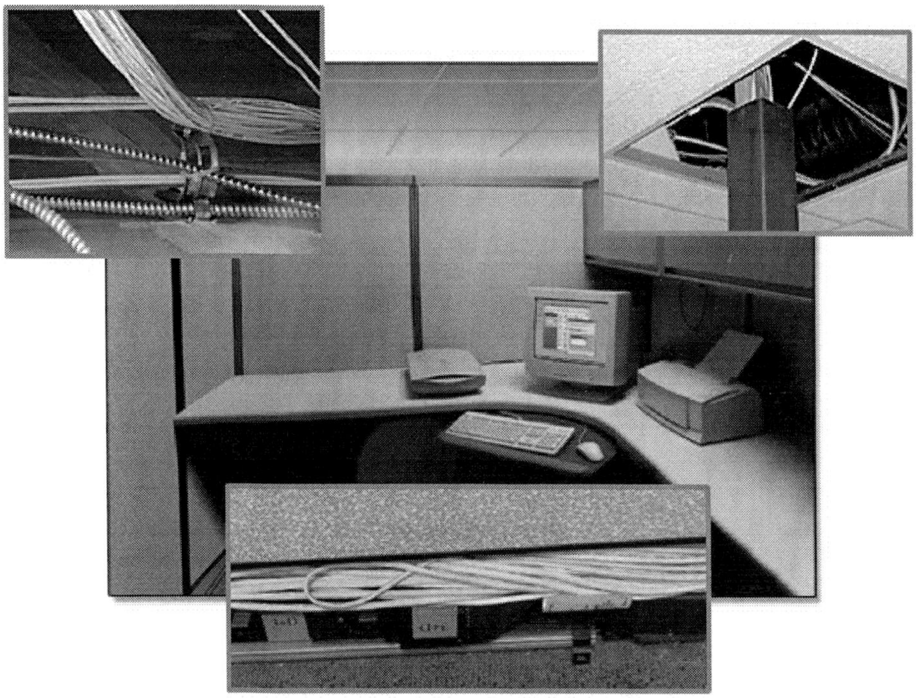

Figure 4-7: *Plenum and PVC cable.*

PVC Cable

Polyvinyl chloride (PVC)-jacketed cabling is inexpensive and flexible. However, when PVC burns, it gives off noxious or poisonous gases. Additionally, PVC jacketing is not formed tightly to the conductors it contains. Tests show that fire can travel within PVC cable, passing through firebreaks.

ACTIVITY 4-1

Identifying Bounded Network Media

Scenario:

In this activity, you will identify the major types of bounded network media.

1. **Match the media type with its definition.**

___	IEEE 1394	a.	Multiple insulated conductors clad in a protective and insulating outer jacket carry the signal. Wires are grouped in colored pairs.
___	Fiber optic	b.	A shielded cable similar to STP with either four or six conductors that can be used to connect up to 63 devices to form a small local network.
___	Twisted pair	c.	The least sensitive of any cable type, light pulses from a laser or high-intensity LED carry the signal through the core.
___	Coaxial	d.	A central copper conductor carries the signal. It is surrounded by braided or foil shielding designed to reduce electromagnetic interference. A dialectic insulator separates the conductor from the shield.

2. **Identify the type of network cabling shown in the illustration.**

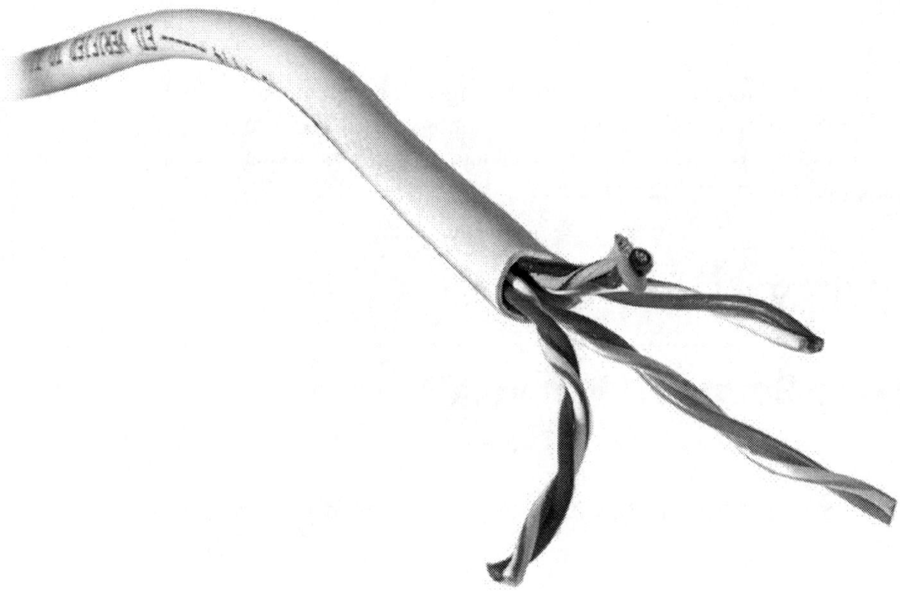

a) Twisted pair

b) Coax

c) Fiber optic

3. **Identify the type of network cabling shown in the illustration.**

a) Unshielded twisted pair
b) Shielded twisted pair
c) Coax
d) Fiber optic

4. **Select the reason or reasons that plenum cable is permitted in air handling spaces and can be run through firebreaks.**

a) It does not give off noxious or poisonous gases when burned.
b) It gives off noxious or poisonous gases when burned.
c) Fire cannot travel through the cable because the jacket is closely formed to the conductors.
d) Fire can travel through the cable because the jacket loosely surrounds the conductors.
e) It is stiffer than PVC cable.

ACTIVITY 4-2

Identifying Local Network Media

Scenario:

In this activity, you will identify the network media used on your local classroom network.

1. **Identify the cable type used to connect your computer to the classroom network.**

2. **Identify the types of connectors used in the classroom network.**

3. **Your instructor will provide samples of a variety of media and connector types. Identify each of the media and connectors.**

TOPIC B

Unbounded Network Media

In the previous topic, you examined bounded network media. Network media can be bounded or unbounded. In this topic, you will examine the other broad class of network media—unbounded media.

While most computer networks still run over wires or fiber optics—bounded network media—unbounded network media, which sends its data signals through the air instead of cables, is growing in popularity. Unbounded media technologies have two distinct advantages for businesses over bounded media: first, they are generally easier to install and reconfigure; and second, they afford client machines a lot of mobility. Unfortunately, they are usually not as secure as bounded media, as the signals are subject to interception. To implement wireless technologies properly, you'll need to understand their advantages and compensate for their disadvantages in your network environments.

Wireless Communication

Definition:

Wireless communication is a type of communications in which signals are transmitted without using bounded media of any sort. Instead, signals are transmitted as electromagnetic energy, such as radio, microwave, or light pulses. Wireless communication enables users to move around while remaining connected to the network.

Wireless communication permits connections between areas where it would be difficult or impossible to install wires, such as in hazardous areas, across long distances, or inside historic buildings.

Example:

Figure 4-8: *Wireless communications.*

Point-to-Point and Broadcast

Wireless connections can be point-to-point or broadcast. Typically, point-to-point wireless connections are used to link distant buildings or networks as part of a CAN, MAN, or WAN. Broadcast wireless connections cover wide areas over short distances and are used to enable LAN communications within a building or small geographical area.

Radio Networking

Definition:

Radio networking is a form of wireless communications in which signals are sent via radio frequency (*RF*) waves in the 10 KHz and 1 GHz range. Radio networking is subject to electrical interference from power lines, a building's metal structural components, and atmospheric conditions.

Radio networking can be broadcast or spread spectrum.

Radio Type	Description
Broadcast	*Broadcast radio* is a form of RF networking that is nondirectional, uses a single frequency for transmissions, and comes in low- and high-power versions. Low-power RF transmissions travel a short distance, often no more than 70 meters, but are inexpensive and relatively easy to install. High-power RF transmissions travel considerably farther; however, specially trained technicians are often required to install this more expensive type of system.
Spread Spectrum	*Spread spectrum* is a form of radio transmission in which the signal is sent over more than one frequency. This technique makes eavesdropping on the signal more difficult. Additionally, distinguishing between the signal and background noise is often easier. Spread spectrum uses either frequency hopping or direct sequencing techniques to distribute the signal across the radio spectrum. In *frequency hopping spread spectrum (FHSS)*, a signal is sent on one channel at a time. At predetermined fixed intervals, the channel changes. Both the sender and receiver use the same selection and order of frequencies so that communication is possible even as the frequency changes. FHSS does not significantly reduce noise or improve the signal to noise ratio. If, by chance, some frequencies are less noisy than others, communication across the less-noisy channels will be improved as compared to the more-noisy channels. *Direct sequence spread spectrum (DSSS)* uses multiple channels simultaneously to send data. Additionally, error detection and correction (EDAC) techniques are used to reduce data transmission errors. In DSSS, a single data signal is converted into multiple digital data signals called chips. The set of chips is sent across a wide band of adjacent channels. Upon receiving the data, the receiver combines and converts the signals back into the original. Because of the included EDAC information, the signal can often be reconstructed even if only some of the channels are received clearly.

Regulatory agencies place limits on which frequencies and how much power can be used to transmit signals. In the United States, the Federal Communications Commission (FCC) is the agency that regulates radio transmissions.

Example:

Figure 4-9: *Radio networking.*

Eavesdroppers are less likely to be successful at listening in on an FHSS transmission than a normal radio transmission. It is not likely that parties outside of the sender and receiver would know the selection and order of frequencies being used to communicate.

Infrared Transmission

Definition:

Infrared transmission is a form of wireless transmission over unbounded media in which signals are sent via pulses of infrared light. Receivers need an unobstructed view of the sender to successfully receive the signal, though the signal can reflect off hard surfaces to reach the recipient. Many infrared-compatible devices follow the standards set forth by the Infrared Data Association (IrDA).

Example:

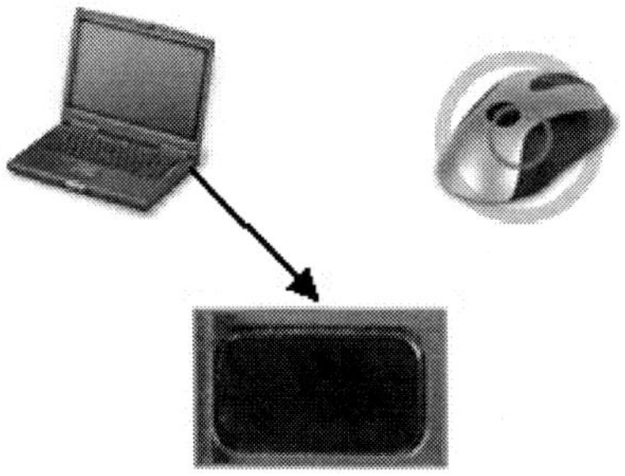

Figure 4-10: *Transferring information over an infrared connection.*

Transmission Rates

Infrared wireless networking offers transmission rates reaching 10 Mbps to 16 Mbps. Infrared compatible devices, such as a wireless mouse and keyboard, are limited to distances of approximately 3 feet and for that reason such devices are often used in WPANS. Direct transmission and short distances between devices virtually eliminates eavesdropping and signal tampering, which makes IrDA a secure transmission medium.

IrDA User Profile Properties

In Windows XP, the IrDA implementation supports five user profiles:

- File transfer (IrOBEX) enables file transfer between IrDA devices.
- Printing (IrLPT) enables printing between IrDA devices such as laptops and IrDA printers.
- Image Transfer (IrTran-P) enables easy image transfer between digital cameras and Windows devices.
- Dial-up networking (IrCOMM) enables dial-up Internet access through IR-enabled cell phones.
- LAN access and peer-to-peer networking (IrNET) enables network access through IR-enabled access points.

Microwave Transmission

Definition:

Microwave transmission is a form of wireless transmission over unbounded media in which signals are sent via pulses of electromagnetic energy in the microwave region of the spectrum. Receivers need an unobstructed view of the sender to successfully receive the signal. Signals can be reflected off satellites to increase transmission distance.

Example:

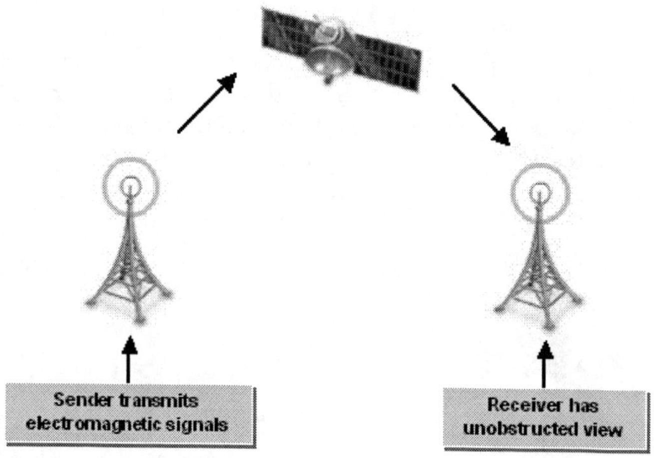

Figure 4-11: *Microwave transmission.*

Activity 4-3

Identifying Wireless Transmission Technologies

Scenario:

In this activity, you will identify and distinguish between the various types of unbounded media used to create wireless links between network nodes.

---

1. **Select the characteristic(s) of unbounded media.**
   a) Uses a physical conductor.
   b) Installs easily in hazardous areas.
   c) Physical shielding protects against noise.
   d) Uses electromagnetic energy.
   e) Some media require line of sight.

2. **Which form of unbounded media uses nondirectional RF signals to transmit signals?**
   a) radio
   b) Infrared
   c) Microwave

3. **In frequency hopping spread spectrum (FHSS), a data signal is:**
   a) Divided into multiple chips; each chip is transmitted across a different frequency.
   b) Sent over a single high-frequency RF transmission band.
   c) Transmitted across a single frequency for a set period, after which the signal is sent over a new, randomly selected frequency.
   d) Less likely to be intercepted but not significantly less susceptible to noise.

4. **True or False? Infrared transmissions require that the receiver and the sender have an unobstructed view of each other.**
   __ True
   __ False

TOPIC C

Noise Control

You have examined both bounded and unbounded transmission media, the conduits over which network communications flow. The flow of network communications can be impaired by interference such as noise. In this topic, you will examine noise and noise control techniques that help maximize the data flow on your network media.

Any number of things can cause interference with the transmissions on your network—radio, TV, cell phones, and radar to name a few. The one constant is that noise always slows a network's performance and reduces its reliability. When the receiving node has to try to make sense of a lot of extra signals, it ends up asking the sending node to resend the data—many times. In order to establish a network where noise is minimized, you need to understand the sources of noise and how to protect against them.

Electrical Noise

Definition:

Electrical noise is unwanted signals that are introduced into network media. Noise interferes with the proper reception of transmitted signals. Noise can come from natural sources, such as solar radiation or electrical storms, or from man-made sources, such as electronic interference from nearby motors or transformers.

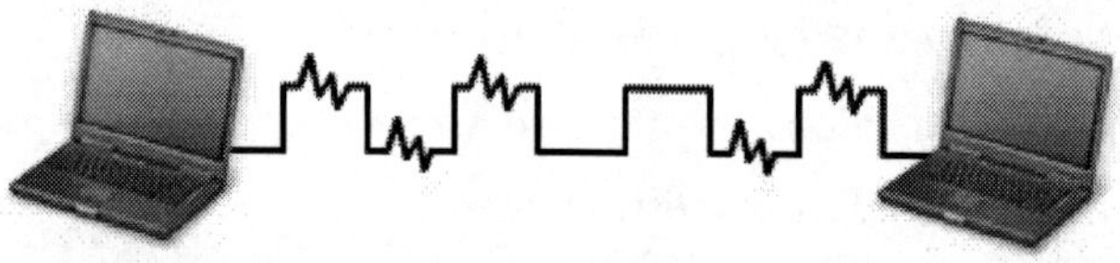

Figure 4-12: *Electrical noise.*

Example: Sources of Electrical Noise

There are many sources of noise.

Noise Source	Description
Ambient noise	Ambient noise can come from many sources, including solar disturbances that affect the earth's magnetosphere, or nearby radio broadcasting towers. These naturally occurring forms of noise affect both bounded and unbounded media, with longer segments being more affected than shorter ones.
Power wires	Nearby high-tension power lines or a building's own electrical wiring can create electrical noise. Network cables that run parallel to electric wires are more susceptible than those that run perpendicular.

Noise Source	Description
Electric motors	Electric motors, such as those used in elevators, refrigerators, water fountains, and Heating, Ventilating, and Air Conditioning (HVAC) equipment, create noise while running, but it is worse when they start up. Motors require a huge amount of electricity to start up, causing a burst of noise. These bursts can create short temporary outages that resolve themselves when the motor reaches full speed or stops.
Electricity-based heat-generating devices	Like electric motors, electric heating elements use a lot of electricity and thus cause a significant amount of noise while running.
Fluorescent, neon, and high-intensity discharge (HID) lights	Lighting devices that use these technologies produce a large amount of electrical noise, generally due to the transformers and ballasts required to make these lights work. Interior overhead lights, building security lights, and decorative lighting can create enough noise during operation to interfere with networking signals traveling over either bounded or unbounded media.

How Noise Affects Device Power

In addition to the noise that leaks into data networking media, noise can affect the electricity that powers computing devices. Surges or dips in the electric current result, which can damage equipment, cause application or operating system software crashes, or even system restarts.

Electric motors, heating elements, solar disturbances, or other natural disasters can cause transient power problems. Most devices include power conditioning components that handle at least some of these power fluctuations. However, sensitive equipment should be protected through the use of specialized power conditioning devices, such as a universal power supply (UPS) or surge protector.

Shielding

Definition:

Shielding is any grounded conductive material placed around the data media to block the introduction of noise into the media. It deflects noise to ground. Because of this, the connection between the ground and the shield is called a *drain*. Shields are drained in only one location to prevent a ground loop, a phenomenon in which the shield generates noise in the data signal.

Example:

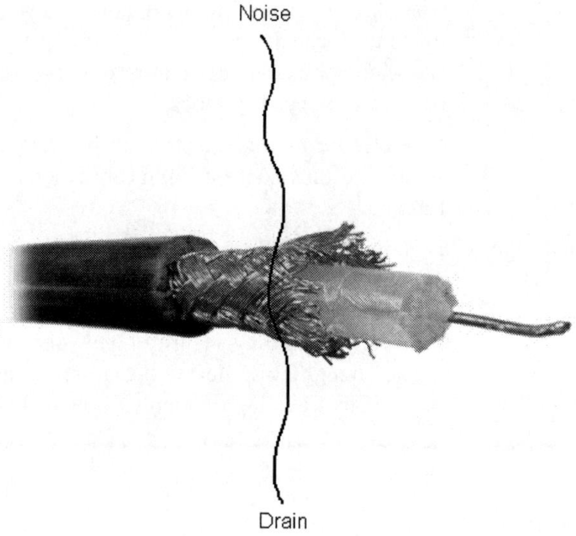

Figure 4-13: *Shielding.*

Differential Signaling

Definition:

Differential signaling is a noise reduction technique in which the signals from two inputs are compared; signals that are identical on the two inputs are ignored, while those that are different on the inputs are accepted. Quite often, noise is the same on both conductors of a network cable. With differential signaling, such noise can be easily cancelled out.

Example:

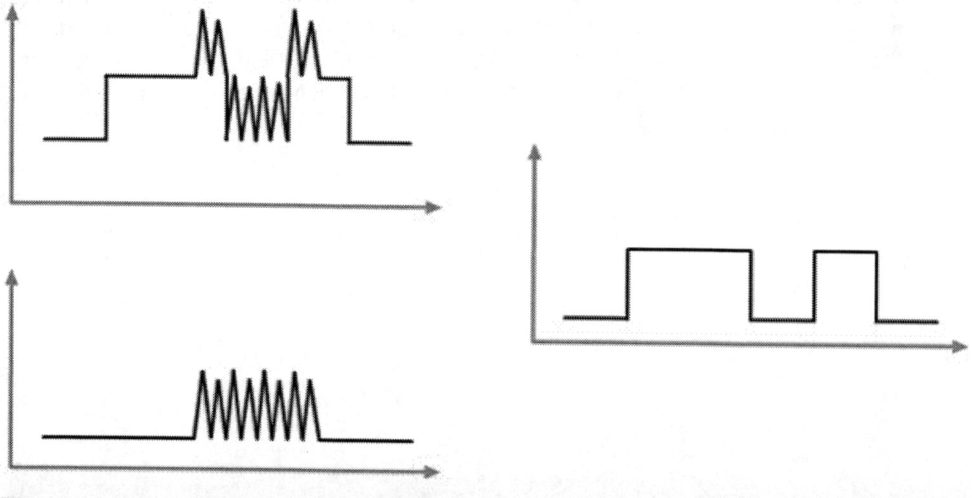

Figure 4-14: *Differential signaling.*

Noise Control with Twisted Pair

The twists in the twisted pair cable determine how resistant to noise the cable will be. When noise is introduced into a twisted pair cable in which the pairs are tightly twisted, the noise is deflected and has minimal affect on the signal. When noise is introduced into a twisted pair cable in which the pairs are loosely twisted, the noise impinges on the conductor and adversely affects the signal.

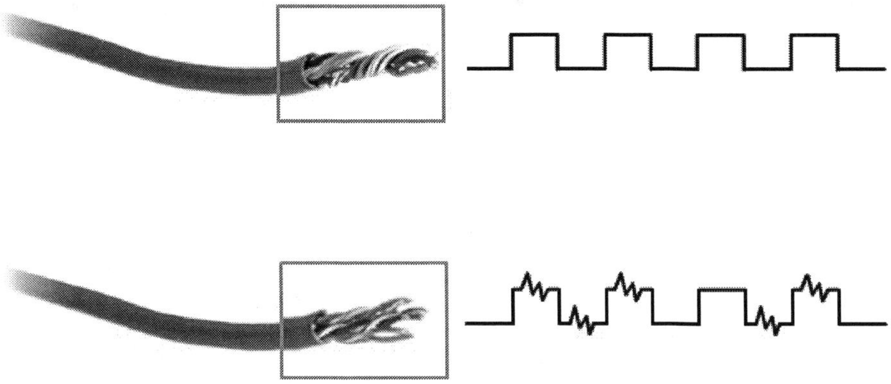

Figure 4-15: *Noise control with twisted pair.*

Twists and Connectors

The primary difference between Category 3 and Category 5 twisted pair is the number of twists per inch, with Cat 5 being more tightly wound. To fully support the network speeds for which they are rated, however, you must take care when installing connectors to these cables. You can't unwind the pairs too much or you will eliminate the noise-canceling benefits of the twists. The more twists per foot and the more consistently the twists are arranged, the more resistant to noise a cable will be.

As a rule, you should not unwind more than 3/8 of an inch (about 10 mm) for Category 5 cable. Category 3 cable is a bit more forgiving. Category 6 cable requires special connectors that maintain the twists inside the connector.

Termination

Termination is the application of a resistor or other device to the end of a cable. Adding such a *terminator* ensures that the end of the cable doesn't represent an abrupt change in impedance, which would be a source of signal reflections and noise. The electrical characteristics of a terminator must match the cable and other components.

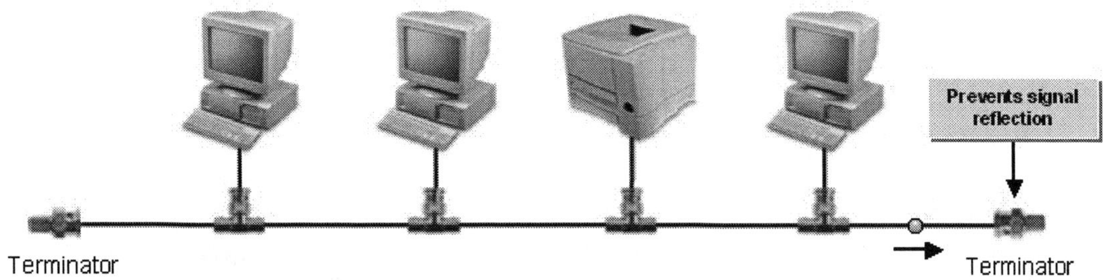

Figure 4-16: *Termination.*

In older networking technologies, you had to install terminators yourself. They are now typically built into the networking devices you use.

Matching Impedance

Generally, you must match the impedance of all devices and cables to achieve proper signal flow. Signals can reflect off the points where impedance changes, such as at a connector between devices or cable segments of mismatched impedance. Signals flow smoothly across connections when impedances match.

A cable's impedance is typically marked on its outer jacket. If such a measure is a concern for a particular networking device, you will find markings on its case or in its manual stating the device's impedance.

Grounding

Grounding is the connection of a shield or conductor to an electrical ground point, such as a pipe or wire that is in contact with the earth. Grounding at one point in a segment helps prevent noise on the data conductor by shunting noise signals to ground. Connecting to ground at multiple points can introduce noise onto the line, degrading network performance.

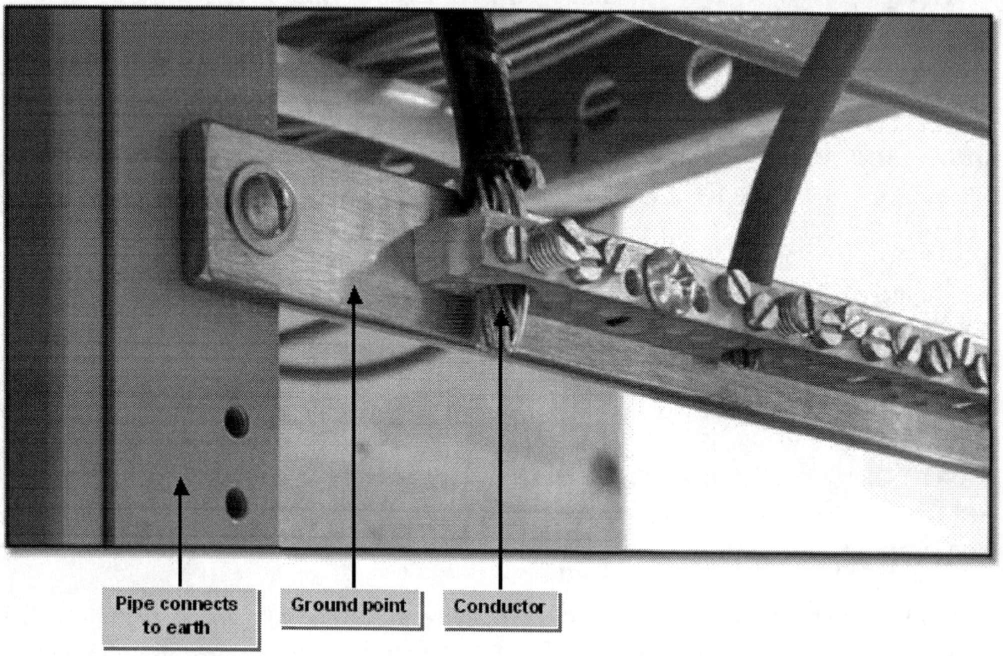

Figure 4-17: *Grounding.*

Grounding for Safety

Electrical devices often must be connected to a ground point for safety. In these situations, the ground connection serves as a way to direct high voltages safely away from humans and other devices, sending it instead into the ground. Building codes typically permit you to ground power circuits to water pipes or to conduits at multiple points.

Isolated Grounds

You should ground networking and other sensitive electronic equipment to dedicated ground points rather than to pipes and conduits. Electricians refer to this sort of ground connection as an isolated ground and will use an orange socket for such circuits.

Media Installation Techniques

The installation techniques you follow can affect the amount of noise injected onto a network cable. To limit noise on data cables caused by media installation techniques, follow the guidelines given in the following table.

Installation Technique	Considerations
Separate data and electric cables	Do not run data and electricity cables in the same trays, raceways, and conduits. Avoid running these cables parallel to each other. Furthermore, avoid running network cables parallel to each other when you can, as crosstalk is worst when cables run parallel.
Fluorescent lights	Keep network cables at least 20 inches from fluorescent lights. If you must run data cables across or near these lights, do so in such a way that exposes the smallest length of cable to the light as you can.
Power ground	Make sure to ground all equipment and electrical circuits according to the manufacturer's instructions and local building codes.
Connector installation	Follow standards, specifications, and manufacturer's directions when installing network cables. Do not unwind conductor pairs any more than required or allowed. Make sure connectors are firmly attached and electrically connected.

ACTIVITY 4-4

Investigating Electrical Noise Control Measures

Scenario:

In this activity, you will identify methods for electrical noise control.

1. **Choose the statement that defines electrical noise.**
    a) Solar radiation or man-made sources of data signals.
    b) Unwanted signals introduced onto network media.
    c) The reception of transmitted signals from man-made sources.
    d) Unwanted signals that impede the proper reception of interference.

2. **Select the items that are sources of electrical noise.**

   a) Fluorescent lights

   b) Solar storms

   c) Wind storms

   d) HVAC equipment

   e) Water current

3. **True or False? Differential signaling is an electrical noise reduction technique for distinguishing between the signal on two conductors.**

   __ True

   __ False

4. **Installing a resistor or other device on the end of a cable to prevent signal reflections and noise is called:**

   a) Impedance

   b) Grounding

   c) Terminating

   d) Ohms

TOPIC D

Network Connectivity Devices

Network media, both bounded and unbounded, carry the data across your network. To move data around the network on the media, network connectivity devices are needed. In this topic, you will examine the network connectivity devices and their purposes.

Network connectivity devices make networks happen. Network connectivity devices connect clients to the network and assist in moving data around a network in the most efficient manner. In some cases, network devices can boost the data signal to increase the distance your data transmissions can travel before they are so degraded that they are unusable at their destination.

Network Interface Cards (NICs)

Definition:

A *network interface card (NIC)* is a device that serves as an intermediary between the computer's data bus and the network. To connect to a network, a PC must have a NIC. NICs can be built into the motherboard of the computer, connected through a USB, PC Card, or FireWire port, or can be an internal adapter card that is installed into one of the computer's expansion slots.

A NIC can also be called a network adapter or network card.

Example:

Figure 4-18: *An internal network interface card.*

Activity 4-5

Identifying the Local Network Card

There is a simulated version of this activity available on the CD-ROM that shipped with this course. You can run this simulation on any Windows computer to review the activity after class, or as an alternative to performing the activity as a group in class. The activity simulation can be launched either directly from the CD-ROM by clicking the Interactives link and navigating to the appropriate one, or from the installed data file location by opening the C:\Data\Simulations\Lesson#\Activity# folder and double-clicking the executable (.exe) file.

Scenario:

In this activity, you will identify the local network adapter card.

What You Do	How You Do It
1. **Open the Local Area Connection Properties dialog box.**	a. **Choose Start→Control Panel→Network Connections.**
	b. **Right-click Local Area Connection and choose Properties.**
2. **Identify the network card type.**	a. In the Connect Using area, **identify the network adapter type.** 
	b. **Click Cancel.**

Transceivers

Definition:

A *transceiver* is a device that both sends and receives data. In networking, transceivers are used to connect a computer's NIC to the network media. Most modern transceivers are built into the network card.

Older transceivers were external boxes, some of which had to clamp on and pierce the jacket of the media to make contact with its conductors.

Example:

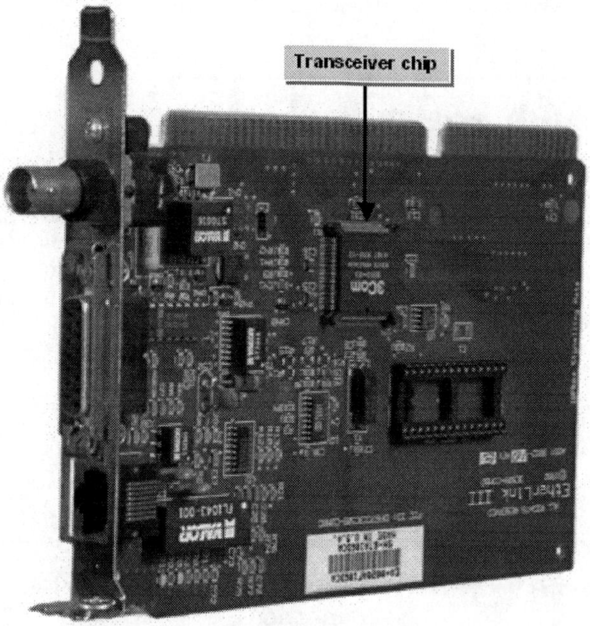

Figure 4-19: *A transceiver on a network interface card.*

Premise Wiring

Premise wiring is the cables, connectors, and connection points that make a network functional.

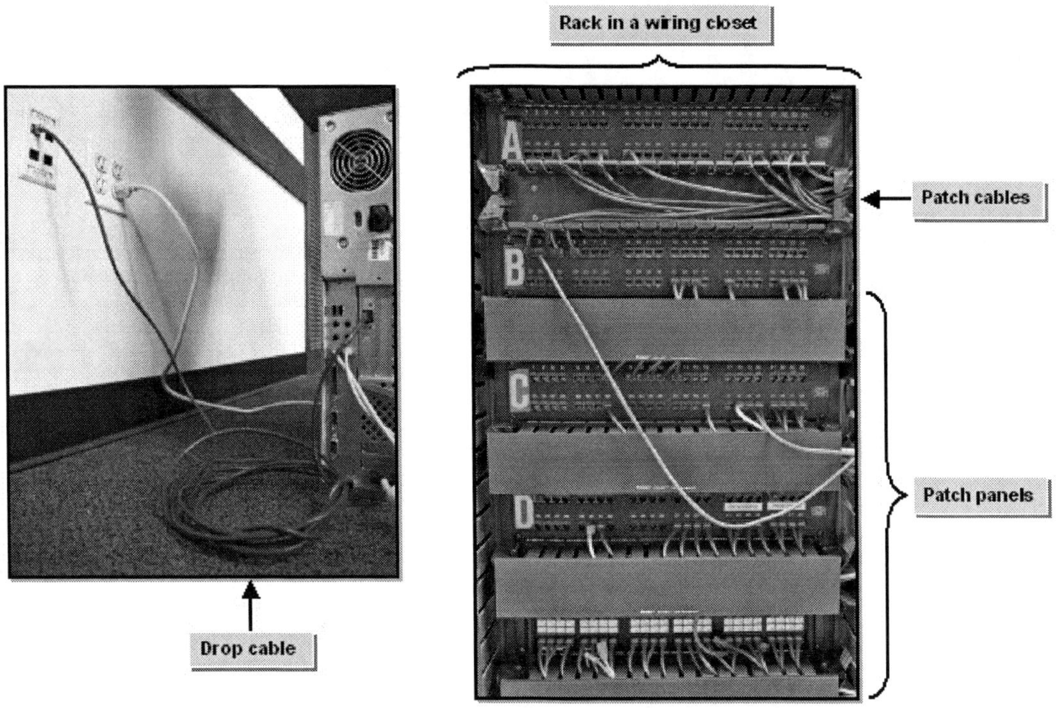

Figure 4-20: *Some premise wiring components.*

Premise Wiring Component	Description
Drop cable	The wire that runs to a PC, printer, or other device connected to the network.
Patch panel	A connection point for drop and patch cables. Typically, a patch panel has one or more rows of RJ-45 or other connectors. Drop cables are connected to the connectors. Cables run between the connectors to connect drop cables as needed.
Patch cable	A cable that is plugged into the patch panel to connect two drops. A patch cable might or might not be a crossover cable, one in which the transmit conductor at one end is connected to the receive conductor at the other.
Cross connects	Individual wires that connect two drops at a patch panel. Cross connects are rarely used in modern networks. However, they are still frequently used with telephone wiring.
Wiring closet	A small room in which patch panels are installed. Drop cables radiate out from the wiring closet to the components on the network.

Repeaters

Definition:

A *repeater* is a device that regenerates a signal to improve transmission distance. By using repeaters, you can exceed the normal limitations on segment lengths imposed by the various networking technologies.

Repeaters are used frequently with coax media, such as cable TV, and were also deployed in networks that used coax cabling. Most networks today use twisted pair cabling, and repeaters are no longer a commonly used network device.

Example:

Figure 4-21: *A repeater.*

The 5-4-3 Rule

There is a limit to how many repeaters you can install before timing problems prevent the proper reception of network signals. You can connect up to five segments using four repeaters; however, only three of those segments can contain nodes. This numeric relation is called the "5-4-3 rule."

Hubs

Definition:

A *hub* is a networking device used to connect the drops in a physical star topology network into a logical bus topology. Hubs support transmission speeds of 10 Mbps and 100 Mbps, though it is typical to find auto-sensing hubs, which will provide either transmission speed. For example, if three computers are connected to a hub and two of the computers have 100-Mbps network cards installed and one has a 10-Mbps card installed, the 10/100-Mbps auto-sensing hub will "sense" the slower transmission of 10 Mbps, and the network will run at 10 Mbps.

Two common types of hubs are passive and active. A passive hub simply receives data transmitted from a device to one port and broadcasts it out to the devices connected on all other ports. An active hub, however, regenerates the signal much like a repeater.

In addition to active and passive, hubs can be managed or switching.

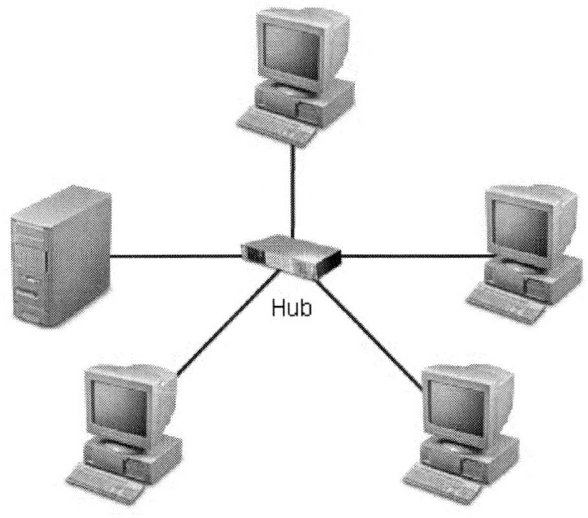

Figure 4-22: *A hub.*

Example: Managed Hub

A managed hub, also called an intelligent hub, is one that includes functions that enable you to monitor and configure its operation. Typically, you connect to the hub using special software or via a dedicated management port. Managed hubs are also called intelligent hubs.

Example: Switching Hub

A switching hub reads the destination address of a packet and directs it to the correct port. Switching hubs are slower than other types because they must process each packet. Many switching hubs support load balancing in that ports can be addressed dynamically to different segments based on traffic patterns.

Switches

Definition:

A *switch* is a networking device used to connect the drops in a physical star topology network into a logical bus topology. Switches forward packets to the correct port based on MAC addresses. Switches work with pairs of ports, connecting two segments as needed. Most switches can work with multiple pairs of ports simultaneously to improve performance.

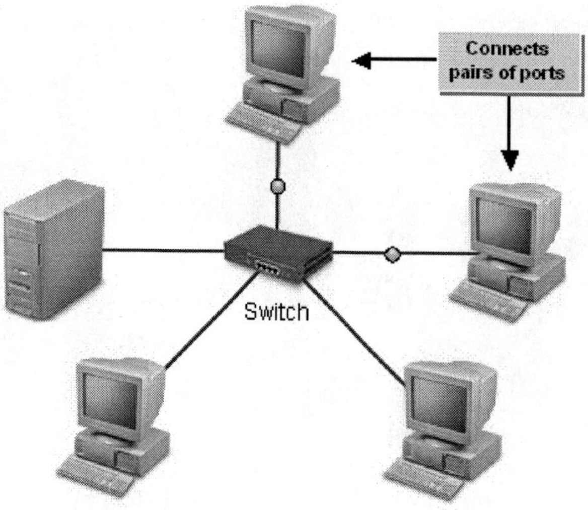

Figure 4-23: *A switch.*

Example: Switch Types

There are several switch types.

Type	Description
Cut-through	A packet is forwarded as soon as it is received. No error checking or processing of the packet is performed. This switch performs the address table lookup immediately upon receiving the destination address field in the frame header. The first bits in a frame are sent out the outbound port on a switch before the bits are received. This switching method does not allow the switch to discard frames that are corrupt and fail error checking in an Ethernet frame.
Fragment-free	The first 64 bytes of each packet are scanned for evidence of damage by a collision. If none is found, the packet is forwarded. Otherwise, it is discarded. By discarding fragments, this type of switch can reduce network congestion. It is similar to the cut-through switching method, but the switch waits to receive 64 bytes before it forwards the first bytes of the outgoing frame.
Store-and-forward	The switch calculates the CRC value for the packet's data and compares it to the value included in the packet. If they match, the packet is forwarded. Otherwise, it is discarded. This is the slowest type of switch. The switch receives the entire frame before the first bit of the frame is forwarded. This allows the switch to inspect the frame check sequence (FCS) before forwarding the frame. (Broadly speaking, FCS refers to error checking in the trailer of an Ethernet frame.)

Full Duplex Support

Because a switch forms a miniature network between a node and itself, there is no chance of data collisions. Thus, it does not need to use a conventional media access method, such as CSMA/CD. Instead, providing the node's NIC is properly configured, the switch can support a full duplex connection with each node over which data can be sent and received simultaneously.

Full duplex operation may not be enabled by default on your NICs and switches. Taking the time to enable this feature can improve performance, as much as doubling throughput on your network.

Bridges

Definition:

A *bridge* is a network device that divides a logical bus network into subnets. Bridges examine the MAC address of each packet. If the packet is destined for a node connected to a different port, the bridge forwards the packet. If the packet is addressed to a node on its own segment, the bridge does not forward the packet. This arrangement reduces traffic between segments and improves overall network performance.

Example:

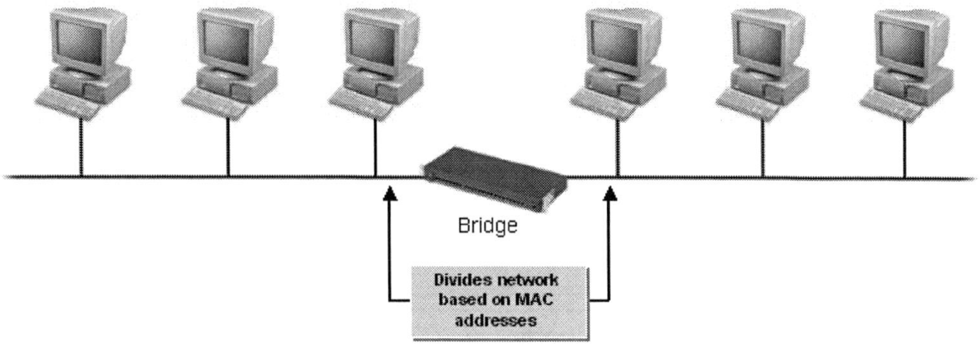

Figure 4-24: *A bridge.*

Manual and Learning Bridges

With older bridges, you had to configure the subnet addresses associated with each port using special software. Learning bridges eliminated this configuration burden by examining the network traffic. By watching the source addresses of packets, these bridges could determine the addresses of the subnets connected to each port and configure themselves automatically.

Spanning Tree Algorithm

In general, you should place a bridge so that no more than 20 percent of network traffic needs to cross the bridge. If you need to improve performance, especially in cases where more traffic needs to cross than the recommended limit, you can connect multiple bridges between segments. However, when you do so, you risk creating bridging loops.

A bridging loop is created when multiple bridges are used and become misconfigured (manually or through mislearning network addresses). In such cases, packets can be forwarded endlessly between subnets when the different bridges each think the packet is destined for a remote port.

To prevent bridging loops, you can implement bridges that support the Spanning Tree Algorithm (STA). With STA, each port is assigned a value. When a bridge forwards a packet, it attaches the appropriate value to the packet. When another bridge receives the packet, it examines the port value. If it is higher than the values assigned to its ports, it won't forward the packet.

Routers

Definition:

A *router* is a networking device that connects multiple networks that use the same protocol. Routers send data between networks by examining the network addresses contained in the packets they process. Routers can work only with *routable protocols*, which are network protocols that provide separate network and node addresses. A router can be a dedicated device or can be implemented as software running on a node, typically with two NICs.

Example:

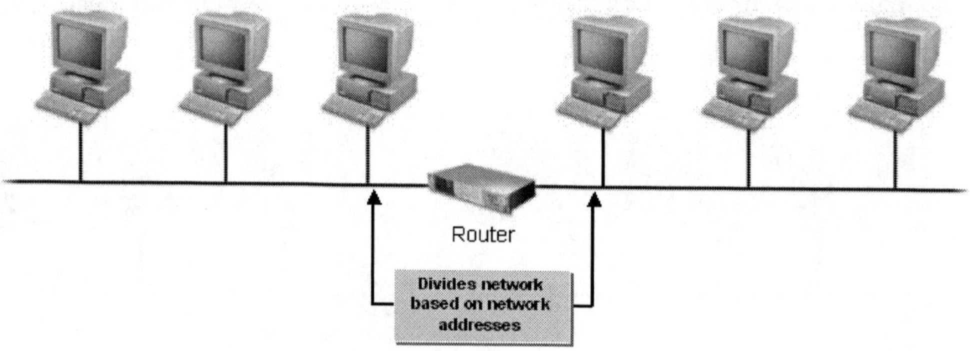

Figure 4-25: *A dedicated router.*

Wireless Access Points

Definition:

A *wireless access point* is a device that provides connection between wireless devices and can connect to wired networks. They have a network interface to connect to the wired network and an antenna or infrared receiver necessary to receive the wireless signals. Many include security features that enable you to specify which wireless devices can make connections to the wired network.

Example:

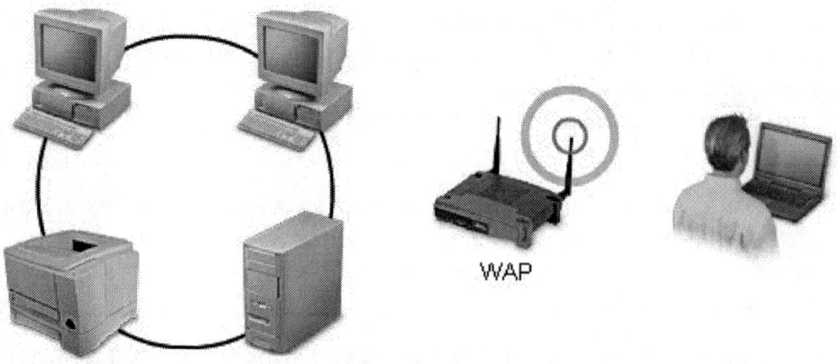

Figure 4-26: *A wireless access point.*

Gateways

Definition:

A *gateway* is a device, software, or a system that converts data between incompatible systems. Gateways can translate data between different operating systems, between different email formats, or between totally different networks.

It is important not to confuse a gateway with the default gateway in TCP/IP which just forwards IP data packets.

Example:

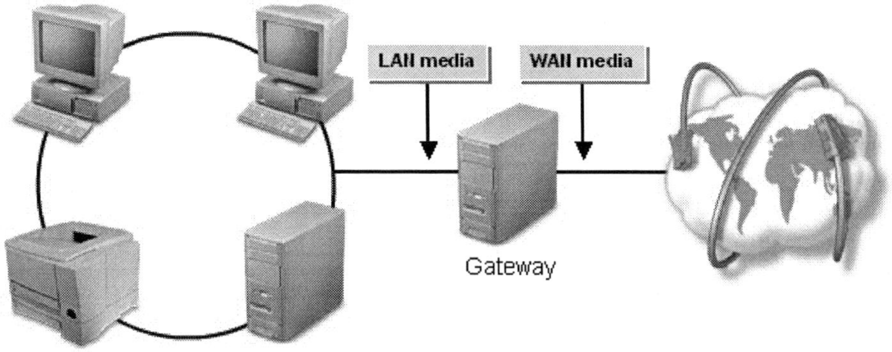

Figure 4-27: *A gateway.*

ACTIVITY 4-6

Investigating Network Connectivity Devices

Scenario:

In this activity, you will identify the primary types of network connectivity devices.

1. **You need to connect multiple networks. You want data to be sent between networks, only as needed. All your networks use the same protocol. Which networking device would best meet your needs?**
    a) Router
    b) Bridge
    c) Gateway
    d) Switch

2. A device that connects drops, turning a physical star into a logical bus network, while connecting only those ports required for a particular transmission is called a:

   a) Hub

   b) Router

   c) Gateway

   d) Switch

---

3. True or False? A gateway subdivides a LAN into subnets.

   __ True

   __ False

---

4. Which of the following are components of premise wiring?

   a) Drop cables

   b) Routers

   c) Patch cables

   d) Patch panels

---

5. You work for a small tech company that supports small, local businesses. You receive a call from an insurance sales office in which users have complained that file sharing on their peer-to-peer network is slow. The manager recently replaced a 10-Mbps hub with an auto-sending 10/100 Mbps hub, but users still complain that the network is too slow. You have been asked to evaluate the situation and make recommendations The network consists of one 10/100-Mbps auto-sensing, six-port hub, but you discover that transmission speeds are limited to 10 Mbps. What upgrades will you suggest to increase transmission speeds to 100 Mbps?

ACTIVITY 4-7

Troubleshooting Network Connectivity

Scenario:

In this activity, you will identify the cause of network connectivity problems.

1. **Some of your network users are complaining that they cannot access a network printer. You perform a physical network inspection and discover the situation shown in the graphic.**

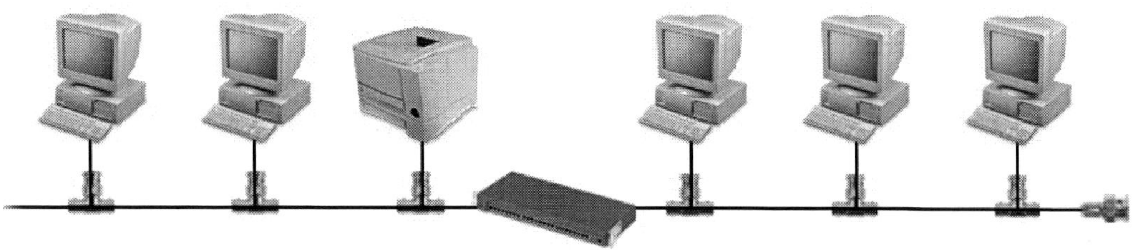

What type of network topology is this? What component of the network has failed?

2. **Which network device(s) will be affected? Why?**

3. You receive a call from a network user who has lost all network connectivity. You examine the network components on the user's station and segment and discover the situation shown in the graphic.

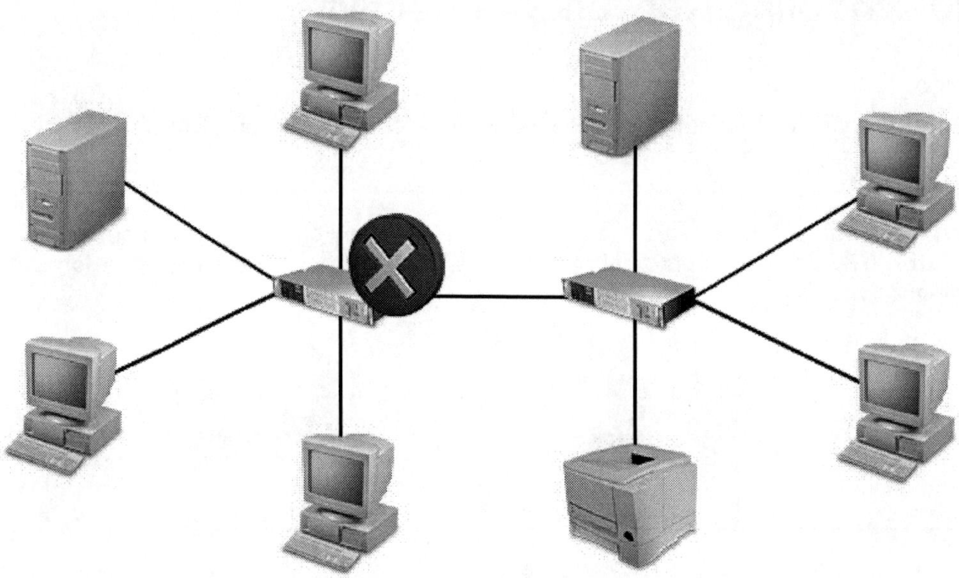

What type of network topology is this? Which network component has failed?

---

4. Which network device(s) will be affected? Why?

---

5. Another network user calls complaining that he can't connect to a server. You try to connect to various network devices and examine the network components and discover the situation shown in the graphic.

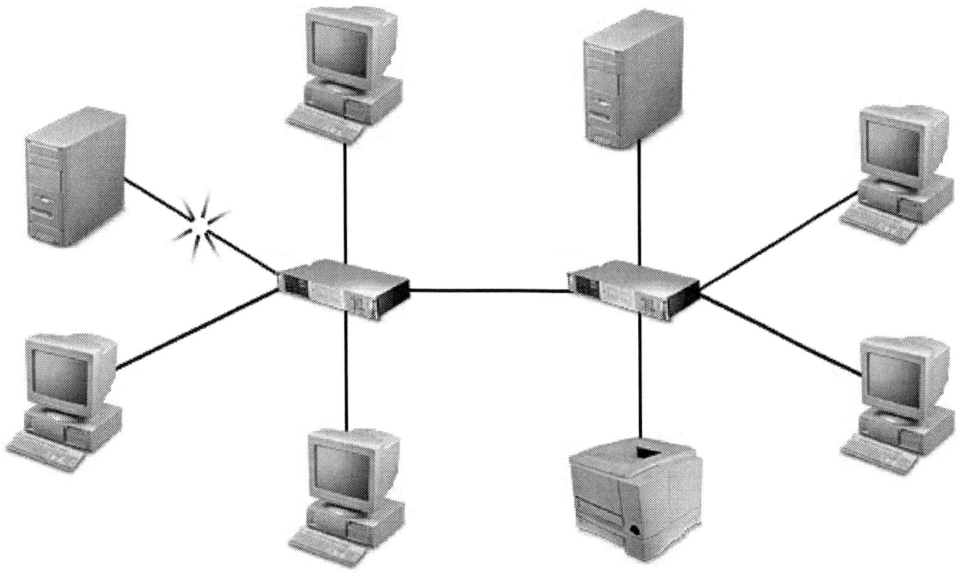

What type of network topology is this? What is the cause of the connectivity failure?

6. Which network device(s) will be affected? Why?

7. Your company's network is spread across several locations within the city. One of your network operations centers has experienced a power surge and you are concerned about the effect on network connectivity. You try to connect to various network devices and discover the situation shown in the graphic.

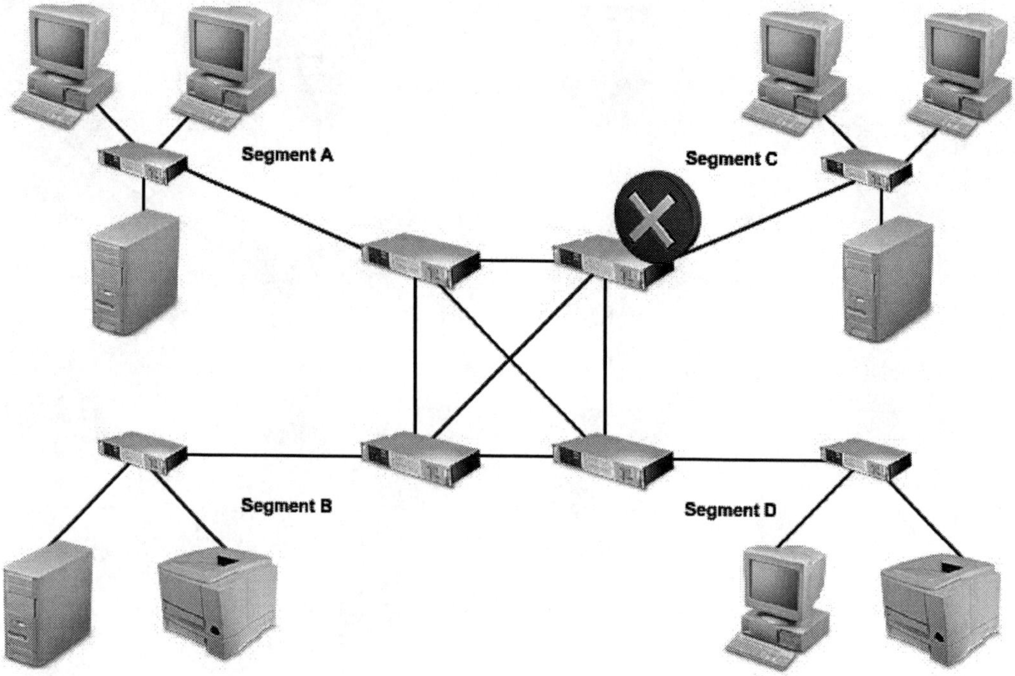

What type of network is this? Which network device has failed?

---

8. What area of the network will be affected?

---

9. Your company occupies part of a floor in a large office building. The office suite adjacent to your location has recently been vacated and you are going to expand into the empty space. You have hired a contractor to run new cable for both your telephone and network infrastructure into the new space. After users have moved into the new space, they begin complaining that network performance is not comparable to the existing network. You examine the cable installation and notice that "CAT 1" is printed on all the cable. What is the most likely cause of the network connectivity problems?

---

10. How can you correct the situation?

---

11. Your network uses UTP CAT 5 cable throughout the building. There are a few users who complain of intermittent network connectivity problems. You cannot determine a pattern for these problems that relates to network usage. You visit the users' workstations and find that they are all located close to an elevator shaft. What is a likely cause of the intermittent connectivity problems?

12. How might you correct the problem?

13. You have been called in as a network consultant for a small company. The company's network uses a star-wired bus with individual nodes connected to a series of hubs, which are then connected together. Network performance seems slow and unreliable. You run network diagnostics and discover that the network media on all segments is saturated with traffic and that there is a high number of collisions. The company does not have the budget to completely re-wire the network or replace a large number of network interface cards. What are options you can recommend to improve performance on this network?

14. What are the factors you should consider when making your decision?

Lesson 4 Follow-up

In this lesson, you examined network media and networking devices. These components form the infrastructure of your network. Just as people don't commute without a road, train, or subway, your data cannot move from computer to computer without media and devices.

1. **Which will you use more frequently in your networks: bounded or unbounded media? Which is better?**

2. **Of the various networking devices, which offers you the best mix of features and functionality?**

NOTES

LESSON 5
Network Implementations

Lesson Time
2 hour(s), 15 minutes

Lesson Objectives:

In this lesson, you will identify the major types of network implementations.

You will:

- Identify the purpose and components of the OSI model.
- Identify ways that network clients access network resources.
- Identify the components of an Ethernet network implementation.
- Identify the components of a Token Ring network implementation.
- Identify the components of a FDDI network implementation.
- Identify the components of a wireless network implementation.

LESSON 5

Introduction

In the previous lesson, you learned about the different types of transmission media, noise control, and the various types of network connectivity options. These components are all combined together to create different types of network implementations. In this lesson, you will examine the major types of network implementations available today.

Networking is a fundamental aspect of all computer infrastructure. The ability to link and communicate between clients, servers, and mainframes is vital for the dissemination of voice and data traffic. As a network specialist, your ability to identify and utilize the various types of networks will enable you to successfully expand and manage your network.

This lesson covers the following CompTIA Network+ (2005) certification objectives:

- Topic A:
  - Objective 2.2: Identify the seven layers of the OSI (Open Systems Interconnection) model and their functions.
  - Objective 2.3: Identify the OSI layers at which the following network components operate: hubs, switches, bridges, routers, NICs (network interface cards), and WAPs (wireless access points).
- Topic C:
  - Objective 1.2: Specify the main features of 802.2 (Logical Link Control) and 802.3 (Ethernet) networking technologies, including speed, access method (CSMA/CA and CSMA/CD), topology, and media.
  - Objective 1.3: Specify the characteristics (for example, speed, length, topology, and cable type) of the following cable standards: 10BASE-T and 10BASE-FL; 100BASE-TX and 100BASE-FX; 1000BASE-T, 1000BASE-CX, 1000BASE-SX, and 1000BASE-LX; and 10 GBASE-SR, 10 GBASE-LR, and 10 GBASE-ER.
- Topic D:
  - Objective 1.2: Specify the main features of 802.5 (Token Ring) networking technologies, including speed, access method, topology, and media.
  - Objective 4.7: Given a troubleshooting scenario involving a network with a particular physical topology (for example, bus, star, mesh, or ring) and including a network diagram, identify the network area affected and the cause of the stated failure.
- Topic E:
  - Objective 1.2: Specify the main features of FDDI (Fiber Distributed Data Interface) networking technologies, including speed, access method, topology, and media.
  - Objective 2.14: Identify the basic characteristics (for example, speed, capacity, and media) of the WAN (wide area network) technology FDDI (Fiber Distributed Data Interface).
  - Objective 4.7: Given a troubleshooting scenario involving a network with a particular physical topology (for example, bus, star, mesh, or ring) and including a network diagram, identify the network area affected and the cause of the stated failure.
- Topic F:
  - Objective 1.2: Specify the main features of 802.11 (wireless) networking technologies, including speed, access method, topology, and media.
  - Objective 1.6: Identify the purposes, features, and functions of WAPs (wireless access points).
  - Objective 1.7: Specify the general characteristics (for example, carrier speed, frequency, transmission type, and topology) of the Bluetooth wireless technology.

— Objective 1.8: Identify factors that affect the range and speed of wireless service (for example, interference, antenna type, and environmental factors).
— Objective 2.15: Identify the basic characteristics of satellite and wireless Internet access technologies.
— Objective 2.17: Identify the following security protocols and describe their purpose and function: WEP (Wired Equivalent Privacy) and WPA (Wi-Fi Protected Access).
— Objective 4.8: Given a network troubleshooting scenario involving an infrastructure (wired or wireless) problem, identify the cause of the stated problem (for example, bad media, interference, network hardware, or environment).

TOPIC A

The OSI Model

In this lesson, you will examine various network implementations. Many network implementations are built on common network standards. In this topic, you will learn how these devices utilize an important common standard, the OSI model.

The theories behind the seven layers of the OSI model and how the model handles data packets have been implemented in many types of networks. Being able to identify the various OSI layers and their purpose will enable you to design and troubleshoot different types of networks effectively and quickly.

The OSI Model

The *Open Systems Interconnection (OSI) model* is a seven-layer framework that defines and describes how software or hardware operating at that layer will act on the data packet being sent. The model consists of two functional blocks: application support and network support.

The OSI model was originally developed in the early 1980s by the ISO, which continues to maintain the standard.

The application block is made up of the upper three layers: Application, Presentation, and Session. It is responsible for connecting software programs to the network.

The network block consists of the lower four layers: Transport, Network, Data-link, and Physical. This block is responsible for moving data on the network.

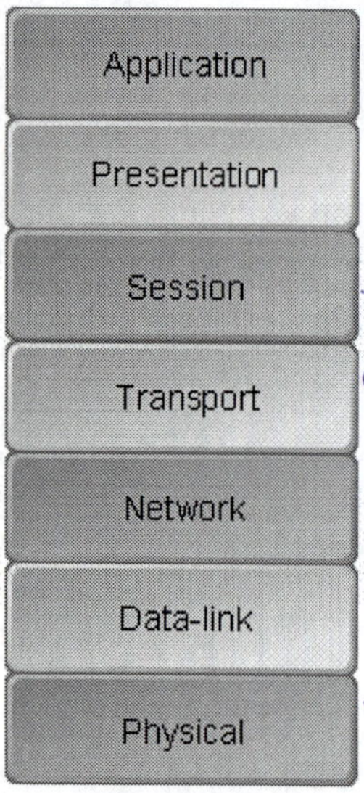

Figure 5-1: *The OSI model.*

CompTIA Network+ Exam Objectives

An Appendix is available to assist you in mapping CompTIA Network+ exam objectives to the course content. You can download the Appendix at the end of this lesson.

OSI Mnemonic

It can be difficult to remember the order of the layers, so in the past, a lot of schools taught them from the top down, using the mnemonic device "All People Seem To Need Data Processing."

The OSI Layers

The OSI model comprises seven layers.

Layer	Description
Layer 7: *Application layer*	Provides services and utilities that enable application programs to access a network and its resources. This enables applications to save files to the network server or print to network printers. The Application layer also advertises resources that each system has available for network use. Examples of technologies at this layer include: HTTP, DNS, FTP, Gopher, NFS, NTP, SMTP, SNMP, and Telnet.
Layer 6: *Presentation layer*	Translates data so that it can be moved on the network. This translation is only an intermediary format, and will change at lower layers. The Presentation layer also adds services such as data compression and encryption. Examples of technologies at this layer include: MME, SSL, TLS, GIF, JPEG, and TIFF.
Layer 5: *Session layer*	Establishes a connection between network devices, maintaining that connection and then terminating it when appropriate. It controls how, when, and for how long a device transmits. Examples of technologies at this layer include: sockets and session establishment in TCP.

Layer	Description
Layer 4: *Transport layer*	Ensures reliable data transmission by breaking up big data blocks into smaller packets that can be sent more efficiently on the network. Because these smaller packets might get out of order during transmission and arrive out of sequence, the Transport layer adds a sequence number so that the original order can be reconstructed. Lastly, the Transport layer is responsible for doing some error correction and sending acknowledgements. Gateways can operate at this layer and at higher layers of the OSI model. Examples of technologies at this layer include: TCP, UDP, IPSec, PPTP, and L2TP.
Layer 3: *Network layer*	Addresses and ensures delivery of packets across a network. This is where the protocol address is attached to the data packet. Routing devices within the Network layer make their decisions based on the protocol address, not the MAC address. Routers and some switches operate at this layer. Examples of technologies at this layer include: IP, ARP, ICMP, DHCP, RIP, OSPF, and IGMP.
Layer 2: *Data-link layer*	Ensures that individual frames get from one device to another without error. After sending frames, the Data-link layer waits for acknowledgements from receiving devices. The Data-link layer attaches the MAC address and makes MAC-level routing decisions. Examples of technologies at this layer include: PPP and SLIP. The Data-link layer can be divided into two sections, or categories: *Logical Link Control (LLC)* and *Media Access Control (MAC)*. The LLC sub-layer enables multiple upper-layer protocols to share the same media. It controls how frames are placed on the media by controlling the Physical layer device. The LLC checks the CRC, and either ACKs or NACKs the data. It also controls data flow so that the input doesn't flood. The MAC sub-layer manages the media access method—don't confuse it with the MAC address. In a contention-based network, the MAC sub-layer is responsible for the carrier sense; in a token passing network, it's responsible for the token. Bridges and some switches operate at this layer.
Layer 1: *Physical layer*	Moves bits of data on and off the physical cabling media. Where the upper layers deal with data bits, the Physical layer deals with voltages and frequencies. Physical-layer devices set the electrical characteristics of the transport—they receive a fully formatted data packet from the Data-link layer and put it on the media. Network adapters, hubs, and wireless access points operate at this layer. Examples of technologies at this layer include: Ethernet, Fast Ethernet, ATM, token ring, and FDDI.

The OSI Process

When data is sent to a network, it is added to the top layer of the OSI model first. From there, it's forwarded down to the next layer and so on until it's placed on the network media at the bottom of the model.

When data is received, it goes through the reverse process. Each layer strips off the information it needs and sends the data to the next layer.

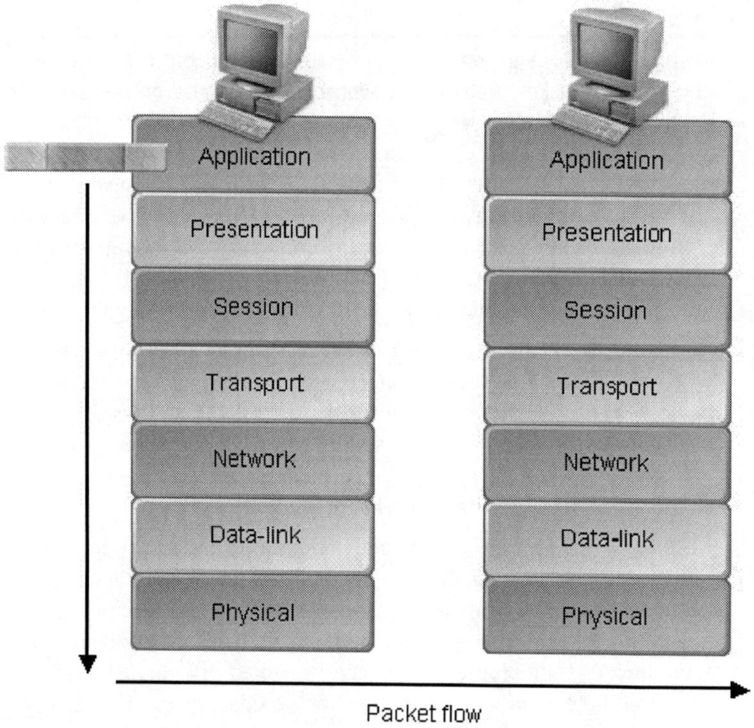

Figure 5-2: *The OSI process.*

ACTIVITY 5-1

Examining the OSI Model

Scenario:

In this activity, you will identify the layers of the OSI model.

1. **Match each layer of the OSI model with a description of its function.**

	Layer		Description
___	Application	a.	Establishes a connection between network devices, maintains that connection, and then terminates it when appropriate.
___	Presentation	b.	Ensures that individual frames get from one device to another without error. After sending frames, waits for acknowledgements from receiving devices.
___	Session	c.	Addresses and delivers packets across a network.
___	Transport	d.	Moves bits of data on and off the physical cabling media.
___	Network	e.	Translates data so that it can be moved on the network.
___	Data-link	f.	Provides services and utilities that enable application programs to access a network and its resources.
___	Physical	g.	Ensures reliable data transmission by breaking up big data blocks into smaller packets that can be sent more efficiently on the network.

2. **At which OSI layer is the MAC address applied to a data packet?**
   a) Layer 1 - Physical layer
   b) Layer 3 - Network layer
   c) Layer 4 - Transport layer
   d) Layer 2 - Data-link layer

3. **Which layer determines how fast data can be sent?**
   a) Layer 6 - Presentation layer
   b) Layer 7 - Application layer
   c) Layer 1 - Physical layer
   d) Layer 4 - Transport layer

4. **What is the highest level of the OSI model at which Telnet operates?**
   a) Data Link
   b) Physical
   c) Application
   d) Presentation
   e) Session

5. **At which layer does a WAP operate?**
   a) Session
   b) Application
   c) Data Link
   d) Network
   e) Presentation

---

6. **Which OSI layer is responsible for establishing connections between two devices?**
   a) Session
   b) Presentation
   c) Application
   d) Physical
   e) Data Link

---

7. **What is the main purpose of Layer 5?**

---

8. **What is the main purpose of Layer 7?**

---

9. **What is the purpose of Layer 1?**

---

10. **At which layer is the MAC address defined?**
    a) Layer 3
    b) Layer 2
    c) Layer 5
    d) Layer 6
    e) Layer 1

---

11. **Which OSI layer usually encapsulates using both a header and a trailer?**
    a) Session
    b) Application
    c) Network
    d) Data Link
    e) Presentation

TOPIC B

Client Network Resource Access

In the previous topic, you learned about the OSI model and how it influences the design and operation of network devices. However, the OSI model is a standard, not an implementation. In this topic, you will examine one implementation of the OSI model, by identifying the ways that clients access resources on a live network.

As a network professional, you will often be asked by end users how to search or browse for a specific network resource. These resource access needs are present on all types of networks, regardless of the specific network implementation. Being able to effectively show end users how to do this will increase their satisfaction with your capabilities and increase their confidence in your abilities.

Network Resources

Definition:

A *network resource* is any device that is external to the client computer and is accessible by multiple users.

Example: Shares

An example of a network resource is a *share*. Disks, folders, or printers can be shared to make them available to other users on the network.

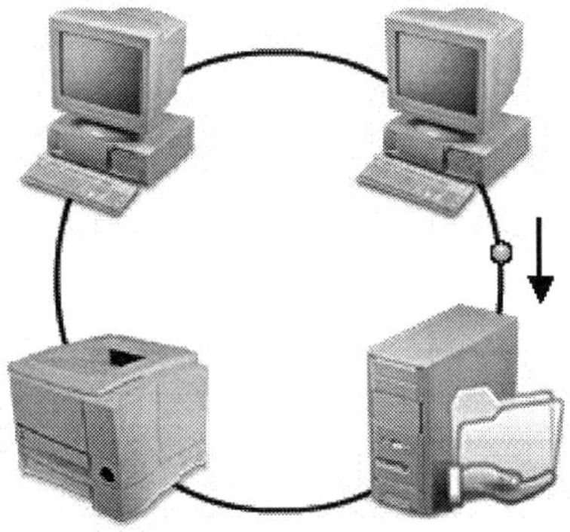

Figure 5-3: *Network resources.*

Network Browsing

Network browsing is the act of searching through an automated information system to locate or acquire a resource without necessarily knowing the existence of that resource. When a user opens My Network Places, the client attempts to contact the network's master browser for a browse list. In the Windows environment, the ability to browse comes from a browse list maintained on one network server elected to be the master browser. Upon contact, the master browser returns a list of online resources.

My Network Places

My Network Places is a graphical user interface (GUI) network browsing feature that enables Windows 2000, Windows XP, and Windows Server 2003 users to browse the network simply by double-clicking the My Network Places icon.

Establishing a Browse List

To establish a browse list in the first place, the master browser listens for server service announcements. When a server comes online, it announces itself and then, approximately every 15 minutes after that, announces again. If the master browser doesn't hear from the server for three announcements (45 minutes), it removes the server from the list. Typically, a server announces that it's being shut down. The master browser then removes it from the list of available servers.

Hidden Shares

When a folder is shared, it becomes visible to all network users, regardless of their rights to the folder. In situations where only administrative access to a folder is desired, an administrator will hide the share by adding a dollar sign ($) to the end of its share name.

This is common practice by administrators, who often need to share confidential information with only a few people. When administrators want to access the hidden share, they simply enter its full path name and are connected to it. Hidden shares can't be found by using the browser.

Windows also has hidden default administrative shares to enable remote administrative access to local resources such as hard disks. For example, the C drive is shared by default as C$.

Mapped Network Drives

Network drive mapping is a method used to link to a directory on one computer so it can be seen on another computer. Instead of typing in the complete path name of a directory to be accessed, simply enter a drive letter that has been assigned to that directory.

Network Searching

Network searching is a built-in function that enables users to find network resources such as printers and servers by name or by location. Network searches can be performed on a specific server, drive, folder, or file.

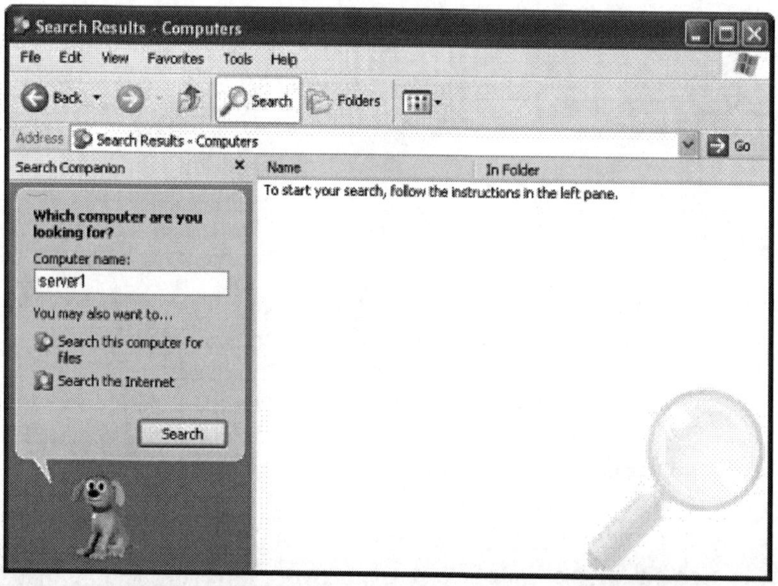

Figure 5-4: *Network searching.*

Browsing Using Active Directory

Active Directory (AD) is an X.500-compliant directory service Microsoft introduced with Windows 2000. Network objects such as users, groups, printers, files, and servers are organized into logical areas and published in the directory. The database may be distributed or replicated between and among other domain servers. Active Directory offers full search capabilities based either on the network object or its attributes. For example, a user could search for a printer on the fourth floor in the sales department instead of searching by the printer name.

Universal Naming Convention

Universal Naming Convention (UNC) is a standard for identifying and locating resources on remote computers. In UNC notation, file names or other resource names begin with double backslash characters (\\). The UNC takes the form *servername*\ *sharename*. A typical UNC path might be *FS01\SharedDocs\Resources.doc.*

ACTIVITY 5-2

Examining Client Network Resource Access

Scenario:

In this activity, you examine the various types of network access methods available to you.

---

1. Shares are ______________________________.

   a) Network resources that are unavailable

   b) Network resources that are available

   c) Disks, folders, or printers that are available to other users on the network.

   d) Ethernet resources

---

2. **To hide a share, you must add a ____________________ to the share name.**

   a) % character

   b) $ character

   c) @ character

   d) # character

---

3. **My Network Places allows you to ______________________________.**

   a) Attach drives to your computer

   b) Control the network

   c) Find other users

   d) Browse the network

---

4. **True or False? A mapped network drive is a directory shared by a network server that appears to be a drive on your local machine.**

   __ True

   __ False

5. **Network searching allows you to ____________________.**

   a) Search for specific items by name or by location

   b) Search for specific items by name only

   c) Search for specific items by location only

   d) Search for online users only

TOPIC C

Ethernet Networks

In the previous topic, you learned about network resources and how to access each type of resource. Resources would not be available if they were not connected in some form of a network. In this topic, you will learn how devices and resources are connected using Ethernet technology.

Ethernet technology is the most popular network technology utilized today. Networks both large and small utilize Ethernet technology to provide both backbone and end-user service. Due to the proliferation of Ethernet technology, you will be required to manage and troubleshoot Ethernet.

Ethernet

Definition:

An *Ethernet* network is a segmented LAN technology that uses Ethernet NICs and twisted pair, coax, or fiber media. Ethernet is used to connect computers, printers, and servers within the same building or campus.

Example:

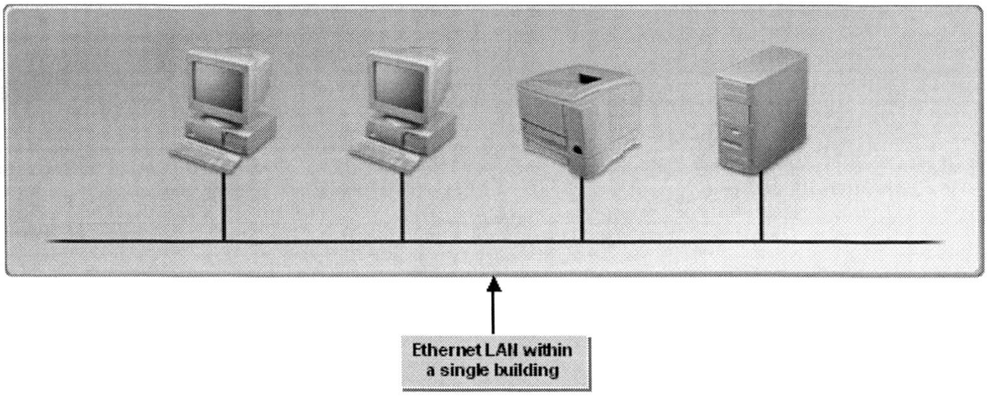

Figure 5-5: *Ethernet.*

Switched Ethernet

Definition:

Switched Ethernet is a LAN technology that connects host computers and network segments by using switches. The switch enables the device to utilize the full bandwidth of the medium.

There are two types of switches. Layer 2 switches operate at the Data-link layer of the OSI model. Layer 3 switches operate at the Network layer of the OSI model.

Example:

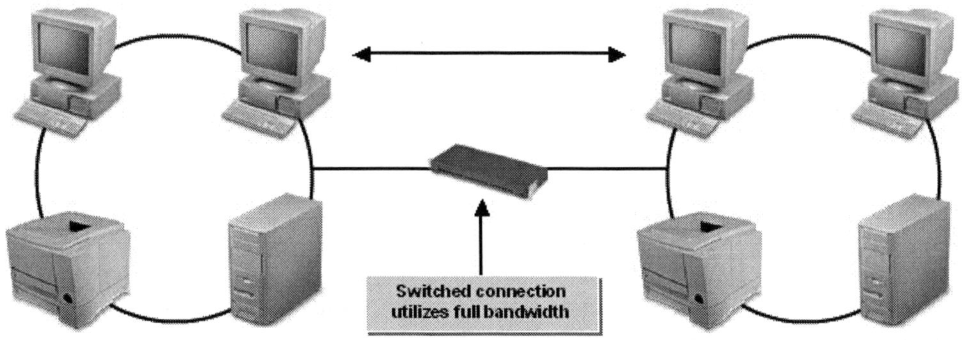

Figure 5-6: *Switched Ethernet.*

Ethernet Frames

Definition:

Ethernet frames control data sent between two nodes. Each frame consists of several fields.

Ethernet Frame Field	Description
Preamble	A pattern of ones and zeros used to signal the start of the frame and provide synchronization timing. The preamble notifies all nodes that there is data to follow. The preamble is 8 bytes in size.
Destination address	The address to which the frame is being sent; it can be a unicast, multicast, or broadcast address. The destination address is 6 bytes in size.
Source address	The address of the node sending—the frame is always a unicast address. The source address is 6 bytes in size.
Frame type	The frame type tells which upper-layer protocol should receive the data after Ethernet processes it. For example, data received as a result of a query to a Web page would have a frame type pointing to the Internet browser software. The frame type is 2 bytes in size.
Data	The payload of the frame (or the information being sent). It must be at least 46 bytes long and can be a maximum of 1500 bytes.
CRC	A 4-byte word generated by the sending node, enabling the receiving node to check the quality of the data it received.

Example:

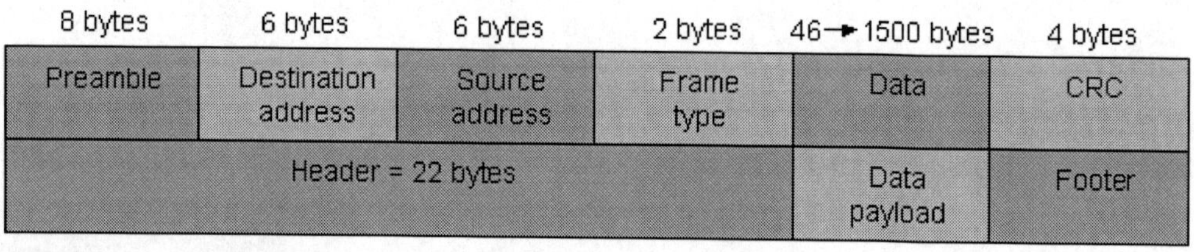

Figure 5-7: *Ethernet frames.*

The IEEE 802.x Standard

The 802.x standards are a family of networking standards developed by the IEEE in 1980 to address the rapid changes in networking technology. The 802.x standards are divided into several subcategories to address different networking requirements.

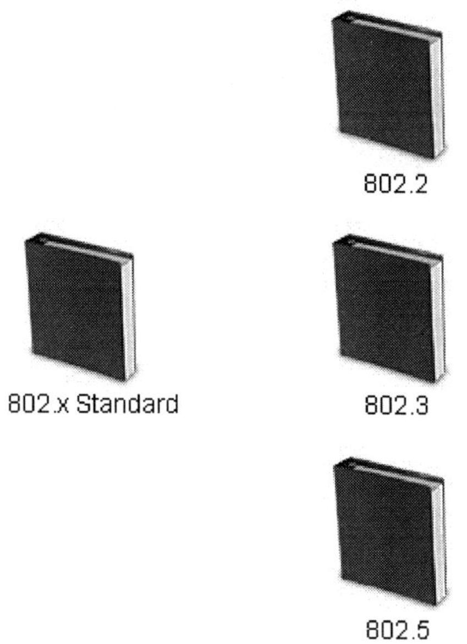

Figure 5-8: *The IEEE 802.x standard.*

802.3 Standards

The original Ethernet network implementation was developed by Xerox in the 1970s. The IEEE issued the 802.3 specification to standardize Ethernet and expand it to include a wide range of cable media. In addition to media type, 802.3 also specifies transmission speed and signal method. This type of network is most efficient in a physical star/logical bus topology.

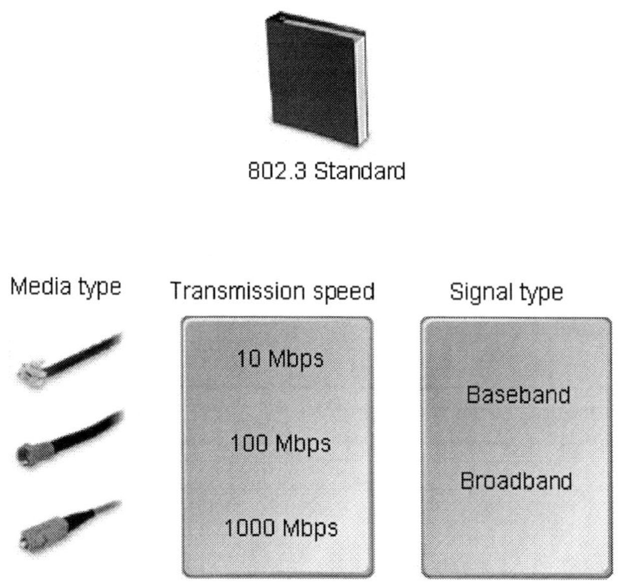

Figure 5-9: *802.3 standards.*

802.2 Standards

The 802.2 standard was developed to address the need for MAC-layer addressing in bridges. The 802.2 standard specifies frame size and rate. Packets can be sent over Ethernet and Token Ring networks using either copper or fiber media.

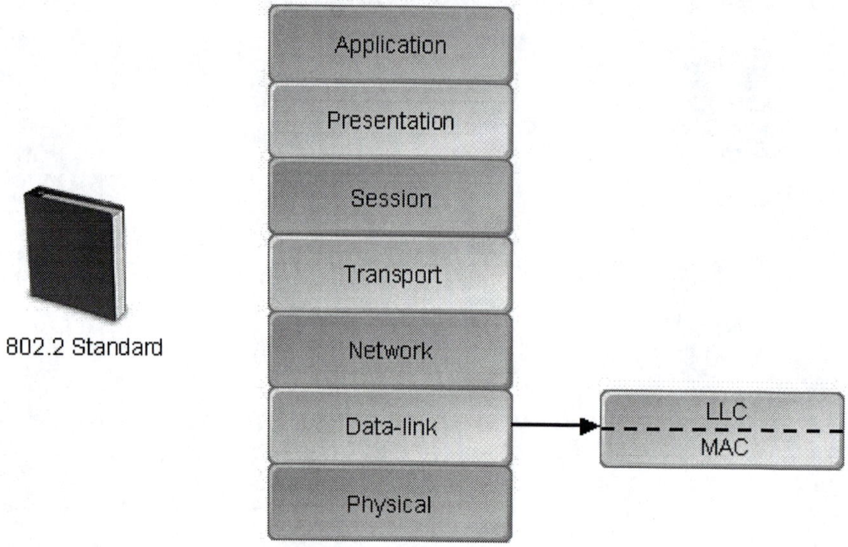

Figure 5-10: *802.2 standards.*

MAC and LLC Sub-Layers

The data link layer is divided into two sub-layers conceptually: the Logical Link Control (LLC) and the Media Access Control (MAC) sub-layers.

- The MAC sub-layer defines how packets are placed on the media. In an Ethernet network, for instance, which uses contention-based media access, the MAC layer controls elements of physical addressing such as error notification, the order of frame delivery, and flow control.
- The LLC sub-layer is responsible for identifying Network layer protocols and for encapsulating those protocols. An LLC header tells the Data Link layer what to do with a packet once it receives a frame.

The 10Base Standards

The 10Base standards describe the type of media used and the speeds at which each type of media operates. The cable standard specification contains three components: a number indicating media speed, the signal type in baseband or broadband, and a code for either copper or fiber media.

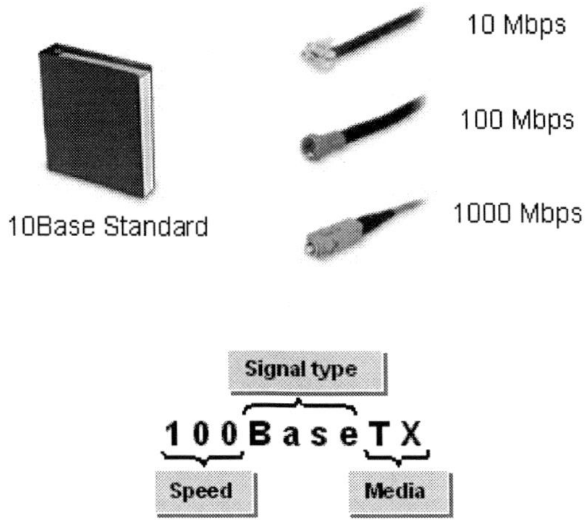

Figure 5-11: *10Base standards.*

Media Type Codes for the 10Base Specifications

Ethernet technology uses a wide variety of media to transmit and receive data.

Code	Physical Media
2	ThinNet coax
5	ThickNet coax
T	UTP or STP cable (could be Category 3, 4, or 5)
F	Fiber optic
FL	Fiber optic link
FB	Fiber optic backbone
FX	Fiber optic using two pairs of multimode fiber
TX	UTP using two pairs of Category 5
T4	UTP using four pairs of Category 3, 4, or 5
CX	Balanced copper media on coax
LX	Long wave light on single-mode fiber
SX	Short wave light on single-mode fiber
SR	Short wave light on multimode fiber
LR	Long range light on single-mode fiber
ER	Extremely long range light on single-mode fiber

Ethernet Speeds, Types, and Specifications

The following table lists the Ethernet speeds, types, and specifications.

Speed	Type of Ethernet	IEEE Standards	IEEE Specifications
10 Mbps	Ethernet	10Base2 10Base5 10BaseFL 10BaseT	802.3
100 Mbps	Fast Ethernet	100BaseFX 100BaseT 100BaseT4 100BaseTX	802.3u
1000 Mbps or 1 Gbps	Gigabit Ethernet	1000BaseCX 1000BaseLX 1000BaseSX 1000BaseT	802.3z
1000 Mbps or 1 Gbps	Gigabit Ethernet	1000BaseT over 5e/6 copper cable	802.3ab
10 Gbps	10 Gigabit Ethernet	10GBaseSR 10GBaseLR 10GBaseER	802.3ae

Ethernet Speed and Cable Length

The following table lists Ethernet speeds and the corresponding cable length.

Speed	Length
10 Mbps • 10Base2 • 10BaseT • 10BaseFL	• 185 meters • 100 meters • 2000 meters
100 Mbps • 100BaseFX • 100BaseT4 • 100BaseTX	• 412 meters/multimode 10,000 meters/single mode • 100 meters • 100 meters
1000 Mbps • 1000BaseCX • 1000BaseLX • 1000BaseSX • 1000BaseT	• 25 meters • 550 meters/multimode 5000 meters/single mode • 550 meters using 50 micron multimode fiber • 75 meters
10 Gbps • 10GBaseSR • 10GBaseLR • 10GBaseER	• 33 meters using 62.5 micron multimode fiber 300 meters using 50 micron multimode fiber • 10,000 meters using single mode fiber • 10,000 meters using single mode fiber

ACTIVITY 5-3

Examining Ethernet Networks

Scenario:

In this activity, you will examine the various types of Ethernet networks.

---

1. **Ethernet is a:**
   - a) Cost-effective network topology
   - b) Segmented LAN topology
   - c) Token-passing network topology
   - d) Topology that uses FDDI NIC cards

---

2. **The four data speeds accommodated by Ethernet are:**
   - a) 10 Mbps, 100 Mbps, 500 Mbps, and 1000 Mbps
   - b) 1 Mbps, 10 Mbps, 100 Mbps, and 10 Gbps
   - c) 10 Mbps, 100 Mbps, 1 Gbps, and 10 Gbps
   - d) 100 Mbps, 10 Gbps, 100 Gbps, and 500 Mbps

---

3. **The maximum amount of data an Ethernet frame can transmit is:**
   - a) 1518 bytes
   - b) 64 bytes
   - c) 100 bytes
   - d) 1500 bytes

---

4. **True or False? The 802.2 standard determines where frames of data start and end.**

   __ True

   __ False

---

5. **Which IEEE standard describes Gigabit Ethernet?**
   - a) 802.3u
   - b) 802.3z
   - c) 802.3
   - d) 802.ae
   - e) 802.5

---

6. **Which of the following do not use copper cabling?**
   a) 100BaseTX
   b) 100BaseCX
   c) 100BaseFX
   d) 100BaseLR

7. **Which fiber optic cable types use single mode?**
   a) 10GBaseER
   b) 10GBaseSR
   c) 10GBaseLR
   d) 10GBaseCX

8. **What is the maximum segment length for 1000BaseSX?**
   a) 25 meters
   b) 100 meters
   c) 550 meters
   d) 3,000 meters

9. **What is the maximum segment length for 100BaseFX?**
   a) 2 kilometers
   b) 5 kilometers
   c) 200 meters
   d) 20 kilometers

10. **What is the maximum segment length for 1000BaseCX?**
    a) 100 meters
    b) 550 meters
    c) 40,000 meters
    d) 25 meters

TOPIC D

Token Ring Networks

In the previous topic, you learned about the most common type of networking technology, Ethernet. However, there are other network implementations that you might encounter, one of which is Token Ring. In this topic, you will identify the characteristics of a Token Ring network implementation.

Over the years, Token Ring technology developed a strong following in high performance industrial networks where contention-based networking, Ethernet, was deemed unacceptable. Being able to manage and troubleshoot a Token Ring network will ultimately help you integrate both Token Ring and Ethernet technology into one functional network.

Token Ring Standards

There are two *Token Ring* standards that are very similar: IBM Token Ring and IEEE 802.5.

Token Ring Characteristics	IBM Token Ring	IEEE 802.5
Transmission speed	4/16 Mbps	4/16 Mbps
Physical topology	Star	Not specified
Number of nodes per ring	STP-260; UTP-72	250
Media type	STP/UTP listed as Category 1, 2, or 3 cable	Not specified
Signaling	Baseband	Baseband
Access method	Token passing	Token passing
Encoding	Differential Manchester	Differential Manchester

Token Ring History

IBM developed Token Ring in the 1970s and the IEEE 802.5 standard was developed in the 1980s. These two standards vary so slightly that they shouldn't even be considered different. The difference between IBM's standard and the IEEE 802.5 standard is that the IBM standard specifies a physical topology and a media type and the 802.5 standard doesn't.

Token States

There are four states that a token can be in while on the network:

1. In the available state, there is no data and the token can be used by any node.
2. In the captured state, the token contains valid data and is passed by the nodes until it reaches its destination.
3. In the acknowledged state, the destination node sends a message to the sending node indicating receipt.
4. In the reserved state, a priority node has reserved the token.

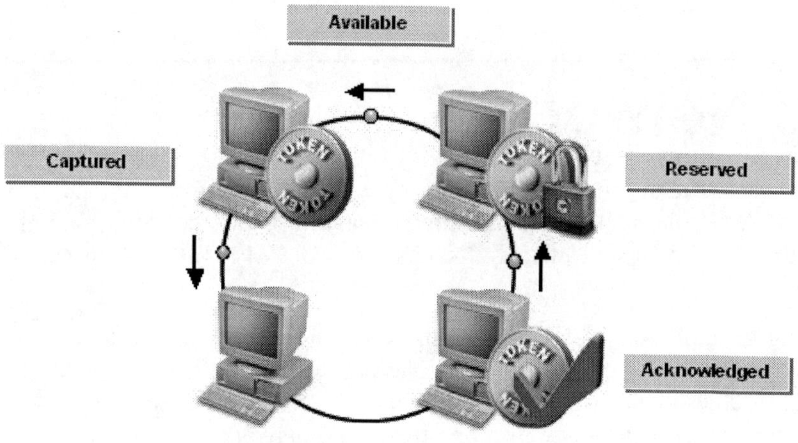

Figure 5-12: *Token states.*

Token State	Description
Available	There is no data in the payload and the token can be captured for use by a node.
Captured	There is a valid data payload. All nodes that receive a captured token evaluate the destination address to determine if the data has reached its destination or needs to be passed again.
Acknowledged	Notification, either positive (ACK) or negative (NACK), sent from the receiving node to the sending node once the token reaches its destination. (ACK indicates good data; NACK indicates bad data.)
Reserved	A priority system used by both IBM and 802.5 Token Ring, in which the token can be reserved.

Token Ring Access Priority

Token Ring networks use a sophisticated priority system that permits certain user-designated, high-priority stations to use the network more frequently. Token Ring frames have two fields that control priority: the priority field and reservation field. Only stations with a priority equal to or higher than the priority value contained in the token can seize that token.

Multi Station Access Units (MSAUs)

Definition:

IBM Token Ring network stations are directly connected to *Multi Station Access Units (MSAUs).* MSAUs can be wired together to form one large ring using patch cables and lobe cables for connections.

Example:

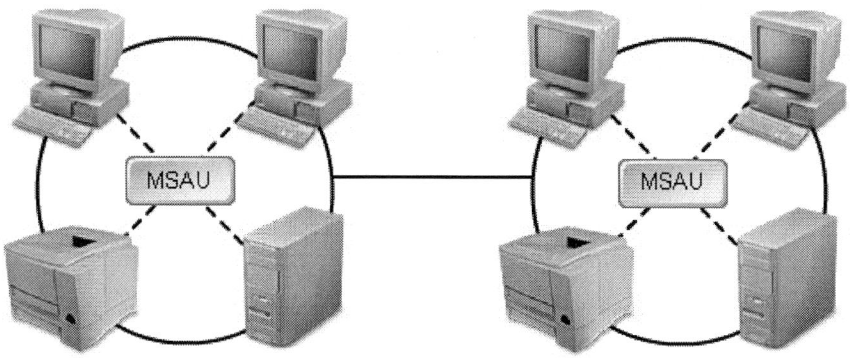

Figure 5-13: *Multi Station Access Units (MSAUs).*

MSAU Functionality

MSAUs also include bypass relays for removing nodes from the ring. The MSAU is responsible for connecting the ring-in and ring-out connections from each client to its neighbors. The MSAU is also responsible for jumping around any disconnected clients and continuing the ring. MSAUs are also called MAUs (Multi-station Access Units).

Token Ring Failure Recovery

Token Ring networks take on a star configuration when a device is turned off or disconnected from the network. In these situations, the MSAU simply bypasses the disconnected device. When a device is online but unresponsive, the MSAU keeps the connection live, but breaks the ring because the device isn't passing data.

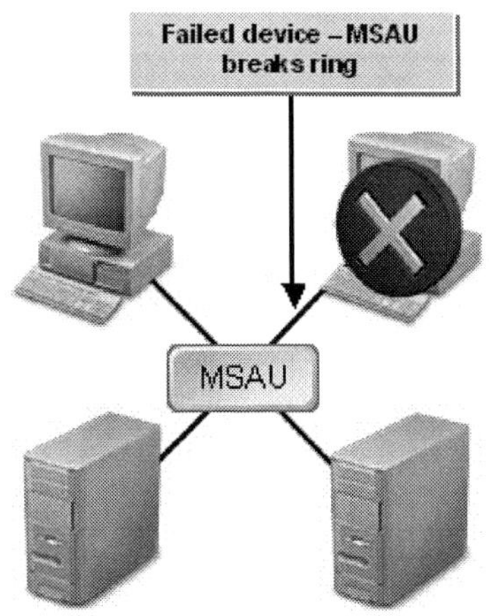

Figure 5-14: *Token Ring failure recovery.*

Beaconing

Beaconing is a process used to ensure that all systems on a ring are responsive. When a ring is established, each device sends a beacon every seven seconds. If a station doesn't get a beacon signal from its neighbor, it notifies the network that the node is down. As a result, traffic is reconfigured to loop back around the failed node.

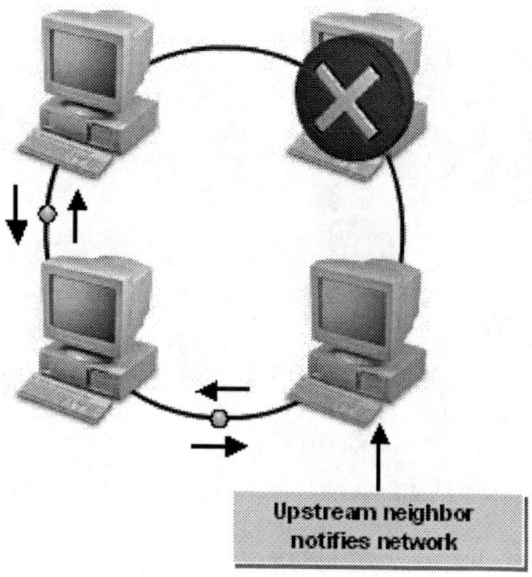

Figure 5-15: *Beaconing.*

ACTIVITY 5-4

Examining Token Ring Networks

Scenario:

In this activity, you will examine the operation of Token Ring networks. Being able to manage and troubleshoot a Token Ring network will ultimately help you integrate both Token Ring and Ethernet technology into one functional network.

---

1. **True or False? IBM Token Ring specifications and IEEE 802.5 specifications both require a Token Ring network to be implemented using a star topology.**

   __ True

   __ False

---

2. **Match the token state with its description.**

___	Captured	a.	A priority system used by both IBM and 802.5 Token Ring.
___	Acknowledgement	b.	There is no data in the payload.
___	Reserved	c.	Positive or negative notification.
___	Available	d.	There is a valid data payload.

---

3. **Which device connects Token Ring clients into a physical star configuration?**

   a) Edge router

   b) Multi Station Access Units

   c) Media Access Units

   d) Hubs

4. You manage a Token Ring network. A user calls and says that she suddenly can't access any network resources. You examine and test various network devices and discover the situation shown in the graphic.

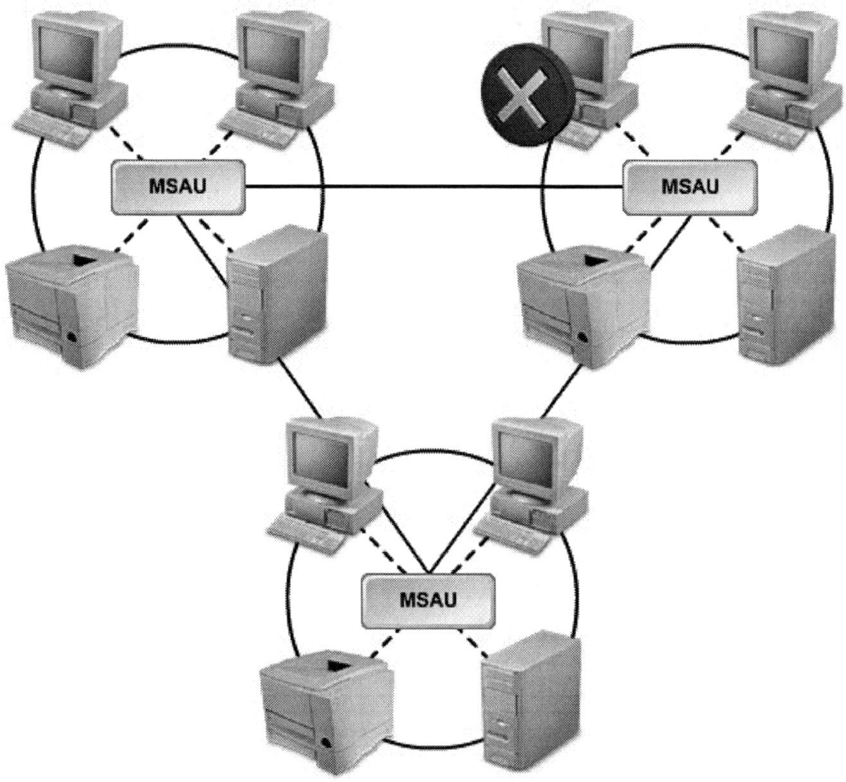

What is the most likely cause of the problem?

---

5. Which network device(s) will be affected? Why?

TOPIC E

Fiber Distributed Data Interface (FDDI) Networks

In the previous topic, you looked at Token Ring networks and how they are used. Another type of network technology that uses a ring topology is Fiber Distributed Data Interface (FDDI). In this topic, you will identify the characteristics of a FDDI network implementation.

As a networking professional, you are likely to encounter FDDI networks in situations that require redundant, high capacity networking with fault tolerance. Understanding FDDI will help you implement and support high capacity networks.

FDDI is commonly pronounced "Fuddy."

FDDI

Definition:

Fiber Distributed Data Interface, or FDDI, is a networking technology that uses a dual fiber ring operating at 100 Mbps. Although FDDI has dual fiber rings, only one ring carries data under normal conditions; the second ring is either idle or carries control signals. Under certain circumstances, if the second ring is not needed for backup, it can also carry data, extending capacity to 200 Mbps.

An extension to FDDI, called FDDI-2, supports the transmission of voice and video information as well as data. Another variation of FDDI, called FDDI Full Duplex Technology (FFDT), uses the same network infrastructure but can potentially support data rates up to 200 Mbps.

Example:

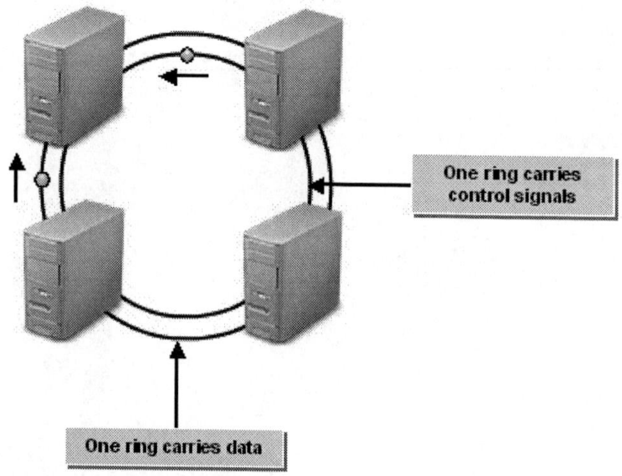

Figure 5-16: *FDDI.*

Dual Ring

The dual ring configuration is important for two reasons. First, an FDDI ring doesn't have a device, such as an MSAU, to remove stations when they're turned off. Second, fiber transceivers can't be configured to reverse; there is receive hardware and transmit hardware. Having two-way data movement on the same cable is simple with copper media, but it's more complex with fiber and requires two media paths, one for each direction.

FDDI Connection Devices

Nodes are connected to the FDDI network in one of two ways. In *dual attached stations (DAS),* nodes are connected directly to both the primary and secondary rings. In *single attached stations (SAS),* nodes are connected to a concentrator, which is connected to both rings.

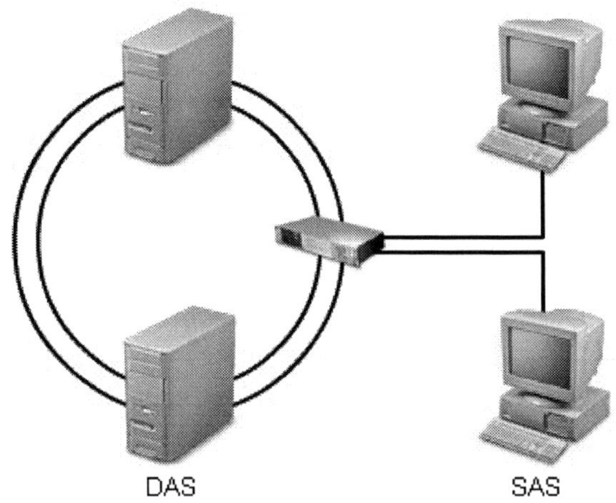

Figure 5-17: *FDDI connectivity.*

Single Attached Stations

The concentrator gives the SAS access to the primary ring. This is advantageous because when a SAS node is removed or turned off, the concentrator simply skips that node.

FDDI Failure Recovery

DAS nodes provide fault tolerance measures that detect loss of connectivity and then loop back the signal—a process known as auto-reconfiguration. By looping back the signal, a node actually reconfigures a network into a single ring. For SAS devices, the concentrator provides fault tolerance through isolation. If a SAS device fails, it's isolated by the concentrator.

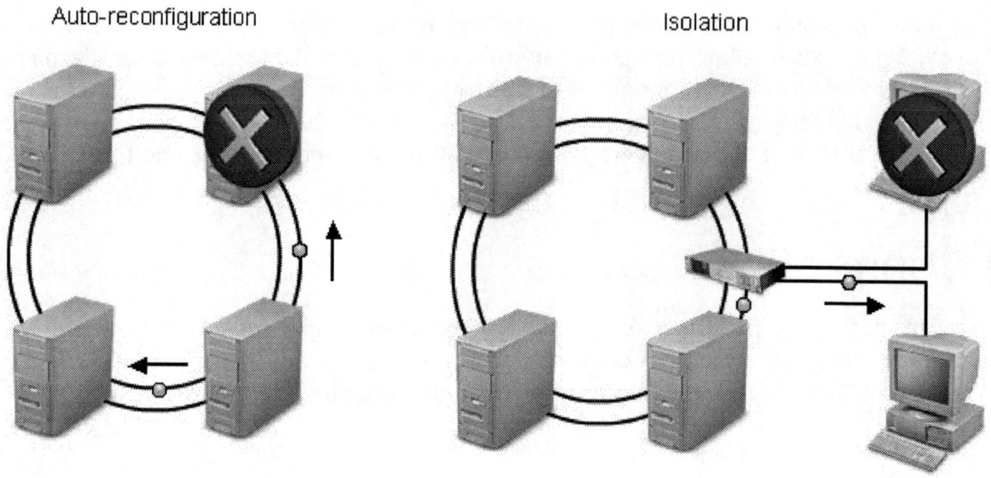

Figure 5-18: *FDDI failure recovery.*

ACTIVITY 5-5

Examining FDDI Networks

Scenario:

In this activity, you will examine the characteristics of FDDI networks and consider FDDI troubleshooting scenarios.

1. **FDDI networks operate at ______________.**
   a) 10 Mbps
   b) 1000 Mbps
   c) 500 Mbps
   d) 100 Mbps

2. **True or False? The second ring of a FDDI network can be utilized in some circumstances to increase total throughput.**
   __ True
   __ False

3. **Dual Attached Stations (DASs) are connected ______________.**
   a) To a concentrator
   b) To an edge router
   c) To both primary and secondary rings
   d) To a backbone router

4. Auto-reconfiguration occurs when ________________________.

   a) There is excessive traffic on the network

   b) There is no traffic on the network

   c) There is a new node added to the network

   d) There is a loss of connectivity to the next station

5. You manage a FDDI network for a financial institution. A municipal construction project is taking place adjacent to one of your network operations centers. You are concerned about the effect on your equipment so you are monitoring your network infrastructure closely. During a periodic test of the network media, you discover the situation shown in the graphic.

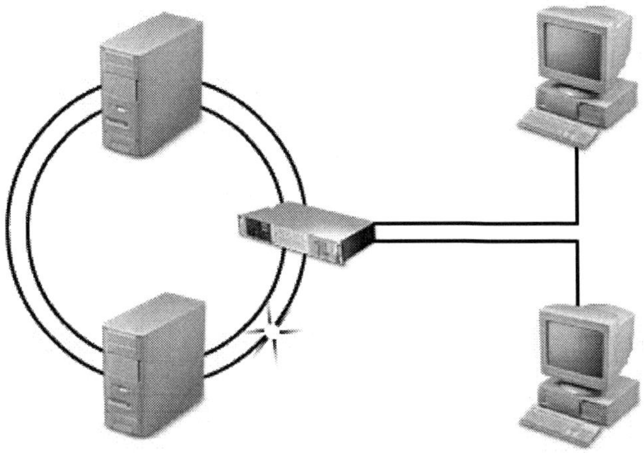

What appears to be the cause of the problem?

6. Which network device(s) will be affected?

TOPIC F

Wireless Technologies and Standards

In the previous topics, you examined the various types of wired networks—that is, networks that use different types of cabling to connect the various nodes. There are also wireless networks that connect without using a physical cable. In this topic, you will identify the components of a wireless network implementation.

Wireless networks are becoming more and more popular because they are relatively easy to install and have a lot of flexibility. Even more important, roaming users in both business and leisure environments want the freedom to work from anywhere without a physical connection to the network. As a networking professional, you will undoubtedly be faced with installing, managing, or troubleshooting a wireless network.

When to Use Wireless Technologies

You will use various types of wireless technologies for different situations.

Wireless Network Type	When to Use
Infrared	Infrared networks use low-frequency light waves to transmit and receive data from individual nodes. Infrared networks are ideal for installations where small areas need to be covered and there are no obstacles in the transmission path.
Radio	Radio networks use high-frequency radio waves to transmit and receive data from individual nodes. Radio networks are ideal for installations where large areas need to be covered and obstacles exist in the transmission path.
Microwave	Microwave networks use high-frequency radio waves to send and receive data from nodes or from satellite transponders. Microwave networks are ideal for installations where large areas need to be covered and no obstacles exist in the transmission path.

Wireless Antenna Types

A wireless antenna receives or transmits Radio Frequency (RF) waves. An antenna transmits by converting electrical energy into a radio frequency wave. When an antenna receives a transmission, it converts the RF wave into electrical energy.

You can choose different antenna types to use in different wireless networking situations. Different styles of antennas vary in their gain, or signal strength, and the shape, or radiation pattern, of the transmission beam. The antenna's gain value is measured in decibels-isotropic, or dBi. An antenna's rating (its gain) is the difference between the 0db isotropic antenna and the actual antenna rating. An isotropic antenna sends a signal equally in all directions (vertical and horizontal). Such an antenna has a 0dBi gain. The rule of thumb is that every 3dBi of gain added doubles the power output of the antenna.

Antennas may be grouped into three broad categories:

- Omni-directional: Radiate radio frequency waves in a 360-degree pattern over a horizontal plane. . A dipole antenna is an example of an omni-directional antenna.
- Semi-directional: Concentrate radio frequency energy into a cone shape called a beam. An example is a Yagi antenna, which offers a fairly focused beam and covers a longer distance than a dipole or omni-directional antenna. A Yagi antenna could be used in a very long area such as an aisle in a warehouse or as a point-to-point antenna from the rooftop corner of one office building to another.
- Highly directional: Radiate radio frequency waves over long distances. Highly directional antennas have a concentrated narrow beam width and are used to provide distanced, highly focused transmission from one point to another. Antenna transmissions are via point-to-point (or line of sight) so they must be aimed at each other precisely. Examples include a parabolic dish antenna and a grid antenna (a grid antenna has a mesh design that allows wind to pass through; it is a better choice in high-wind conditions than a parabolic dish).

For more information on antenna types and antenna characteristics, see **http://en.wikipedia.org/wiki/Category:Radio_frequency_antenna_types**

Polarization

The concept of polarization is important when considering the purchase and implementation of antennas. Polarization refers to the physical position of the antenna and the direction that the antenna radiates wavelengths. Both the sending and receiving antennas must be set to the same polarization.

Infrared Performance Factors

The maximum distance of an infrared wireless installation is affected by all of the following factors:

- Bright sunlight
- Hard obstacles, such as walls, doors, or shelves
- Smoke, dust, or fog

Radio Performance Factors

The maximum distance of a radio wireless installation is affected by all of the following factors:

- The signal characteristics of the antenna, including gain and radiation pattern
- Atmospheric conditions
- Influence of ambient electrical noise
- Conductive obstacles in the path
- The presence of other electrical equipment
- Data rate

Microwave Performance Factors

The maximum distance of a microwave wireless installation is affected by all of the following factors:

- The signal characteristics of the antenna, including gain and radiation pattern
- Line of sight
- Distances between transmission stations

What Is a WAP?

Definition:

A *WAP*, or wireless access point, is a wireless connectivity device that enables multiple wireless nodes to communicate with each other and with other networks. The WAP transfers the broadcast signal to another WAP or onto the network medium. In this way, wireless and wired networks can coexist in the same environment.

Example:

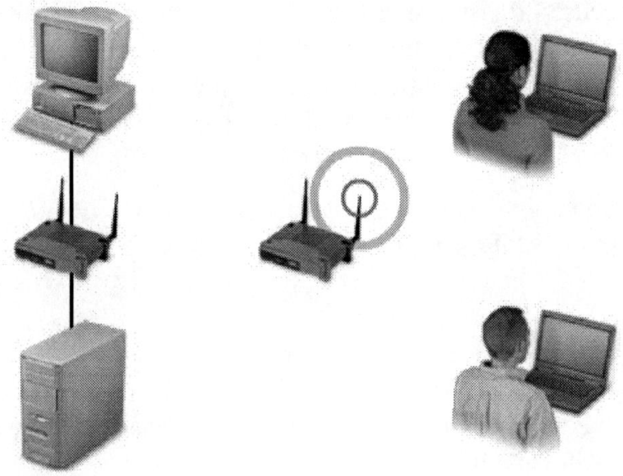

Figure 5-19: *A WAP.*

The IEEE 802.11 Standard

The *802.11* standard is a family of specifications developed by the IEEE for wireless LAN technology. 802.11 specifies an over-the-air interface between a wireless client and a base station or between two wireless clients.

802.11 defines the access method as CSMA/CA. For reliability, it specifies spread spectrum radio devices in the 2.4 GHz band. It provides for both FHSS and DSSS. The 802.11b standard also defines a multichannel roaming mode and automatic data rate selection.

802.11 Standards

The following table describes the 802.11 standards.

Standard	Description
802.11	There are two variations of the 802.11 standard. Both have transmission speeds of 1 or 2 Mbps and a radio frequency of 2.4 GHz. One variation uses FHSS and the other uses DSSS.
802.11a	Specifies speeds up to 54 Mbps in the 4 GHz band. Transmission typically takes place at 6 Mbps, 12 Mbps, and 24 Mbps. 802.11a is not compatible with the wireless standards 802.11b and 802.11g.

Standard	Description
802.11b	Specifies a maximum transmission speed of 11 Mbps and a radio frequency of 2.4 GHz. 802.11b is compatible with 802.11g.
802.11g	Specifies speeds up to 54 Mbps and operates in the 2.4 GHz radio frequency range, similar to 802.11b.

802.11 Modes

There are two components to the 802.11 standard: Infrastructure mode and Ad-hoc mode.

Mode	Description
Infrastructure mode	*Infrastructure mode* utilizes one or more WAPs to connect workstations to the cable backbone. Infrastructure mode wireless networks use either the *Basic Service Set (BSS)* or *Extended Service Set (ESS)* protocol.
Ad-hoc mode	*Ad-hoc mode*, also referred to as *Independent Basic Service Set (IBSS)*, utilizes a peer-to-peer configuration in which each wireless workstation talks directly to other workstations.

Overview of 802.11 Architecture

Several components comprise a wireless architecture: Station (STA), an access point (AP), basic service set (BSS), extended service set (ESS), independent basic service set (IBSS), and distribution system (DS). A wireless STA contains and adapter card, a PC card, or an embedded device to provide wireless connectivity. The AP functions as a bridge between wireless STAs and the existing network backbone for network access.

Wireless LANS (WLANS) are organized into service sets: Basic Service Sets (BSSs), Extended Service Sets (ESSs), and Independent Service Sets (IBSSs).

Basic Service Set (BSS)

A BSS is comprised of one access point connected to a wired network and has one or more wireless stations or clients. A BSS is also referred to as infrastructure mode because it requires an access point to be used in order to transmit data wirelessly. Data is transmitted from the wireless station to the access point and from the access point back to the station. There are no direct, client-to-client data transmissions. All devices in a BSS share a common BSS ID.

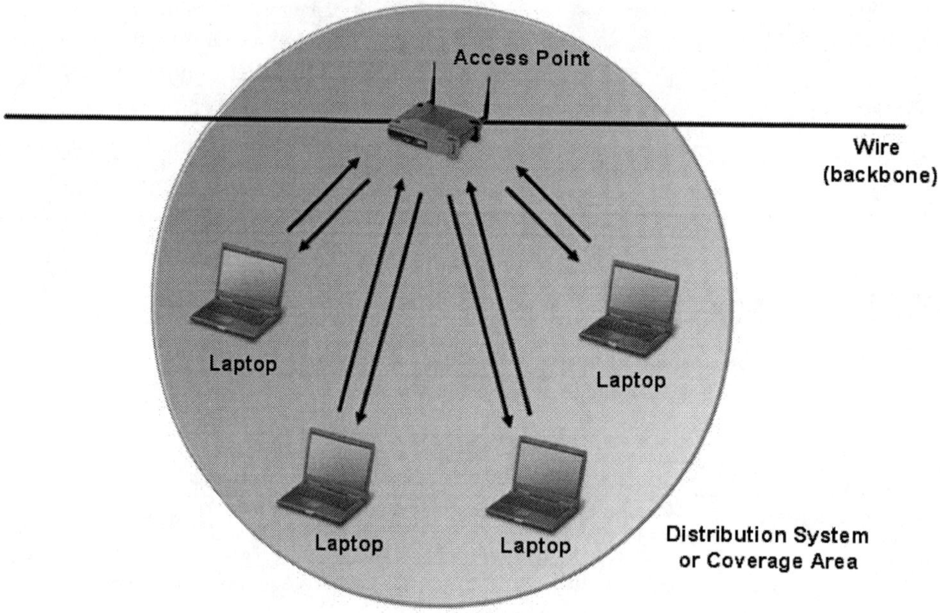

Figure 5-20: *A Basic Service Set architecture.*

Extended Service Set (ESS)

An ESS is comprised of two or more BSSs that are connected to a common distribution system such as a wired network. An ESS must contain at least two wireless access points operating in infrastructure mode, which allows wireless clients to use either AP, depending on the location of the wireless station or client. An ESS enables users to move their mobile devices, such as laptop computers, outside of their home BSS while keeping their connection. It also enables data to be forwarded from one BSS to another through the network backbone.

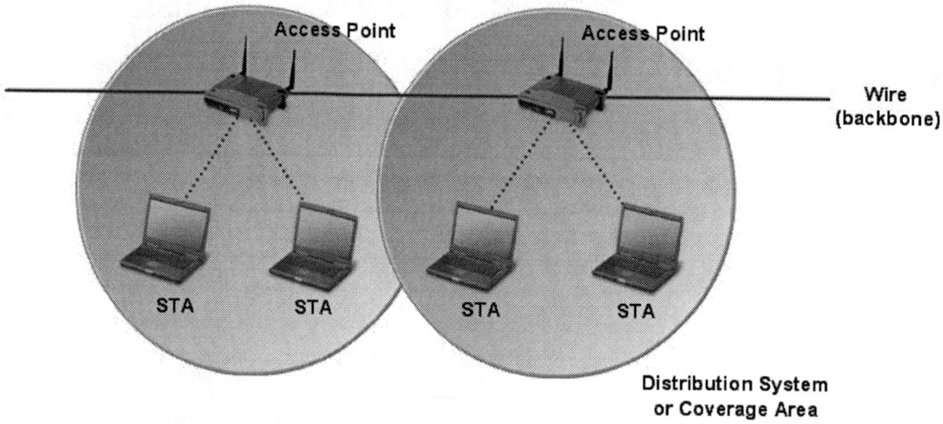

Figure 5-21: *An Extended Service Set architecture.*

Independent Basic Service Set (IBSS)

An IBSS does not contain an AP. It is a peer-to-peer network in which each wireless station or client has its own wireless network adapter and each acts as both a client and a wireless AP. Each station both transmits and receives data. Since the stations in an IBSS are not connected to a wireless AP, it is the responsibility of the station to transmit the data wirelessly from one station to another. All stations or clients participating in an IBSS must have the same SSID so an IBSS must have one unique SSID.

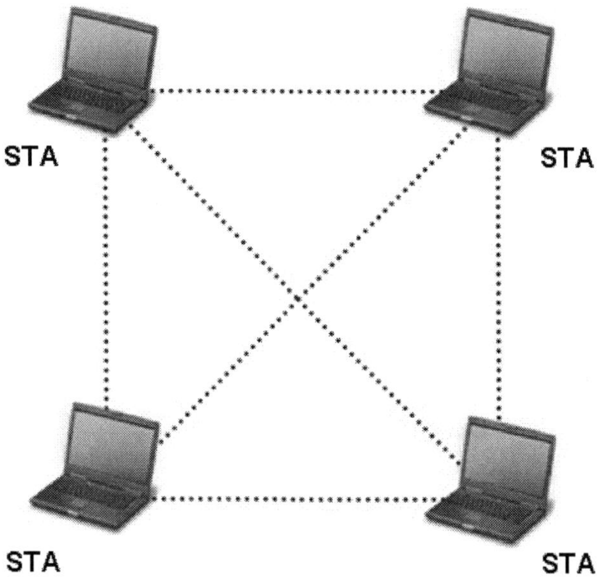

Figure 5-22: *An Independent Basic Service Set architecture.*

Wired Equivalent Privacy (WEP)

To prevent eavesdropping, IEEE 802.11 Wired Equivalent Privacy (WEP) defines an algorithm that gives authorized users the same level of security they would have if they were on a wired network not protected by encryption. WEP offers three security options: Off, or no security; 64-bit, which is basic security; and 128-bit, which is strong security. WEP 128-bit security is the strongest option, but this level of encryption has an impact on network performance. WEP is an option available to an administrator to provide better security for wireless networks. WEP accounts for lost packets, is self synchronizing, and requires little maintenance.

Wi-Fi Protected Access (WPA)

Wi-Fi Protected Access (WPA) is a Wi-Fi standard that was designed to improve upon the security flaws of WEP. The technology is designed to work with existing Wi-Fi products that have been enabled with WEP. WPA provides users with:

- Improved data encryption through the Temporal Key Integrity Protocol (TKIP). TKIP scrambles the keys using a hashing algorithm and, by adding an integrity-checking feature, ensures that the keys haven't been tampered with.

- User authentication, which is considered poor in WEP, through the Extensible Authentication Protocol (EAP). WEP regulates access to a wireless network based on a computer's hardware-specific MAC address, which is relatively easy to figure out, steal, and use (that is, sniffed and spoofed). EAP is built on a more secure public-key encryption system to ensure that only authorized network users can access the network.

Wireless Authentication Methods

There are three methods used for wireless authentication:

Authentication Method	Description
Open system	This is the default for APs and stations. Open system authentication uses null authentication, which means that user names and passwords are not used to authenticate a user. When open system is configured on an AP and a station, the station will find an AP by sending out a probe, and when it finds one, it sends an authentication request to that AP. The AP responds with an authentication success. The station then must associate by sending an association request and when received, the AP will respond with a success association response. Open system authentication enables a station to connect to any wireless AP that has open system authentication enabled, even if the SSID is different from the station.
Shared key	This authentication method verifies the identity of a station by using a WEP key. Both the station and the AP must be configured to use data encryption and the same WEP key. The station also needs to be configured to use a shared key authentication instead of the default setting, open system authentication. Once configured correctly, the communication process begins. The station probes for the AP and initiates an authentication request. Upon receipt of the request, the AP issues a challenge to the station and, in turn, the station accepts the challenge and encrypts the challenge using the WEP key with which it has been configured. It then sends the challenge back to the AP and the AP decrypts the encrypted challenge using its key. If both the station and the AP have the same key, the AP will be able to decrypt the challenge with the matching WEP key. The AP will authenticate the station and the station will initiate an association request and the AP will accept the request.

Authentication Method	Description
802.1x and EAP	This authentication method authenticates the user and not the station. This is done with a RADIUS server. The AP forwards the authentication request to the RADIUS server and the server calls the user credential database (for example, Active Directory in Windows domains) to verify the user. The RADIUS server then passes the identity verification to the AP. The authentication process breaks down as follows: A station initiates an authentication request to the AP. The AP issues an EAP identity request. Once the station receives the request, the station sends an EAP identity response to the AP. The AP forwards the EAP identity response to the RADIUS server. The RADIUS server issues a RADIUS access challenge, which passes through the AP to the station. The station sends a RADIUS challenge response that passes through the AP and the AP forwards it to the RADIUS server. If the RADIUS server can decrypt the challenge and verify the user, it forwards a success response to the AP. The AP forwards an EAP success to the station and the station can then establish an association with the AP.

Bluetooth

Bluetooth 1.1 is a wireless protocol that is used to communicate from one device to another in a small area, usually less than 30 feet. Bluetooth establishes a link using an RF-based media and does not need line-of-sight to make connections. Bluetooth uses the 2.4 GHz spectrum to communicate a 1 Mbps connection between two devices for both a 232 Kbps voice channel and a 768 Kbps data channel. Bluetooth 2.0 will increase overall speed to a data rate of 2.1 to 3 Mbps.

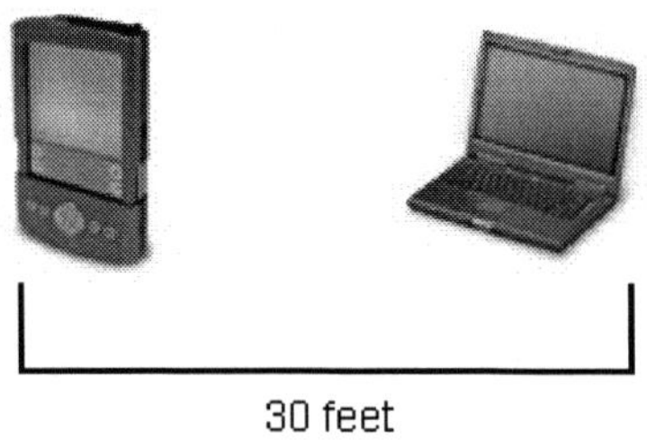

Figure 5-23: *Bluetooth.*

ACTIVITY 5-6

Examining Wireless Technologies and Standards

Scenario:

In this activity, you will examine wireless networks and consider wireless troubleshooting scenarios.

---

1. **True or False? Radio networks are ideal for large area coverage with obstacles.**

   __ True

   __ False

---

2. **Which condition affects the operation of infrared wireless networks?**

   a) Atmospheric conditions

   b) The presence of other electrical equipment

   c) Bright sunlight

   d) Data rate

---

3. **True or False? Infrastructure mode wireless networks use either Basic Service Set or Extended Service Set protocols.**

   __ True

   __ False

---

4. **True or False? Bluetooth is a long-range radio technology designed to simplify communications among Internet devices.**

   __ True

   __ False

---

5. **A user on your network uses a Personal Digital Assistant (PDA) to keep track of her calendar and contact list. She synchronizes the PDA data frequently with her laptop computer via the systems' infrared ports. She complains that she intermittently loses the infrared connection between the two devices. You visit her workstation and find that she is seated in close proximity to a large window. What problem do you suspect?**

---

6. **What can you advise the user?**

---

7. Your company's network has a downtown location and a suburban location. You are using a dish-style microwave antenna for wireless connectivity between the two locations. A luxury hotel is being constructed in the block adjacent to your downtown location. The hotel structure is planned to be lower than your existing microwave installation; nevertheless, you have started to experience connectivity problems with the suburban site. There is a great deal of construction equipment on the site. What is the likely cause of the connectivity issues?

---

8. Your company has installed a wireless network. There are ceiling dome transmitters at various locations in your building, and you have upgraded users' laptop systems with wireless NICs. There is one wireless antenna to serve the warehouse area. The coverage area is adequate; however, users in the warehouse report intermittent connectivity problems as they move in and out of the tall metal storage shelving. What problem do you suspect?

---

9. 5) Your CEO is concerned with security on the new wireless network. Clients, guests, and contractors often enter the building bringing their own laptops equipped with wireless adapters. How can you ensure that only authorized systems connect to your wireless network?

---

10. What is the maximum transmission speed that IrDA 1.1 can support?
    a) 3 Mbps
    b) 10 Mpbs
    c) 11 Mpbs
    d) 4 Mbps
    e) 54 Mbps

---

11. At what radio frequency does Bluetooth operate?
    a) 5 GHz
    b) 2.4 GHz
    c) 54 Mbps
    d) 11 Mbps

---

12. At which radio frequency does IEEE 802.11a operate?
    a) 2.5 GHz
    b) 10 GHz
    c) 5.0 GHz
    d) 2.4 GHz

Lesson 5 Follow-up

In this lesson, you learned about the various types of networks, their characteristics, and how they interoperate. These skills will enable you to accurately configure, manage, and troubleshoot your networks.

1. **What are some of the challenges that you might face in implementing any network topology?**

2. **How might you overcome these challenges?**

LESSON 6

Networking with TCP/IP

Lesson Time
2 hour(s)

Lesson Objectives:

In this lesson, you will identify the components of a TCP/IP network implementation.

You will:

- View the protocols bound to a network interface card in Windows Server 2003.
- View the TCP/IP information for your computer.
- Describe a default IP addressing scheme.
- Create custom IP addressing schemes.
- Identify the major protocols and utilities in the TCP/IP protocol suite.

Lesson 6

Introduction

As you learned previously, one component required for successful network data delivery is a network protocol, which formats the data packets that are sent between computers on the network. In order for two computers to communicate over a network, they must have the same network protocol. In this lesson, you will examine one of the most common network protocols in use today, TCP/IP.

TCP/IP is a protocol that is in use on networks of every size and type, including the biggest network of all, the Internet. No matter what type of network you support, you'll need to understand the characteristics and capabilities of this universal protocol.

This lesson covers the following CompTIA Network+ (2005) certification objectives:

- Topic A:
  - Objective 3.2: Identify the basic capabilities needed for client workstations to connect to and use network resources (for example, media, network protocols, and peer and server services).
- Topic B:
  - Objective 2.4: Characterize the TCP/IP (Transmission Control Protocol/Internet Protocol) network protocol in terms of routing, addressing schemes, interoperability, and naming conventions.
  - Objective 2.5: Identify the components and structure of IP (Internet Protocol) addresses (IPv4) and the required setting for connections across the Internet.
- Topic C:
  - Objective 2.4: Characterize the TCP/IP (Transmission Control Protocol/Internet Protocol) network protocol in terms of routing, addressing schemes, interoperability, and naming conventions.
  - Objective 2.6: Identify classful IP ranges and their subnet masks (for example, Class A, B, and C).
  - Objective 2.8: Identify the differences between private and public network addressing schemes.
- Topic D:
  - Objective 2.4: Characterize the TCP/IP (Transmission Control Protocol/Internet Protocol) network protocol in terms of routing, addressing schemes, interoperability, and naming conventions.
  - Objective 2.7: Identify the purpose of subnetting.
- Topic E:
  - Objective 2.4: Characterize the TCP/IP (Transmission Control Protocol/Internet Protocol) network protocol in terms of routing, addressing schemes, interoperability, and naming conventions.
  - Objective 2.10: Define the purpose, function, and use of the following protocols used in the TCP/IP suite: TCP (Transmission Control Protocol), UDP (User Datagram Protocol), ICMP (Internet Control Message Protocol), ARP/RARP (Address Resolution Protocol/Reverse Address Resolution Protocol), and IGMP (Internet Group Multicast Protocol).
  - Objective 2.11: Define the function of TCP/UDP (Transmission Control Protocol/User Datagram Protocol) ports.
  - Objective 2.12: Identify the well-known ports associated with the following commonly used services and protocols: 20 FTP (File Transfer Protocol); 21 FTP (File

Transfer Protocol); 22 SSH (Secure Shell); 23 Telnet; 25 SMTP (Simple Mail Transfer Protocol); 53 DNS (Domain Name Service); 69 TFTP (Trivial File Transfer Protocol); 80 HTTP (Hypertext Transfer Protocol); 110 POP3 (Post Office Protocol version 3); 119 NNTP (Network News Transport Protocol); 123 NTP (Network Time Protocol); 143 IMAP4 (Internet Message Access Protocol version 4); and 443 HTTPS (Hypertext Transfer Protocol Secure).

TOPIC A

Families of Protocols

Successful network communication between two computers hinges on them sharing a network protocol to perform various functions related to that communication. These functions are divided up into categories based on the OSI model. In this topic, you will examine the different categories of protocols and their functions.

Network protocols are classified into general families that share common features. Some protocols are hybrids—they perform more than one function. Others perform only one function. Computer technology professionals use the OSI model to classify protocols by function. If you understand the different functions that are provided by the network protocol, when there is a communication problem, you can use this knowledge to identify if the problem lies with the network protocol.

Network Protocols

Definition:

Network communication between computers is provided by a *network protocol*—rules by which network operations are conducted. A network protocol is responsible for formatting the data packets that are sent between computers on a network. Two computers must have a network protocol in common in order to communicate directly with one another.

Example:

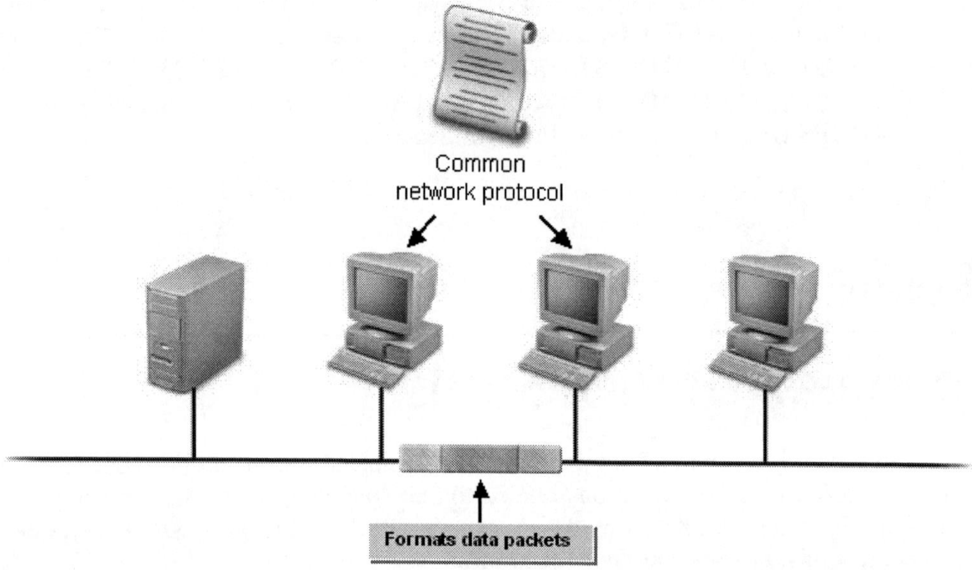

Figure 6-1: *A network protocol provides rules for network communication.*

Network- and Transport-Layer Protocols

The Network and Transport layers contain several protocol families.

Protocol Family	Function
Reliability protocols	Provide a way to ensure that reliable data transfer occurs. For example, a header or trailer might contain a checksum value or request that received data be acknowledged by sending an acknowledgement message back to the sender.
Connection protocols	Used for establishing and maintaining a connectionless or connection-oriented service for upper layers. In a connection-oriented service, the sending and receiving stations maintain constant communication to mediate the transfer of data. Sequencing, flow control, and reliability are monitored by both ends. In a connectionless service, the message is packaged, delivered, and sent. The message is transferred with little, if any, communication between the two parties, other than the message itself.
Routing protocols	Provide a way to ensure that data is transferred to the correct destination. In an unswitched network, routing is virtually unnecessary because the nodes are directly connected. In a switched network, however, the routing function determines which path a packet will take to reach its destination. This function is particularly important and complex in a packet-switched network, because there can be many possible paths to a destination and many intermediary nodes (routers) along the way. Routing protocols determine the strategies used to transmit data through the network.

Application-, Presentation-, and Session-Layer Protocols

The Application, Presentation, and Session layers contain several protocol families.

Protocol Family	Function
Terminal-emulation protocols	Enable computers to behave like a standard terminal so that they can access a host. This typically involves translation of keyboard codes and video-display codes.
File-access and file-transfer protocols	File-access protocols enable nodes to use network files. For example, different network clients might use different file- and path-naming conventions. File-access protocols provide a common means to access network files. File-transfer protocols copy files between network storage and other storage, such as a computer's local disk drive.
Email protocols	Provide for email delivery and handling of related messages.
Remote-action and multiple-session protocols	Remote-action protocols determine whether processes should be performed by a client node or by a server. These protocols are required for setting up a client-server relationship. Multiple-session protocols enable multiple network links to be established.
Network-management protocols	Provide tools for setting up and maintaining the network. As networks interconnect into internetworks and become more complex, more sophisticated network-management tools are necessary.
Task-to-task protocols	Enable software processes to communicate over the network.
Codeset-and-data-structure protocols	Define how data is represented. These protocols translate data for nodes that use different coding schemes.

Protocol Bindings

Assigning a protocol to a network interface card is referred to as protocol *binding*. Multiple protocols can be bound to a single NIC. The NIC can use any of the protocols that are bound to it to communicate with other nodes on the network.

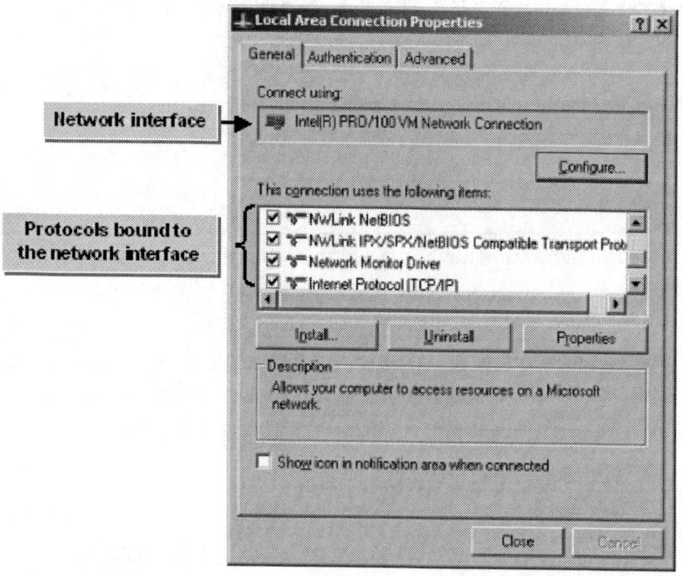

Figure 6-2: *Multiple protocols bound to a single network interface in Windows Server 2003.*

Binding Order

A network interface bound with multiple protocols attempts to connect to a receiving node by testing its available protocols, one by one, until it finds a protocol that the receiving node answers. This isn't the most efficient scenario because the protocol that the node answers might not be the most efficient one—it's simply the first one in the sender's protocol list that the two nodes have in common. In Windows Server 2003, Windows XP Professional, Windows 2000, and Windows NT, you are able to bind protocols to a network interface in a particular order. By setting the binding order to prefer the most frequently used protocol on your network, your system accesses the network in the most efficient manner and does not waste time attempting to use other protocols.

How to View Protocol Bindings

Procedure Reference: View Protocol Bindings

To view the protocols bound to a network interface card on a computer running Windows Server 2003:

1. Choose Start→Control Panel→Network Connections.
2. Right-click the network connection object you want to view.
3. Choose Properties.
4. In the This Connection Uses The Following Items list box, view the protocols bound to your network card.
5. Click OK to close the Properties dialog box for your network connection.

ACTIVITY 6-1

Identifying Families of Protocols

There is a simulated version of this activity available on the CD-ROM that shipped with this course. You can run this simulation on any Windows computer to review the activity after class, or as an alternative to performing the activity as a group in class. The activity simulation can be launched either directly from the CD-ROM by clicking the Interactives link and navigating to the appropriate one, or from the installed data file location by opening the C:\Data\Simulations\Lesson#\Activity# folder and double-clicking the executable (.exe) file.

Conditions:

Your computer is running Windows Server 2003 and is turned on. Your computer name is Computer##, where ## is a two-digit number (for example, Computer01). Your user name is User##, where ## matches your computer number (for example, User01). Your password is !Pass1234. You are logged on as User##.

Scenario:

In this activity, you will identify functions of the families of protocols based on the OSI network model.

What You Do	How You Do It
1. **Verify that the TCP/IP protocol is bound to your NIC.**	a. **Choose Start→Control Panel→Network Connections.**
	b. **Right-click Local Area Connection.**
	c. **Choose Properties.**
	d. In the This Connection Uses The Following Items list box, **verify that TCP/IP is bound to your network card.**

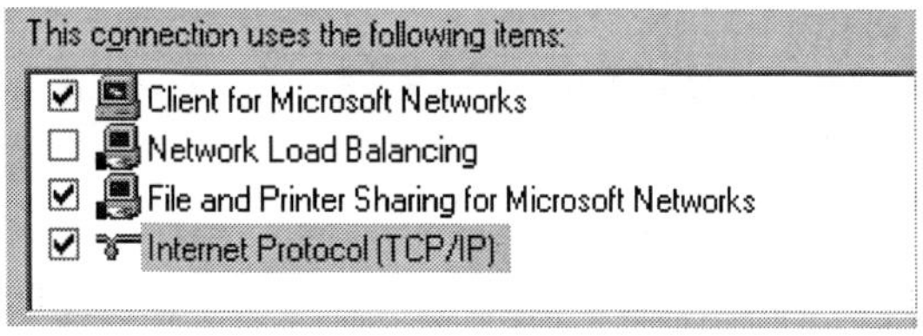

e. **Click OK** to close the Properties dialog box for your network connection.

2. **Match the Network- and Transport-layer protocol families with their functions.**

___	Reliability protocols	a.	Responsible for transmitting data to its correct destination in the most efficient manner.
___	Connection protocols	b.	Ensure that data transfer is successful.
___	Routing protocols	c.	Ensure that the communication is established and maintained during data transfer.

3. **Match the Application-, Presentation-, and Session-layer protocol families with their functions.**

___	Terminal-emulation protocols	a.	Enables network communication of various software processes.
___	Remote-action protocols	b.	Responsible for determining whether the process will be performed by the client or server node.
___	Multiple-session protocols	c.	Translate data between coding schemes for different nodes.
___	Task-to-task protocols	d.	Allow access to a host and translate keyboard and video-display information.
___	Codeset-and-data-structure protocols	e.	Establishes multiple network links.

4. **True or False? If you need to run more than one protocol on your computer, each protocol must be bound to its own NIC.**

___ True

___ False

TOPIC B

The TCP/IP Protocol

TCP/IP is a protocol suite that works at the Network and Transport layers of the OSI model, providing the protocol family functions of reliability, connection, and routing. In this topic, you will identify the components of the TCP/IP protocol.

The TCP/IP protocol suite is most readily associated with the IP address. To properly configure and troubleshoot TCP/IP communication problems, you need to have a good understanding of the characteristics of the TCP/IP address and how it works to enable communication between hosts.

TCP/IP

The *Transmission Control Protocol/Internet Protocol (TCP/IP)* is a nonproprietary, routable network protocol suite that enables computers to communicate over all types of networks. TCP/IP is the native protocol of the Internet and is required for Internet connectivity.

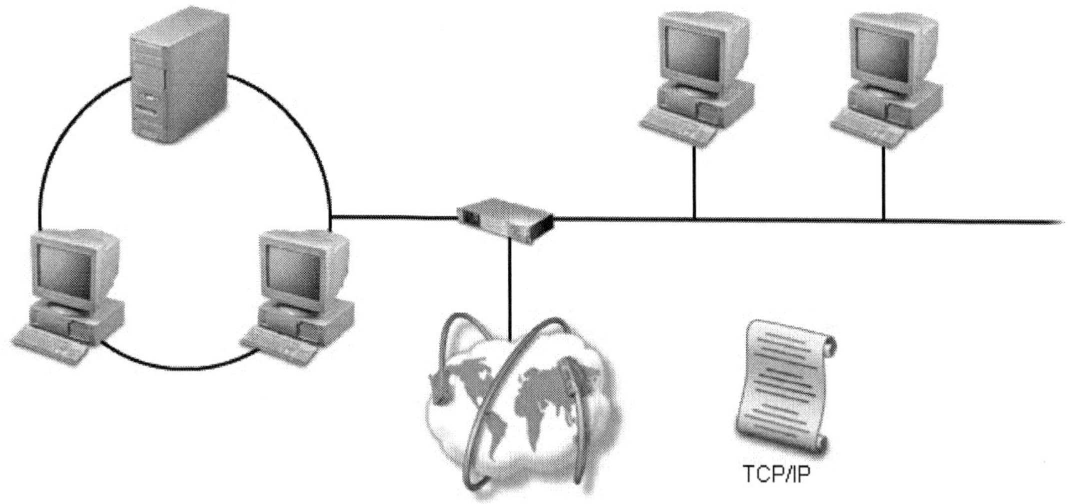

Figure 6-3: *TCP/IP is required for Internet connectivity.*

The TCP/IP protocol suite includes a network/node address structure, tools for static and dynamic address assignment, name resolution services, and utilities for testing and configuration.

The IP Address

An *IP address* is a 32-bit binary number assigned to a computer on a TCP/IP network. Some of the bits in the address represent the network segment; the other bits represent the host itself. For readability, the 32-bit binary IP address is usually separated by dots into four 8-bit octets, and each octet is converted to a single decimal value. Each decimal number can range from 0 to 255, but the first number cannot be 0. In addition, all four numbers cannot be 0 (0.0.0.0) or 255 (255.255.255.255).

Binary 11010000.01111011.00101101.00010010

Decimal 208.123.45.18

Figure 6-4: *An IP address.*

Dotted Decimal Notation

TCP/IP addresses are usually displayed in dotted decimal notation rather than in binary. Dotted decimal notation consists of four decimal numbers separated by three dots. Each decimal number is called an octet and represents eight binary bits. When pronouncing a dotted decimal number, include the separator dots. For example, the IP address 208.123.45.18 is pronounced "two oh eight dot one twenty-three dot forty-five dot eighteen."

An IP Address Is Like a Mailing Address

Some of the numbers in the IP address identify the network segment on which a computer resides, just as a person's mailing address uses a street name to identify the street on which he or she lives. The rest of the numbers in the IP address uniquely identify the computer on the network, just as the house number portion of the mailing address uniquely identifies a specific house on a street.

Binary and Decimal Conversion

Binary is a base 2 numbering system in which any bit in the number is either a zero or one. Each bit has a weight, or place value, which is a power of two. The place value is determined by the bit's location in the binary number. The value of a binary number is the sum of the place values of all the one bits in the number.

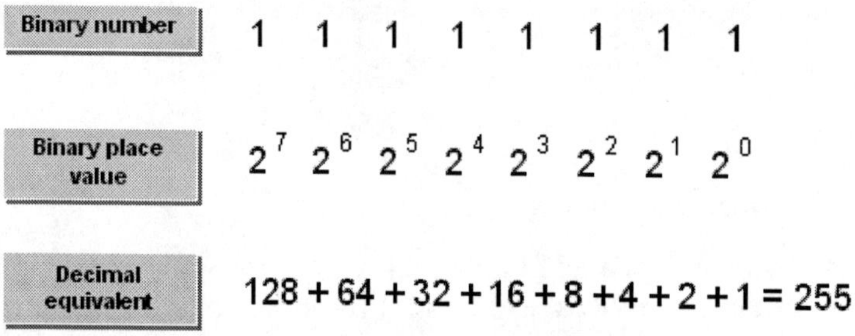

Figure 6-5: *Binary to decimal equivalents.*

Binary to Decimal Conversion Charts

This table shows the decimal values of 2^n, where n=0 through 7.

Exponent Value	Decimal Value
2^0	0
2^1	2
2^2	4
2^3	8
2^4	16
2^5	32
2^6	64
2^7	128

This table shows how to convert 8-bit binary numbers to their decimal equivalents using powers of two.

Binary Number	Conversion	Decimal Value
00000001	$0+0+0+0+0+0+0+2^0$	1
00000011	$0+0+0+0+0+0+2^1+2^0$	3
00000111	$0+0+0+0+0+2^2+2^1+2^0$	7
00001111	$0+0+0+0+2^3+2^2+2^1+2^0$	15
00011111	$0+0+0+2^4+2^3+2^2+2^1+2^0$	31
00111111	$0+0+2^5+2^4+2^3+2^2+2^1+2^0$	63
01111111	$0+2^6+2^5+2^4+2^3+2^2+2^1+2^0$	127
11111111	$2^7+2^6+2^5+2^4+2^3+2^2+2^1+2^0$	255

The Subnet Mask

A *subnet mask* is a 32-bit number that is assigned to each host to divide the 32-bit binary IP address into network and node portions. This makes TCP/IP routable. A subnet mask uses the binary AND operation to remove the node ID from the IP address, leaving just the network portion. Default subnet masks use the value of eight 1s in binary, or 255 in decimal, to mask an entire octet of the IP address.

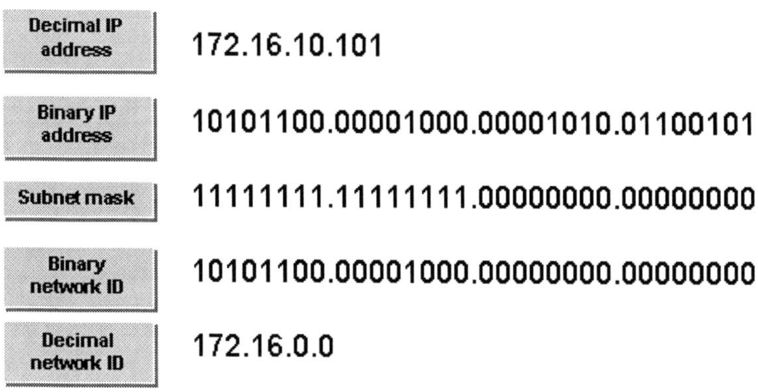

Figure 6-6: *The subnet mask removes the node portion of the IP address.*

Subnet Mask Values

The first number of a subnet mask must be 255; the remaining three numbers can be any of the following values:

- 255
- 254
- 252
- 248
- 240
- 224

- 192
- 128
- 0

Default Subnet Masks

Groups of IP addresses have specific default subnet masks, based on the range of values of the first octet of the IP address.

Default Subnet Mask	Value of First Octet of Address
255.0.0.0	1–126
255.255.0.0	128–191
255.255.255.0	192–223

Subnet Mask Structure

To conform to TCP/IP standards, subnet masks must follow these rules:

- Ones in the mask always start at bit 32, to the left of the mask.
- Zeros in the mask always start at bit 1, to the right of the mask.
- Ones in the mask must be contiguous, with no zeros interspersed between the ones.

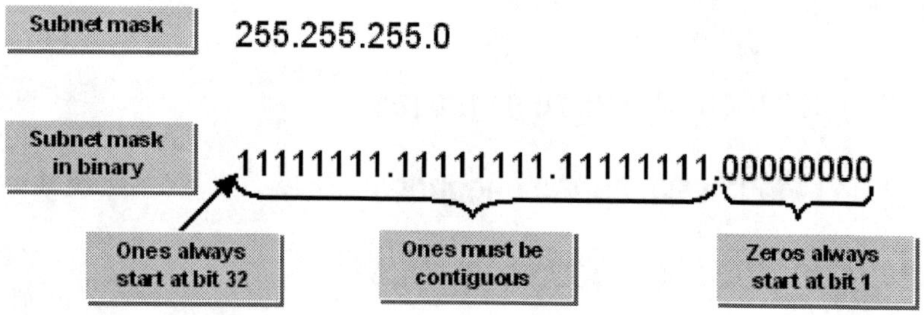

Figure 6-7: *Subnet mask structure.*

Binary ANDing

There are two rules in the binary AND operation:

- Zero AND any value equals zero.
- One AND one equals one.

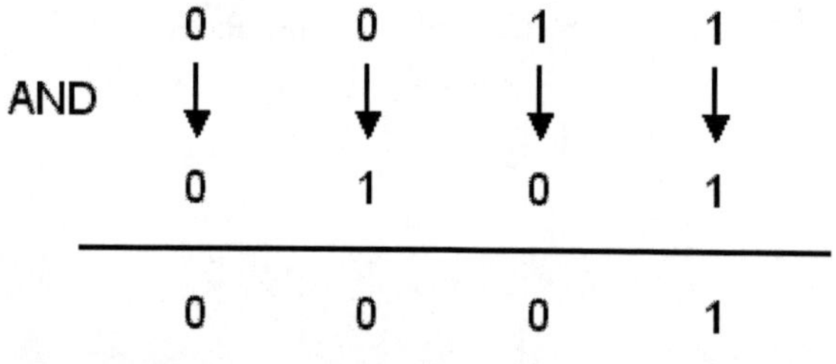

Figure 6-8: *Binary ANDing.*

To apply a subnet mask, you convert both the IP address and the subnet mask to binary. You AND the two binary numbers together. The zeros in the subnet mask convert all the bits in the node portion of the IP address to zeros, leaving the network portion of the address intact.

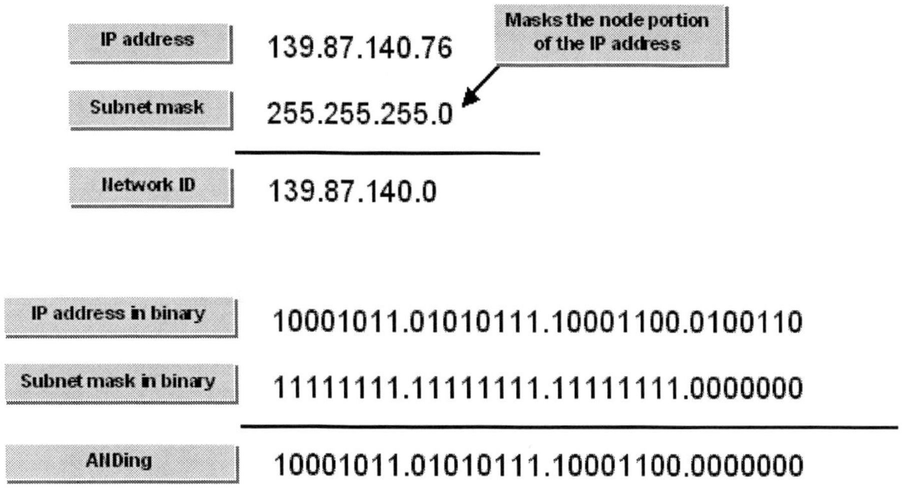

Figure 6-9: *Applying a subnet mask.*

Because the binary value of 255 is all ones (11111111), you can easily identify the network portion of an IP addresses with any of the three default subnet masks applied without converting to binary. However, you can subdivide your IP network address by borrowing part of your network's host addresses to identify subnet addresses. In these cases, the network portion of the IP address is not so easily identified and it may be necessary to convert to binary to determine the network and node portions of the IP address. For more information on custom subnetting, see the Appendix titled Additional IP Addressing and Subnetting Practice.

Distinguishing Local and Remote Addresses

The network client uses the subnet mask to determine whether a data packet is bound for the local subnet or must be routed to a remote subnet. First, the node applies the subnet mask to its own IP address to determine its own network ID. It then applies the subnet mask to the packet's destination address to determine the destination network ID.

Once the node has applied the subnet mask, it compares the two network IDs. If they are the same, then the two nodes are on the same subnet and the node can deliver the packet. If the two networks are different, then the two nodes are remote to each other and the data is routed to the remote network.

The process of determining local and remote addresses based on IP address falls under the Network layer's routing protocol function.

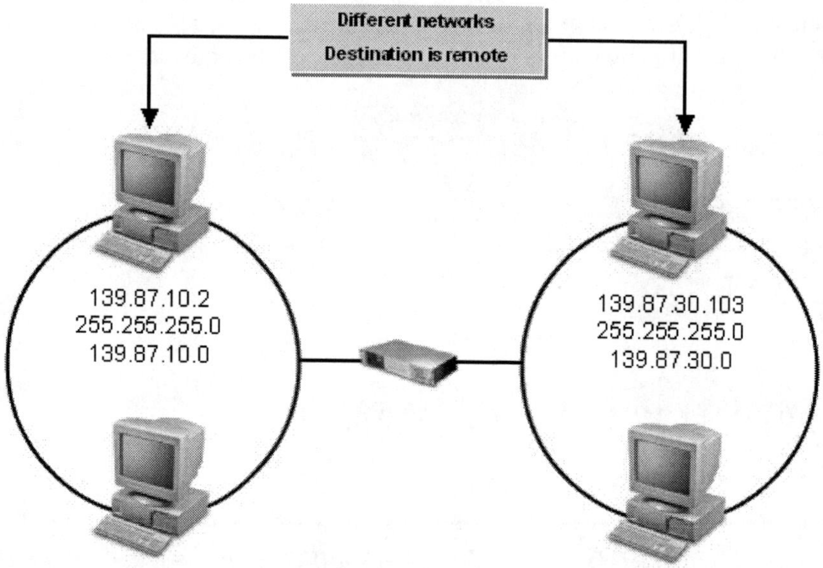

Figure 6-10: *A client compares its network ID to the data packet's destination network ID.*

The Default Gateway

Definition:

The *default gateway* is the IP address of the router that will route remote traffic from the computer's local subnet to remote subnets. Typically, the default gateway is the address of the router that is connected to the Internet. A TCP/IP host does not need a default gateway address if the computer does not need to communicate with computers outside its local subnet.

Example:

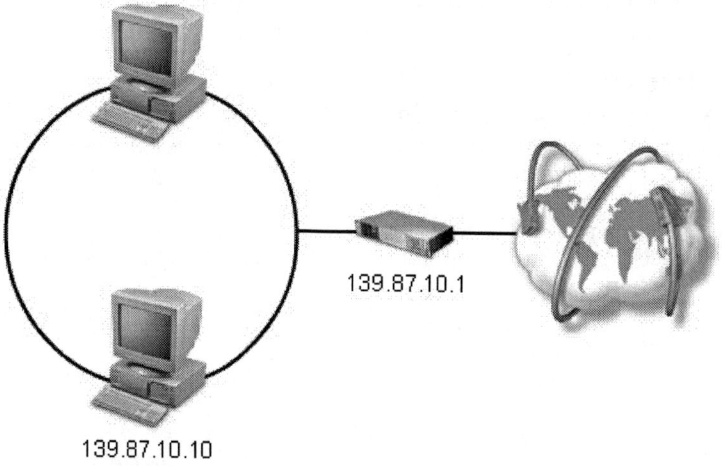

Figure 6-11: *The default gateway routes traffic to remote subnets.*

IP Address Assignment Rules

On a network running the TCP/IP protocol suite:

- Each device that connects to the network must have a unique IP address.
- Each subnet must have its own unique network ID.
- All devices on a subnet must share the same network ID.
- All devices on a subnet have the same subnet mask.

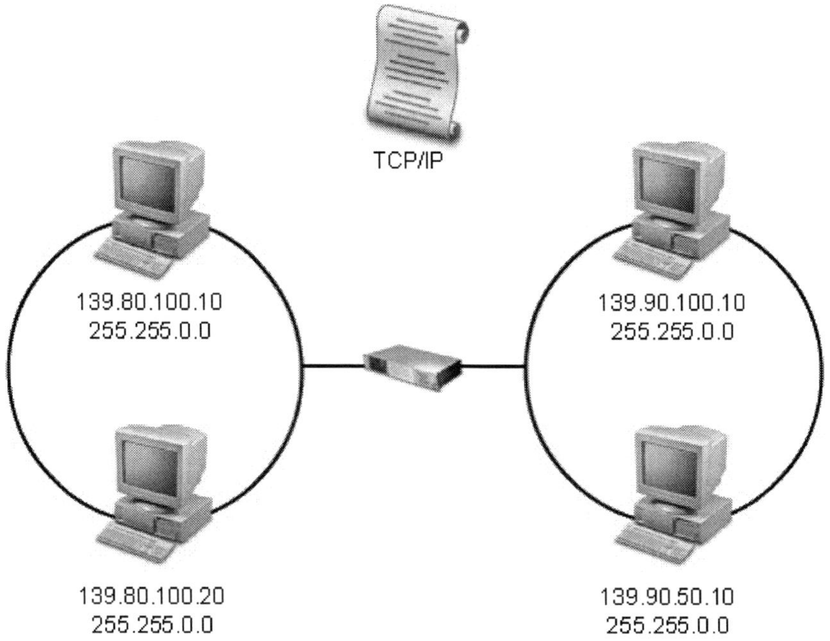

Figure 6-12: *Valid IP addressing.*

For valid node addressing on a TCP/IP network:

- Nodes on a local subnet must have unique node IDs.
- Nodes on different subnets can have the same node IDs if the network IDs are different.
- The node address cannot be all ones or all zeros.
- The IP address 127.0.0.1 is reserved for testing and cannot be used as a node ID.

For more information on IP address assignments, see RF 3330 on Special-Use IPv4 Addresses, and **www.iana.org/assignements/ipvr-address-space**.

How to View TCP/IP Information

Procedure Reference: View TCP/IP Information

To use the Status function to view the TCP/IP information for your computer:

1. Choose Start→Control Panel→Network Connections.
2. Right-click the connection object and choose Status.
3. Select the Support tab to view the addressing information.
4. Click Close.

ACTIVITY 6-2

Identifying the Characteristics of a TCP/IP Protocol Suite Implementation

There is a simulated version of this activity available on the CD-ROM that shipped with this course. You can run this simulation on any Windows computer to review the activity after class, or as an alternative to performing the activity as a group in class. The activity simulation can be launched either directly from the CD-ROM by clicking the Interactives link and navigating to the appropriate one, or from the installed data file location by opening the C:\Data\Simulations\Lesson#\Activity# folder and double-clicking the executable (.exe) file.

Scenario:

In this activity, you will identify the characteristics of a TCP/IP protocol implementation.

What You Do	How You Do It
1. **View the TCP/IP information assigned to your NIC.**	a. **Choose Start→Control Panel→Network Connections.**
	b. **Right-click Local Area Connection and choose Status.**
	c. **Select the Support tab.**
	d. In the Internet Protocol (TCP/IP) section, **view the IP address, subnet mask, and default gateway information.**

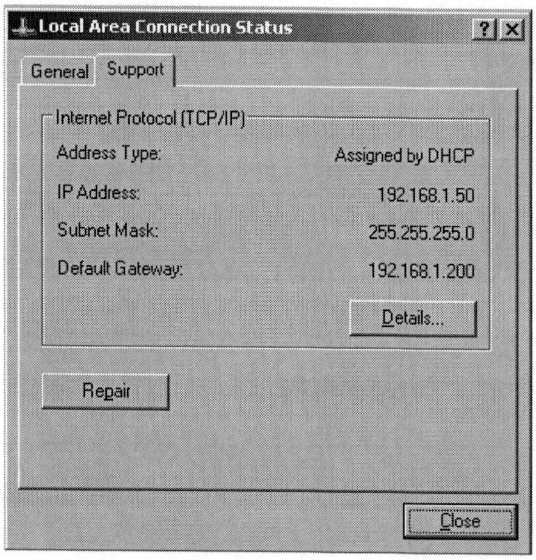

e. **Click Close.**

2. **Identify the required components of TCP/IP addressing.**

   a) Node address

   b) Subnet mask

   c) Gateway address

   d) Name resolution service

---

3. **Match the binary value with its decimal equivalent.**

	Binary		Decimal
___	01100100	a.	100
___	11100000	b.	100.100.2.1
___	11111111.11111111. 11110000.00000000	c.	255.255.240.0
___	01100100.01100100. 00000010.00000001	d.	127.0.0.1
___	01111111.00000000. 00000000.00000001	e.	224

---

4. **Local or Remote? Determine if Node 2 is local or remote to Node 1.**

   Node 1=192.225.16.8

   Node 2=192.225.14.8

   Subnet Mask=255.255.255.0

   ___ Local

   ___ Remote

---

5. **Is the subnet mask 11111111.11111111.10101111.00000000 valid or invalid?**

   ___ Valid

   ___ Invalid

TOPIC C

Default IP Addresses

In the previous topic, you learned about the structure of an IP address. Now you can examine the ways in which IP addresses are assigned. In this topic, you will learn about default IP address classes and how they are distributed.

TCP/IP addresses are controlled to ensure that there are no duplicate addresses worldwide. Companies and Internet service providers (ISPs) lease addresses for their networks and customers to gain Internet access. It's expensive for a company to lease IP addresses for every client that needs Internet access. In order for you to lease only the IP addresses you truly need, you need to first understand the default IP address classes, their reserved purposes, and where to lease the IP addresses you need.

The ICANN

The IP address of every node on the Internet must be unique. An international organization called the *Internet Corporation for Assigned Names and Numbers (ICANN)* controls the leasing and distribution of IP addresses on the Internet. Companies lease their IP addresses from ICANN to ensure that there are no duplicate IP addresses.

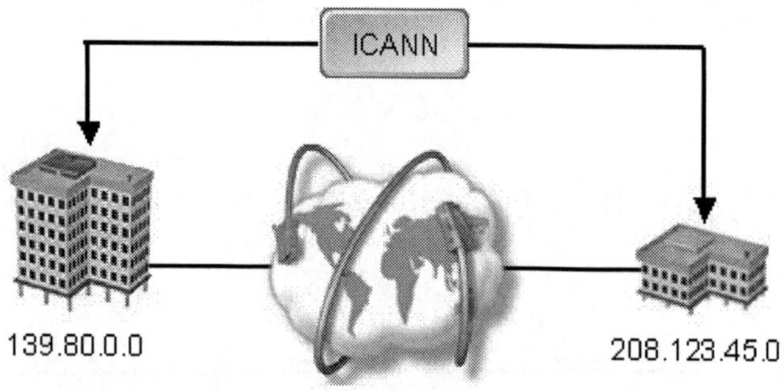

Figure 6-13: *The ICANN.*

In 1993, an international organization called the Internet Assigned Number Authority (IANA) was established to govern the use of Internet IP addresses. Today, that function is taken care of by ICANN.

IP Address Classes

The designers of the TCP/IP suite defined five blocks of addresses, called address classes, for specific network uses and sizes.

Address Class	Description
Class A	*Class A* addresses provide a small number of network addresses for networks with a large number of nodes per network. • Address range: 1.0.0.0 to 127.255.255.255 • Number of networks: 126 (The IP address 127.0.0.1 is reserved.) • Number of nodes per network: 16,777,214 • Network ID portion: First octet • Node ID portion: Last three octets • Default subnet mask: 255.0.0.0
Class B	*Class B* addresses provide a balance between the number of network addresses and the number of nodes per network. • Address range: 128.0.0.0 to 191.255.255.255 • Number of networks: 16,382 • Number of nodes per network: 65,534 • Network ID portion: First two octets, excluding Class A addresses • Node ID portion: Last two octets • Default subnet mask: 255.255.0.0
Class C	*Class C* addresses provide a large number of network addresses for networks with a small number of nodes per network. • Address range: 192.0.0.0 to 223.255.255.255 • Number of networks: 2,097,150 • Number of nodes per network: 254 • Network ID portion: First three octets, excluding Class A and Class B addresses • Node ID portion: Last octet • Default subnet mask: 255.255.255.0
Class D	*Class D* addresses are set aside to support multicast transmissions. Any network can use them, regardless of the base network ID. A multicast server assigns a single Class D address to all members of a multicast session. There is no subnet mask. Class D addresses are routable only with special support from the routers. • Address range: 224.0.0.0 to 239.255.255.255 • Number of networks: N/A • Number of nodes per network: N/A • Network ID portion: N/A • Node ID portion: N/A • Default subnet mask: N/A
Class E	*Class E* addresses are set aside for research and experimentation. • Address range: 240.0.0.0 to 255.255.255.255 • Number of networks: N/A • Number of nodes per network: N/A • Network ID portion: N/A • Node ID portion: N/A • Default subnet mask: N/A

Used only by extremely large networks, Class A addresses are far too big for most companies. Large telephone companies and ISPs leased most Class A network addresses early in the Internet game. In the beginning, Internet designers didn't see a need for extremely large networks on the Internet, just a need for many smaller networks.

Most companies leased Class B addresses for use on Internet-connected networks. In the beginning, there were plenty of Class B addresses to go around, but soon they were depleted.

Because multicasting has limited use, the Class D address block is relatively small.

Class E addresses are not tightly defined. Set aside strictly for research and experimentation purposes, they are not available for use by network administrators.

Special Addresses in Default Address Classes

Because neither the host portion nor the network portion of an IP address can be all 1s or all 0s, certain host addresses in each address class are invalid for individual hosts. For example, in Class A, the host address 10.0.0.0 is not valid because the host portion is all 0s—the address is identical to the network address. Similarly, the Class A address 120.255.255.255 is not valid because the host portion is all 1s. A host address with all 1s has a special purpose; it is used as a broadcast address. The address 127.255.255.255 would be used for broadcasts to the local subnet; the internet broadcast address of 255.255.255.255 is used for broadcasts to all networks.

Available Host and Network Addresses

The number of host addresses or network addresses available on networks in each class depends upon how many bits are in the network portion or host portion of the address. The formula to calculate available host addresses is 2^x-2, where x is the number of host bits. Two addresses in each block are unavailable because host addresses cannot be all ones or all zeros.

Similarly, the formula to calculate available network addresses is 2^y-2, where y is the number of network bits.

Private Nonroutable Addresses

ICANN has set aside three nonroutable address ranges that a company can use internally to enable their network nodes to communicate with one another using TCP/IP. When an Internet router receives a data packet bound for one of these reserved IP addresses, it recognizes the address as nonroutable and does not forward it outside the company. These private IP addresses can be used freely on internal networks; because they are not routable, they do not cause duplicate IP address conflicts on the Internet.

In order for a computer with an assigned nonroutable IP address to access Internet resources or other external networks, the private IP address must be converted to a routable address. Typically, this translation is done by a gateway or by a router.

The nonroutable private address ranges are defined in RFC 1918.

Private IP Address Ranges

The private, nonroutable IP address ranges are:

- 10.0.0.0 to 10.255.255.255
- 172.16.0.0 to 172.31.255.255
- 192.168.0.0 to 192.168.255.255

ACTIVITY 6-3

Identifying Characteristics of Default IP Addressing Schemes

Scenario:

In this activity, you will identify characteristics of default IP addressing schemes.

1. **Match the IP address range with its class.**

___	Class A	a.	224.0.0.0 to 239.255.255.255
___	Class B	b.	240.0.0.0 to 255.255.255.255
___	Class C	c.	128.0.0.0 to 191.255.255.255
___	Class D	d.	192.0.0.0 to 223.255.255.255
___	Class E	e.	1.0.0.0 to 127.255.255.255

2. **Select the IP address classes that can be assigned to hosts.**

   a) Class A

   b) Class B

   c) Class C

   d) Class D

   e) Class E

3. **True or False? To implement TCP/IP on your network, you must lease a block of IP addresses from ICANN.**

   __ True

   __ False

4. **True or False? To route traffic to Internet destinations, you must lease a block of IP addresses from ICANN if you do not receive them from an ISP.**

   __ True

   __ False

5. **How many bits comprise an IP address?**

    a) 16

    b) 32

    c) 10

    d) 8

6. **True or False? The two parts of an IP address are the network and host.**

    ___ True

    ___ False

7. **True or False? The IP address 127.0.0.0 is a valid address to use on a network.**

    ___ True

    ___ False

TOPIC D

Custom IP Addresses

In the previous topic, you learned about the default IP address ranges. Administrators can also create customized IP address schemes. In this topic, you will learn how to construct custom IP addressing schemes.

Because of the fixed number of default networks and hosts on Class B and Class C networks, many companies were forced to either lease Class B networks and then divide them up into multiple subnetworks within their company, or combine multiple smaller subnets into one highly subnetted network using Class C networks to facilitate the total number of nodes. As a network administrator, you will need to know how to create subnets that still meet the requirements of a valid IP addressing scheme and are fully functional on the Internet.

TCP/IP Subnets

Definition:

A *TCP/IP subnet* is a class of leased addresses that has been divided up into smaller groups to serve the network's needs. A custom TCP/IP subnet has a custom subnet mask ANDed to the IP address, so that what the node sees as its local network is a subset of the whole default network address block. A default gateway is configured for each subnet to route traffic between the subnets.

Example:

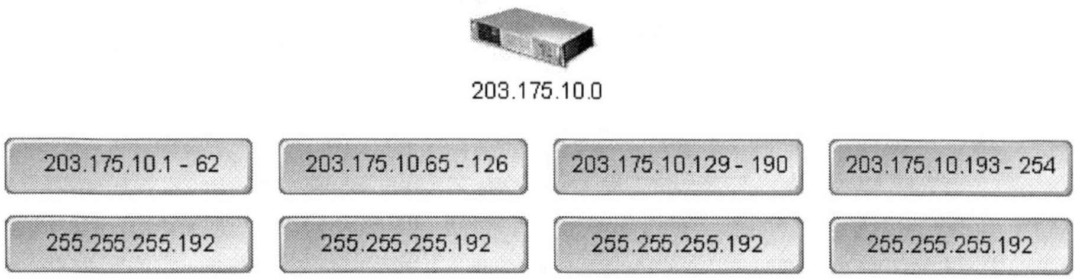

Figure 6-14: *TCP/IP subnets.*

Custom Subnet Masks

Use a custom subnet mask to separate a single IP address block into multiple subnets. The custom subnet mask borrows node bits in a contiguous block from the left side of the node portion of the address, and uses them as network bits. This divides a single network address into multiple networks, each containing fewer nodes.

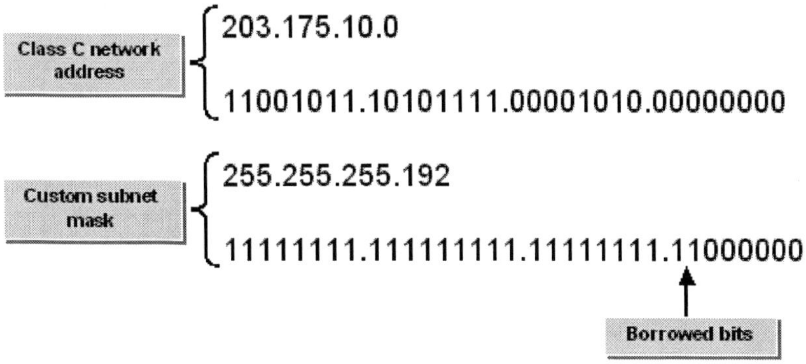

Figure 6-15: *Subnetting a classful address.*

Custom Subnet Masks on a Class C Network

This table shows all the possible custom subnet masks on a Class C network.

Last Octet of New Mask (Binary)	New Mask (Decimal)	Number of Added Networks	Nodes per Network
10000000	255.255.255.128	2	126
11000000	255.255.255.192	4	62
11100000	255.255.255.224	8	30
11110000	255.255.255.240	16	14
11111000	255.255.255.248	32	6
11111100	255.255.255.252	64	2
11111110	255.255.255.254	Not allowed in Class C	

Last Octet of New Mask (Binary)	New Mask (Decimal)	Number of Added Networks	Nodes per Network
11111111	255.255.255.255	Not allowed in Class C	

Determining Available Host Addresses

The number of host addresses on a custom subnet is a function of the total number of address bits available for host addressing. The formula is 2^x-2, where x is the number of host bits. Two addresses in each block are unavailable because host addresses cannot be all ones or all zeros.

So, with a subnet mask of 255.255.255.248 (11111111.11111111.11111111.11111000 in binary), three bits are available for host addresses (2^3=8), less two unavailable addresses leaves a total of six available host addresses per network.

Limitations on Default IP Addresses

Because classful networks provide fixed numbers of node addresses, it is difficult to match IP address leases to a company's need without waste. A company with only 300 nodes could potentially lease an entire Class B network, thus depriving the industry of thousands of usable IP addresses. Companies can conserve the limited IP addresses by leasing them only for those routers and hosts that connect directly to the Internet, and by using nonroutable addresses internally.

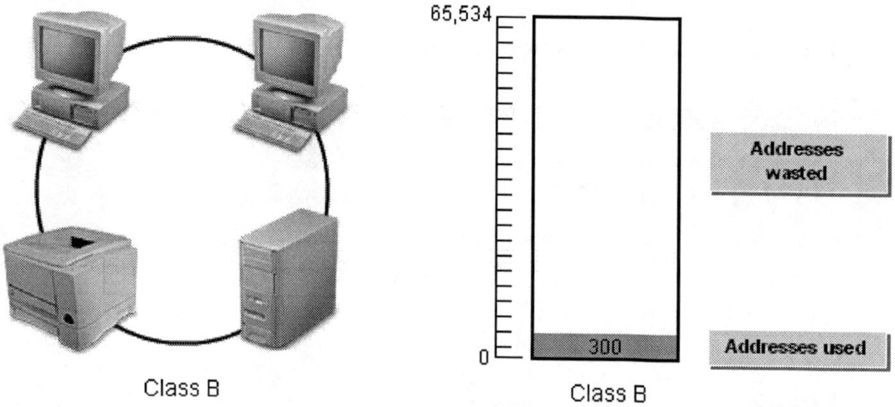

Figure 6-16: *Limitations on classful addresses.*

Variable Length Subnet Masks (VLSMs)

Definition:

In a standard subnet, the number of addresses is identical within each subnet. The custom subnet mask must accommodate the subnet with the greatest number of nodes. This can waste addresses on the smaller subnets. A *variable length subnet mask (VLSM)* can be used to create subnets containing different numbers of nodes. A VLSM applies the custom subnet mask that provides the number of nodes required for each subnet.

The downside of carefully tailoring a subnet mask to each subnet is that you limit your capacity for future node growth on each subnet. Ideally, you want some room for future growth, but predicting how much growth you need is more of an art than an exact science.

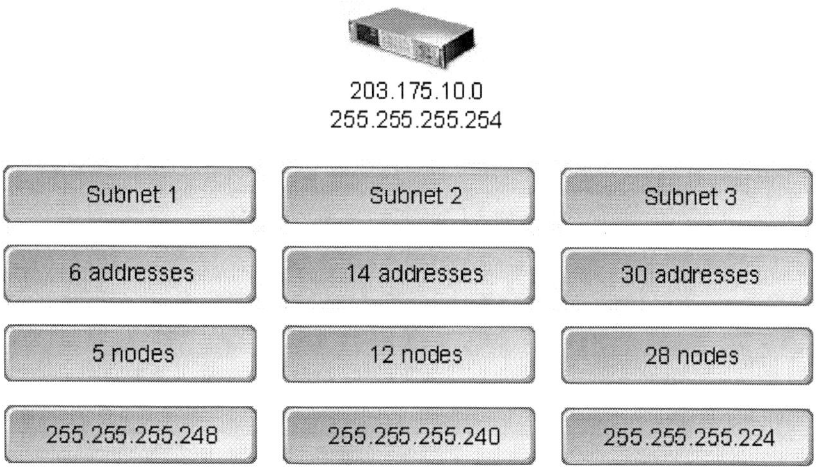

Figure 6-17: *Variable length subnet masks.*

Example: VLSMs on a Class C Network

A Class C network might contain 3 subnets, with 5 hosts on subnet 1, 12 hosts on subnet 2, and 28 hosts on subnet 3. You could use a custom subnet mask of 255.255.255.224 to allow each subnet to have 30 addresses. However, applying this subnet mask would waste 25 IP addresses on subnet 1, 18 IP addresses on subnet 2, and 2 IP addresses on subnet 3. By applying the variable subnet mask of 255.255.255.248 to subnet 1, 255.255.255.240 to subnet 2, and 255.255.255.224 to subnet 3, you only waste 1 IP address on subnet 1, and 2 IP addresses on each of subnets 2 and 3.

Classless Inter Domain Routing (CIDR)

Classless Inter Domain Routing (CIDR) is a subnetting method that treats a VLSM as a 32-bit binary word. The mask bits can move in one-bit increments to provide the exact number of nodes and networks required. CIDR notation combines the network address with a single number to represent the number of one bits in the mask. With CIDR, multiple class-based networks can be represented as a single block.

CIDR can also be referred to as classless routing or supernetting. Because of its efficiencies, CIDR has been rapidly adopted, and the Internet today is largely a classless address space.

A CIDR Application

The CIDR address 192.168.12.0/23 applies the network mask 255.255.254.0 to the 192.168.0.0 network, starting at 192.168.12.0. On a VLSM-enabled router, this single routing entry can define a supernet that includes the address range from 192.168.12.0 to 192.168.13.255. Compare this to traditional class-based networking, where this range of addresses would require separate routing entries for each of two Class C networks—192.168.12.0 and 192.168.13.0—each using the default Class C subnet mask of 255.255.255.0.

CIDR Subnet Masks

This table shows the value of each possible CIDR subnet mask. The /24, /16, and /8 CIDR masks correspond with the classful ranges of Class C, Class B, and Class A, respectively.

CIDR Mask (Number of Network Bits)	Number of Possible Nodes	Standard Subnet Mask in Dotted Decimal
/32	N/A	255.255.255.255
/31	N/A	255.255.255.254
/30	2	255.255.255.252
/29	6	255.255.255.248
/28	14	255.255.255.240
/27	30	255.255.255.224
/26	62	255.255.255.192
/25	126	255.255.255.128
/24	254	255.255.255.0
/23	510	255.255.254.0
/22	1,022	255.255.252.0
/21	2,046	255.255.248.0
/20	4,094	255.255.240.0
/19	8,190	255.255.224.0
/18	16,382	255.255.192.0
/17	32,766	255.255.128.0
/16	65,534	255.255.0.0
/15	131,070	255.254.0.0
/14	262,142	255.252.0.0
/13	524,286	255.248.0.0
/12	1,048,574	255.240.0.0
/11	2,097,150	255.224.0.0
/10	4,194,304	255.192.0.0
/9	8,386,606	255.128.0.0
/8	16,777,214	255.0.0.0
/7	33,554,430	254.0.0.0
/6	67,108,862	252.0.0.0

CIDR Mask (Number of Network Bits)	Number of Possible Nodes	Standard Subnet Mask in Dotted Decimal
/5	134,217,726	248.0.0.0
/4	268,435,544	240.0.0.0
/3	536,870,910	224.0.0.0
/2	1,073,741,824	192.0.0.0
/1	N/A	

How to Calculate the Base Network ID of a Custom Subnet

When dealing with classful IP addresses, everything is relatively well laid out. As long as the default subnet masks are used, network IDs can be compared in decimal form with no conversion. Once the subnet mask is changed, the subnetted octet needs to be converted to determine how many bits have been borrowed for network bits.

Procedure Reference: Calculate the Base Network ID of a Custom Subnet

To calculate the base network ID of a custom subnet:

1. Isolate the octet that has shared network and node bits. This is the only octet you need to focus on. The other octets will be either all network bits or all node bits.
2. Convert the shared octet for the IP address to binary.
3. Apply the mask from the shared octet of the subnet mask to the shared octet of the IP address to remove the node bits.
4. Convert the shared portion of the IP address back to decimal.

Example: Calculating a Base Network ID

To determine the base network ID of the IP address 206.234.120.87 /20:

1. Isolate the octet that has shared network and node bits.

   The subnet mask for /20 is 11111111 11111111 11110000 00000000

   The third octet is shared between nodes and networks.
2. Convert the shared octet for the IP address to binary; add leading zeros as needed to create an 8-bit number.

   The third octet is 120; the binary equivalent is 1111000. Add a leading zero to create an 8-bit number.

   206.234.01111000.87
3. Apply the mask from the shared octet of the subnet mask to the shared octet of the IP address to remove the node bits.

   Because the fourth octet is node bits, all of it will change to zeros. The first and second octets are totally network bits and will drop through the mask.

   206.234.01111000.87

255.255.11110000.0

206.234.01110000.0

4. Convert the shared portion of the IP address back to decimal.

   01110000 = 112

   The base network ID is 206.234.112.0.

Windows Calculator

The Calculator accessory that is built in to Windows operating systems can be very useful when converting decimal and binary numbers. Switch the Calculator to Scientific view, type a number, and use the Dec and Bin radio buttons to convert the number from one format to another.

DISCOVERY ACTIVITY 6-4

Selecting Network IDs

Scenario:

You've been asked to implement TCP/IP on a divided network. There are three subnets separated by two Layer 3 network devices and no Internet connection. Subnet 1 has 120 nodes, Subnet 2 has 1,350 nodes, and Subnet 3 has 240 nodes. You need to select the appropriate network IDs.

---

1. **How many individual network IDs do you need?**

   a) One

   b) Two

   c) Three

   d) Four

---

2. **If you were going to use default subnet masks for the networks, which default subnet would be applied to each network?**

   a) Subnets 1, 2, and 3 would all use 255.255.0.0.

   b) Subnets 1, 2, and 3 would all use 255.255.255.0.

   c) Subnets 1 and 2 would use 255.255.0.0 and Subnet 3 would use 255.255.255.0.

   d) Subnets 1 and 3 would use 255.255.255.0 and Subnet 2 would use 255.255.0.0

   e) Subnets 2 and 3 would use 255.255.0.0 and Subnet 1 would use 255.255.255.0.

---

3. **Which is a valid example of an appropriate network address and subnet mask for Subnet 1?**

   a) IP address: 192.168.10.0; Subnet mask: 255.255.255.0

   b) IP address: 172.16.0.0; Subnet mask: 255.255.0.0

   c) IP address: 192.168.10.0; Subnet mask: 255.255.0.0

   d) IP address: 172.16.0.0; Subnet mask: 255.255.255.0

Discovery Activity 6-5

Calculating Base Network IDs

Scenario:

In this activity, you will calculate base network IDs for custom subnets that use CIDR notation.

1. **Select the correct base network ID for 203.121.45.6 /22.**

   a) 203.121.45.0

   b) 203.224.45.0

   c) 203.121.44.0

   d) 203.121.45.6

2. **Select the correct base network ID for 10.10.123.164 /27.**

   a) 10.10.123.0

   b) 10.10.123.164

   c) 10.10.123.160

   d) 10.10.120.0

TOPIC E

The TCP/IP Protocol Suite

So far we've discussed TCP/IP as an addressing scheme—that's what most users think TCP/IP is. However, the TCP/IP protocol is actually a suite of complimentary protocols and standards that work together to provide the functionality that TCP/IP networks have become famous for. In this topic, you will learn about the protocols and standards that can be used on a TCP/IP network.

The TCP/IP protocol suite includes many services that make running TCP/IP as your network's routable protocol very enticing, even if you don't need to connect to the Internet. The TCP/IP protocol suite defines how applications on separate nodes establish a connection and track communications. To ensure that your network is receiving the benefits that the TCP/IP suite of protocols and standards provide, you need to learn what those services are and how they can benefit your network.

The TCP/IP Network Model

TCP/IP is a four-layer network model that loosely follows the seven-layer OSI model. The Application layer maps to the Application, Presentation, and Session layers in the OSI model. The Transport layer maps to the Transport layer in the OSI model. The Internet layer maps to the Network layer in the OSI model, and the Network layer maps to the Data-link and Physical layers in the OSI model.

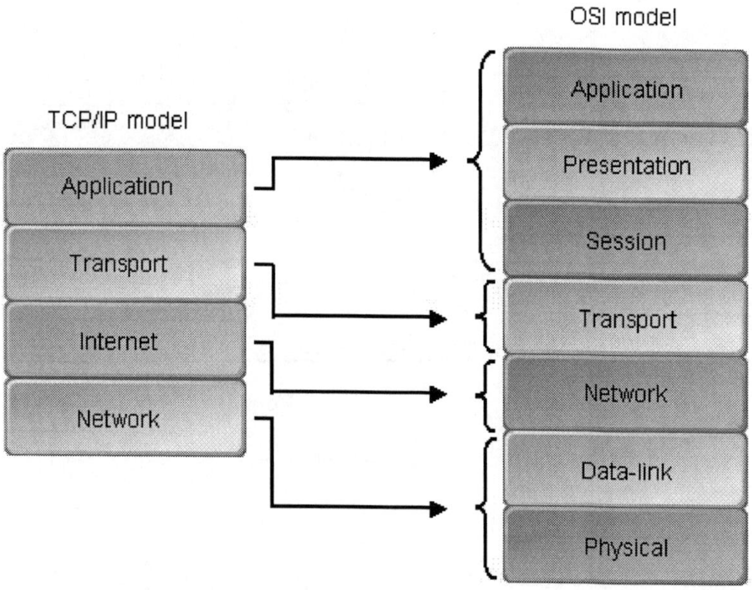

Figure 6-18: *TCP/IP networking layers compared to the OSI model.*

Layers in the TCP/IP Protocol Suite

Each layer in the TCP/IP model provides services similar to the OSI model.

TCP/IP Layer	Provides
Application	Utilities such as socket services and NetBIOS over TCP/IP.
Transport	Connection and communication services.
Internet	Addressing and routing services.
Network	Services that send and receive frames from the network.

TCP and UDP Transport Protocols

The TCP/IP suite includes two transport-layer protocols: *Transmission Control Protocol (TCP)* and *User Datagram Protocol (UDP)*. TCP is a connection-oriented, guaranteed-delivery protocol. It sends data, waits for an ACK, and fixes erroneous data. UDP is a connectionless, best-effort-delivery protocol. It sends data but does not take responsibility for the data's integrity.

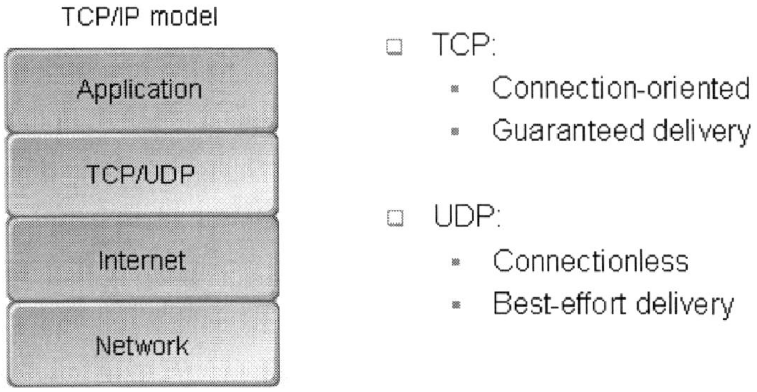

Figure 6-19: *TCP and UDP.*

Store and Forward

Because UDP is connectionless, it can send data in a *store and forward* fashion. That is, it can send data to a server or a router where the data is stored until the next hop becomes available.

TCP Analogy

Mr. TCP's boss gives him a letter to send to a client. TCP sends it certified mail with delivery confirmation and waits by the mailbox. In a few days, he gets a notice in the mail that the letter was delivered. However, if the notice doesn't come in a timely manner, Mr. TCP knows he has to resend the letter.

UDP Analogy

Ms. UDP's boss gives her a letter to send which she sends via regular mail. She doesn't wait by the mailbox or give the letter a second thought. She assumes that it reached its destination. If Ms. UDP's letter didn't reach its destination, the receiving party has to call UDP's boss and ask for the letter to be resent. Ms. UDP has done her best job and is out of the picture.

The Internet Protocol (IP)

The *Internet Protocol (IP)* primarily serves to assign the correct destination address to a data packet. When a service establishes a connection to the receiving node at the Transport layer, it resolves the name of the receiving node to that node's IP address. The IP address is then passed from the Transport layer to the Internet layer, and IP uses the subnet mask to determine if the receiving node is on the same subnet or a remote network, and delivers the packet.

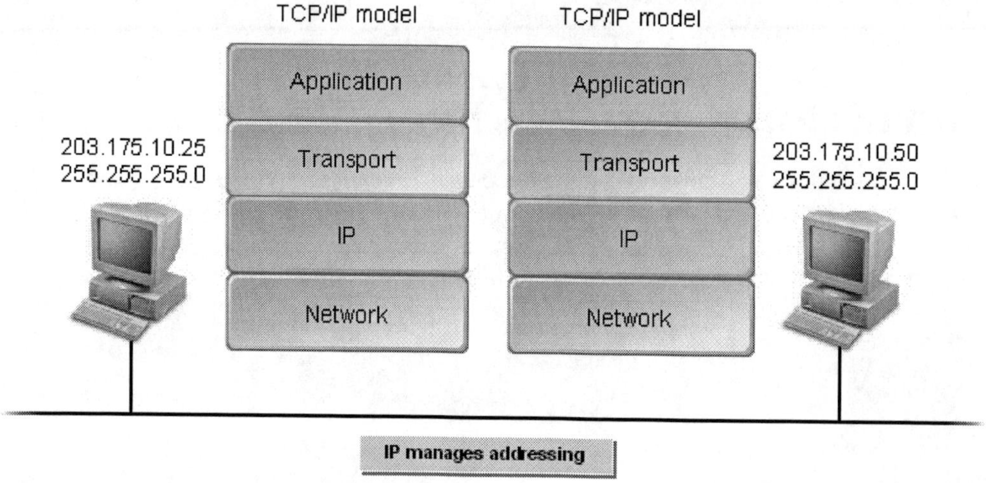

Figure 6-20: *The Internet Protocol.*

The Address Resolution Protocol (ARP)

Address Resolution Protocol (ARP) supports the Internet Protocol by resolving IP addresses to MAC addresses. First, ARP receives an IP address from the Internet Protocol. If ARP has the MAC address in its cache, it returns it to IP. If not, it issues a broadcast to resolve the IP address. The target node responds with a unicast that includes its MAC address. ARP adds the MAC address into its cache and then sends it to IP as requested.

The ARP broadcast is very efficient and doesn't create a lot of network traffic.

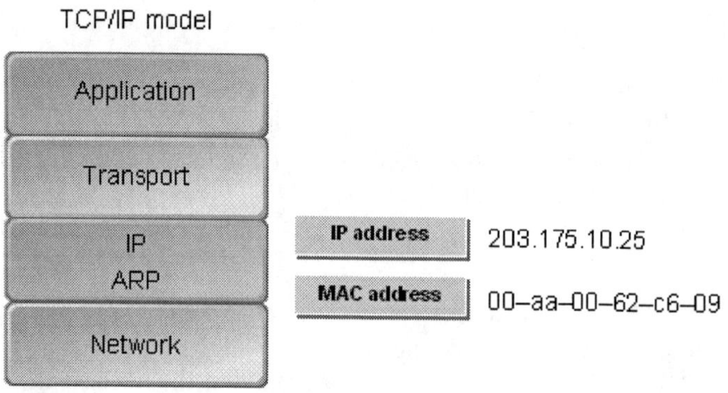

Figure 6-21: *ARP.*

The Destination MAC Address

If IP needs to deliver a packet to an IP address on the local subnet, it needs to obtain the MAC address of the destination node directly from ARP. However, if IP needs to deliver a packet to an IP address on a remote subnet, it only needs the MAC address of the default gateway, not of the final destination node. Once IP sends the packet to the default gateway, the default gateway will undertake its own MAC address resolution process to locate the MAC address of the next hop, and then forward the packet to other routers and networks as needed. Because the first step in the route to the destination is always on the local network, ARP resolution broadcasts can be confined to the local subnet.

Reverse Address Resolution Protocol (RARP)

The *Reverse Address Resolution Protocol (RARP)* is a protocol that allows a node on a local area network to discover its IP address from a router's ARP table or cache. With RARP, a network administrator creates a table on the LAN's router that maps each node's MAC address to its corresponding IP addresses. When a node is added to the network, its RARP client program requests its IP address from the RARP server on the router. If that entry has been set up in the router table, the RARP server returns the IP address to the node, which stores it for future use.

RARP is available for Ethernet, FDDI, and Token Ring LANs.

The Internet Control Message Protocol (ICMP)

The *Internet Control Message Protocol (ICMP)* is a service added to the IP protocol that attempts to report on the condition of a connection between two nodes. ICMP messages notify a sender of network conditions by reporting IP errors. If a TCP/IP node is sending data so fast that the receiving node's buffers flood, the receiving node sends an ICMP source quench message to slow down the data from the sending node.

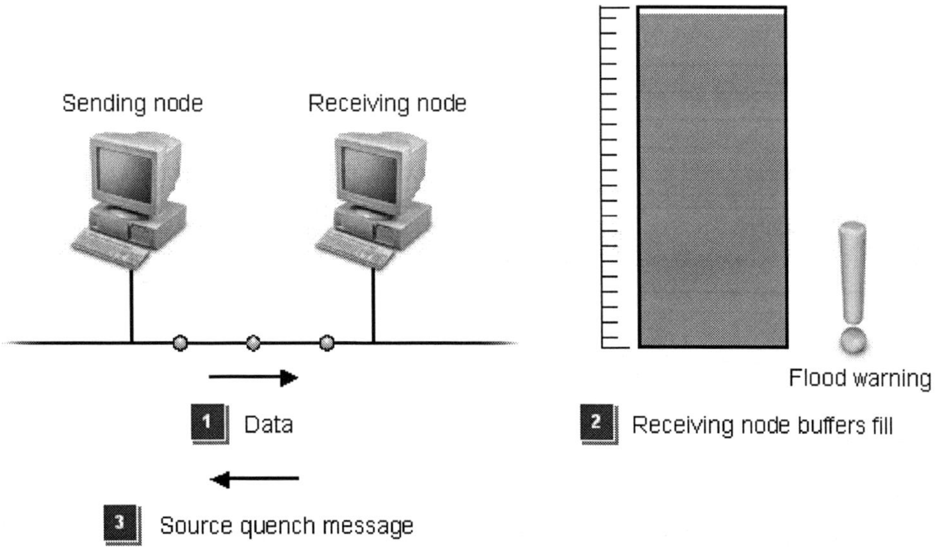

Figure 6-22: *The ICMP reports on the condition of a connection between two nodes.*

The Internet Group Management Protocol (IGMP)

The *Internet Group Management Protocol (IGMP)* supports multicasting in a routed environment. The routers have to support IGMP and multicast packet routing. IGMP on the node responsible for the multicast traffic sends a message to the router informing it of the multicast session in progress. The router uses IGMP to poll its interfaces for members of the multicast group, and then forwards the multicast transmission to the group members.

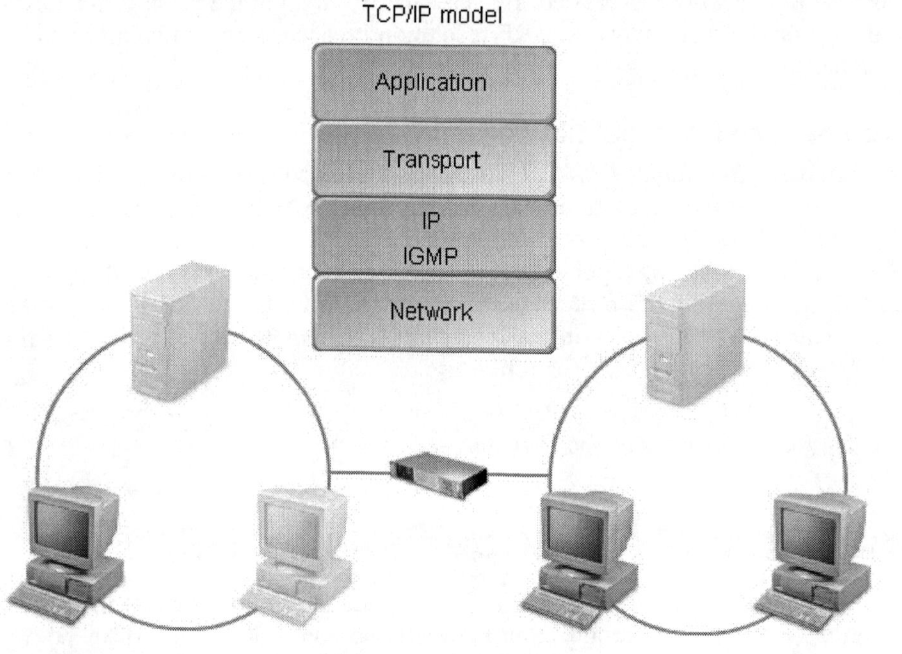

Figure 6-23: *IGMP directs multicast traffic to members of the selected group.*

Ports

Definition:

In TCP and UDP networks, a *port* is the endpoint of a logical connection. Client computers connect to specific server programs through a designated port. All ports are assigned a number in a range from 0 to 65,535. The IANA separates port numbers into three blocks: well-known ports, which are preassigned to system processes by IANA; registered ports, which are available to user processes and are listed as a convenience by IANA; and dynamic ports, which are assigned by a client operating system as needed when there is a request for service.

Example:

The three blocks of port numbers are:

- Well-known ports: 0 to 1,023
- Registered ports: 1,024 to 49,151
- Dynamic or private ports: 49,152 to 65,535

Well-Known Port Numbers

Different services are assigned unique port numbers. This allows nodes to ex data with multiple services at the same time. This table lists some of the most well-known port numbers. Well-known ports and other port number assignment. available online at **www.iana.org/assignments/port-numbers**.

Port Number	Service Name	Service
7	echo	Ping
20	ftp-data	File Transfer [Default Data]
21	ftp	File Transfer [Control]
22	ssh	SSH (Remote Login Protocol)
23	telnet	Telnet
25	smtp	Simple Mail Transfer Protocol
42	namesrv	Host Name Server
53	dns	Domain Name Service
69	tftp	Trivial File Transfer Protocol
80	http	World Wide Web HTTP
88	kerberos	Kerberos Authentication Service
103	x400	X.400 Standard
110	pop3	Post Office Protocol – Version 3
115	sftp	Simple File Transfer Protocol
119	nntp	Network News Transfer Protocol
123	ntp	Network Time Protocol
137	netbios	NetBIOS Name Service
143	imap	Internet Message Access Protocol
161	snmp	Simple Network Management Protocol
194	irc	Internet Relay Chat
389	ldap	Lightweight Directory Access Protocol
443	https	HTTP-Secure

Sockets

Definition:

A *socket* is a piece of software within an operating system that connects an application with a network protocol, so that the application can request network services from the operating system. In TCP/IP, the socket links the IP address with the port number of the service. The socket address uses the form {*protocol, local-address, local-process*}.

Example: A Socket Address

In the socket address `{tcp, 193.44.234.3, 53}`

- TCP is the protocol.
- 193.44.234.3 is the local IP address.

- 53 is the port number of the local process, which in this example is DNS.

Activity 6-6

Identifying Features of the TCP/IP Protocol Suite

Scenario:

In this activity, you will identify features of the TCP/IP protocol suite.

1. **Match the OSI layers with the TCP/IP layers.**

___	Application, Presentation, Session	a.	Network
___	Transport	b.	Transport
___	Network	c.	Application
___	Data-link, Physical	d.	Internet

2. **True or False? UDP is a connectionless, best-effort-delivery protocol.**

   ___ True

   ___ False

3. **True or False? ARP uses a multicast session to resolve any IP address to MAC address it does not have in its cache.**

   ___ True

   ___ False

4. **Which is a function of the ICMP protocol?**

   a) Use to control multicast sessions.

   b) Can request that a sender speed up or slow down data traffic based on network conditions.

   c) Resolves IP addresses to MAC addresses.

   d) Provides best-effort data delivery.

5. **Match the port number ranges with their reserved block.**

___	Well-known ports	a.	1 to 1023
___	Registered ports	b.	49,152 to 65,535
___	Dynamic or private ports	c.	1024 to 49,151

6. **For the socket address example {tcp, 110.105.25.5, 23}, identify the components.**

___	tcp	a.	The port number of the local service.
___	110.105.25.5	b.	The IP address of the local computer.
___	23	c.	The protocol.

Lesson 6 Follow-up

In this lesson, you examined one of the most common network protocols in use today, TCP/IP. When you implement the TCP/IP protocol on your network, you allow your computers' communications to be routed across different segments of your network, as well as to communicate over the Internet.

1. **In your network, which communications would be best served by TCP and which by UDP?**

2. **For what applications does your organization require IGMP to support multicasting?**

NOTES

LESSON 7
TCP/IP Services

Lesson Time
2 hour(s)

Lesson Objectives:

In this lesson, you will identify the major services deployed on TCP/IP networks.

You will:

- Configure a computer to get its IP address statically and dynamically.
- Identify host name resolution methods on a TCP/IP network.
- Identify NetBIOS name resolution methods.
- Identify common TCP/IP utilities and their functions.
- Identify the primary upper-layer services in use on a TCP/IP network.
- Identify TCP/IP interoperability services.

Lesson 7

Introduction

In the previous lesson, you learned how the TCP/IP protocol suite uses IP addresses to create networks and enable communication. The TCP/IP protocol suite also includes services that make managing your TCP/IP network more effective. In this lesson, you will learn how the services that are part of the TCP/IP protocol suite can be used on your network.

To manage a TCP/IP network, you need to understand IP addressing theory. But you also have to be able to implement your addressing scheme, and to support it on an ongoing basis. To do that, you'll need to understand and use the TCP/IP services and tools that enable you to configure, monitor, and troubleshoot your TCP/IP network.

This lesson covers the following CompTIA Network+ (2005) certification objectives:

- Topic A:
  - Objective 2.4: Characterize the TCP/IP (Transmission Control Protocol/Internet Protocol) network protocol in terms of routing, addressing schemes, interoperability, and naming conventions.
  - Objective 2.9: Identify and differentiate between the following IP (Internet Protocol) addressing methods: static, dynamic, and self-assigned (APIPA (Automatic Private Internet Protocol Addressing)).
  - Objective 4.1: Given a troubleshooting scenario, select the appropriate network utility from the following: Ping, Ipconfig/Ifconfig, and Winipcfg.
  - Objective 4.2: Given output from a network diagnostic utility (for example, those utilities listed in objective 4.1), identify the utility and interpret the output.
  - Objective 4.6: Given a scenario, determine the impact of modifying, adding, or removing network services (for example, DHCP (Dynamic Host Configuration Protocol)) for network resources and users.
- Topic B:
  - Objective 2.4: Characterize the TCP/IP (Transmission Control Protocol/Internet Protocol) network protocol in terms of routing, addressing schemes, interoperability, and naming conventions.
  - Objective 2.13: Identify the purpose of network services and protocols (for example, DNS (Domain Name Service)).
  - Objective 4.6: Given a scenario, determine the impact of modifying, adding, or removing network services (for example, DNS) for network resources and users.
- Topic C:
  - Objective 2.4: Characterize the TCP/IP (Transmission Control Protocol/Internet Protocol) network protocol in terms of routing, addressing schemes, interoperability, and naming conventions.
  - Objective 2.13: Identify the purpose of network services and protocols (for example, WINS (Windows Internet Name Service)).
  - Objective 4.6: Given a scenario, determine the impact of modifying, adding, or removing network services (for example, WINS) for network resources and users.
- Topic D:
  - Objective 2.4: Characterize the TCP/IP (Transmission Control Protocol/Internet Protocol) network protocol in terms of routing, addressing schemes, interoperability, and naming conventions.
  - Objective 4.1: Given a troubleshooting scenario, select the appropriate network utility from the following: Tracert, Netstat, Nbtstat, Nslookup, and Arp.

- Objective 4.2: Given output from a network diagnostic utility (for example, those utilities listed in objective 4.1), identify the utility and interpret the output.

- Topic E:
  - Objective 2.4: Characterize the TCP/IP (Transmission Control Protocol/Internet Protocol) network protocol in terms of routing, addressing schemes, interoperability, and naming conventions.
  - Objective 2.10: Define the purpose, function, and use of the following protocols used in the TCP/IP suite: FTP (File Transfer Protocol); TFTP (Trivial File Transfer Protocol); SMTP (Simple Mail Transfer Protocol); HTTP (Hypertext Transfer Protocol); HTTPS (Hypertext Transfer Protocol Secure); POP3/IMAP4 (Post Office Protocol version 3/Internet Message Access Protocol version 4); Telnet; NTP (Network Time Protocol); and NNTP (Network News Transport Protocol).
- Topic F:
  - Objective 2.4: Characterize the TCP/IP (Transmission Control Protocol/Internet Protocol) network protocol in terms of routing, addressing schemes, interoperability, and naming conventions.
  - Objective 2.10: Define the purpose, function, and use of the following protocols used in the TCP/IP (Transmission Control Protocol/Internet Protocol) suite: SFTP (Secure File Transfer Protocol); SSH (Secure Shell); SCP (Secure Copy Protocol); LDAP (Lightweight Directory Access Protocol); and LPR (Line Printer Remote).
  - Objective 2.13: Identify the purpose of the following network services and protocols: SNMP (Simple Network Management Protocol), NFS (Network File System), Zeroconf (Zero configuration), SMB (Server Message Block), LPD (Line Printer Daemon), and Samba.

TOPIC A

IP Address Assignment Methods

In the previous lesson, you learned that each node that wants to communicate on a TCP/IP network is assigned an IP address. Those IP addresses can be assigned manually by an administrator or automatically without user intervention. In this topic, you will learn the different methods for assigning IP addresses to your nodes, and how to use tools that support IP address assignment.

Depending on the scope and size of your network, it may be just as easy to manually assign IP addresses to all your nodes as it is to install and maintain a service to do it for you. By understanding the different methods available to you for assigning IP addresses to the nodes on your network, you can choose the method that best suits the needs of your network and the time you have available for administration.

Static and Dynamic Addressing

TCP/IP address information can be assigned to nodes on the network statically, by manually entering addressing information on each individual network node. Or, it can be provided dynamically, by using the Dynamic Host Configuration Protocol (DHCP) service.

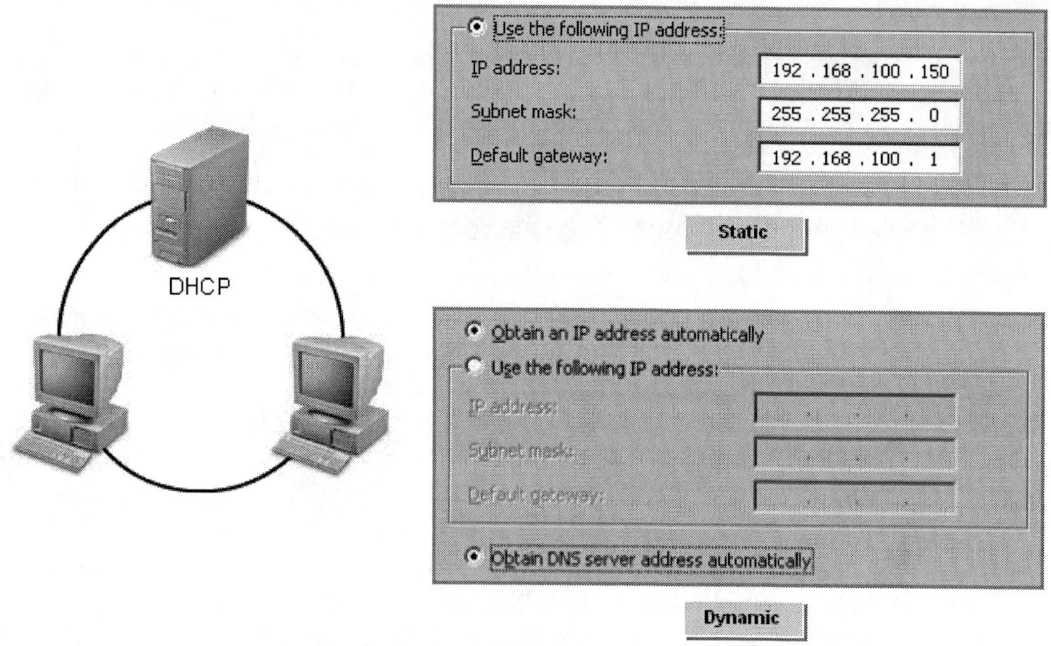

Figure 7-1: *Static and dynamic addressing.*

On Windows systems, static IP configuration information is entered in the Internet Protocol (TCP/IP) Properties dialog box for each network connection object.

Static IP Address Assignment

Configuring TCP/IP statically on a network requires an administrator to visit each node to manually enter IP address information for that node. If the node moves to a different subnet, the administrator must manually reconfigure the node's TCP/IP information for its new network location. In a large network, configuring TCP/IP statically on each node can be very time consuming, and can be prone to errors that disrupt communication.

Uses for Static Addresses

Static addresses are typically only assigned to systems with dedicated functionality, such as router interfaces, network-attached printers, or server systems that host network applications.

Dynamic Host Configuration Protocol (DHCP)

DHCP is a network service that provides automatic assignment of IP addresses and other TCP/IP configuration information on network nodes that are configured as DHCP clients. DHCP requires a DHCP server configured with at least one DHCP scope. The scope contains a range of IP addresses and a subnet mask, and can contain other options, such as a default gateway address. When the scope is enabled, it automatically leases TCP/IP information to DHCP clients for a defined lease period.

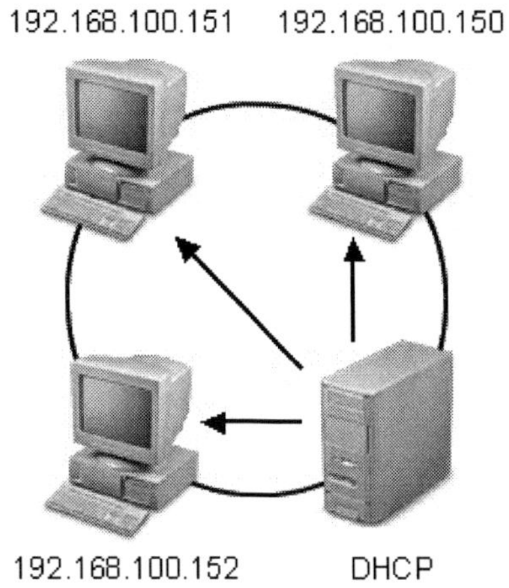

Figure 7-2: *DHCP.*

The DHCP Lease Process

There are several steps in the DHCP lease process.

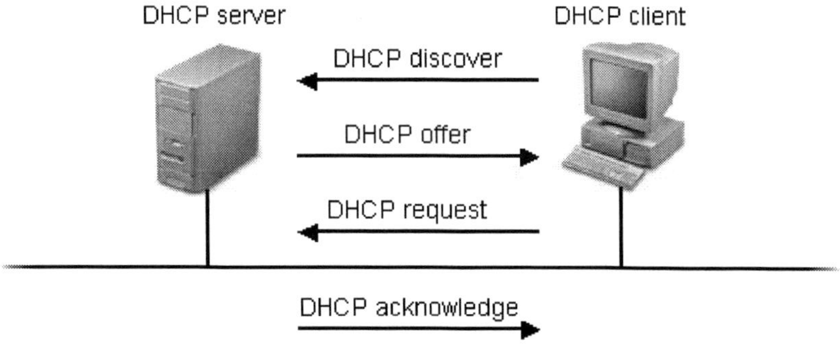

Figure 7-3: *The DHCP lease process.*

Process Step	Description
Node comes online	A node configured to use DHCP comes online and loads a simple version of TCP/IP.
DHCP discover	The node issues a BootP (Bootstrap Protocol) broadcast, called a DHCP discover, to the network's broadcast address of 255.255.255.255 to find out if any DHCP servers are online.
DHCP offer	All DHCP servers that are online respond with a directed lease offer packet, called a DHCP offer.

Process Step	Description
DHCP request	The node selects the first offer it receives and returns a request to lease the address, called a DHCP request.
DHCP ack	The DHCP server acknowledges the request with a packet called a DHCP ack, and starts the lease.
Unused offers expire	When the unused offers expire, all other servers return the IP addresses they offered to the available pool in their DHCP scopes.

All DHCP servers respond to clients the same way despite which vendor they're manufactured by because the process follows a standard methodology.

DHCP Relay Agent

BootP is a local broadcast that can't be sent through network routers. As an administrator of a TCP/IP network using DHCP, you must either have a DHCP server on each subnet, configure the router to forward the broadcasts, or configure a *DHCP relay agent*. A DHCP relay agent is a server service that captures the BootP broadcast and forwards it through the router as a unicast transmission to the DHCP server on a remote subnet. The DHCP server returns an offer to the relay agent, which in turn presents the offer to the client. Once the client has its lease, it also has the DHCP server's IP address, so it doesn't need to use the agent to renew the lease.

Recovering IP Addresses

The DHCP lease process is important to the overall performance of a DHCP system. By leasing addresses to clients instead of permanently assigning them, a DHCP server can recover addresses leased to offline clients.

Automatic Private IP Addressing (APIPA)

Automatic Private IP Addressing (APIPA) is a service that enables a DHCP client computer to configure itself automatically with an IP address in the range of 169.254.0.1 to 169.254.255.254 if no DHCP servers respond to the client's DHCP discover broadcast. APIPA enables DHCP clients to initialize TCP/IP and communicate on the local subnet even in the absence of an active DHCP scope. APIPA addresses are not routable, so computers with APIPA addresses cannot communicate outside the local subnet.

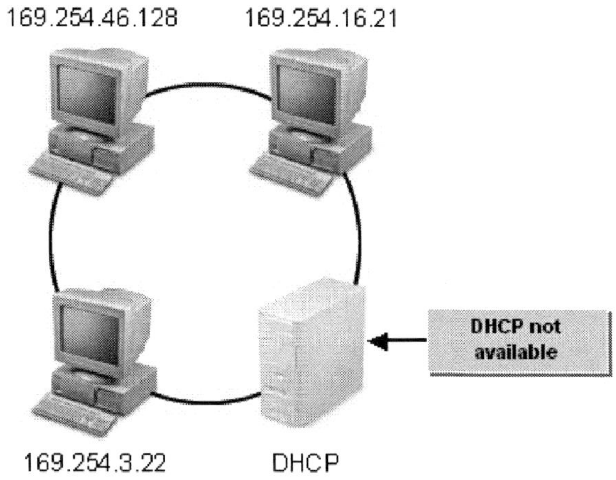

Figure 7-4: *APIPA.*

APIPA is available on Windows 2000, Windows Me, Windows 2003, and Windows XP systems. Because APIPA requires no administrative configuration, APIPA addressing could be used for small office or home networks where local subnet communication is all that is required.

The Ping Utility

You can use the *ping* command to verify the network connectivity of a computer. Ping checks the host name, IP address, and that the remote system can be reached. Ping uses ICMP ECHO_REQUEST datagrams to check connections between hosts by sending an echo packet, then listening for reply packets.

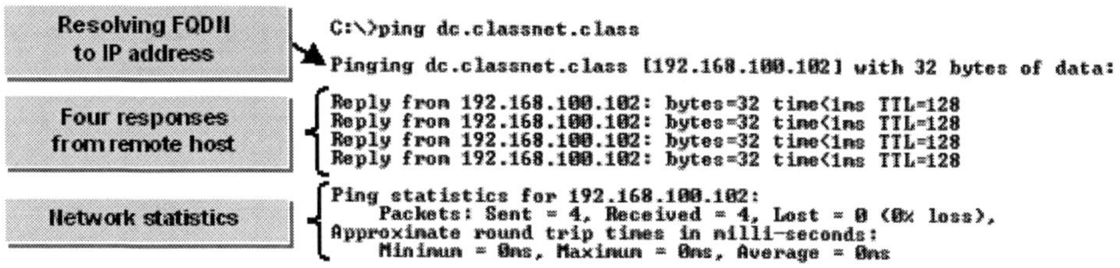

Figure 7-5: *Results of a ping on a Windows system.*

Ping Options

You can ping by computer name or by IP address. You can also ping the loopback address (127.0.0.1) to test whether TCP/IP has initialized on an individual system. If the computer has a default gateway, you can ping remote systems.

To list other options for the ping command, enter `ping` at the command prompt. Some of the options include setting the packet size, changing the *time to live (TTL)* value, and specifying how many times to ping the host.

Ping Blocking

As a security measure, some public Internet hosts and Internet routers might be configured to block incoming packets that are generated by the ping command. (They might also block packets from other TCP/IP diagnostic utilities such as the tracert command.) Pinging these hosts will fail even if the host is online. Keep this in mind when you try to ping large public Internet sites such as **www.yahoo.com** or **www.microsoft.com**; if you are trying to determine if one of these sites is up and available, a better method is simply to use a web browser to connect to the site directly.

IP Configuration Utilities

Use the IP configuration utility for your operating system to see TCP/IP configuration information.

Utility Name	Operating Systems and Function
Winipcfg	Supported on Windows Me, Windows 98, and Windows 95. Displays the network card driver, adapter address, IP address, subnet mask, and default gateway. The More Info button displays additional information about the IP configuration.
Ipconfig	Supported on Windows Server 2003, Windows XP, Windows 2000, Windows NT, and NetWare. Displays connection-specific DNS suffix, IP address, subnet mask, and default gateway. Must be run from a command line. To display additional information about the IP configuration, use the `/all` parameter with the command.
Ifconfig	Supported on Linux and UNIX. Displays the status of the currently active network interface devices. Using options, you can dynamically change the status of the interfaces and change the IP address.

Ipconfig Commands

The Ipconfig utility provides switches that enable you to manage dynamic address leases.

- `ipconfig /release` forces the release of an IP address of a network connection.
- `ipconfig /renew` requests the renewal of an IP address for a network connection. The system first attempts to obtain a DHCP address, and then will revert to APIPA addressing.

How to Assign IP Addresses

Procedure Reference: Assign IP Addresses

To configure a network interface with the Internet Protocol (TCP/IP) installed on a Windows Server 2003 computer to use a particular IP address assignment:

1. Choose Start→Control Panel→Network Connections.
2. Right-click the network connection you wish to configure for IP address assignment.

3. Choose Properties.
4. In the This Connection Uses The Following Items list, select Internet Protocol (TCP/IP).
5. Click Properties.
6. To use automatic IP addressing for IP address, subnet mask, and default gateway, select Obtain An IP Address Automatically. To manually configure a static IP address, subnet mask, and default gateway, select Use The Following IP Address.
7. If you selected Use The Following IP Address, in the IP Address, Subnet Mask, and Default Gateway text boxes, enter the TCP/IP information for your network.
8. To use automatic IP addressing pointing to a DNS server, select Obtain DNS Server Address Automatically. To manually configure a static DNS server address, select Use The Following DNS Server Addresses.
9. If you selected Use The Following DNS Server Addresses, in the Preferred DNS Server and Alternate DNS Server text boxes, enter the DNS server addresses for your network.
10. Click OK to close the Internet Protocol (TCP/IP) Properties dialog box.
11. Click OK to close the Properties dialog box for your selected network connection.

ACTIVITY 7-1

Manually Assigning IP Addresses

There is a simulated version of this activity available on the CD-ROM that shipped with this course. You can run this simulation on any Windows computer to review the activity after class, or as an alternative to performing the activity as a group in class. The activity simulation can be launched either directly from the CD-ROM by clicking the Interactives link and navigating to the appropriate one, or from the installed data file location by opening the C:\Data\Simulations\Lesson#\Activity# folder and double-clicking the executable (.exe) file.

Setup:

Your computer is currently configured to lease an IP address from the classroom DHCP server.

This activity uses internal IP addresses in the 192.168.1.x range for demonstration purposes. An ISP would not allocate addresses in this range.

Scenario:

You are a network administrator for a small company with leased addresses from their ISP in the range of 192.168.1.1 to 192.168.1.49. Their subnet mask is 255.255.255.0. The IP address of the DNS server for their company is 192.168.1.200. The DNS server is also the default gateway. They have asked you to configure their computers to use the IP addresses given to them by their ISP.

What You Do | **How You Do It**

1. **Configure your computer with the static IP address.**
    - IP address = 192.168.1.##, where ## is your student number
    - Subnet mask = 255.255.255.0
    - Default gateway = 192.168.1.200
    - DNS server = 192.168.1.200

a. **Choose Start→Control Panel→Network Connections.**

b. **Right-click Local Area Connection.**

c. **Choose Properties.**

d. In the This Connection Uses The Following Items box, **select Internet Protocol (TCP/IP).**

e. **Click Properties.**

f. **Select Use The Following IP Address.**

g. In the IP Address box, **type *192.168.1.##***, where ## is your student number.

h. **Click in the Subnet Mask box.** The default subnet mask for the IP address autopopulates.

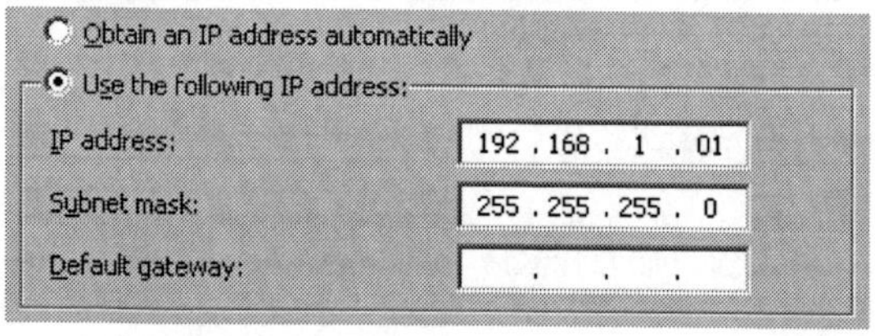

i. In the Default Gateway box, **type *192.168.1.200***

j. **Verify that Use The Following DNS Server Addresses is selected.**

k. In the Preferred DNS Server box, **type *192.168.1.200***

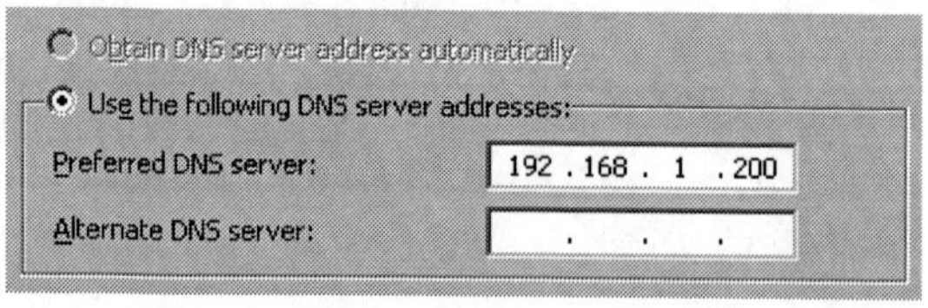

l. **Click OK** to close the Internet Protocol (TCP/IP) Properties dialog box.

m. **Click Close** to close the Local Area Connection Properties dialog box.

---

2. **Verify your IP information.**

a. **Choose Start→Command Prompt.**

b. At the command prompt, **enter** ***ipconfig /all***

```
Ethernet adapter Local Area Connection:

   Connection-specific DNS Suffix  . :
   Description . . . . . . . . . . . : 3Com 3C905TX-based Ethernet Adapter (Gene
ric)
   Physical Address. . . . . . . . . : 00-60-08-CD-34-64
   DHCP Enabled. . . . . . . . . . . : No
   IP Address. . . . . . . . . . . . : 192.168.1.1
   Subnet Mask . . . . . . . . . . . : 255.255.255.0
   Default Gateway . . . . . . . . . : 192.168.1.200
   DNS Servers . . . . . . . . . . . : 192.168.1.200
```

c. **Verify that the Local Area Connection object shows the IP address, subnet mask, default gateway, and DNS server information you entered.**

---

3. **Test your ability to communicate over TCP/IP with the DNS server (192.168.1.200).**

a. At the command prompt, **enter** ***ping 192.168.1.200***

```
C:\Documents and Settings\user01>ping 192.168.1.200

Pinging 192.168.1.200 with 32 bytes of data:

Reply from 192.168.1.200: bytes=32 time<1ms TTL=128
Reply from 192.168.1.200: bytes=32 time<1ms TTL=128
Reply from 192.168.1.200: bytes=32 time<1ms TTL=128
Reply from 192.168.1.200: bytes=32 time<1ms TTL=128

Ping statistics for 192.168.1.200:
    Packets: Sent = 4, Received = 4, Lost = 0 (0% loss),
Approximate round trip times in milli-seconds:
    Minimum = 0ms, Maximum = 0ms, Average = 0ms
```

b. **Minimize the command prompt window.**

ACTIVITY 7-2

Using APIPA

There is a simulated version of this activity available on the CD-ROM that shipped with this course. You can run this simulation on any Windows computer to review the activity after class, or as an alternative to performing the activity as a group in class. The activity simulation can be launched either directly from the CD-ROM by clicking the Interactives link and navigating to the appropriate one, or from the installed data file location by opening the C:\Data\Simulations\Lesson#\Activity# folder and double-clicking the executable (.exe) file.

Scenario:

You have a small business with a few computers that need to communicate with one another. You do not need Internet access, nor have you any leased IP addresses. You need to configure the computers to communicate with one another using the TCP/IP protocol.

What You Do	How You Do It
Instructor Only Step:	
1. **Deactivate the classroom DHCP scope.**	a. **Choose Start→Administrative Tools→ DHCP.** b. **Expand your DHCP server object.** c. **Select and then right-click the scope object.** d. **Choose Deactivate.** e. **Click Yes.** f. **Minimize DHCP.**
2. **Configure your computer to use APIPA.**	a. **Choose Start→Control Panel→Network Connections.** b. **Right-click Local Area Connection.** c. **Choose Properties.** d. In the This Connection Uses The Following Items box, **select Internet Protocol (TCP/ IP).** e. **Click Properties.**

f. **Select Obtain An IP Address Automatically.**

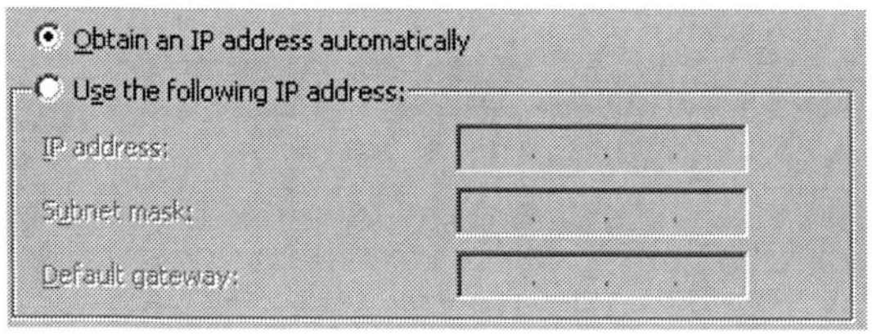

g. **Select Obtain DNS Server Address Automatically.**

h. **Click OK.**

i. **Click Close.**

---

3. **Verify your IP information.**

a. **Maximize the command prompt window.**

b. At the command prompt, **enter *ipconfig /all***

APIPA configuration can take a moment because the system first attempts to contact a DHCP server before self-assigning the APIPA address. If ipconfig /all shows your IP address and subnet mask as null (all zeros), wait a minute and run ipconfig /all again or type in ipconfig /renew.

c. **Verify that the Local Area Connection shows the IP address and subnet mask from the 169.254.0.0 APIPA network.**

```
Ethernet adapter Local Area Connection:

    Connection-specific DNS Suffix  . :
    Description . . . . . . . . . . . : Intel(R) PRO/100 VM Network Connection
    Physical Address. . . . . . . . . : 00-0B-CD-3D-DE-83
    DHCP Enabled. . . . . . . . . . . : Yes
    Autoconfiguration Enabled . . . . : Yes
    Autoconfiguration IP Address. . . : 169.254.211.27
    Subnet Mask . . . . . . . . . . . : 255.255.0.0
    Default Gateway . . . . . . . . . :
```

---

4. **Test your ability to communicate over TCP/IP with the DNS server (192.168.1.200).**

a. At the command prompt, **enter *ping 192.168.1.200***

b. Because you are using a nonroutable APIPA address, you cannot communicate with the DNS server. **Verify that the destination is unreachable.**

```
C:\Documents and Settings\user01>ping 192.168.1.200

Pinging 192.168.1.200 with 32 bytes of data:

Destination host unreachable.
Destination host unreachable.
Destination host unreachable.
Destination host unreachable.

Ping statistics for 192.168.1.200:
    Packets: Sent = 4, Received = 0, Lost = 4 (100% loss),
```

5. **Test your ability to communicate with another computer on the APIPA network.**

a. At the command prompt, **enter *ping 169.254.#.#*,** where ## is the address of another computer in the classroom.

```
C:\Documents and Settings\user01>ping 169.254.124.201

Pinging 169.254.124.201 with 32 bytes of data:

Reply from 169.254.124.201: bytes=32 time<1ms TTL=128
Reply from 169.254.124.201: bytes=32 time<1ms TTL=128
Reply from 169.254.124.201: bytes=32 time<1ms TTL=128
Reply from 169.254.124.201: bytes=32 time<1ms TTL=128

Ping statistics for 169.254.124.201:
    Packets: Sent = 4, Received = 4, Lost = 0 (0% loss),
Approximate round trip times in milli-seconds:
    Minimum = 0ms, Maximum = 0ms, Average = 0ms
```

ACTIVITY 7-3

Assigning IP Addresses with DHCP

There is a simulated version of this activity available on the CD-ROM that shipped with this course. You can run this simulation on any Windows computer to review the activity after class, or as an alternative to performing the activity as a group in class. The activity simulation can be launched either directly from the CD-ROM by clicking the Interactives link and navigating to the appropriate one, or from the installed data file location by opening the C:\Data\Simulations\Lesson#\Activity# folder and double-clicking the executable (.exe) file.

Scenario:

You work for a large company that has implemented DHCP to control the assignment of TCP/IP information to its network nodes. There are some computers that are configured for automatic IP address assignment, but are receiving their addresses from APIPA.

What You Do	How You Do It
Instructor Only Step:	
1. Activate the classroom DHCP scope.	a. Maximize DHCP.
	b. Right-click Scope.
	c. Choose Activate.
	d. Close DHCP.
2. Force your computer to lease an IP address from the DHCP server.	a. In the command prompt window, **enter** ***ipconfig /renew***
3. Test your ability to communicate over TCP/IP with the DNS server (192.168.1.200).	a. At the command prompt, **enter** ***ping 192.168.1.200***
	b. Because you are using DHCP-issued IP information, you can communicate with the DNS server. **Enter** ***exit*** to close the command prompt window.

TOPIC B

Host Name Resolution

Each network node that has an IP address assigned also has a descriptive name that can be used to identify it on the network. These descriptive names are easier for users to remember and use than 32-bit IP addresses. In this topic, you will learn about host name resolution for TCP/IP networks.

Without host name resolution services, you have to connect to other computers and websites using IP addresses. When you have host name resolution services configured on your network, you can connect to other computers and websites using their names. For the user, it is much easier to remember a descriptive name like www.ourglobalcompany.com, than its assigned 32-bit IP address of 67.137.6.152.

Host Names

Definition:

A *host name* is the unique name given to a network node on a TCP/IP network. The host name combined with the host's domain name forms the node's *fully qualified domain name (FQDN)*. The FQDN is mapped to the network node's IP address by a name resolution service so that users can use names instead of IP addresses to communicate with other network nodes and the Internet.

FQDNs are written using standard dot-delimited notation. That is, a dot separates each section of the name. The maximum length of an FQDN is 255 characters; each dot-delimited section can be up to 63 characters long.

A network node may have more than one host name assigned to it. Its primary name is its host name; the other names are called canonical names (CNAMEs), also known as aliases.

Example:

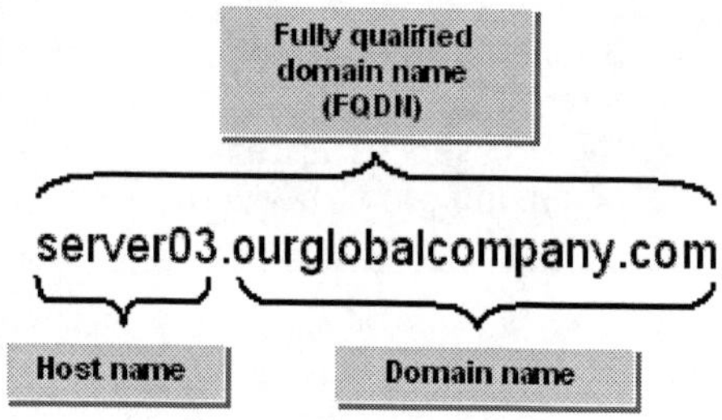

Figure 7-6: *A host name.*

ACTIVITY 7-4

Identifying the Local Host Name

There is a simulated version of this activity available on the CD-ROM that shipped with this course. You can run this simulation on any Windows computer to review the activity after class, or as an alternative to performing the activity as a group in class. The activity simulation can be launched either directly from the CD-ROM by clicking the Interactives link and navigating to the appropriate one, or from the installed data file location by opening the C:\Data\Simulations\Lesson#\Activity# folder and double-clicking the executable (.exe) file.

Scenario:

In this activity, you will use different tools to identify your computer's host name.

What You Do	How You Do It

1. **Identify the host name and FQDN by using System Properties.**

   a. **Click Start.**

   b. **Right-click My Computer and choose Properties.**

   c. **Select the Computer Name tab.**

   d. **Identify the computer's FQDN.**

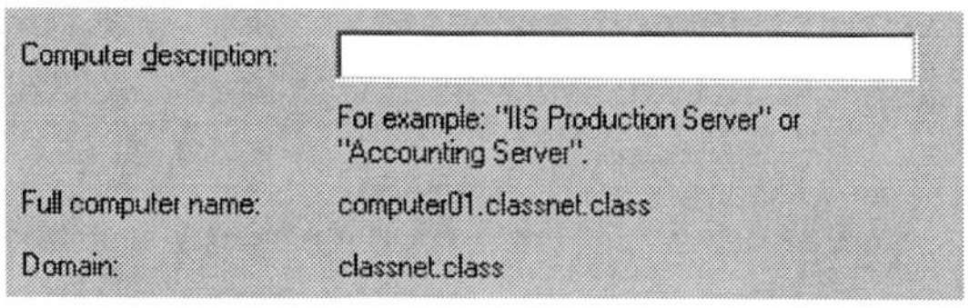

   e. **Identify the host name portion of the FQDN.**

   f. **Click Cancel.**

2. **Identify the host name by using the hostname command.**

   a. **Open a command prompt window.**

   b. **Enter *hostname***

```
C:\Documents and Settings\User01>hostname
computer01
```

3. **Identify the FQDN by using the ipconfig command.**

   a. **Enter *ipconfig /all***

   b. **Identify the host name.**

```
Host Name . . . . . . . . . . . . : computer01
Primary Dns Suffix  . . . . . . . : classnet.class
Node Type . . . . . . . . . . . . : Unknown
IP Routing Enabled. . . . . . . . : No
WINS Proxy Enabled. . . . . . . . : No
DNS Suffix Search List. . . . . . : classnet.class
```

   c. **Identify the DNS suffix.**

   d. **Close the command prompt window.**

The Domain Name System (DNS)

The *Domain Name System (DNS)* is a TCP/IP name resolution service that translates FQDNs into IP addresses. It consists of a system of hierachical databases that are stored on separate DNS servers on all the networks that connect to the Internet. All these servers work together to resolve FQDNs. On internal networks, a local DNS service can resolve host names without using external DNS servers.

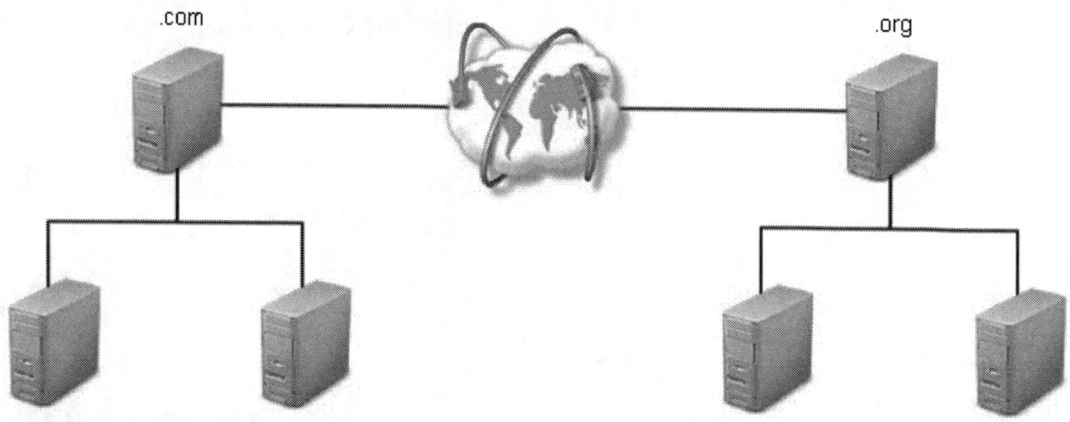

Figure 7-7: *DNS.*

DNS Components

The DNS database is divided logically into a hierarchical grouping of domains. It is divided physically into files called zones. The zone files contain the actual IP-to-host name mappings for one or more domains. The zone file is stored on the DNS server that is responsible for resolving host names for the domains contained in the zone. For example, a zone might be responsible for mapping host names to IP addresses within the ourglobalcompany domain within the .com namespace. Each network node in that domain will have a host record within the domain's zone file. The record includes the node's host name, FQDN, and assigned IP address.

For example, a host named 2003srv in the ourglobalcompany.com domain might have an IP address of 67.137.6.152. That host would have a host record that maps the 2003srv.ourglobalcompany.com name to the IP address of 67.137.6.152. That host record will appear in the ourglobalcompany.com zone file on the DNS server that is responsible for the ourglobalcompany.com domain.

Static vs. Dynamic Records

Records can be entered into a DNS database either statically or dynamically. A static record is entered manually by an administrator and does not change unless manually updated by the administrator. A dynamic record is added based on a request from the network node itself and can change dynamically. For example, if a client is using DHCP to get its IP address, each time it leases a new address, it can request that its DNS host record be updated.

Common DNS Record Types

Each network node might have three records in DNS:

- An A record, which is the host record and maps the host name to its IP address.
- A PTR, or pointer, record, which maps the IP address to host name for reverse lookup functionality.

- A CNAME record, which maps multiple canonical names (aliases) to one A record.

The DNS Hierarchy

DNS names are built in a hierarchical structure. The top of the structure contains the root name, which is represented by a period. Below that is the top-level domain name, then the first-level domain name, and so on, until the fully qualified domain name for an individual host is complete.

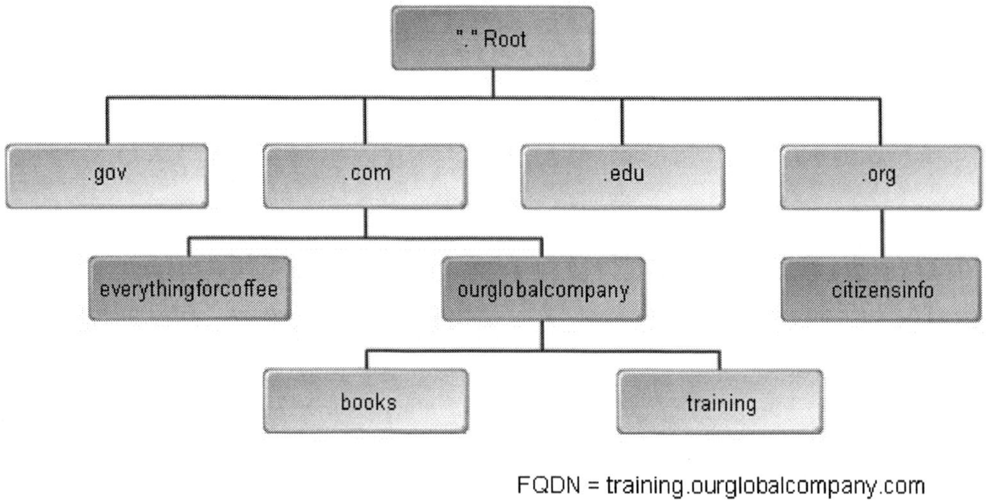

Figure 7-8: *The DNS hierarchy.*

The DNS Name Resolution Process

In the DNS process, DNS servers work together as needed to resolve names on behalf of DNS clients.

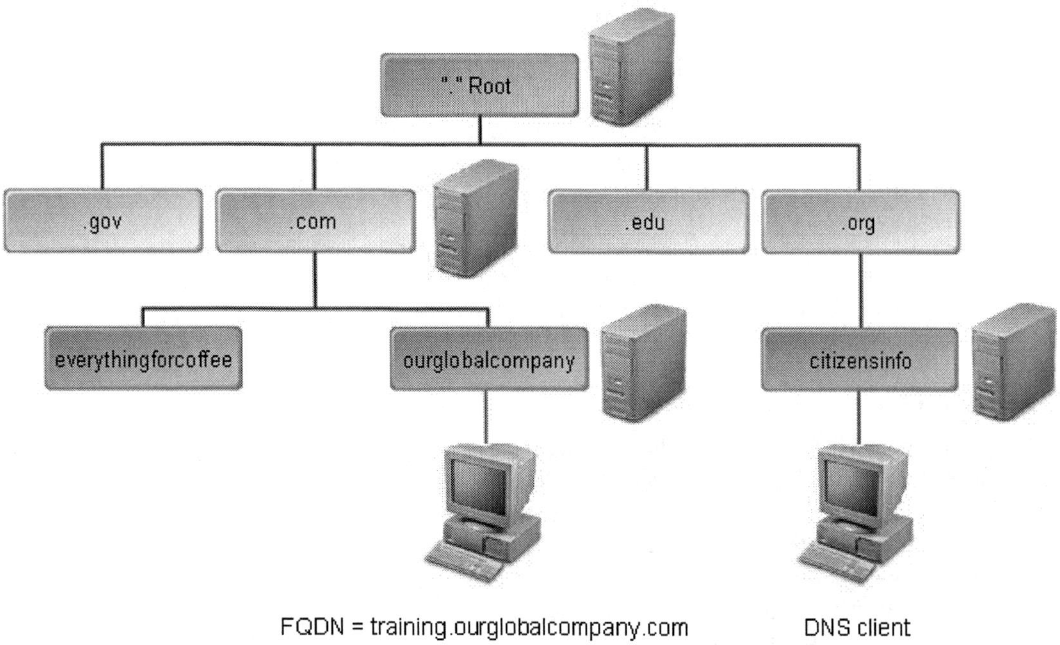

Figure 7-9: *The DNS name resolution process.*

Process Step	Description
Client request	When a client needs to resolve a DNS name, it sends a name resolution request to the IP address of its preferred DNS server.
Preferred DNS server	If the preferred DNS server has the requested name in its DNS cache entries or its local DNS database, it returns the IP address to the client.
Root server	If it doesn't have the address, it contacts the root server, asking it which DNS server has the entries for the appropriate top-level domain.
Top-level domain address	The root server returns the IP address for the DNS server responsible for the appropriate top-level domain.
Top-level domain server	The preferred DNS server then contacts the top-level domain's DNS server to resolve the name. If the top-level domain can resolve the name, it sends the desired IP address back to the preferred DNS server.
Other domain servers	If the top-level domain cannot resolve the name because of additional levels in the FQDN, it sends the IP address of the second-level DNS server.
Host name resolution	This communication between DNS servers continues until it reaches the level in the DNS hierarchy where a DNS server can resolve the host name.
Host address	The preferred DNS server provides the client with the IP address of the target host.

Recursive and Iterative Name Queries

There are two kinds of DNS queries: recursive and iterative. A recursive query is when the client requests that its preferred DNS server find data on other DNS servers. A recursive request starts with the client requesting a name to be resolved to an IP address to its preferred DNS server. If the preferred server can't resolve the name, it sends a request, on behalf of the client, to another DNS server.

An iterative query occurs when the client requests only the information a server already has in its cache for a particular domain name. If the receiving server can't resolve the request, it notifies the client, but does not forward the request on to any other server.

Recursive queries usually take place between end-user client systems and their preferred DNS servers. Once the recursive query is in process, queries between DNS servers are usually iterative.

Primary and Secondary DNS Servers

When configuring a client's DNS settings, it is common to specify both a primary and a secondary DNS server to provide a more reliable name resolution process. When two DNS servers are listed, the client queries the primary server first. If the primary server doesn't answer, the client queries the secondary server. If the primary server returns a Name Not Found message, the query is over and the client doesn't query the secondary server. This is because both DNS servers can do recursive and iterative queries, and both the primary and secondary servers should be able to contact the same resources. If one can't find it, the other won't be able to either.

The HOSTS File

A *HOSTS file* is a plain text file configured on a client machine containing a list of IP addresses and their associated host names, separated by at least one space. Comments may be included after the host name if preceded by the # symbol and separated from the host name by at least one space.

The HOSTS file provides an alternative method of host name resolution. An external client can use a HOSTS file to resolve names on your internal network without needing access to your internal DNS server. You have to manually configure each host name entry in a HOSTS file and they require a lot of maintenance, so it is recommended that you use it only when other methods of host name resolution aren't supported, or temporarily for troubleshooting purposes.

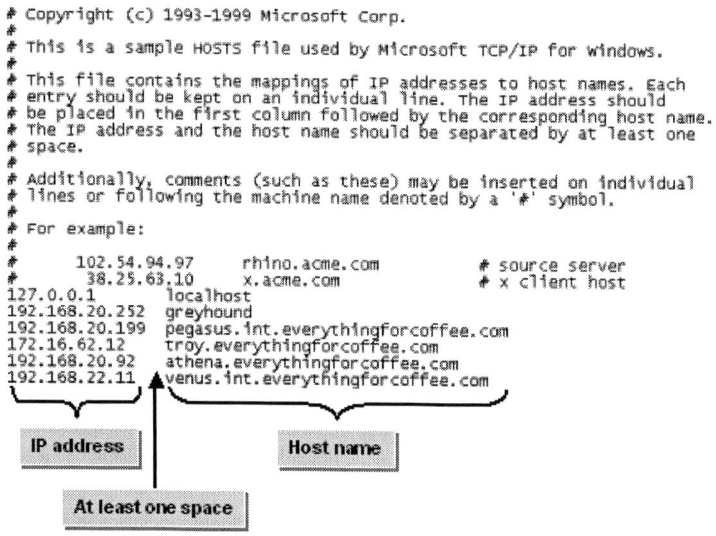

```
# Copyright (c) 1993-1999 Microsoft Corp.
#
# This is a sample HOSTS file used by Microsoft TCP/IP for Windows.
#
# This file contains the mappings of IP addresses to host names. Each
# entry should be kept on an individual line. The IP address should
# be placed in the first column followed by the corresponding host name.
# The IP address and the host name should be separated by at least one
# space.
#
# Additionally, comments (such as these) may be inserted on individual
# lines or following the machine name denoted by a '#' symbol.
#
# For example:
#
#      102.54.94.97     rhino.acme.com          # source server
#       38.25.63.10     x.acme.com              # x client host
127.0.0.1        localhost
192.168.20.252   greyhound
192.168.20.199   pegasus.int.everythingforcoffee.com
172.16.62.12     troy.everythingforcoffee.com
192.168.20.92    athena.everythingforcoffee.com
192.168.22.11    venus.int.everythingforcoffee.com
```


Figure 7-10: *A HOSTS file statically maps host names to IP addresses.*

ACTIVITY 7-5

Viewing a Sample HOSTS File

There is a simulated version of this activity available on the CD-ROM that shipped with this course. You can run this simulation on any Windows computer to review the activity after class, or as an alternative to performing the activity as a group in class. The activity simulation can be launched either directly from the CD-ROM by clicking the Interactives link and navigating to the appropriate one, or from the installed data file location by opening the C:\Data\Simulations\Lesson#\Activity# folder and double-clicking the executable (.exe) file.

Setup:

The sample HOSTS file on your system is located in the C:\Windows\system32\drivers\etc folder.

Scenario:

In this activity, you will open the sample HOSTS file provided with Windows Server 2003.

What You Do	How You Do It
1. **Open the sample HOSTS file.**	a. **Choose Start→Run.** b. **Type *C:\Windows\system32\drivers\etc* and click OK.** c. **Double-click the HOSTS file.** d. In the Open With dialog box, **select Notepad and click OK.**
2. **What is the only active entry in the HOSTS file?**	
3. **What are the three components of this entry?**	
4. **Why are the other entries not active?**	
5. When you have finished examining the file, **close the open windows.**	a. **Close Notepad.** b. **Close the C:\Windows\system32\drivers\etc window.**

ACTIVITY 7-6

Discussing DNS Names and Name Resolution

Scenario:

In this activity, you will identify components of DNS and the name resolution process.

1. **Which are fully qualified domain names?**
    a) www.everythingforcoffee.com
    b) \\fs001\data\new\accounts.mdb
    c) data1.electrocon.dom.\users\home
    d) citizensinfo.org

2. **What is the name of the top of the DNS hierarchy?**
    a) Host record
    b) Zone
    c) Root
    d) First-level domain

3. **True or False? If a preferred DNS server can't resolve a client's name request, it contacts the DNS server immediately above it in the hierarchy.**
    __ True
    __ False

4. **True or False? An advantage of using a HOSTS file for DNS name resolution services is that updates to the file are automatic.**
    __ True
    __ False

TOPIC C

NetBIOS Name Resolution

Host name resolution is one type of name resolution service. NetBIOS name resolution is another. In this topic, you will learn how NetBIOS names are resolved on a network.

In addition to host names, Microsoft networks can use NetBIOS names to communicate. These names also need to be resolved to protocol addresses for communication to occur successfully. When you understand the NetBIOS name resolution process and components, you will be able to provide support for NetBIOS communication on your network.

NetBIOS Names

Definition:

NetBIOS names are a 16-byte common name format developed by IBM and Microsoft to identify network devices. Fifteen bytes represent characters in the name; the hidden 16th byte is a code to denote the type of service provided by the device. NetBIOS names must be unique on the network.

Unlike DNS names, NetBIOS names don't give any hints as to the device's location.

Example:

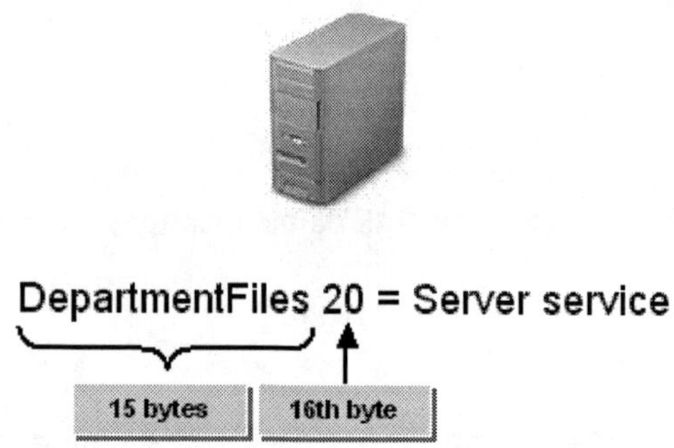

Figure 7-11: *NetBIOS names provide a simple way for users to refer to a network device.*

NetBIOS Service Codes

The 16th byte of each NetBIOS name represents a specific service that can be running on the node. This table provides all the NetBIOS service codes.

Suffix in Hex	Network Service
00	Workstation service
03	Messenger service
06	Remote access server service
20	Server service
21	Remote access client service

Suffix in Hex	Network Service
1B	Domain master browser
1C	Domain controller
1D	Master browser
1E	Browser election service

NetBIOS Broadcast Name Resolution

For data delivery, NetBIOS names must be resolved to MAC addresses. The original NetBIOS name resolution method was to broadcast a name and wait for a response from the device with the name. The resolved MAC address is then cached on the local machine for later use. As networks grow, the amount of traffic generated by NetBIOS broadcasts can slow down the network.

One disadvantage of broadcast name resolution is the increased network traffic. Another is that because most routers do not pass broadcast packets, clients cannot use broadcast name resolution to resolve names on remote subnets.

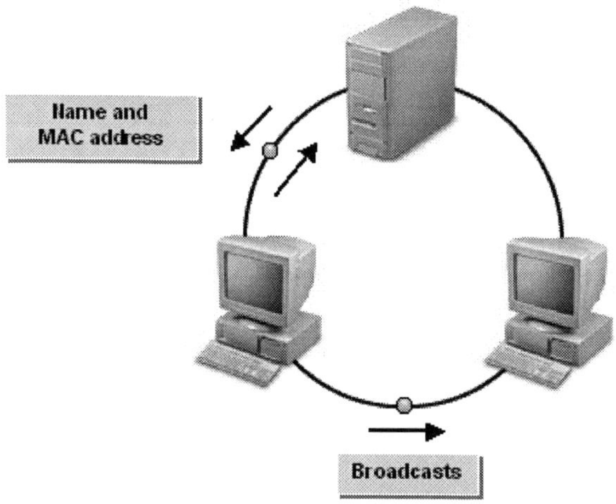

Figure 7-12: *NetBIOS name resolution by broadcast.*

Windows Internet Name Service (WINS)

The *Windows Internet Name Service (WINS)* is Microsoft's NetBIOS name server, which was developed to reduce the number of NetBIOS name resolution broadcasts. The WINS server uses a name resolution table to map NetBIOS names to protocol addresses. WINS clients are configured with the IP address of the WINS server, so that they automatically register their names in the WINS database when they come online. They can also resolve names by targeted requests to the WINS server.

Other manufacturers have NetBIOS name servers available as well. These are generically referred to as NetBIOS Name Servers (NBNS).

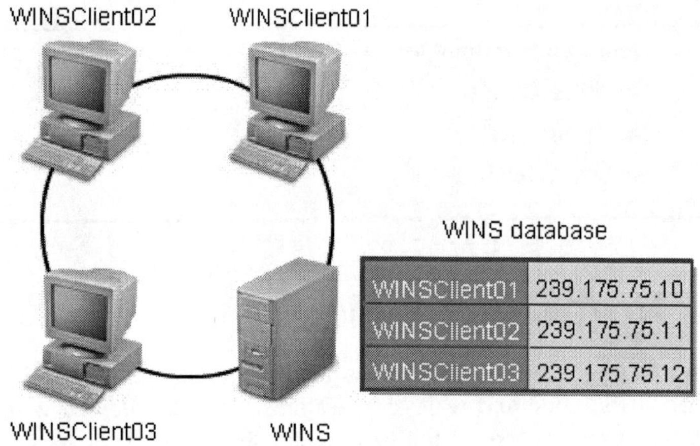

Figure 7-13: *WINS.*

The WINS Name Registration Process

When a WINS client starts up, it contacts the WINS server to register its name for a fixed lease period. It keeps the name until it shuts down properly and releases the name, or until its lease expires. If another client starts up and attempts to register the same name while the first computer's lease is still valid, the second computer's name registration fails.

All Microsoft clients using Windows 9x or later support WINS name resolution.

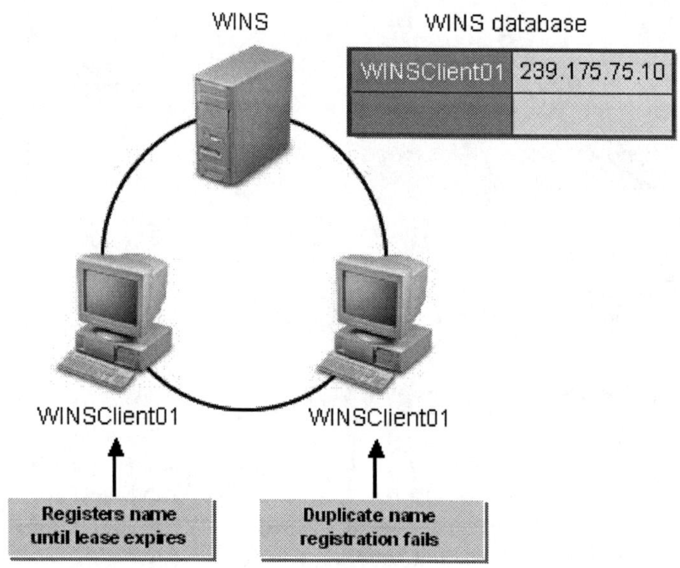

Figure 7-14: *The WINS name registration process.*

A WINS client can renew its name registration before its lease expires. If a WINS client is shut down improperly, the WINS server automatically removes its name registration after the period expires.

The LMHOSTS File

An *LMHOSTS* file is a text file that contains NetBIOS name–to–IP address mappings, each on a separate line. The IP address is listed first, then a space, and then the associated NetBIOS name. A comment may be included on any line if it is preceded by the # symbol and separated from the NetBIOS name by at least one space or tab. If you do not have a WINS server, the LMHOSTS file is a manual alternative to broadcast-based name resolution.

LMHOSTS stands for LAN Manager HOSTS. LAN Manager was Microsoft's first network software product. It used NetBIOS naming. Microsoft developed the LMHOSTS format to resolve NetBIOS names in the same way that the HOSTS file could be used to resolve host names.

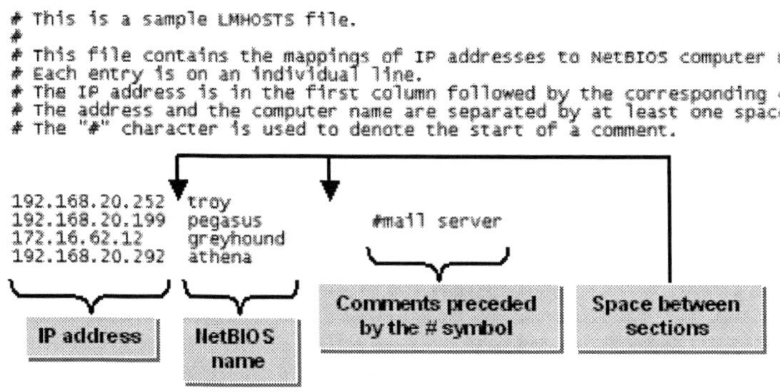

Figure 7-15: *A sample LMHOSTS file.*

Local and Centralized LMHOSTS Files

Like the HOSTS file, LMHOSTS files can be manually created and copied individually to each NetBIOS client. This requires a lot of maintenance, because every time a mapping changes, each file must be updated.

Unlike HOSTS files, however, the LMHOSTS file can be centralized. You can store the master copy of the file, containing the complete list of name mappings, on a server and configure the individual LMHOSTS files on clients with special tags that cause the clients to find and load the mappings from the network version of LMHOSTS. In this case, when mappings change, they only have to be updated in the central copy of the file.

ACTIVITY 7-7

Viewing a Sample LMHOSTS File

There is a simulated version of this activity available on the CD-ROM that shipped with this course. You can run this simulation on any Windows computer to review the activity after class, or as an alternative to performing the activity as a group in class. The activity simulation can be launched either directly from the CD-ROM by clicking the Interactives link and navigating to the appropriate one, or from the installed data file location by opening the C:\Data\Simulations\Lesson#\Activity# folder and double-clicking the executable (.exe) file.

Setup:

The LMHOSTS.SAM file on your system is located in the C:\Windows\system32\drivers\etc folder.

Scenario:

In this activity, you will open the LMHOSTS.SAM file provided with Windows Server 2003.

What You Do	How You Do It
1. **Open the LMHOSTS.SAM file.**	a. **Choose Start→Run.** b. **Type** ***C:\Windows\system32\drivers\etc*** **and click OK.** c. **Double-click the LMHOSTS.SAM file.** d. **Click Select The Program From A List and click OK.** e. In the Open With dialog box, **select Notepad and click OK.**
2. **Are there any active entries in the sample file?**	
3. **Identify the components of one of the sample entries.**	
4. When you have finished examining the file, **close the open windows.**	a. **Close Notepad.** b. **Close the C:\Windows\system32\drivers\etc window.**

The NetBIOS Name Resolution Process

When a WINS client needs an address for a name, it first checks its NetBIOS cache to see if it already has the address. If not, it sends a query request to the WINS server. If the WINS server has an entry, it returns it. If it doesn't, it responds negatively. Then the WINS client broadcasts for the name. If it doesn't receive a response to its broadcast, it checks for an entry in its LMHOSTS file.

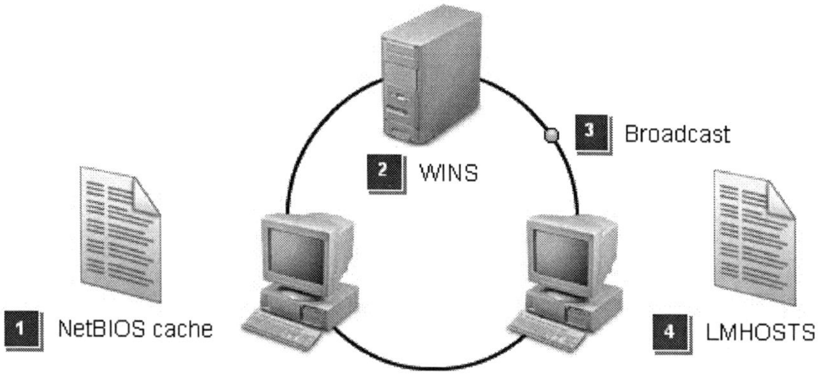

Figure 7-16: *Resolving a NetBIOS name.*

Non-WINS Clients

WINS also supports adding non-WINS-enabled client's names, such as names of UNIX servers, through manual entries. A static database entry is added on the WINS server, enabling WINS clients to resolve the names of non-WINS clients that can't register automatically with the WINS server.

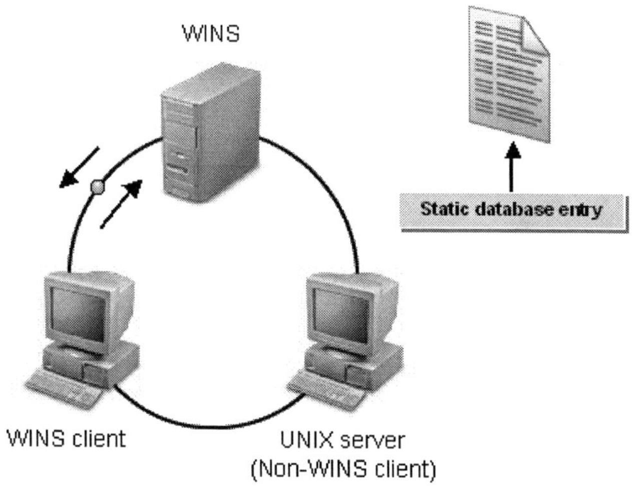

Figure 7-17: *Non-WINS clients.*

WINS Proxy Agents

A WINS proxy agent enables non-WINS clients to use WINS for name resolution. The proxy agent captures the client's NetBIOS broadcast request for name resolution, and forwards it to the WINS server. The WINS server responds to the proxy agent and the proxy agent sends the response to the client. WINS proxy agents have to be on the same subnet as the non-WINS clients. They must be configured with the IP address of the WINS server, so that they can send unicast name requests across routers to the server.

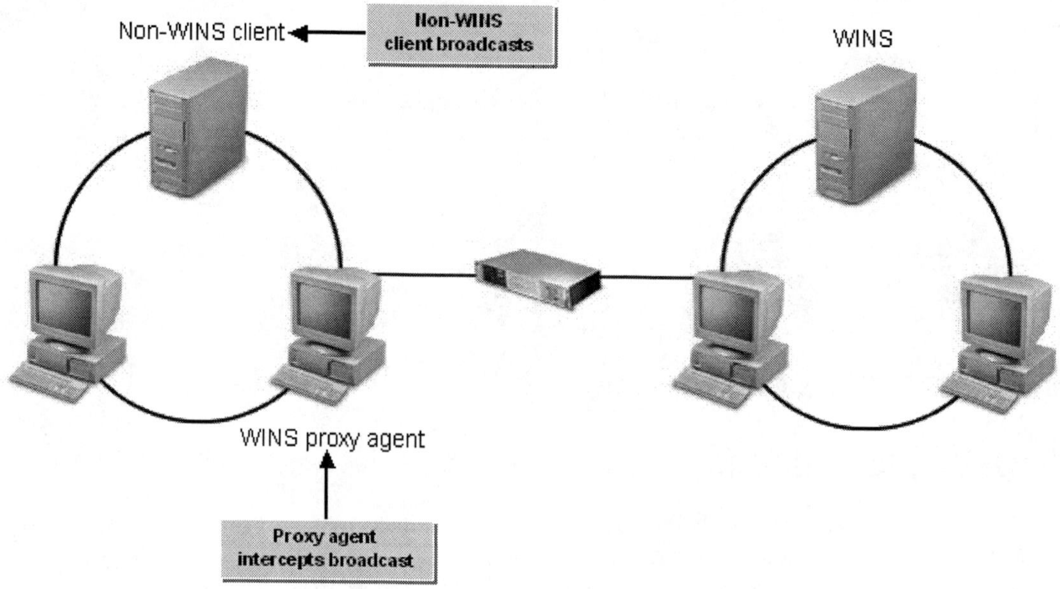

Figure 7-18: *Non-WINS clients can use a WINS proxy agent to resolve NetBIOS names.*

ACTIVITY 7-8

Identifying NetBIOS Name Resolution Methods

Scenario:

In this activity, you will identify NetBIOS name resolution methods.

1. **How many standard characters are allowed in a NetBIOS name?**
   a) Twelve. An additional byte is reserved for the service identifier.
   b) Fifteen. An additional byte is reserved for the service identifier.
   c) Sixteen. An additional byte is reserved for the service identifier.
   d) Eight. An additional byte is reserved for the service identifier.

2. **True or False? Systems that cannot automatically register NetBIOS names with a WINS server, such as those running UNIX, can use a WINS proxy agent.**
   __ True
   __ False

3. **Put the steps of the NetBIOS name resolution process in the correct order.**

   Check LMHOSTS file

   Broadcast for name

   Check NetBIOS name cache

   Query WINS server

TOPIC D

TCP/IP Utilities

The TCP/IP protocol suite provides a host of utilities that can be used to troubleshoot and configure connectivity and name resolution. In this topic, you will learn how the utilities included with the TCP/IP protocol suite can be used to help you ensure smooth connectivity in your TCP/IP network.

TCP/IP utilities allow you to gather information about how your systems are using and communicating over TCP/IP. These utilities can provide critical information when communication is not working properly and you need to figure out the cause.

The Tracert Utility

The *Tracert* (or Traceroute) utility determines the route data takes to get to a particular destination. The ICMP protocol sends out Time Exceeded messages to each router to trace the route. Each time a packet is sent, the time-to-live (TTL) value is reduced before the packet is forwarded. This allows TTL to count how many hops it is to the destination.

If you run the tracert command repeatedly for the same destination, you will normally see different results. This is because TCP/IP is auto-correcting and takes the fastest route possible across the global network of Internet routers.

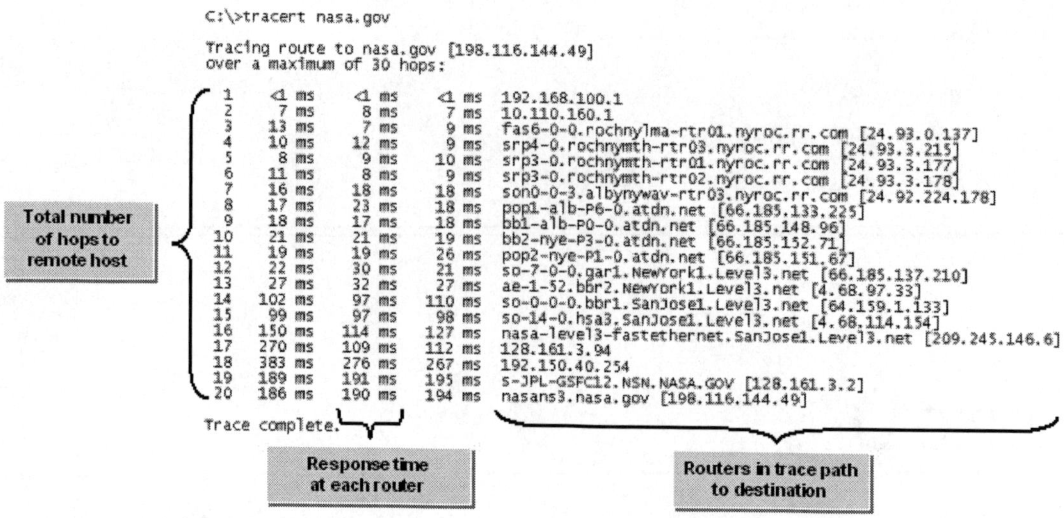

Figure 7-19: *Results of a tracert to nasa.gov on a Windows system.*

Troubleshooting with Tracert

Using the tracert command as a troubleshooting tool, you can see how far the packets are getting and how long (in milliseconds) each router took to respond to the ICMP packet. A long response time indicates a routing problem at that point in the route.

Network Firewalls

If a network firewall is configured to not allow a tracert or ping through, you might not be able to trace the route all the way to the end; it might appear to end at the firewall. If you get the message Destination Unreachable, a router isn't able to figure out how to get to the next destination. Even though it doesn't tell you what is wrong, it alerts you to the router where the problem is occurring.

Tracert Options

There are various options that you can use with the tracert command.

Option	Description
`-d`	If you're having trouble resolving host names when using `tracert`, use the `-d` option to prevent Tracert from trying to resolve host names. It also speeds up response time since it isn't spending time resolving host names.
`-h max_hops`	The default number of hops Tracert will attempt to reach is 30. Using the `-h` option, you can specify more or fewer hops for it to check.
`-j` *[router]* *[local_computer]*	With loose source routing, you specify the destination router and your local computer using the `-j` option. It lets you trace the round trip rather than the default, which is to get to the destination.

Option	Description
`-w timeout`	If many of your responses on the `tracert` are timing out, you can increase the number of milliseconds to wait before continuing. If, after increasing the value, destinations are then reachable, you probably have a bandwidth issue to resolve.

The Netstat Utility

The *Netstat* utility shows the status of each active network connection. Netstat will display statistics for both TCP and UDP, including protocol, local address, foreign address, and the TCP connection state. Because UDP is connectionless, no connection information will be shown for UDP packets.

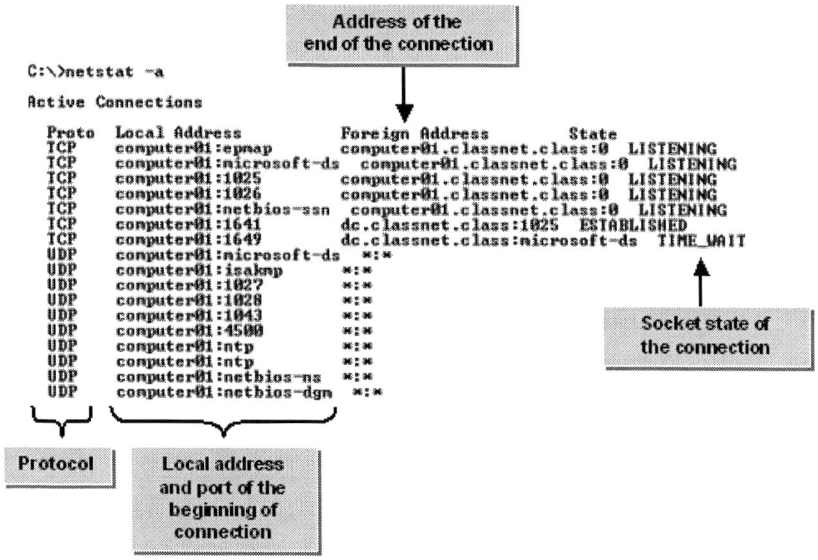

Figure 7-20: *Results of the netstat command on a Windows system.*

Netstat Versions

On UNIX systems, Netstat is a full-featured program with options arranged into groups—each of which shows a particular type of information about the operation of the TCP/IP protocol suite. On Windows systems, Netstat is more limited in function but still shows important information about the active connections.

Netstat Options

There are several options available to use with the netstat command.

Option	Displays
`-a`	All connections and listening ports.
`-e`	Ethernet statistics.
`-n`	Addresses and port numbers in numerical form.
`-o`	The process ID associated with each connection.

Option	Displays
`-p [proto]`	Connections for the protocol specified in place of `[proto]` in the command syntax. The value of the `[proto]` variable may be TCP, UDP, TCPv6, or UDPv6.
`-r`	The routing table.
`-s`	Statistics grouped by protocol—IP, IPv6, ICMP, ICMPv6, TCP, TCPv6, UDP, and UDPv6.
`[interval]`	Refreshes and redisplays the statistics specified in the command at the stated number of seconds specified in place of `[interval]` in the code syntax. Ctrl+C stops the command from refreshing.

Socket States

Netstat will display one of several states for each socket.

Socket State	Description
SYN_SEND	Connection is active and open.
SYN_RECEIVED	Server just received synchronize flag set (SYN) from the client.
ESTABLISHED	Client received server's SYN and session is established.
LISTEN	Server is ready to accept connection.
FIN_WAIT_1	Connection is active, but closed.
TIMED_WAIT	Client enters this state after FIN_WAIT_1.
CLOSE_WAIT	Passive close. Server just received FIN_WAIT_1 from a client.
FIN_WAIT_2	Client just received acknowledgement of its FIN_WAIT_1 from the server.
LAST_ACK	Server is in this state when it sends its own FIN.
CLOSED	Server received acknowledgement (ACK) from client and connection is closed.

A SYN packet contains information regarding the return path for the data.

The Nbtstat Utility

Nbtstat is a Windows utility that is used to view and manage NetBIOS over TCP/IP (NetBT) status information. It can display NetBIOS name tables for both the local computer and remote computers, and also the NetBIOS name cache. With Nbtstat, you can refresh the NetBIOS name cache as well as the names registered with the WINS server.

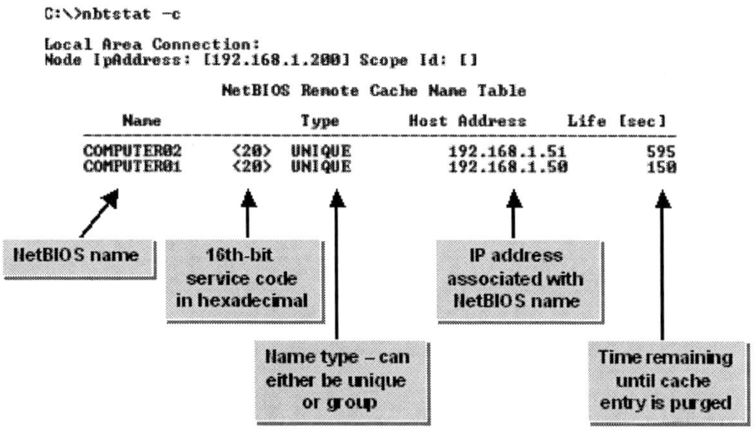

Figure 7-21: *The NetBIOS name cache on a workstation.*

Nbtstat Options

There are several case-sensitive options you can use with the nbtstat command.

Option	Description
`-a [`*`RemoteName`*`]`	Displays the NetBIOS name table of the remote computer specified by name.
`-A [`*`IPAddress`*`]`	Displays the NetBIOS name table of the remote computer specified by IP address.
`-c`	Displays the NetBIOS name cache of the local computer.
`-n`	Lists the local NetBIOS name table along with service code, type, and status.
`-r`	Lists NetBIOS names resolved by broadcast and via WINS.
`-R`	Purges the cache and reloads static entries from the LMHOSTS file.
`-S`	Lists NetBIOS connections and their state with destination IP addresses.
`-s`	Lists NetBIOS connections and their state, converting destination IP addresses to computer NetBIOS names.
`-RR`	Sends name release packets to the WINS server and then starts refresh.

The Nslookup Utility

The *Nslookup* utility is used to test and troubleshoot domain name servers. Nslookup has two modes. Interactive mode enables you to query name servers for information about hosts and domains, or to print a list of hosts in a domain. Non-interactive mode prints only the name and requested details for one host or domain. Non-interactive mode is useful for a single query.

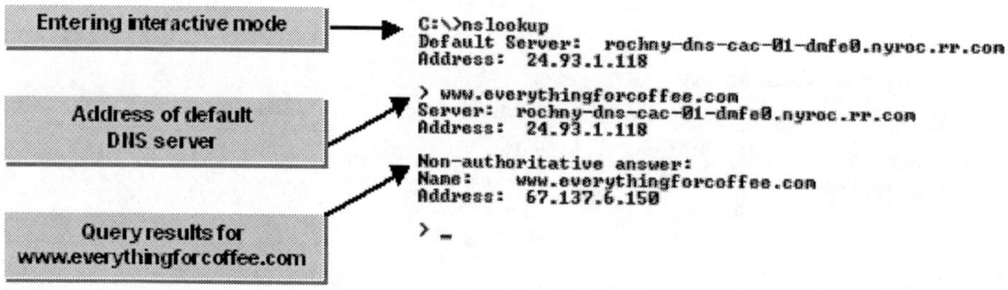

Figure 7-22: *Results of an nslookup query for www.everythingforcoffee.com on a Windows system.*

Nslookup Support

Nslookup is available on UNIX, and on all Windows systems except for Windows 9x and Windows Me.

Nslookup Syntax

The syntax for the nslookup command is `nslookup [-option ...] [computer-to-find | - [server]]`.

To enter the interactive mode of Nslookup, type `nslookup` without any arguments at a command prompt, or use only a hyphen as the first argument and specify a domain name server in the second. The default DNS name server will be used if you don't enter anything for the second argument.

To use non-interactive mode, in the first argument, enter the name or IP address of the computer you want to look up. In the second argument, enter the name or IP address of a domain name server. The default DNS name server will be used if you don't enter anything for the second argument.

The Dig Utility

The Domain Information Groper (Dig) is a UNIX utility used to gather information from DNS servers. Dig sends domain name query packets to name servers to display the DNS records for the given host or domain.

The Arp Utility

The *arp* command supports the ARP service of the TCP/IP protocol suite. It enables an administrator to view the ARP cache and add or delete cache entries. Any added entry becomes permanent until it is deleted or the machine is shut down.

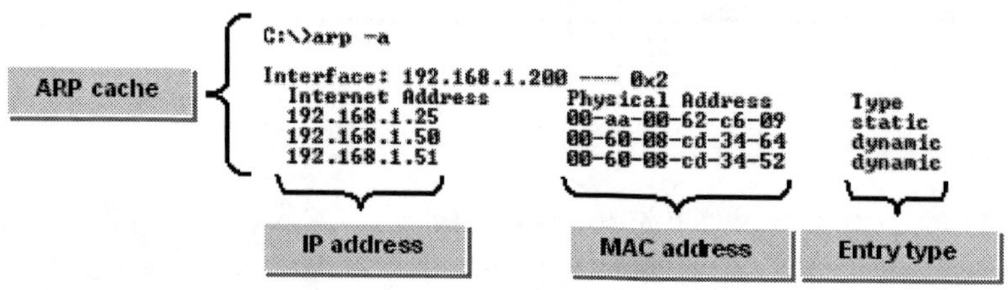

Figure 7-23: *The arp command.*

Arp Options

There are several options available for use with the arp command.

Option	Description
inet_addr	Used with other options to specify an Internet address.
eth_addr	Used with other options to specify a physical address.
if_addr	Used with other options to specify the Internet address of the interface whose ARP table should be modified.
-a	Displays the current ARP entries in the cache. Can add inet_addr to specify a particular IP address.
-g	Displays the same information as the -a option.
-N if_addr	Displays the ARP entries for the network interface specified by if_addr.
-d	Deletes a single host entry if followed by if_addr. Deletes all host entries if followed by *.
-s inet_addr eth_addr	Add a host. The Internet address is set by adding an inet_addr value and the physical address is set by adding an eth_addr value.

ACTIVITY 7-9

Using TCP/IP Diagnostic Utilities

There is a simulated version of this activity available on the CD-ROM that shipped with this course. You can run this simulation on any Windows computer to review the activity after class, or as an alternative to performing the activity as a group in class. The activity simulation can be launched either directly from the CD-ROM by clicking the Interactives link and navigating to the appropriate one, or from the installed data file location by opening the C:\Data\Simulations\Lesson#\Activity# folder and double-clicking the executable (.exe) file.

Scenario:

In this activity, you will use several TCP/IP diagnostic utilities.

What You Do	How You Do It
1. **Use the tracert command to trace the route from your workstation to the DNS server.**	a. **Choose Start→Command Prompt.** b. To view the syntax of the tracert command, in the command prompt window, **enter *tracert /?*** c. In the command prompt window, **enter *tracert -d 192.168.1.200***

d. **Verify that there was only one hop.**
There is only one hop to the DNS server because it is on the same local network as your workstation.

```
C:\Documents and Settings\User01>tracert -d 192.168.1.200

Tracing route to 192.168.1.200 over a maximum of 30 hops

  1    <1 ms    <1 ms    <1 ms  192.168.1.200

Trace complete.
```

e. To clear the screen, **enter *cls***

---

2. **Use the netstat command to identify the connections that are active on your system.**

a. To view the syntax of the netstat command, in the command prompt window, **enter *netstat /?***

b. In the command prompt window, **enter *netstat -a***

c. To clear the screen, **enter *cls***

---

3. **Use the nbtstat command to see the names in your NetBIOS name cache.**

a. To view the syntax of the nbtstat command, in the command prompt window, **enter *nbtstat /?***

b. In the command prompt window, **enter *nbtstat -c***

c. To clear the screen, **enter *cls***

---

4. **Use the nslookup command to obtain the host name of the DNS server.**

a. To enter nslookup interactive mode, in the command prompt window, **enter *nslookup***

b. To view nslookup command syntax, **enter *help***

c. **Enter *set querytype=ptr***

d. Enter ***192.168.1.200***

```
> set querytype=ptr
> 192.168.1.200
Server:  dc.classnet.class
Address:  192.168.1.200

200.1.168.192.in-addr.arpa       name = dc.classnet.class
```

e. To exit nslookup, **enter *exit***

f. To clear the screen, **enter *cls***

---

5. **Use the arp command to view the entries in your system's ARP cache.**

a. To view the syntax of the arp command, in the command prompt window, **enter *arp /?***

b. In the command prompt window, **enter *arp -a***

c. To close the command prompt window, **enter *exit***

ACTIVITY 7-10

Determining Which TCP/IP Utility to Use

Scenario:

In this activity, you will examine problems and decide which TCP/IP utility would be best to assist you in determining the problem.

---

1. **Match the TCP/IP utility with its function.**

___	Tracert	a.	Used to manage the cache of MAC addresses.
___	Netstat	b.	Used to determine the route that data takes to get to a specific destination.
___	Nbtstat	c.	Used to test and troubleshoot DNS servers.
___	Nslookup	d.	Used to display information about a computer's active TCP and UDP connections.
___	Arp	e.	Used to view and manage NetBIOS name cache information.

2. **You're working the help desk and get a call that a user can't access the UNIX host at 150.150.32.157. You are on the same subnet as the user and the UNIX host, and try to ping the UNIX host. You can successfully do so. You can also ping the user's workstation. When you ask the user to enter ping 150.150.32.157, all they get is a series of Destination Unreachable messages. What should you do?**

   a) Log in to the UNIX host and enter netstat -a to see if it is listening on the correct port.

   b) Use the ipconfig /release and /renew commands to update the workstation's IP address lease.

   c) From the problem workstation, enter arp -a to list the ARP cache.

   d) Use nslookup to query the DNS server for the UNIX host.

---

3. **You're a network administrator and have been receiving complaints that users aren't able to post files to or download files from an FTP server. What might you do to determine the status of the server?**

   a) Ping the server's IP address.

   b) Log on to the FTP server and enter netstat -a to see if its listening on the correct port.

   c) At a workstation, enter arp -d to delete the entry to the FTP server. Then, manually add the corrected entry.

   d) Use the nbtstat command to list statistics about the FTP server's NetBT connections.

---

4. **You are a networking administrator. Two Microsoft XP workstations have the same IP address, which results in an IP address conflict. Which command will you use to determine which two computers have the same IP address?**

   a) ipconfig /all

   b) ifconfig /all

   c) Netstat -e

   d) Arp -a

   e) Arp -d

---

5. **You want to add a static IP address to MAC address mapping to the local ARP table. Which command will you use?**

   a) arp -d

   b) arp -a

   c) arp -g

   d) arp inet_addr

   e) arp -s

---

6. **You want to view active connections on your system. Which command will you use?**

   a) tracert

   b) Nbtstat

   c) arp -a

   d) Netstat -a

   e) Ping -t

---

7. **You want to view the IP information on a Linux workstation. Which command will you use?**
   a) Ipconfig /all
   b) winipcfg
   c) Ping
   d) Ifconfig

8. **You are a network administrator and several users call you complain that they cannot reach the company's website. They can, however, reach other websites. Which command will you use first to identify the problem?**
   a) arp -a
   b) Nbtstat
   c) Tracert
   d) Ipconfig /all
   e) ping

TOPIC E

TCP/IP Upper-Layer Services

The TCP/IP protocol suite also includes services that work at the upper layers of the protocol stack. In this topic, you will learn about the different upper-layer services and the functions they can provide to your network.

Once network communication has been established at the lower layers of the protocol stack, users want to use applications to complete tasks over that communication link. These tasks include transferring and sharing files, reading and sending email, reading and posting messages on a newsgroup, and browsing the World Wide Web. TCP/IP upper-layer services make accomplishing these tasks possible. By understanding the function of each of the TCP/IP upper-layer services, you can choose the appropriate service for the desired user task.

File Transfer Protocol (FTP)

The *File Transfer Protocol (FTP)* enables the transfer of files between a user's workstation and a remote host. With FTP, a user can access the directory structure on a remote host, change directories, search and rename files and directories, and download and upload files. The FTP daemon or service must be running on the remote host and an FTP utility may need to be installed on the client. FTP commands must be entered in lowercase. There are both DOS and UNIX commands.

A daemon is a background process that performs a specific operation. Daemon is a UNIX term, though daemons are supported on other operating systems. Daemons on Windows are referred to as system agents or services.

To access most FTP servers, the client needs to connect using a valid user name and password. Some FTP servers allow limited access through an anonymous connection. To use this option, log on using the user name *anonymous*, and enter your email address for the password.

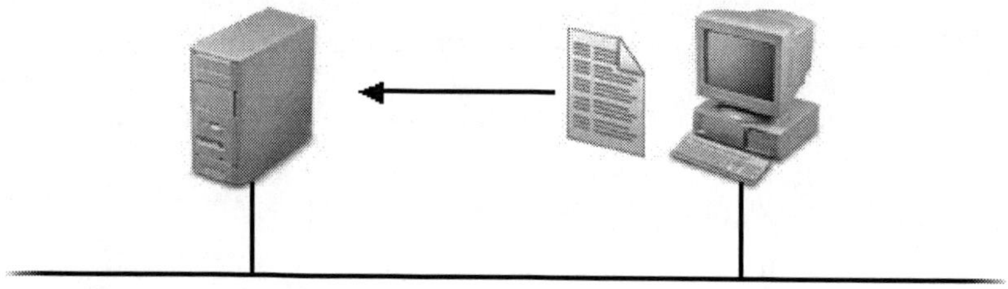

Figure 7-24: *FTP.*

FTP Options

FTP is defined in RFC 959. It uses two TCP port connections: Port 20 is used for data and port 21 is used for commands. There are several options you can use with the FTP command-line utility.

FTP Option	Is Used To
`-v`	Prevent showing remote server command responses.
`-n`	Suppress auto-logon at initial connection.
`-i`	Disable interactive prompting when transferring multiple files.
`-d`	Debug, displaying all commands passed between the FTP client and server.
`-g`	Disable wildcard character support.
`-s: [`*`filename`*`]`	Run all the FTP commands contained in the `[`*`filename`*`]` file.
`-a`	Allow use of any local interface during data connection binding.
`-w: [`*`windowsize`*`]`	Override the default transfer buffer size.

TFTP and SFTP

Trivial File Transfer Protocol (TFTP) is a simple version of FTP that uses UDP as the transport protocol. Simple File Transfer Protocol (SFTP) was another early unsecured file transfer protocol that has since been declared obsolete.

Internet Browsers and FTP

Most Internet browsers can support FTP in a GUI mode. A connection to an FTP site can be made by browsing the Internet, logging on, and connecting. Once connected, you can drag files on and off the FTP site the same way you would from Windows Explorer. There are also a number of third-party FTP utilities that can be used for connecting and loading files to your FTP site.

ACTIVITY 7-11

Using the Command-Line FTP Utility

There is a simulated version of this activity available on the CD-ROM that shipped with this course. You can run this simulation on any Windows computer to review the activity after class, or as an alternative to performing the activity as a group in class. The activity simulation can be launched either directly from the CD-ROM by clicking the Interactives link and navigating to the appropriate one, or from the installed data file location by opening the C:\Data\Simulations\Lesson#\Activity# folder and double-clicking the executable (.exe) file.

Setup:

There is an FTP site set up on the classroom server. The classroom server is named dc.classnet.class.

Scenario:

In this activity, you will use the command-line FTP utility to transfer a file from the classroom FTP server to your local computer.

What You Do	How You Do It
1. **Connect to the classroom FTP server.**	a. **Open a command prompt window.**
	b. **Enter *ftp***
	c. **Enter *open dc.classnet.class***
	d. **Enter *anonymous*** as the user name.
	e. **Press Enter** to submit a blank password.

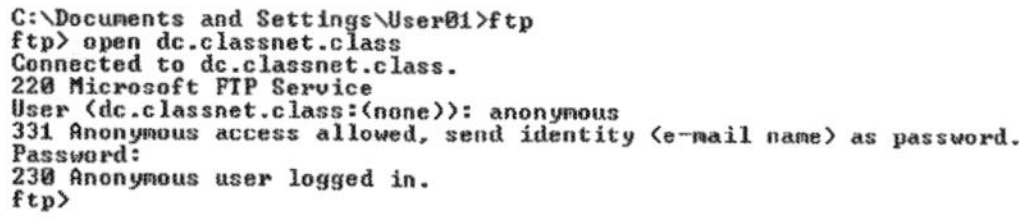

What You Do	How You Do It
2. **Download a file from the FTP server.**	a. **Enter *dir*** to list the files available on the FTP server.

b. **Enter *get FTP_Sample.txt* to download the file to the current directory on your local computer.**

```
ftp> dir
200 PORT command successful.
150 Opening ASCII mode data connection for /bin/ls.
01-03-05  12:30PM                        50 FTP_Sample.txt
226 Transfer complete.
ftp: 55 bytes received in 0.00Seconds 55000.00Kbytes/sec.
ftp> get FTP_Sample.txt
200 PORT command successful.
150 Opening ASCII mode data connection for FTP_Sample.txt(50 bytes).
226 Transfer complete.
ftp: 50 bytes received in 0.00Seconds 50000.00Kbytes/sec.
ftp> _
```

c. **Enter *close* to disconnect.**

d. **Enter *bye* to return to the command prompt.**

---

3. **Verify the transfer.**

a. **Enter *dir***

b. **Verify that the file appears in the current directory listing.**

```
 Directory of C:\Documents and Settings\User01

02/04/2005  10:03 AM    <DIR>          .
02/04/2005  10:03 AM    <DIR>          ..
02/03/2005  11:15 AM    <DIR>          Desktop
01/31/2005  04:03 PM    <DIR>          Favorites
02/04/2005  10:03 AM                50 FTP_Sample.txt
02/04/2005  10:04 AM    <DIR>          My Documents
01/31/2005  10:11 AM    <DIR>          Start Menu
01/31/2005  10:13 AM                 0 Sti_Trace.log
               2 File(s)             50 bytes
               6 Dir(s)   1,638,330,368 bytes free
```

c. **Close the command prompt window.**

Activity 7-12

Using a Browser as an FTP Client

There is a simulated version of this activity available on the CD-ROM that shipped with this course. You can run this simulation on any Windows computer to review the activity after class, or as an alternative to performing the activity as a group in class. The activity simulation can be launched either directly from the CD-ROM by clicking the Interactives link and navigating to the appropriate one, or from the installed data file location by opening the C:\Data\Simulations\Lesson#\Activity# folder and double-clicking the executable (.exe) file.

Scenario:

In this activity, you will use the Internet Explorer web browser to transfer a file using FTP.

What You Do	How You Do It
1. **Open Internet Explorer.**	a. **Choose Start→All Programs→Internet Explorer.**
	b. In the Internet Explorer message box, **check In The Future, Do Not Show This Message and click OK.**

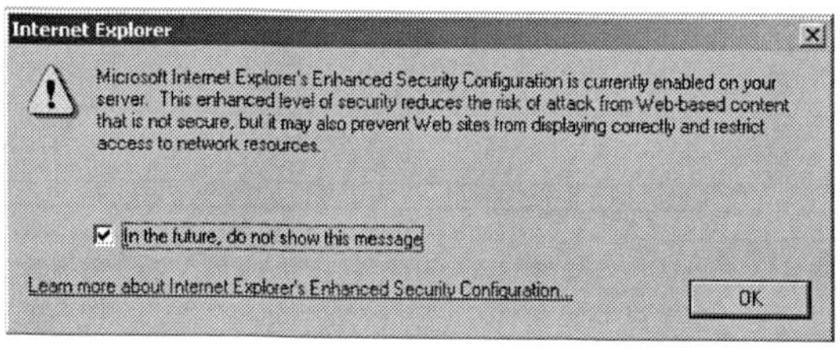

What You Do	How You Do It
2. **Connect to the classroom FTP server.**	a. **Select the text in the Address bar.**
	b. **Enter *ftp://dc.classnet.class***

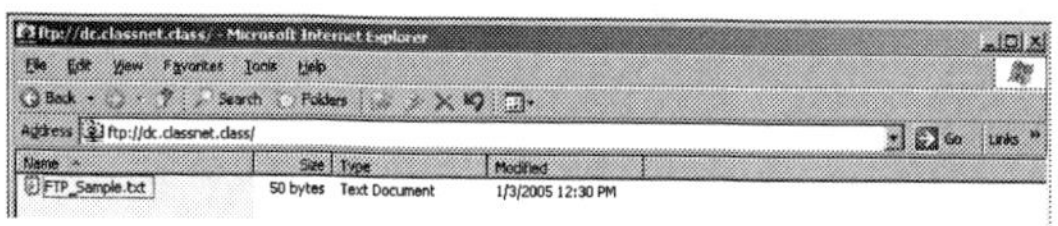

3. **Transfer the file.**

a. **Double-click the FTP_Sample.txt file** to open the file in a new window.

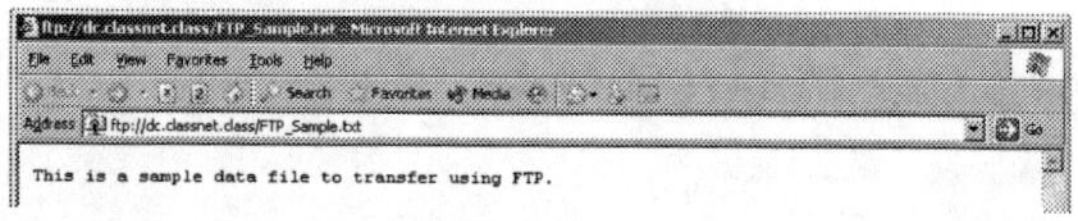

b. **Choose File→Save As.**

c. **Click Save** to save the file to the local My Documents folder.

d. **Close the FTP_Sample.txt window.**

e. **Close Internet Explorer.**

---

4. **Verify the transfer.**

a. **Choose Start→My Computer.**

b. **Open the Address list and select My Documents.**

c. **Verify that the file appears in the local My Documents folder.**

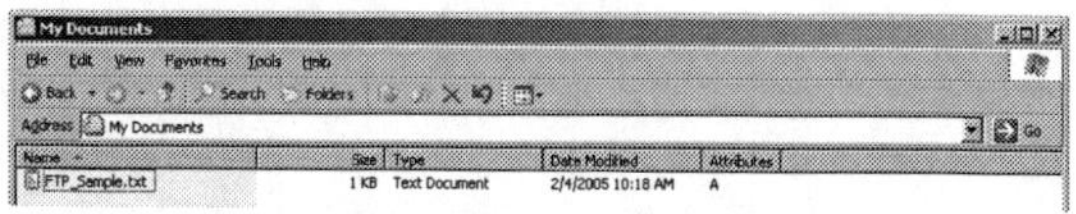

d. **Close the My Documents window.**

Telnet

Telnet is a terminal emulation protocol that enables a user at one site to simulate a session on a remote host as if the terminal were directly attached. It does this by translating keystrokes from the user's terminal to instructions recognized by the remote host, and then carrying the output back and displaying it in a format native to the user's terminal. You can connect to any host that is running a Telnet daemon or service.

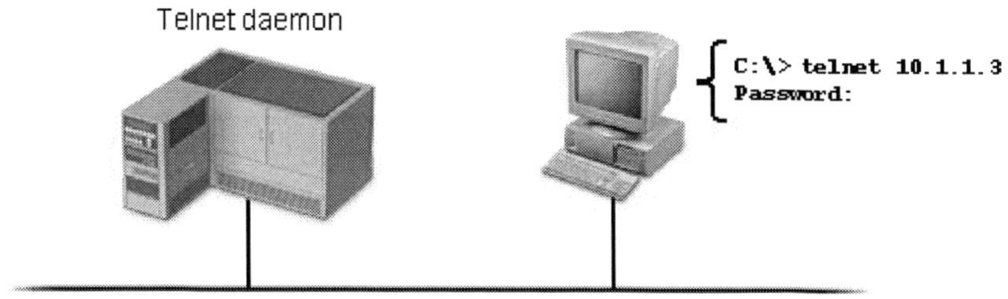

Figure 7-25: *Telnet.*

Telnet Servers

Many systems, such as a UNIX host or an IBM mainframe running TCP/IP, include Telnet daemons. There is also a Telnet server service in Windows 2000 Server, Windows XP, and Windows Server 2003.

Telnet Defaults

As defined in RFC 854, Telnet uses the following defaults:

- Port 23. However, you can specify a different port if the host to which you are connecting is configured to use a different port.
- Twenty-five lines in the buffer, but can be configured for up to 399 lines.
- VT100 (Video Terminal 100) as the default terminal emulation, but some versions allow you to configure your system with VT220, VT52, and TTY (TeleTYpe) terminal emulation support.

Windows Telnet Client

Windows includes a basic Telnet client utility. It is installed when you install TCP/IP on your Windows system. It includes VT100, VT52, and TTY terminal emulation. It does not include the Telnet daemon or service, but the Telnet service can be enabled on Windows Server computers.

Network Time Protocol (NTP)

Network Time Protocol (NTP) is an Internet standard protocol that synchronizes the clock times of computers in a network. Synchronization is done to the millisecond against the U.S. Naval Observatory master clocks. NTP runs continuously in the background on a computer. It sends periodic time requests to servers to obtain the server time stamp and then adjusts the client's clock based on the server time stamp received.

RFC 1305 defines the latest version of NTP.

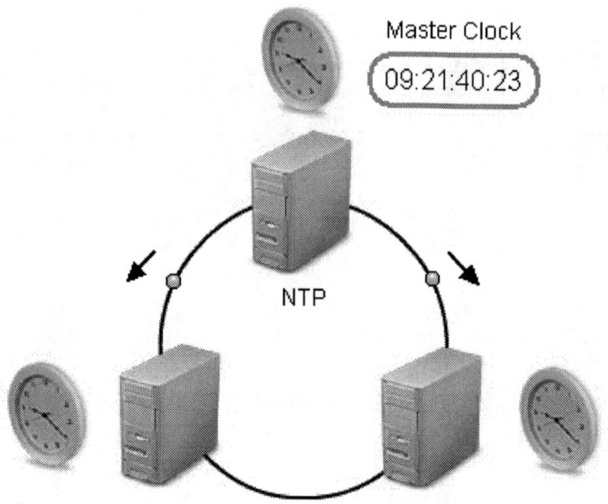

Figure 7-26: *NTP.*

Master Clock Locations

The master time clocks are located in Washington, D.C., and Colorado Springs, Colorado.

Simple Mail Transfer Protocol (SMTP)

TCP/IP has two services that operate in the Application layer of the OSI model and support the sending and receiving of email—Simple Mail Transfer Protocol (SMTP) and Post Office Protocol version 3 (POP3).

Simple Mail Transfer Protocol (SMTP) is used to send email from a client to a server or between servers. It uses a store-and-forward process. In SMTP, the sender starts the transfer. SMTP can store a message until the receiving device comes online. At that point, it contacts the device and hands off the message. If all devices are online, the message is sent quickly.

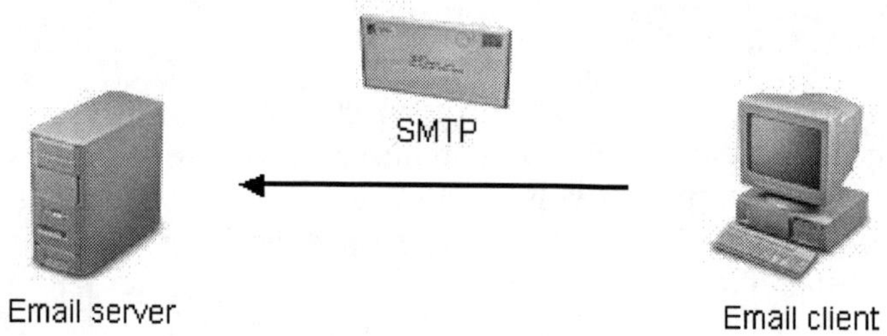

Figure 7-27: *Sending mail to a server through SMTP.*

Using SMTP on Unreliable WAN Links

Because of SMTP's store and forward capability, it's used to send data through unreliable WAN links if delivery time isn't critical. Data is sent to the endpoint and continues to hop from server to server until it eventually reaches its destination. For example, Windows Server 2003 and Windows 2000 Server support using SMTP for replication of Active Directory traffic across unreliable links.

Post Office Protocol Version 3 (POP3)

Post Office Protocol version 3 (POP3) is a protocol used to retrieve email messages from a mailbox on a mail server. With POP3, the email messages wait in the mailbox on the server until the client retrieves them. The client starts the transfer on a set schedule, or can transfer messages manually. Once the messages are retrieved and downloaded to the client, they are generally deleted from the server unless the client configures options to leave the messages on the server. The client then works with the email messages locally.

Because POP3 is designed by default to download messages to the local computer and delete them from the email server, it is not the best email protocol to use when users must access their email from multiple computers. When users access their email from multiple computers using POP3, they end up with their email messages downloaded and split among the computers they use instead of in one central location. Or, if they leave their messages on the server, they will have to delete old messages manually to avoid exceeding mailbox size limits, which may also lead to messages being split across multiple computers.

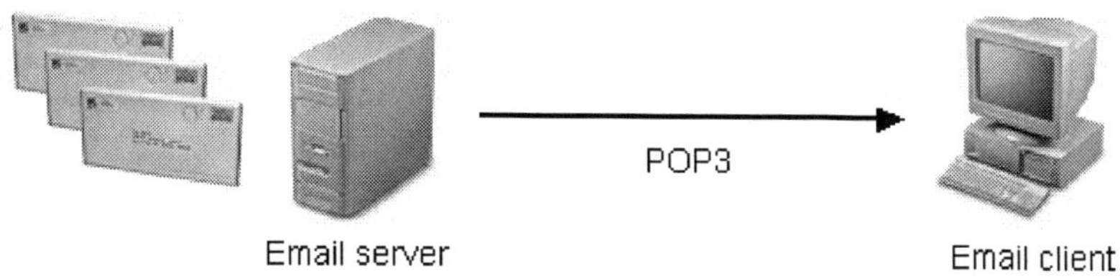

Figure 7-28: *Retrieving mail from a server through POP3.*

Internet Mail Access Protocol (IMAP4)

Internet Mail Access Protocol version 4 (IMAP4) is also used to retrieve messages from a mail server. With IMAP4, messages can also remain on the server while the client works with them as if they were local. IMAP4 enables users to search through messages by keywords, and to choose which messages to download locally. Messages in the user's mailbox can be marked with different status flags, such as deleted or replied to. The messages and their status flags stay in the mailbox until explicitly removed by the user. Unlike POP3, IMAP4 enables users to access folders other than their mailbox.

Because IMAP4 is designed to store messages on the server, it is easier for users to access their email messages—both new and saved—from multiple computers.

IMAP was developed at Stanford University in 1986.

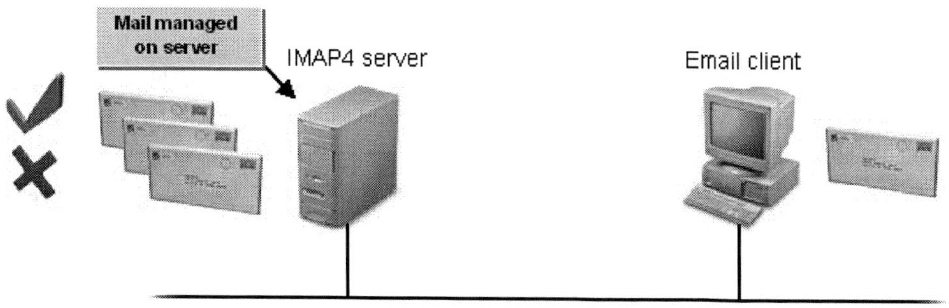

Figure 7-29: *Working with email on an email server using IMAP4.*

Network News Transfer Protocol (NNTP)

Network News Transfer Protocol (NNTP) is a protocol used to post and retrieve messages from the worldwide bulletin board system called USENET. USENET contains more than 14,000 forums, called newsgroups, on just about every imaginable topic. With NNTP, postings to newsgroups are stored in a database and individual users, called subscribers, select only those items they wish to read.

USENET is a contraction of User's Network.

NNTP is defined in RFC 977. How articles are transmitted to the news servers is specified in RFC 1036.

UNIX-to-UNIX Copy Protocol (UUCP) is a UNIX protocol and utility that enabled computers to send files to one another over a direct serial connection or through modems. UUCP was the original USENET protocol. For most file transfer applications, it has been superseded by FTP, SMTP, and NNTP.

Figure 7-30: *NNTP.*

Hypertext Transfer Protocol (HTTP)

Hypertext Transfer Protocol (HTTP) is the TCP/IP service that enables clients to connect and interact with websites. It defines how messages are formatted and transmitted, as well as what actions web servers and the client's browser should take in response to different commands. HTTP is a stateless protocol; each command is executed independently of any prior commands. HTTP supports persistent connections to web resources to reduce reconnection times, as well as pipelining and buffering to help in the transfer process.

One of the main reasons that it is difficult to implement websites that react intelligently to user input is that HTTP is stateless. This shortcoming of HTTP is being addressed in a number of add-on technologies, such as ActiveX, Java, JavaScript, and cookies.

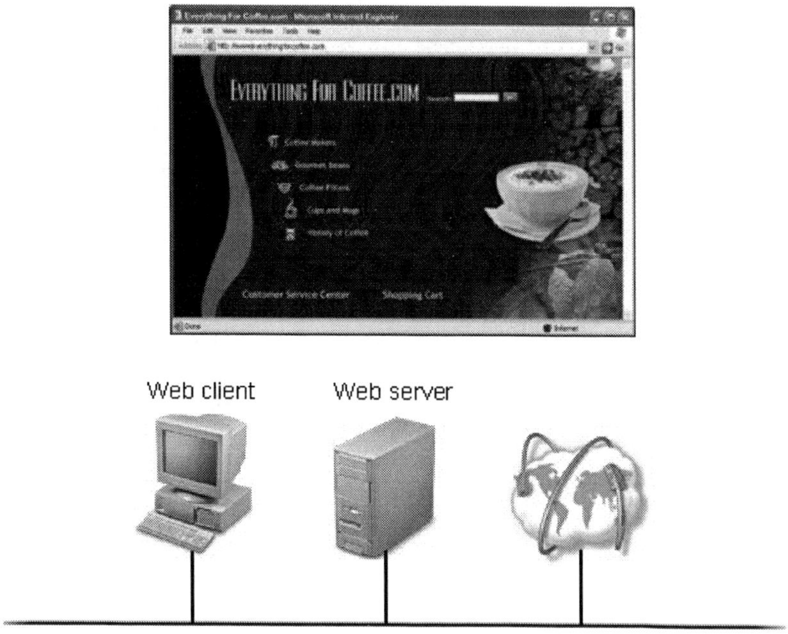

Figure 7-31: *HTTP.*

HTML

The other main standard that controls how the World Wide Web works is *Hypertext Markup Language (HTML)*, which covers how web pages are formatted and displayed.

ACTIVITY 7-13

Using HTTP to View a Website

There is a simulated version of this activity available on the CD-ROM that shipped with this course. You can run this simulation on any Windows computer to review the activity after class, or as an alternative to performing the activity as a group in class. The activity simulation can be launched either directly from the CD-ROM by clicking the Interactives link and navigating to the appropriate one, or from the installed data file location by opening the C:\Data\Simulations\Lesson#\Activity# folder and double-clicking the executable (.exe) file.

Setup:

There is a website installed on the classroom web server. The classroom web server is named dc.classnet.class.

Scenario:

In this activity, you will use HTTP to view the classroom website.

What You Do	How You Do It
1. **Connect to the classroom website.**	a. **Open Internet Explorer.** b. **Select the text in the Address bar.** c. **Enter *http://dc.classnet.class*** 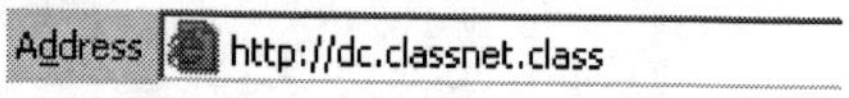 d. **Verify that the classroom web page loads.** 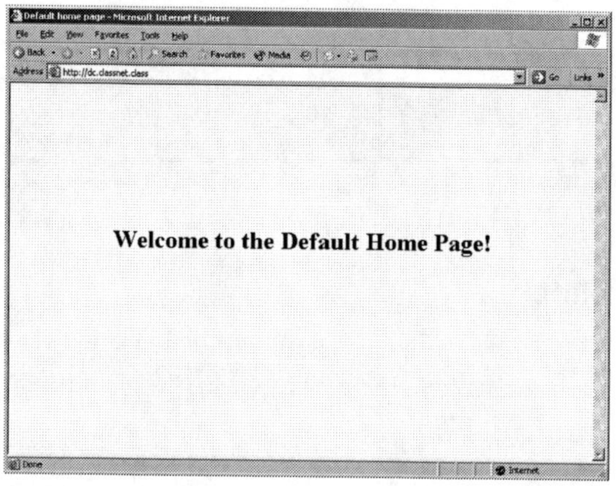
2. If your classroom has Internet connectivity, **use Internet Explorer to view other websites.**	a. **Connect to the websites of your choice.** b. When you are done, **close Internet Explorer.**

HTTPS

Hypertext Transfer Protocol Secure (HTTPS) is a secure version of HTTP that supports web commerce by providing a secure connection between web browser and server. HTTPS uses the Secure Sockets Layer (SSL) security protocol to encrypt data. Not all web browsers and servers support HTTPS.

HTTPS is also referred to as Hypertext Transfer Protocol over Secure Sockets Layer, or HTTP over SSL.

Figure 7-32: *HTTPS.*

ACTIVITY 7-14

Identifying Primary TCP/IP Upper-Layer Services

Scenario:

In this activity, you will identify the functions of the primary upper-layer services in use on a TCP/IP network.

---

1. **Your sales department wants to sell supplies over the Internet and wants to make sure that the transactions are secure. Which protocol should be configured on the web server?**

    a) FTP

    b) HTTPS

    c) NNTP

    d) SMTP

---

2. **Your company has a production floor with several shared computers. The production staff needs to be able to check their email from whichever computer is free. Which email protocol should you use?**

    a) UUCP

    b) NTP

    c) IMAP4

    d) NNTP

---

3. True or False? Telnet is a terminal emulation program that allows users to connect to the USENET system and read newsgroup messages.

   __ True

   __ False

4. Your sales force needs to retrieve sales prospective documents and upload completed sales order forms to corporate headquarters while they are on the road. What service should you use?

   a) Telnet

   b) NNTP

   c) NTP

   d) FTP

TOPIC F

TCP/IP Interoperability Services

The TCP/IP protocol suite includes services with the purpose of providing interoperability between systems both similar and dissimilar. In this topic, you will learn about the different TCP/IP interoperability services and the functions they can provide to your network.

Networks are established so that individual devices can communicate with each other and share resources. Most networks are made up of devices that are not natively compatible. When these devices are running TCP/IP, you can use the interoperability services that run on TCP/IP to create a network where dissimilar systems can securely communicate and share resources.

Line Printer Remote (LPR) and Line Printer Daemon (LPD)

Line Printer Remote (LPR) and *Line Printer Daemon (LPD)* can be used with TCP/IP for network printing. The LPR client sends a print request to the IP address of the LPD print server. The server places the print request in its print queue and prints the job when the printer becomes available.

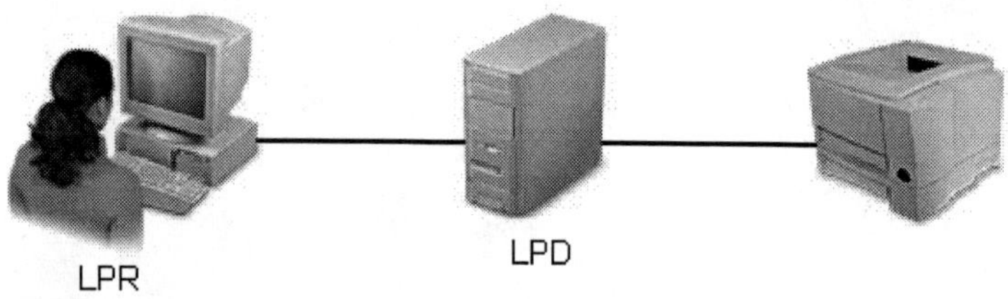

Figure 7-33: *LPR and LPD.*

Network File System (NFS)

Network File System (NFS) is a client/server application that enables users to access shared files stored on different types of computers and work with those files as if they were stored locally. It also allows a user to share local files and act as a file server for other client computers. NFS is independent of the computer, operating system, network architecture, and transport protocol.

NFS was designed by Sun Microsystems in the 1980s as a way to create a file system on diskless clients.

On TCP/IP networks, NFS uses an interface called the Virtual File System (VFS) that runs on top of TCP/IP.

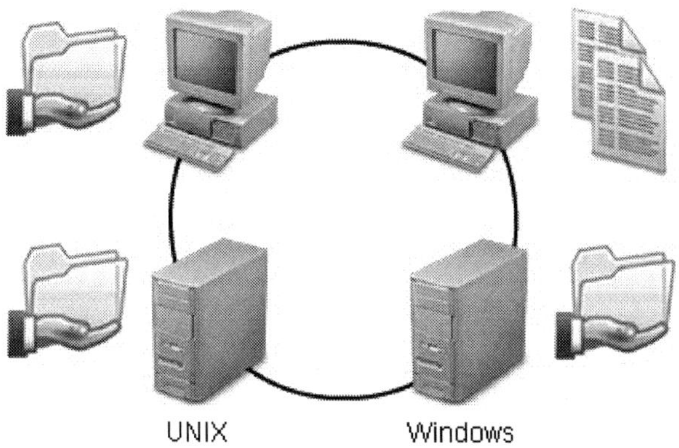

Figure 7-34: *A computer can access shared network files and share its own files using NFS.*

Secure Shell (SSH)

Secure Shell (SSH) is a program that enables a user or application to log on to another computer over a network, execute commands, and manage files. It provides strong authentication methods and secure communications over insecure channels. It replaces UNIX-based remote connection programs that transmit passwords unencyrpted. With the SSH `slogin` command, the entire login session, including the password, is encrypted and protected against attack.

Figure 7-35: *Secure Shell (SSH) provides secure communications over insecure channels.*

SSH was developed by SSH Communications Security Ltd.

SSH encrypts all traffic (including passwords) to effectively eliminate eavesdropping, connection hijacking, and other network-level attacks, such as IP spoofing, IP source routing, and DNS spoofing. When you implement SSH with encryption, any attacker who has managed to gain access to your network can only force SSH to disconnect. They cannot play back the traffic or hijack the connection.

Secure Shell works with many different operating systems, including Windows, UNIX, and Macintosh systems.

SSH is a replacement for the UNIX-based rlogin command, which can also establish a connection with a remote host, but transmits passwords in cleartext.

SSH1 and SSH2

There are two versions of Secure Shell available: SSH1 and SSH2. SSH1 and SSH2 are two different protocols and encrypt different parts of the data packet. SSH2 is more secure. To authenticate systems, SSH1 employs user keys, to identify users; host keys, to identify systems; session keys, to encrypt communication in a single session; and server keys, which are temporary keys that protect the session key. SSH2 does not use server keys. SSH2 includes a secure replacement for FTP called Secure File Transfer Protocol (SFTP). Because of the different protocol implementation, SSH1 and SSH2 are not compatible with each other.

Note that the SFTP acronym is used both for Secure File Transfer Protocol as well as for the obsolete Simple File Transfer Protocol.

Secure Copy Protocol (SCP)

Secure Copy Protocol (SCP) uses SSH to securely transfer computer files between a local and a remote host, or between two remote hosts. SCP can also be implemented as a command-line utility that uses either the SCP protocol or the SFTP protocol to perform secure copying.

Figure 7-36: *SCP.*

Server Message Block (SMB)

Server Message Block (SMB) is a protocol used for sharing resources such as files, printers, and serial ports between computers. In a TCP/IP network, NetBIOS clients, such as Windows systems, use NetBIOS over TCP/IP to connect to servers, and then issue SMB commands to complete tasks such as accessing shared files and printers. SMB can also run over IPX/SPX and NetBEUI.

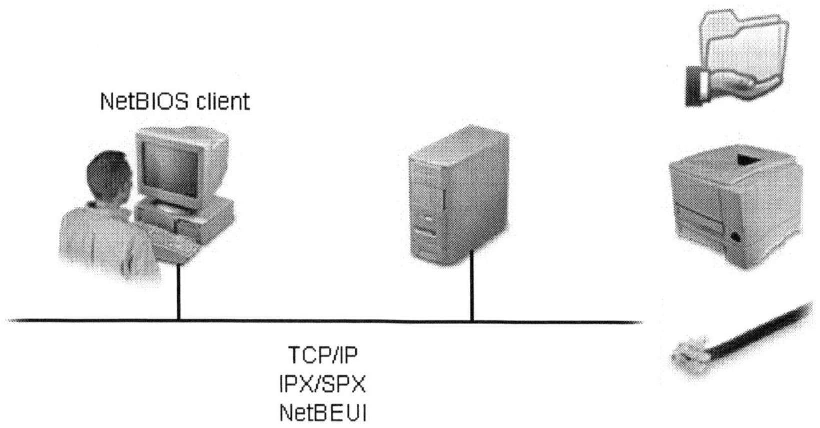

Figure 7-37: *SMB enables resource sharing in mixed environments.*

Samba

Although the SMB protocol is primarily used in Microsoft networks, there are products that use SMB to enable file sharing across different operating system platforms. Samba is a well-known open-source product that uses SMB to enable UNIX and Windows machines to share directories and files.

Lightweight Directory Access Protocol (LDAP)

Lightweight Directory Access Protocol (LDAP) is a protocol that defines how a client can access information, perform operations, and share directory data on a directory server. It was designed for use specifically over TCP/IP networks, and on the Internet in particular. In most implementations, LDAP relies on the DNS service. DNS enables clients to find the servers that host the LDAP directory, and then the LDAP servers enable clients to find directory objects.

Microsoft's Active Directory directory service implements the LDAP standard and supports LDAP versions 2 and 3. The Novell directory services NDS and eDirectory are also LDAP compliant.

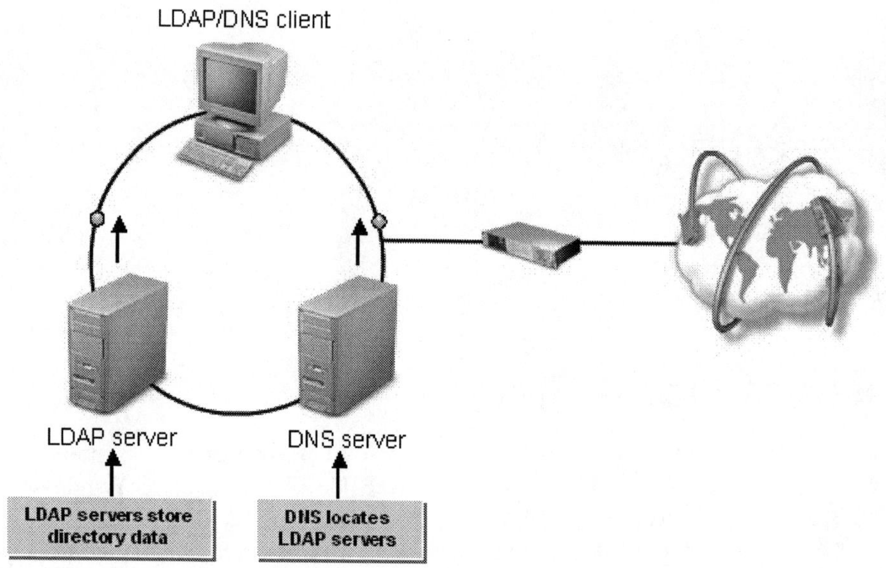

Figure 7-38: *LDAP.*

Simple Network Management Protocol (SNMP)

Simple Network Management Protocol (SNMP) is an Application-layer service used to collect information from network devices for diagnostic and maintenance purposes. SNMP includes two components: management systems and agent software, which is installed on network devices such as servers, routers, and printers. The agents send information to an SNMP manager. The SNMP manager can then notify an administrator of problems, run a corrective program or script, store the information for later review, or query the agent about a specific network device.

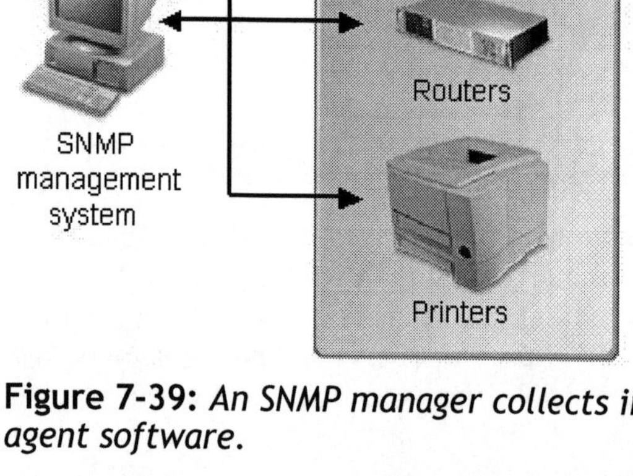

Figure 7-39: *An SNMP manager collects information on network hardware from SNMP agent software.*

SNMP Traps

When an SNMP agent sends data to the management system without first being queried, it's referred to as a *trap*. The SNMP agent traps events and sends the information to the management system. Many administrators use traps to indicate that a device is overworked or on the verge of failure. The administrator setting up the SNMP system can configure conditions under which the agent sends a trap—for example, when the CPU usage exceeds a specified level or when the hard drive is becoming full. There are several other traps that can be configured based on the agent software provided by the manufacturer.

SNMP MIBs

An SNMP Management Information Base (MIB) is a custom database containing system information for a device—essentially, a list of equipment specifications. The MIB database contains all the agent counters that a management system can monitor for the device. Because MIBs are specific to a particular device, they differ from manufacturer to manufacturer, and from device to device. Typically, a manufacturer provides the MIB for their devices. The custom MIBs enable a single monitoring management system to monitor a wide range of agents. As long as the manufacturers write the MIBs correctly, the SNMP system can manage the devices.

MIBs are registered by the ISO to control their development.

Zeroconf (Zero Configuration Networking)

Zero Configuration Networking (Zeroconf) is a proposed set of standards that provides for automatic configuration and IP address allocation on both Ethernet and wireless networks. Zeroconf networks can exist without central control or configuration services such as DHCP or DNS. Zeroconf protocols can use configuration information if it is available, but do not require it.

Zeroconf technology networks must include methods for four functions:

- Network-layer address assignment.
- Automatic address assignment by multicast.
- Translation between network names and network addresses.
- Location or discovery of network services by name and protocol.

Zeroconf protocols typically use MAC addresses as parameters because they are unique and available on most network devices.

Universal Plug and Play (UPnP) is another emerging technology that provides for automatic configuration and IP address allocation on networks.

Zeroconf Implementations

The use of addresses in the 169.254.0.0 /16 address range for automatic configuration has been implemented in Microsoft's APIPA addressing and in the Rendezvous product from Apple Computer, Inc. For more information, see **www.zeroconf.org**.

ACTIVITY 7-15

Identifying TCP/IP Interoperability Services

Scenario:

In this activity, you will identify TCP/IP interoperability services.

1. **If you desire to monitor network devices on your TCP/IP network for diagnostic purposes, which upper-layer TCP/IP service would you implement?**
   a) Zeroconf
   b) SNMP
   c) SMB
   d) NFS
   e) LPR/LPD

2. **Which two services work together to securely transfer computer files between a local and a remote host, or between two remote hosts?**
   a) LPR and LPD
   b) SMB and NFS
   c) SCP and SSH
   d) NFS and LDAP
   e) NFS and SSH

3. **True or False? To establish connections between client workstations and network printers in TCP/IP networks, LPR is installed on the client and LPD is installed on the print server.**
   __ True
   __ False

4. **Samba, which enables UNIX and Windows machines to share printers and files, is what type of a service?**
   a) NFS
   b) SCP
   c) LDAP
   d) SMB

5. **Zeroconf networks provide which automatic configuration services?**
   a) Multicast address assignment
   b) User account creation
   c) Printer sharing
   d) Name resolution

Lesson 7 Follow-up

In this lesson, you learned how the services that are part of the TCP/IP protocol suite can be used on your network. By implementing TCP/IP services and utilities on your network, you can automate the IP configuration of your devices, enable dissimilar systems to communicate and share resources securely, resolve host names to IP addresses, and support and maintain aspects of your TCP/IP implementation.

1. **What TCP/IP services and utilities do you currently implement in your organization?**

2. **What TCP/IP services and utilities, not currently implemented, would your company benefit from?**

NOTES

LESSON 8
Other Network Protocols

Lesson Time
1 hour(s), 15 minutes

Lesson Objectives:

In this lesson, you will identify characteristics of a variety of network protocols.

You will:

- Identify the characteristics of a NetBEUI protocol implementation.
- Identify the characteristics of an IPX/SPX protocol implementation.
- Identify the characteristics of an AppleTalk protocol implementation.
- Identify the components of an IPv6 implementation.

Lesson 8

Introduction

In the previous lessons, you identified the characteristics of the TCP/IP version 4 protocol. There are other protocols besides TCP/IP that you might encounter in older networks or in mixed networks. In this lesson, you will identify the characteristics of several other network protocols.

Although TCP/IP version 4 is the de facto standard protocol in most networks today, you might encounter other protocols, especially in older networks or in mixed networks that run multiple protocols. As a networking professional, you will need to understand the characteristics of a variety of protocols in order to support and maintain the networks that run them.

This lesson covers the following CompTIA Network+ (2005) certification objectives:

- Topic A:
  - Objective 2.4: Characterize the NetBEUI (Network Basic Input/Output System Extended User Interface) network protocol in terms of routing, addressing schemes, interoperability, and naming conventions.
- Topic B;
  - Objective 2.4: Characterize the IPX/SPX (Internetwork Packet Exchange/Sequenced Packet Exchange) network protocol in terms of routing, addressing schemes, interoperability, and naming conventions.
  - Objective 4.5: Given a troubleshooting scenario between a client and a NetWare server environment, identify the cause of the stated problem.
- Topic C:
  - Objective 2.4: Characterize the AppleTalk/AppleTalk over IP (Internet Protocol) network protocols in terms of routing, addressing schemes, interoperability, and naming conventions.
  - Objective 2.13: Identify the purpose of network services and protocols—for example, AFP (Apple File Protocol).
  - Objective 3.1: Identify the basic capabilities (for example, client support, interoperability, authentication, file and print services, application support, and security) of the AppleShare IP (Internet Protocol) server operating system to access network resources.
  - Objective 3.4: Given a remote connectivity scenario comprised of a protocol, an authentication scheme, and physical connectivity, configure the connection. Include a connection to an AppleShare IP (Internet Protocol) server.
- Topic D:
  - Objective 2.5: Identify the components and structure of IP (Internet Protocol) addresses (IPv6) and the required setting for connections across the Internet.

TOPIC A

The NetBEUI Protocol

In this lesson, you will identify the characteristics of a variety of network protocols. One protocol you might encounter on older Microsoft networks is NetBEUI. In this topic, you will identify the characteristics of a NetBEUI implementation.

If you work with older Microsoft operating systems or network implementations, you're almost guaranteed to encounter the NetBEUI protocol. You will need to understand this protocol and its limitations so that you can support those networks appropriately.

NetBEUI

NetBIOS Extended User Interface (NetBEUI) is a legacy protocol commonly found in older Windows networks. NetBEUI is fast and simple, and requires no administrative configuration. It relies on NetBIOS broadcast traffic for node discovery and name resolution. However, this makes NetBEUI relatively inefficient, because the broadcasts create more network traffic overhead than other protocols.

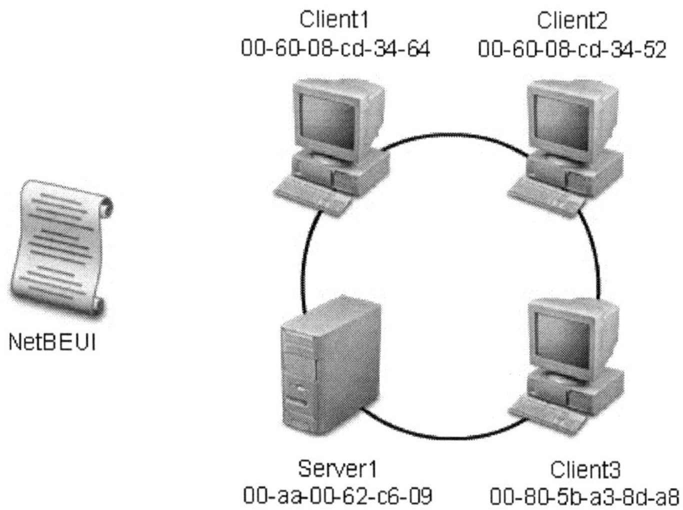

Figure 8-1: *NetBEUI.*

NetBEUI is implemented at the Data-link layer of the OSI model. NetBEUI identifies each node both by a NetBIOS node name and by the node's MAC address. Because the MAC address has no location element, NetBEUI is not routable.

CompTIA Network+ Exam Objectives

An Appendix is available to assist you in mapping CompTIA Network+ exam objectives to the course content. You can download the Appendix at the end of this lesson.

Operating Systems that Support NetBEUI

NetBEUI was developed by Microsoft and IBM for implementation on small networks. It was the default networking protocol in the original Windows network operating systems, including Windows for Workgroups and Windows NT 3.1. NetBEUI is an optional protocol that can be installed in many other versions of Windows. NetBEUI is no longer supported in Windows XP and Windows Server 2003.

Activity 8-1

Identifying Characteristics of NetBEUI

Scenario:

In this activity, you will identify the characteristics of the NetBEUI protocol.

1. **On what type of network are you most likely to find the NetBEUI protocol?**
   a) On networks running the Windows Server 2003 operating system.
   b) On networks running the Windows NT 4.0 operating system.
   c) On networks running Linux or UNIX.
   d) On home networks running Windows XP Professional.

2. **NetBEUI's reliance on broadcast traffic makes it:**
   a) Complex to install and administer.
   b) Simple to install and administer.
   c) Efficient in comparison to other protocols.
   d) Inefficient in comparison to other protocols.

3. **Because NetBEUI is implemented at the Data-link layer, it:**
   a) Is suitable for large internetworks.
   b) Requires administrative configuration.
   c) Requires no name resolution.
   d) Is not routable.

TOPIC B

The IPX/SPX Protocol

In the previous topic, you examined NetBEUI, which is a protocol you might encounter on older Microsoft networks. Another older protocol, which you might encounter on Novell networks, is IPX/SPX. In this topic, you will identify the characteristics of an IPX/SPX protocol implementation.

Just as you might encounter NetBEUI if you support older Microsoft networks, you're likely to encounter IPX/SPX on Novell networks running older versions of NetWare. Or, you might see its Microsoft counterpart, NWLink, on mixed Novell/Microsoft networks. If you support these types of networks, it will be important for you to understand the capabilities and configuration parameters of these two related protocols.

IPX/SPX

Internetwork Packet Exchange/Sequenced Packet Exchange (IPX/SPX) is a proprietary, routable network protocol developed by Novell for use in versions 3 and 4 of the Novell NetWare network operating system. IPX/SPX includes two protocols. IPX is a connectionless, Network-layer protocol that provides best-effort data delivery. SPX is a connection-oriented, Transport-layer protocol that provides guaranteed data delivery.

Novell developed IPX/SPX based on work done at the Xerox Palo Alto Research Center (PARC)

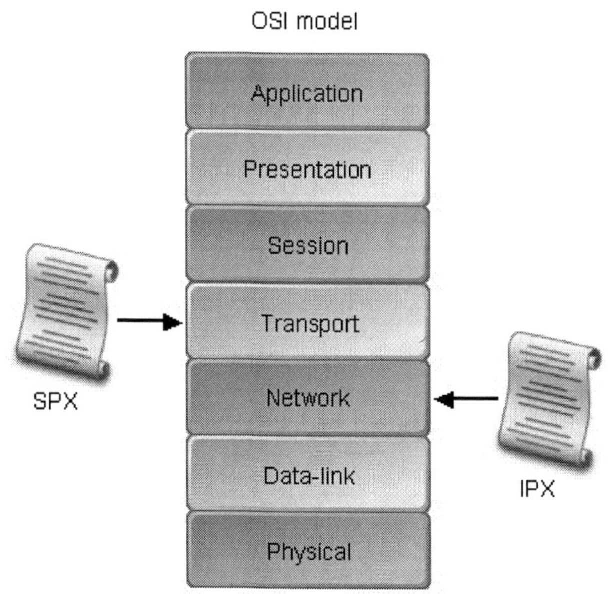

Figure 8-2: *IPX/SPX.*

NWLink

Microsoft developed its own version of the IPX/SPX protocol, NWLink, for compatibility and interoperability between Microsoft and Novell networks. NWLink can also be used in standalone Microsoft Windows networks.

IPX/SPX and TCP/IP

IPX/SPX is a routable, multilayered protocol like TCP/IP. IPX corresponds to the IP protocol in the TCP/IP suite; SPX corresponds to TCP. IPX/SPX and its Microsoft counterpart, NWLink, have been replaced by TCP/IP in almost all network implementations, because of the need for most networks to connect to the Internet. TCP/IP is the native protocol in current versions of NetWare, but IPX/SPX is supported for backward compatibility.

NetWare Client Software

Although installing the IPX/SPX or the NWLink protocols enables nodes to establish a network connection, it does not enable users to log in to NetWare servers. To log in and authenticate to Novell NetWare servers, you must install network client software, such as the Novell Client for Windows or Microsoft's Client Services for NetWare.

Service Advertisement Protocol (SAP)

Servers on an IPX/SPX network use a broadcast transmission called a Service Advertisement Protocol (SAP) to inform the network of services they have available. SAP broadcasts also help routers keep their tables of server services current. By default, all servers broadcast every 60 seconds. Workstations can issue SAP requests, which cause all servers on a local network to respond with a SAP broadcast. When a workstation logs on to the network, it sends a GET Nearest Server SAP broadcast and attaches to the first server that responds.

IPX/SPX Node Addresses

All IPX/SPX nodes are assigned a 12-byte IPX internetwork number represented by 24 hexadecimal digits. The first 8 hex digits represent the external network address, and identify the cable segment. The next 12 hex digits represent the node address, and are unique to each network adapter. The final 4 hex digits represent the socket number, which identifies the service or application running on the node. Because the address contains both a network identifier and a node identifier, IPX/SPX is fully routable.

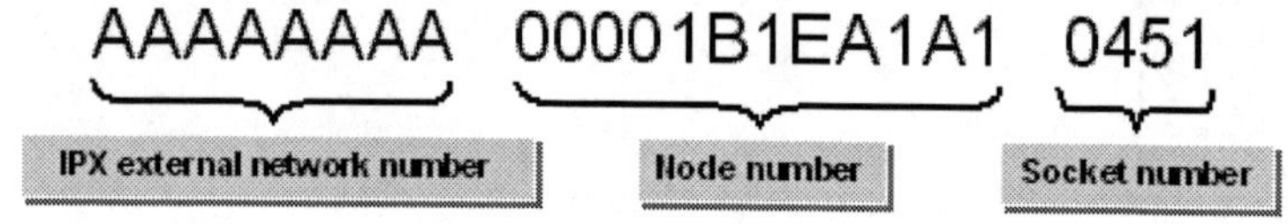

Figure 8-3: *IPX/SPX node addresses.*

IPX/SPX socket numbers are similar in function to TCP port numbers.

Hexadecimal Numbering

Hexadecimal numbering is a notational system that assigns 16 separate alphanumeric values to represent the first 16 half-bytes of binary data. Hexadecimal numbers can include the alphanumeric values from 0 to 9 and A to F. When converted to hexadecimal notation, long binary values, such as the 12-byte IPX address, can be represented more meaningfully and using fewer characters than in raw binary notation.

This table gives the conversion values for decimal, hexadecimal, and binary notation.

Decimal	Hexadecimal	Binary
0	0	0000
1	1	0001
2	2	0010
3	3	0011
4	4	0100
5	5	0101
6	6	0110
7	7	0111
8	8	1000
9	9	1001
10	A	1010
11	B	1011
12	C	1100
13	D	1101
14	E	1110
15	F	1111

PRACTICE ACTIVITY 8-2

Converting Values for Decimal, Hexadecimal, and Binary Notations

Objective:

Scenario:

1. Convert the IP address: 10.170.10.20 to binary.

   Answer:* *00001010.10101010.00001010.00010100

2. Convert the IP address: 172.40.100.64 to binary.

   Answer:* *10101100.00101000.01100100.01000000

3. Convert the following binary sequence to an IP address octet: 11000000.10101000.00011000.01100100

   Answer:* *192.168.48.100

4. Convert the IP address 192. 104.50.100 to a hexadecimal sequence.

   Answer: C0 68 32 64

5. Convert the hexadecimal sequence 8E 0F 24 82 into an IP address and into binary.

   Answer: As an IP address, 142.15.36.130

   Answer: As binary: 10001110.00001111.00100100.10000010

IPX/SPX Server Addresses

Servers on an IPX/SPX network are uniquely identified both by an eight-character name and also by an eight-digit hexadecimal internal network number. Both are assigned during installation. The internal network number can be random, or it can be manually assigned. The internal network number enables the server to route between multiple network cards with different external network addresses.

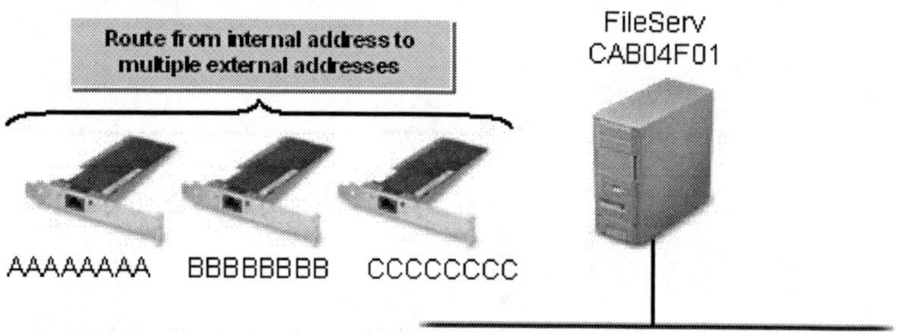

Figure 8-4: *IPX/SPX server addresses.*

The internal network number does not have to be configured unless the server is hosting network applications. If the internal network number is not needed, it should be set to all zeros.

IPX Frame Types

There are four IPX/SPX frame types, each corresponding to a different Ethernet standard. When a node is first connected to an IPX/SPX network, it can automatically detect the frame type. If no frames are detected, the node defaults to its preferred frame type. Or, the frame type can be manually configured. Nodes that use different frame types cannot communicate, which is a common cause of communications failure on IPX/SPX networks. A server can be configured to route between multiple frame types.

The different IPX/SPX frame types are used with different versions of network software.

Frame Type	Description
IEEE 802.2	Preferred frame type for Netware 3.12 and later.
IEEE 802.3	Preferred frame type for NetWare 3.11 and earlier.
Ethernet II	Ethernet version that preceded IEEE 802.x.
Ethernet SNAP (SubNetwork Access Protocol)	Used for AppleTalk connectivity.

IPX/SPX also supports a Token Ring or 802.5 frame type for use on Token Ring networks, as well as a Token Ring SNAP frame type.

ACTIVITY 8-3

Installing the NWLink Protocol

There is a simulated version of this activity available on the CD-ROM that shipped with this course. You can run this simulation on any Windows computer to review the activity after class, or as an alternative to performing the activity as a group in class. The activity simulation can be launched either directly from the CD-ROM by clicking the Interactives link and navigating to the appropriate one, or from the installed data file location by opening the C:\Data\Simulations\Lesson#\Activity# folder and double-clicking the executable (.exe) file.

Setup:

You are logged on as your User## user account. This account has administrative privileges on your Windows Server 2003 computer.

Scenario:

Your Windows-based network includes some legacy Novell NetWare servers that run the IPX/SPX protocol. Windows servers that need to communicate with the NetWare servers will need the NWLink protocol installed.

What You Do	How You Do It
1. **Open the properties of the Local Area Connection.**	a. **Choose Start→Control Panel→Network Connections.**
	b. **Right-click Local Area Connection and choose Properties.**

2. **Add the NWLink network protocol.**

a. **Click Install.**

b. **Select Protocol and click Add.**

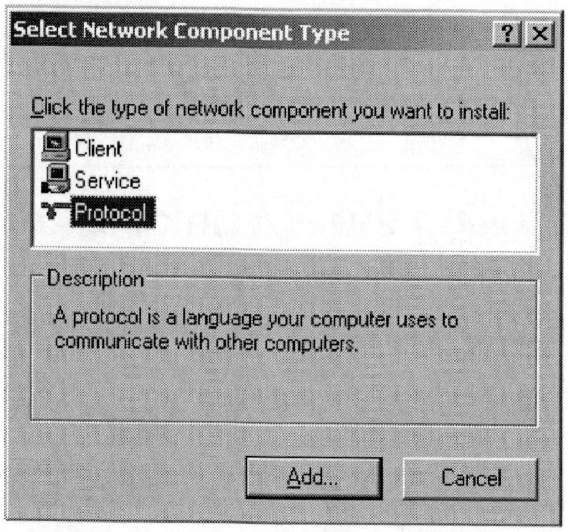

c. In the Network Protocol list, **select NWLink IPX/SPX/NetBIOS Compatible Transport Protocol and click OK.**

d. **Verify that the protocol appears in the properties of the Local Area Connection.**

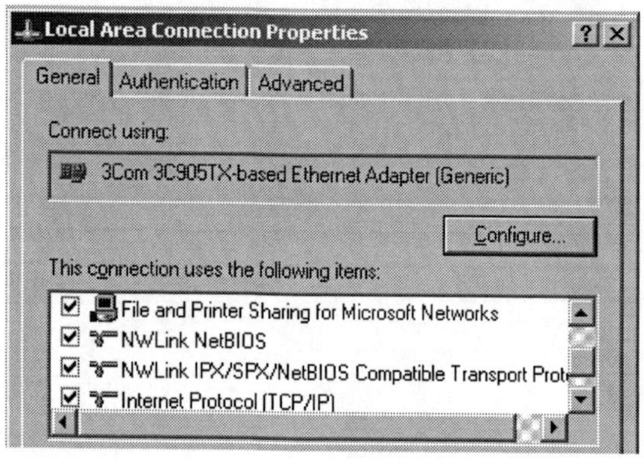

---

3. **Verify automatic frame type detection.**

a. **Select NWLink IPX/SPX/NetBIOS Compatible Transport Protocol and click Properties.**

b. **Verify that the adapter is set to Auto Frame Type Detection and click OK.**

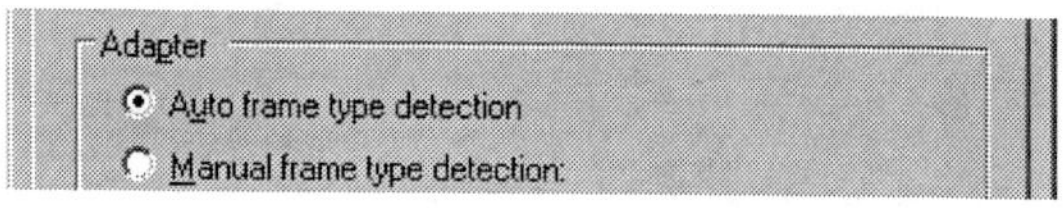

c. In the Local Area Connection Properties dialog box, **click Close.**

TOPIC C

The AppleTalk Protocol

In previous topics, you learned about protocols you might encounter on particular types of older networks or mixed networks. The AppleTalk protocol is one that you might see on networks that contain Macintosh workstations. In this topic, you will identify the characteristics of an AppleTalk protocol implementation.

The Macintosh operating system might not be as ubiquitous as Windows, but it is fairly common in certain environments, such as schools or graphic-design firms. As a network professional, if you work in these environments, you'll be called upon to support their network functions. On older Macintosh networks, this might mean supporting the AppleTalk protocol. You will need to understand this legacy protocol's characteristics and limitations in order to support and configure it effectively.

AppleTalk

AppleTalk is a routable protocol found in older Macintosh networks. AppleTalk networks have a hierarchical structure consisting of nodes, which are individual network devices; networks, which are physical or logical cable segments; zones, which are administratively created workgroups that facilitate resource sharing and resource access; and sockets, which are addressable locations within nodes. AppleTalk supports various physical network topologies, such as TokenTalk, EtherTalk, and FDDITalk.

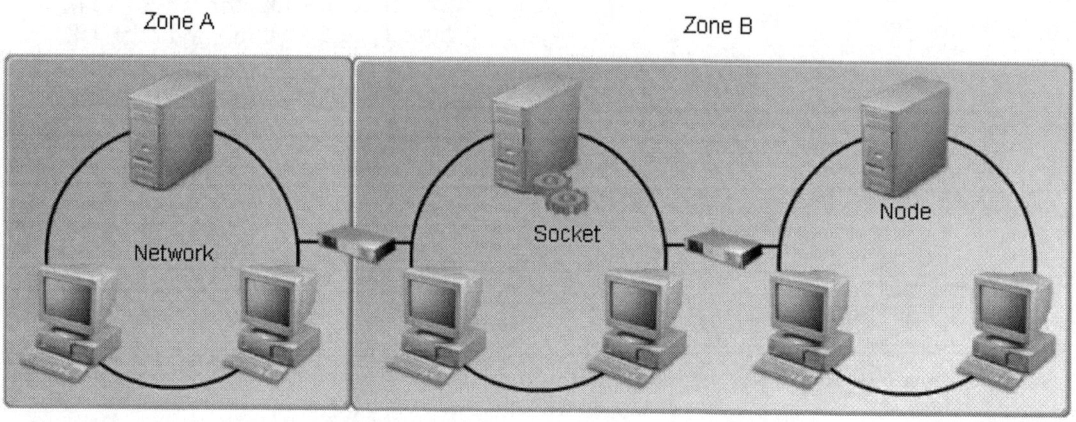

Figure 8-5: *AppleTalk.*

Windows and AppleTalk Interoperability

Windows server computers include support for the AppleTalk protocol, which enables network connectivity between Windows servers and AppleTalk nodes and enables Windows servers to function as AppleTalk routers. However, for Macintosh clients to authenticate to Windows server computers, the Windows servers must also be running the Services for Macintosh network component. Services for Macintosh provides both file services and print services for Macintosh clients.

AppleTalk Addressing

There is a different addressing scheme for each of the AppleTalk network components.

Component	Addressing
Zones	Zone membership is assigned by the network administrator, who assigns a descriptive name to the zone. Members of a zone don't need to be on the same network or physical segment.
Networks (non-extended)	A non-extended network is a single cable segment assigned a unique 10-bit network ID in the decimal range from 1 to 1023. All nodes on a subnet or cable segment share the same network number but must have unique node IDs. Nodes detect their network address when they come online.
Networks (extended)	An extended network is the combination of multiple logical networks assigned to the same cable segment. Nodes on a segment are assigned multiple network numbers as long as they stay in a cable range. This circumvents AppleTalk's 254-node limit. In a cable range, network numbers are assigned in blocks and the combination of the node and extended network address must be unique to the network.
Nodes	Nodes randomly generate their own unique 8-bit addresses in the range from 1 to 254, and confirm that the address is available by broadcasting an address request. The combination of node and network number makes the complete address unique.

Component	Addressing
Sockets	A node can maintain up to 254 sockets. Socket numbers can be assigned statically or dynamically. Static socket numbers are reserved for well-known services. Dynamic sockets are assigned at a node's request to track a communication process.

The AppleTalk Protocol Suite

The AppleTalk protocol suite consists of a number of related protocols, some of which function in the upper OSI layers.

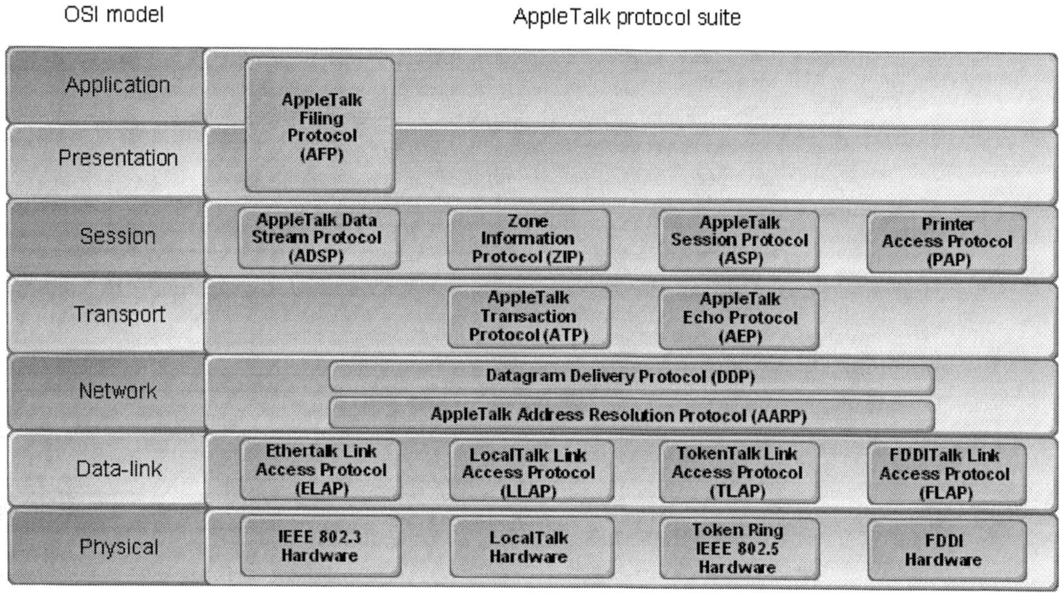

Figure 8-6: *The AppleTalk protocol suite.*

Protocol	Description
AFP	AppleTalk Filing Protocol (AFP) is an Application- and Presentation-layer protocol used by workstations to exchange data across a network. It enables network resources to be mapped as local resources. AFP enables clients to access resources on servers running the AppleShare file and print service.
ADSP	AppleTalk Data Stream Protocol (ADSP) is a Session-layer protocol that establishes and maintains full duplex connections between nodes. It also handles data sequencing and ensures that data packets aren't duplicated.
ZIP	Zone Information Protocol (ZIP) is a Session-layer protocol that provides an AppleTalk node with information about its zone and network.
ASP	AppleTalk Session Protocol (ASP) is a Session-layer protocol that maintains communication sessions between network nodes and provides the framework used by clients to send commands to servers.
PAP	Printer Access Protocol (PAP) is used by clients to send data to print servers and by AppleTalk servers to exchange data with each other.

Other protocols in the AppleTalk suite function at the lower OSI layers.

Protocol	Description
ATP	AppleTalk Transaction Protocol (ATP) is a Transport-layer protocol used to manage transactions between two sockets on different nodes. (A transaction consists of requests and responses.)
AEP	AppleTalk Echo Protocol (AEP) is the AppleTalk equivalent of the Ping utility, and is used to test a node's reachability. AEP uses the statically assigned socket number 4. It is implemented at the Transport layer.
DDP	At the Network layer, Datagram Delivery Protocol (DDP) is the main routing protocol that provides best-effort, connectionless data delivery. It transfers and receives data. When a node sends data, DDP gets the data from upper layers and creates a DDP header containing the source and destination addresses. It then passes the packet to the Data-link layer. When the node receives the data, DDP examines the addresses in the DDP header to determine if the data is bound for a socket on the local machine or a remote network. DDP also maintains a list of all local and remote cable addresses and any known routes to those addresses.
AARP	Like all protocols, AppleTalk uses the MAC address of the node for packet addressing. At the Network layer, the AppleTalk Address Resolution Protocol (AARP) protocol enables a node to locate the MAC address of the next hop in the route.
Data-link-layer access protocols	At the Data-link layer, AppleTalk provides four link access protocols: EtherTalk Link Access Protocol (ELAP), LocalTalk Link Access Protocol (LLAP), TokenTalk Link Access Protocol (TLAP), and FDDITalk Link Access Protocol (FLAP).
Physical-layer components (EtherTalk, TokenTalk, FDDITalk, LocalTalk)	At the Physical layer, AppleTalk supports Ethernet, Token Ring, FDDI, and LocalTalk network hardware.

AppleTalk and TCP/IP Interoperability

Legacy AppleTalk networks can interoperate with TCP/IP-based networks. Apple and other third-party vendors provide AppleTalk over IP support to enable AppleTalk clients to communicate with servers on TCP/IP networks. The AppleShare IP file-sharing service enables AppleShare servers to provide web, file, and print resources to clients on TCP/IP networks. TCP/IP is supported natively in current Macintosh operating systems.

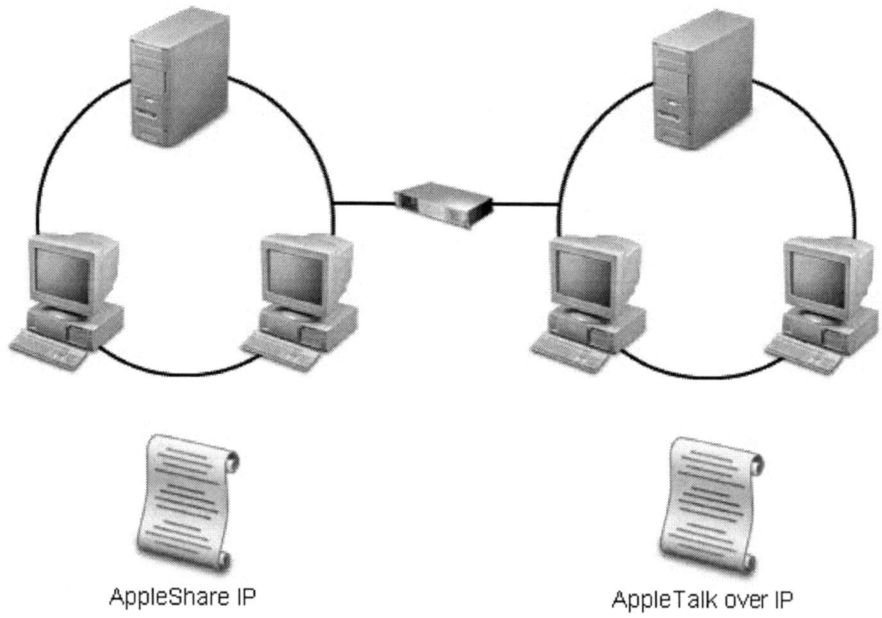

Figure 8-7: *AppleTalk and TCP/IP interoperability.*

AppleShare IP Features

The Apple Share IP server product provides a bundled set of LAN and Internet services to both Macintosh clients over AppleTalk and TCP/IP, and Windows clients running TCP/IP. It provides file and print services, a web server, an FTP server, built-in support for Windows file sharing, and mail services that support Internet standard mail protocols. It also includes an integrated administration console for managing AppleShare users, groups, and security.

Windows users who connect to an AppleShare IP server must have the same user name and password on Windows and on AppleShare IP. The AppleShare IP server uses the SMB protocol for file sharing, and will appear in the Network Neighborhood or My Network Places browsing tool on Windows systems. Windows clients can also connect to AppleShare IP servers by mapping drives or by using the Start→Run command and entering the AppleShare IP server name or IP address. Macintosh clients can use the Chooser to locate the AppleShare IP server.

AppleShare IP runs on Mac OS Server version 8 and version 9. The AppleShare IP functions and features are now integrated into the current Mac OS X Server product.

ACTIVITY 8-4

Installing the AppleTalk Protocol

There is a simulated version of this activity available on the CD-ROM that shipped with this course. You can run this simulation on any Windows computer to review the activity after class, or as an alternative to performing the activity as a group in class. The activity simulation can be launched either directly from the CD-ROM by clicking the Interactives link and navigating to the appropriate one, or from the installed data file location by opening the C:\Data\Simulations\Lesson#\Activity# folder and double-clicking the executable (.exe) file.

Scenario:

Your Windows-based network includes some legacy Macintosh clients that run the AppleTalk protocol. Windows servers that need to communicate with the Macintosh clients will need the AppleTalk protocol installed.

What You Do	How You Do It
1. **Open the properties of the Local Area Connection.**	a. **Choose Start→Control Panel→Network Connections.** b. **Right-click Local Area Connection and choose Properties.**
2. **Add the AppleTalk network protocol.**	a. **Click Install.** b. **Select Protocol and click Add.** c. In the Network Protocol list, **select AppleTalk Protocol and click OK.** d. **Verify that the protocol appears in the properties of the Local Area Connection and click Close.** 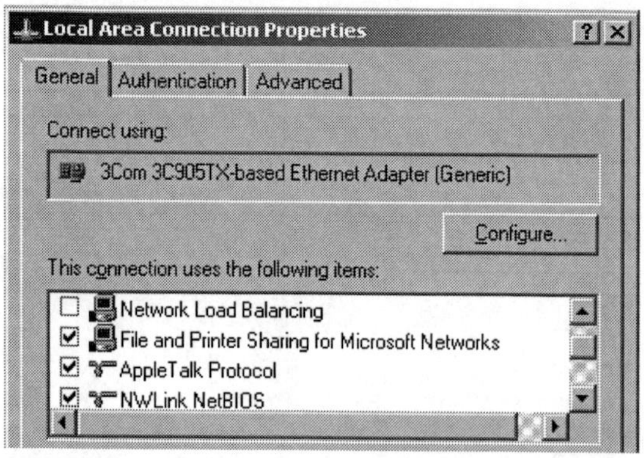

3. You administer an older mixed AppleTalk/Windows network. Windows users are complaining that they cannot locate the AppleShare IP server. You can see the server in the Chooser on your Macintosh client. How can you help the Windows clients connect?

4. A Windows 98 user is complaining that he cannot log on to the AppleShare IP server. No other Windows clients are having difficulty. What should you check?

TOPIC D

The IP Version 6 (IPv6) Protocol

In the previous topics, you looked at legacy protocols that might be implemented on older or mixed networks. In contrast, IP version 6 (IPv6) is in development as a new networking standard. In this topic, you will identify the components of an IPv6 protocol.

Any network professional who supports TCP/IP networking is aware of the limitations of the IPv4 addressing scheme. IPv6 is one option available to network administrators who need to overcome these limitations. If you support or configure networks that include this new standard protocol, you will need to understand its characteristics as well as how it can interoperate with existing IP implementations.

The IP Version 4 (IPv4) Address Space

The current version of TCP/IP is IP version 4, or IPv4. Although the theoretical address space of IPv4 is vast, its 32-bit address length and reliance on classful addressing inherently limits the number of actual addresses that are available. Classless subnetting, which uses the address space more efficiently, has been widely adopted, but the ultimate solution is to create a larger IP address space.

Limitations of IPv4

Limitations of IPv4 include:

- The 32-bit address space itself, which provides a theoretical maximum of 2^{32}, or approximately 4,295 billion, separate addresses.
- The division of the address space into fixed classes, the result being that node addresses falling between classes or between subnets are unavailable for assignment.
- The depletion of Class A and Class B network address assignments.
- The unassigned and unused address ranges within existing Class A and Class B blocks.

IPv6

IP version 6, or IPv6, is a proposed Internet standard that increases the available pool of IP addresses by implementing a 128-bit binary address space. IPv6 also includes new efficiency features, such as simplified address headers, hierarchical addressing, support for time-sensitive network traffic, and a new structure for unicast addressing.

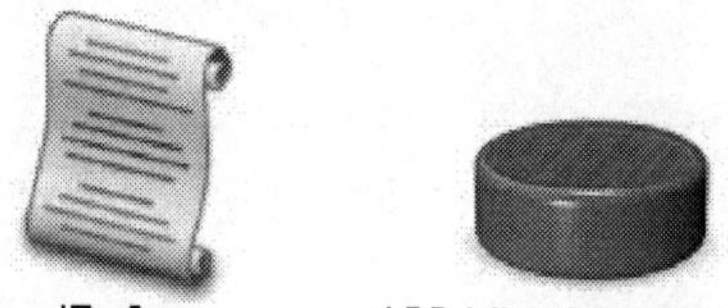

Figure 8-8: *IPv6.*

IPv6 is not compatible with IPv4, so at present it is narrowly deployed on a limited number of test and production networks. Full adoption of the IPv6 standard will require a general conversion of IP routers to support interoperability.

For more information on IPv6, see the IETF's IP Version 6 Working Group charter at **www.ietf.org/html.charters/ipv6-charter.html**.

Simplified Headers

One of the goals of IPv6 is to keep the IP headers as small as possible, to make access to the address more efficient and quicker. Non-essential information in IPv6 headers is moved to optional extension headers.

Hierarchical Addressing

In IPv6, address blocks are automatically assigned hierarchically by routers. Top-level routers have top-level address blocks, which are automatically divided and assigned as routers and segments are added. This divides the address space logically instead of randomly, making it easier to manage.

Time-Sensitive Data Support

A new field in the IP header of IPv6 packets enables IP to guarantee the allocation of network resources when requested by time-dependent services such as voice and video transmission.

Unicast Address Structure

IPv6 replaces classful addresses with a more flexible and logical unicast addressing structure. There are different categories of unicast addresses that serve different functions. Each network interface on a typical IPv6 host will be logically multihomed, which means that it will have more than one type of unicast address assigned.

Unicast Address Type	Description
Global addresses	Globally routable public addressess. Also known as aggregatable global unicast addresses, they are designed to be summarized to produce an efficient routing infrastructure. Global addresses are the equivalent of the entire IPv4 public address space.
Site-local addresses	Addresses used for internal networks that aren't routable on the Internet. The equivalent of the IPv4 private, nonroutable address blocks.
Link-local addresses	Addresses that are used to communicate, automatically assigned on private network segments with no router. The equivalent of APIPA addressing in IPv4.
IPv6 transitional addresses	Addresses are used on mixed networks to support routing of IPv6 data across IPv4 networks. This class will be phased out when all routers convert to IPv6.

IPv6 Addresses

The IPv6 address space provides an enormous number of possible address combinations. The 128-bit decimal address is divided into eight 16-bit blocks, which are expressed in hexadecimal, and divided by colons. To simplify the notation, blocks of zeros can be compressed. A sample IPv6 address might appear as fe80::260:8ff:fecd:3452.

Every IPv6 node is logically multihomed, which means that each network adapter always has at least two IPv6 addresses assigned.

For more information on IPv6 address types and address assignment on Windows systems, see the Internet Protocol Version 6 Technology Center on the Microsoft website at **www.microsoft.com/windowsserver2003/technologies/ipv6/default.mspx**.

- 128-bit decimal address:
  1111111010000000000000000000000000000000000000000000000000000000
  0000001001100000000010001111111111111110110011010011010001010010
- Divided into eight 16-bit blocks:
  1111111010000000.0000000000000000.0000000000000000.0000000000000000.
  0000001001100000.0000100011111111.1111111011001101.0011010001010010
- Expressed in hexadecimal:
  fe80:00000000:00000000:00000000:0260:08ff:fecd:3452
- Blocks of 0s are compressed:
  fe80::260:8ff:fecd:3452

Figure 8-9: *IPv6 addresses.*

The IPv6 Address Space

A 128-bit address provides 2^{128} possible different address combinations, which is approximately equal to the number 34 followed by 37 zeros. The actual number is 340,282,366,920,938,464,464,274,607,431,768,211,456.

ACTIVITY 8-5

Installing IPv6

There is a simulated version of this activity available on the CD-ROM that shipped with this course. You can run this simulation on any Windows computer to review the activity after class, or as an alternative to performing the activity as a group in class. The activity simulation can be launched either directly from the CD-ROM by clicking the Interactives link and navigating to the appropriate one, or from the installed data file location by opening the C:\Data\Simulations\Lesson#\Activity# folder and double-clicking the executable (.exe) file.

Scenario:

Your company will be implementing the IPv6 protocol on a test network. An infrastructure team will be installing the IPv6-compatible routers; your job is to add the protocol to the test systems and verify the installation.

What You Do	How You Do It
1. **Open the properties of the Local Area Connection.**	a. **Choose Start→Control Panel→Network Connections.**
	b. **Right-click Local Area Connection and choose Properties.**

2. **Add the IPv6 network protocol.**

   a. **Click Install.**

   b. **Select Protocol and click Add.**

   c. In the Network Protocol list, **select Microsoft TCP/IP Version 6 and click OK.**

   d. **Verify that the protocol appears in the properties of the Local Area Connection and click Close.**

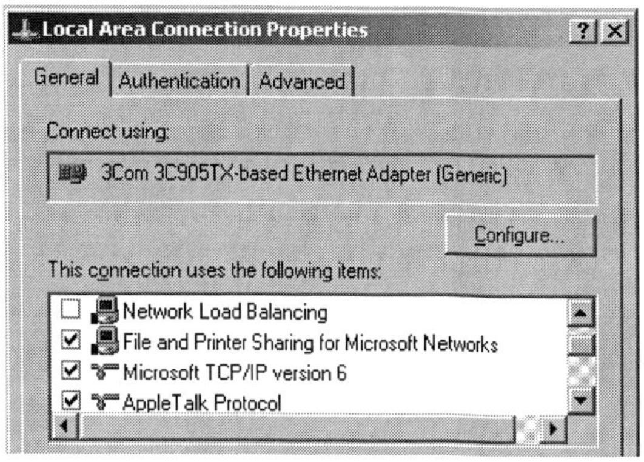

---

3. **Test the IPv6 configuration.**

   a. **Choose Start→Command Prompt.**

   b. To list the IPv6 network interfaces, **enter *netsh interface ipv6 show interface***

   c. To display the automatically-configured IPv6 network addresses, **enter *netsh interface ipv6 show address***

   d. To ping the IPv6 loopback address, **enter *ping ::1***

   e. **Close the command prompt window.**

Lesson 8 Follow-up

In this lesson, you identified the characteristics of a variety of network protocols. As a networking professional, you will need to understand the characteristics of those protocols in order to support and maintain the networks that run them.

1. **Have you ever encountered a network running a protocol other than TCP/IP? Which protocol?**

2. **Which of the protocols discussed in this lesson do you think you are most likely to encounter in your role as a network professional, and why?**

LESSON 9

Local Area Network (LAN) Infrastructure

Lesson Time
2 hour(s)

Lesson Objectives:

In this lesson, you will identify the components of a LAN implementation.

You will:

- Identify the functions of bridges and switches in LAN networking.
- Identify the components of LAN routing topology.
- Identify the components of a static routing implementation.
- Identify the components of a dynamic routing implementation.
- Identify the methods for controlling data movement with filters and VLANs.

Lesson 9

Introduction

In previous lessons, you have learned general information about a number of different network components and technologies. These technologies can be deployed either in local area networks (LANs) or wide area networks (WANs). In this lesson, you will identify the components of a LAN implementation.

The LAN is the fundamental unit of computer networking—computers in close proximity connected together to share resources between groups. No matter where your career as a network professional takes you, you'll always need to have a thorough understanding of the components of a LAN implementation.

This lesson covers the following CompTIA Network+ (2005) certification objectives:

- Topic A:
  - Objective 1.6: Identify the purposes, features, and functions of switches and bridges.
- Topic B:
  - Objective 1.6: Identify the purposes, features, and functions of routers.
- Topic C:
  - Objective 1.6: Identify the purposes, features, and functions of routers.
- Topic D:
  - Objective 1.6: Identify the purposes, features, and functions of routers.
- Topic E:
  - Objective 1.6: Identify the purposes, features, and functions of switches and routers.
  - Objective 2.3: Identify the OSI (Open Systems Interconnection) layers at which switches and routers operate.
  - Objective 3.7: Given a connectivity scenario, determine the impact on network functionality of a particular security implementation (for example, port blocking and filtering, authentication, and encryption).
  - Objective 3.8: Identify the main characteristics of VLANs (virtual local area networks).

TOPIC A

Bridges and Switches

In this lesson, you will identify the components of a LAN implementation. Bridges and switches are often implemented in LANs. In this topic, you will identify the functions of bridges and switches in LAN networking.

Next to hubs, bridges and switches are the most fundamental LAN connectivity devices, so it's very likely that you will encounter them in the network environments you support. In addition, bridges and switches provide features and functions that make them slightly more complex to manage than a simple Ethernet hub. Understanding the capabilities of these LAN devices will prepare you to support bridged and switched network environments on the job.

The Bridge Routing Table

Bridges eavesdrop on network traffic and capture the source address for each data packet that is sent on the local network. From this capture, the bridge dynamically builds a table (known as a *bridge routing table*) of all the MAC addresses on each of its interfaces. The nodes' MAC addresses in the routing table correspond to the bridge interfaces that support those nodes. This system makes bridges self-configuring and easy to install and administer.

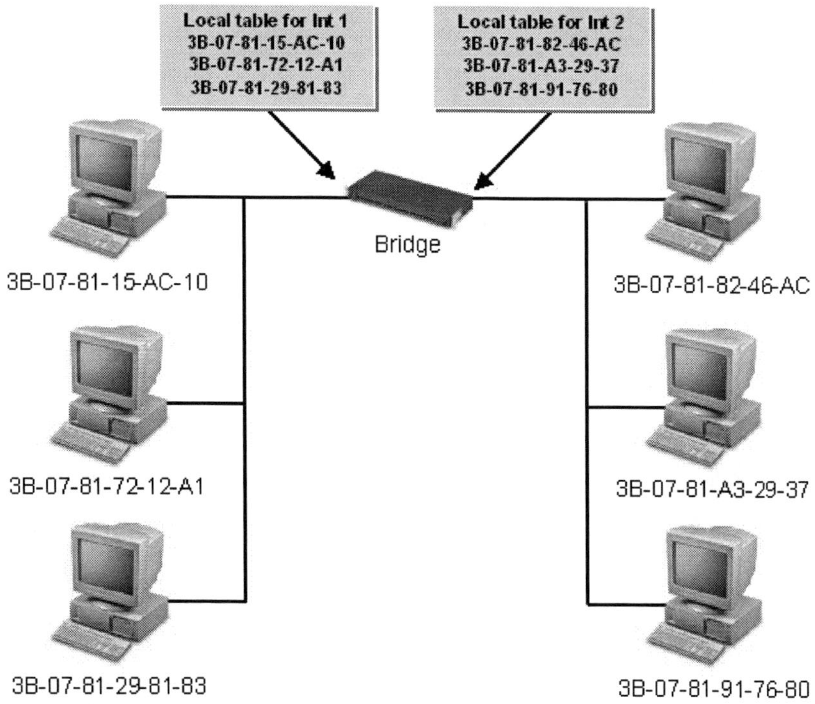

Figure 9-1: *A bridge routing table.*

Bridge Broadcasting

Bridges are designed to stop unicast transmissions bound for the local subnet from moving on to the remote subnet. This keeps local traffic within the local network. However, because broadcasts don't have a single address, the bridge sends internetwork broadcasts to every interface. In networks with heavy broadcast traffic, a bridge does very little to quiet it down.

A lot of network services need broadcasts to operate, but there are also non-broadcast-based services that don't. When choosing which network services to implement in a network, try to choose those that don't use broadcasts.

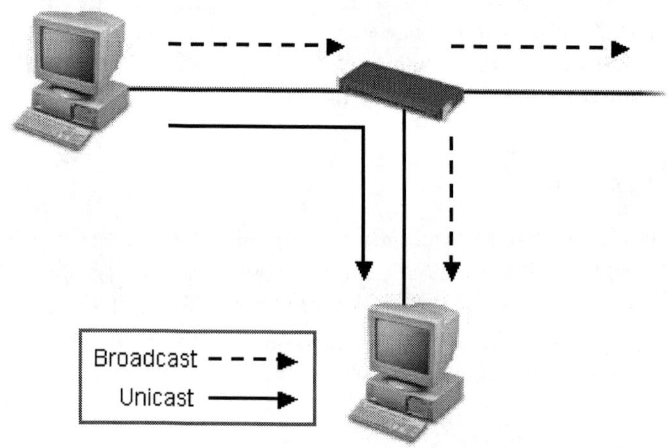

Figure 9-2: *Bridge broadcasting.*

Types of Bridges

There are several types of bridges that you can deploy in your network.

Type of Bridge	Description
Transparent	Bridges with the same type of network, such as Ethernet, on all interfaces are called transparent bridges because they don't change or affect the data at all—they just forward unchanged packets between networks.
Source-route	Source-route bridges were designed for use in Token Ring networks. These bridges make decisions about how to forward packets based on routing information included in the packet.
Translational	When a company needs two types of networks, such as Ethernet and Token Ring, to exchange data, a translational bridge can be placed in between the two networks. Translational bridges connect dissimilar network types using an interface that supports requirements of each network. The interface contains circuitry that supports both network types. Translational bridges have to change data into a format compatible with the new network. This includes changing and supporting the access method.

Type of Bridge	Description
Remote	Remote bridges connect different networks across a remote connection. A remote bridge's primary function is to reduce unnecessary traffic sent across the remote link and preserve bandwidth for valuable data. The remote bridge connects to another bridge, placing data on the remote network. Remote bridges can use CAN/MAN or WAN connections, but keep in mind that most times, a remote link has less bandwidth than the local LAN does. Remote bridges are simpler and easier to configure than routers and can connect across public media like a leased phone line, fiber optic link, or wireless media. When using a remote bridge to connect across any on-demand connection, the bridge will be configured to make and drop the connection as needed.

Switch Performance

Switches are designed to add functionality and increase performance on LANs. The main purpose of a switch is to optimize performance by providing users with greater access to bandwidth. Switches inspect data packets as they are received from the source device and forward packets only to the port that connects to the destination device. The traffic between two devices can be isolated to allow the switch port and destination device to operate in full duplex mode. Because a switch forwards data directly to the intended destination, it significantly increases network performance.

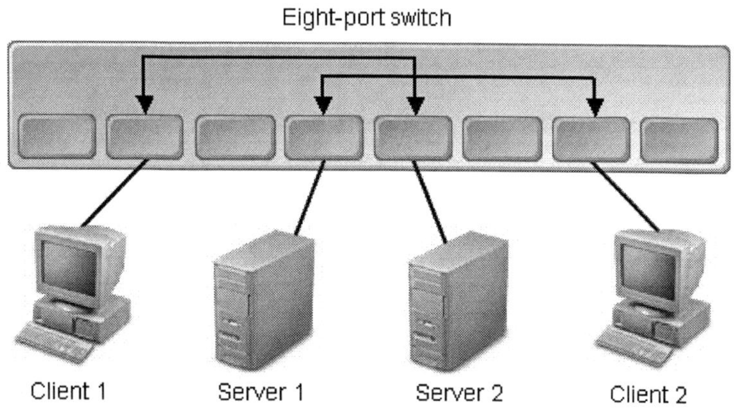

Figure 9-3: *Connections within a switch isolate traffic between two ports.*

ACTIVITY 9-1

Exploring Bridge and Switch Functionality

Scenario:

In this activity, you will identify the functions of bridges and switches in LAN implementations.

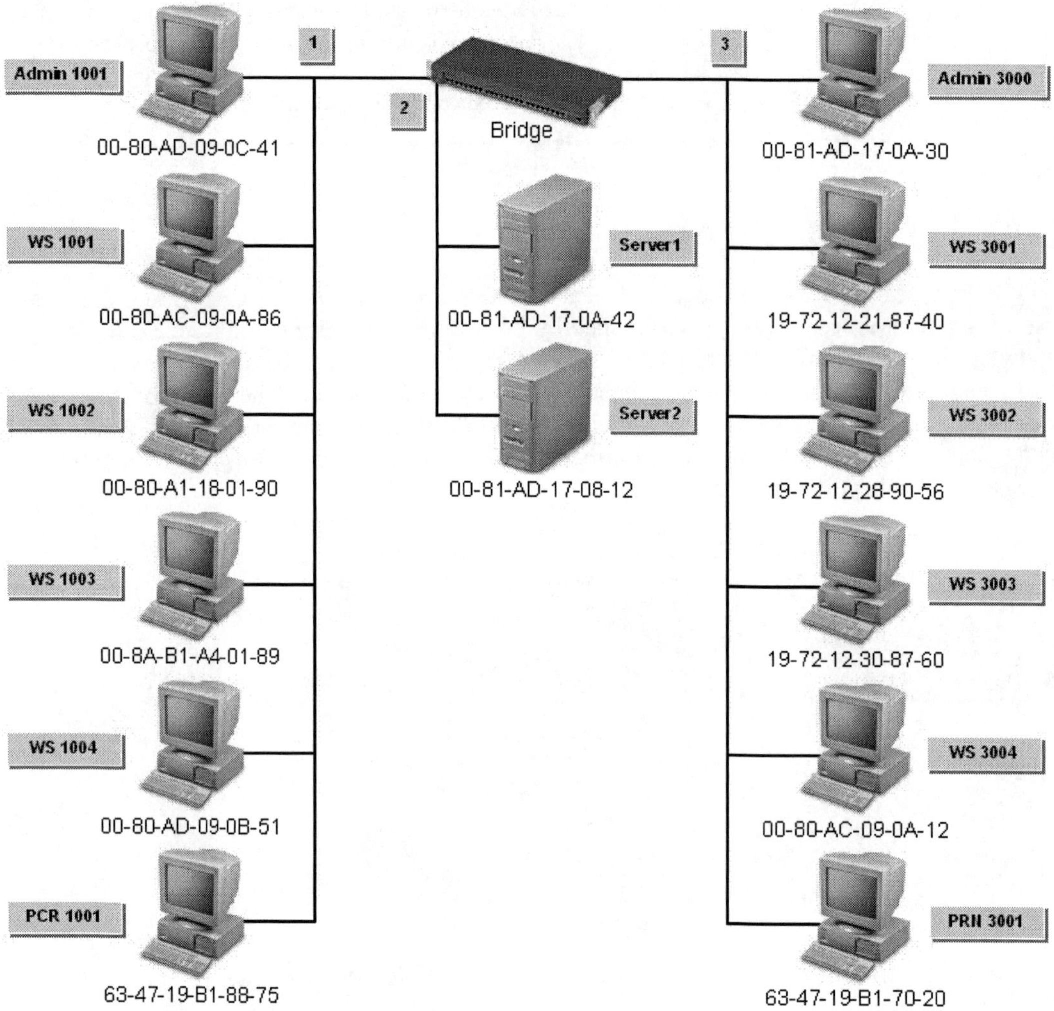

Figure 9-4: *A sample bridged network.*

1. **In the sample bridged network, which of the following MAC addresses would a bridge add to its routing table for its Interface 1?**

   a) 00-80-AD-09-0C-41

   b) 63-47-19-B1-70-20

   c) 00-80-A1-18-01-90

   d) 00-81-AD-17-0A-42

   e) 19-72-12-28-90-56

2. **In the sample bridged network, which of the following MAC addresses would a bridge add to its routing table for its Interface 3?**

   a) 00-81-AD-17-0A-42

   b) 00-80-A1-18-01-90

   c) 00-80-AC-09-0A-12

   d) 63-47-19-B1-70-20

   e) 00-80-0A-09-0C-41

3. **Match the bridge type with the description.**

___	Remote bridge	a.	Used to connect an Ethernet and a Token Ring network.
___	Translational bridge	b.	Used to divide a network without modifying data.
___	Transparent bridge	c.	Used across a CAN, MAN, or WAN connection.
___	Source-route	d.	Used in Token Ring networks.

4. **True or False? A switch improves network performance by isolating traffic between two ports.**

   __ True

   __ False

5. **True or False? Unlike bridges, switches do not flood broadcasts.**

   __ True

   __ False

TOPIC B

IP Routing Topology

In the previous topic, you examined bridges and switches and their role in a LAN implementation. Routers are another common LAN infrastructure device. In this topic, you will identify the components of LAN routing topology.

Bridges and switches function well in many network situations, but in most large TCP/IP networks, you'll need the more advanced traffic-control capabilities of a router. Because routers are the workhorses of all internetworks, including the Internet, you'll need to understand routing basics no matter what kind of network you support.

The Routing Process

When a router receives data, it reads the data's IP address and tries to find the best path. The router looks in a table or map of the network. Once it decides on a route, it removes the old destination MAC address and attaches the new MAC address of the next hop in the data's path. The data's ultimate destination IP address never changes. By enabling the router to change the MAC address, the data can move through multiple local networks.

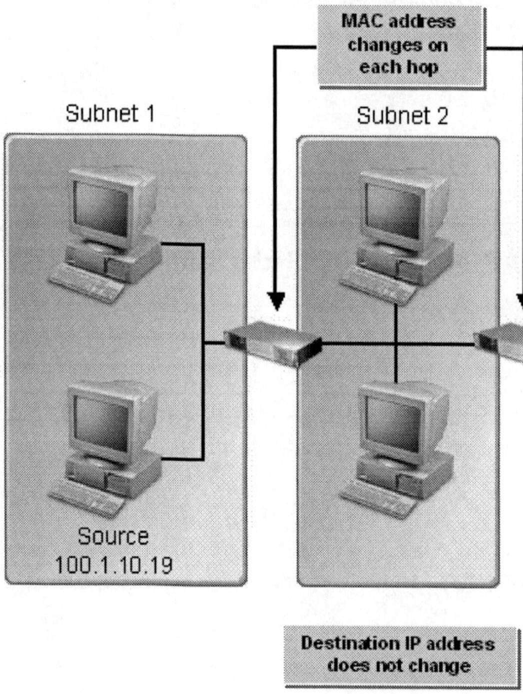

Figure 9-5: *The routing process.*

Routers vs. Switches

When computers communicate with different networks through switches, they're limited to adjacent networks because switches use the MAC address. Routers, on the other hand, are designed to interconnect multiple networks and support connectivity to distant networks. They use a map of the network to make decisions on where to forward data packets. Routers seem to be complicated devices, but their sole job is to determine the next hop for data.

Another advantage that a router has over a switch is that it can read the port number and determine not only the data's destination but also what kind of data it is (because it's aware of the IP address). Broadcasts can either be forwarded or dumped, based on the rule of the router. Most routers dump broadcasts.

Software-Based Routing in Windows Server

Although not as common as hardware-based routers, Windows Server computers with two or more network interface cards installed can use the Routing and Remote Access software to function as routers. For testing purposes, instead of installing two NICs, you can install a software-based interface called the Microsoft Loopback Adapter on your Windows system, which can simulate the presence of a separate NIC.

Small Office Routers

Routing in a small office/home office (SOHO) network does not require the same level of router hardware as large networks and the Internet. There are several popular, relatively inexpensive, and easy to implement router products that are designed to support both wired and wireless SOHO networks, available from companies such as D-Link, Linksys, and NETGEAR.

Autonomous Systems (AS)

Definition:

An *autonomous system (AS)* is a self-contained network or group of networks connected to the Internet that deploys a single protocol and has a single administration. All the routers in the AS share and conform to a single routing policy. An AS can connect to other networks or other autonomous systems, but does not share routing information outside the AS.

Example:

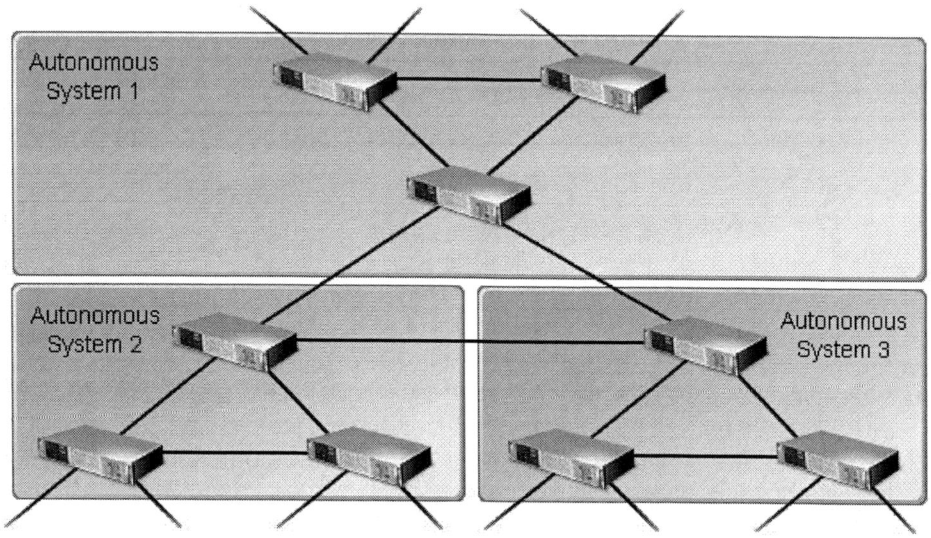

Figure 9-6: *Autonomous systems.*

Router Roles in Autonomous Systems

Routers can play three different roles in autonomous systems.

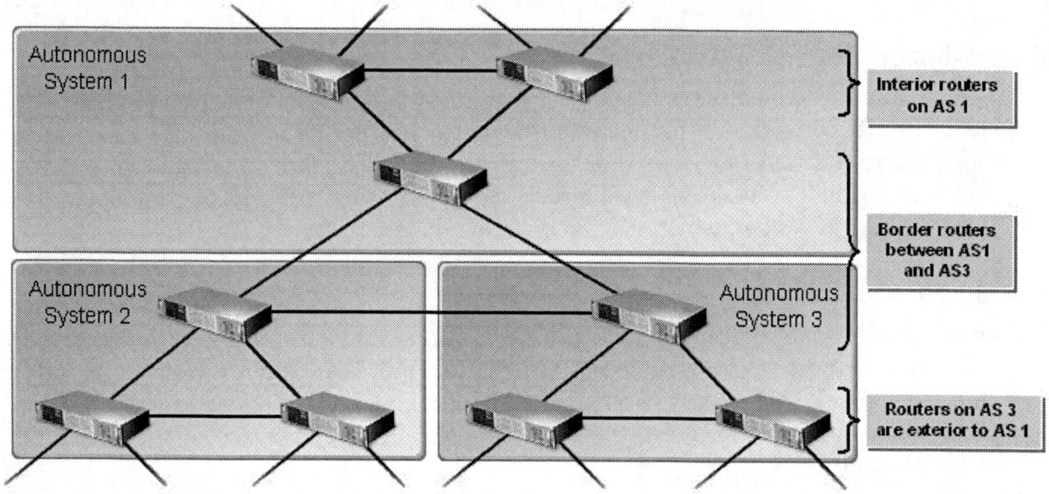

Figure 9-7: *Router roles.*

Router Role	Description
Interior router	*Interior routers* are arranged inside the AS and are completely controlled by the AS administrator. All interfaces on an interior router are connected to subnets inside the AS. Interior routers do not provide connections to other networks.
Exterior router	An *exterior router* is any router entirely outside the AS. These routers only matter to the AS if they handle data from the AS.
Border router	*Border routers* are situated on the edge of an AS. They have one or more interfaces inside the AS and one or more interfaces that provide a connection to remote networks. Border routers are usually managed by the administrator of one AS and can be placed between two private networks or between a private network and a public network like the Internet.

Routing Inside an Autonomous System

When routing inside a network, data starts at a workstation and doesn't leave the AS. That means that when any node sends data, it can only send it to a node on the same local network. Nodes use the ARP protocol to obtain the local destination's MAC address. When a node needs to send data to a remote network, it sends it to the IP address configured as the node's default gateway. When a node sends data to an address on its own subnet, it sends it directly to the address. When a node needs to send data to a node anywhere inside the AS, all routers in the AS should be aware of the path to the destination node.

Routing Between Adjacent Networks

Adjacent networks share border routers, and because any router inside the AS knows a direct path to the adjacent network, it knows how to deliver data to the correct border router. That border router then passes the data on to the appropriate network. This configuration gives an AS a single point of contact between adjacent networks.

Routing Between Distant Networks

Distant networks aren't directly aware of the location of a destination network. You've experienced a distant network if you've sent a request to the Internet for a web page. There is no way that any AS router can possibly know all of the details in the path to the website. In this situation, the routers send the data to the default gateway. If the router serving as the default gateway doesn't know the destination location, it transmits the packet to its own default gateway. The data moves from default gateway to default gateway until it either reaches a router that knows a route to the destination, or the TTL expires and the packet expires on the network.

Activity 9-2

Installing Multiple Network Adapters

There is a simulated version of this activity available on the CD-ROM that shipped with this course. You can run this simulation on any Windows computer to review the activity after class, or as an alternative to performing the activity as a group in class. The activity simulation can be launched either directly from the CD-ROM by clicking the Interactives link and navigating to the appropriate one, or from the installed data file location by opening the C:\Data\Simulations\Lesson#\Activity# folder and double-clicking the executable (.exe) file.

Scenario:

You work for a small company that plans to implement software-based routing by using Windows Server 2003 routing features. You need set up the computer for testing in the lab by installing and configuring the loopback adapter as a second network connection. The second adapter will be the interface to the 172.16.0.0 network. You will also need to configure your primary adapter with a static address.

What You Do	How You Do It
1. **Install the Microsoft Loopback Adapter.**	a. **Choose Start→Control Panel→Add Hardware.**
	b. **Click Next.**
	c. After the hardware search is complete, **select Yes, I Have Already Connected The Hardware and click Next.**

d. At the bottom of the Installed Hardware list, **select Add A New Hardware Device and click Next.**

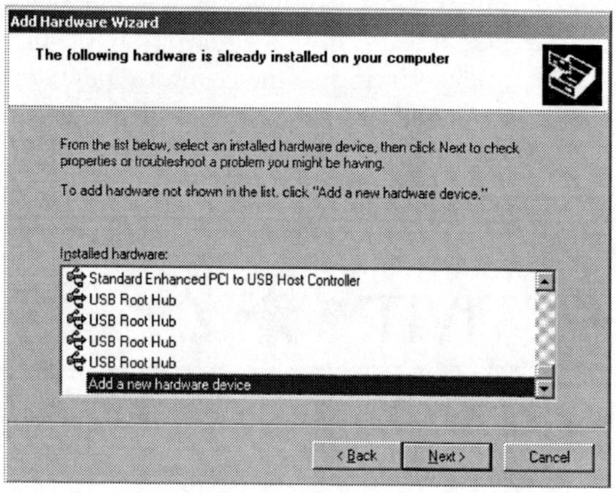

e. **Select Install The Hardware That I Manually Select From A List (Advanced) and click Next.**

f. **Select Network Adapters and click Next.**

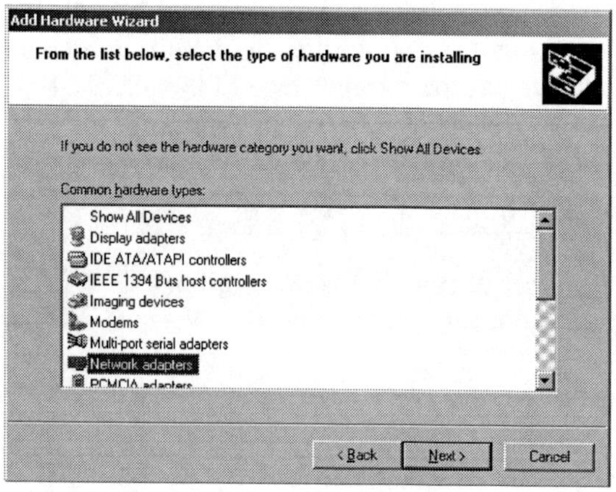

g. Under Manufacturer, **verify that Microsoft is selected.** Under Network Adapter, **select Microsoft Loopback Adapter and click Next.**

h. **Click Next** to begin the installation.

i. When the installation is complete, **click Finish.**

2. **Configure the new network interface.**

a. **Choose Start→Control Panel→Network Connections.**

b. **Right-click Local Area Connection 2 and choose Properties.**

c. **Select Internet Protocol (TCP/IP) and click Properties.**

d. **Select Use The Following IP Address.**

e. In the IP Address text box, **type *172.16.0.##***, where ## is your assigned number.

f. **Press Tab** to auto-populate the subnet mask.

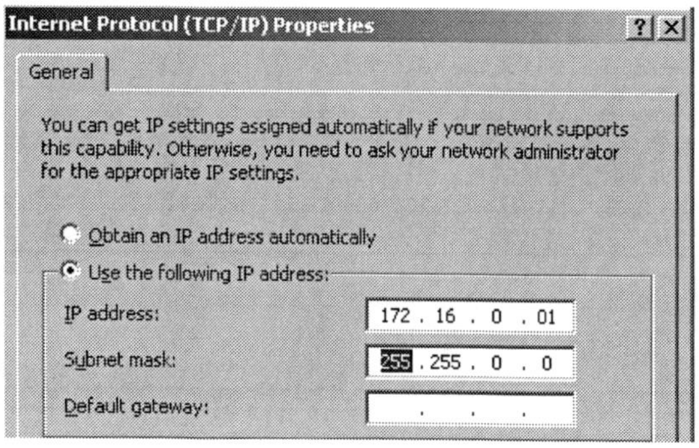

g. **Click OK and then click Close.**

3. **Configure the Local Area Connection with a static IP address.**

   a. **Choose Start→Control Panel→Network Connections.**

   b. **Right-click Local Area Connection.**

   c. **Choose Properties.**

   d. In the This Connection Uses The Following Items box, **select Internet Protocol (TCP/IP).**

   e. **Click Properties.**

   f. **Select Use The Following IP Address.**

   g. In the IP Address box, **type *192.168.1.##*,** where ## is your student number.

   h. **Click in the Subnet Mask box.**

   i. In the Default Gateway box, **type *192.168.1.200***

   j. **Verify that Use The Following DNS Server Address is selected.**

   k. In the Preferred DNS Server Address box, **type *192.168.1.200***

   l. **Click OK** to close the Internet Protocol (TCP/IP) Properties dialog box.

   m. **Click Close** to close the Local Area Connection Properties dialog box.

ACTIVITY 9-3

Enabling Routing on Windows Server 2003

There is a simulated version of this activity available on the CD-ROM that shipped with this course. You can run this simulation on any Windows computer to review the activity after class, or as an alternative to performing the activity as a group in class. The activity simulation can be launched either directly from the CD-ROM by clicking the Interactives link and navigating to the appropriate one, or from the installed data file location by opening the C:\Data\Simulations\Lesson#\Activity# folder and double-clicking the executable (.exe) file.

Setup:

Routing and Remote Access is installed on Windows Server 2003 by default.

Scenario:

You work for a small company that plans to implement software-based routing by using Windows Server 2003 routing features. You are going to test a router in a lab environment to simulate the production router. You need to enable routing on the server that you will be testing.

What You Do	How You Do It
1. Enable the router.	

a. Choose Start→Administrative Tools→Routing And Remote Access.

b. Select Computer## (Local).

c. Choose Action→Configure And Enable Routing And Remote Access.

d. Click Next.

e. Select Custom Configuration and click Next.

f. Check LAN Routing and click Next.

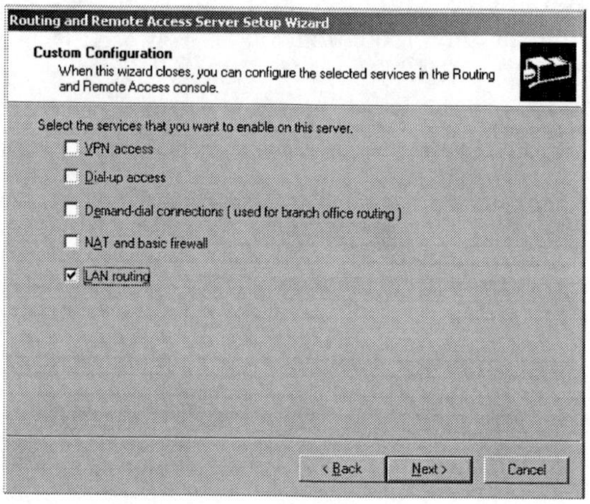

g. Click Finish.

h. Click Yes to start the Routing And Remote Access service.

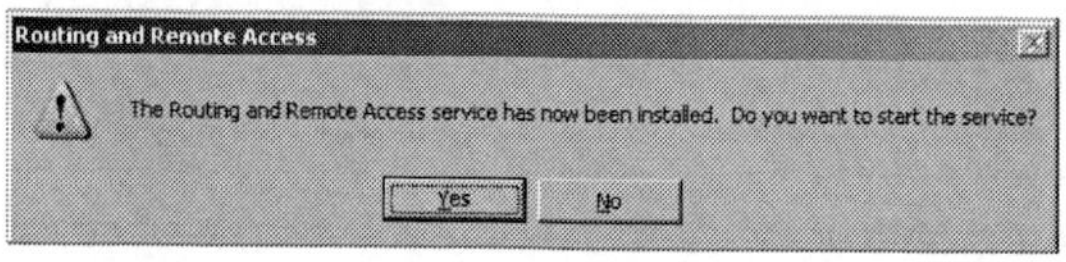

2. **Verify the router configuration.**

a. After the routing service starts and the router object expands, **select Network Interfaces** to verify that both your network connections are listed.

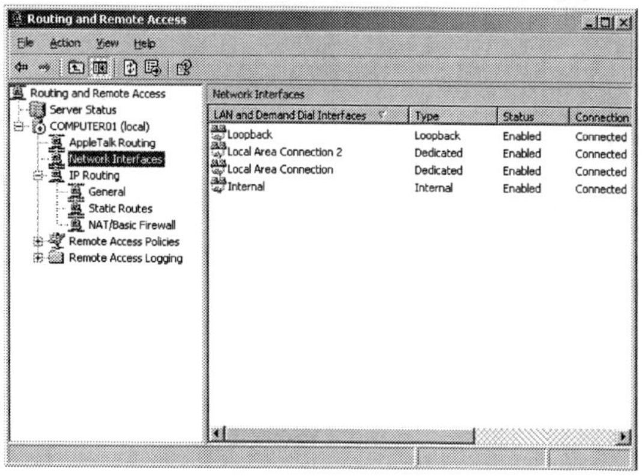

b. Under IP Routing, **select General** to verify that both your IP addresses appear.

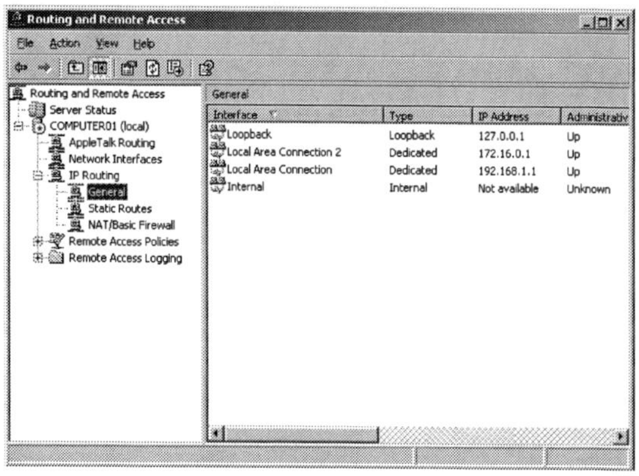

c. **Close Routing And Remote Access.**

TOPIC C

Static IP Routing

In the previous topic, you identified the components of LAN routing topology. There are two general types of routing implementations: static and dynamic. In this topic, you will identify the components of a static routing implementation.

Even though static routing, like static IP addressing, isn't something you deploy on large networks, the concepts of static routing still form the basis of all routing structures. Understanding the elements of static routing will help you deploy and manage any type of routed environment.

Routing Tables

Definition:

A *routing table* is a database created manually or by a route discovery protocol that contains network locations as perceived by a specific router. Each router uses its routing table to forward a packet to another network or router until the packet reaches its destination. You can specify the number of *hops* that packets can take from sender to receiver.

Example: Routing Table Information

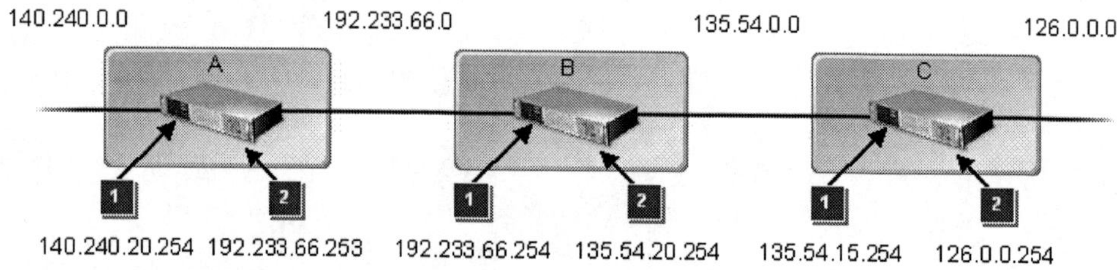

Figure 9-8: *A sample network with three routers.*

The following table lists the routing entries for router A.

Table 9-1: *Routing Entries for Router A.*

Destination	Next Hop	Type	Cost	Interface
140.240.0.0	140.240.20.254	Direct	1	1
192.233.66.0	192.233.66.253	Direct	1	2
135.54.0.0	192.233.66.254	Remote	2	2
126.0.0.0	192.233.66.254	Remote	3	2

Route Cost

The action of forwarding a packet from one router to the next is called a hop. The number of hops along a route between two networks constitutes that route's *cost*. However, a cost can also consist of other specifications, such as speed. Typically, a router maintains the most cost-effective route in its table.

Static Routing Tables

Static routing tables are manually configured on the router. They're easy to set up and are sometimes used on a small network. Also, as long as a network is relatively unchanging, static routing tables are ideal for an extranet situation where the border router of the AS is pointed toward the border router of the partner company.

The advantage of static routing is that it doesn't cause extra network traffic sending routing table updates to other routers. It provides extra security from other systems' rogue routers sending information to the AS routers. Also, the routing table can be configured to cover only the necessary portion of the network. That way the router doesn't expend resources maintaining a dynamic routing table.

The biggest disadvantage to static routing tables is that they require manual maintenance. Any network changes have to be updated manually on all routers affected by the change. Because of this, it's critical to maintain detailed documentation when using static routing tables.

Routing Entry Components

There are several components to each entry in a routing table.

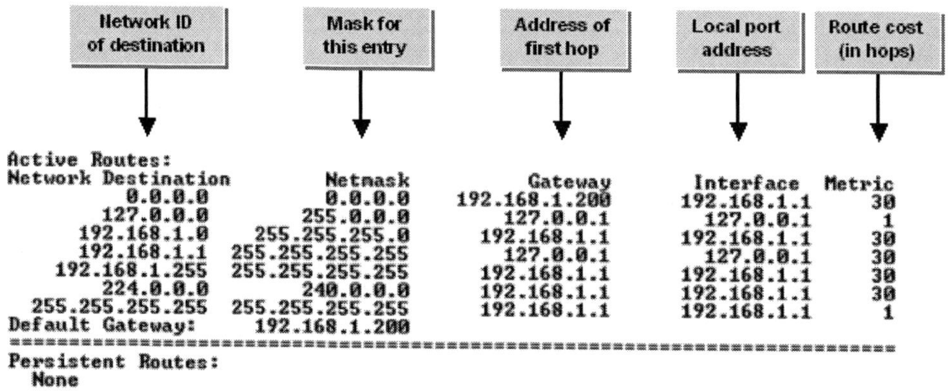

Figure 9-9: *Routing entry components.*

Routing Field	Description
Network destination (network address)	The destination field contains the network ID of the destination address and is the search point when processing the routing table. It can be listed as a complete address but the router will be more efficient if the destination entries are listed as network IDs. This way only one entry is added to the routing table for an entire subnet no matter how many nodes are on it.
Network mask	The network mask is specific to a routing entry. It determines how much of a packet's destination address must match the network destination field of the routing entry before that route is used to deliver the packet.
Gateway	The gateway field indicates the address to which the packet is delivered on its first hop. It can be the local loopback address, a local IP address, the host's own default gateway address, or the address of another adjacent router.

Routing Field	Description
Interface	The interface is the IP address of the local port that the host uses to send the data. Once the destination entry is found, the data is sent to the interface entry listed on the same line as the destination.
Metric	The metric is the cost of the route, and it's determined by the number of hops. The metric is used to determine which route to use when there are multiple routes to a destination.

Routing Table Entries

Routing table entries fall into four general categories:

- Direct network routes, for subnets to which the router is directly attached.
- Remote network routes, for subnets that are not directly attached.
- Host routes, for routes to a specific IP address.
- Default routes, which are used when a better network or host route isn't found.

All IP host computers have a routing table with default entries so that the host can deliver packets to common destinations.

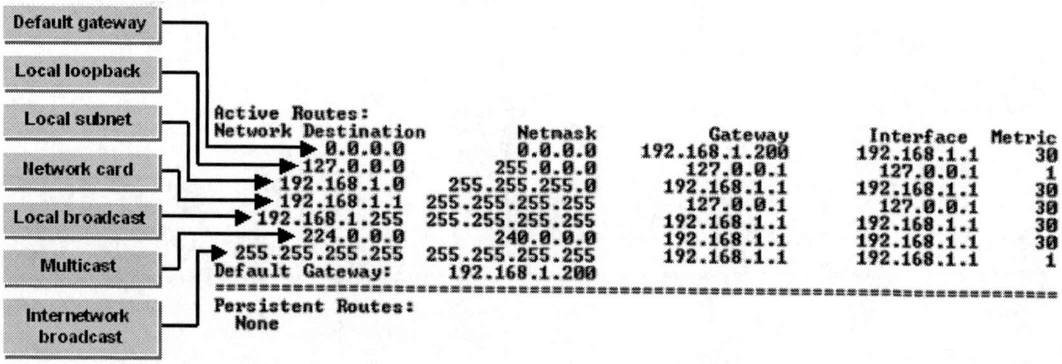

Figure 9-10: *Typical default routing table entries.*

Routing Entry	Description
Default gateway (destination: 0.0.0.0)	The default gateway entry appears if the local host has been configured with a default gateway address.
Local loopback (destination: 127.0.0.0)	The local loopback entry provides a delivery route for packets addressed to the local loopback address (127.0.0.1).
Local subnet (destination: network portion of local IP address plus host address of all .0)	The local subnet entry identifies the route to the local network. A sample destination address is 140.125.0.0.
Network interface (destination: local IP address)	The network interface entry identifies the route to the host's local network card. A sample destination address is 140.125.10.25.

Routing Entry	Description
Subnet broadcast address (destination: network portion of local IP address plus host address of all .255)	The subnet broadcast entry identifies the route for broadcasts on the local subnet. A sample destination address is 140.125.255.255.
Multicast broadcast address (destination: 224.0.0.0)	The multicast broadcast entry identifies the route for sending multicasts.
Internetwork broadcast address (destination: 255.255.255.255)	The internetwork broadcast entry identifies the route for broadcasts to the entire network. However, most routers will not pass these broadcasts.

The Route Command

Routes to destinations that are not in the default routing table must be added manually. On a Windows Server 2003 computer, you can use the route command to manage the static routing table.

Command	Function
`route print`	Display the routing table entries.
`route add`	Add static entries.
`route delete`	Remove static entries.
`route change`	Modify an existing route.

ACTIVITY 9-4

Examining Routing Entries

There is a simulated version of this activity available on the CD-ROM that shipped with this course. You can run this simulation on any Windows computer to review the activity after class, or as an alternative to performing the activity as a group in class. The activity simulation can be launched either directly from the CD-ROM by clicking the Interactives link and navigating to the appropriate one, or from the installed data file location by opening the C:\Data\Simulations\Lesson#\Activity# folder and double-clicking the executable (.exe) file.

Setup:

Routing has been enabled in Routing and Remote Access.

Scenario:

You want to identify the default routing entries on the Windows Server 2003 computer that you have enabled as a router.

What You Do	How You Do It
1. **Open the routing table.**	a. **Choose Start→Command Prompt.**

b. Enter *route print*

```
Microsoft Windows [Version 5.2.3790]
(C) Copyright 1985-2003 Microsoft Corp.

C:\Documents and Settings\User01>route print

IPv4 Route Table
===========================================================================
Interface List
0x1 ........................... MS TCP Loopback interface
0x10003 ...00 0e 7f 65 a4 85 ...... Broadcom NetXtreme Gigabit Ethernet for hp
0x10004 ...02 00 4c 4f 4f 50 ...... Microsoft Loopback Adapter
===========================================================================
===========================================================================
Active Routes:
Network Destination        Netmask          Gateway       Interface  Metric
          0.0.0.0          0.0.0.0    192.168.1.200    192.168.1.1     20
        127.0.0.0        255.0.0.0        127.0.0.1      127.0.0.1      1
       172.16.0.0      255.255.0.0       172.16.0.1     172.16.0.1     30
       172.16.0.1  255.255.255.255        127.0.0.1      127.0.0.1     30
   172.16.255.255  255.255.255.255       172.16.0.1     172.16.0.1     30
      192.168.1.0    255.255.255.0      192.168.1.1    192.168.1.1     20
      192.168.1.1  255.255.255.255        127.0.0.1      127.0.0.1     20
    192.168.1.255  255.255.255.255      192.168.1.1    192.168.1.1     20
        224.0.0.0        240.0.0.0       172.16.0.1     172.16.0.1     30
        224.0.0.0        240.0.0.0      192.168.1.1    192.168.1.1     20
  255.255.255.255  255.255.255.255       172.16.0.1     172.16.0.1      1
  255.255.255.255  255.255.255.255      192.168.1.1    192.168.1.1      1
Default Gateway:     192.168.1.200
===========================================================================
Persistent Routes:
  None
```

c. When you have finished examining the routing entries, **close the command prompt window.**

2. **Which route determines the destination for packets to the 172.16.0.0 network? What adapter will they be delivered to?**

3. **Which interfaces will receive internetwork broadcasts? How can you tell?**

4. **Why is there no route to the 0.0.0.0 network destination on the 172.16.0.## interface?**

5. **If you wanted packets to a specific network to be routed to the 172.16.0.## network interface instead of to the default gateway, what would you do?**

TOPIC D

Dynamic IP Routing

In the previous topic, you identified the components of a static routing implementation. Routing can also be implemented dynamically. In this topic, you will identify the components of a dynamic routing implementation.

Dynamic routing, like dynamic IP addressing, is the technology of choice in most larger network environments. As a network professional, you should understand dynamic routing technologies and how they are implemented so that you can support routed environments of all sizes and types.

Dynamic Routing

Routers that support dynamic routing perform route discovery operations to build and update the routing tables themselves. Dynamically built routing tables can show a more accurate picture of the network as it changes than static tables can because the routers, not the administrator, update the tables. This is a huge advantage on large networks with many routers or multiple paths to multiple endpoints.

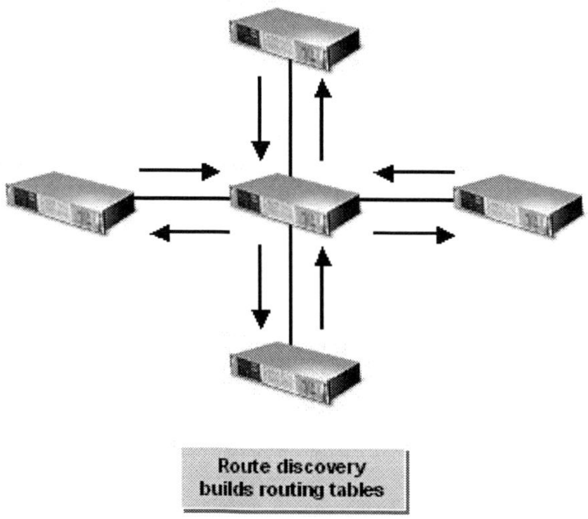

Figure 9-11: *Dynamic routing.*

efficient

Distance-Vector Routing

In distance-vector routing, each router passes a copy of its routing table to its adjacent neighbors. The neighbor adds the route to its own table, incrementing the metric to reflect the extra distance to the end network. The distance is given as a hop count; the vector component specifies the address of the next hop. When a router has two routes to the same network, it selects the one with the lowest metric, assuming that it's faster to route through fewer hops.

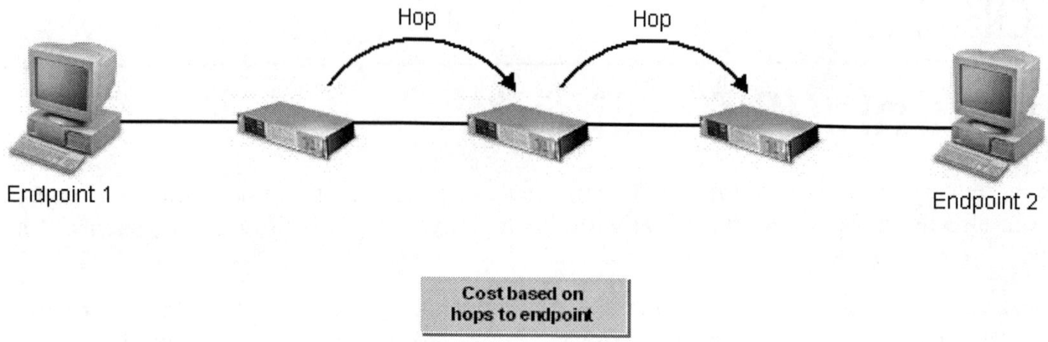

Figure 9-12: *Distance-vector routing.*

Implementing Distance-Vector Routing

Distance-vector routing is easy to set up—all you need to configure are the router's local interfaces. The rest is configured through discovery. The drawback to distance-vector routing is that there isn't a way to differentiate between different routes based on bandwidth and quality. Typically, this is acceptable for routers inside an AS where the links and bandwidth are the same. However, when routing between multiple autonomous systems where WAN links might be involved, distance-vector treats all links the same, giving the same priority to a dial-up line with a 56 Kbps bandwidth as it does to a T1 line with 1.544 Mbps bandwidth.

Link-State Routing

Link-state routing attempts to build and maintain a more complex route database with more information about the network. Routers can exchange information about a route, such as its quality, bandwidth, and availability. This way the routers can make a decision about sending data through the network based on more than hop count.

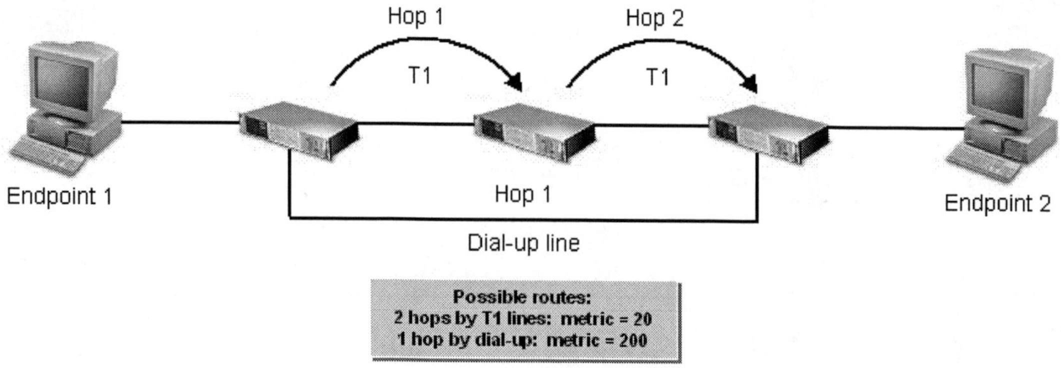

Figure 9-13: *Link-state routing.*

Link-State vs. Distance-Vector Routing

To understand the difference between the link-state and distance-vector algorithms, consider a routing situation in which a packet can be delivered over a single dial-up connection or over two separate T1 links. Distance-vector prefers the dial-up based on hop count alone; link-state prefers the two-hop route through the higher bandwidth connections. Also, link-state is more complicated to set up and maintain than distance-vector. An administrator has to configure more information about the routers' local routes. However, link-state routers are a must in situations with multiple routes through different types of connections, such as border routers.

Convergence

In dynamic routing, when network topology or conditions change, each router must first learn of the change and then calculate the effect and update its routing tables. Convergence is the period of time between the network change and the router updates. During convergence, data delivery can be unreliable.

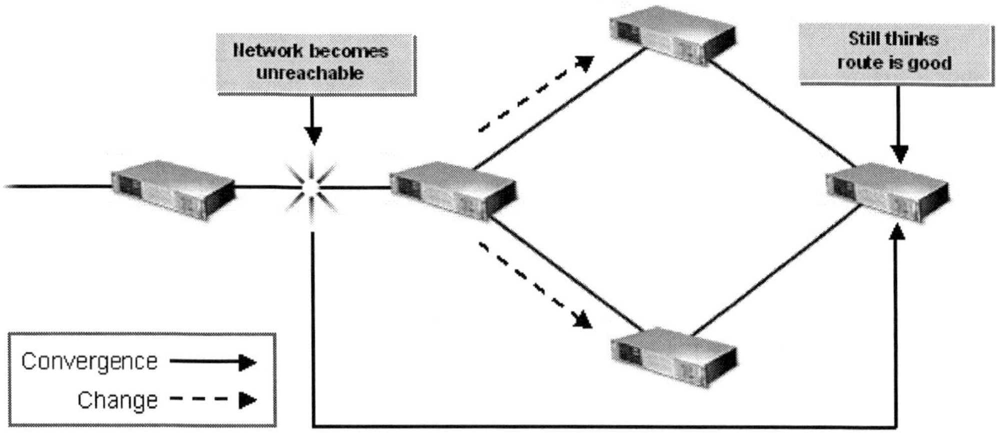

Figure 9-14: *Convergence.*

Count-to-Infinity Loops

A count-to-infinity loop can occur when a router or network goes down if one of the remaining routers does not realize that a route can no longer be reached. Routers broadcast incorrect information and update each other's routing tables to create an endless cycle of hop count recalculation. This cycle continues to infinity, which is configured as 16 hops in most routing implementations.

Example: A Count-to-Infinity Loop

For example, imagine four routers that connect five networks. In calculating the cost to network E, router 3 figures its cost to be one hop, router 2 figures two hops, and router 1 figures three hops. If router 4 fails, router 3 must recalculate its routing table using information from other routing partners. However, it still thinks that network E can be reached, and uses information advertised from router 2 to calculate its table. According to router 2, network E is two hops away, so router 3 broadcasts that its cost to network E is three hops. Router 1 receives the new information from router 3, updates its table, and then broadcasts its information. Router B recalculates accordingly and the loop continues.

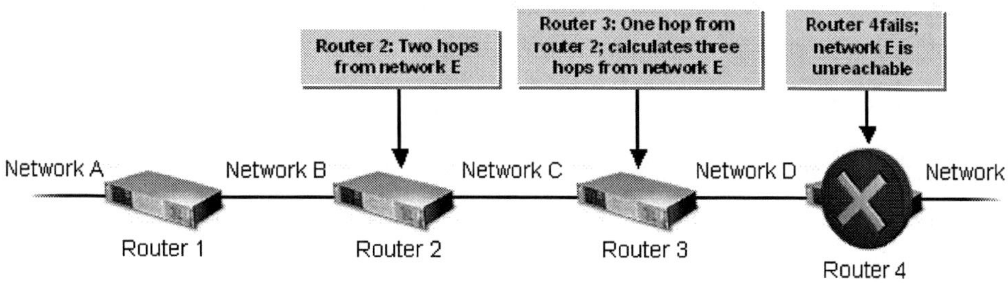

Figure 9-15: *Count-to-infinity loops.*

Split Horizon and Poison Reverse

One workaround to the count-to-infinity problem is the *split horizon* method, where a router does not include in its broadcasts any routes to the router from which it discovered its own location.

Another workaround to the count-to-infinity problem is called *poison reverse*. Unlike in split horizon, routers using poison reverse broadcast routes back to the router from which they calculated their own location, but instead of giving a true hop count, they broadcast a hop count of 16, which means they are inaccessible.

Split horizon and poison reverse are not used together. Split horizon is enabled when poison reverse is disabled, and vice versa.

Routing Loops

Routing loops occur when two routers discover different routes to the same location that include each other but never reach the endpoint. Data caught in a routing loop circles around until its TTL expires. Routing loops can be difficult to detect and to troubleshoot; the best prevention is proper router configuration.

Example: A Routing Loop

For example, data is sent to router A. Router A decides that the best way to get to the endpoint is to send the data to router B. Router B decides that the best way to send the data to the endpoint is to send it to router C. Router C decides that the best way to send the data to the endpoint is to send it to router A. Router A sends the data to router B and the loop starts all over again.

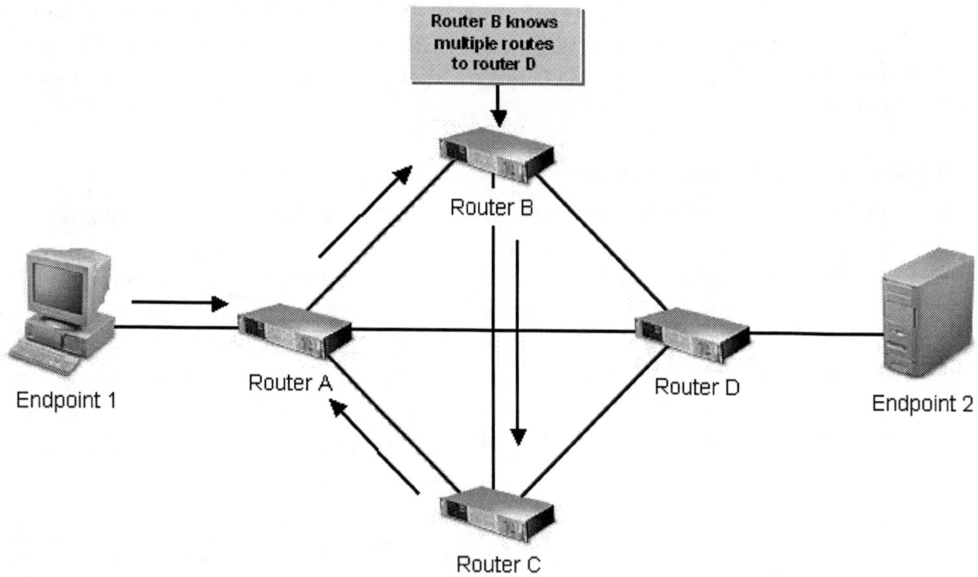

Figure 9-16: *Routing loops.*

Router Discovery Protocols

Router discovery protocols are the language that routers use to talk to each other.

For more information on RIP II, see RFC 1387 "RIP Version 2 Protocol Analysis." You might also be interested in RFCs 1388 and 1389 for RIP II information.

Protocol	Description
Routing Information Protocol	*Routing Information Protocol (RIP)* is a simple distance-vector protocol that is easy to configure, works well inside simple autonomous systems, and is best deployed in small networks with few numbers of routers in an environment that does not change much. Most equipment that supports RIP is lower in cost than those that support more complicated router protocols. RIP broadcasts the entire routing table, including known routes and costs, every 30 seconds. This places a lot of router discovery traffic on the network. When RIP builds its routing table, it does not support multiple routes to the same network. The router will record the route with the lowest metric to a location and remove the others. RIP is subject to count-to-infinity loops and does not support many of the new features expected on modern networks. It does not support multicast addresses or Variable Length Subnet Masks (VLSMs). RIP was replaced with RIP version 2.
RIP II	RIP II enhances RIP by supporting the following features: • Next Hop Addressing—Includes IP address information in routing tables for every router in a given path to avoid sending packets through extra routers. • Authentication—Enables password authentication and the use of a key to authenticate routing information to a router. • Subnet mask—Supports more subnets and hosts on an internetwork by supporting VLSMs and including length information in routing information. • Multicast packet—Decreases the workload of non–RIP II hosts by communicating only with RIP II routers. RIP II packets use 224.0.0.9 as their IP multicast address. Most hosts and routers support RIP I, so be sure that the RIP II mode you configure works with your current RIP configuration.
Interior Gateway Routing Protocol	*Interior Gateway Routing Protocol (IGRP)* is a distance-vector routing protocol developed by Cisco as an improvement over RIP and RIP II. It was designated as a protocol best deployed on interior routers within an AS. IGRP introduced a composite metric, enabling an administrator to manually configure and add to the hop count up to six metric values to give extra value to the metric. Because of this, IGRP can support multiple routes to the same network and can even support load balancing across routes with identical metrics.

Protocol	Description
Enhanced Interior Gateway Routing Protocol	*Enhanced Interior Gateway Routing Protocol (EIGRP)* is more of a modernization of IGRP than an improvement. It includes features that support VLSM and classful and classless subnet masks. Additional updates reduce convergence times and improve network stability during changes. To ensure that EIGRP is a viable solution for interior routing, EIGRP removed routing protocol dependence on the network protocol. This means that routing tables can be built for several different protocols—even protocols that haven't been deployed yet, such as IPv6.
Open Shortest Path First	On IP internetworks, link-state routing is usually accomplished by the *Open Shortest Path First (OSPF)* protocol (RFCs 1245, 1246, 1850, and 2178). Each OSPF router uses the information in its database to build the shortest possible path to destinations on the internetwork. Although OSPF uses less bandwidth than distance-vector protocols, it requires more memory and CPU resources.

RIP vs. OSPF

The following table compares the characteristics of RIP and OSPF.

Characteristic	RIP	OSPF
Size of metric	16—This means that a RIP network cannot be larger than 16 hops. This maximum is further reduced when costs other than 1 are used for certain routes.	Limited only by the number of bits in the metric field (64,000). Because OSPF does not suffer from the count-to-infinity problem, it can be the basis for much larger internetworks, and administrators can assign costs to optimize routing without limiting the size of the network.
Maximum number of routers	15—This value is related to the allowable metric size.	65,535. This value is related to the allowable metric size.
Variable-length subnets	Only with RIP II. RIP treats subnets as part of the internal structure of the network and assumes that all subnets are of equal length. With RIP, all subnets must be contiguous, connected, and hidden from remote networks.	Supported by default. Because OSPF treats the subnet mask as part of the protocol information, the restrictions that affect RIP do not apply.

Characteristic	RIP	OSPF
Convergence	Poison reverse or split horizon must be used to counteract count-to-infinity problem. RIP must calculate all routes before sending the information throughout the network.	Link State Acknowledgements (LSAs) provide rapid convergence among tables; no count-to-infinity problem arises. OSPF passes along LSAs as soon as they are received, meaning that nodes can adjust their routing tables at practically the same time.
Traffic	The entire routing table is broadcast every 30 seconds.	A partial routing table (Hello packet) is broadcast only to direct connections every 30 minutes.

ACTIVITY 9-5

Implementing Dynamic Routing

There is a simulated version of this activity available on the CD-ROM that shipped with this course. You can run this simulation on any Windows computer to review the activity after class, or as an alternative to performing the activity as a group in class. The activity simulation can be launched either directly from the CD-ROM by clicking the Interactives link and navigating to the appropriate one, or from the installed data file location by opening the C:\Data\Simulations\Lesson#\Activity# folder and double-clicking the executable (.exe) file.

Scenario:

Your company has grown and static routing no longer meets your needs. You plan to implement dynamic routing and you need to install the routing protocol on your Windows Server 2003 router.

What You Do	How You Do It
1. Add the RIP II routing protocol.	a. Choose Start→Administrative Tools→ Routing And Remote Access.
	b. Under IP Routing, select General.
	c. Choose Action→New Routing Protocol.

d. **Select RIP Version 2 For Internet Protocol and click OK.**

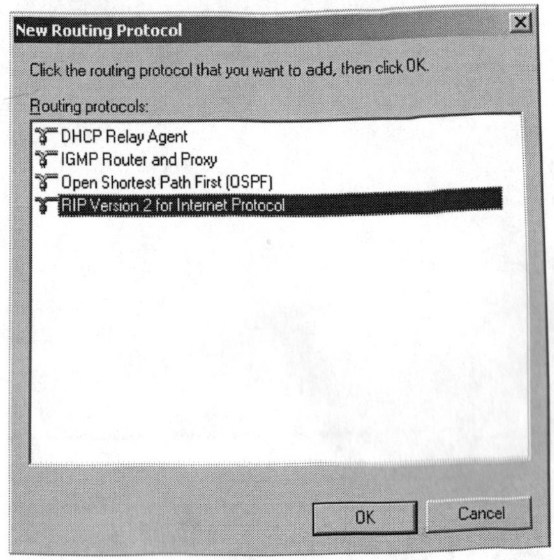

2. **Add the RIP interfaces.**

a. Under IP Routing, **select RIP.**

b. **Choose Action→New Interface.**

c. With Local Area Connection selected, **click OK.**

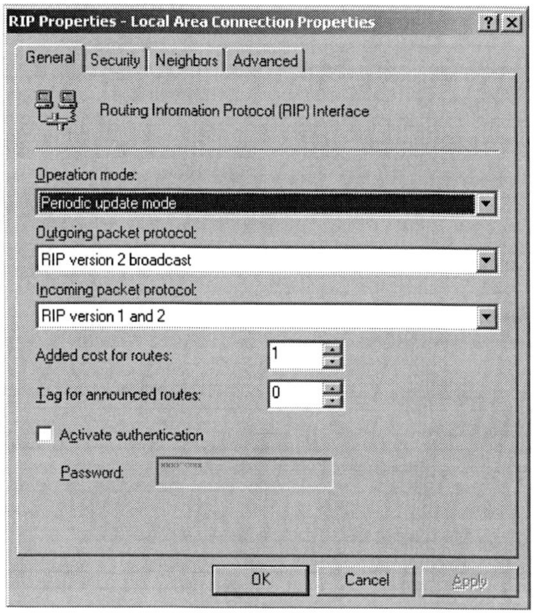

d. **Click OK** to accept the default settings.

e. **Choose Action→New Interface.**

f. With Local Area Connection 2 selected, **click OK.**

g. **Click OK** to accept the default settings.

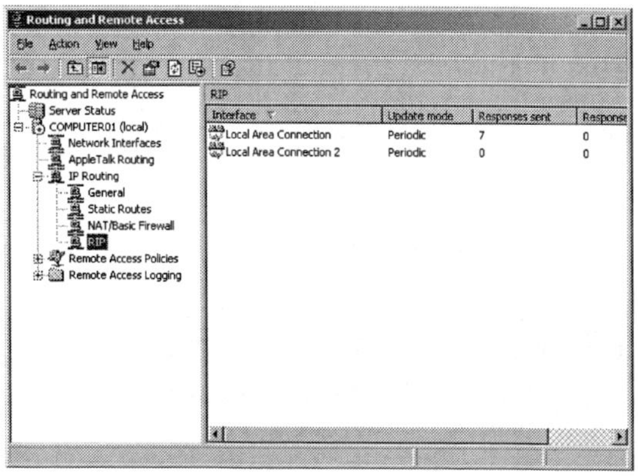

3. **Examine the dynamic routes.**

a. With RIP selected, **choose Action→Show Neighbors.**

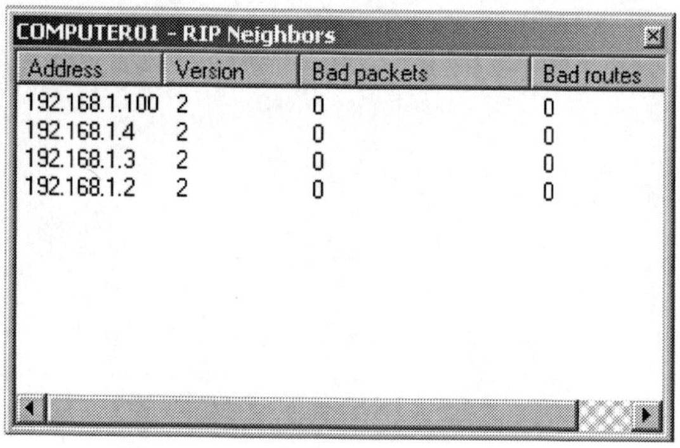

b. You have neighbor routers running the RIP protocol. **Close the RIP Neighbors window.**

TOPIC E

Controlling Data Movement with Filters and VLANs

In the previous topics in this lesson, you examined the functions of bridges, switches, and routers in LAN implementations. Filters and VLANs are two other LAN infrastructure technologies that add data control to basic LAN connectivity. In this topic, you will identify the methods for controlling data movement with filters and VLANs.

Once you understand the basic operation of switches and routers within your LAN, you're ready to start considering implementing some of their more advanced capabilities. Both routers and switches provide additional features that can help you and your organization control the data on your network and improve efficiency. Because these data-movement techniques are quite widely deployed, you should be familiar with their underlying principles so you can be prepared to support and implement them in your networks.

Data Filtering with Routers

A routed network can filter data based on more than the data's MAC address. Routers operate at layer 3 of the OSI model and can read protocol information. They can make decisions to block or pass data based on network ID, node ID, or port number. Some routers can even make decisions based on what is in the data.

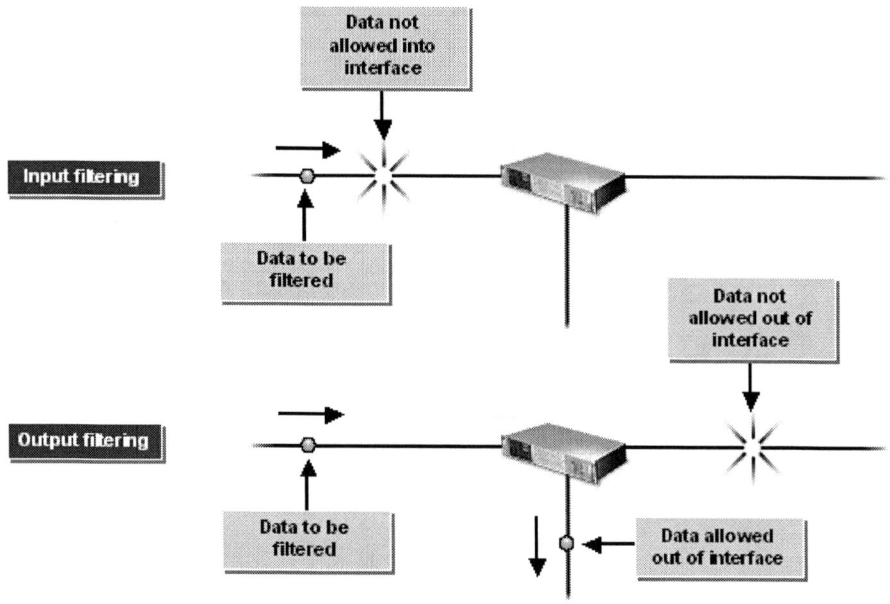

Figure 9-17: *Data filtering with routers.*

Each of a router's interfaces can filter either input or output. Input filtering stops undesirable data from entering the router through the filtered interface. The router only has to evaluate the interface where the packet enters.

Output filtering stops data from leaving through the filtered interface. Filtered data can enter through any interface, as long as an input filter isn't applied, but the output filters of every interface are evaluated. This means that output filtering uses more router resources than input filtering.

Virtual LANs (VLANs)

A *virtual LAN (VLAN)* is a point-to-point logical network with no real physical characteristics. The network's central point is typically a highly configurable device called a *VLAN switch* that can build any logical network in any required configuration, even when computers are on different physical segments.

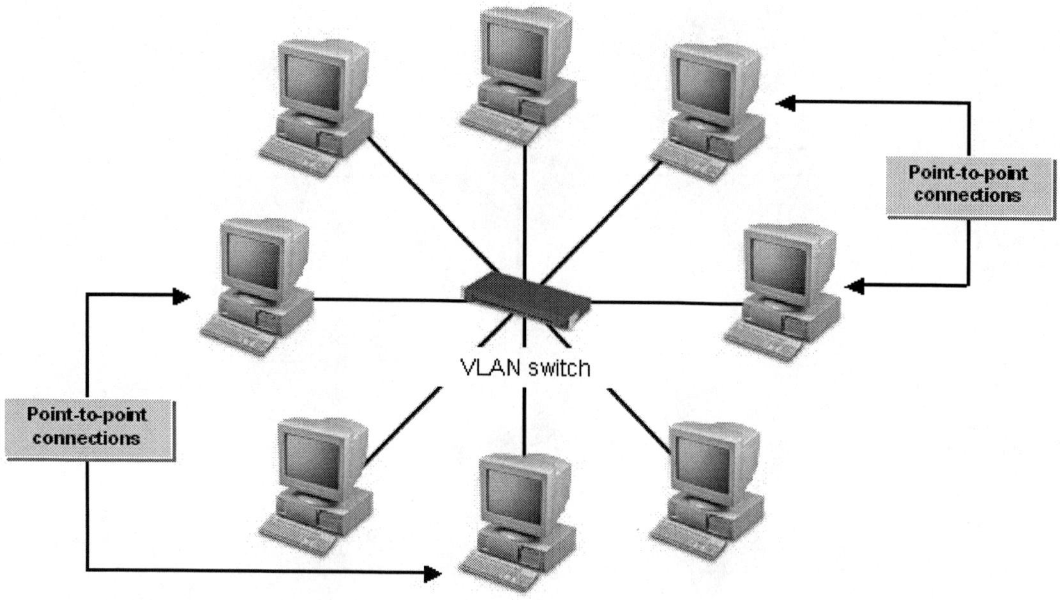

Figure 9-18: *A VLAN.*

Advantages of a VLAN

A VLAN network's biggest advantage is that once the physical network is built, it can be reconfigured for optimal performance by simply changing the VLAN's configuration; the network doesn't have to be rewired. For example, if a given node sends most of its traffic to an endpoint in a separate subnet, that node can be removed from its current subnet and placed in the endpoint's subnet—all without changing a single cable and without the user's knowledge. VLANs lend themselves to remote administration because an administrator can telnet into the VLAN device rather than physically visit it, as long as the physical point-to-point configuration doesn't change.

Also, VLAN switches are relatively expensive but the advantages and improvements in network performance quickly outweigh the cost.

VLAN Switch Functions

When a network is built in a physical configuration, physical segments and subnets are built into the network during its installation. Changes to the design requirements mean physical changes such as re-running cable or deploying more or different hardware.

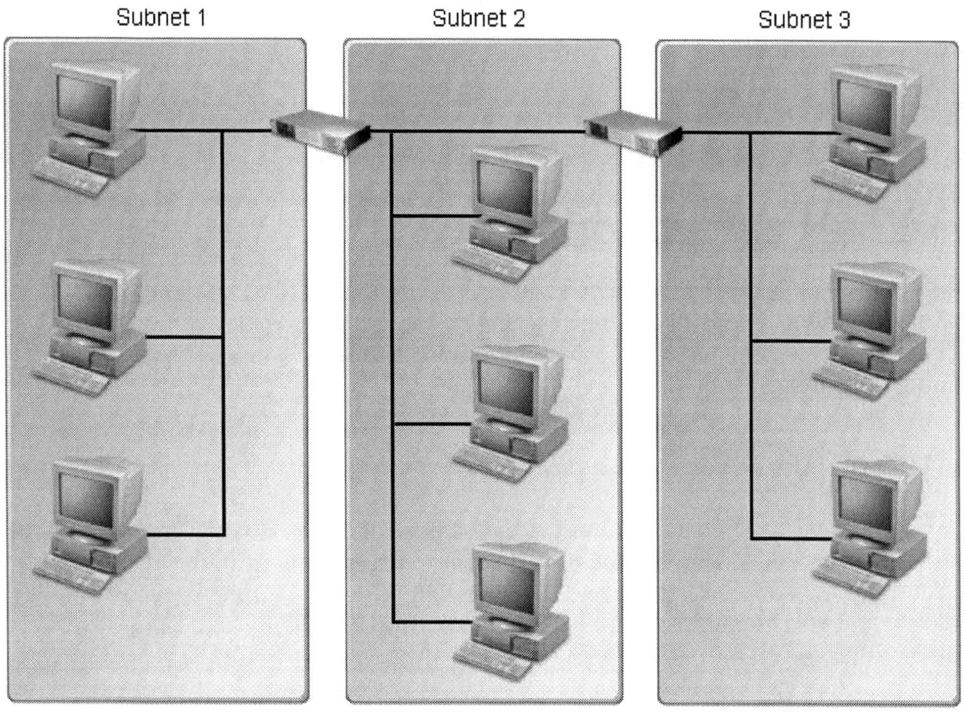

Figure 9-19: *Physical segmentation.*

The VLAN switch enables the network administrator to lay the network out in a logical configuration with a pure star topology. All segments have equal point-to-point connections. The VLAN switch can tie any of its interfaces together into a logical subnet with all the characteristics of a physical subnet. This enables an administrator to control the IP addresses, MAC contention domains, and interior routing with the VLAN switch configuration.

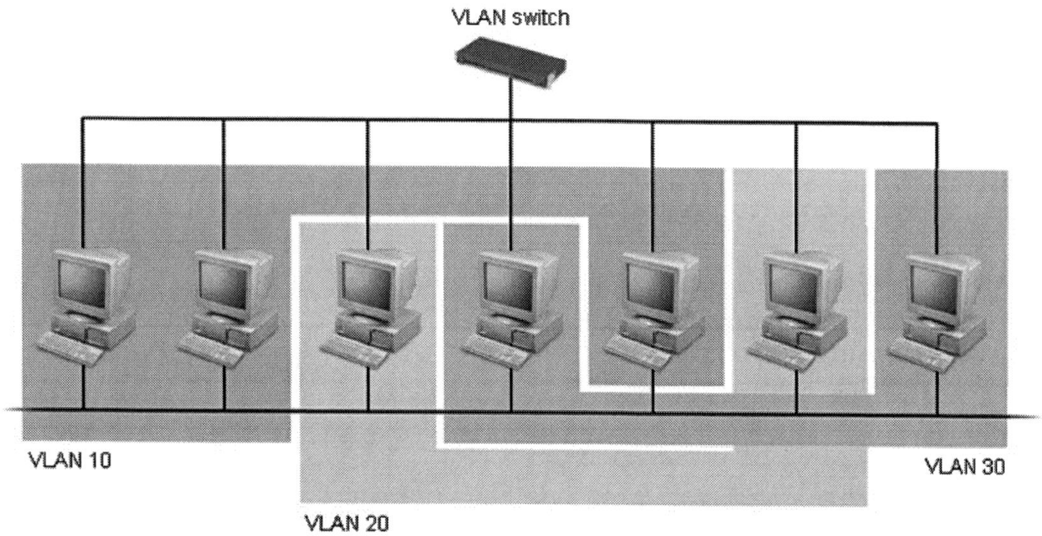

Figure 9-20: *Logical segmentation.*

Layer 2 VLAN Operation

VLANs have a component that operates at layer 2 of the OSI model. In layer 2 operation, each VLAN interface is a switched port so each node is tied to a contention domain of one. Like a private switch port, there is no other device to compete with for the media. A VLAN switch passes only data bound for the MAC address on the port, and broadcasts for the node's subnet.

Layer 3 VLAN Operation

VLANs also have a component that operates at layer 3, like a router. To configure layer 3 operation, an administrator groups nodes together and the nodes are assigned a VLAN identifier inside the switch. This ID is used to segment the network into its subnets. The logical subnets determine the broadcast domains and the data filters.

Routing in a VLAN

When a VLAN switch receives data, it routes the data based on the destination IP address, just like a router does. However, because all the routed subnets are configured in the VLAN, there are no local routes more than two hops away. Exterior routes are handled the same way they're handled in a regular routed network—they're sent to a default gateway and routed to distant networks.

ACTIVITY 9-6

Implementing Data Filtering

There is a simulated version of this activity available on the CD-ROM that shipped with this course. You can run this simulation on any Windows computer to review the activity after class, or as an alternative to performing the activity as a group in class. The activity simulation can be launched either directly from the CD-ROM by clicking the Interactives link and navigating to the appropriate one, or from the installed data file location by opening the C:\Data\Simulations\Lesson#\Activity# folder and double-clicking the executable (.exe) file.

Setup:

Routing And Remote Access is open.

Scenario:

You wish to protect your internal network by using your router to prevent incoming traffic from remote routes on your second network adapter. You need to configure the filter on your Windows Server 2003 router.

What You Do	How You Do It
1. **Open the properties of the network interface.**	a. In Routing And Remote Access, under IP Routing, **select General.**
	b. In the right pane, **select Local Area Connection 2.**
	c. **Choose Action→Properties.**

2. **Configure the filter.**

a. On the General page, **click Inbound Filters.**

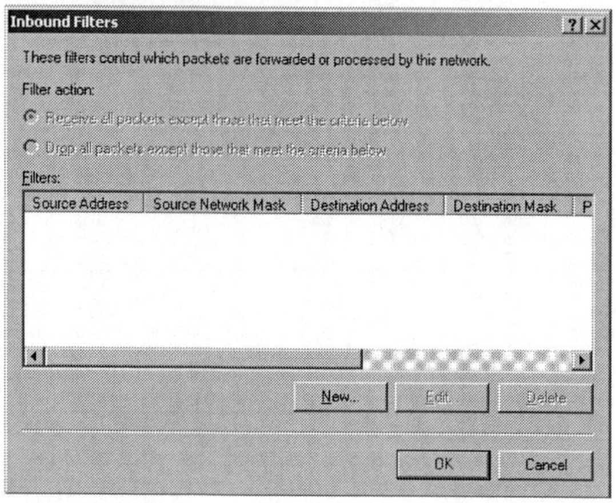

b. **Click New.**

c. **Check Source Network.**

d. Under Source Network, in the IP Address text box, **type *192.168.0.0***

e. In the Subnet Mask text box, **type *255.255.0.0***

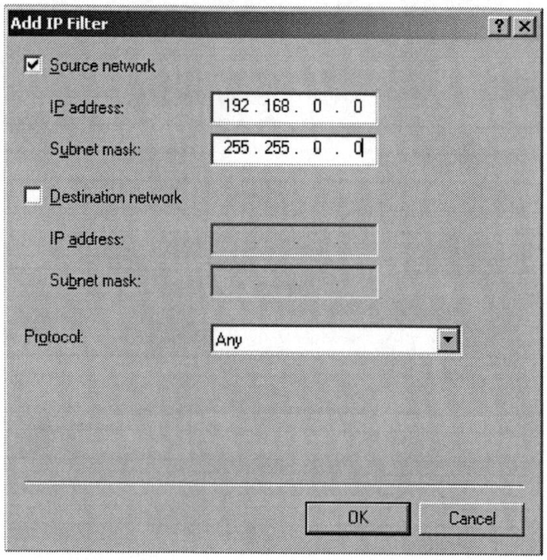

f. **Click OK.**

g. Under Filter Action, **select Drop All Packets Except Those That Meet The Criteria Below.**

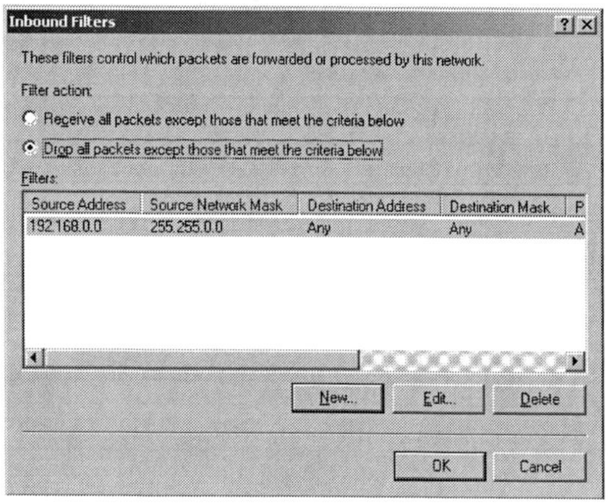

h. **Click OK twice.**

i. **Close Routing And Remote Access.**

Lesson 9 Follow-up

In this lesson, you identified the components of a LAN implementation. Because the LAN is the fundamental unit of computer networking, all networking professionals will need a thorough understanding of LAN technologies.

1. **Of the LAN infrastructure technologies discussed in this lesson (bridges, switches, static routing, dynamic routing, filtering, and VLANs), which ones do you expect to work with the most? Why?**

2. **What do you see as the pros and cons of implementing static routing versus dynamic routing?**

Notes

LESSON 10

Wide Area Network (WAN) Infrastructure

Lesson Time
1 hour(s), 30 minutes

Lesson Objectives:

In this lesson, you will identify the components of a WAN implementation.

You will:

- Identify the major WAN switching technologies.
- Identify the major transmission technologies for WANs.
- Identify the major WAN connectivity methods.
- Identify major Voice over Data systems.

Lesson 10

Introduction

In the previous lesson, you identified the components of a LAN implementation. The other major network implementation category is the wide area network (WAN). In this lesson, you will identify the components of a WAN implementation.

There aren't very many local networks these days that don't have some kind of wide-area connection to a distant network. And virtually every network connects in one way or another to the biggest WAN of them all, the Internet. As a networking professional, you'll need to understand the infrastructure of these WAN connections so that you can ensure WAN connectivity in the networks you support.

This lesson covers the following CompTIA Network+ (2005) certification objectives:

- Topic A:
  - Objective 2.14: Identify the basic characteristics (for example, speed, capacity. and media) of the following WAN (wide area network) technologies: packet switching and circuit switching.
- Topic B:
  - Objective 1.4: Recognize the RJ-11 (Registered Jack) media connector and describe its uses.
  - Objective 1.6: Identify the purposes, features, and functions of ISDN (Integrated Services Digital Network) adapters.
  - Objective 2.14: Identify the basic characteristics (for example, speed, capacity, and media) of the following WAN technologies: ISDN (Integrated Services Digital Network); T1 (T-Carrier level 1)/E1/J1; T3 (T-Carrier level 3)/E3/J3; OCx (Optical Carrier); and X.25.
  - Objective 2.15: Identify the basic characteristics of the following Internet access technologies: xDSL (Digital Subscriber Line); broadband cable (cable modem); POTS/PSTN (Plain Old Telephone Service/Public Switched Telephone Network); satellite; and wireless.
  - Objective 3.4: Given a remote connectivity scenario comprising a protocol, an authentication scheme, and physical connectivity, configure the connection. Include connection to the following servers: UNIX/Linux/MAC OS X Server; NetWare; Windows; and AppleShare IP (Internet Protocol).
  - Objective 4.4: Given a troubleshooting scenario involving a client accessing remote network services, identify the cause of the problem (for example, file services, print services, authentication failure, protocol configuration, physical connectivity, or SOHO (Small Office/Home Office) router).
- Topic C:
  - Objective 1.6: Identify the purposes, features, and functions of the following network components: CSU/DSU (Channel Service Unit/Data Service Unit) and modems.
  - Objective 2.13: Identify the purpose of network services and protocols (for example, ICS (Internet Connection Sharing)).

TOPIC A

WAN Switching Technologies

In this lesson, you will identify the components of a WAN implementation. WAN switching technologies are one component of a WAN. In this topic, you will identify the major WAN switching technologies.

Data can move through WAN links in a number of different ways. These different switching methods can have a great effect on network characteristics such as performance and reliability. You'll need to understand the impact a given switching technology can have on your network implementation.

Circuit Switching Networks

In *circuit switching networks,* a single path from one endpoint to another is built when a connection is needed. Once the path is established, all data follows that path and is subject to the same network conditions. When the connection isn't needed any more, it is dropped and the resources again become available for network use. Because of this, there is no guarantee that data will follow the same path through the network in different sessions.

In general, circuit switching networks are a bit less expensive than dedicated lines.

In circuit switching networks, the word "circuit" refers to the path between endpoints.

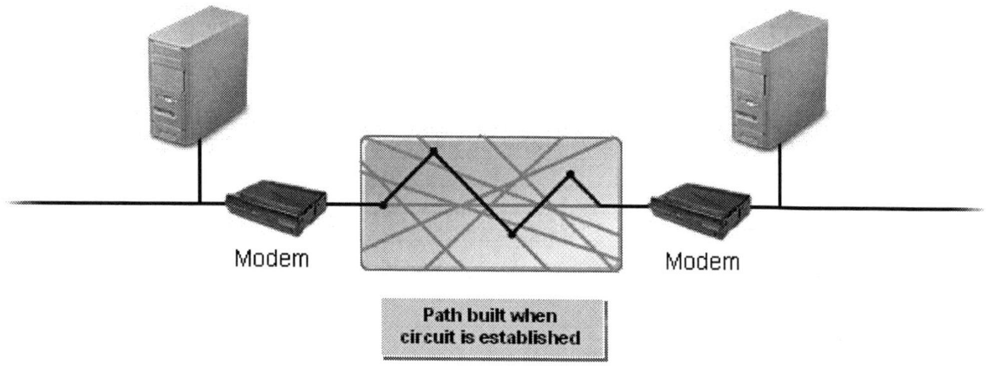

Figure 10-1: *Circuit switching networks.*

CompTIA Network+ Exam Objectives

An Appendix is available to assist you in mapping CompTIA Network+ exam objectives to the course content. You can download the Appendix at the end of this lesson.

Virtual Circuits

Virtual circuits are a routing technique that connects endpoints logically through a provider's network. These logical paths are assigned to identities rather than physical locations and can be either permanent or switched.

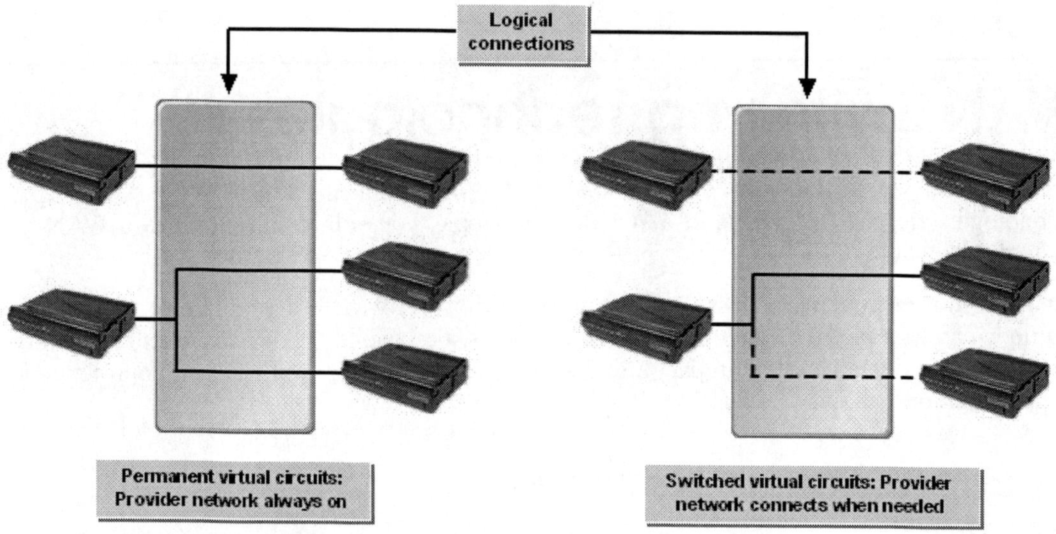

Figure 10-2: *Virtual circuits.*

Permanent Virtual Circuits

Permanent virtual circuits (PVCs) are usually associated with leased lines. They connect two endpoints and are always on, which is why they're referred to as permanent. When a PVC is established, it's manually built and maintained by the telephone company (telco). The telco identifies the endpoints with a Data Link Connection Identifier (DLCI, pronounced del-see). PVCs provide a fast, reliable connection between endpoints because the connection is always on. Customers pay a fixed price per month for the connection.

Switched Virtual Circuits

Switched virtual circuits (SVCs) are associated with dial-up and demand-dial connections. SVCs provide more flexibility than PVCs and allow a single connection to an endpoint to be connected to multiple endpoints as needed. When a network device attempts to connect to the WAN, the SVC is requested and the carrier establishes the connection. Customers typically pay by connection time (like a long distance phone call) and the monthly charge is less than that for a PVC. SVCs are useful when you need a part-time connection. But keep in mind that connection time can be slow, and if usage increases, so can an SVC's cost.

Packet Switching Networks

Packet switching networks move data through the network packet by packet. Each packet takes the best route available at any given time rather than following an established circuit. Each data packet contains all of the routing and sequencing information required to get it from endpoint to endpoint, where the data is reassembled. The packet switching concept assumes that a network is constantly changing and adjustments can be made to compensate for network congestion or dead links.

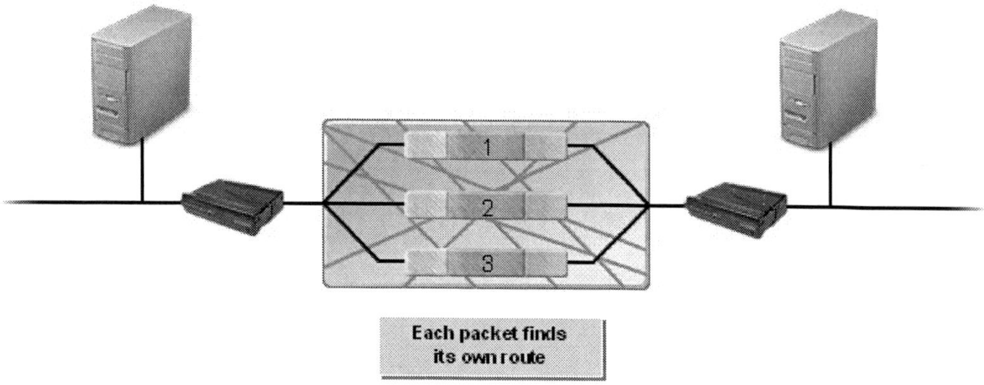

Figure 10-3: *Packet switching networks.*

Cell Switching Networks

Cell switching networks are very similar to packet switching networks except that data is divided into fixed-length cells instead of variable-length packets. If data doesn't fill up an entire cell, the remainder of the data space is filled with blank data or filler data until the cell reaches its fixed size. The advantage of cell switching over packet switching is its predictability. Cell switching technologies make it easy to keep track of how much data is moving on a network.

ACTIVITY 10-1

Exploring the WAN Environment

Scenario:

In this activity, you will examine various aspects of the WAN environment.

1. **Which methods use the same path for all data traffic between two endpoints in a single session?**
    a) Packet switching
    b) Circuit switching
    c) Virtual circuits
    d) Cell switching

2. **Which method uses a fixed-length packet?**
    a) Packet switching
    b) Virtual circuits
    c) Cell switching
    d) Switched virtual circuits

3. **True or False? Virtual circuits are always switched.**

    __ True

    __ False

4. **Which switching technology is used on the Internet?**

    a) Cell switching

    b) Circuit switching

    c) Packet switching

TOPIC B

WAN Transmission Technologies

In the previous topic, you identified the major WAN switching technologies. Transmission technologies are another component of a WAN implementation. In this topic, you will identify the major transmission technologies for WANs.

The transmission method on your WAN might affect overall network performance—and network cost—more than any other single factor. From the slowest dial-up to the fastest fiber-optic service, you'll need to understand the capabilities and limitations of your network's transmission method.

Dial-Up Connections

Dial-up lines are local loop *Public Switched Telephone Network (PSTN)* connections that use modems, existing phone lines, and existing long-distance carrier services to provide low-cost, low-bandwidth WAN connectivity and remote network access. Dial-up lines are generally limited to 56 Kbps, and are sometimes used as backups for higher-bandwidth WAN services.

Another term for PSTN is Plain Old Telephone Service, or POTS.

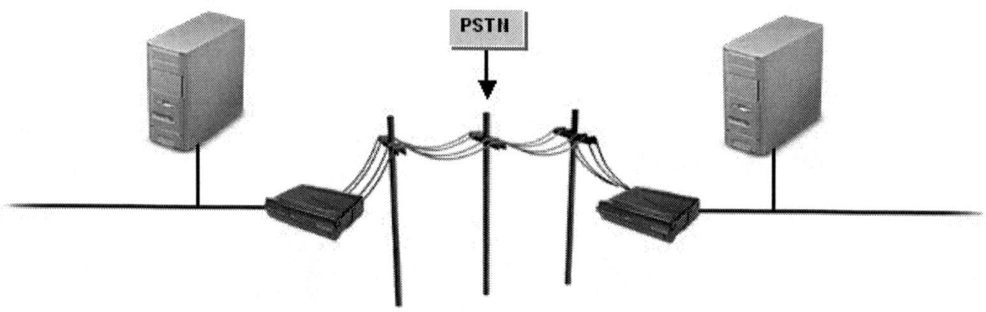

Figure 10-4: *Dial-up connections.*

Dial-up Hardware

You can keep hardware requirements simple and use a modem attached to a serial port on a PC, or you can use a specialized modem card installed in the server to support multiple phone connections.

RJ-11 Connectors

RJ-11 connectors are four- or six-wire connectors that are used to connect telephones and modems to telephone outlets. The RJ-11 connector looks much like the RJ-45 connector that's used to connect network cards to LANs. When you're looking at an RJ-11 and RJ-45 connector, the RJ-11 connector is smaller.

Benefits and Drawbacks of Dial-up

Dial-up lines have two major drawbacks: they're slow and they can have considerable connection wait time (because the modem has to dial and establish a connection before data can be sent across the network). Despite those limitations, dial-ups are popular because they provide enough bandwidth to get the job done at a very low cost, and because the telephone infrastructure is already in place and is universally available.

Dedicated and Leased Data Lines

Dedicated lines and *leased lines* are essentially the same; the telephone company provides a dedicated connection between two endpoints that companies use to provide a high-quality connection between two locations.

With dedicated or leased lines, bandwidth availability varies with the technology, but is usually between 56 Kbps and 1.544 Mbps. A company can lease the connection for a fixed fee, typically based on the distance between endpoints. Leasing a line can be advantageous because the customer is guaranteed a set minimum bandwidth with a minimum connection time.

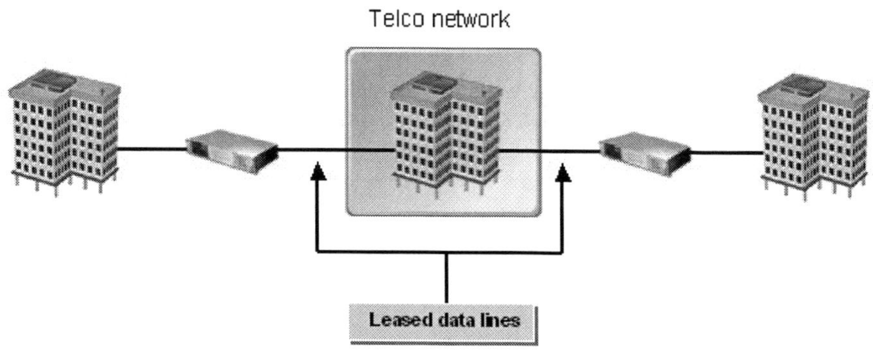

Figure 10-5: *Leased data lines.*

Integrated Services Digital Network (ISDN)

Integrated Services Digital Network (ISDN) is a digital circuit switching technology that carries both voice and data over digital phone lines or PSTN wires. Connections are made on demand by dialing another ISDN circuit's telephone number. ISDN is a channelized service and has two interface modes: Basic Rate Interface (BRI) or Primary Rate Interface (PRI), which includes more data channels to provide higher bandwidth.

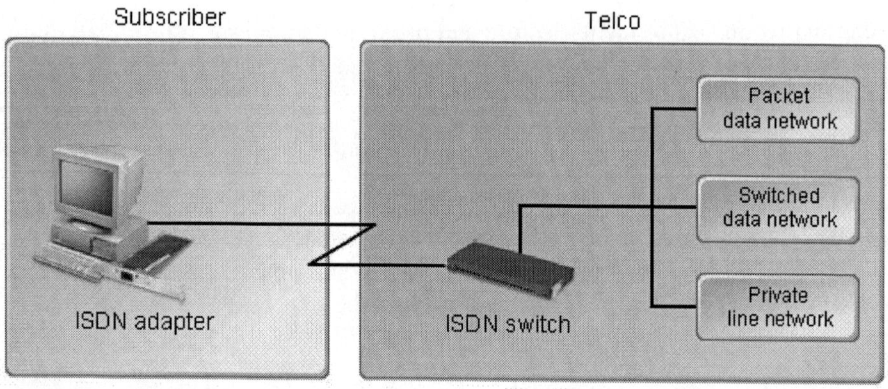

Figure 10-6: *ISDN.*

Channels

Channel services use multiple communication channels, tied logically together within a set bandwidth, to form a single communication path of bandwidth equal to the sum of the individual channels' bandwidths. In other words, they combine all of their individual bandwidths to make one channel with a lot of bandwidth. Channels that carry data are called bearer channels, or B channels, and the channel used to set up, control, and take down the connection is called the delta channel, or D channel. BRI-ISDN uses two 64 Kbps B channels and one 16 Kbps D channel for a total data bandwidth of 128 Kbps. It's used primarily for remote connections. PRI-ISDN uses twenty-three 64 Kbps B channels and one 64 Kbps D channel for a total bandwidth of 1.544 Mbps. It's used primarily for multi-user WAN connections. As demand for higher bandwidth connections to the Internet grew, BRI-ISDN was deployed to many small businesses and homes. However, ISDN, for the most part, has been replaced by ADSL technology.

ISDN Hardware

ISDN hardware includes terminal equipment (TE), terminal adapters (TAs), network termination (NT) devices, line termination equipment, and exchange termination equipment. ISDN lines terminate at a customer's premises using an RJ-45 connector in a configuration called a U-interface, which is usually connected to a network termination unit (NTU). The NTU can directly connect to ISDN-aware equipment, such as phones or ISDN NICs in computers. This type of equipment is called terminal equipment type 1 (TE1).

Cable Access

Cable Internet access uses a cable television connection and a specialized interface device known as a cable modem to provide high-speed Internet access to homes and small businesses. Cable access is contention-based, with users arranged in contention groups off nodes that split the television and data signals at the cable provider's end. The speed of the network varies depending on how populated the node is.

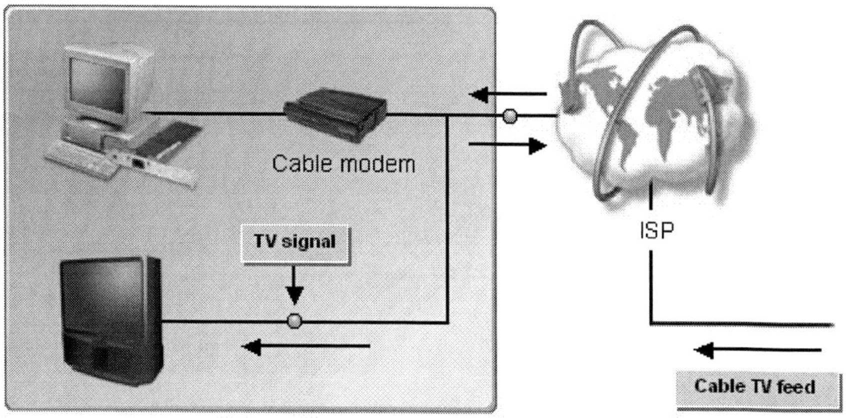

Figure 10-7: *Cable Internet access.*

Cable Connectivity Devices

Cable modems are the hardware devices that provide the specialized connectivity required to connect to the provider's cable systems. They connect to a customer's machine or network with an interface that appears to the computer system as a LAN card. Most cable companies support a cable modem access limit of 10 Mbps and require a 10 MB NIC. However, a cable modem usually functions reliably up to 27 Mbps. This is what makes a cable modem approximately 1,000 times faster than a 28.8 modem.

Cable Access Speeds

User perceptions of access speed are usually based on download times rather than upload times. With cable access, because of the variation of speed between nodes, it's common to see download speeds vary by more than 1 Mbps between a cable system in one part of town and a different cable system in a more populated, very heavily implemented part of town. Many cable access providers offer differing service levels, where subscribers can pay a fee for a higher maximum download speed. At a minimum, most cable companies try to guarantee a 150 Kbps download speed from their test sites.

Digital Subscriber Line (DSL)

Digital Subscriber Line (DSL) is a broadband Internet connection method that transmits digital signals over existing phone lines. It has become a popular way to connect small businesses and households to the Internet because it is affordable and provides a relatively high download speed—typically, 1.5 Mbps. However, distance and the quality of the lines affect the total bandwidth available to a customer.

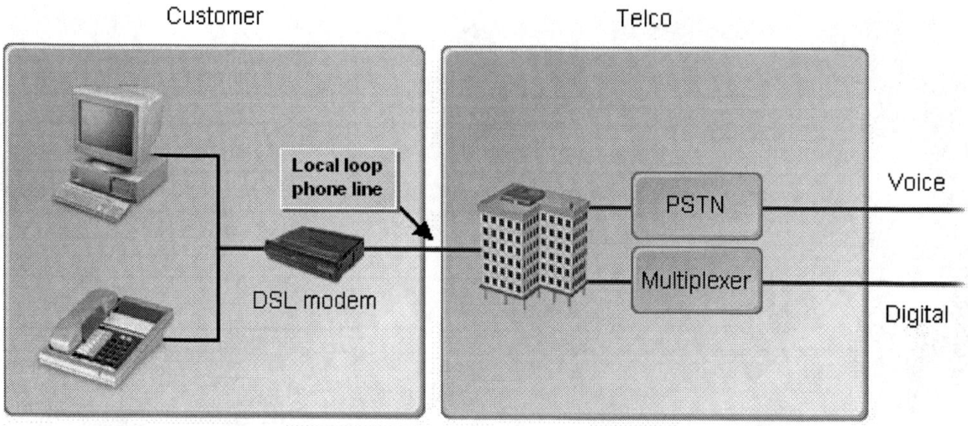

Figure 10-8: *Digital Subscriber Line (DSL).*

DSL Connection Lines

DSL connects over standard, unconditioned, copper phone lines that are tested and certified for the maximum speed. It has a hard limit of 18,000 feet from the telco's switch. The section between the central office and the customer is called the local loop.

DSL Channels

Like ISDN, DSL uses bearer channels but DSL bearer channels refer to transmission direction. When the bearer channel carries data from the central office to the customer it's called a downstream bearer channel. When data moves from the customer to the central office, it does so on what's called the duplex bearer channel.

DSL Technologies

Two popular DSL technologies are currently in use in networks: Asymmetric Digital Subscriber Line (ADSL) and High-speed Digital Subscriber Line (HDSL). ADSL is popular for Internet browsing and has different speed channels—1.544 Mbps to 6.1 Mbps for downstream channels and 16 Kbps to 640 Kbps for the duplex channel. HDSL uses the same speed for both channels—640 Kbps to 1.544 Mbps. Even though HDSL has slower downstream speeds, a lot of companies prefer HDSL as a lower cost alternative to T1 or PRI-ISDN for connecting networks.

DSL Connectivity Devices

A customer's network is connected to the phone line with a DSL modem. The modem converts analog signals to digital signals, compresses data, and creates the normal-voice telephone. It supports both voice phone conversations and data transfers simultaneously on the same lines.

Another modem, called a splitter, is located on the telco's end, separating the digital and voice signals. It sends digital signals to the Digital Subscriber Line Access Multiplexer (DSLAM), which combines signals from each customer into a single, high-speed backbone that feeds into the telco's network. Each local loop connection is point-to-point.

X.25 Switched Networks

X.25 is a legacy packet switching network technology developed in the 1970s to move data across the less-than-reliable long-distance public carriers available at that time. X.25 emphasizes reliable delivery, and because of that involves a lot of overhead and sacrifices performance. X.25, like many switched network protocols, is implemented on top of leased lines or other local connection technologies.

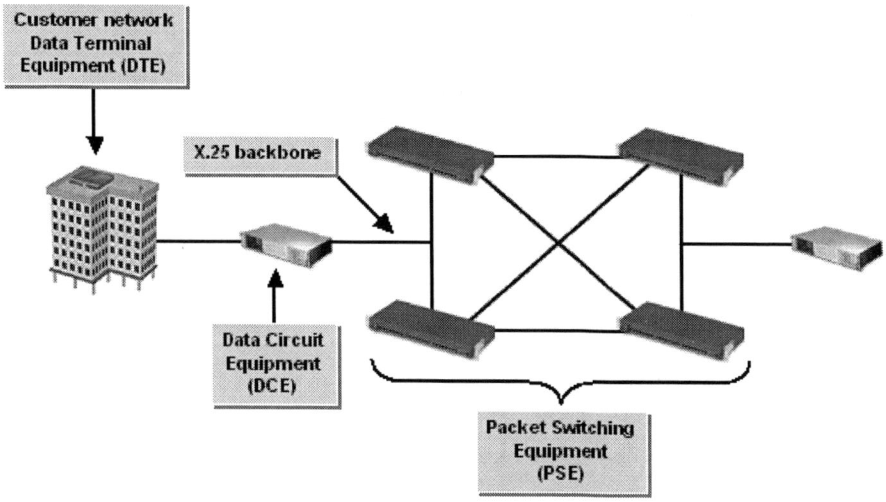

Figure 10-9: *X.25.*

X.25 Hardware

In an X.25 network, an endpoint is called Data Terminal Equipment (DTE). The DTE can be a card installed in either a PC or a server that interfaces with a router, or it can be a standalone unit. The DTE is connected to the Data Circuit Equipment (DCE), which connects the customer to the X.25 backbone. The backbone of the network is made up of Packet Switching Equipment (PSE).

Frame Relay

Frame relay is a packet switching implementation first offered in 1992 by AT&T and Sprint as a more efficient alternative to X.25. It was originally developed to support PRI-ISDN networks, but has been found to be functional on several other network types. Frame relay relies on a relatively clean carrier and, therefore, doesn't have the error-correction overhead that X.25 does. Frame-relay network connections are usually PVC but can be SVC.

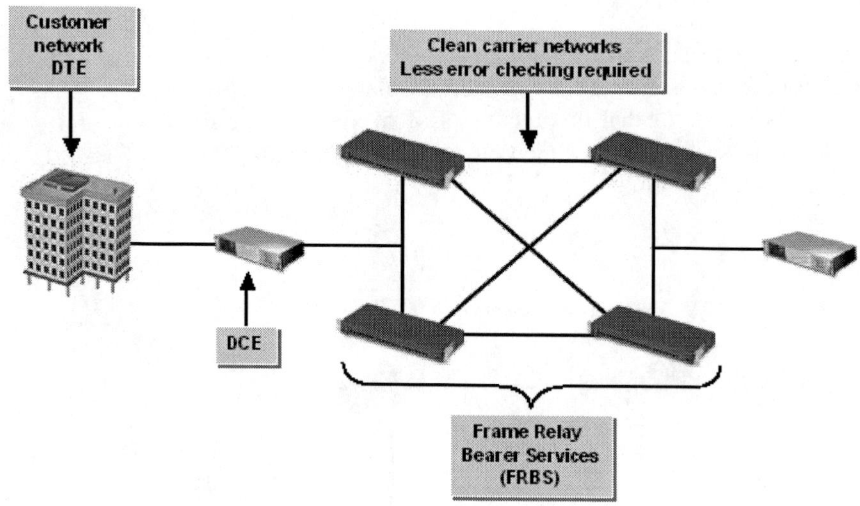

Figure 10-10: *Frame relay.*

Provisioning a Frame Relay Connection

Like X.25, frame relay uses DTE and DCE to connect to the appropriate frame relay network, referred to as the Frame Bearer Service (FRBS). Inside the FRBS—or frame network cloud—is a network of switches that makes connections between endpoints. Frame relay allows a virtual circuit to be established between two DTE devices. DTE equipment can consist either of a single network device or a router. DCE typically is a CSU/DSU that sends signals to an edge system (ES), a switch on the frame network.

Keep in mind that you never see the complexity of the communication happening inside the cloud because frame relay communicates using virtual circuits. There are two types of virtual circuits: permanent and switched. Permanent virtual circuits (PVCS) are created by the telco inside their devices and the circuit is constant. Switched virtual circuits (SVCS) act more like a telephone conversation. The circuit is established when data needs to be transmitted and when the data "conversation" is over, the connection is closed.

Asynchronous Transfer Mode (ATM)

Asynchronous Transfer Mode (ATM) is a versatile, cell switching network technology designed for deployment in LANs, WANs, and telephone networks. ATM LAN implementations are uncommon because they are expensive and complex. However, ATM WAN networks have become reasonably popular because of their versatility and high bandwidth. ATM networks are made up of switches, which transport the 53-byte ATM data cells between networks, and endpoints, which terminate customer equipment.

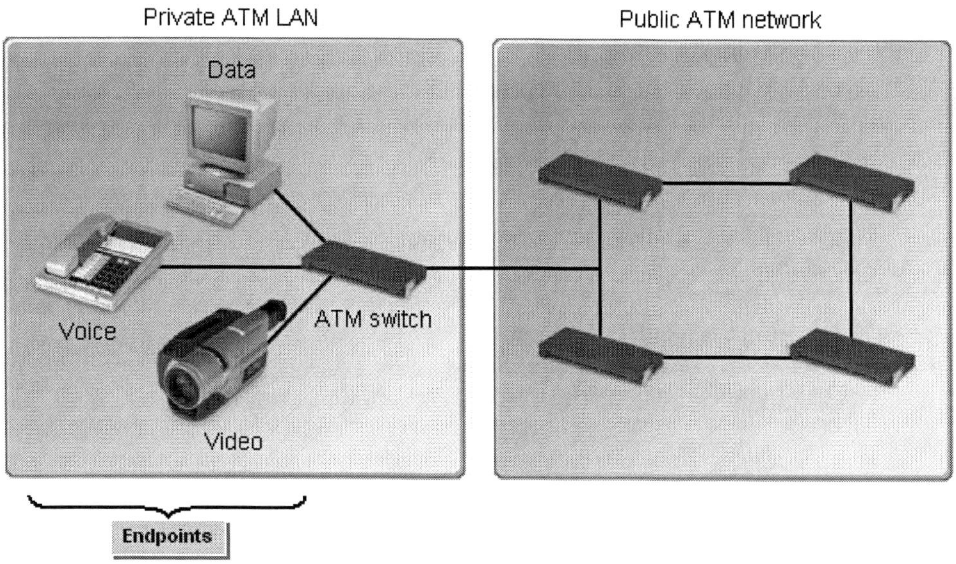

Figure 10-11: *ATM.*

ATM Features

ATM versatility comes from its wide array of features, including:

- A wide range of fast bandwidth options—155 Mbps to 622 Mbps are commonly deployed, but ATM can support 51.84 Mbps to 2.488 Gbps.
- Capability to carry data, voice, and video simultaneously on the same channels.
- The fixed 53-byte cell size enables ATM to be implemented in hardware, reducing overhead and drain on resources required to move network data.
- Built in Quality of Service (QoS) features designed to aid in the flow of data between endpoints: Traffic Contracting and Traffic Shaping. Traffic Contracting guarantees a set data rate assigned to an endpoint. When an endpoint connects to an ATM network, it enters into a contract with the network for service quality. The ATM network won't contract more service than it can provide. Traffic Shaping optimizes network data flow. It includes controlling bursts and optimizing bandwidth allocation.
- A connection-oriented protocol that provides guaranteed data delivery without adding extra overhead on a clean network.
- Support for real-time and non-real-time data. Real time is used for time-sensitive data, such as voice or video, and travels at a higher priority than non-real-time data.
- Support for both SVC and PVC networks. (Because of connection time, SVC isn't very popular.)

ATM Switch Categories

ATM switches fall into two categories: User-to-Network Interface (UNI) and Network-to-Network Interface (NNI). NNI is an ATM switch that is totally inside an ATM network. The UNI, referred to as a user device, is actually an ATM border device used to connect one ATM network to another ATM network or a LAN. Single devices can be attached to the ATM network, but it's not often done.

ATM Connections

ATM is not a channelized service and doesn't waste channels assigned to nodes that aren't talking. For example, when a PRI-ISDN allocates three channels to an offline device, it sends three spaces of filler data to hold the channel space for the node it was promised to. In the same situation, ATM would make that bandwidth available to other nodes, exhibiting traffic contracting to allocate the bandwidth as needed but not over-allocate it.

An ATM switch makes virtual connections with other switches to provide a data path from endpoint to endpoint. The individual connections are called Virtual Channels (VCs). The VC supports the connection-oriented transport between endpoints and is identified by the Virtual Channel Identifier (VCI). VCs with a common path are tied together into Virtual Paths (VPs) and are identified by a Virtual Path Identifier (VPI). Multiple VPs can be joined together to form a Transmission Path (TP).

T-Carrier Systems

The T-Carrier system was designed to carry multiplexed telephone connections. T1 and T3 are the two most common T-service levels. T-services can be used to support a point-to-point WAN where the telco sets up a dedicated connection between two T-service endpoints. This connection is always on and the customer pays by link distance.

T-services connect a customer's office with the telco's network. The internal connection is over frame relay. The T-service can also connect an office to the telco for remote access. Individual remote clients dial in to a number and then the telco routes them to the office through the T-service. This way, a server can service multiple dial-in connections without having many modems.

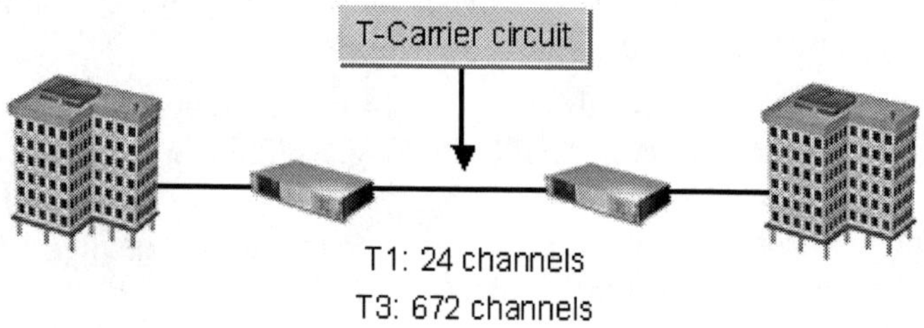

Figure 10-12: *The T-Carrier system.*

T-Carrier Transfer Speeds

A T1 line has 24 channels with speeds of 64 Kbps and can carry 24 concurrent conversations by converting each one into digital format and placing it on a channel. Commercial T-services are available to support DS1 and DS3 as T1 and T3 services. Fractional T-services are available, which enable a company to lease only part of the T-service. T1 supports 24 channels at 1.544 Mbps total bandwidth; T3 supports 672 channels for 44.736 Mbps (equal to 28 T1 lines).

For a listing of the specifications for all the T-Carrier line rate designations, see **http://en.wikipedia.org/wiki/T-carrier**.

Digital Signal Hierarchy Standards

The T-Carrier system is the most common physical implementation of the ANSI Digital Signal Hierarchy (DSH) specifications. DSH is a channelized data transmission standard used to multiplex several single data or voice channels for a greater total bandwidth. It was established in the 1980s, primarily for use with digital voice phones.

DSH defines a hierarchy of DSx specifications numbered DS0 to DS5. The basic DS0 level specifies a single voice channel of 64 Kbps. A DS1 signal bundles 24 DS0 channels and uses a T1 carrier line. In T-Carrier implementations, DSH systems have become the standard building block of most channelized systems in the United States today.

CEPT Standards

Another channelized specification standard was developed by the International Telecommunications Union (ITU), based on recommendations of the Conference of European Postal and Telecommunications Administration (CEPT). CEPT uses a 64 Kbps channel like DSH does, but starts with the CEPT-1 specification that uses 30 channels instead of 24 (all of CEPT's specifications use a different number of channels). Because of this, Europe's version of T-Carriers aligns its channels with CEPT specs and are called E-Carriers. For example, E1 and E3 are the European equivalents of T1 and T3 lines. Japan uses the J-Carrier hierarchy. J1 and J3 are the equivalents.

Synchronous Optical Network (SONET)

Synchronous Optical Network (SONET) is a standard for synchronous data transport over fiber optic cable. The key advantages of SONET are its excellent bandwidth management, built-in fault recovery features, and support for data transfer speeds up to 2.48 Gbps. SONET has two specifications: the OC spec for fiber optic cabling and the STS spec for copper wire, although SONET over copper has severe limits. SONET is deployed in a self-healing dual-fiber ring topology, similar to FDDI.

SONET's transmission bandwidths range from 51.84 Mbps to 2.48 Gbps. The hardware actually operates at speeds in the 10 Gbps range, but the SONET standard hasn't been expanded to include it yet. SONET is most widely used inside service providers to act as a high speed backbone for other systems, like frame relay and ATM.

The Optical Carrier (OC) System

The Optical Carrier (OC) system is a channelized technology based on the same 64 Kbps channel as DSH but with a base rate of 810 channels. The OC standard is open-ended, enabling manufacturers to add to it as they develop hardware that supports faster speeds. These added specifications aren't part of the standard but do follow the pattern. The following table lists OC standard specifications.

OC Specification	Number of Channels	Data Rate
OC1	810	51.84 Mbps
OC3	2,430	155.52 Mbps
OC9	7,290	466.56 Mbps
OC12	9,720	622.08 Mbps
OC18	14,580	933.12 Mbps
OC24	19,440	1.244 Gbps
OC36	26,160	1.866 Gbps
OC192	155,520	9.95 Gbps

The STS System

The Synchronous Transport Signal (STS) system is the electrical signal component of the SONET system. It is both the specification for implementing SONET over copper and the frame type for SONET optical transmissions. The channel numbers and bandwidth for STS are identical to those for the OC system. However, because electrical noise is such a problem in copper wiring, bandwidths beyond STS9 (OC9) are impossible. The most common copper implementations inside a controlled environment are STS1 and STS3, but even then the copper wire is limited to 100 meters.

Synchronous Digital Hierarchy (SDH)

SDH is another optical communications standard that is based upon SONET and implemented widely outside the U.S. The first level of the SDH hierarchy is designated as STM1, and is the equivalent of OC3 in the SONET standard.

SONET Network Components

A SONET network is divided into three areas. Each area is controlled by the same integrated management.

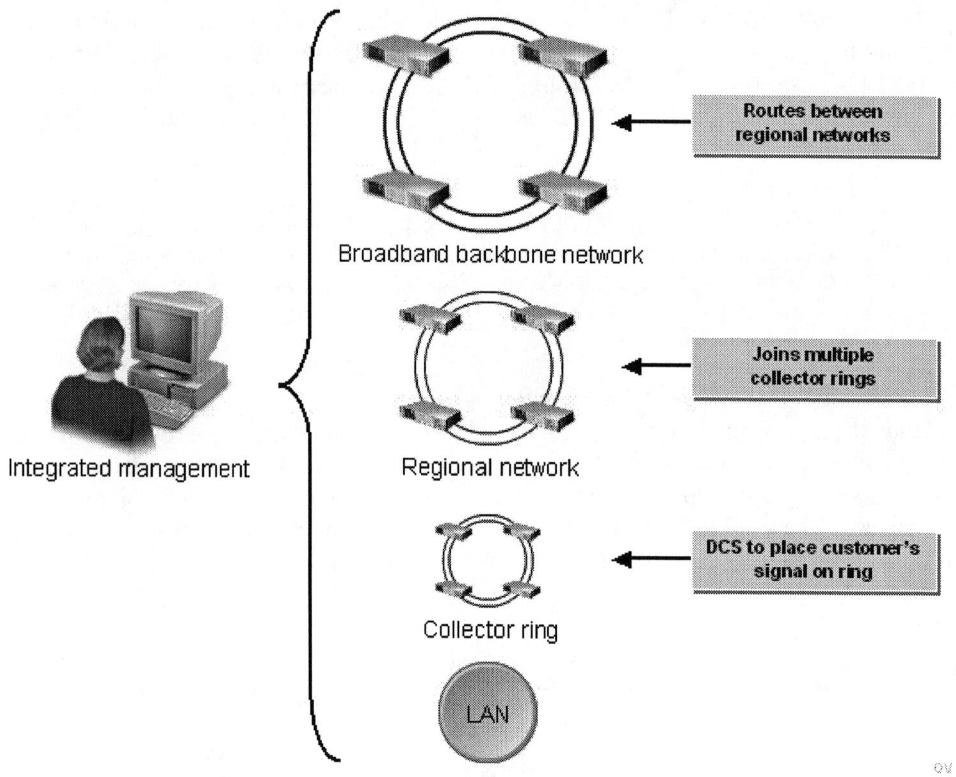

Figure 10-13: *SONET network components.*

Area	Description
Local collector ring	The local collector ring is closest to users and made up of Digital Cross Connect Switches (DCSs) placed at the customer location or tied to the customer location via a T-Carrier. The DCS acts like a concentrator to place the customer's signal onto the SONET ring. It supports connections from different speed technologies and from multiple customers. Almost any technology can be connected to the ring— ATM, T1 or T3 lines, ISDN, or even DSL voice.
Regional network	By managing the bandwidth on the regional network, the regional network becomes extremely efficient. When data moves between two networks supported by the same regional network, the connection can be made most efficiently through the regional network. The regional network joins multiple collector rings by using Add/Drop Multiplexers (ADMs). The ADM allows data from the collector rings to be added to the regional ring. Data that isn't getting off the ring simply passes through the ADM.
Broadband backbone network	The backbone network routes data between regional networks. It can route very big blocks of data simultaneously, which makes it highly efficient. It does not route individual channels.

Unbounded WAN Media

Unbounded media such as satellite linkups are employed for truly long-range WAN transmission. Often the signal is transferred from bounded media to a satellite link at some point in the transmission, and transmitted back down to a physical link at the other end of the transmission for data delivery.

One example of direct unbounded WAN transmissions is satellite Internet access. Depending upon their satellite provider, satellite TV customers can choose to receive Internet access through the same satellite dish that receives their TV signal.

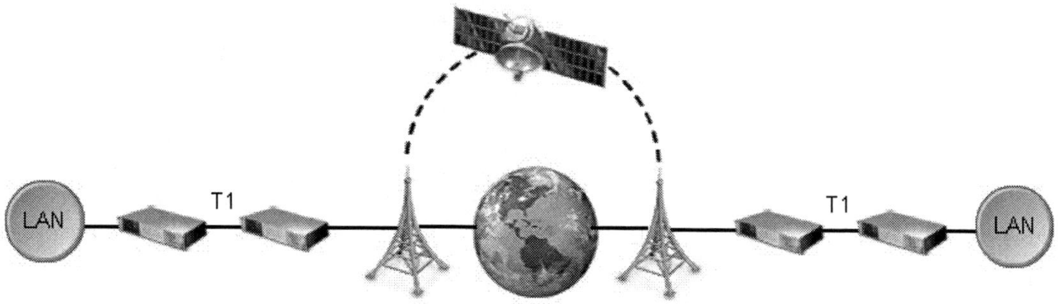

Figure 10-14: *Unbounded WAN media.*

Satellite Transmissions

With satellite services, the speeds average around 1 Mbps for uploads and 2 Mbps for downloads. However, unlike other wireless options such as 802.11b and 802.11g, satellite connections can be slow or delayed, so satellite transmissions do not work well with traffic bursts. Although satellite speeds are increasing, they still are no match for wireless LANS. However, a satellite-based network offers immense geographical coverage.

ACTIVITY 10-2

Installing a Modem

There is a simulated version of this activity available on the CD-ROM that shipped with this course. You can run this simulation on any Windows computer to review the activity after class, or as an alternative to performing the activity as a group in class. The activity simulation can be launched either directly from the CD-ROM by clicking the Interactives link and navigating to the appropriate one, or from the installed data file location by opening the C:\Data\Simulations\Lesson#\Activity# folder and double-clicking the executable (.exe) file.

Scenario:

You are going to use dial-up Internet connectivity for your home computer. Before you create your Internet connection, you will need to install a modem.

What You Do	How You Do It
1. **Enter your modem dialing code.**	a. **Choose Start→Control Panel→Phone And Modem Options.**
	b. In the What Area Code (Or City Code) Are You In Now? text box, **type *585***
	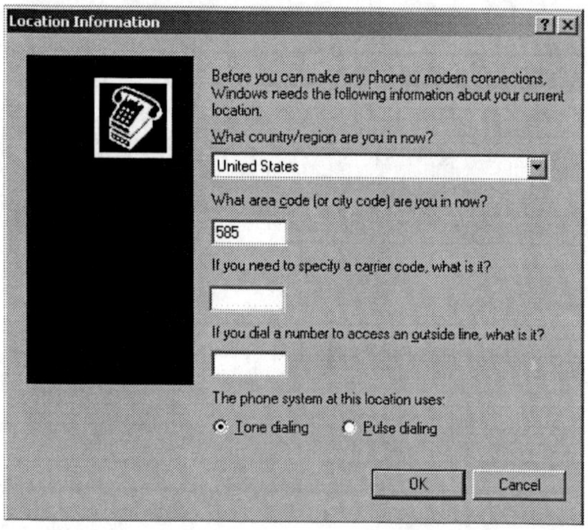
	c. **Click OK.**

2. **Install the modem.**

a. **Select the Modems tab.**

b. **Click Add.**

c. **Check Don't Detect My Modem; I Will Select It From A List and click Next.**

d. Under Models, **select Standard 28800 bps Modem and click Next.**

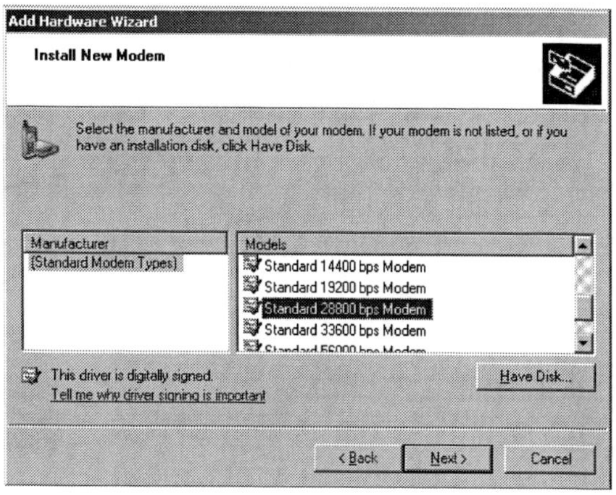

e. **Select COM 1 and click Next.**

f. When the installation is complete, **click Finish.**

g. **Verify that the modem appears in the Modem list and click OK.**

ACTIVITY 10-3

Creating a Dial-Up Connection

There is a simulated version of this activity available on the CD-ROM that shipped with this course. You can run this simulation on any Windows computer to review the activity after class, or as an alternative to performing the activity as a group in class. The activity simulation can be launched either directly from the CD-ROM by clicking the Interactives link and navigating to the appropriate one, or from the installed data file location by opening the C:\Data\Simulations\Lesson#\Activity# folder and double-clicking the executable (.exe) file.

Scenario:

To connect to your dial-up Internet service provider, you will need a dial-up connection to the Internet. The ISP's local access number is 555-1234.

What You Do	How You Do It
1. Create the dial-up connection.	a. **Choose Start→Control Panel→Network Connections.**

b. **Choose New Connection Wizard.**

c. **Click Next.**

d. **Verify that Connect To The Internet is selected and click Next.**

e. **Verify That Connect Using A Dial-up Modem is selected and click Next.**

f. In the ISP Name text box, **type *My Dial-up* and click Next.**

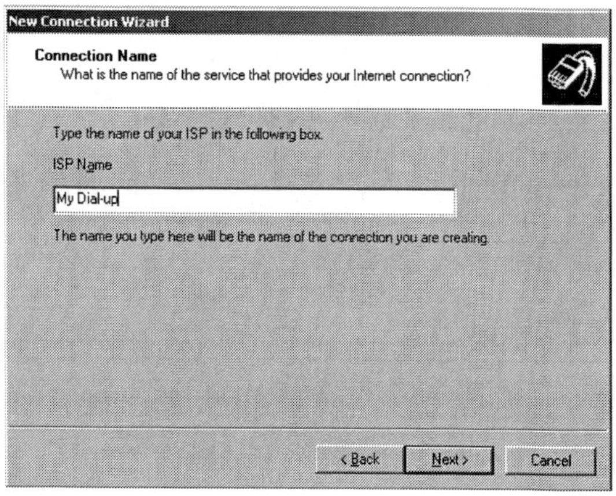

g. In the Phone Number text box, **type *555-1234* and click Next.**

h. **Verify that Anyone's Use is selected and click Next.**

i. **Type *User* as the user name and leave the Password and Confirm Password text boxes blank.**

j. **Uncheck Make This The Default Internet Connection and click Next.**

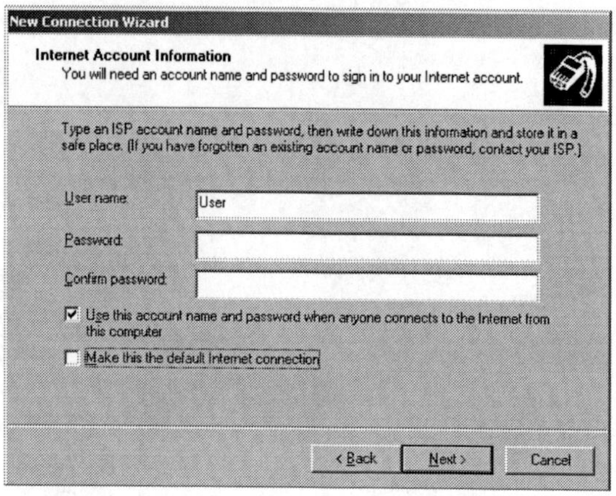

k. **Click Finish.**

---

2. **Verify the connection properties.**

a. In the Connect My Dial-up dialog box, **click Properties.**

b. **Verify that the connection will use the standard 28800 bps modem and that the phone number is 555-1234.**

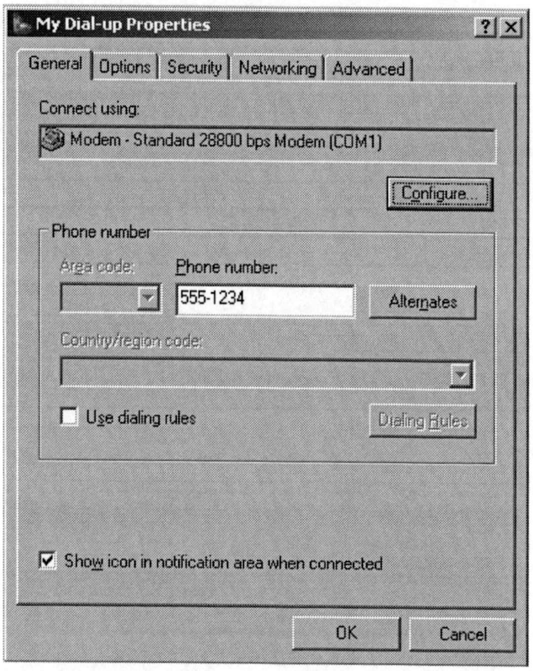

c. **Click Cancel twice.**

TOPIC C

WAN Connectivity Methods

In previous topics, you identified WAN switching and transmission technologies. Another WAN component is the WAN connectivity method. In this topic, you will identify the major WAN connectivity methods.

Once you've decided how you're going to transmit your WAN data, you have one last issue to deal with: How do you connect your self-contained LAN to a WAN that uses completely different technologies? Understanding the various WAN connectivity devices and methods will help you implement your WAN connection appropriately.

Multiplexers in WAN Connectivity

A multiplexer (mux) can be used to combine multiple data signals onto WAN transmission media, such as fiber or T1 lines, to use the physical link in the most efficient way possible. The mux usually can demux as well, to serve as a single point of connectivity to the network for both directions of data flow.

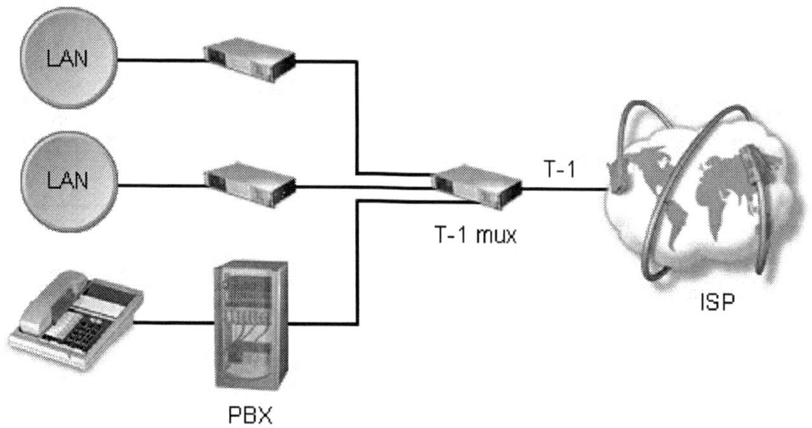

Figure 10-15: *A mux in a WAN link.*

Disadvantage of TDM

A mux that uses time-division multiplexing (TDM) to share the channel among devices divides the bandwidth fairly. However, if a time slice is allocated to a node that doesn't have data to send, the node's time channel is sent empty, wasting that part of the bandwidth.

Channel Service Unit/Data Service Unit (CSU/DSU)

Definition:

A *Channel Service Unit/Data Service Unit (CSU/DSU)* is a combination of two WAN connectivity devices that work together to terminate the ends of a digital T1 or T3 line from a telephone company network. The DSU receives the signal from the LAN and passes it to the CSU. The CSU converts the signal format to make it compatible with the digital data service (DDS) on the WAN line.

The DSU and CSU can be deployed separately, which means that different LAN types can terminate with different DDS systems. In this case, the customer typically owns or leases the DSU, while the WAN provider retains the CSU. Alternatively, the DSU and CSU can be combined in a single device.

Example:

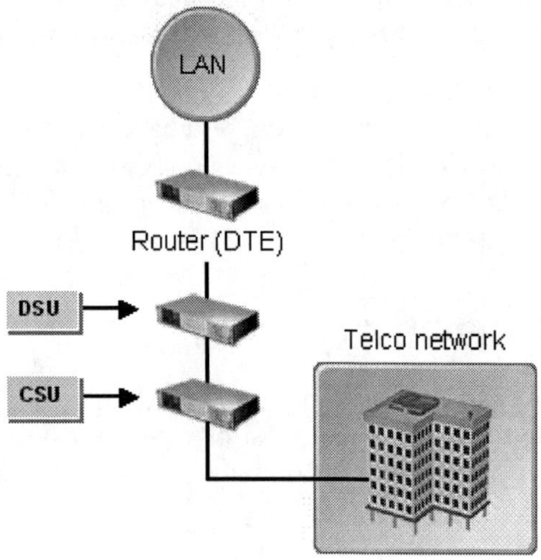

Figure 10-16: *A CSU/DSU.*

A CSU/DSU has the same function in connecting a LAN interface with a digital WAN that a modem does in connecting a computer or LAN to a standard analog phone line.

Telephone Modem Standards

Current modem standards are set by the International Telecommunications Union (ITU). The following table lists some of the most common standards.

ITU Standard	Speed
V.32	9,600 bps synchronous; 4,800 bps asynchronous
V.32 bis	14.4 Kbps synchronous and asynchronous
V.34	28.8 Kbps
V.34 bis	33.6 Kbps
V.42	57.6 Kbps; specifies standards for error checking
V.42 bis	57.6 Kbps; specifies standards for compression
V.90	56 Kbps upstream; 33.6 Kbps downstream because downstream data is modulated

ITU Standards Notation

ITU standards are called "vee-dot" standards because they come from Series V, "Data Communication over the Telephone Network," of the ITU's recommended standards. V dot standards sometimes appear with *bis* or *terbo* in the notation. These are French words that mean second and third.

For more information on the ITU and Series V standards, see the ITU website at **www.itu.org**

Modems vs. Interfaces

Some network connectivity devices are commonly called modems when they are more properly classified as a type of network interface device. For example, cable modems actually appear to the computer system as a specialized network interface card, as do ISDN adapters. These are not modems because they do not modulate and demodulate between analog and data signals; they are interfaces between two digital systems.

Internet Connection Sharing (ICS)

Internet Connection Sharing (ICS) is a WAN connectivity method for Windows computer systems that connects multiple computers to the Internet by using a single Internet connection. The computer that is connected to the Internet is called the ICS host; the other computers are ICS clients.

The ICS host must have two network connections:

- A local area connection, automatically created by installing a network adapter that connects to the computers on your home or small-office network.
- An external connection, linking the home or small-office network and the Internet. ICS is enabled on this connection.

When you enable ICS, the LAN connection to the internal network is given a new static private IP address and configuration. The ICS host assigns new dynamic private IP addresses to the ICS clients.

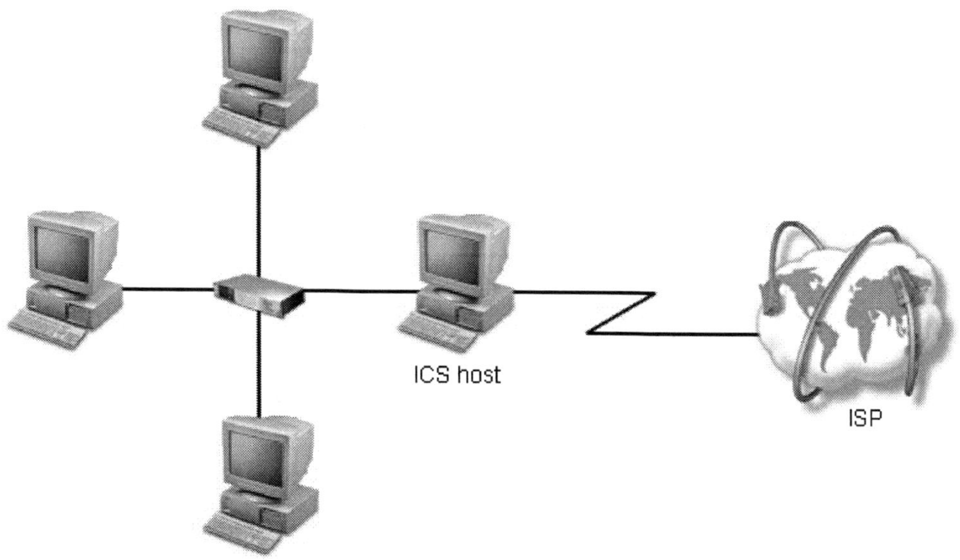

Figure 10-17: *ICS.*

The Internet connection on the ICS host can use standard dial-up, or a high-speed broadband ISDN, DSL, or cable modem connection. ICS is most effective with a high-speed connection, but dial-up performance is usually acceptable.

Other ICS Requirements

ICS is supported in Windows XP and Windows Server 2003. There are several other network configuration requirements for an ICS connection. Because the ICS host provides dynamic addressing and DNS proxy services to the ICS clients, there must not be any active DNS or DHCP servers on the network, and the ICS clients must be configured for dynamic IP addressing. Also, the logon credentials for the Internet connection on the ICS host must be shared for all users. See the Windows Help system for more information.

ACTIVITY 10-4

Examining ICS Configuration on Windows Server 2003

There is a simulated version of this activity available on the CD-ROM that shipped with this course. You can run this simulation on any Windows computer to review the activity after class, or as an alternative to performing the activity as a group in class. The activity simulation can be launched either directly from the CD-ROM by clicking the Interactives link and navigating to the appropriate one, or from the installed data file location by opening the C:\Data\Simulations\Lesson#\Activity# folder and double-clicking the executable (.exe) file.

Scenario:

You are thinking of implementing ICS to connect your small home office to the Internet. You want to see how difficult the ICS configuration on your host computer will be.

What You Do	How You Do It
1. **View the ICS properties for your computer's Internet connection.**	a. **Choose Start→Control Panel→Network Connections.**
	b. **Right-click My Dial-up and choose Properties.**
	c. **Select the Advanced tab.**
	d. The dial-up connection will be the shared Internet connection. **Check the Allow Other Network Users To Connect Through This Computer's Internet Connection check box.**

e. The Local Area Connection will be the internal network connection. From the Home Networking Connection drop-down list, **select Local Area Connection.**

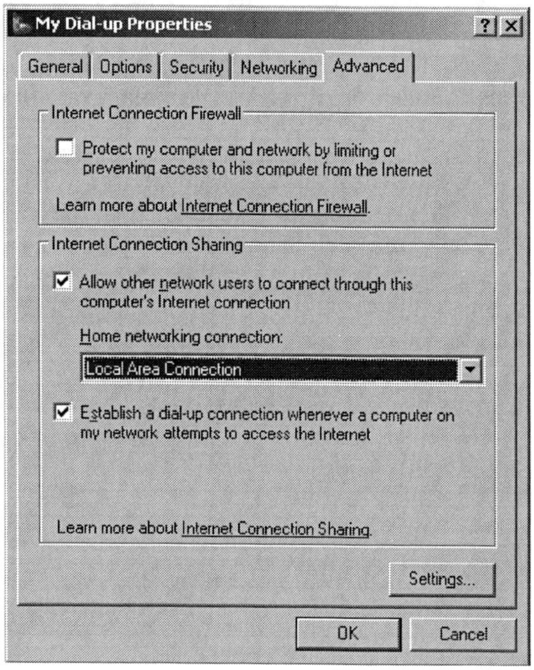

f. **Click Cancel.**

---

2. **If you enabled ICS on this host, what would be the effect on the network configuration?**

---

3. **What are some of the other configuration requirements for ICS?**

TOPIC D

Voice Over Data Systems

In previous topics, you identified the data-transmission technologies used in WAN implementations. Another aspect of WAN implementations is voice-transmission technology. In this topic, you will identify major Voice over Data systems.

A WAN implementation is valuable for moving data efficiently over long distances. But once your WAN is in place, you might find that it's useful for moving other kinds of data as well, including voice data that is currently transported over standard telephone systems. Most network professionals today will implement some form of the rapidly evolving Voice over Data technology, so you should understand its fundamentals.

Voice Over Data Systems

Definition:

Voice over Data systems are communications systems that replace traditional telephone links by transmitting analog voice communications over digital WAN networking technologies. The digital WANs provide more bandwidth and better quality of service than analog phone systems, and there is no long-distance service cost.

Because voice communications are time sensitive, the Voice over Data system must ensure that packets arrive complete and in close proximity to each other. In a Voice over Data system, voice agent software interfaces with an analog voice device to convert the voice to a data signal and to translate the dialing destination to a network address.

Example:

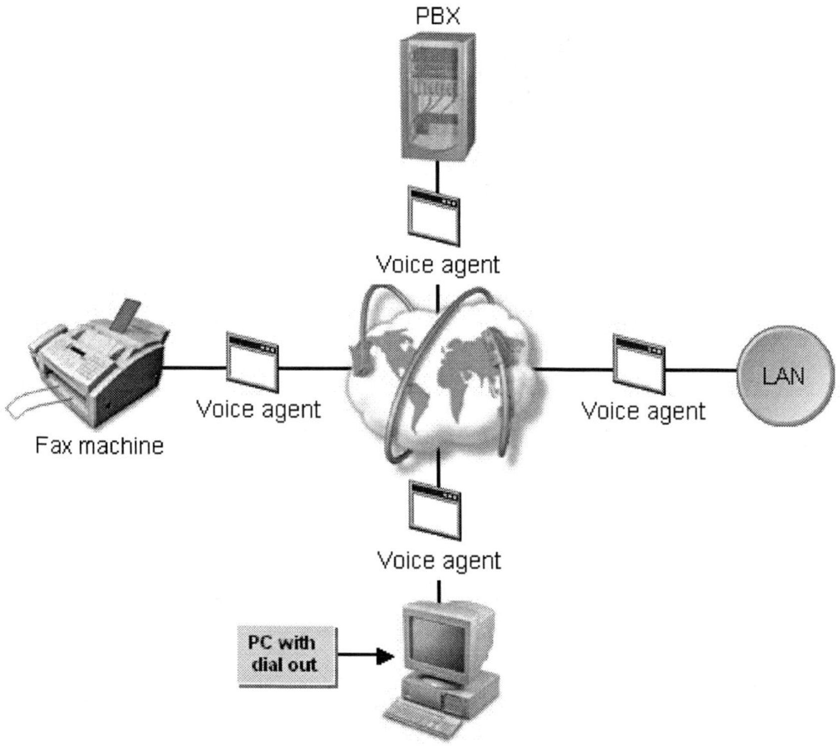

Figure 10-18: *Voice over Data.*

Voice Over IP (VoIP)

Voice over IP (VoIP) is a Voice over Data implementation in which voice signals are transmitted over IP networks. The phone instrument is the addressed device. It can be an IP telephone unit or a VoIP interface at a *Private Branch Exchange (PBX)*, which enables the phone system to access the IP network at a single point. A dial plan map translates between PBX dial numbers and IP addresses; if a dialed phone number is found in the map, VoIP routes the call to an IP host.

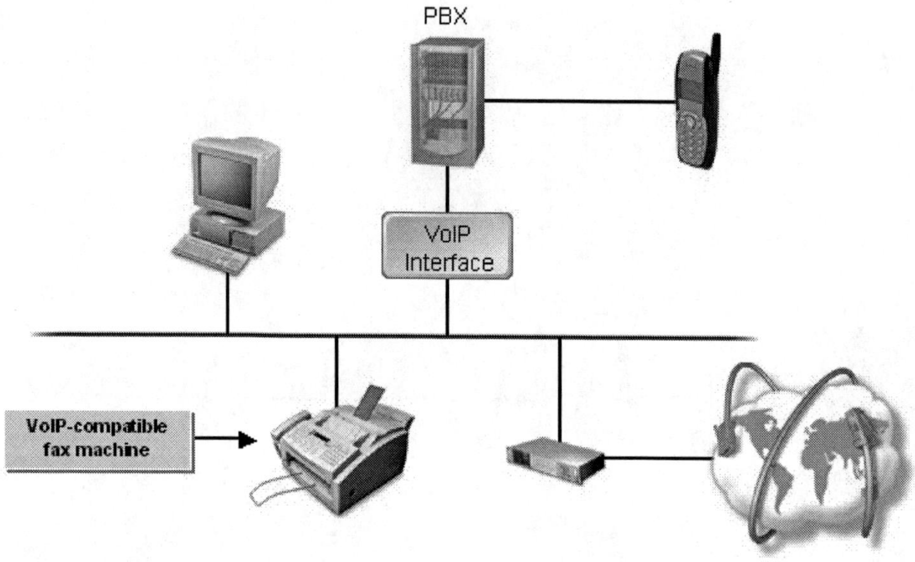

Figure 10-19: *VoIP.*

Advantages and Limitations of VoIP

VoIP is being rapidly adopted because it relies on the existing, robust router infrastructure of IP networks and the near-universal implementation of the IP protocol. It also eliminates per-call costs because it uses the existing Internet connectivity channel. It does have some drawbacks. The major problem is that IPv4 does not provide for time-sensitive data. On a busy network, voice data is packet switched with other network data and delivery can slow down or become unreliable.

Voice over Frame Relay (VoFR)

Voice over Frame Relay (VoFR) is an alternative to VoIP in which voice traffic is routed over a frame relay WAN. It creates either a permanent or switched end-to-end connection through the network requested by the VoFR access equipment. It can use either PVCs or SVCs, but PVCs are preferred because there is no lag in connection time. Once an SVC connection is made, however, the user is unaware of the frame relay routing. The VoFR industry is not well standardized; features and compatibilities can vary greatly between vendors, so it is best to implement a single-vendor solution.

Voice over ATM (VoATM)

Voice over ATM (VoATM) is an alternative to VoIP in which voice traffic is routed over an ATM network. One advantage of ATM is that it already includes priority for time-sensitive data, along with high backbone speeds. Inside telco networks, ATM is implemented over SONET at 10 Gbps data rates.

ACTIVITY 10-5

Discussing Voice Over Data Systems

Scenario:

In this activity, you will discuss the characteristics of Voice over Data systems.

1. **What are advantages of Voice over Data systems as compared to traditional telephone systems?**
   - a) Reduced long-distance costs
   - b) Increased bandwidth
   - c) Increased quality of service
   - d) Dedicated circuit switching

2. **What component of a VoIP system translates between phone numbers and IP addresses?**
   - a) The voice agent
   - b) The dial plan map
   - c) The PBX
   - d) The router
   - e) The DNS server

3. **Which component of a VoIP system converts the voice data to a digital signal?**
   - a) The telephone instrument
   - b) The dial plan map
   - c) The voice agent
   - d) The router
   - e) The PBX

Lesson 10 Follow-up

In this lesson, you identified the components of a WAN implementation. Because almost every LAN uses WAN technologies to connect to other networks, including the Internet, understanding WAN infrastructure helps you ensure WAN connectivity on the networks you support.

1. **Of the WAN switching, transmission, and connectivity technologies discussed in this lesson, which ones do you expect to work with most frequently? Why?**

2. **What do you see as the future for Voice over Data systems? In your opinion, what are their benefits and drawbacks?**

NOTES

LESSON 11
Network Security

Lesson Time
2 hour(s), 30 minutes

Lesson Objectives:

In this lesson, you will identify major issues and technologies in network security.

You will:

- Identify the major categories of network threats.
- Identify the elements of a virus protection plan.
- Identify the components of local network security.
- Identify network authentication methods.
- Identify major data encryption methods and technologies.
- Identify the primary techniques used to secure Internet connections.

Introduction

This course covers the fundamental concepts and skills needed by network administrators and support personnel. One of the most basic tasks in supporting a network is securing it. In this lesson, you will identify the major issues and technologies involved in network security.

Each day, the number and complexity of threats against computer network security increases. In response to these threats, there are more and more security tools and techniques available to increase network security. As a networking professional, your organization and your users will all be looking to you to ensure that your network environment provides the appropriate level of security, without compromising network performance.

This lesson covers the following CompTIA Network+ (2005) certification objectives:

- Topic B:
  - Objective 3.10: Identify the purpose, benefits, and characteristics of antivirus software.
- Topic D:
  - Objective 2.18: Identify authentication protocols (for example, Kerberos and EAP (Extensible Authentication Protocol)).
  - Objective 3.7: Given a connectivity scenario, determine the impact on network functionality of a particular security implementation (for example, port blocking/filtering, authentication, and encryption).
- Topic E:
  - Objective 2.17: Identify the following security protocols and describe their purpose and function: IPSec (Internet Protocol Security) and SSL (Secure Sockets Layer).
  - Objective 3.7: Given a connectivity scenario, determine the impact on network functionality of a particular security implementation (for example, port blocking/filtering, authentication, and encryption).
- Topic F:
  - Objective 1.6: Identify the purposes, features, and functions of firewalls.
  - Objective 2.13: Identify the purpose of network services and protocols, such as NAT (Network Address Translation).
  - Objective 3.5: Identify the purpose, benefits, and characteristics of a firewall.
  - Objective 3.6: Identify the purpose, benefits, and characteristics of a proxy service.

TOPIC A

Network Threats

In this lesson, you will identify major issues and technologies in network security. The starting point for understanding any type of network security measure is understanding the threats it is designed to combat. In this topic, you will identify the major categories of network threats.

To secure your network, you have to protect against threats, but you can't protect against threats you don't understand or recognize. That's why "know your enemy" should be the watchword of any network security professional. To properly develop, deploy, and maintain a network security plan, a network administrator has to understand the different types of threats and how they can affect the network.

Unauthorized Access

Definition:

Unauthorized access is any type of network or data access that is not explicitly approved by the organization. It can be a deliberate attack by an outsider, a misuse of valid privileges by an authorized user, or it can be inadvertent. Unauthorized access does not necessarily result in data loss or damage, but it is the first step in mounting a number of attacks against the network.

Example:

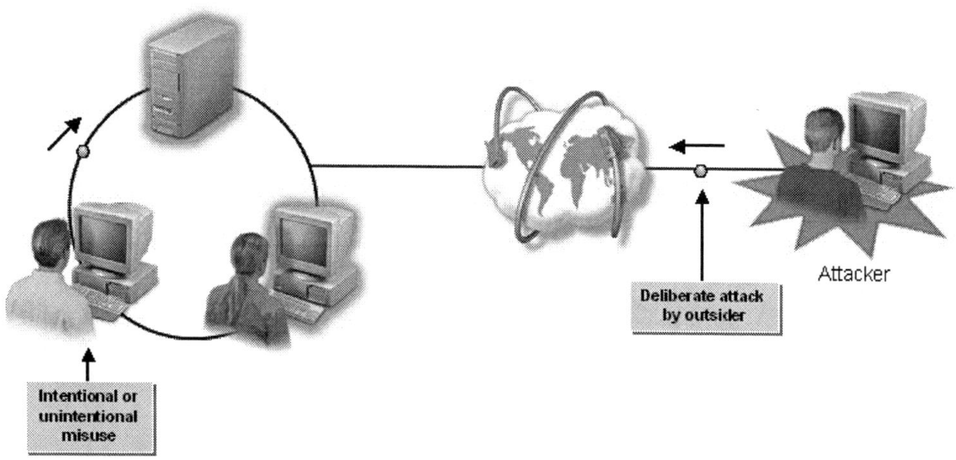

Figure 11-1: *Unauthorized access.*

Data Theft

Definition:

Data theft is a type of attack in which unauthorized access is used to obtain protected network information. The attacker can use stolen credentials to authenticate to a server and read data stored in files. Or, the attacker can steal data in transit on the network media by using a hardware- or software-based "*sniffer*," which is a device or program that monitors network communications and captures data.

Example:

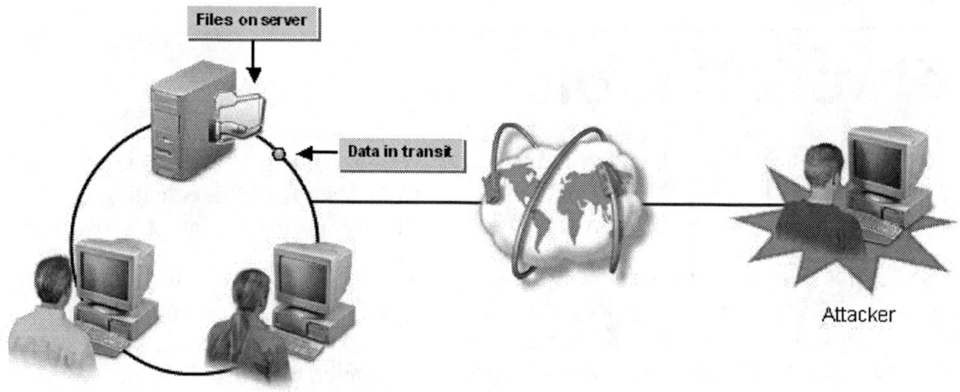

Figure 11-2: *Data theft.*

Password Attacks

Definition:

A *password attack* is any type of unauthorized effort to discover a user's valid password. The attacker can steal the password or guess the password. Once the attacker has obtained a valid password, the attacker can use it to gain unauthorized access to the network.

Example:

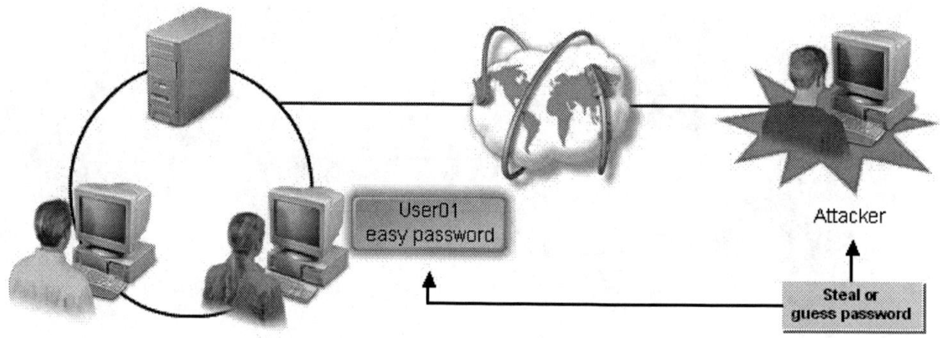

Figure 11-3: *Password attacks.*

Brute Force Password Attacks

Definition:

A *brute force password attack* is a method of guessing passwords by using software that systematically generates password combinations until a valid one is found. Brute force password attacks, given enough time and sufficiently complex password-cracking software, will usually succeed.

Example:

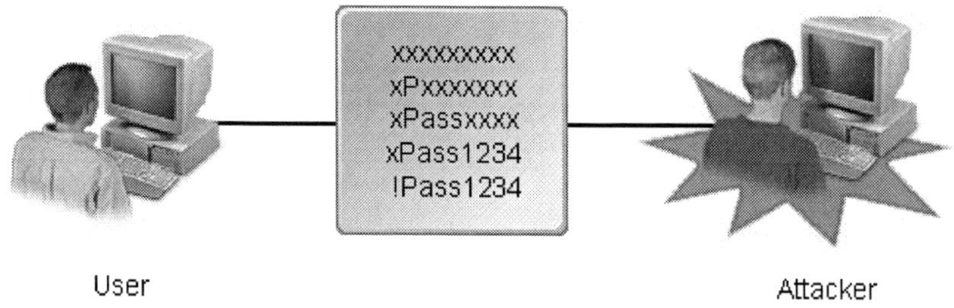

Figure 11-4: *Brute force password attacks.*

Trojan Horse Attacks

Definition:

A *Trojan horse attack* is an attempt to gain unauthorized access through the use of a *Trojan horse* program, which masquerades as valid software. The Trojan horse is often delivered as an email attachment; the user runs the Trojan horse thinking it is a harmless or approved file. The Trojan horse then performs unauthorized functions such as stealing or corrupting passwords, credit card information, or data.

Example:

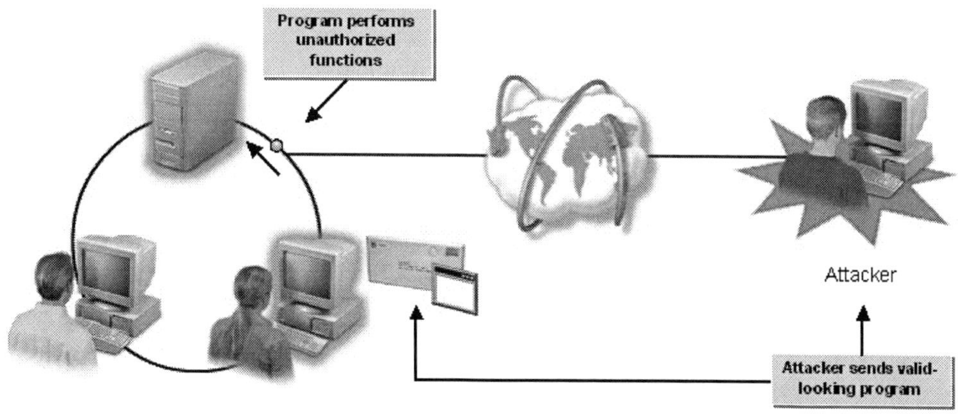

Figure 11-5: *Trojan horse attacks.*

Spoofing Attacks

Definition:

A *spoofing* attack is a type of attack in which a device outside the network uses an internal network address to masquerade as a device inside the network. Because network devices often authenticate by address only, rather than by password, the external device can use a legitimate internal address to authenticate on the network and obtain network information.

Example:

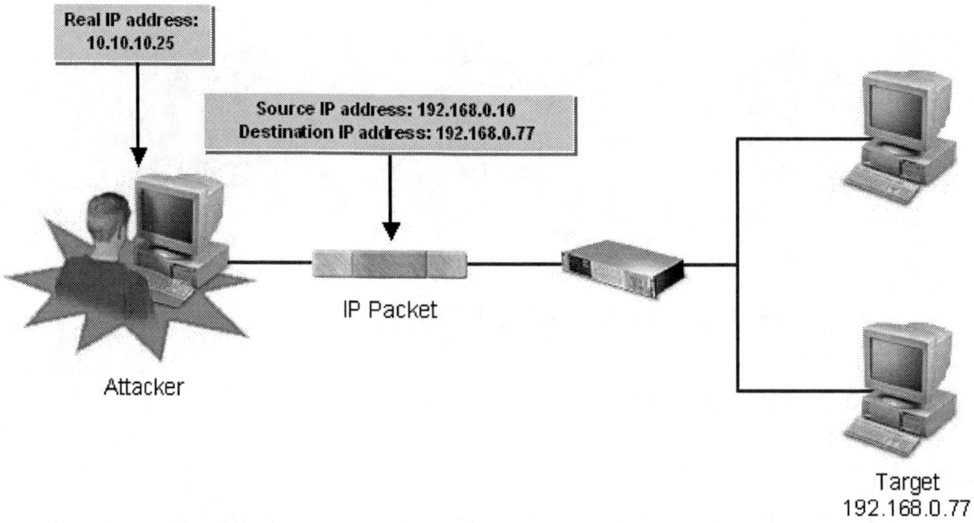

Figure 11-6: *Spoofing.*

The Spoofing Process

In a basic spoofing attack, the attacker:

1. First, identifies a target within the network.
2. Then, identifies a host that has a trust relationship with the target.
3. Next, disables the legitimate host that is communicating with the target.
4. Steals the trusted device's network address and identity.
5. Finally, uses the stolen identity to redirect data from the target to a host under the attacker's control.

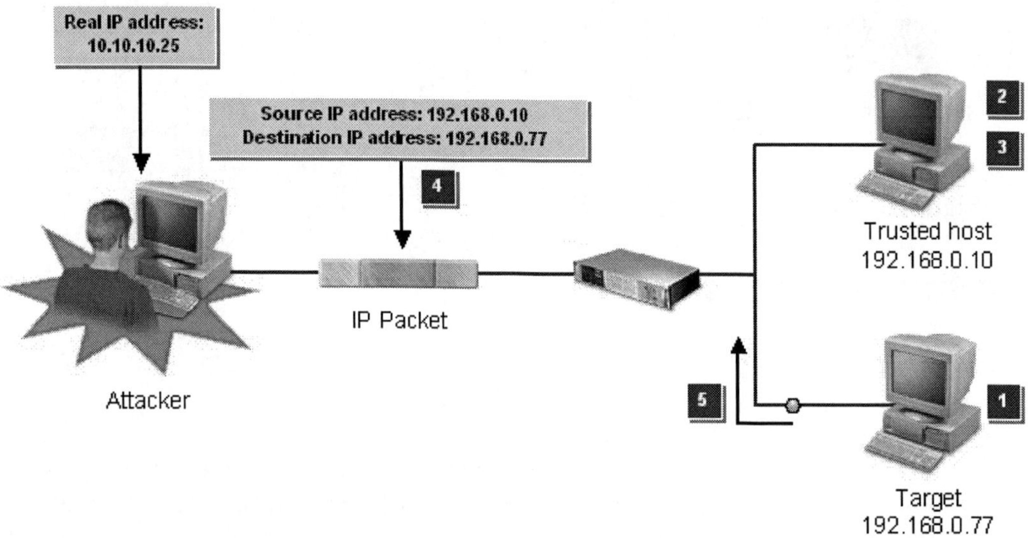

Figure 11-7: *The spoofing process.*

Session Hijacking Attacks

Definition:

Session hijacking is a type of spoofing in which the attacker takes over an existing network communication session between two devices after the session has already been authenticated. The hijacker can either read network packets as they pass between the legitimate hosts, or disable one host and pose as one of the original parties in the session.

Example:

Figure 11-8: *Session hijacking.*

Man-in-the-Middle Attacks

Definition:

A *man-in-the-middle attack* is a data-theft technique in which the attacker interposes a device between two legitimate hosts to gain access to their data transmissions. The intruder device deceives both the sender and receiver by responding to the transmissions in both directions. Unlike spoofing and hijacking, the attacker can actively manipulate the communication, rather than listening passively, and can gain access to a variety of data, including user names, passwords, network configuration, and the contents of network packets.

Example:

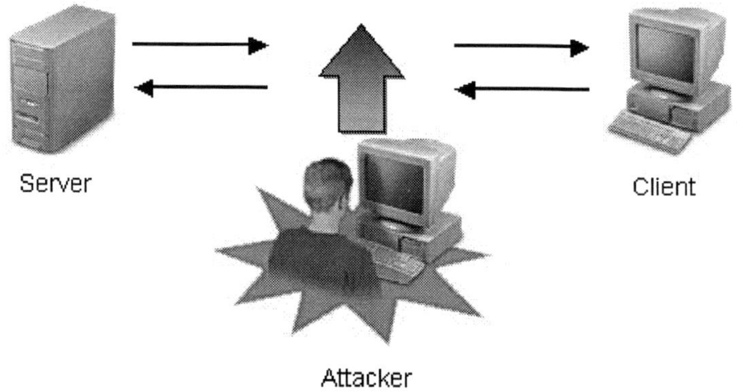

Figure 11-9: *Man-in-the-middle attacks.*

Denial of Service (DoS) Attacks

Definition:

A *Denial of Service (DoS) attack* is an attack that is mounted for the purpose of disabling systems that provide network services, rather than to steal data or inflict damage. The targets of the attack can be network servers or network routers. The DoS attack prevents the system from responding to legitimate requests, thus impeding network functions.

A DoS attack is usually mounted through one of three methods:

- Flooding a network with data to consume all available bandwidth.
- Sending data designed to exploit known flaws in a network application.
- Sending multiple service requests to a target system to consume its resources.

Example:

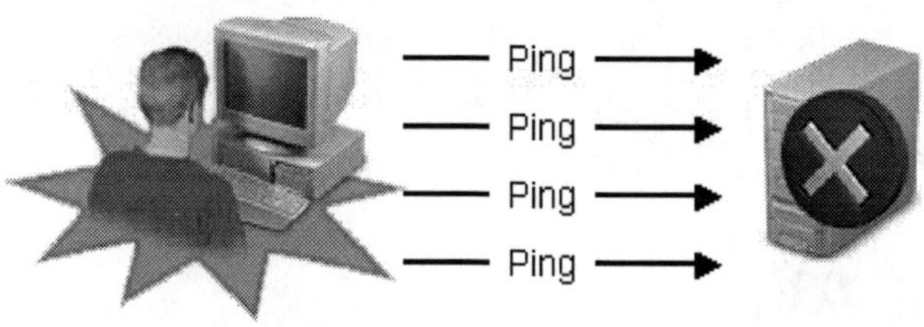

Figure 11-10: *DoS attacks.*

Smurf Attacks

Smurf attacks are a type of denial of service attack that exploits vulnerabilities in the Internet Control Message Protocol (ICMP) by overloading a host with ping requests and clogging a network with traffic. Essentially, smurf attackers create a false ICMP Echo Request (ping) packet that uses the address of the targeted host as the source and a network broadcast address as the destination. When a smurf attack is launched, every machine on the destination network returns a packet to the victim. In well-orchestrated attacks, an attacker could cause the complete crash of the target operating system as well as create substantial traffic that can cripple a network.

Distributed Denial of Service (DDoS) Attacks

Definition:

A *Distributed Denial of Service (DDoS) attack* is a type of DoS attack that uses multiple computers on disparate networks to launch the attack from many simultaneous sources. The attacker introduces unauthorized software called a *zombie* or *drone* that directs the computers to launch the attack.

Example:

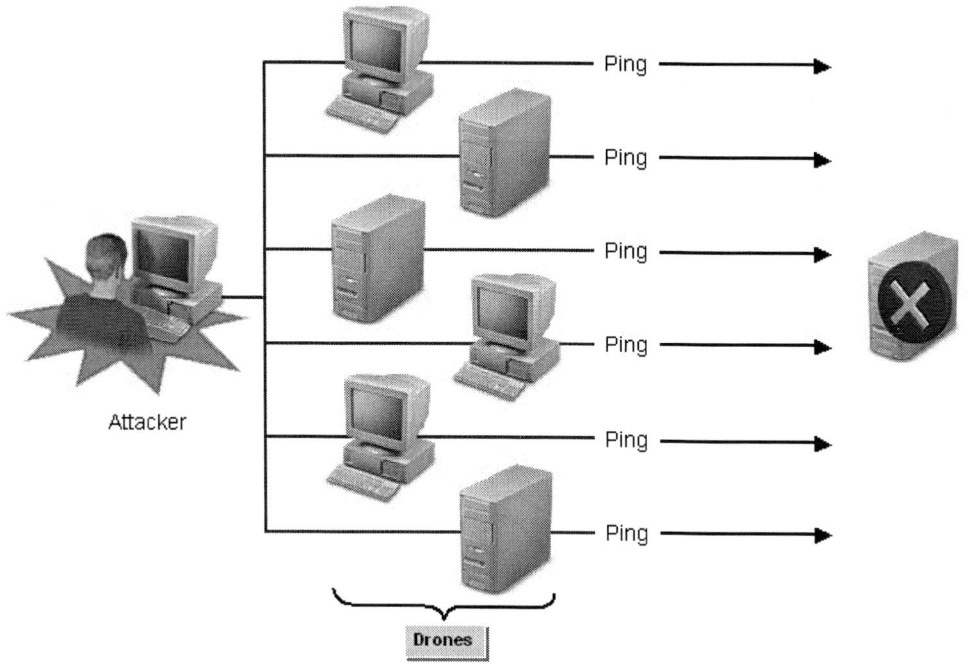

Figure 11-11: *DDoS attacks.*

Viruses

Definition:

A *virus* is a self-propagating unauthorized software program. Many viruses are able to move from one computer to another and create copies of themselves. A virus can carry payload code that enables the virus to perform additional tasks, which can be either benign or destructive. Many viruses have a malicious payload, and virus threats are among the most serious on networks today.

Purpose of Virus Attacks

Unlike other attacks, which have the specific purpose of denying services, stealing data, or obtaining access, virus attacks often have no specific target or goal. Rather, the attacker may get satisfaction merely from seeing the virus propagate and cause damage.

Example:

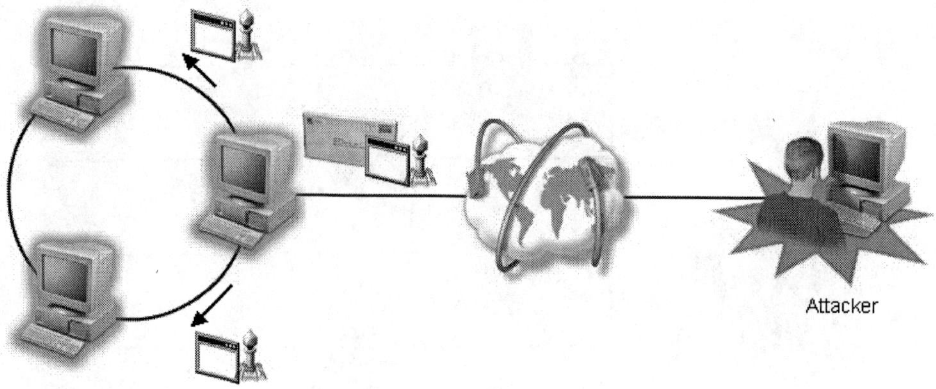

Figure 11-12: *Viruses.*

Social Engineering Attacks

Definition:

A *social engineering attack* is a non-technical attack in which the attacker attempts to obtain information directly from network users by employing deception and trickery. The attacker tries to use legitimate-sounding means to persuade a user to provide passwords, sensitive data, or even money. The attack can come through email or over the phone, and is often a precursor to another type of attack. Social engineering attacks prey upon the users least likely to recognize them and most likely to suffer directly from their effects.

Example:

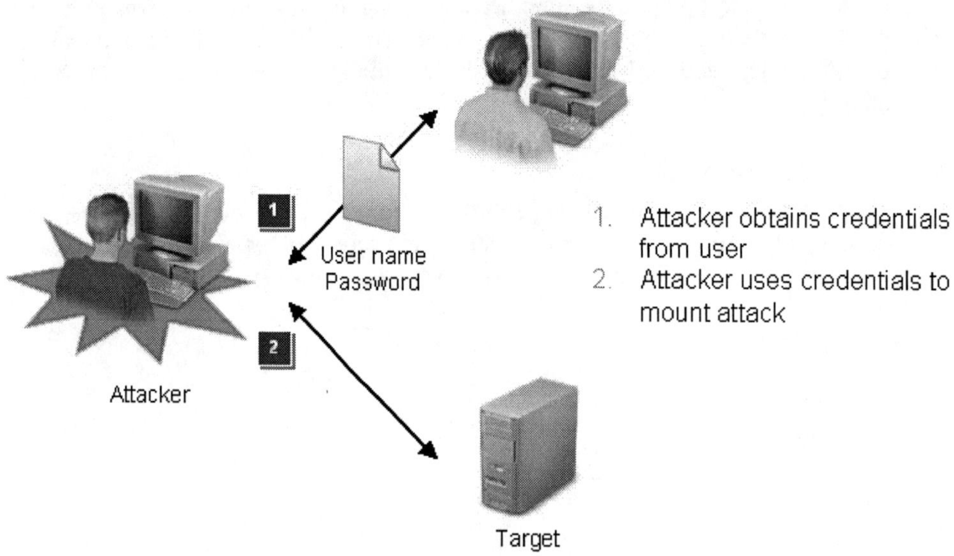

Figure 11-13: *Social engineering attacks.*

Example: Phishing

Phishing is a type of social engineering attack that is becoming more and more common. In a phishing attack, the attacker sends an email that seems to come from a respected bank or other financial institution. The email claims that the email recipient needs to provide an account number, social security number, or other private information to the email sender in order to "verify an account." Ironically, the phishing attack often claims that the "account verification" is necessary for security reasons. If the email recipient sends back the information, the attacker can use it to steal the user's financial identity. Individuals should never provide personal financial information to someone who requests it, whether through email or over the phone; legitimate financial institutions never solicit this information from their clients.

Data Protection Methods

By balancing the potential security threat with the cost of implementing and maintaining a secure network, a security professional both ensures the proper level of data protection and guards against loss of network functionality.

Guidelines

To protect data on your network, follow these guidelines:

- Deploy intruder-detection and virus-protection software to monitor for unauthorized software activity, such as the presence of viruses, password-cracking software, or Trojan horses.
- Limit physical access to the network to prevent the introduction of hardware-based sniffers or unauthorized hosts.
- Require the use of strong, complex user passwords. Change passwords on a regular basis.
- Employ strong authentication and encryption measures on data stored on network servers.
- To guard against IP spoofing, use more than one form of authentication between devices.
- Encrypt data during network transmission so that it cannot be read by sniffers.
- Conceal network address information with various technologies, including firewalls, Internet proxies, and address translation, to protect against spoofing and hijacking.
- Train users to recognize and deter social engineering attacks.

Wireless Security

Wireless networking offers both mobility and convenience to users, but it comes at a security cost. If you do not take the time to configure authentication and data encryption options, you leave your system vulnerable to attack. Wireless access point detection—often referred to as war driving or LAN-jacking—is a fairly simple process given the number of sniffing tools freely available on the Internet. There are three main ways to detect the presence of an AP and its SSID. One way is to send a probe request to the network broadcast address (FF:FF:FF:FF:FF:FF) with a zero length SSID. Many APs will respond with information such as an SSID. Another technique is to watch for AP beacon frames. Yet another option is to monitor station associations and reassociations. Perhaps the best way to protect a wireless network is to become your own investigator and download wireless sniffing tools and use them to crack your machine or network.

Example:

As a security professional, Sue is concerned about threats against her company from hackers as well as from internal users. She has deployed several safeguards against outside intruders, including enterprise-wide virus-protection software. She has also deployed a firewall.

There are company-wide security policies in place to make sure that outside parties, such as clients and vendors, cannot enter the building or use equipment without an escort. Internally, Sue has implemented strong authentication measures so that users cannot log on or access server data without valid credentials and strong passwords.

The most sensitive company data must be encrypted in storage and in transit, but universal data encryption affected network performance and was unacceptable to many users. Sue also sends out regular bulletins to make sure users understand proper security procedures, and provides users with information to help them recognize viruses, hoaxes, and other suspicious network activities.

ACTIVITY 11-1

Identifying Network Threats

Scenario:

In this activity, you will identify various types of network threats.

1. **Response time on the website that hosts the online version of your product catalog is getting slower and slower. Customers are complaining that they cannot browse the catalog items or search for products. What type of attack do you suspect?**
   a) A Trojan horse attack
   b) A spoofing attack
   c) A social engineering attack
   d) A Denial of Service (DoS) attack

2. **Jason arrives at work in the morning and finds that he can't log on to the network. The network administrator says his account was locked at 3 A.M. due to too many unsuccessful logon attempts. What type of attack do you suspect?**
   a) A man-in-the-middle attack
   b) A password attack
   c) A virus attack
   d) A hijacking attack

3. **Which of these examples can be classified as social engineering attacks?**

   a) A customer contacts your help desk asking for her user name and password because she cannot log on to your e-commerce website.

   b) A user gets a call from a person who states he is a help desk technician. The caller asks the user to go to an external website and download a file so that the technician can monitor the user's system.

   c) The CEO of your company calls you personally on the phone to ask you to fax salary data to her personal fax number. The fax number she gives you is listed in the company directory, and you recognize her voice.

   d) A user receives an email that appears to be from a bank; the bank says they need the user's name, date of birth, and social security number to verify account information.

4. **Which are considered legitimate network security measures?**

   a) Requiring complex passwords.

   b) Installing antivirus software.

   c) Denying users the ability to log on.

   d) Preventing users from storing data on network servers.

   e) Restricting physical access to the network.

TOPIC B

Virus Protection

In the previous topic, you identified the major categories of network threats. In the remaining topics, you will identify some of the methods you can use to protect against those threats. Viruses are among the most common network threats. In this topic, you will identify the elements of a virus protection plan.

Because viruses are such a common and serious type of network threat, a good virus defense plan is critical to securing network systems of any size and type. All networks will encounter viruses; as a network professional, you need to understand how a virus protection plan can limit viruses and control their spread.

Virus Infection Methods

Viruses are an insidious threat because of their ability to replicate themselves and thus spread to multiple systems. Viruses can use different propagation methods:

- A virus on a hard disk can attach itself to removable media, such as a floppy disk, which is then shared.
- A virus on the Internet can attach itself to a file. When a user downloads and runs the file, the virus is activated.

- A virus can attach to email. When a user opens or runs the attachment, the virus is activated.

Virus Types

Viruses can be categorized into several types.

Virus Type	Description
Boot sector	The original floppy disk–based virus. Writes itself into the boot sector of a floppy disk. When a system attempts to boot from the disk, the virus is moved onto the system. Once on the system, the virus attempts to move itself to every disk placed in the system.
File infecting	Infects executable programs and uses operating system resources to propagate itself. It often destroys the executable file unless it's well written.
Macro	A macro is a group of application-specific instructions that executes as a group within a specific application. A macro virus uses other programs' macro engines to propagate or dump its payload. True macro viruses don't actually infect files or data, but attach themselves to the file's template, document, or macro code. Microsoft Office products have been popular targets for macro viruses.
Mailer and mass mailer	A mailer virus sends itself to other users through the email system. It simply rides along with any email that is sent. A mass mailer virus searches the email system for mailing lists and sends itself to all users on the list. Often, the virus doesn't have a payload; its purpose is to disrupt the email system by swamping it with mail messages in a form of DoS attack.
Polymorphic	This type of virus can change as it moves around, acting differently on different systems. It can sometimes even change the virus code, making it harder to detect.
Script	A small program that runs code using the Windows scripting host on Windows operating systems. It's written as script in Visual Basic or JavaScript and executes when the script runs. Scripts are often distributed by email and require a user to open them.
Stealth	A stealth virus moves and attempts to conceal itself until it can propagate. After that, it drops its payload.
Worm	A self-contained program, similar to a virus, that spreads and can exist without a carrier file. It detects a connection and establishes communications with other devices on its own. It propagates on any network connection or email system.

See **support.microsoft.com/?scid=kb;en-us;187243** for more information on macro viruses in Microsoft products.

Hoaxes

A *hoax* is any type of incorrect or misleading information that is disseminated to multiple users through unofficial channels. Hoaxes can be relatively benign, such as an email letter containing misinformation about historical facts. However, hoaxes often improperly alert users to the existence of unsubstantiated virus threats. Users then react in two ways; first, by widely disseminating the hoax email, clogging communications systems and possibly triggering a DoS condition. Secondly, users react by following instructions in the hoax that direct them to defend or secure their computer in an improper or unapproved manner. The hoax email might, for example, use social engineering methods that direct users to delete legitimate files, or to go to websites and download files that might themselves contain actual viruses.

Antivirus Software

Definition:

Antivirus software is an application that scans files for executable code that matches patterns, known as *signatures* or *definitions,* that are known to be common to viruses. The antivirus software also monitors systems for activity that is associated with viruses, such as accessing the boot sector. Antivirus software is typically deployed on the gateway computers at the perimeter of the network as well as on individual desktop systems.

Antivirus Software Vendors

Two major antivirus software vendors are Symantec (**www.symantec.com**) and McAfee (**www.mcafee.com**).

Example:

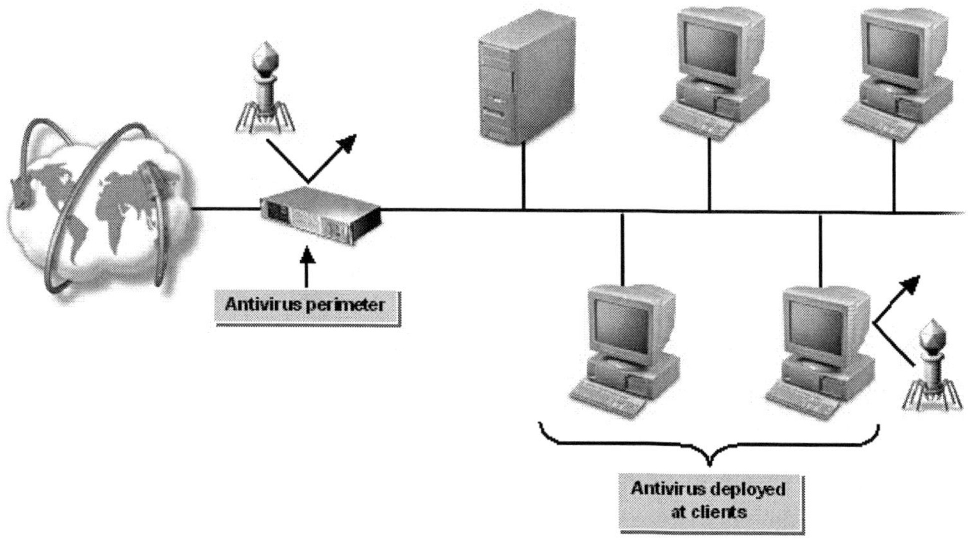

Figure 11-14: *Antivirus software.*

Updating Virus Definitions

The antivirus software vendor maintains and updates the libraries of virus definitions; the customer must periodically update the definitions on all systems where the software is installed. Most vendors provide an automatic update service that enables customers to obtain and distribute current virus definitions on a schedule. Periodically, administrators should manually check to verify that the updates are current. When there is a known active threat, administrators should also manually update definitions.

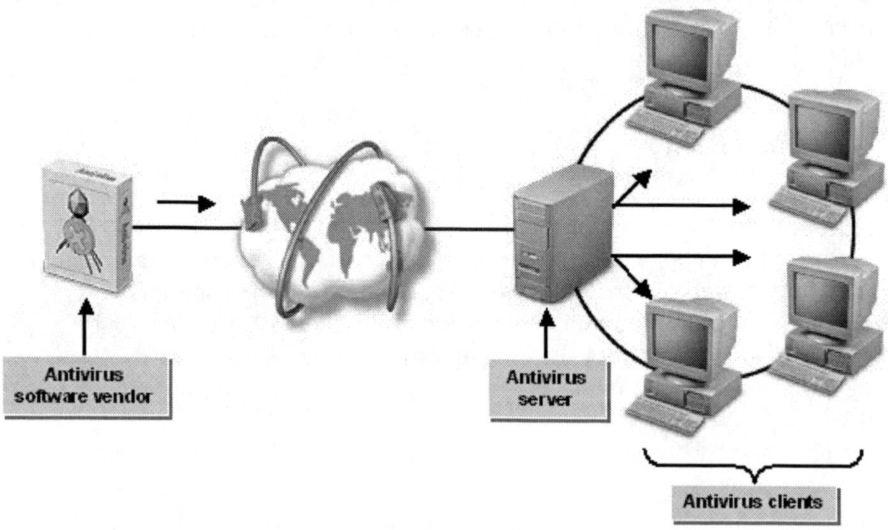

Figure 11-15: *Updating virus definitions.*

Enterprise Virus Solutions

Some vendors offer enterprise virus suites that include virus protection for all systems in a company, automatic updating, and the ability to download and distribute updates from a central server. Distributing the updates from a local server instead of obtaining them directly from the vendor enables the antivirus administrator to review and verify virus definitions before they are deployed.

Internet Email Virus Protection

Because almost all computer systems today are connected to the Internet, Internet email is a source of serious virus threats. Companies can implement Internet email virus protection by:

- Screening the Internet gateway computers for viruses.
- Employing good desktop antivirus software.
- Scanning incoming email between the Internet and the email server.
- Scanning email again at the desktop.
- If a virus attack is detected, disabling all Internet connections and isolating affected systems.

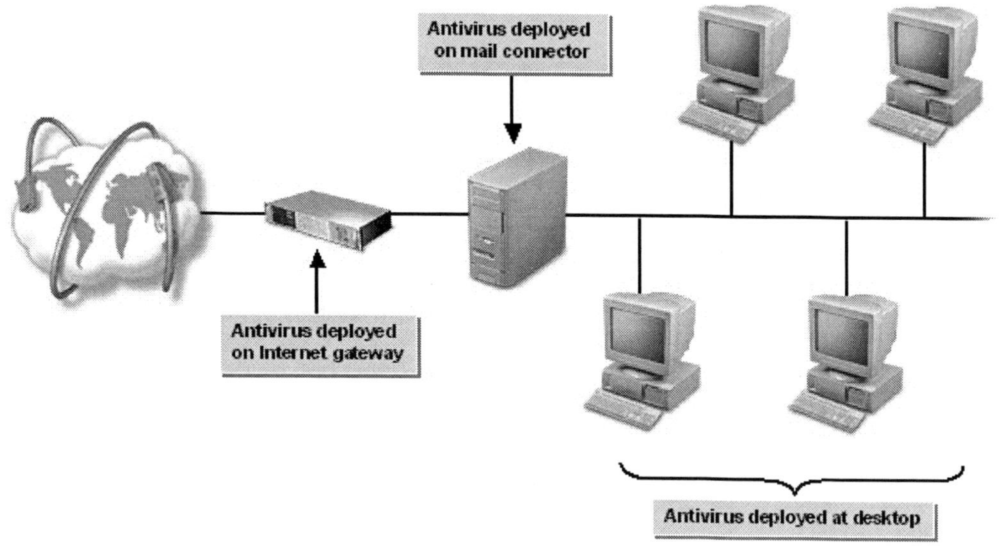

Figure 11-16: *Internet email virus protection.*

ACTIVITY 11-2

Discussing Virus Protection Plans

Scenario:

In this activity, you will identify components of a virus protection plan.

1. **What is a macro virus?**

    a) A virus that is transmitted via email.

    b) A virus that uses a specific program's command language.

    c) A virus that attacks the boot sector.

    d) A virus that runs in the Windows scripting host.

2. **Why is a hoax dangerous?**

    a) The hoax is an actual virus that has the potential to cause damage.

    b) Propagation of the hoax can create DoS conditions.

    c) Users are annoyed by the hoax.

    d) The hoax can include elements of a social engineering attack.

3. **When should a virus administrator manually check for virus updates?**

   a) When an known threat is active.

   b) After each automatic update.

   c) Never.

   d) On a daily basis.

---

4. **You manage a small office network with a single gateway to an Internet service provider. The ISP maintains your corporate email on its own email server. There is an internal server for file and print services. As the administrator for this network, where should you deploy antivirus software?**

   a) On the desktop systems.

   b) On the gateway system.

   c) On the email server.

   d) On the file and print server.

TOPIC C

Local Security

This lesson covers major issues and technologies related to network security. One component of a total security plan is implementing security on the local network. In this topic, you will identify the components of local network security.

In your organization's quest to ensure security for its users, systems, and data, you will implement security measures on different levels and on different components of your network. You'll need to secure from the inside out as well as from the outside in. Configuring appropriate security on local network components secures from the inside out, and is an important piece of an overall security plan.

Share-Level and User-Level Security

There are two primary models for implementing security on local networks: share-level security and user-level security.

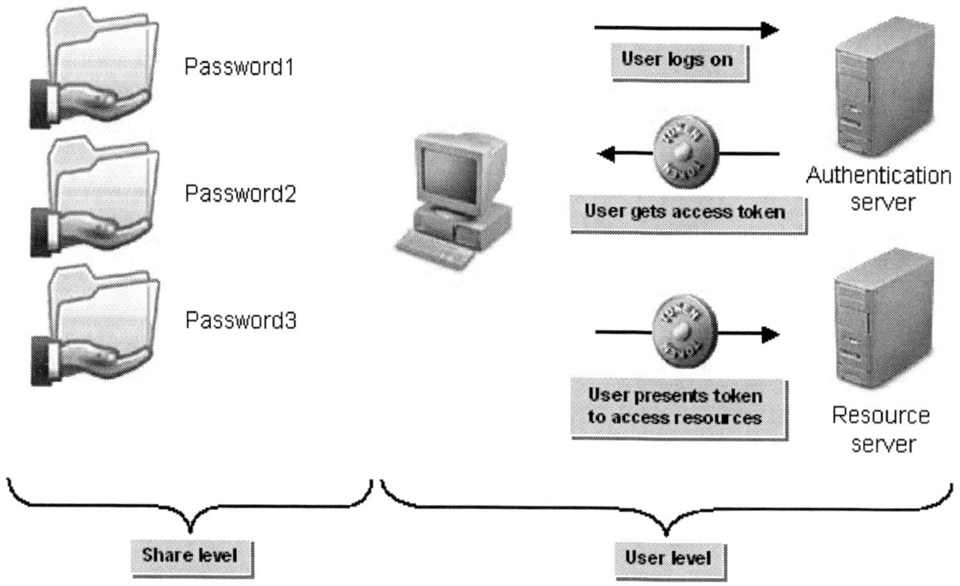

Figure 11-17: *Share-level and user-level security.*

In share-level security, access is controlled separately for each network resource. Any user who has the authentication information to a resource (usually a password) can use that resource. If the password is compromised, it must be re-created and redistributed to legitimate users.

Workgroup computers running Windows 95 and Windows 98 implemented a share-level security model.

In user-level security, all security settings, rights, and permissions are associated with specific user accounts. When the user is authenticated, the system builds an access token containing that user's security profile. Then, an access-control system checks the contents of the token to determine whether the user can access a given resource. User-level security has superseded share-level security in most network implementations.

Rights

Definition:

A *right* is a security setting that controls whether or not a user can perform a system-wide function such as shutting down a computer or logging on to a server. Rights are assigned to user or group accounts, not to a particular object or resource.

Example:

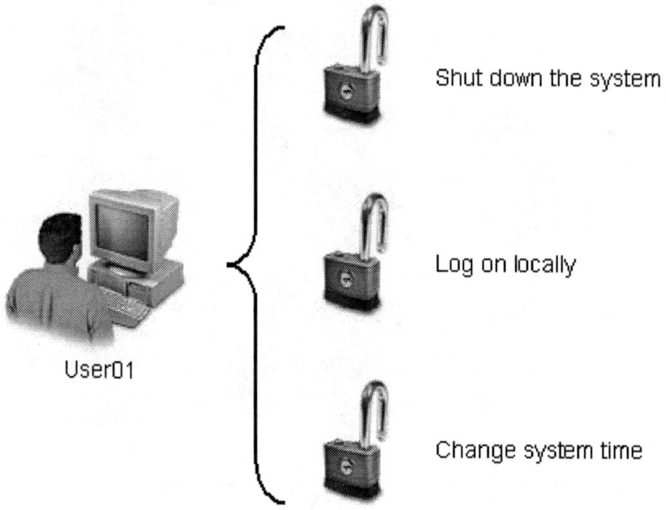

Figure 11-18: *Rights.*

Permissions

Definition:

A *permission* is a security setting that determines the level of access a user or group account has to a particular resource. Permissions can be associated with a variety of resources, such as files, printers, shared folders, and network directory databases. Permissions can typically be configured to allow different levels of privileges, or to deny privileges to users who should not access a resource.

Example:

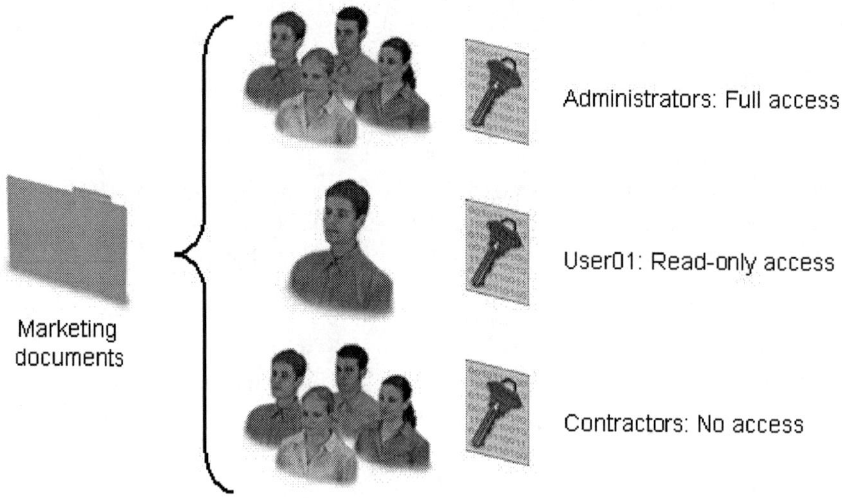

Figure 11-19: *Permissions.*

The NTFS File System

On Windows operating systems, file-level security is supported on drives that are formatted to use the NTFS file system. NTFS permissions can be applied either to folders or to individual files. NTFS permissions on a folder are inherited by files and subfolders within it. There are several levels of NTFS permissions, which can determine, for example, whether users can read files or run applications; write to existing files; and modify, create, or delete files.

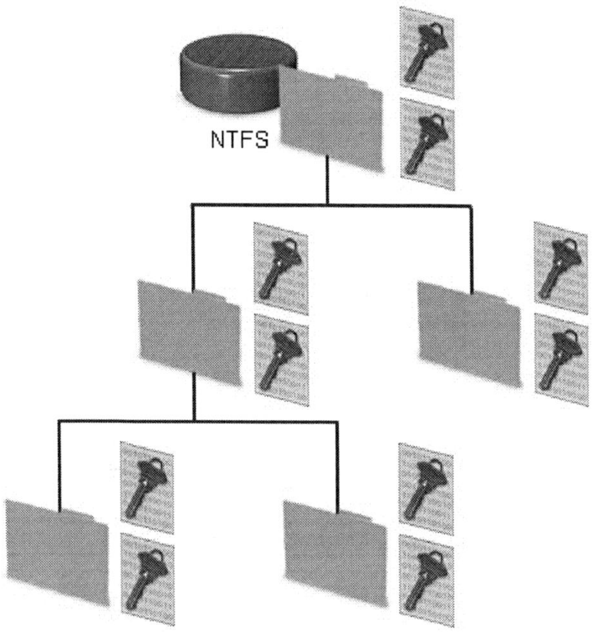

Figure 11-20: *The NTFS file system.*

NTFS File and Folder Permissions

You can set NTFS file and folder permissions on the Security tab of the Properties dialog box for the file or folder. The standard permissions for both files and folders include Read, Write, Read & Execute, Modify, and Full Control. The following tables describe the file and folder permissions in more detail.

Folder Permission	Enables You To
Read	Display the folder's data, attributes, owner, and permissions.
Write	Write to a folder, append to the folder, and read or change its attributes.
List Folder Contents	Display the data from the folder and from files within the folder; display attributes, the owner, and permissions; and run files in the folder or the programs associated with them. Is not inherited by files within the folder.
Read & Execute	Similar to List Folder Contents but is inherited by files within the folder.
Modify	Read, write, modify, and execute files in the folder, and change the attributes of the folder or of files within it.

Folder Permission	Enables You To
Full Control	Read, write, modify, and execute files in the folder; change attributes and permissions; and take ownership of the folder or of files within it.

File Permission	Enables You To
Read	Display the file's data, attributes, owner, and permissions.
Write	Write to the file, append to the file, and read or change its attributes.
Read & Execute	Display the file's data, attributes, owner, and permissions, and run the file or the program associated with the file.
Modify	Read, write, modify, and execute the file, and change its attributes.
Full Control	Read, write, modify, and execute the file; change its attributes and permissions; and take ownership of the file.

Users and Groups

Rights and permissions can be assigned to individual user accounts. However, this is an inefficient security practice, because so many permission assignments must be duplicated for users with similar roles, and because individual users' roles and needs can change frequently. It is more efficient to create groups of users with common needs, and assign the rights and permissions to the user groups. As individual users' needs change, the users can be placed in groups with the appropriate security configuration.

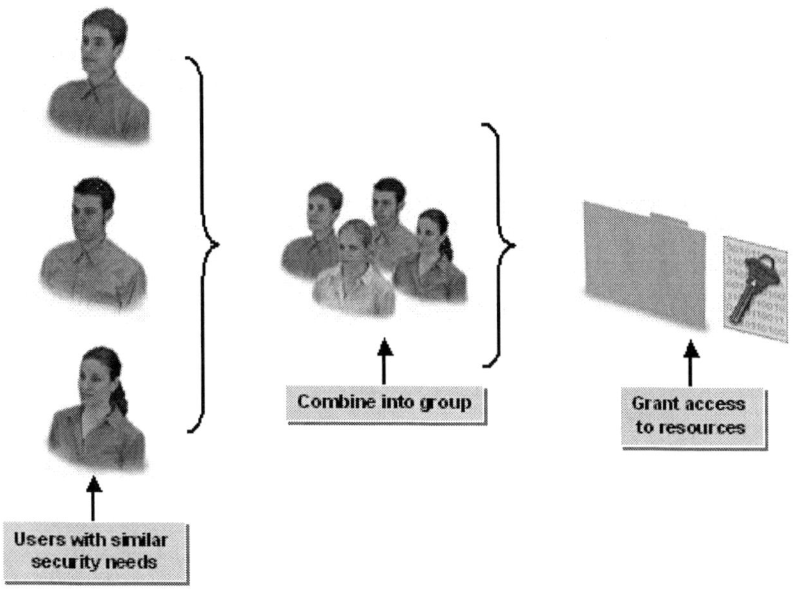

Figure 11-21: *Users and groups.*

Effective Permissions

Permissions are cumulative. This means that when a user is a member of multiple groups that each have permissions to a resource, the user's total effective permission is the combination of all the separate permission assignments.

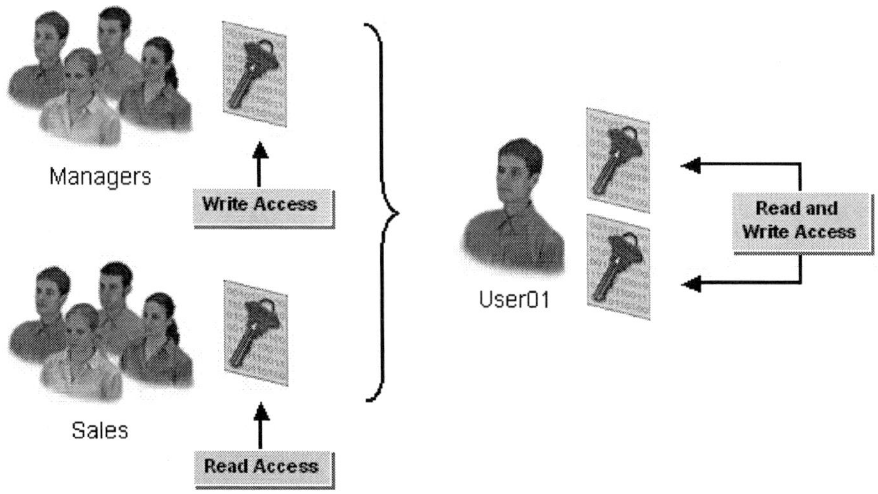

Figure 11-22: *Effective permissions.*

The Deny Permission

In Microsoft Windows, permissions are cumulative except for the Deny permission, which overrides all other permissions.

Share and File System Permissions

On most Windows systems, you can set NTFS permissions on individual files and folders. When you share a folder for network use, you can assign a separate set of permissions to the shared folder.

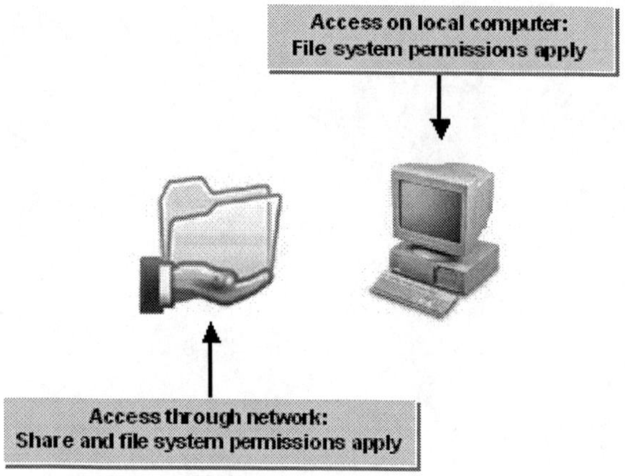

Figure 11-23: *Share and file system permissions.*

If a user accesses the folder while logged on to the local system where it is stored, only the local file permissions pertain. If a user accesses the folder through the network share, the share permissions are applied first, and then the file-level permissions are applied. The user's effective access is the most restrictive of the two sets of permissions.

Share Permissions

The share permissions on Windows systems are Read, Change, and Full Control.

ACTIVITY 11-3

Implementing Local Security

There is a simulated version of this activity available on the CD-ROM that shipped with this course. You can run this simulation on any Windows computer to review the activity after class, or as an alternative to performing the activity as a group in class. The activity simulation can be launched either directly from the CD-ROM by clicking the Interactives link and navigating to the appropriate one, or from the installed data file location by opening the C:\Data\Simulations\Lesson#\Activity# folder and double-clicking the executable (.exe) file.

Data Files:

- C:\Data\Security\Confidential.doc

Setup:

There is a user account named Test## that has a password of !Pass1234. This user does not have local administrative privileges. The password for the default Administrator account is also !Pass1234. All administrative accounts are in the Administrators group on your computer.

Scenario:

In a folder on your system, you have a file containing confidential company data. You need to protect the contents of this file. All users should be able to open this file when they are logged on to the local system. Only Administrators should be able to change the file. And you are the only user who should be able to access the file from across the network.

What You Do	How You Do It
1. **Verify that you can open the confidential file.**	a. **Choose Start→All Programs→Accessories→Windows Explorer.**
	b. **Click the plus signs to expand My Computer, Local Disk (C:), and Data.**
	c. The Security folder contains a confidential file. **Select the Security folder.**
	d. To verify that you can read the file, **double-click Confidential.**
	e. To close WordPad, **click the Close box.**

2. **Set the file system permissions.**

a. In the left pane of Windows Explorer, **right-click the Security folder and choose Properties.**

b. **Select the Security tab.**

c. In the Group Or User Names list, **select Users.**

d. Under Permissions For Users, **examine the default permissions.** The default permissions do not permit users to make changes to the file.

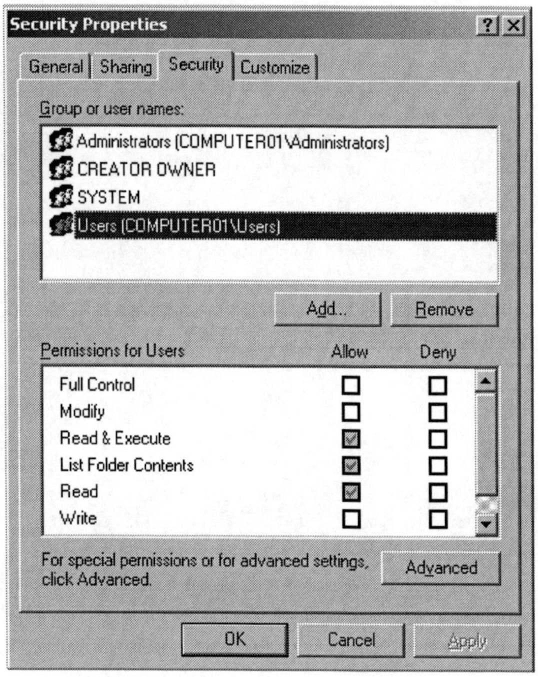

e. In the Group Or User Names list, **select Administrators.**

f. Under Permissions For Administrators, **examine the default permissions.** By default, Administrators have Full Control to the file.

---

3. **Share the folder and set the share permissions.**

a. In the Security Properties dialog box, **select the Sharing tab.**

b. **Select Share This Folder.**

c. **Verify that the default share name is Security.**

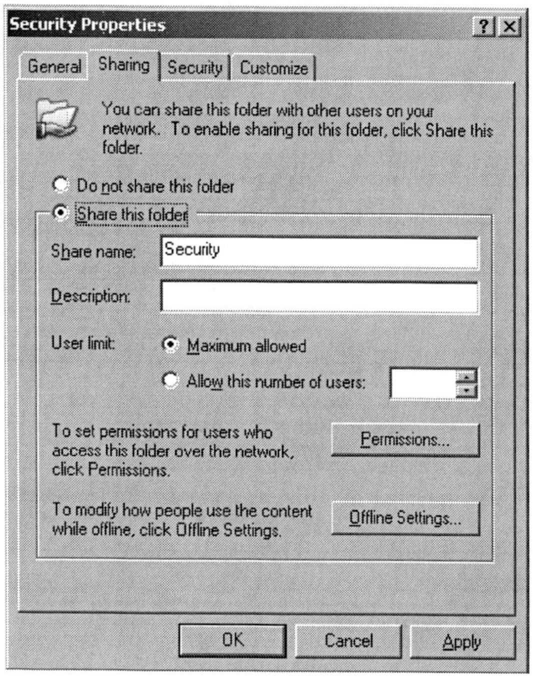

d. **Click Permissions.**

e. **Click Add.**

f. In the Enter The Object Names To Select box, **type *Computer##\Administrators* and then click Check Names.**

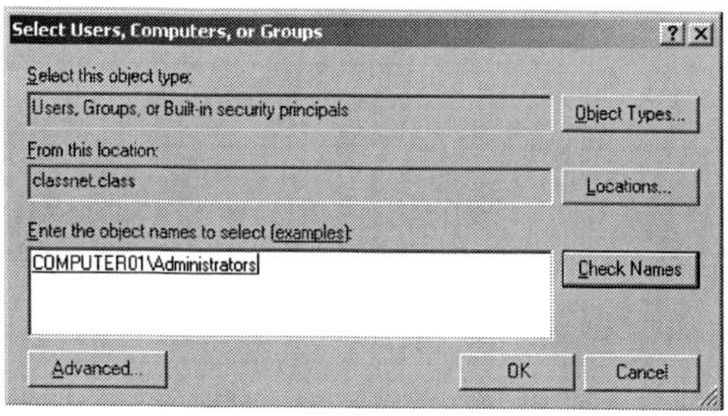

g. **Click OK.**

h. In the Permissions For Security dialog box, in the Group Or User Names list, **verify that Administrators is selected.**

i. In the Permissions For Administrators area, **check the Allow box for the Full**

	Control permission. j. In the Group Or User Names list, **select Everyone.** k. Removing the Everyone group from the permissions list will remove permissions for users who are not in the Administrators group. **Click Remove.** l. **Click OK twice.** m. **Close Windows Explorer.**
4. **Log on as a non-administrative user.**	a. **Choose Start→Log Off.** b. **Click Log Off.** c. To open the Log On To Windows dialog box, **press Ctrl+Alt+Del.** d. In the User Name text box, **type *Test##*** e. In the Password text box, **type *!Pass1234*** f. **Verify that CLASSNET appears in the Log On To box and click OK.**
5. As a non-administrative user, **test the file system permissions.**	a. **Open Windows Explorer.** b. **Expand My Computer, Local Disk (C:), and Data, and select the Security folder.** c. **Double-click Confidential.** d. In WordPad, **type *This is a test*.** e. **Click the Save button.**

	f. Access to change the file is denied. In the message box, **click OK.**  g. **Close WordPad.** h. When prompted to save changes, **click No.** i. **Close Windows Explorer.** j. **Log off.**
6. At another computer, **log on as Test##.**	a. **Switch places with another student.** b. At the new computer, **log on as Test##.**
7. At another computer, **test the share permissions as a non-administrative user.**	a. **Choose Start→Run.** b. To test the share permissions, you need to open the shared Security folder on Computer##. In the Open text box, **type** ***\\computer##\security*** **and click OK.** c. Access is denied because this user account does not have the correct share permissions. To close the message box, **click OK.** 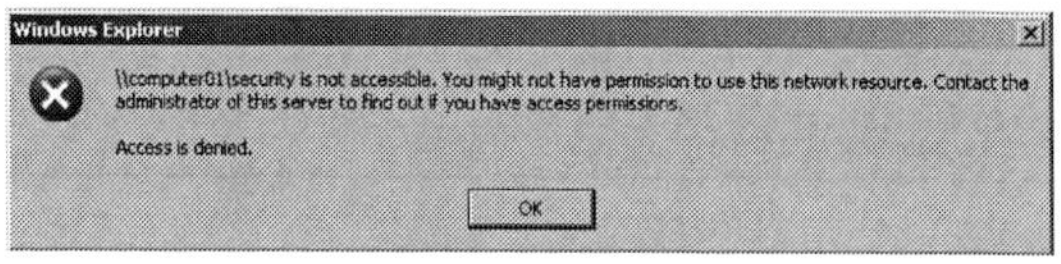 d. **Log off.** e. **Return to your own computer and log on as User## with a password of !Pass1234.**

TOPIC D

Network Authentication Methods

In the previous topic, you saw various security settings that affect local computers. In a network environment, there are also security settings that control how users and computers authenticate to the network. In this topic, you will identify network authentication methods.

Authentication is the first line of defense against attack or intrusion into network systems. There are many authentication systems, each with different requirements and capabilities. To manage authentication on your network effectively, you'll need to understand these different systems and what each one can provide for your organization.

Strong Passwords

Definition:

A *strong password* is a password that meets complexity requirements that are set by a system administrator and documented in a password policy. Strong passwords increase the security of systems that use password-based authentication by protecting against password guessing and brute force password attacks.

Password complexity requirements should meet the security needs of an individual organization, and can specify:

- The minimum length of the password.
- Required characters, such as a combination of letters, numbers, and symbols.
- Forbidden character strings, such as the user account name or dictionary words.

Example:

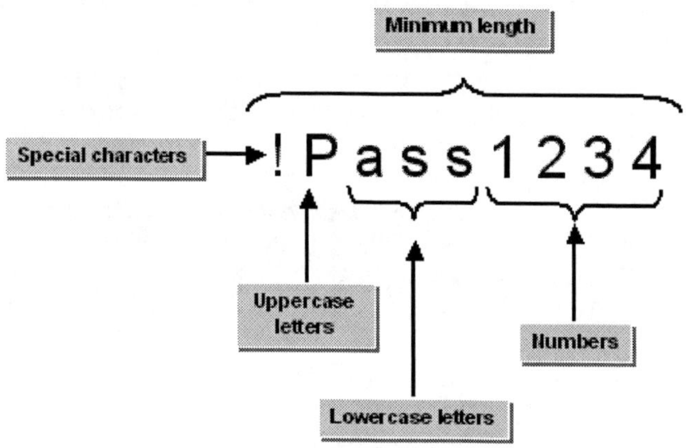

Figure 11-24: *Strong passwords.*

Authentication by Assertion

Authentication based entirely on a user name/password combination is sometimes called *authentication by assertion,* because once the client has a valid set of credentials, it can use them to assert its identity to obtain access to a resource.

Password Policies and Policy Tools

The types of password policies and the complexity settings they can include vary from organization to organization and from system to system. An official password policy can be a simple document maintained by a human resources or information technology department and publicized to employees, or it can be a system configuration setting within an application or operating system. For example, in all current Windows systems, password complexity requirements are controlled by security settings in a policy object, and can be viewed in a policy-editing tool. On local Windows systems, the Local Security Settings console displays the security configuration of the local computer.

Kerberos

Kerberos is an Internet standard authentication protocol that links a user name and password to an authority that can certify that the user is valid and also verify the user's ability to access resources. A Kerberos Authentication Server (KAS) issues and verifies client credentials; other systems in the Kerberos structure trust the KAS. Kerberos enables secure authentication between insecure systems and networks.

See **http://web.mit.edu/kerberos/www/dialogue.html** for more information on Kerberos.

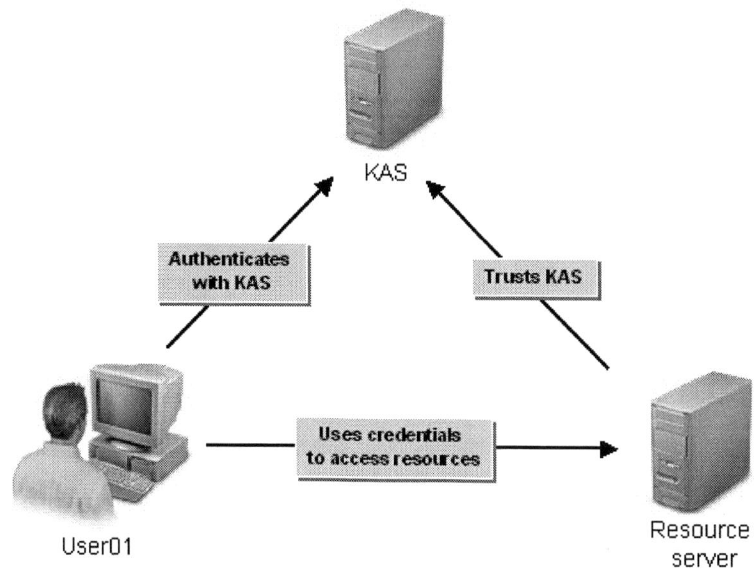

Figure 11-25: *Kerberos.*

Kerberos Implementations

Kerberos is a nonproprietary authentication standard that was originally developed by the Massachusetts Institute of Technology (MIT) to ensure secure interoperability between UNIX-based systems. Kerberos is platform independent and can be implemented in a variety of environments. Separate Kerberos authorities can trust each other to enable cross-environment authentication and resource access. The Microsoft Active Directory service uses Kerberos-based authentication.

The Kerberos Process

A Kerberos client uses a Kerberos authentication process to establish a secure connection with a service.

1. The client's logon request is sent to the KAS and the account is verified.
2. The KAS returns a Ticket Granting Ticket (TGT), which is used to establish the user session. It also returns a session key, which is used to encrypt further service requests within the current session.
3. When a client needs network services, it presents the TGT to the KAS.
4. The KAS issues a session ticket that is valid for that service.
5. The client submits the service ticket to the service provider to access the network resource. The client does not need to re-authenticate.

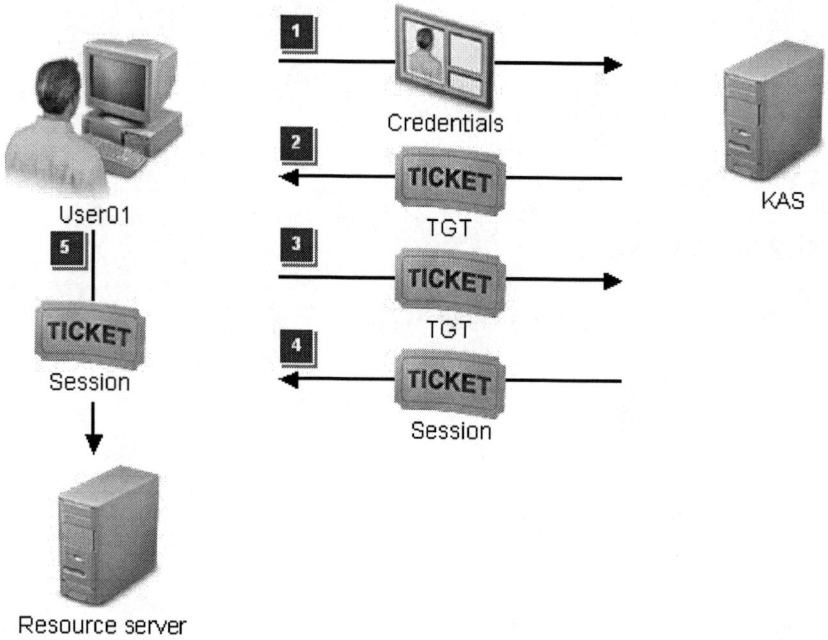

Figure 11-26: *The Kerberos process.*

Extensible Authentication Protocol (EAP)

Extensible Authentication Protocol (EAP) is an authentication protocol that enables systems to use hardware-based identifiers, such as fingerprint scanners or smart card readers, for authentication. EAP categorizes the devices into different EAP types depending on each device's authentication scheme. The EAP method associated with each type enables the device to interact with a system's account database. Users might need to provide a password in addition to the physical authentication.

Microsoft 2003 supports MD-5 challenge, Smart Card or other Certificate (TLS), Protected EAP (PEAP), and Secured Password (EAP-MSCHAP v2).

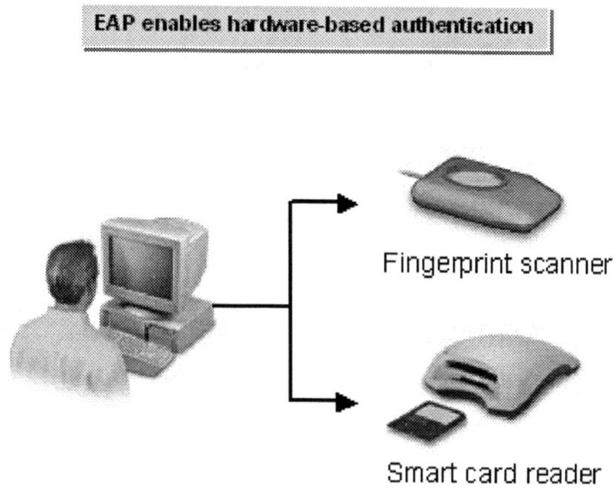

Figure 11-27: *EAP.*

IEEE 802.1x

The IEEE 802.1x is a standard for securing wireless networking by implementing EAP as the authentication protocol over either a wired or wireless Ethernet LAN. IEEE 802.1x employs an authentication service, such as RADIUS, to secure wireless clients, removing the need to implement security features in WAPs, which typically do not have the memory or processing resources to support complex authentication functions.

EAP Implementation in Windows

Current Windows systems support EAP authentication for both wired and wireless network connections, as well as for dial-up and other remote connections.

ACTIVITY 11-4

Examining Strong Passwords

There is a simulated version of this activity available on the CD-ROM that shipped with this course. You can run this simulation on any Windows computer to review the activity after class, or as an alternative to performing the activity as a group in class. The activity simulation can be launched either directly from the CD-ROM by clicking the Interactives link and navigating to the appropriate one, or from the installed data file location by opening the C:\Data\Simulations\Lesson#\Activity# folder and double-clicking the executable (.exe) file.

Scenario:

To support the security needs on your network, you want to enforce the use of strong passwords. You decide to verify that the default password settings in Windows Server 2003 require complex passwords.

What You Do	How You Do It
1. **Examine the policy setting for password complexity.**	a. **Choose Start→Administrative Tools→Local Security Policy.**
	b. In the left pane, **expand Account Policies and select Password Policy.**
	c. In the right pane, **verify that Password Must Meet Complexity Requirements is enabled.**

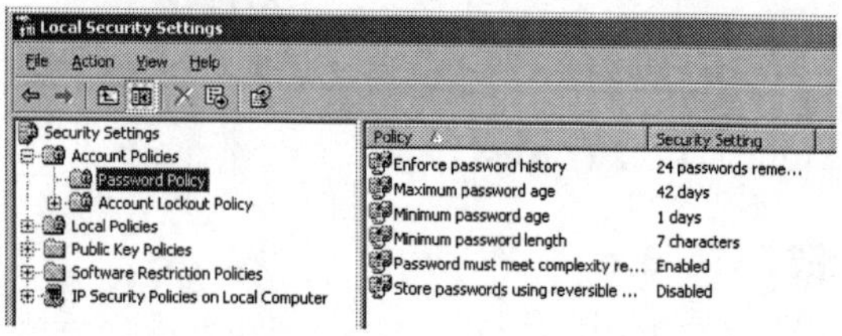

2. **Use Help to determine the specific complexity requirements.**

   a. **Choose Help→Help Topics.**

   b. **Select the Search tab.**

   c. In the Type In The Word(s) To Search For text box, **type *complexity* and click List Topics.**

   d. **Double-click Password Must Meet Complexity Requirements** to display details for that policy.

   e. In the right pane, **examine the password complexity requirements, and then close the Help window.**

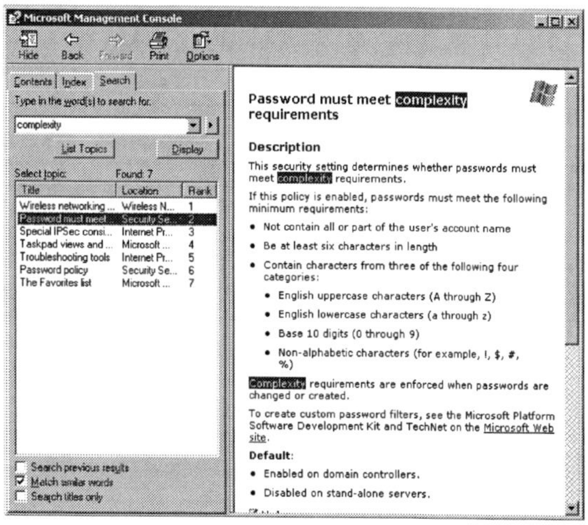

   f. **Close the Local Security Settings window.**

3. **Test the current password policy with a new user on your system.**

a. **Choose Start→Administrative Tools→ Computer Management.**

b. In the left pane, **expand Local Users And Groups and select the Users folder.**

c. **Choose Action→New User.**

d. In the New User dialog box, in the User Name text box, **type *LocalUser***

e. In the Password text box, **type *password***

f. In the Confirm Password text box, **type *password***

g. **Click Create.**

h. An error message is generated because the password is not complex. **Click OK** to close the error message.

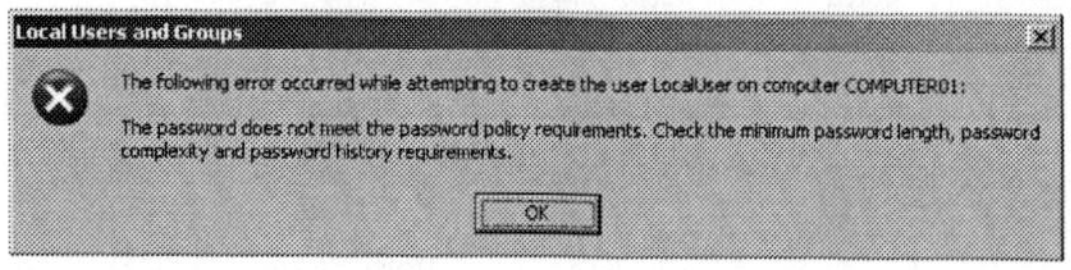

i. In the Password text box, **type *!Pass1234***

j. In the Confirm Password text box, **type *!Pass1234***

k. **Click Create.**

l. **Click Close.**

m. **Close the Computer Management window.**

TOPIC E

Data Encryption

In the previous topic, you saw that secure client authentication prevents unauthorized network access. For complete security, client data should be secured as well. Data encryption is one way to secure client information. In this topic, you will identify major data encryption methods and technologies.

As fast as digital communications are secured, attackers will test the security method and attempt to breach the systems. To stay one step ahead of the hackers and protect the data in your organization, you'll need to have an understanding of the fundamentals of data encryption and the choices you have for implementing data encryption in your network.

Key-Based Encryption Systems

All data encryption depends on the use of a key to control how information is encoded and decoded. There are two main categories of key-based encryption.

- In *shared-key,* or *symmetric, encryption* systems, the same key is used both to encode and to decode the message. The secret key must somehow be communicated securely between the two parties to the communication.
- In *key-pair,* or *asymmetric, encryption* systems, each party has two keys: a *public key*, which anyone can obtain, and a *private key*, known only to the individual. Anyone can use the public key to encrypt data; only the holder of the associated private key can decrypt it.

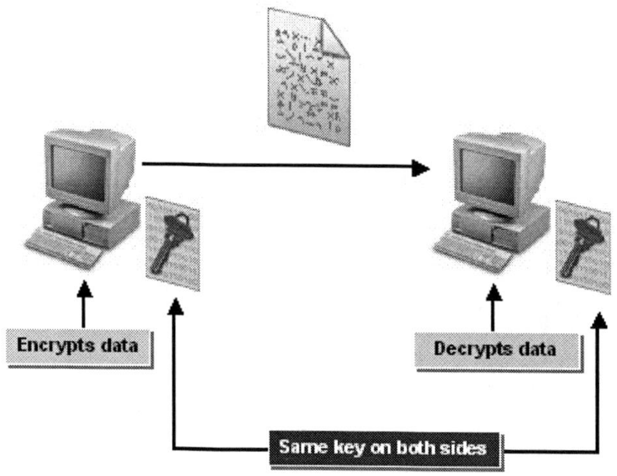

Figure 11-28: *Shared-key encryption.*

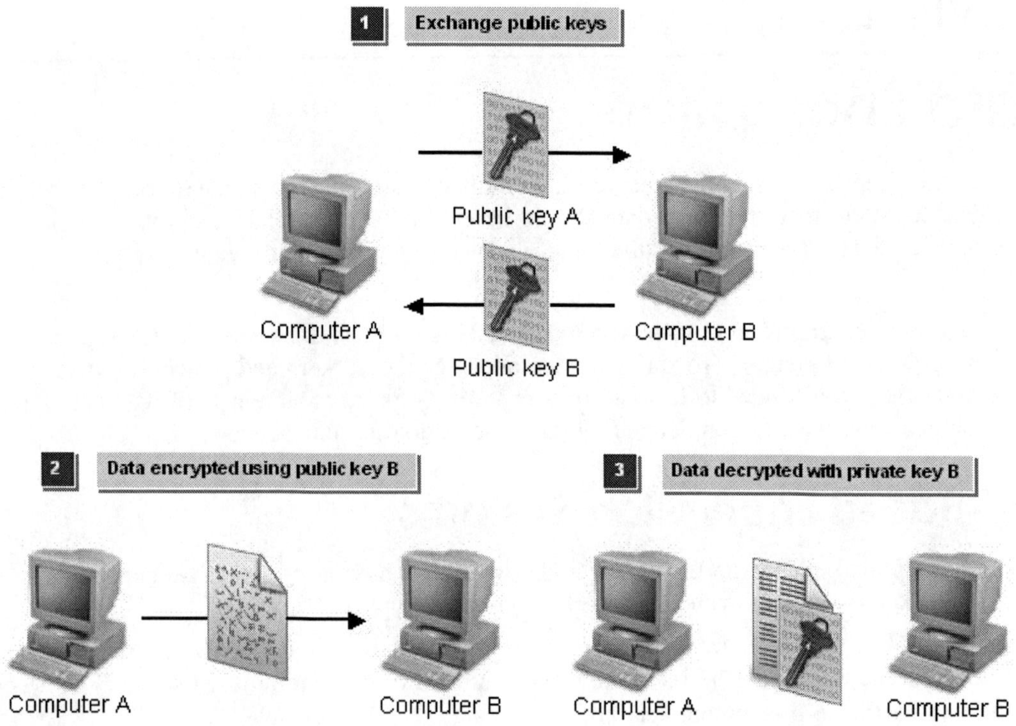

Figure 11-29: *Public-key encryption.*

Data Encryption Standard (DES)

Data Encryption Standard (DES) is a shared-key encryption standard that is based on a 56-bit encryption key that includes an additional 8 parity bits. DES applies the encryption key to each 64-bit block of the message. *Triple DES* or *3DES* is a more-secure variant of DES that uses three separate DES keys to repeatedly encode the message.

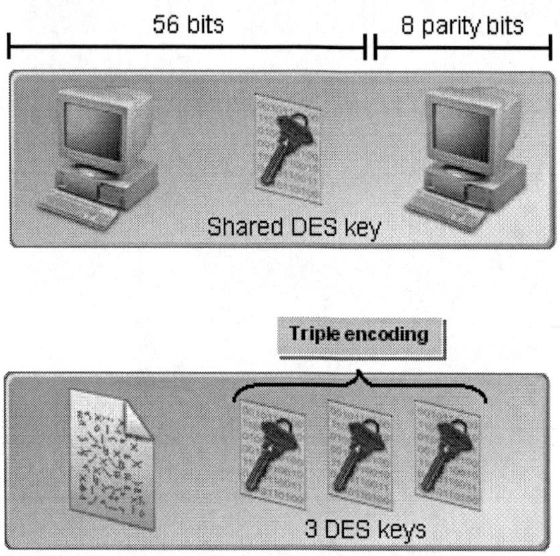

Figure 11-30: *DES and Triple DES.*

Digital Certificates

Definition:

A *digital certificate* is an electronic document that associates credentials with a public key. Both users and devices can hold certificates. The certificate validates the certificate holder's identity and is also a way to distribute the holder's public key. A server called a *Certificate Authority (CA)* issues certificates and the associated public/private key pairs.

Example:

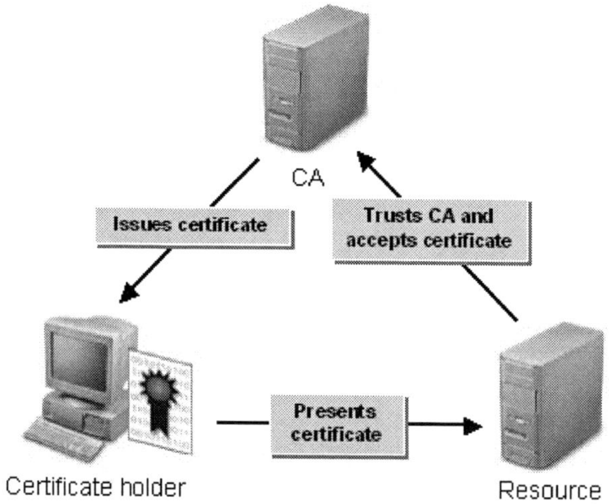

Figure 11-31: *Digital certificates.*

Public Key Infrastructure (PKI)

Definition:

Public key infrastructure (PKI) is a hierarchical system that is composed of CAs, certificates, software, services, and other cryptographic components, for the purpose of authenticating and validating data and entities—for example, to secure transactions over the Internet. A PKI issues and maintains public/private key pairs and certificates.

The PKI hierarchy consists of at least one top-level CA called the root CA. It can include additional, subordinate CAs. The root CA issues itself a self-signed certificate. It is then possible for the root CA to provide certificates and key pairs directly to clients. However, it is more typical for the root CA to issue certificates to subordinate CAs, which handle the client certificates.

Example:

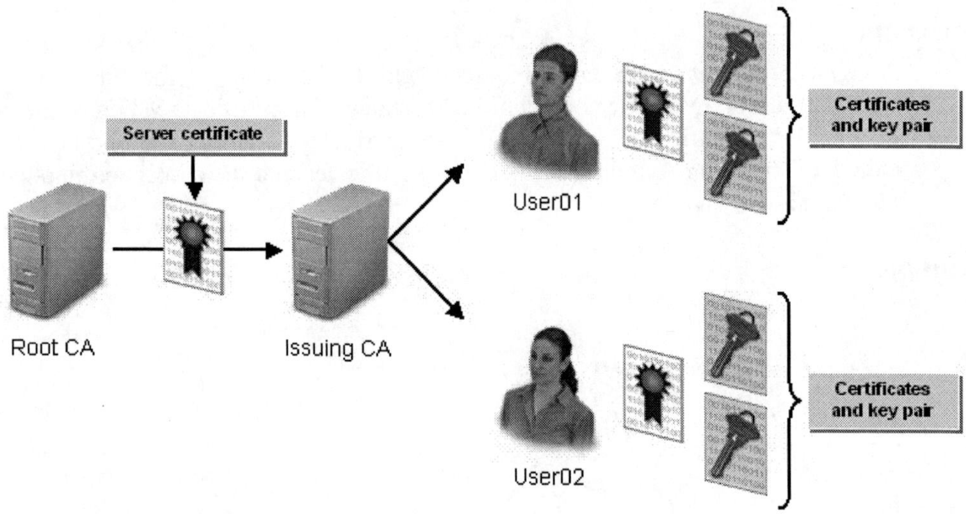

Figure 11-32: *PKI.*

Public and Private Root CAs

A private root CA is set up for internal use by a particular organization. Although it follows the hierarchical PKI structure, certificates from a private root CA are not available outside the organization that maintains it.

A public root CA is set up by a commercial vendor or other public authority for the express purpose of providing a common authentication structure between different organizations and entities. For example, an e-commerce website might contract with a public CA provider, such as VeriSign, to obtain a certificate to demonstrate to customers that its website is secure and reliable.

The Certificate Encryption Process

Certificates can be used for data encryption. In the certificate encryption process:

1. A security principal obtains a certificate and public/private key pair from a CA.
2. The party who is encrypting the data obtains the user's public key from the user or from the CA's certificate repository.
3. The encrypting party uses the public key to encrypt the data and sends it to the other user.
4. The other user uses the private key to decrypt the data.

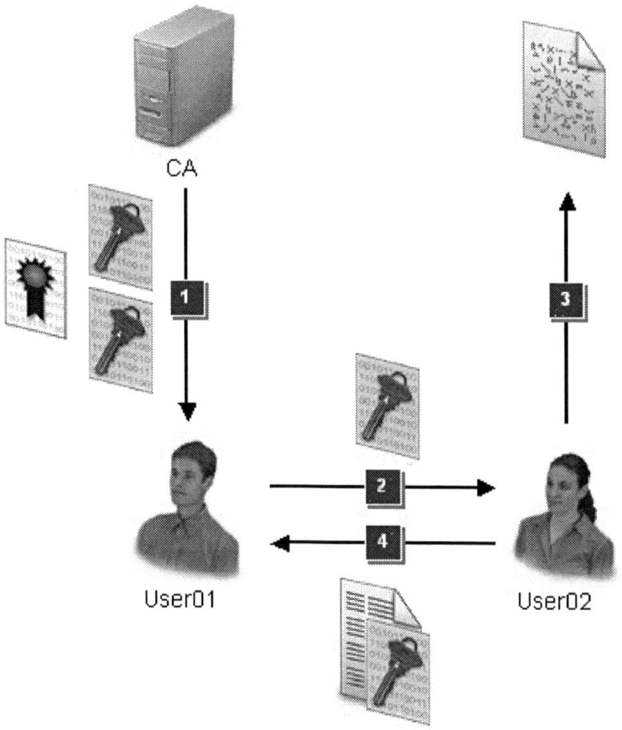

Figure 11-33: *The certificate encryption process.*

Encrypting File System (EFS)

The Encrypting File System (EFS) is a file-encryption tool available on Windows systems that have partitions formatted with NTFS. EFS encrypts file data by using digital certificates. If a CA is not available to issue a file-encryption certificate, the local system can issue a self-signed encryption certificate to users who want to encrypt files. Unlike NTFS permissions, which control access to the file, EFS protects the contents of the data. With EFS, you can keep data secure even if NTFS security is breached—for example, if an attacker steals a laptop computer and moves the laptop's hard drive to another system to bypass the NTFS security.

The Certificate Authentication Process

Certificates are also used to verify a user's identity. In the certificate authentication process:

1. A security principal obtains a certificate and a public/private key pair from a CA.
2. The security principal uses the certificate to identify itself to other users or devices.
3. If the receiver trusts the issuing CA, the receiver checks the CA's Certificate Revocation List (CRL) to see if the certificate is still valid, or if it has been revoked.
4. If the certificate is valid, the receiver accepts it.
5. Otherwise, if the certificate appears in the CRL, or if the receiver cannot contact the CA, the receiver rejects the certificate.

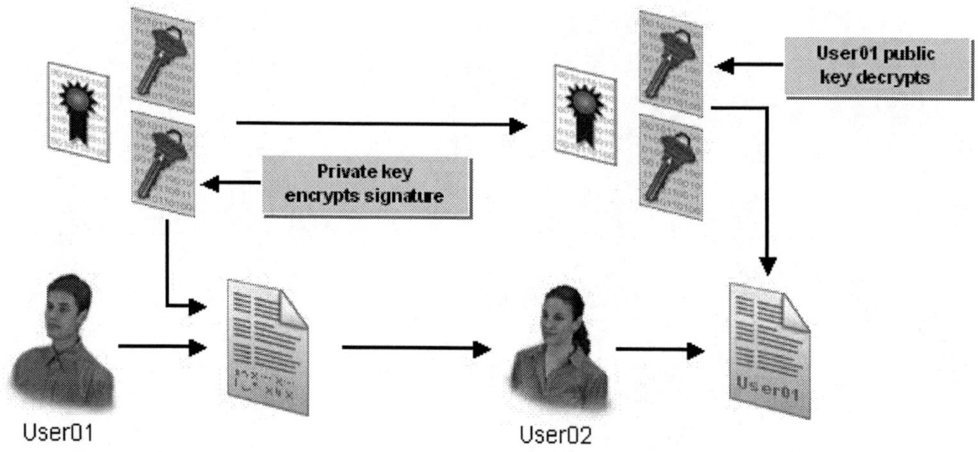

Figure 11-34: *The certificate authentication process.*

Digital Signature

A sender can verify its identity by attaching a small piece of encrypted data, called a *digital signature,* to a message. The digital signature is encrypted with the sender's private key; the receiver decrypts it by using the public key as obtained from the certificate repository. Because only the public key associated with the sender can decrypt the signature, it verifies the sender's identity and proves that the data has not been altered in transit.

IP Security (IPSec)

IP Security (IPSec) is a versatile, nonproprietary suite of security standards that provides end-to-end authentication and encryption for secure communications sessions on IP networks. IPSec negotiates the highest common level of security between two endpoints, and establishes a *Security Association (SA)* that contains the security parameters for a session. SAs enable a node to have multiple IPSec sessions, each with its own security level.

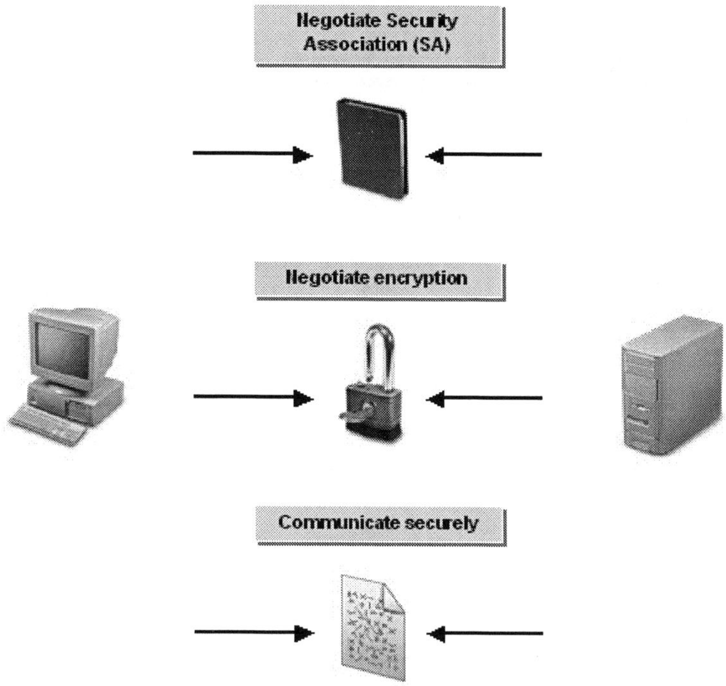

Figure 11-35: *IPSec.*

IPSec Levels

There are three IPSec levels.

IPSec Level	Description
Client	The lowest level is Client (Respond Only). The client negotiates security if the server requests it.
Server	The middle level is Server (Request Security). The server requests a secure session if the client can support it, but will accept an open session.
Secure Server	The highest level is Secure Server (Require Security). The session fails if the client cannot negotiate security with the server.

The "client" and "server" in the IPSec levels refer to which node initiates the session.

IPSec Policies

The IPSec level for a communication session is determined by IPSec policies that are set on each system. Each of the endpoints must have an IPSec policy with at least one matching security method in order for the communication to succeed.

IPSec policies are composed of rules, and each rule has five components.

Rule Component	Description
IP filters	IP filters describe the protocol, port, and source or destination computer the rule applies to.
Filter action	The filter action specifies how the system should respond to a packet that matches a particular filter. The system can permit the communication, or request or require security.
Authentication method	The authentication method enables the computers establish a trust relationship. Possible methods include Kerberos, digital certificates, or a preshared key configured as part of the rule.
Tunnel setting	The tunnel setting enables the computers to encapsulate data in a tunnel inside the transport network.
Connection type	The connection type determines if the rule applies to local network connections, remote access connections, or both.

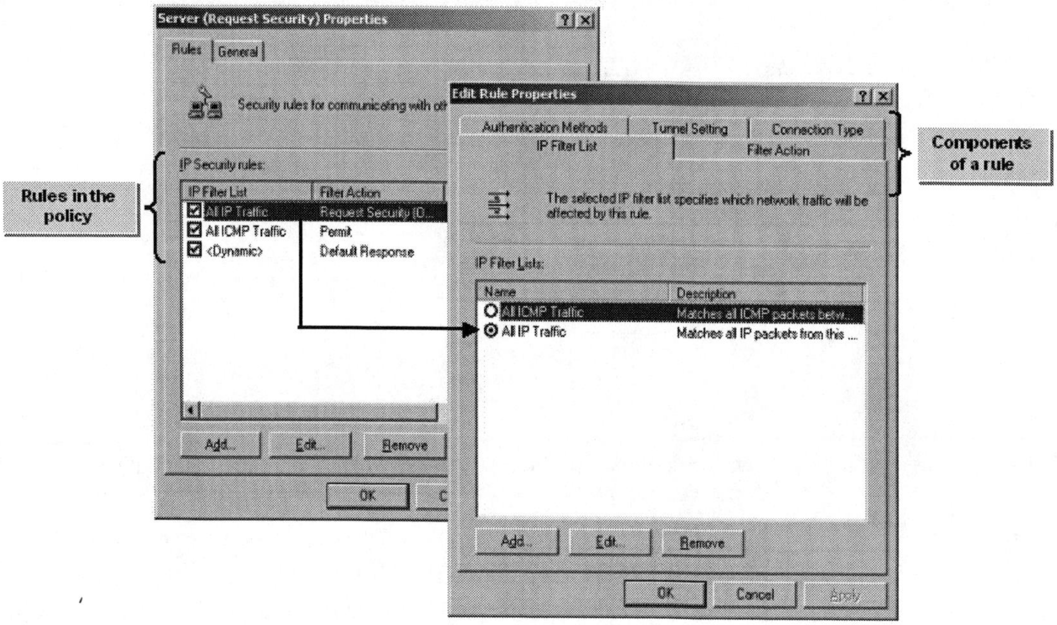

Figure 11-36: *IPSec policies on Windows Server 2003.*

Secure Sockets Layer (SSL)

Secure Sockets Layer (SSL) is a security protocol that combines digital certificates for authentication with RSA public-key data encryption. SSL is a server-driven process; a client that supports SSL does not need a registered certificate to connect securely to an SSL-enabled server. SSL is widely deployed on the web; a website that supports the secure HTTPS protocol must have an SSL security certificate.

RSA Encryption

The RSA encryption algorithm—named for its inventors, Rivest, Shamir, and Adelman—is a well-known and widely implemented public-key data encryption standard. Mathematically, it is based on the difficulty of factoring extremely large numbers. Most web browsers, including Internet Explorer and Netscape Navigator, support RSA encryption.

The SSL Process

The SSL process starts with a client requesting a session from a server. The server sends its digital certificate and public key to the client. The server and client negotiate an encryption level. The client then generates and encrypts a session key using the server's public key, and returns it to the server. The client and server then use the session key for data encryption.

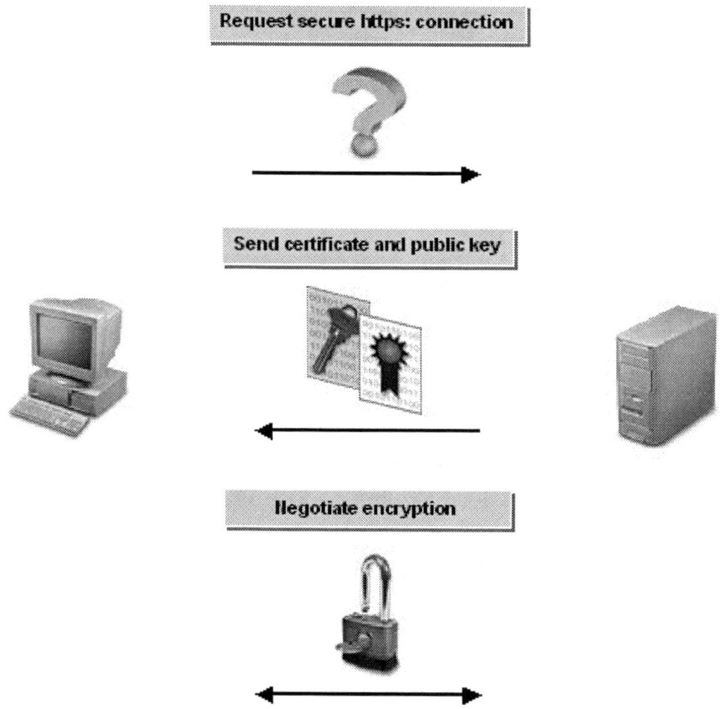

Figure 11-37: *SSL.*

ACTIVITY 11-5

Encrypting Data with EFS

There is a simulated version of this activity available on the CD-ROM that shipped with this course. You can run this simulation on any Windows computer to review the activity after class, or as an alternative to performing the activity as a group in class. The activity simulation can be launched either directly from the CD-ROM by clicking the Interactives link and navigating to the appropriate one, or from the installed data file location by opening the C:\Data\Simulations\Lesson#\Activity# folder and double-clicking the executable (.exe) file.

Data Files:

- C:\Data\Encrypt\Prospects\Clients.doc

Setup:

There is a C:\Data\Encrypt\Prospects folder on your hard drive that contains a file named Clients.doc.

You are logged on as your User## account. You have another user account named Test##. The password for both accounts is !Pass1234.

Scenario:

You have a private file on your laptop whose contents you want to protect. You want to make sure the file is secure from other users even if the file permissions are compromised.

What You Do	How You Do It
1. **Open the Clients.doc file** to verify that you can access it.	a. **Choose Start→All Programs→Accessories→Windows Explorer.**
	b. **Expand My Computer, Local Disk (C:), Data, and Encrypt.**
	c. **Select the Prospects folder.**
	d. **Double-click Clients.doc.**
	e. The file is open in WordPad. **Close WordPad.**
2. **Encrypt the Prospects folder and its contents.**	a. In the left pane, **right-click the Prospects folder and choose Properties.**
	b. On the General tab of the Prospects Properties dialog box, **click Advanced.**
	c. **Check Encrypt Contents To Secure Data.** 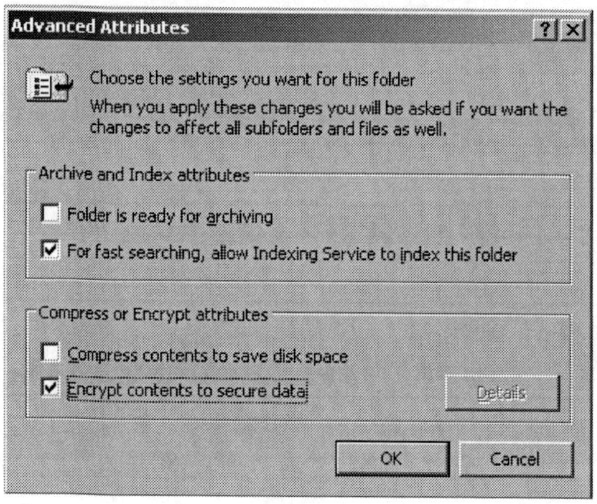
	d. **Click OK twice.**

e. **Verify that Apply Changes To This Folder, Subfolders, And Files is selected and click OK.**

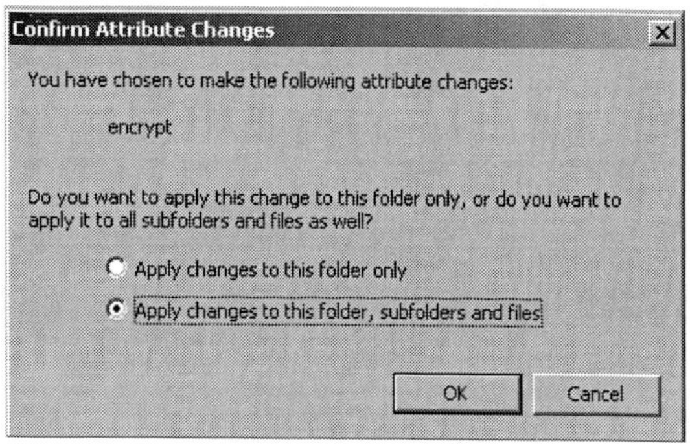

f. Windows Explorer displays the encrypted folder in an alternate color. **Close Windows Explorer.**

---

3. **Log on as a different user.**

   a. **Choose Start→Log Off.**

   b. **Click Log Off.**

   c. **Press Ctrl+Alt+Del.**

   d. **Log on as your Test## account with a password of !Pass1234.**

---

4. **Test the encryption.**

   a. **Open Windows Explorer.**

   b. **Expand My Computer, Local Disk (C:), Data, and Encrypt.**

   c. **Select the Prospects folder.**

   d. **Double-click Clients.doc.**

e. Access is denied. **Click OK** to close the message box and WordPad.

f. **Close Windows Explorer.**

5. **Log back on as User##.**	a. **Log off as Test##.**
	b. **Log back on as User## with a password of !Pass1234.**

ACTIVITY 11-6

Examining Default IPSec Policies

There is a simulated version of this activity available on the CD-ROM that shipped with this course. You can run this simulation on any Windows computer to review the activity after class, or as an alternative to performing the activity as a group in class. The activity simulation can be launched either directly from the CD-ROM by clicking the Interactives link and navigating to the appropriate one, or from the installed data file location by opening the C:\Data\Simulations\Lesson#\Activity# folder and double-clicking the executable (.exe) file.

Scenario:

You are considering implementing IPSec on your network on a limited basis. You will need to decide if you need to create custom policies, or if the default settings will be sufficient. You decide to begin by examining the contents of the policies that are available by default.

What You Do	How You Do It
1. Open the IPSec Security Policy Management MMC snap-in.	a. Choose Start→Run.
	b. Type *mmc* and click OK.
	c. Maximize the Console1 window.
	d. Maximize the Console Root window.
	e. Choose File→Add/Remove Snap-In.
	f. Click Add.
	g. Select IP Security Policy Management and click Add.
	h. Verify that Local Computer is selected and click Finish.

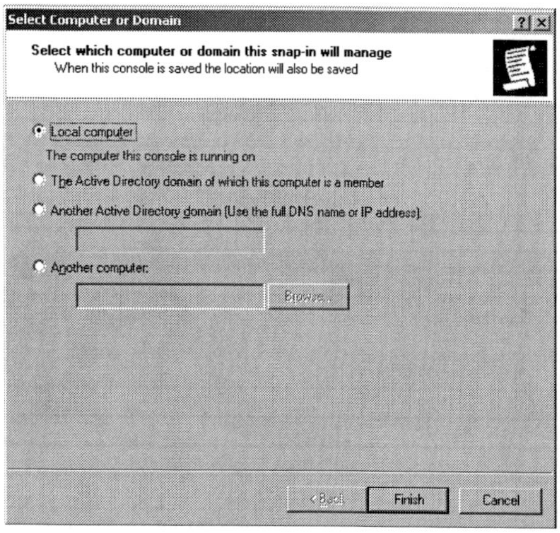

What You Do	How You Do It
	i. Click Close and then click OK.
2. Examine the rules in a policy.	a. In the console tree, select IP Security Policies On Local Computer.

b. **Verify that the three default policies appear in the right pane.**

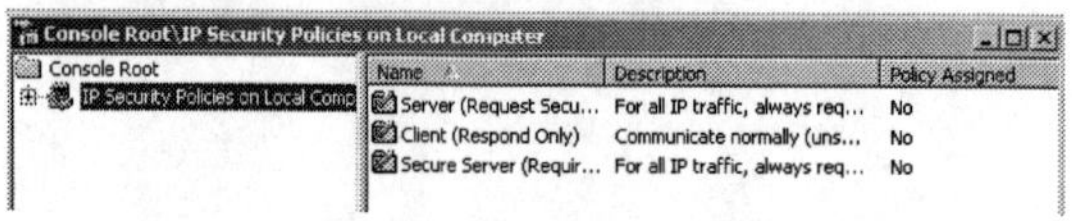

c. **Double-click Server (Request Security).**

d. There are three IP security rules in this default policy. The Filter List, Filter Action, and Authentication settings for each rule are visible. **Scroll to view the Tunnel Endpoint and Connection Type for each rule.**

---

3. **Examine the contents of a rule.**

a. With the first rule selected, **click Edit.**

b. The Edit Rule Properties dialog box has pages for each of the five components of the rule. The IP Filter List tab is visible. **Select the Filter Action tab.**

c. **Select the Authentication Methods tab.**

d. **Select the Tunnel Setting tab.**

e. **Select the Connection Type tab.**

f. **Click Cancel twice.**

g. **Close the MMC console window.**

h. When prompted to save settings, **click No.**

ACTIVITY 11-7

Installing a Root Certificate Authority (CA)

There is a simulated version of this activity available on the CD-ROM that shipped with this course. You can run this simulation on any Windows computer to review the activity after class, or as an alternative to performing the activity as a group in class. The activity simulation can be launched either directly from the CD-ROM by clicking the Interactives link and navigating to the appropriate one, or from the installed data file location by opening the C:\Data\Simulations\Lesson#\Activity# folder and double-clicking the executable (.exe) file.

Setup:

The installation source files for Windows Server 2003 are available on the network at \\dc\2003install.

Scenario:

You work for a small company that wants to use certificates on its secure internal network for authentication and data encryption. As the enterprise network administrator, you are responsible for installing the root CA server. Other department administrators will install subordinate CAs to issue certificates.

What You Do	How You Do It
1. **Install Certificate Services.**	a. **Choose Start→Control Panel→Add Or Remove Programs.**
	b. **Click Add/Remove Windows Components.**
	c. **Check Certificate Services.**
	d. In the Microsoft Certificate Services message box, **click Yes.**

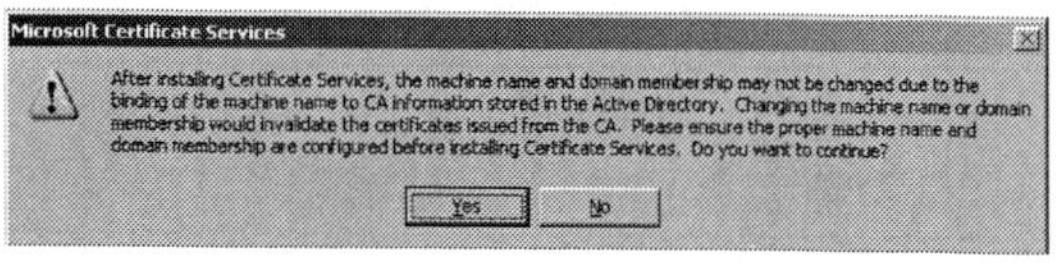

	e. **Click Next.**
	f. **Select Stand-alone Root CA and click Next.**

g. In the Common Name For This CA text box, **type *RootCA##* and click Next.**

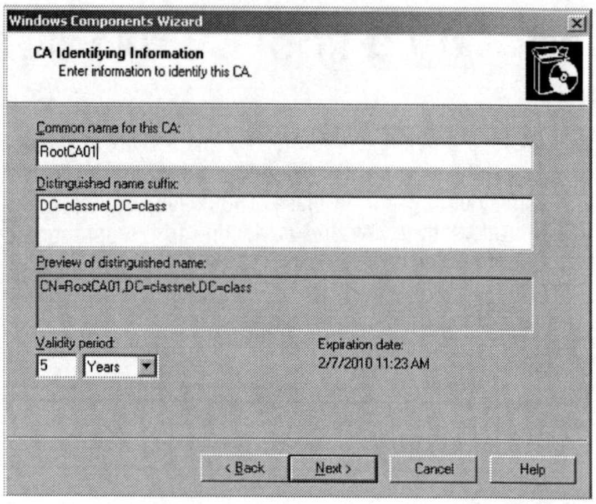

h. **Click Next** to accept the default database and log locations.

i. When prompted for the installation CD-ROM, **click OK.**

j. In the Copy Files From text box, **type *\\dc\2003install* and click OK.**

k. In the Microsoft Certificate Services message box, **click OK.**

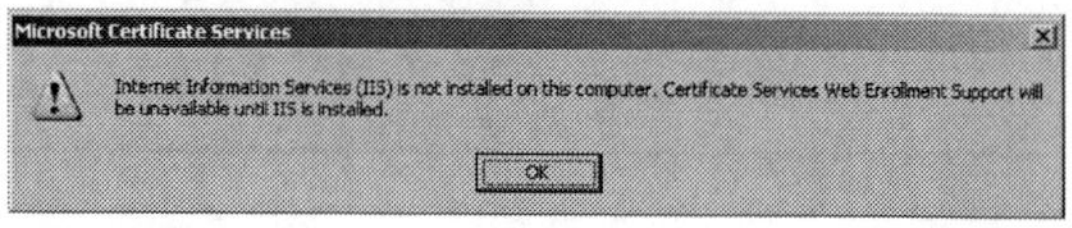

l. When the installation is complete, **click Finish.**

m. **Close Add Or Remove Programs.**

---

2. **Verify the installation.**

a. **Choose Start→Administrative Tools→Certification Authority.**

b. **Select the RootCA## object.**

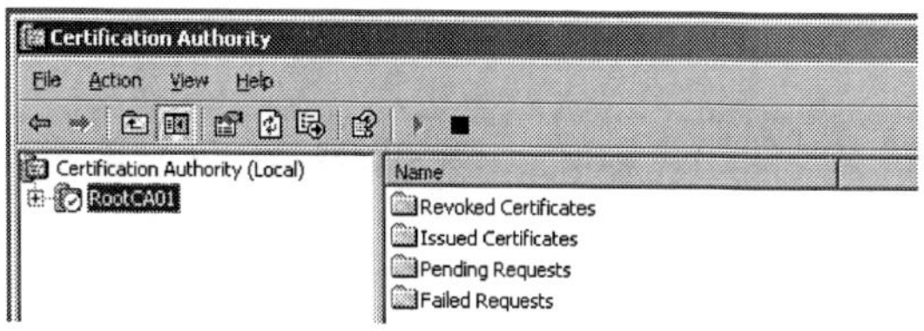

c. **Choose Action→Properties.**

d. **Click View Certificate.**

e. The certificate is self-issued by the root CA and expires in five years. **Click OK twice.**

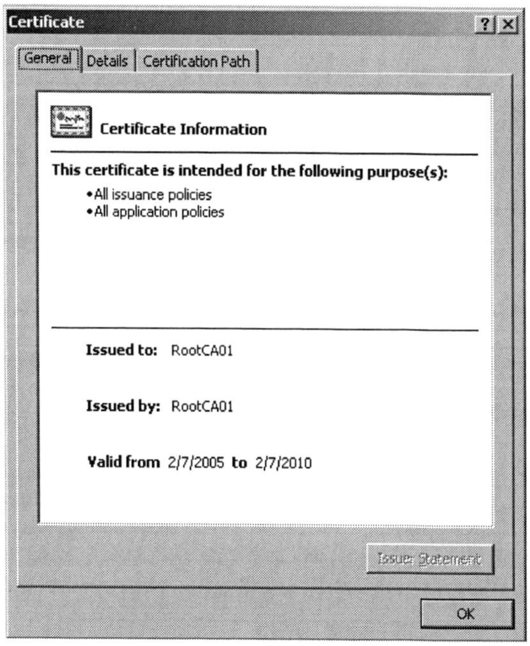

f. **Double-click Issued Certificates.**

g. This CA has not yet issued any certificates. **Close Certification Authority.**

TOPIC F

Internet Security

In the previous topics in this lesson, you have learned how various components of security can protect communications on a variety of networks. Connections to the Internet have their own specific security considerations. In this topic, you will identify the primary techniques used to secure Internet connections.

Every company and organization today wants to connect to the Internet. At the same time, every organization has a valid concern about the risks involved in connecting to this huge, open, public network. As a network administrator, you need to be aware of the specific tools and techniques that companies use to protect themselves from outside attacks as well as from Internet misuse internally.

Network Address Translation (NAT)

Definition:

Network address translation (NAT) is a simple form of Internet security that conceals internal addressing schemes from the public Internet. A router is configured with a single public IP address on its external interface and a nonroutable address on its internal interface. A NAT service running on the router or on another system translates between the two addressing schemes. Packets sent to the Internet from internal hosts all appear is if they came from a single IP address, preventing external hosts from identifying and connecting directly to internal systems.

Example:

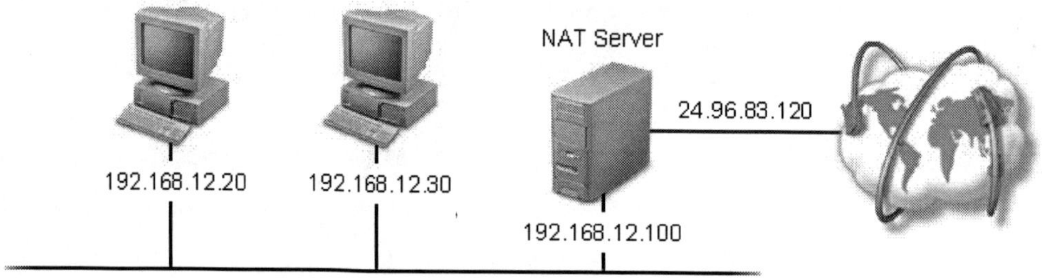

Figure 11-38: *NAT.*

NAT Implementations

NAT can be implemented as software on a variety of systems, or in hardware in a dedicated device such as a router. Internet Connection Sharing (ICS) in Windows systems includes a simple software-based NAT implementation, but requires a separate device, such as a modem, to provide actual Internet connectivity. Hardware-based NAT devices, such as cable modems and DSL routers, often have extended functionality and can double as Internet access devices.

The NAT Process

The NAT process translates external and internal addresses based on port numbers.

Step	Description
Client request	An internal client sends a request to an external service, such as a website, using the external destination IP address and port number.
Source address Conversion	The NAT device converts the source address in the request packet to its own external address, and adds a reference port number to identify the originating client.
Data return	The service returns data to the NAT device's external address using the reference port number.
Internal source identification	NAT uses the reference port number to identify the correct internal source address.
Data delivery	NAT readdresses the packet to the internal system and delivers the data.

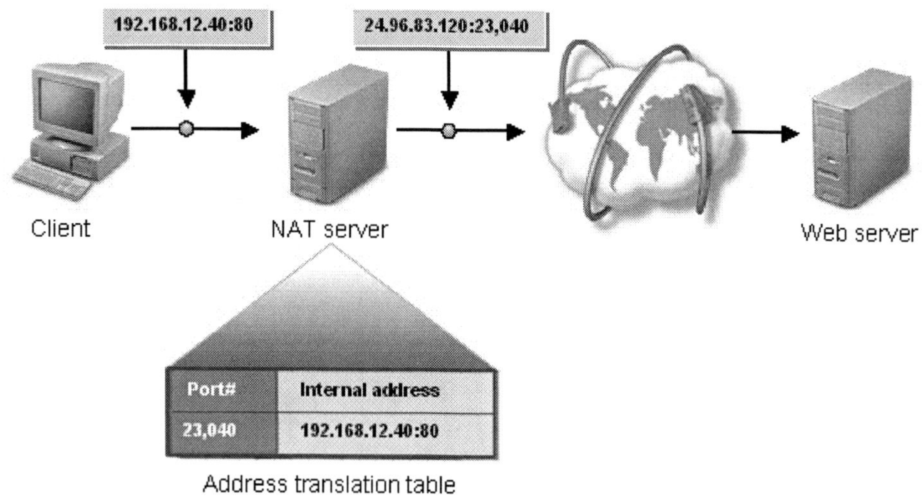

Figure 11-39: *The NAT process.*

Firewalls

Definition:

A *firewall* is a software program or hardware device that protects networks from unauthorized data by blocking unsolicited traffic. Firewalls allow incoming or outgoing traffic that has specifically been permitted by a system administrator, and incoming traffic that is sent in response to requests from internal hosts. Firewalls use complex filtering algorithms that analyze incoming packets based on destination and source addresses, port numbers, and data type.

Firewalls themselves do not provide network address translation, but can be implemented in conjunction with a NAT device. Also, some products do incorporate both types of functionality.

Firewalls are universally deployed between private networks and the Internet. They can also be used between two separate private networks, or even on individual systems, to control data flow between any two sources.

Example:

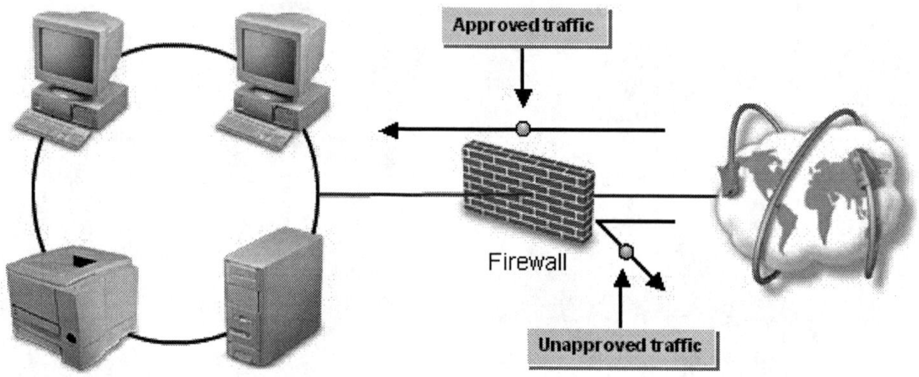

Figure 11-40: *A firewall.*

Demilitarized Zones (DMZs)

Definition:

A *demilitarized zone (DMZ)* is a small section of a private network that is located between two firewalls and made available for public access. A DMZ enables external clients to access data on private systems, such as web servers, without compromising the security of the internal network as a whole. The external firewall enables public clients to access the service; the internal firewall prevents them from connecting to protected internal hosts.

Example:

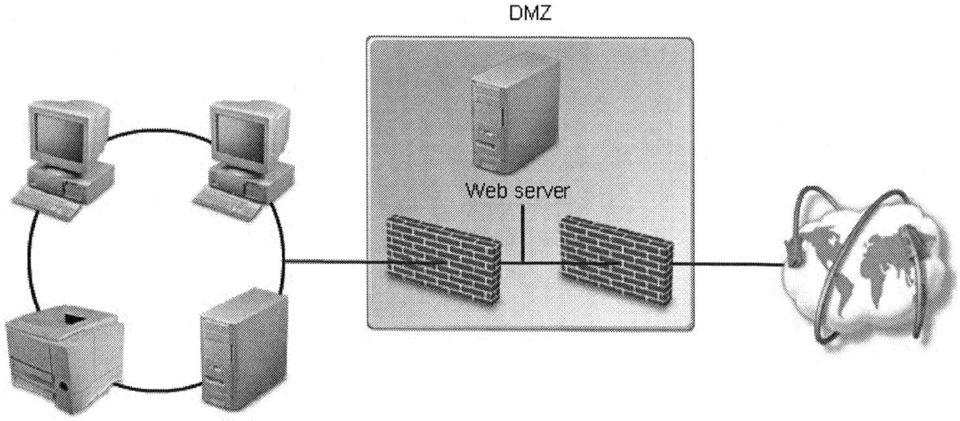

Figure 11-41: *A DMZ.*

Internet Proxies

Definition:

An *Internet proxy* is a system that isolates internal networks from the Internet by downloading and storing Internet files on behalf of internal clients. It intercepts requests for web-based or other external resources that come from internal clients, and, if it does not have the data in its cache, generates a completely new request packet using itself as the source. In addition to providing security, the data cache can also improve client response time and reduce Internet traffic by providing frequently used pages to clients from a local source.

A proxy server combines NAT, firewall, and caching functionality.

Example:

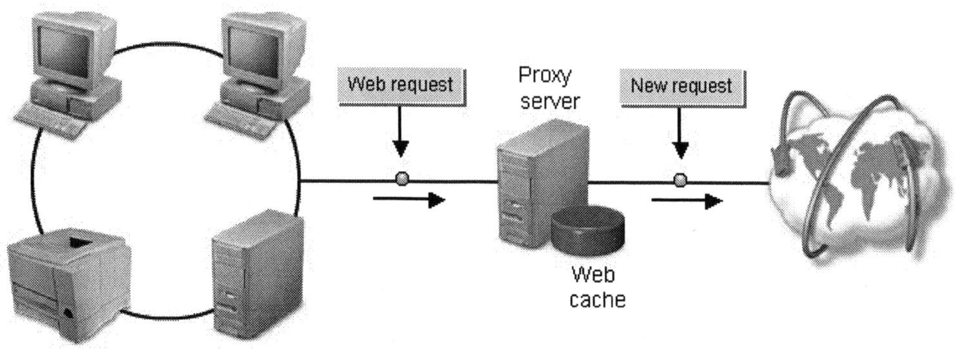

Figure 11-42: *An Internet proxy.*

Proxies vs. NAT

Both Internet proxies and NAT devices readdress outgoing packets. However, NAT simply replaces the original source address on the packet. Proxies actually examine the packet contents and then generate a new request packet, thus providing an additional level of protection between the original requesting client and the external network.

Proxies for Different Services

Depending on your traffic level and network needs, different proxies can be configured for different external services. For example, one proxy server can handle HTTP requests, while another server can handle FTP content.

Website Caching

The caching process enables Web proxies to cache web data for clients.

Step	Description
Client request	The client requests data from a website.
Packet intercepted	The proxy server intercepts the packet, generates a new request, and transmits it to the website.
Download content	The proxy server downloads all requested content, caches it, and sends it to the client.
Verify cache	If a client requests the same data, the proxy server intercepts the request, verifies that the files are current based on the TTL values in its cache index, and sends the cached data to the client.
Update cache	If the files are not current, the proxy server updates the cache contents from the external website and updates the TTL on the cache.
Purge cache	The proxy server purges its cache once the TTL value on an indexed item expires.

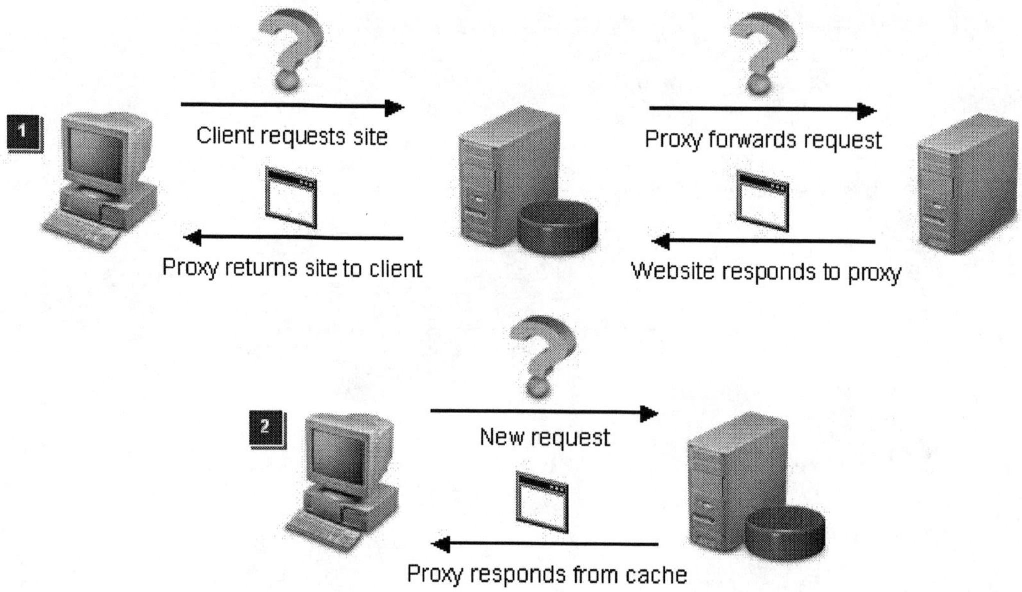

Figure 11-43: *Website caching.*

Keeping the Cache Current

One danger of using a proxy server is that if an external website updates its contents before the TTL of the cache on the web proxy expires, a client might get outdated information from the web proxy's cache. Proxy servers can use either passive or active caching to ensure that cache data is current. In passive caching, the proxy server does not cache any data marked as time sensitive, but sends repeated requests to external sites to ensure that data is current. In active caching, the proxy server profiles cache indexes of websites based on the volume of use. The proxy server actively refreshes the cache contents for sites that have had multiple hits from internal clients.

Another technique the proxy server can use is to request time stamps from the external website, compare them to the stamp in its cache, and download only new data. The time stamp requests generate only a small amount of traffic and eliminate unnecessary content downloads.

Web Proxy Features

Web proxies can incorporate a number of enhanced features.

Feature	Description
User security	Enables an administrator to grant or deny Internet access based on user name or group membership.
Gateway services	Enables proxies to translate traffic between protocols.
Auditing	Enables administrators to generate reports on users' Internet activity.
Remote access services	Provides access to the internal network for remote clients.
Content filtering	Evaluates the content of websites based on words or word combinations, and blocks content that an administrator has deemed undesirable.

ACTIVITY 11-8

Examining Proxy Settings

There is a simulated version of this activity available on the CD-ROM that shipped with this course. You can run this simulation on any Windows computer to review the activity after class, or as an alternative to performing the activity as a group in class. The activity simulation can be launched either directly from the CD-ROM by clicking the Interactives link and navigating to the appropriate one, or from the installed data file location by opening the C:\Data\Simulations\Lesson#\Activity# folder and double-clicking the executable (.exe) file.

Setup:

There is a dial-up connection on your system called My Dial-up.

Scenario:

You are considering implementing a proxy server for HTTP and one for FTP on your local network. You would like to understand how to configure proxy settings so that the clients' web browsers are aware of the proxy on both local and dial-up connections.

What You Do	How You Do It
1. In Internet Explorer, **open the Connections settings.**	a. **Choose Start→Internet Explorer.**
	b. **Choose Tools→Internet Options.**
	c. **Select the Connections tab.**

2. **Examine the LAN proxy settings.**

a. **Click LAN Settings.**

b. **Check Use A Proxy Server For Your LAN.**

c. You can now enter a single proxy address. **Click Advanced.**

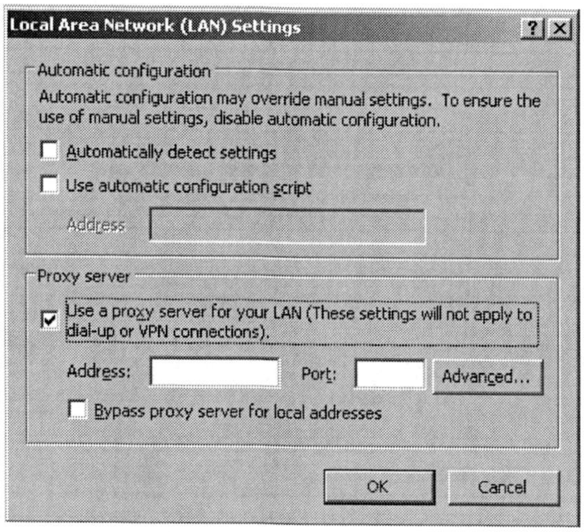

d. The Proxy Settings dialog box enables you to configure separate proxies. **Click Cancel twice.**

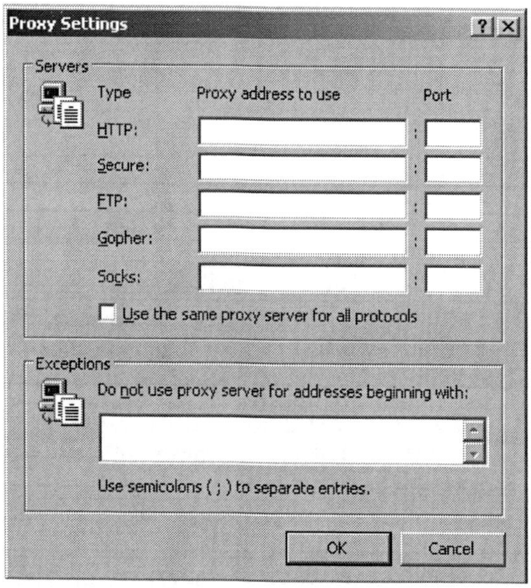

---

3. **Examine the dial-up proxy settings.**

a. Under Dial-up And Virtual Private Network Settings, **select My Dial-up and click Settings.**

b. You can configure the proxy settings for this connection here. **Click Cancel.**

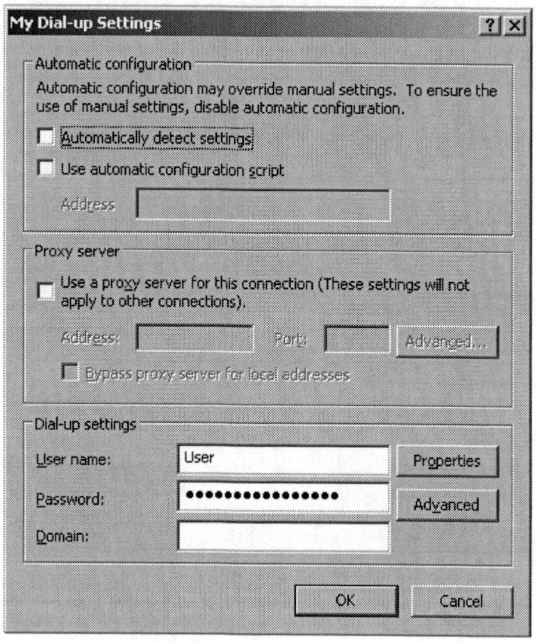

c. **Click Cancel** to close the Internet Options dialog box.

d. **Close Internet Explorer.**

Lesson 11 Follow-up

In this lesson, you identified the major issues and technologies involved in network security. With more and more network threats appearing every day, your responsibility as a networking professional will be ensuring that your network environment provides the appropriate level of security, without compromising network performance.

1. **Give some examples of network threats that you are familiar with from your professional experience or from media reports. What impact did these threats have? How were they resolved?**

2. **Which of the security measures discussed in this lesson are you most familiar with, and which do you think you are most likely to implement or support in your network environments?**

LESSON 12
Remote Networking

Lesson Time
2 hour(s), 30 minutes

Lesson Objectives:

In this lesson, you will identify the components of a remote network implementation.

You will:

- Identify the major architectures in remote networking implementations.
- Identify common terminal services network implementations.
- Identify the components of remote access networking implementations.
- Identify the major components of a VPN implementation.

LESSON 12

Introduction

In previous lessons, you examined the technologies for implementing and securing networks where users and computers have a direct network connection. Many networks also include remote users, who connect to the network through indirect, remote-networking technologies. In this lesson, you will identify the components of a remote network implementation.

Almost every organization needs to support remote users. Whether it's the company CEO who is always on the road, the salesperson with a home office, or the technologist who dials in from an occasional offsite conference, all your remote users need reliable, secure access to your network from their offsite locations. As a network professional, you'll need to understand all the components that are required for remote network implementations so that you can support your remote users effectively.

This lesson covers the following CompTIA Network+ (2005) certification objectives:

- Topic A:
  - Objective 2.16: Define the function of RAS (remote access services).
  - Objective 3.4: Given a remote connectivity scenario comprising a protocol, an authentication scheme, and physical connectivity, configure the connection. Include connections to the following servers: UNIX/Linux/MAC OS X Server, NetWare, Windows, and AppleShare IP (Internet Protocol).
- Topic B:
  - Objective 2.16: Define the function of RDP (Remote Desktop Protocol).
  - Objective 3.4: Given a remote connectivity scenario comprising a protocol, an authentication scheme, and physical connectivity, configure the connection. Include connections to the following servers: UNIX/Linux/MAC OS X Server, NetWare, Windows, and AppleShare IP (Internet Protocol).
- Topic C:
  - Objective 2.16: Define the function of the following remote access protocols and services: RAS (remote access services), PPP (Point-to-Point Protocol), SLIP (Serial Line Internet Protocol), and PPPoE (Point-to-Point Protocol over Ethernet)
  - Objective 2.18: Identify authentication protocols, such as CHAP (Challenge Handshake Authentication Protocol), MS-CHAP (Microsoft Challenge Handshake Authentication Protocol), PAP (Password Authentication Protocol), and RADIUS (Remote Authentication Dial-In User Service).
  - Objective 3.4: Given a remote connectivity scenario comprising a protocol, an authentication scheme, and physical connectivity, configure the connection. Include connections to the following servers: UNIX/Linux/MAC OS X Server, NetWare, Windows, and AppleShare IP (Internet Protocol).
- Topic D:
  - Objective 2.16: Define the function of the following remote access protocols and services: VPN (virtual private network) and RDP (Remote Desktop Protocol).
  - Objective 2.17: Identify and describe the purpose and function of L2TP (Layer 2 Tunneling Protocol).
  - Objective 3.4: Given a remote connectivity scenario comprising a protocol, an authentication scheme, and physical connectivity, configure the connection. Include connections to the following servers: UNIX/Linux/MAC OS X Server, NetWare, Windows, and AppleShare IP (Internet Protocol).

TOPIC A

Remote Network Architectures

In this lesson, you will identify the components of remote network implementations. Many remote network implementations have similar configurations, or architectures. In this topic, you will identify the major architectures used in remote networking implementations.

The needs of remote users are often different than the needs of in-house network users. Several common implementation schemes have evolved to meet the most prevalent user requirements. As a network professional, you might be asked to provide connectivity to remote users. You need to understand the types of connectivity provided by various remote network architectures so that you can provide remote users with the functionality they need.

Remote Networking

Definition:

Remote networking is a type of network communication that enables users to access resources that are not at their physical locations. The remote computer uses an established connection mechanism to attach to the network. Remote networking can be as simple as enabling a user to dial in to a single machine, or it can be a full-service connection with the same functionality the user would have at the office. Remote networking can take one of three basic forms: remote access, remote control, and terminal services.

CompTIA Network+ Exam Objectives

An Appendix is available to assist you in mapping CompTIA Network+ exam objectives to the course content. You can download the Appendix at the end of this lesson.

Remote Networking Limitations

The biggest limit to remote networks is the connection bandwidth. Dial-up connections are common, but support exists for ISDN, xDSL, and other high-speed connections, if the service is available to the remote user.

Example:

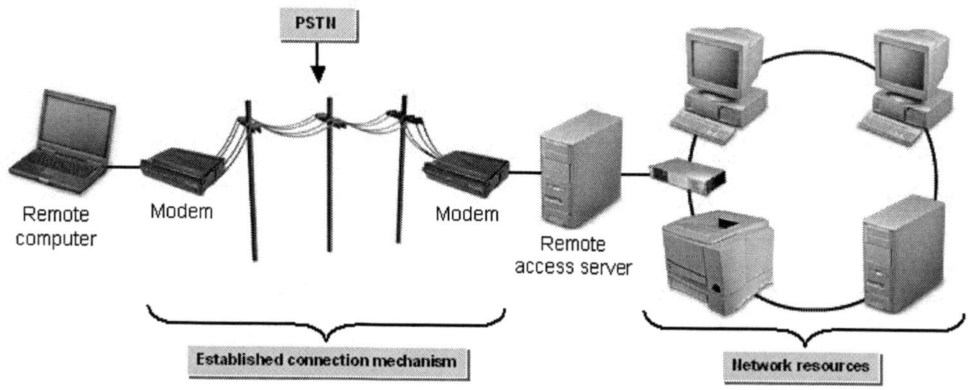

Figure 12-1: *Remote networking.*

Remote Access Networking

In remote access networking, a remote node uses a remote connection to attach to a network. Once attached, the node acts as if it were on the same physical network, except that most of the time the connection is slower because of bandwidth constraints. Most remote access connections are made to a dial-in or remote access server. The server provides security and logs users in to the network. All network traffic to and from the remote node goes through the server.

Remote Access Services (RAS) Servers

Remote access services (RAS) servers are available from many sources. Microsoft's implementation is called Routing and Remote Access Services (RRAS). On Microsoft networks, using RRAS instead of a third-party remote access server means that the user can dial in and authenticate with the same account he or she uses at the office. With third-party remote access servers, there must be some mechanism in place to synchronize the user names and passwords.

In Windows NT 4.0, the service was commonly referred to as RAS.

RAS Server Vendors

Microsoft's RRAS is included with Windows NT Server 4.0, Windows 2000 Server, and Windows Server 2003. Third-party remote access servers are available from vendors such as Perle, Citrix, and Patton.

ACTIVITY 12-1

Configuring Windows RRAS as a Dial-Up Server

There is a simulated version of this activity available on the CD-ROM that shipped with this course. You can run this simulation on any Windows computer to review the activity after class, or as an alternative to performing the activity as a group in class. The activity simulation can be launched either directly from the CD-ROM by clicking the Interactives link and navigating to the appropriate one, or from the installed data file location by opening the C:\Data\Simulations\Lesson#\Activity# folder and double-clicking the executable (.exe) file.

Setup:

The Routing and Remote Access service has been started. The computer is configured to act as a LAN router. A standard 28800 bps modem driver has been installed.

Scenario:

In this activity, you will configure Routing and Remote Access Services to support remote dial-up clients.

What You Do	How You Do It
1. **Configure your computer to act as a dial-up RAS server.**	a. **Choose Start→Administrative Tools→Routing And Remote Access.**

b. **Select your computer and choose Action→Properties.**

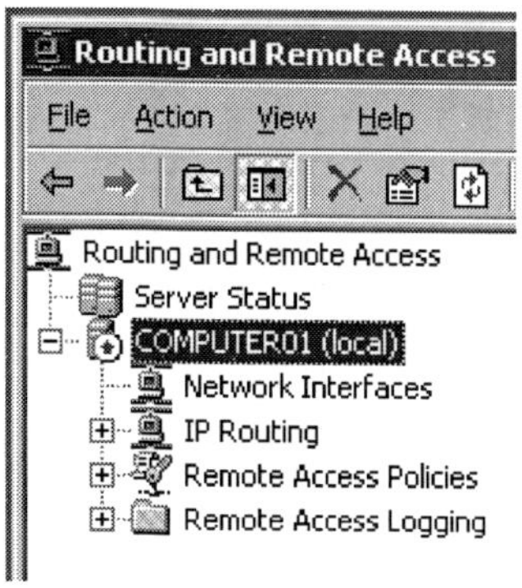

c. On the General tab, **check Remote Access Server and click OK.**

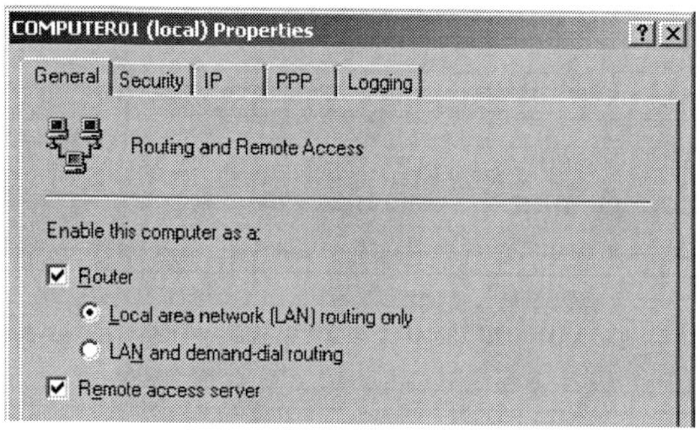

d. To restart the router, **click Yes.**

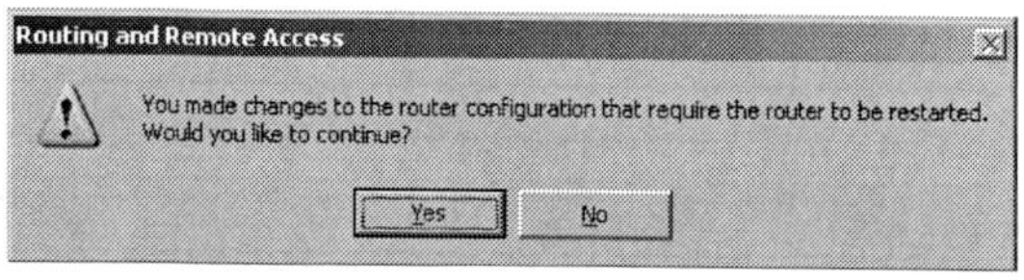

---

2. **Verify the dial-up configuration.**

a. **Select Ports.**

b. Several remote access ports have been enabled. **Choose Action→Properties.**

c. **Verify that a RAS modem port has been enabled on your modem device and click Cancel.**

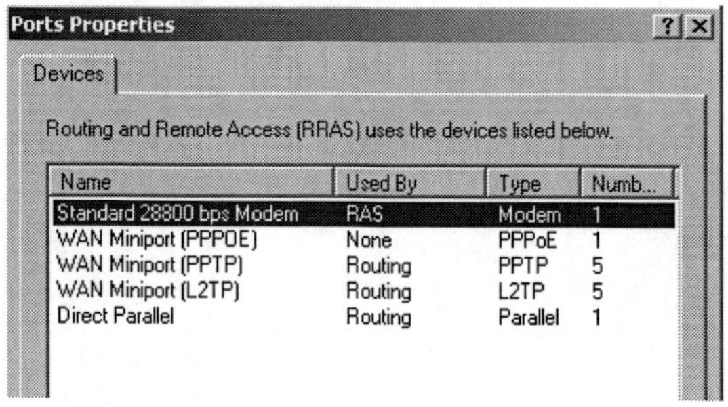

d. **Close Routing And Remote Access.**

Remote Control Networking

Remote control uses a special software package that enables a remote client to take over a host computer on the network. Once connected, the remote client can send keyboard and mouse data and receive screen information. However, all job processing and execution happens on the host computer. Remote control can be deployed across a WAN link or on a local network. Many companies use it as a help desk solution, providing technicians with access to user machines without leaving the help desk.

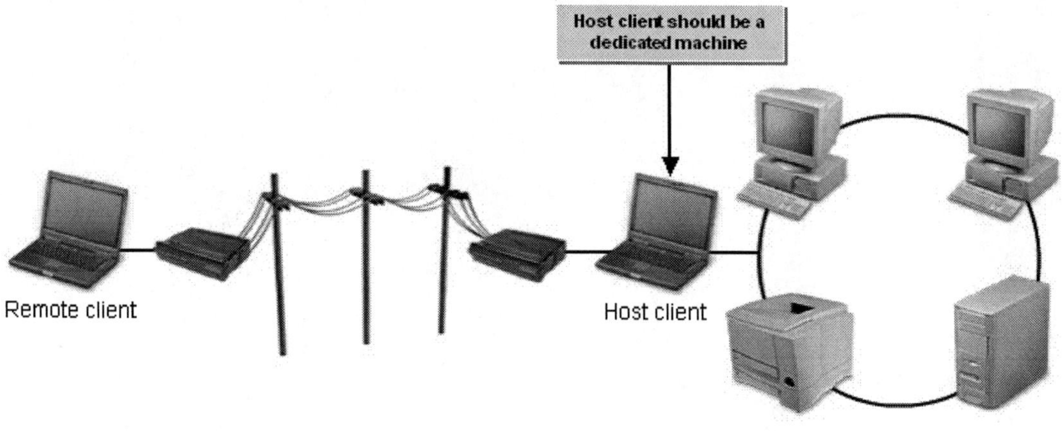

Figure 12-2: *Remote control networking.*

Remote Control Solutions

Remote control networking solutions include Windows Remote Desktop and Remote Assistance, Symantec pcAnywhere, GoToMyPC, LogMeIn, and WebEx AccessAnywhere.

Network Access Through Remote Control

One use for remote control networking is to use the host computer as an access point to a remote network. When a host computer is used to access a network, the host should be a dedicated machine.

ACTIVITY 12-2

Enabling and Creating Remote Desktop Connections

There is a simulated version of this activity available on the CD-ROM that shipped with this course. You can run this simulation on any Windows computer to review the activity after class, or as an alternative to performing the activity as a group in class. The activity simulation can be launched either directly from the CD-ROM by clicking the Interactives link and navigating to the appropriate one, or from the installed data file location by opening the C:\Data\Simulations\Lesson#\Activity# folder and double-clicking the executable (.exe) file.

Scenario:

In this activity, you will work with Remote Desktop Connections.

What You Do	How You Do It
1. **Enable Remote Desktop Connections on your computer.**	a. **Choose Start→Control Panel→System.**
	b. **Select the Remote tab, and check Allow Users To Connect Remotely To Your Computer.**
	c. In the Remote Sessions information box, **click OK.**

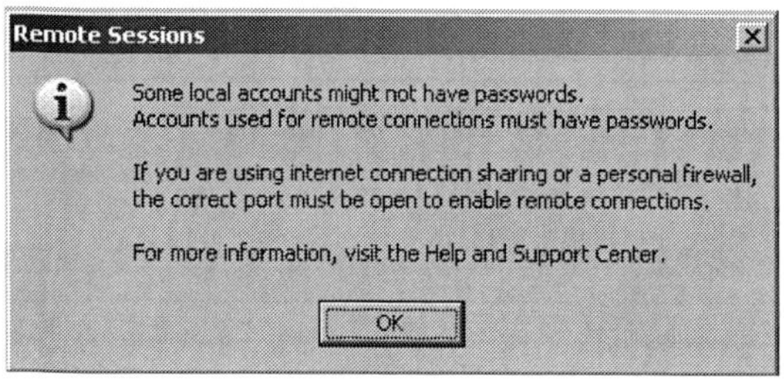

What You Do	How You Do It
2. **Specify the users to be granted remote access to your computer.**	a. In the Remote Desktop area, **click Select Remote Users.**
	b. **Click Add, and click Locations.**

c. **Select Entire Directory, and click OK.**

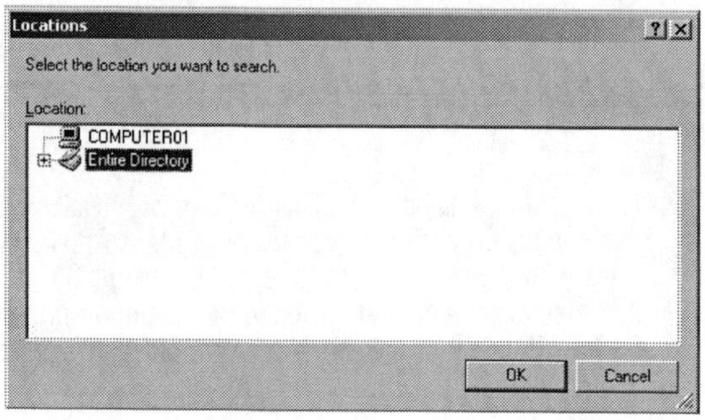

d. **Click Advanced, and click Find Now.**

e. **Select User01 through User100, and click OK.**

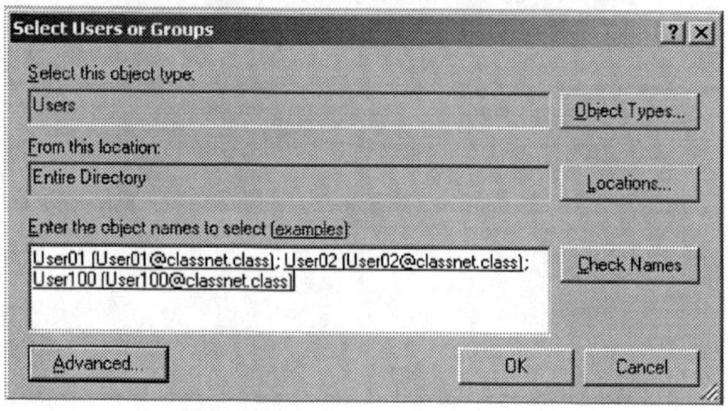

f. **Click OK three times.**

3. **Connect to another computer with Remote Desktop Connection.**

a. **Choose Start→All Programs→ Accessories→Communications→Remote Desktop Connection.**

b. In the Computer text box, **type *Computer##*** where the ## is one higher than your computer's number. For instance, if you were using Computer02, you would type Computer03. If your computer has the highest number in the class, you should type Computer01.

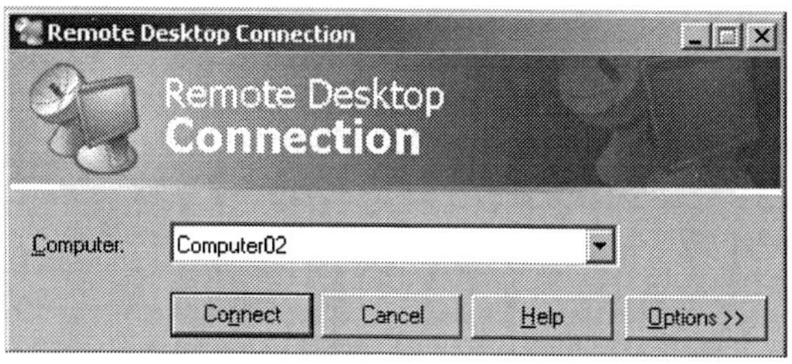

c. **Click Connect.**

d. In the Password text box, **type *!Pass1234* and press Enter.**

e. **Observe the remote session toolbar across the top of the screen.**

f. **Click the Restore button.**

g. You are now connected and can view the remote computer's desktop. In the Remote Desktop window, **scroll down to show the Start menu and the taskbar.**

h. Although you are logged on to a remote computer, you logged on with your own user name. **Click the Start button, and verify that your user name is displayed at the top of the Start menu.**

Step	Action
4. **Create a file on the remote computer.**	a. In the Remote Desktop window, **right-click an open area of the desktop, and choose New→Text Document.** b. **Name the document *remote##.txt*,** where ## is your computer number.
5. **Verify that a new file exists on the local hard drive.**	a. On your taskbar, **choose Start→Windows Explorer.** b. **Expand My Computer, Local Disk (C:), and Documents And Settings.** c. **Expand the User## folder**, where ## is one less than your computer number. For example, if you were using Computer02, then you would expand User01. If you are using Computer01, you should expand the User## with the highest number. d. **Select Desktop, and verify that a text file is listed.** e. **Close Windows Explorer.**
6. **Open the CD drive on the remote computer.**	a. In the Remote Desktop window, **open Windows Explorer.** b. **Expand My Computer, right-click the CD drive, and choose Eject.** c. **Close Windows Explorer.**
7. **End the Remote Desktop session.**	a. In the Remote Desktop window, **choose Start→Log Off.** b. In the Log Off Windows box, **click Log Off.** c. **Close any open windows on your desktop.**

Terminal Services

Terminal services are included in a special server software package built to establish virtual sessions that emulate a remote host. A client logs on to a server, starts a session, and appears to the host as a remote terminal. The main advantage of terminal services is that one host can support multiple sessions. Terminal servers need to be pretty robust since they're running all the services requested by the client, which acts like a dedicated terminal and does very little processing of its own.

As companies began implementing terminal services in this manner, the term "thin client" first came into use.

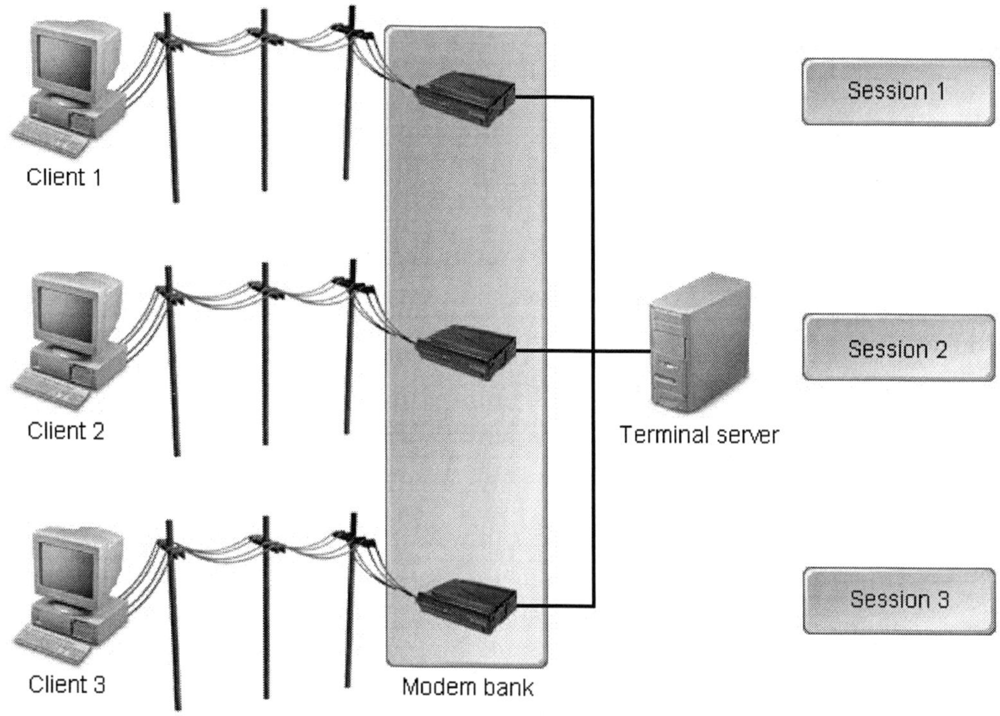

Figure 12-3: *Terminal services.*

Deployment Options

The low demands on the client have led a lot of companies to deploy terminal services as a way of extending the life of their outdated computers. It's possible for a terminal server to support hundreds of sessions. By spending money on a big server and using older clients, companies can sometimes save a lot of upgrade money. These days, $100,000 goes a long way when buying a server, but even at today's lower prices, it will buy only around 75 workstations.

ACTIVITY 12-3

Investigating Remote Networking Architectures

Scenario:

In this activity, you will identify common remote networking architectures.

1. **Match the remote networking technology with its description.**

___	Remote access	a.	Is often used as a troubleshooting or help desk tool.
___	Remote control	b.	Enables several computers to connect simultaneously.
___	Terminal services	c.	Lets traveling users work as if they are in the office.

2. **Which remote access method is best for accessing applications?**

   a) Remote access

   b) Remote control

   c) Terminal services

TOPIC B

Terminal Services Implementations

In the previous topic, you identified the major architectures used in remote networking—remote access, remote control, and terminal services. In this topic, you will identify common terminal services components and network implementations.

Terminal services has become a popular remote networking architecture because it provides flexible functionality at a relatively low cost. The flexibility of terminal services enables companies to deploy applications to remote users in many different ways. As a network professional, you need to understand the different ways that terminal services can be implemented so that you can support your remote users.

Thin Clients

Definition:

A *thin client* is any machine that uses a thin client protocol to connect to a server in order to access and run applications. When a thin client connects to an application server, it starts a session that emulates a complete PC environment that has allocated memory and CPU resources. The session appears to the client to be a working Windows desktop, in which the client can run and shut down software and run several applications at once.

Thin Client Configuration

Hardware for thin clients can range from the minimal components found in dedicated thin client machines to standard workstations. Thin clients can also use different operating systems, such as UNIX and Windows XP Professional, or even no operating system at all.

Example:

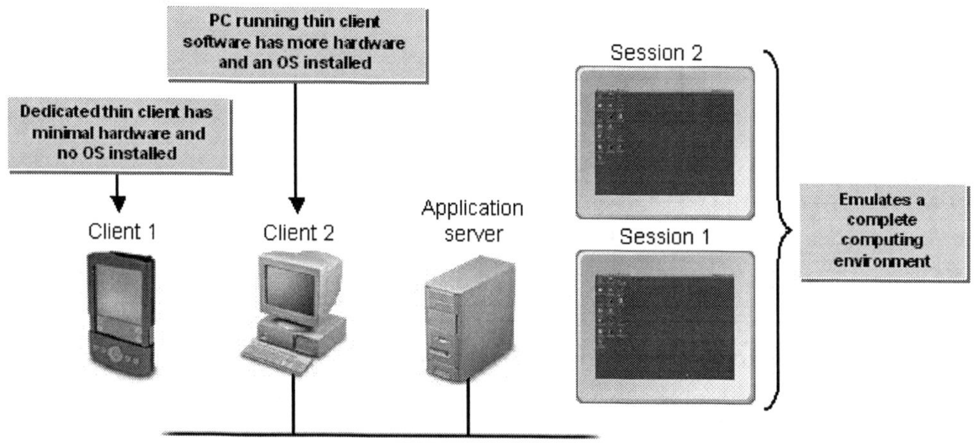

Figure 12-4: *Thin clients.*

History of Thin Clients

Thin client is a term that flooded the industry back in the late 1990s when the 486-DX and 100s gave way to the new class of Pentium computers. Many companies spent huge sums of money to purchase and deploy client machines near the end of the 486 era—when a business computer was thought to have a three- to five-year life cycle and cost around $2,000. When Pentiums hit the market, both software and hardware were changing so fast that many analysts recommended annual leases and replacements to keep up with the fast pace of the new IT era. This was simply not cost effective for companies. The thin client offered two things for those who needed the new technology but wanted to control costs:

- The lives of existing workstations could be extended by configuring them as clients to the new class of application servers.
- A class of desktop PCs, called thin client desktops, was released. These desktops were stripped down to the bare components and marketed in the $700 price range, a significant savings over the $2,000 price tag for a standard desktop.

Thin Client Components

The thin client consists of four basic parts:

- Input devices, usually a keyboard and a mouse.
- An output device, usually a monitor.
- A network connection.
- Thin client software.

The thin client software strips off keystrokes and mouse movements, and redirects them to the application server. It also receives video data from the application server and displays it on the screen.

A PC running thin client software can run applications locally as well as on the application server. A dedicated thin client runs applications only on the application server.

A dedicated thin client has no hard drives or installed operating systems, and uses a boot ROM to boot up and attach to the server. It then downloads and runs the thin client software from the server, and then reconnects to the application server to launch a session for the user.

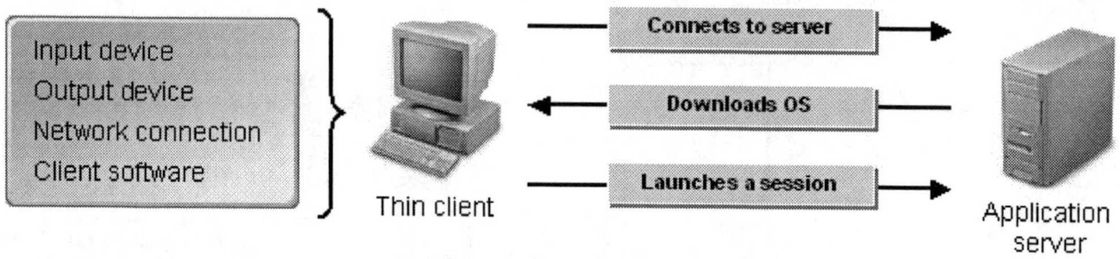

Figure 12-5: *Basic thin client components and actions.*

Comparing Host-Based and Thin Client Computing

This probably sounds like the computer industry has come full circle, back to the days of host-based networking and green-screen dumb terminals, but there is one specific difference—the software that runs on the application server is standard, off-the-shelf software. While the UNIX environment is built around custom-written software, the thin client environment is built around the same software that normally runs on a desktop PC.

Thin Client Benefits

Thin client saves money on desktop purchases, but it also:

- Supports remote clients that dial in through low-bandwidth connections. Because the only data that moves between the remote client and the server is the keystrokes and the screens, there is much less traffic. Similar to when applications located in one remote office need to be run by users at another office location, thin client applications can be run across a smaller WAN connection, saving money in the long run. For example, when 16 users need to run an application across a WAN, a single 56 K dedicated line would not handle the traffic, but it would handle 16 thin client connections.
- Provides added security for banks and public facilities. Thin clients that are set up without 3.5" floppy drives or CD-ROM drives prevent users from loading or removing software and data from the client machine. This configuration is common in banks, public libraries, and schools.

- Runs database applications in which the database can be queried on the application server and then only the results of the query passed to the user.
- Reduces the administrative overhead associated with maintaining client desktops. Every time a client boots up, its OS is refreshed and the user can't install any applications such as AOL or Winamp. Administrators don't have to spend a lot of time fixing configuration issues. Any updates are made at the application server once and will cover all clients that download the software.

Microsoft Terminal Services

Microsoft's thin client application server is called Terminal Server. It is available on Windows NT Server, Windows 2000 Server, and Windows Server 2003. All versions include application mode, which allows users to run applications on the server. Windows 2000 Server and Windows Server 2003 also offer administration mode, which provides fewer connections and less functionality but does not require the purchase of licenses.

Terminal Services provides client access to all Windows-compatible applications by opening a user session on the server. All application execution, data processing, and data storage is handled by the Terminal Server. Microsoft's terminal emulation software can be installed on almost any client operating system, from DOS to Windows XP Professional. Even handheld PCs running Windows CE can connect to a Terminal Server and run applications.

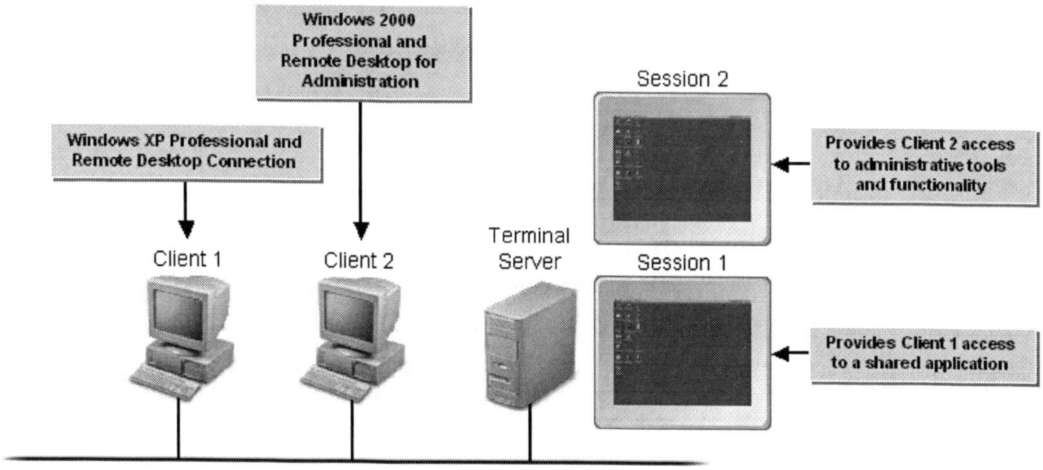

Figure 12-6: *Microsoft Terminal Services.*

Terminal Services Protocol Support

Windows XP Professional and Windows Server 2003 include support for Remote Desktop Protocol (RDP) version 5.2, as well as the Citrix Independent Computing Architecture (ICA) protocol via the Citrix MetaFrame add-on.

Windows Terminal Services Features

Terminal Services includes several related features and components.

Feature	Description
Remote Desktop for Administration	On Windows Server 2003 systems, this feature provides two server-side connections, which can be used to access administrative tools. You do not need to install Terminal Server in order to use Remote Desktop for Administration unless you need more than two incoming connections to the server.
Remote Desktop Connection	The latest version of the Terminal Services client software. It not only enables a thin client connection to a Terminal Server, it also enables users to take advantage of locally available resources, such as drives, peripherals, and even the Clipboard.
Remote Desktop Protocol (RDP) version 5.2	*Remote Desktop Protocol (RDP)* provides the remote input and output capabilities that are the basis for the functionality of both Terminal Server and Remote Desktop. Independent of network topology and protocol, RDP uses separate virtual channels to carry client keystrokes and mouse actions to the server and the resulting server screens back to the client. At the client, keyboard and mouse actions are redirected from the client to the server. RDP version 5.2 provides enhanced performance over previous versions. When a client is accessing an application resident on the Terminal Server, only a screen view of the application data is transmitted, not the actual data, which reduces the bandwidth required for the remote session.
Session Directory	Provides for automatic reconnection of disconnected remote sessions.
Remote Desktop Users group	Enables administrators to grant users remote access to other computers via policy management.
Licensing	Microsoft licenses Terminal Server separately from the Windows 2000 Server or Windows Server 2003 operating system. If a company is deploying 200 clients, it will need 200 client access licenses (CALs) and 200 Terminal Server access licenses. The licensing model provides for both user and device licensing, instead of only device licensing. This reduces licensing costs in situations where a single user might connect via several devices, such as a PC, a laptop, and a PDA, because one user license can be used with any of the devices.

Remote Desktop is a scaled-down version of Remote Desktop for Administration that is included with Windows XP Professional. Remote Desktop enables a Windows XP Professional computer to host incoming connections from a remote location.

Terminal Services in Windows 2000

In Windows 2000 Server, you can install Terminal Services in one of two modes: Application server and Remote Administration server. The Remote Administration mode of Terminal Services in Windows 2000 Server is the equivalent of Remote Desktop for Administration in Windows Server 2003. It provides two Terminal Server connections to enable administrators to connect to the server and run Windows 2000 administrative tools remotely. It does not support application sharing.

RDP Drivers

RDP uses drivers at both the server and the client. At the server, RDP virtual drivers receive the keyboard and mouse data. The data is processed, and an RDP video driver transforms the display output into network packets that are returned to the client. Back at the client, RDP receives the display packets and converts them into the corresponding graphical API calls.

RDP Features and Capabilities

The following table lists the main features and capabilities of RDP.

RDP Feature	Description
Encryption	Using the RC4 stream cipher from RSA Security, RDP packets can be encrypted with a 56- or 128-bit key.
Bandwidth reduction	RDP uses data compression and caching to reduce the amount of data that is transmitted during a remote session.
Extensibility	RDP supports up to 64,000 separate virtual channels, as well as multipoint transmission capabilities.
Roaming disconnect	Users can disconnect from a terminal session without logging off and later reconnect to the existing session from either the same device or a different one. If a disconnection results from a network failure, the user is returned to the existing session upon reconnection.
Clipboard mapping	Text and graphics can be transferred between local applications and terminal sessions, as well as between multiple terminal sessions.
Print redirection	Users can print terminal session data to a local or network printer.
Sound redirection	Sounds from the remote computer can be transferred and played on the RDP client.
Resource redirection	Local disk drives, serial ports, and smart cards are recognized and can be used by a terminal session.

Citrix MetaFrame

Citrix MetaFrame is a terminal services application that runs on most Windows platforms. It provides client connectivity for Windows, Macintosh, Linux, and UNIX desktops. Citrix has digital independence, which means that it can run any application from any desktop over any network media. The Citrix client is independent of hardware platform and can operate on any 386 or later PC as well as most Macintosh platforms. Citrix supports LAN/WAN-to-web connectivity.

Citrix MetaFrame runs on Windows NT Server, Windows 2000 Server, Windows Server 2003, and Windows XP Professional.

Citrix MetaFrame must be installed on a properly installed and licensed Terminal Server. It is configured in a cluster called a server farm, which contains one or more servers and is managed as a single system. The server farm provides clients with a single point of contact for all services. Server farms balance work among the resources of multiple servers to provide the highest possible performance levels. You can add to the server farm without the need to reconfigure existing servers.

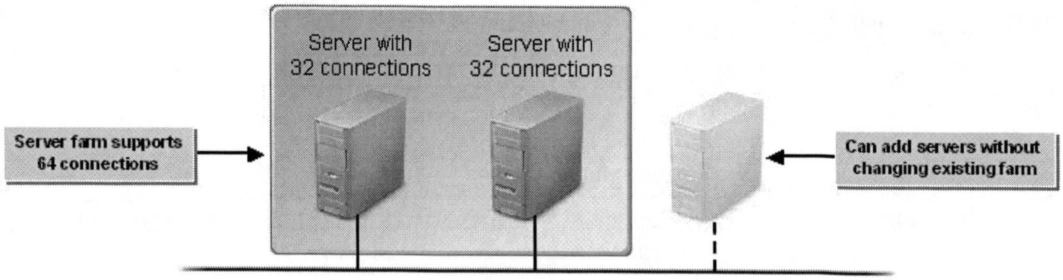

Figure 12-7: *Citrix MetaFrame is deployed in a server farm.*

Citrix Clients

Because of Citrix's digital independence, almost anything can be a Citrix client, including PC desktops, net appliances, web browsers, or mobile devices. Net appliances are dedicated thin client workstations that have a keyboard, mouse, and video, but no hard drives or CD-ROM drives (they might or might not have floppy drives). The net appliance's OS is embedded in a ROM chip, it has lower CPU power, and its entire job is to connect to a MetaFrame server. Even though it is a low-power device, it can run any application on the server.

Web browser support is provided through the Citrix NFuse web server application. Websites that provide the applications are set up, and a client connects to the site with any ActiveX-enabled browser. Like a thin client on a LAN, the applications run on the web server and not the browser machine. Mobile devices that use wireless connectivity services can access and run applications from laptops, cell phones, PDAs, or Windows CE handhelds.

Citrix Independent Computing Architecture (ICA)

The Citrix *Independent Computing Architecture (ICA)* protocol is a remote terminal protocol used by Citrix MetaFrame and MetaFrame XP software as an add-on to Microsoft Terminal Services. ICA enhances and expands on the core thin-client functionality found in Terminal Services, and provides client support for additional protocols and services.

Web-Based Remote Access

With the advent of global businesses and the Internet's immense popularity, providing access to services and data via web browsers is a substantial part of remote access. The main benefit of properly deployed web-based services is that a client doesn't need special software installed to access web-based applications and data.

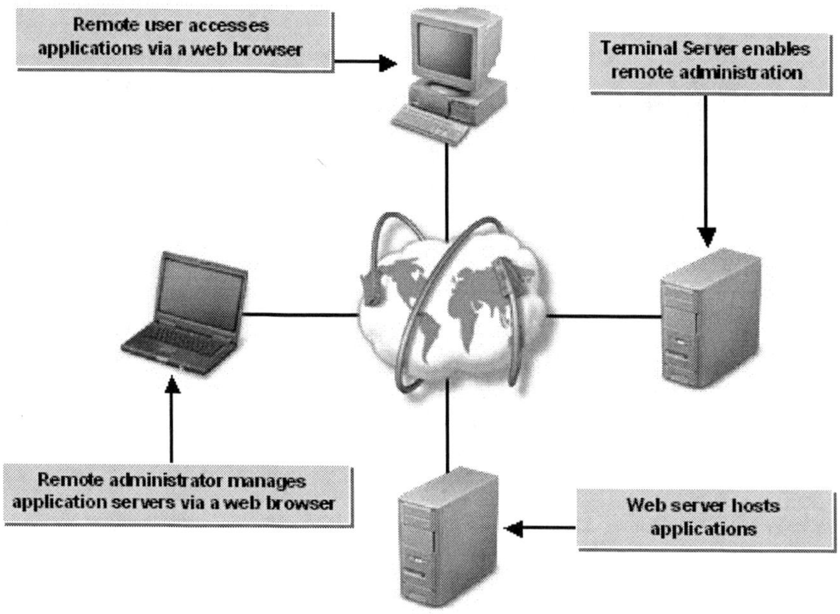

Figure 12-8: *Web-based remote access.*

Web-Based Access in Windows

In Windows Server 2003 and Windows XP Professional, web-based remote access is available through the Remote Desktop Web Connection. The remote machine requires only Internet Explorer 5 or higher, while the web server requires Remote Desktop Web Connection to be installed and running.

Another web-based access feature in Windows Server 2003 is called Web Interface For Remote Administration. Designed for remote management of application servers, it enables administrators to access a server (via secure HTTP on port 8098) from any computer running Internet Explorer 6 or higher. On the application server, which cannot be a domain controller, Web Interface For Remote Administration must be installed.

ACTIVITY 12-4

Installing Microsoft Terminal Server

There is a simulated version of this activity available on the CD-ROM that shipped with this course. You can run this simulation on any Windows computer to review the activity after class, or as an alternative to performing the activity as a group in class. The activity simulation can be launched either directly from the CD-ROM by clicking the Interactives link and navigating to the appropriate one, or from the installed data file location by opening the C:\Data\Simulations\Lesson#\Activity# folder and double-clicking the executable (.exe) file.

Scenario:

In this activity, you will install Terminal Server on your Windows Server 2003 machine.

What You Do	How You Do It
1. Install Terminal Server.	a. **Choose Start→Control Panel→Add Or Remove Programs.**
	b. **Click Add/Remove Windows Components, and check Terminal Server.**
	c. In the Configuration Warning information box, **click Yes.**

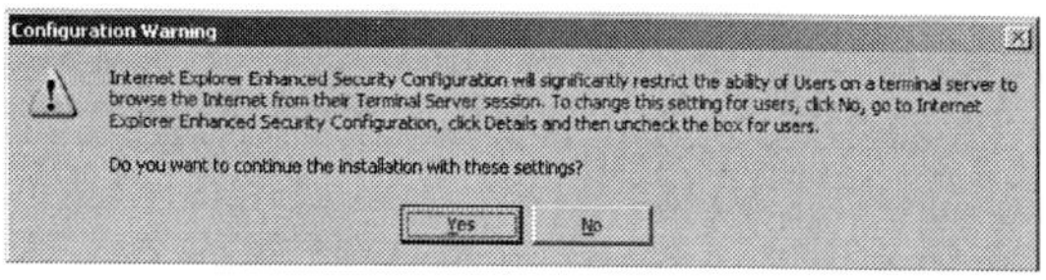

d. **Click Next.**

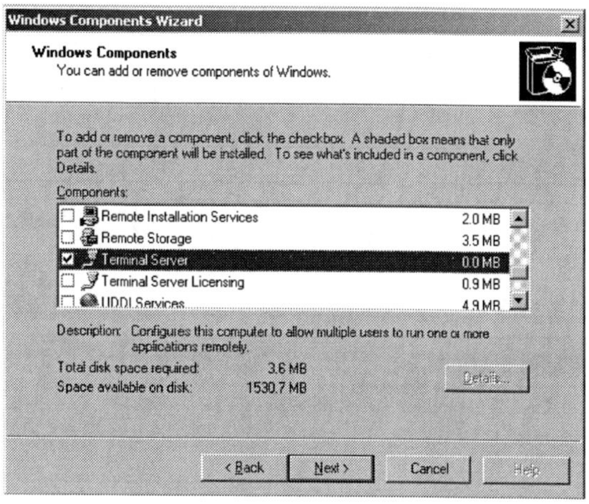

e. **Read the information presented, and click Next.**

Verify that Full Security is selected, and click Next.

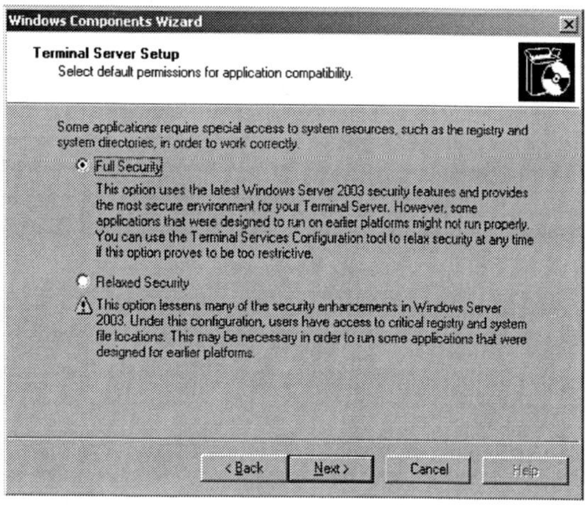

g. **Click Finish, and then click Yes** to restart the computer.

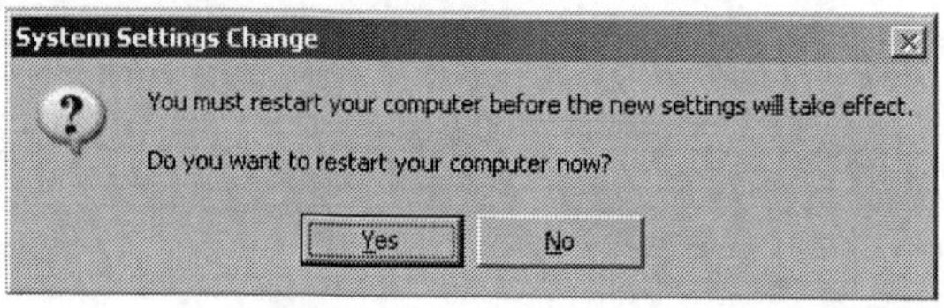

h. If necessary, **click Next** to continue restarting the computer.

i. When the computer restarts, **log on to the Classnet domain as User##.**

j. **Observe the checklists for continuing the setup of Terminal Services, and then close the Help window.**

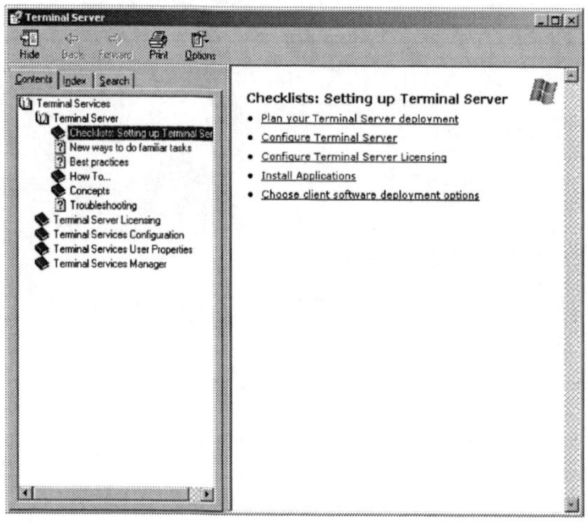

2. **Verify the Terminal Server installation.**	a. **Choose Start→Administrative Tools→Terminal Services Manager.**
	b. **Click OK** to close the Terminal Services Manager information box.
	c. **Expand This Computer, then expand your computer name.**
	d. **Verify that a console session for your user is active.**
	e. **Close Terminal Services Manager.**

TOPIC C

Remote Access Networking Implementations

In the previous topic, you identified Terminal Services components and implementations. Another popular remote networking architecture is remote access networking. In this topic, you will identify the components commonly found in remote access networking implementations.

For many, remote access networking is a way of life. From telecommuters to traveling sales reps to the manager attending an annual conference, these remote users need a reliable way to get to network services while they are not in the office environment. As a network professional, you need to recognize the components commonly used in remote access networking so that you can support your remote users.

Remote Access Protocols

Definition:

A *remote access protocol* is a type of protocol that enables users to log on to a computer or network within an organization from an external location. Remote access protocols can provide direct dial-in connections via modems, or they can provide connections via ISPs and the Internet.

Example:

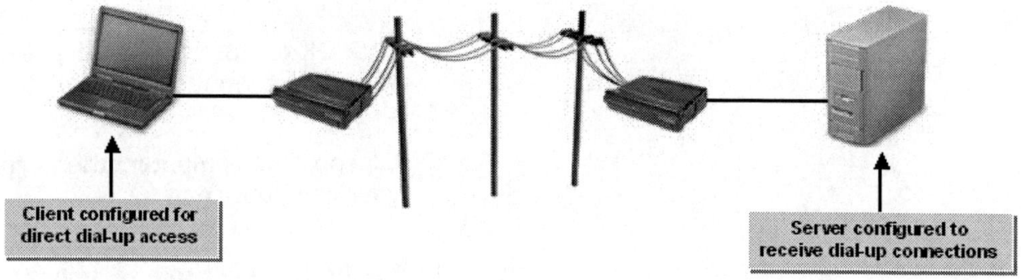

Figure 12-9: *Remote access protocols.*

Serial Line Internet Protocol (SLIP)

Serial Line Internet Protocol (SLIP) is a legacy remote access protocol used for sending IP bytestreams over serial lines such as modem/phone connections. With SLIP transmissions, both ends of the communication channel need to convert data to and from IP datagrams. SLIP has been used with UNIX-based systems since 1984. Its use has mostly been superseded by protocols that provide more features, but some ISPs continue to use SLIP because of its longevity.

SLIP is defined in RFC 1055.

SLIP is sometimes referred to as a packet-framing protocol. With SLIP, each IP datagram is appended with a SLIP END character to distinguish it from other datagrams.

Point-to-Point Protocol (PPP)

Point-to-Point Protocol (PPP) is the current Internet standard for sending IP datagram packets over serial point-to-point links. It can be used in synchronous and asynchronous connections. It supports the use of the NetBEUI, IP, IPX, and AppleTalk network protocols by encapsulating data with the Network Control Protocol (NCP).

PPP can dynamically configure and test remote network connections, and is often used by Windows clients to connect to Windows networks and the Internet. It also provides encryption for passwords, paving the way for secure authentication of remote users. To log on to a remote session via PPP, you need to enable a remote authentication protocol.

A PPP server needs to be configured to provide PPP services.

PPP is defined in RFC 1661.

Comparing SLIP and PPP

The following table compares the functionality of the SLIP and PPP protocols.

SLIP	PPP
Supports only IP datagrams.	Supports NetBEUI, IPX, and AppleTalk, in addition to IP.

SLIP	PPP
Manual configuration of IP addresses.	Dynamic IP address configuration supported.
No packet addressing or identification.	Packet addressing and identification available.
No error detection or correction.	Error detection and correction supported.
No data compression.	Data compression supported.
No encryption of passwords.	Password encryption supported.
Slower, due to lack of compression and error handling.	Faster, even though there is more overhead.

PPPoE

Point-to-Point Protocol over Ethernet (PPPoE) is a standard that provides the features and functionality of PPP to DSL or cable modem connections that use Ethernet to transfer signals from the carrier to the client. In addition, it contains a discovery process that determines a client's Ethernet MAC address prior to establishing a connection.

EAP

Extensible Authentication Protocol (EAP) is an extension of PPP that provides support for additional authentication methods, such as tokens, smart cards, certificates, and so forth.

The Remote Access Authentication Process

There are several steps that must occur to authenticate a remote dial-up connection.

Step	Description
Step 1	A remote user initiates a dial-up session.
Step 2	The remote computer dials a remote access server.
Step 3	The remote access server answers the call, establishing the physical link between the two computers.
Step 4	The remote access server requests that the client authenticate itself by using a remote authentication protocol. • If the client does not agree to provide the requested authentication data, the server refuses to create a connection and the call is terminated. • If the client agrees to send the authentication data, the server establishes a connection and authentication begins.
Step 5	The server and client use the agreed-upon authentication protocol to communicate authentication credentials. • If the server does not accept the authentication credentials provided by the client, the server closes the connection and the call is terminated. • If the server accepts the authentication credentials provided by the client, the server allows the client to access resources.

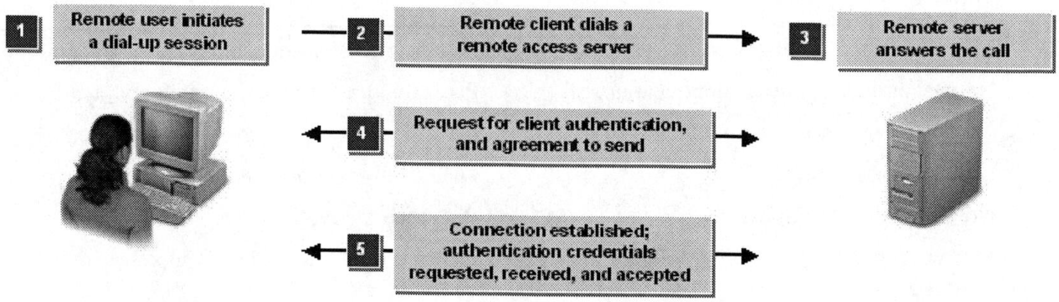

Figure 12-10: *Remote access authentication.*

Password Authentication Protocol (PAP)

Password Authentication Protocol (PAP) is an authentication method that sends client IDs and passwords as cleartext. It is generally used when a remote client is connecting to a non-Windows PPP server that does not support password encryption. When the server receives a client ID and password pair, it compares them to its local list of credentials. If a match is found, the server accepts the credentials and allows the remote client to access resources. If no match is found, the connection is terminated.

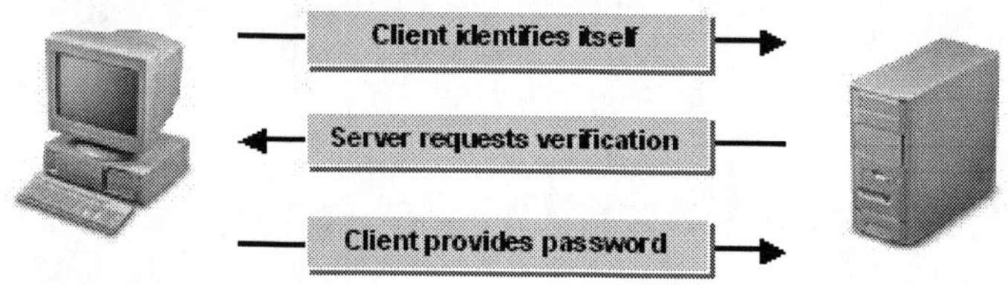

Figure 12-11: *PAP.*

SPAP

Shiva Password Authentication Protocol (SPAP) enables remote connections between Windows and Shiva machines.

Challenge Handshake Authentication Protocol (CHAP)

Challenge Handshake Authentication Protocol (CHAP) is an encrypted authentication method that enables connections from any encrypted authentication method the server requests. CHAP was developed so that passwords would not have to be sent in plain text. It is generally used to connect to non-Microsoft servers. CHAP uses a combination of MD5 hashing and a challenge-response mechanism, and accomplishes authentication without ever sending passwords over the network.

CHAP does not support PAP or SPAP unencrypted authentication.

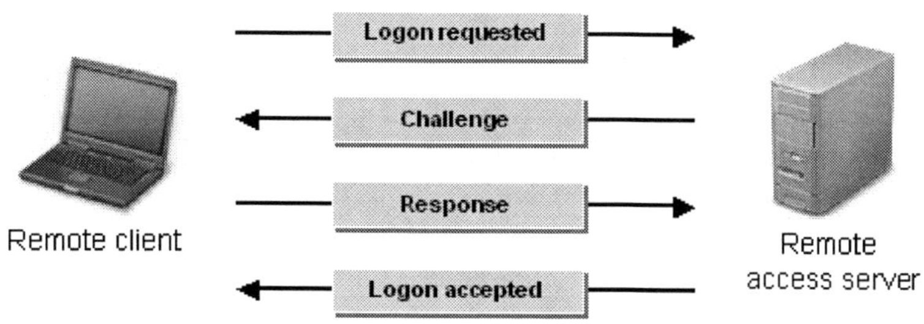

Figure 12-12: *CHAP.*

MS-CHAP and MS-CHAPv2

MS-CHAP is a Microsoft extension of CHAP that is specifically designed for authenticating remote Windows workstations. MS-CHAPv2 provides all of the functionality of MS-CHAP, in addition to additional security features such as two-way authentication and stronger encryption keys.

The CHAP Process

In the challenge-response authentication process, the password is never sent across the network.

Step	Description
Step 1	The remote client requests a connection to the remote access server.
Step 2	The remote server sends a challenge sequence, which is usually a random value.
Step 3	The remote client uses its password as an encryption key to encrypt the challenge sequence and sends the modified sequence to the server.
Step 4	The server encrypts the original challenge sequence with the password stored in its local credentials list and compares the results with the modified sequence received from the client. • If the two sequences do not match, the server closes the connection and the call is terminated. • If the two sequences match, the server allows the client to access resources.

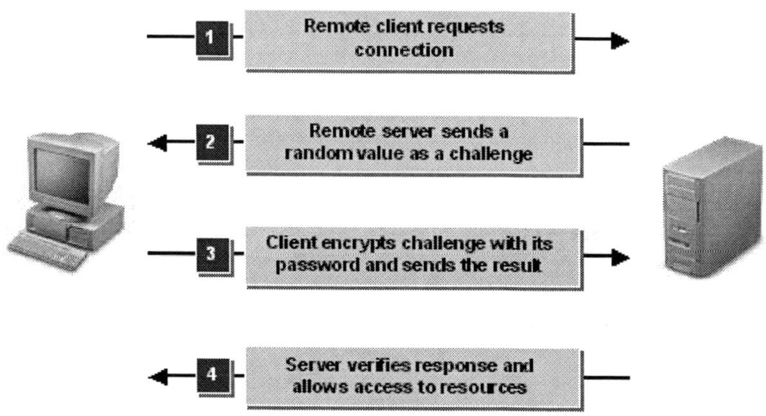

Figure 12-13: *The challenge-response process.*

Remote Authentication Dial-In User Service (RADIUS)

Remote Authentication Dial-In User Service (RADIUS) is a protocol that enables one server to provide standardized, centralized authentication of remote users. When a network contains several remote access servers, you can configure one of the servers to be a RADIUS server, and all of the other servers as RADIUS clients. The RADIUS clients will pass all authentication requests to the RADIUS server for verification. User configuration, remote access policies, and usage logging can be centralized on the RADIUS server.

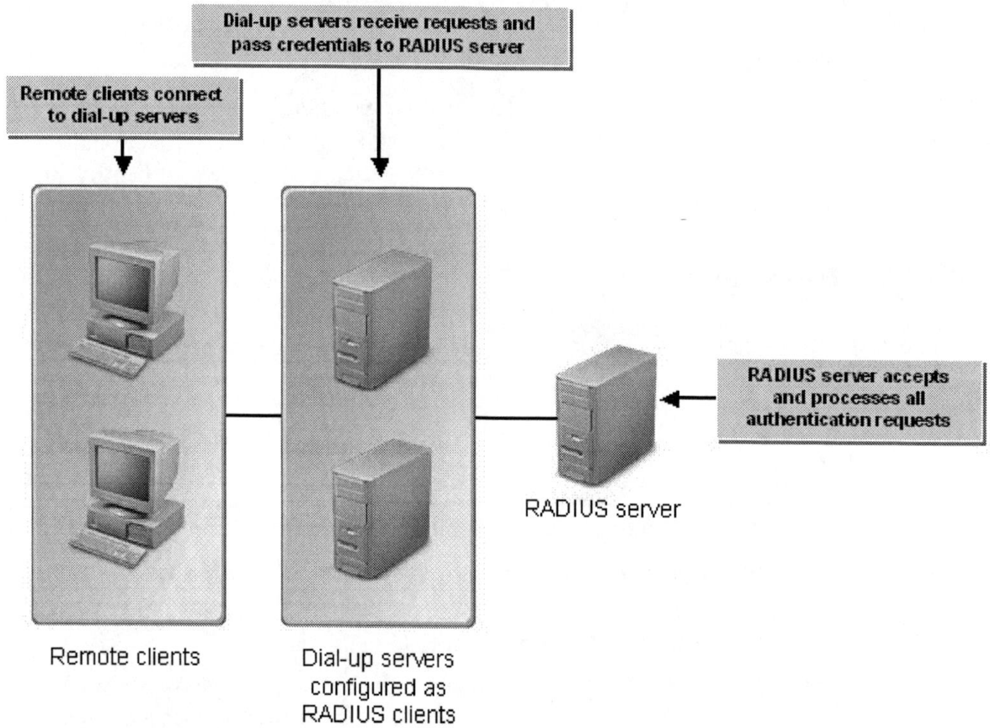

Figure 12-14: *RADIUS.*

RADIUS Implementation in Windows

In Windows, RADIUS implementation is accomplished through the Internet Authentication Service.

ACTIVITY 12-5

Implementing a Remote Access Solution

There is a simulated version of this activity available on the CD-ROM that shipped with this course. You can run this simulation on any Windows computer to review the activity after class, or as an alternative to performing the activity as a group in class. The activity simulation can be launched either directly from the CD-ROM by clicking the Interactives link and navigating to the appropriate one, or from the installed data file location by opening the C:\Data\Simulations\Lesson#\Activity# folder and double-clicking the executable (.exe) file.

Scenario:

You plan to implement RADIUS for remote authentication in your enterprise. You want to test RADIUS in a lab environment before deploying it in production. On a test RRAS system, you will install a RADIUS server and reconfigure a RRAS server to use RADIUS authentication.

For simplicity in this exercise, you will install IAS on the system you previously configured as a RRAS remote-access server. Normally you would install the IAS server and the remote-access RRAS server on separate systems, because the remote-access RRAS server acts as a client of the IAS server.

What You Do	How You Do It
1. **Identify the authentication methods supported by RRAS.**	a. **Choose Start→Administrative Tools→ Routing And Remote Access.**
	b. **Select your computer and choose Action→Properties.**

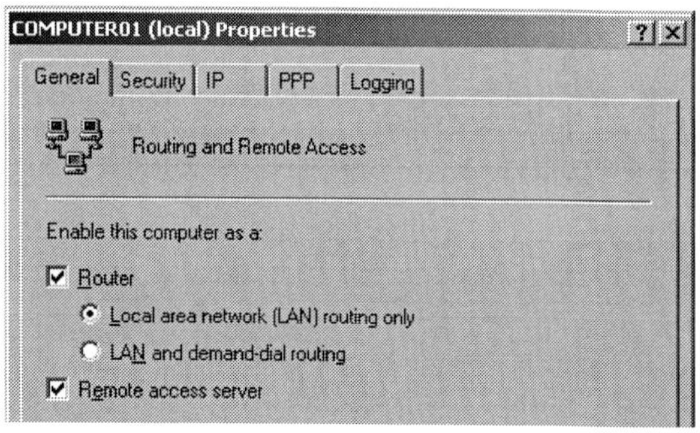

c. **Select the Security tab.**

d. **Click Authentication Methods.**

e. Examine the methods, then click Cancel twice.

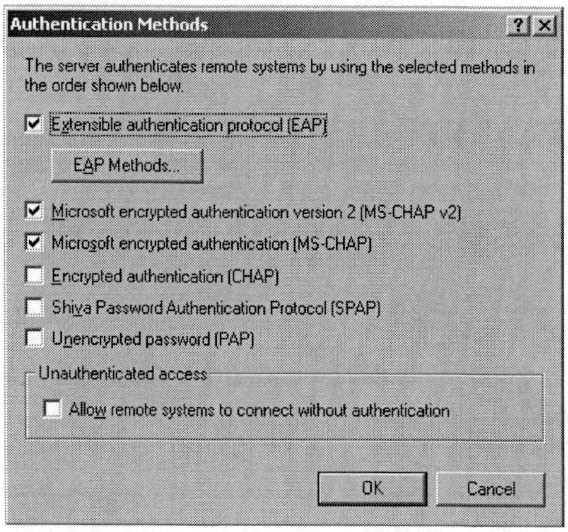

f. Minimize the RRAS console.

---

2. Install the Internet Authentication Service.

a. Choose Start→Control Panel→Add Or Remove Programs.

b. Click Add/Remove Windows Components.

c. Select (but do not check) Networking Services, and click Details.

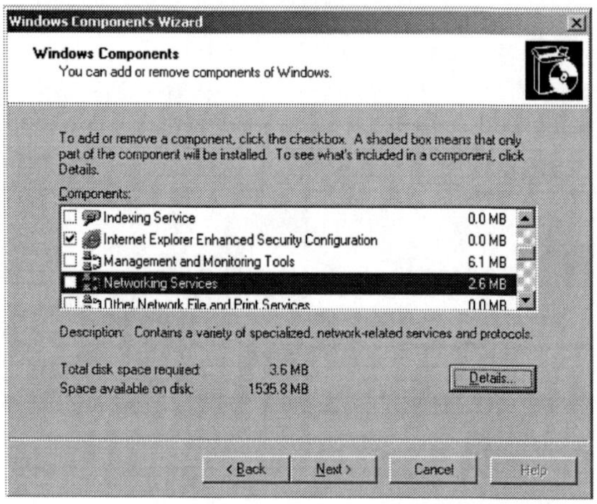

d. **Check Internet Authentication Service.**

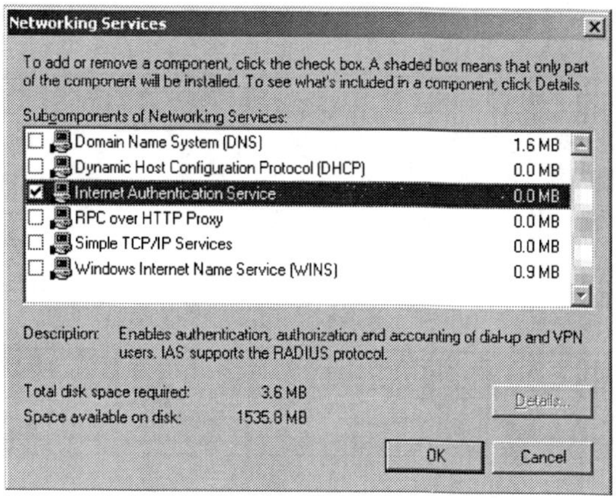

e. **Click OK, click Next, and then click Finish.**

f. **Close the Add Or Remove Programs window.**

3. **Set up the RADIUS server.**	a. **Choose Start→Administrative Tools→Internet Authentication Service.**
	b. **Right-click RADIUS Clients and choose New RADIUS Client.**
	c. In the Friendly Name text box, **type *##dialup*,** where ## corresponds to your computer number.
	d. In the Client Address text box, **type the IP address of your computer and click Next.**
	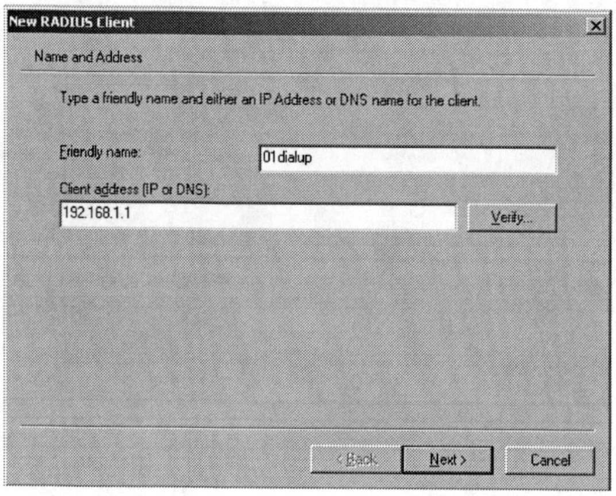
	e. In the Shared Secret text box, **type *Network+***
	f. In the Confirm Shared Secret text box, **type *Network+***
	g. **Click Finish.**
	h. **Close the Internet Authentication Services console.**
4. **Reconfigure your RRAS server to use RADIUS authentication.**	a. **Switch to the RRAS console.**
	b. **Right-click the RRAS server and choose Properties.**
	c. **Select the Security tab.**

d. From the Authentication Provider drop-down list, **select RADIUS Authentication.**

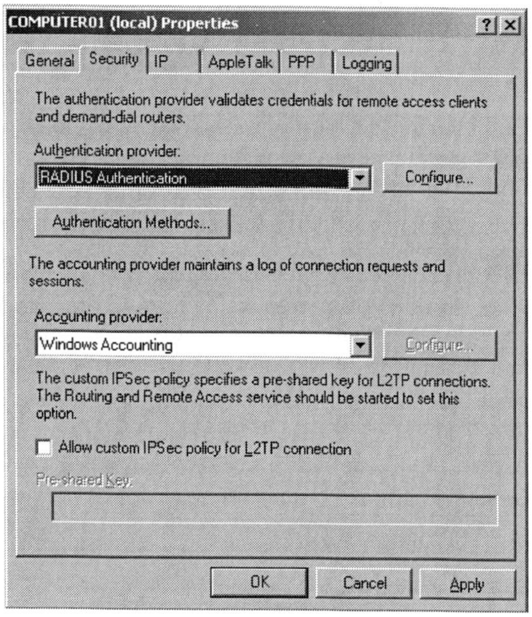

e. **Click OK.**

f. **Click Yes.**

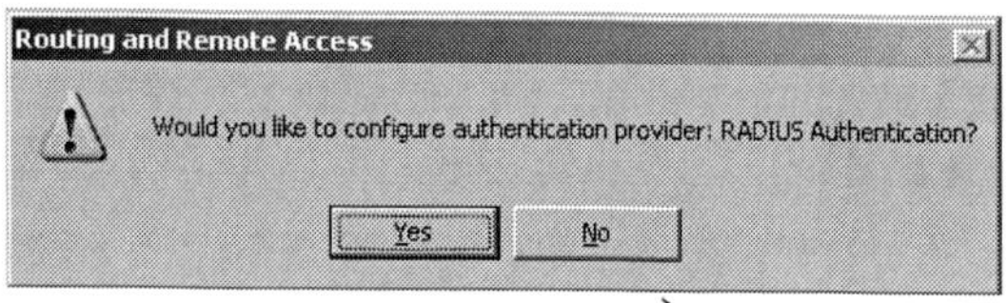

g. **Click Add.**

h. In the Server Name text box, **type your computer name.**

i. **Click OK three times.**

j. **Right-click the RRAS server and choose All Tasks→Stop.**

k. **Right-click the RRAS server and choose All Tasks→Start.**

TOPIC D

Virtual Private Networking

In the last topic, you identified remote access networking components and implementations. In some organizations, the sheer number of remote users makes the implementation of traditional remote access networking cost-prohibitive. This is where VPNs come into the picture. In this topic, you will identify the major components of VPN implementations.

Although standard dial-up implementations continue to be popular, other considerations, such as security and the number of remote users to be supported, require additional measures to provide remote connections. Instead of implementing a WAN, many larger companies opt to take advantage of public networks like the Internet, but then the issue of securing data transmissions becomes more important. One of the main solutions to counter the security risks found on public networks is to implement a virtual private network (VPN) within the public network. As a network professional, you need to recognize the components found in VPN implementations so that you can support your remote users.

Tunneling

Definition:

Tunneling is a data-transport technique in which a data packet from one protocol, called the passenger protocol, is transferred inside the frame or packet of another protocol, called the carrier protocol. This enables data from one network to pass from one endpoint of a tunnel to the other through the infrastructure of another network. The carrier protocol can encapsulate and route nonroutable passenger protocols, or it can provide additional security by hiding passenger data from the carrier network.

Example:

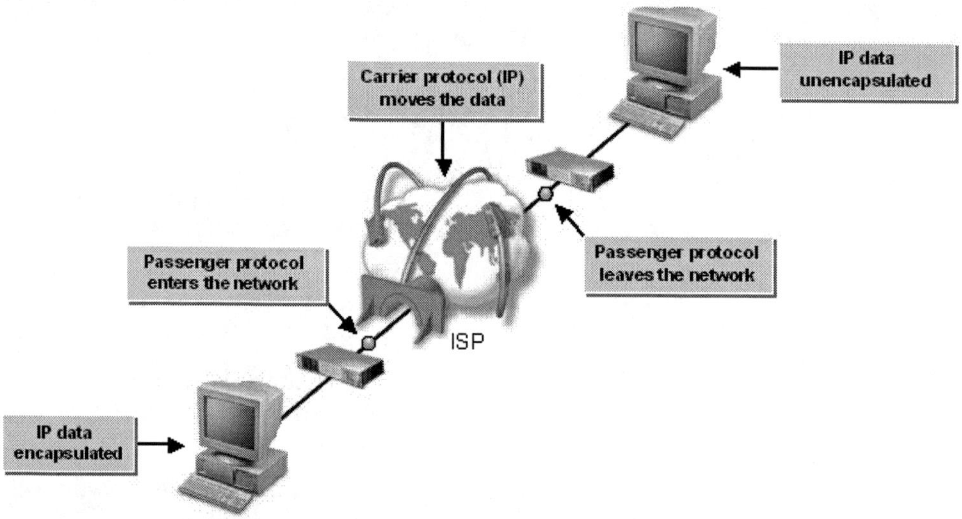

Figure 12-15: *Tunneling.*

Tunnel Types

Essentially, there are two tunnel types: voluntary and compulsory.

- Voluntary tunnels are created between client endpoints at the request of the client. When a user runs a software application that supports encrypted data communications, the client establishes an encrypted tunnel to the other end of the communication session, whether it is on a local network or the Internet.
- A WAN carrier establishes compulsory tunnels with no involvement from client endpoints. Clients send data between endpoints, and all data is tunneled without affecting the client at all. Compulsory tunnels can be in place permanently (static), or they can be put in place based on data or client type (dynamic).

VPNs

Definition:

A *virtual private network (VPN)* is a private network that is configured by tunneling through a public network such as the Internet. VPNs provide secure connections between endpoints, such as routers, clients, or servers, by using tunneling to encapsulate and encrypt data. Special *VPN protocols* are required to provide the VPN tunneling, security, and data encryption services.

A VPN endpoint is called a Point of Presence (PoP).

Example:

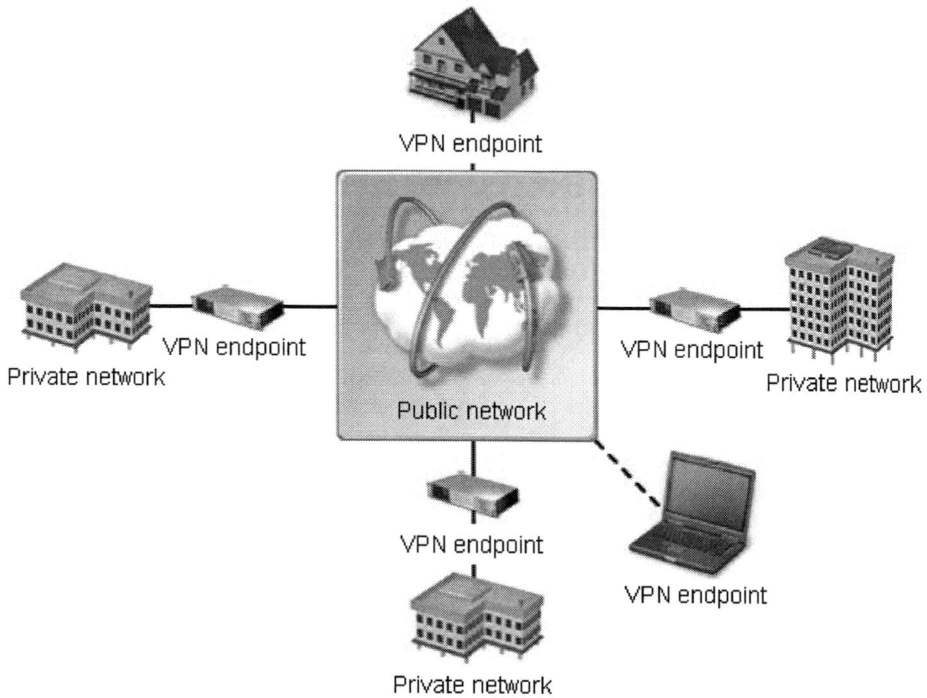

Figure 12-16: *VPN.*

Example:

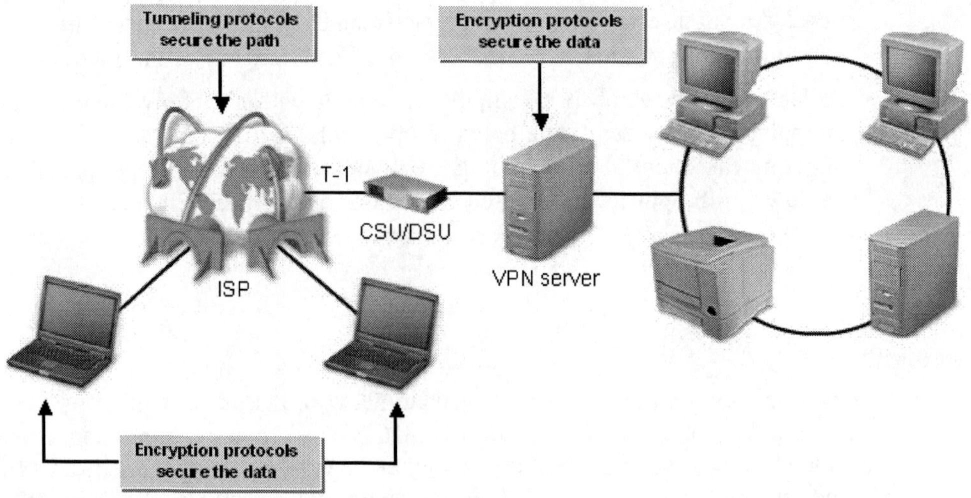

Figure 12-17: *VPN protocols.*

VPN Advantages

The biggest reason that most companies implement VPNs is cost. The cost to maintain a VPN is generally lower than other remote access technologies. For instance, if a remote access technology depends on long-distance or toll-free calls, a company's phone bill can become enormously expensive. Another reason for implementing VPNs is versatility. One VPN PoP connected to a T1 or T3 line to the service provider can accommodate hundreds of simultaneous connections from any type of client using any type of connection.

Point-to-Point Tunneling Protocol (PPTP)

Point-to-Point Tunneling Protocol (PPTP) is a Microsoft VPN protocol that increases the security of PPP by providing tunneling and data encryption for PPP packets. It uses the same authentication types as PPP, and is the most widely supported VPN method among older Windows clients. PPTP encapsulates any type of network protocol and transports it over IP networks.

Layer Two Tunneling Protocol (L2TP)

Layer Two Tunneling Protocol (L2TP) is an Internet-standard protocol for tunneling PPP sessions across a variety of network protocols, such as IP, frame relay, or ATM. L2TP was specifically designed to provide tunneling and security interoperability for client-to-gateway and gateway-to-gateway connections. L2TP tunnels appear as IP packets, so IPSec Transport Mode provides authenticity, integrity, and confidentiality security controls.

L2TP is defined in RFC 2661.

L2TP has wide vendor support because it addresses the IPSec shortcomings of client-to-gateway and gateway-to-gateway connections.

VPN Support in Windows

Windows RRAS supports both PPTP and L2TP.

VPN Data Encryption

In most VPNs, data encryption is accomplished by either MPPE or IPSec.

Data Encryption Method	Description
MPPE	MPPE is often used with PPTP. It provides strong (128-bit key) and standard (56- or 40-bit key) data encryption. MPPE requires the use of MS-CHAP, MS-CHAPv2, or EAP remote authentication, because the keys used for MPPE encryption are derived from the authentication method.
IPSec	IPSec in Tunnel Mode is often used with L2TP. Data encryption is accomplished by IPSec, which uses DES or 3DES encryption to provide data confidentiality. IPSec can also be used on its own to provide both tunneling and encryption of data.

VPN Types

VPNs can be one of three types.

VPN Type	Description
Access VPNs	Provide remote access to single users via dial-up, ISDN, xDSL, or cable modem connections.
Intranet VPNs	Connect sections of a network, such as remote offices tying into a corporate headquarters.
Extranet VPNs	Connect networks belonging to different companies for the purposes of sharing resources.

VPNs can also be classified by their implementation.

Implementation	Description
Hardware-based	Usually use encrypting routers.
Firewall-based	Use a firewall's security mechanisms.
Software-based	Can be used when the VPN endpoints are not controlled by the same organization.

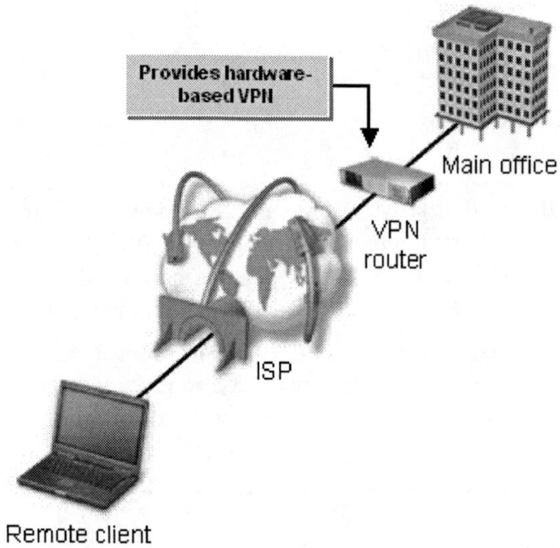

Figure 12-18: *An access VPN.*

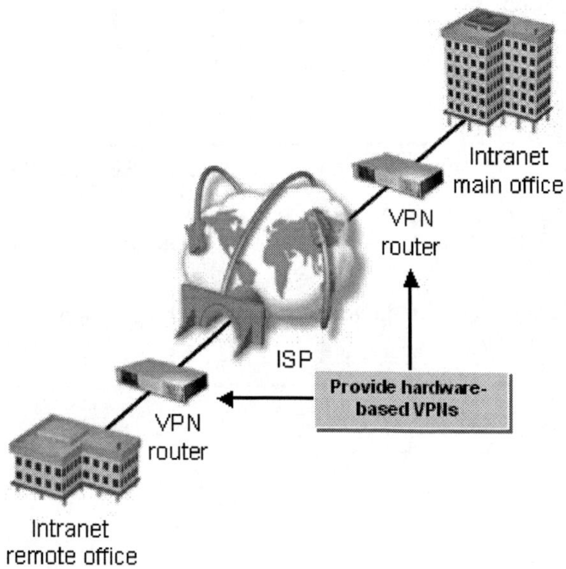

Figure 12-19: *An intranet VPN.*

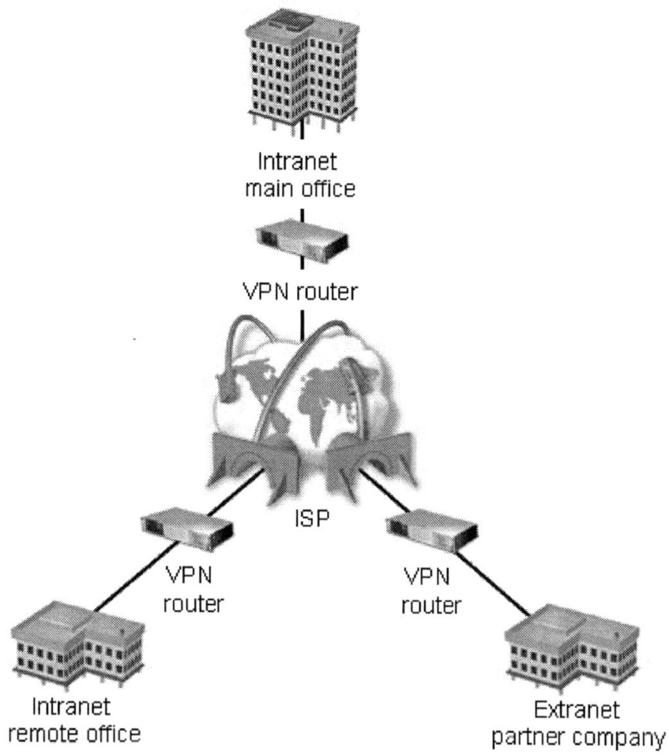

Figure 12-20: *An extranet VPN.*

ACTIVITY 12-6

Investigating VPNs

Setup:

Routing And Remote Access is running.

Scenario:

In this activity, you will identify components and characteristics of VPNs.

What You Do	How You Do It
1. Enable VPN support on RRAS.	a. In the Routing And Remote Access console, in the left pane, **select Ports.**
	b. The ports are displayed in the right pane. The WAN Miniport entries use either PPTP or L2TP. There are five of each that are available for routing. **Choose Action→ Properties.**
	c. **Select the first WAN miniport that uses PPTP and click Configure.**
	d. **Check Remote Access Connections (Inbound Only) and click OK.**
	e. **Select the first WAN miniport that uses L2TP and click Configure.**
	f. **Check Remote Access Connections (Inbound Only) and click OK.**
	g. In the Ports Properties dialog box, **click OK.**
	h. **Verify that the Used By column for the two ports displays RAS And Routing, and click OK.**
	i. **Close the RRAS console.**

2. **True or False? VPNs can only be implemented over the Internet.**

__ True

__ False

3. **What provides the security for most VPNs?**

a) Encapsulation

b) Remote authentication

c) Encryption

d) Firewalls

4. **Which VPN protocol provides both encapsulation and encryption?**
   a) PPTP
   b) SSL
   c) IPSec
   d) MPPE
   e) L2TP

5. **Which VPN type is most likely to be used by satellite offices?**
   a) Access VPN
   b) Intranet VPN
   c) Extranet VPN

ACTIVITY 12-7

Troubleshooting Remote Connectivity

Scenario:

In this activity, you will discuss ways to resolve various remote connectivity problems.

1. **Your company hosts a VPN server using the L2TP protocol with IPSec encryption. A user trying to connect from his home PC consistently fails, although he can connect when he brings his laptop home from the office. What do you suspect is the cause of the failure?**

2. **What should you do to correct the situation?**

3. **A user attempts to establish a dial-up connection with your company's RRAS server. The connection consistently fails with an authentication error. You ask the user to examine the properties of his dial-up connection object. Under Logon Security, in the Allow These Protocols section, only PAP is checked. What is the most likely cause of the failure?**

4. What should you do to correct the situation?

5. You provide help desk support for an ISP. A home user has called to say that he is trying to dial in but the system reports that there is no dial tone. His home phone is on the same line, and he obviously has a dial tone on the phone instrument. He could connect yesterday. What could be the problem?

6. You work for a large ISP that provides a number of PoP phone numbers for each metropolitan area where you provide service. A Chicago-based user is trying to connect using the first local dial-up number listed in your service guide, but receives an error that the remote system is busy or not responding. There is a high amount of traffic on your network, but all systems are functioning. What should you suggest to the user?

7. You maintain a Microsoft RRAS server with several incoming phone lines to support network access for remote dial-up clients, and VPN service for Internet users. A home user running Linux can connect to the Internet through his local ISP, but cannot connect to your RRAS server. What should you check on the RRAS server?

8. How might you enable the user to connect?

Lesson 12 Follow-up

In this lesson, you identified the components of a remote network implementation. As a network professional, you'll need to understand the technologies involved in remote network implementations so that you can support your remote users effectively.

1. What experience do you have with remote networking implementations? What technologies were used?

2. Which of the remote networking technologies discussed in this lesson do you think you are most likely to encounter in your organization?

LESSON 13
Disaster Recovery

Lesson Time
1 hour(s), 45 minutes

Lesson Objectives:

In this lesson, you will identify major issues and technologies in disaster recovery.

You will:

- Identify the components of a disaster recovery plan.
- Identify the primary tools and technologies used to back up and recover data.
- Identify tools and technologies used to implement fault tolerance.

Lesson 13

Introduction

In previous lessons, you examined technologies to implement and secure networks and to support remote networking. No matter how carefully constructed a network is, though, unforeseen events can occur that will damage network resources, including data. In this lesson, you will identify major issues and technologies related to disaster recovery.

You can't prevent every possible catastrophic event. As a network professional, you will be called on to assist in the maintenance of the network and in the protection of the data stored on it. And, if the worst ever does happen, your managers, users, and clients will look to you to help get the network running again.

This lesson covers the following CompTIA Network+ (2005) certification objectives:

- Topic A:
  - Objective 3.12: Identify the purpose and characteristics of disaster recovery, including backup/restore, offsite storage, hot and cold spares, and hot, warm, and cold sites.
- Topic B:
  - Objective 1.4: Recognize and describe the uses of USB (Universal Serial Bus) media connectors.
  - Objective 3.12: Identify the purpose and characteristics of disaster recovery, including backup/restore and offsite storage.
- Topic C:
  - Objective 3.11: Identify the purpose and characteristics of fault tolerance, such as power, link redundancy, storage, and services.

Topic A

Planning for Disaster Recovery

In this lesson, you will identify major issues and technologies related to disaster recovery. The first step most organizations will take is to create a disaster recovery plan so that they have it in place before any disaster occurs. In this topic, you will identify the components of a disaster recovery plan.

Networks are vulnerable to a multitude of threats—not only from hackers, but also from natural disasters and plain old-fashioned decay. Insurance can replace hardware, and administrators can rebuild the network, but lost data is gone for good, and many companies can't survive that. Having a solid disaster recovery plan in place will help ensure that your organization recovers efficiently from any type of disaster.

LESSON 13

Disasters and Disaster Recovery

Definition:

A *disaster* is a catastrophic loss of system functioning due to a cause that cannot reasonably be prevented. Disasters can affect personnel, buildings, devices, communications, resources, and data. *Disaster recovery* is the administrative function of protecting people and resources while bringing a failed network or system back online as quickly as possible. The first priority is to ensure the safety of personnel, and then to ensure continuity of business functions.

Example:

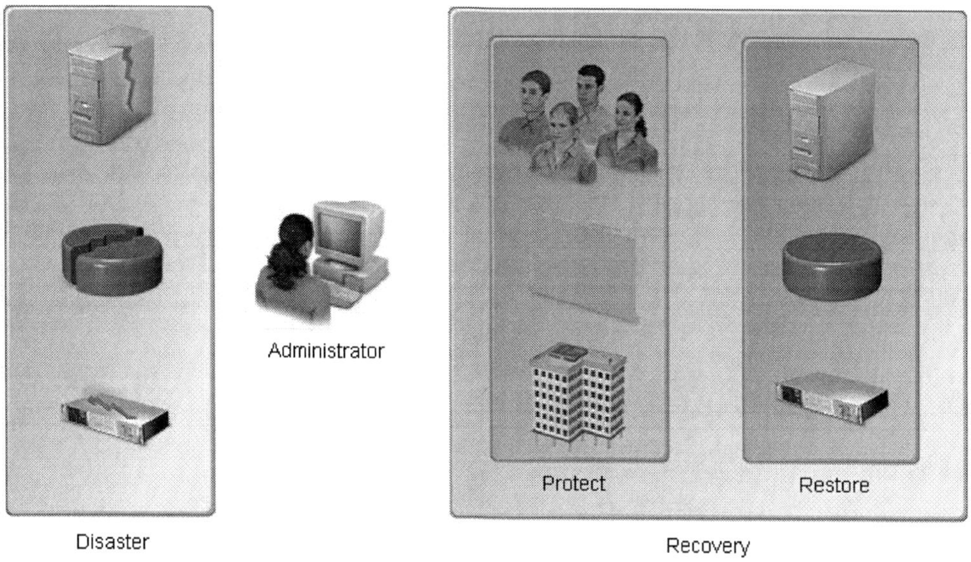

Figure 13-1: *Disaster recovery.*

Disaster Categories

Disasters that can affect network functioning fall into one of three main categories.

Disaster Category	Description
	Natural disasters include fires, storms, floods, and other destructive forces. Natural disasters involve the involuntary destruction of network hardware. Data loss is usually related to destruction of network infrastructure and hardware. The best defense against this type of disaster is excellent documentation and physical security for data backups. In the worst-case scenario, nothing remains of the office after the disaster, and the network has to be completely rebuilt from documentation alone.

Disaster Category	Description
 Data destruction	Data loss due to causes other than natural disaster is much easier to recover from. This kind of data loss includes accidental deletion, malicious destruction, or a virus attack. Again, the key is a good quality data backup.
 Equipment failure	Most day-to-day network disasters relate to failure of network hardware. Not only can hardware failure cause a loss of data, but it can also cause a loss of productivity in the office. Defense against equipment failure can be as simple as having a relationship with a vendor who can get replacement parts quickly or contracting a service provider that stocks parts. Many companies keep high-risk spares on hand in order to quickly replace failures. One major mistake that many administrators make is to standardize an exotic piece of hardware or rely too heavily on older hardware that might be hard to replace. If a network goes down because older equipment fails, it could be down for an unacceptable length of time while a replacement is found or the network is reconfigured.

Disaster Recovery Plans

Definition:

A *disaster recovery plan* is a policy and set of procedures that documents how people and resources will be protected in case of disaster, and how the organization will recover from the disaster and restore normal functioning. The plan should be developed and implemented cooperatively between different functional groups.

The disaster recovery plan incorporates many components, including:

- A complete list of responsible individuals.
- A critical hardware and software inventory.
- Detailed instructions on how to reconstruct the network.

A complete disaster recovery plan will be highly detailed and completely customized to suit the needs and circumstances of a particular organization. This section provides only a broad overview of the components and considerations involved in constructing a recovery plan.

Example:

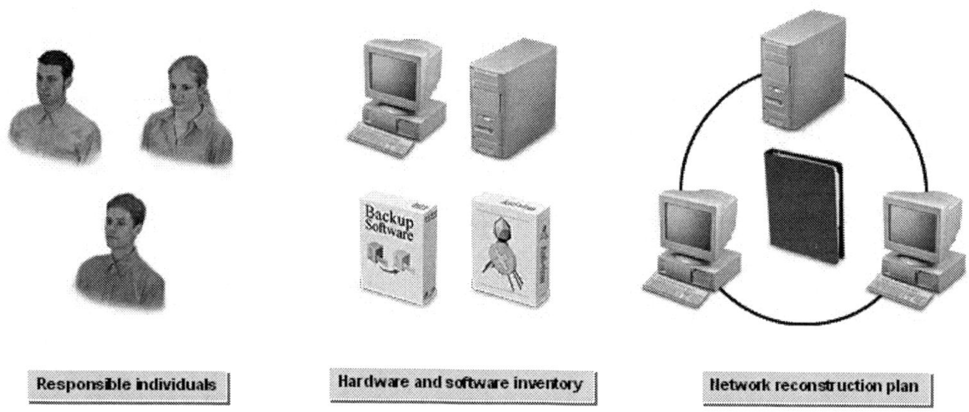

Figure 13-2: *Disaster recovery plans.*

Group Roles in Plan Development

The network administrator has the biggest responsibility for drafting, testing, and documenting the plan. Corporate managers and administrators should contribute to the plan, and should understand their role in implementing the plan, if needed. Vendors and regular contractors should understand their responsibilities and what service levels they will guarantee.

Responsible Individuals

A documented contact list of the individuals responsible for various elements of the network speeds the disaster recovery process.

Responsible Individuals	Information to Include
Network administrators	Office, home, pager, and cell phone numbers, and home addresses. Document each person's role on the network.
Office managers	Office and human resources managers, department supervisors, and anyone who might have a say in network reconstruction.
Security officials	Anyone with access to safes or storage locations containing offsite data, and contacts for data and records storage companies. Also include how to recover offsite data. Include public fire and safety authorities if your disaster situation could affect public safety.
Vendors	Vendors your company deals with regularly and the type of equipment they provide. List sales contacts, cell phone numbers, and home numbers, if possible.
Service providers and contractors	Contractors used regularly and all providers of customized software or custom services.
Manufacturer technical contacts	Contact numbers and websites for manufacturers of all network software and hardware. Include account numbers applicable to the company.

Responsible Individuals	Information to Include
Past IT personnel	Anyone who had a hand in building the network. It's a last resort, but they could contract in to help rebuild, or at least provide guidance or information not otherwise available.

Critical Hardware and Software Inventory

Your hardware and software inventory provides insurance documentation and helps determine what you need to rebuild the network.

Hardware Inventory Entry	Information to Include
Standard workstation	A basic description of a standard client workstation. Include minimum requirements and the installed operating system as well as how many workstations of this type are deployed.
Specialty workstation	A description of any specialty workstations deployed. Include a brief description of their roles and special configurations implemented on them.
Basic server	A list of the basic server configuration used and the role of these servers. List their internal hardware and any special configurations. Include a configuration list for the operating system.
Specialty server	A list of any specialty servers existing on the network. List their role and any special configuration implemented on them. Detail the server configuration containing the tape backup, including the brand and model of tape drive.
Connectivity hardware	A list of all connectivity hardware in as much detail as possible. List at least the brand and model numbers, but try to describe each feature so that replacements can be made without researching older hardware.
Backup hardware	Document critical information about the backup hardware, such as the vendor and model number of a tape drive.

The critical inventory also includes software elements.

Software Inventory Entry	Information to Include
Operating system software	A list of all operating system software, including both desktop and server operating systems. Include documentation on licensing and copies of the bulk licenses, if possible. Many vendors retain records of software licenses sold to their customers. If this is the case, include this fact in your documentation.
Productivity and application software	A list of all off-the-shelf productivity software, including any applications installed on client machines and servers.

Software Inventory Entry	Information to Include
Maintenance utilities	Documentation of which utilities are used to maintain the network, especially backup software and software configuration.
Backup documentation	Records of when backups were taken, what backups contain, where backups are stored, and credentials needed to restore backups. Document the backup software and version. Special setup and configuration considerations need to be documented, too.
Overall corporate inventory	If your company maintains an overall asset inventory, attach a copy. Many companies use the inventory as a base to track hardware and maintenance. This usually includes most of the information needed.

The Network Reconstruction Plan

The network reconstruction plan provides all the steps needed to bring the network back online, even if the original administrators are unavailable.

Plan Component	Description
Network diagram	A network diagram will include not only a drawing of the physical network layout, but also should include the configuration for all servers and the software environment. The administrator's passwords and service account passwords need to be documented so that the system is accessible after the restore. Decryption or recovery agents and digital certificates need to be documented as well.
Fall-back plan	A *fall-back plan* is an alternate design that can be implemented temporarily to enable critical network elements to function. It should include a list of minimum required hardware and software as well as implementation instructions. It might also include a plan to convert a *hot site*, *warm site*, or *cold site* into a functional network. You might also maintain *hot spare* or *cold spare* replacement equipment for critical systems and servers.
Data restoration plan	Finally, you must document a data restoration plan detailing exactly how to retrieve and restore data backups in the correct sequence.

Hot, Warm, and Cold Sites; Hot and Cold Spares

Backup site locations and replacement equipment can be classified as hot, warm, or cold, depending on how much configuration would be necessary to bring the location or spare equipment online.

- A hot site is a fully configured alternate network that can be online quickly after a disaster.
- A warm site is a business site that performs noncritical functions under normal conditions, but which can be rapidly converted to a key operations site if needed.
- A cold site is a predetermined alternate location where a network can be rebuilt after a disaster.
- A hot spare is a fully configured and operational piece of backup equipment that can be swapped into a system with little to no interruption in functionality.
- A cold spare is a duplicate piece of backup equipment that can be configured to use as an alternate if needed.

Documenting Security Information

Many administrators have the valid concern that writing down security information, such as administrative and service account passwords, provides opportunities for security breaches. However, a network is useless when restored if there is no administrative access. The security information must be in the recovery documentation, but it can be stored securely and accessed separately by the appropriate individuals; it certainly doesn't need to be distributed to everyone working on or reviewing the plan.

Maintaining the Plan

A network is a living entity—most companies don't stay the same. A disaster recovery plan needs to reflect changes to the organization. You should formally review the disaster recovery plan at least twice a year, and informally review it quarterly. A formal review should include office managers, corporate staff, and IT managers. An informal review can be done by the appropriate administrator and his or her staff. A formal review makes many employees, including corporate personnel, aware of the review. During a review, check administrative passwords, recovery agents, and changes to the backup scheme. Review time is also a good time to train new IT personnel on the recovery plan.

Once the plan has been reviewed and accepted, it needs to be distributed to the appropriate people. To ensure that you can access the plan in the event of an actual disaster, at least one copy must be stored offsite in a secure but known location, such as a remote corporate office. If your company uses an offsite data storage location, consider keeping a copy there. Key managers might also keep copies of the plan at their homes.

ACTIVITY 13-1

Discussing Disaster Recovery Plans

Scenario:

In this activity, you will examine various aspects of disaster recovery plans.

1. **Which are common components of a disaster recovery plan?**
   - a) A list of employees' personal items
   - b) Contact information for key individuals
   - c) An inventory
   - d) Plans to reconstruct the network

2. **Which of these groups should you include in your disaster recovery contact list?**
   - a) Security officials
   - b) Vendors, contractors, and manufacturers
   - c) Network administrators and corporate managers
   - d) All current employees

3. **Company X pays a small monthly rental fee for a warehouse with phone and power hookups that they can use as a:**
   - a) Hot site
   - b) Cold site
   - c) Warm site
   - d) Hot spare
   - e) Cold spare

4. **Which are components of a critical hardware inventory?**
   - a) Servers and workstations
   - b) Connectivity devices
   - c) Hand tools
   - d) Operating system software

5. **Match the component of the network reconstruction plan with its description.**

___	Network diagram	a.	Information about the layout, configuration, and security credentials for the network.
___	Fall-back plan	b.	An alternate network design to implement temporarily.
___	Data restoration plan	c.	Details how you will retrieve and restore backups.

PRACTICE ACTIVITY 13-2

Designing a Disaster Recovery Plan

Objective:

To design a disaster recovery plan for a typical home kitchen.

Scenario:

Because you live in a known flooding area, you are concerned about the possibility of damage to major household items such as your kitchen appliances. Because you have adequate property insurance and flood insurance, you are comfortable that you will be able to replace any items in case of loss, but you would like to make that process as smooth as possible by preparing an advance plan.

---

1. **What are the critical components of your kitchen?**

---

2. **Build a simple inventory and vendor list.**

---

3. **Where will you store the manufacturers' documentation for your appliances?**

---

4. **Is there an alternate source for manuals and documentation?**

---

5. **Do you have a fall-back plan if water does damage your kitchen?**

---

6. **Draw a floor plan of your kitchen.**

---

7. **Reflect on the process of developing this plan. What were the difficulties? What aspects do you think would be most useful for you?**

TOPIC B

Data Backup

In the previous topic, you identified the components and technologies involved in creating and maintaining a disaster recovery plan. You saw that one of the key elements of that plan was restoring data from backups. In this topic, you will identify the primary tools and technologies used to back up and recover data.

Consider the value of the data stored on your network. A week's worth of changes and additions to files or to a database can have greater value to a company than the entire network on which it is stored. As companies use networks for more and more of their business communications and data storage, the value of the information kept on these networks increases dramatically. The cost of replacing lost data far outweighs the cost of the backup systems that protect it. That is why implementing and maintaining proper backups is one of the most serious duties of the network administrator.

Backup Policies

Each organization will need to maintain a backup policy that documents its own backup requirements, procedures, and systems. The policy should include specifications for all the components of the backup plan, including the backup software, hardware, media, schedule, and testing plans, as well as designating administrative responsibility for the system.

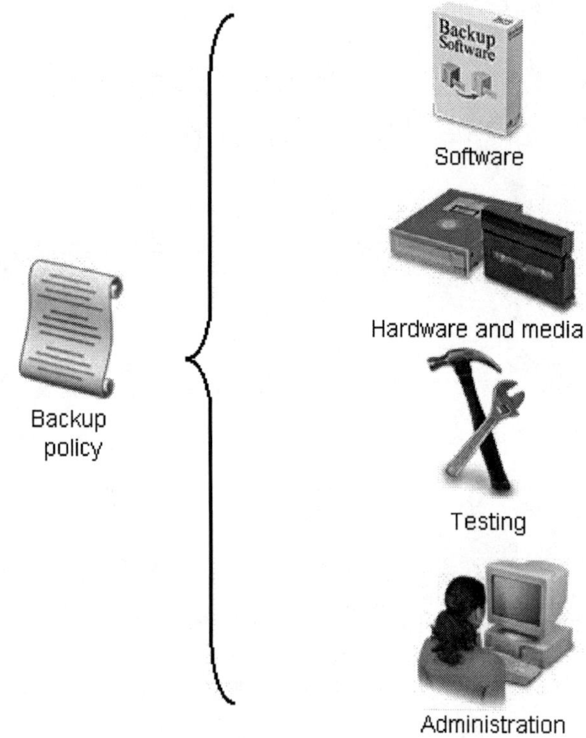

Figure 13-3: *Backup policies.*

Backup Policy Considerations

When you devise a backup policy and implement a backup system, you should consider these factors:

- Hardware and media—What is appropriate for your environment? How do you balance cost against performance?
- Software—Can you use the utilities built into your operating system, or will you need a dedicated third-party backup application?
- Backup administration—Who is responsible for performing backup functions?
- Backup frequency—How much data you can afford to lose determines how often you will back up.
- Backup methods—Which of several backup media-rotation schemes is appropriate for your organization?
- Backup types—Which of several schemes will you use for backing up new and existing data efficiently? What is the balance between partial and complete backups?
- Backup set—How many tapes or other media will you need for each backup?
- Backup scheduling—What time of day and when during the week will you run the backups? Will users be logged on? Will files be open?
- Media identification—What are the standards for labeling backup media?
- Media storage—Where will backup media be kept? Onsite or offsite, or in multiple locations?
- Recovery testing—When and how will you perform test restorations of data? Who is responsible?

- Maintenance—What scheduled maintenance or replacement is required for the hardware, software, and media? When will this be performed? How will you budget for it?
- Restoration timeline—Do you have a complete plan for recovering all lost data? How long is recovery expected to take?

Backup Media Types

Backups can be stored on almost any type of media. Different types of magnetic tape cartridges are the most popular media, but you can also choose optical drives, such as recordable CD or DVD drives, or additional hard disk drives. Additionally, you can consider using various types of portable or removable hard drives or USB drives, or even removable Zip drive products from Iomega.

Magnetic Tape Formats

There are several popular formats for magnetic tape cartridges. The following table lists some of the most common.

Media Type	Characteristics
Digital audio tape (DAT)	Storage capacity: Around 1 GB to 70 GB Size: 4 mm, about the size of an audio tape Use: Used by many different-sized networks.
Digital linear tape (DLT)	Storage capacity: 15 GB to 300 GB or more Size: ½-inch cartridges Used: The de facto standard. Used mainly by mid- to large-size networks.
Quarter-inch cartridge (QIC)	Storage capacity: Around 80 MB to 10 GB Size: Original width was ¼ inch; available in 3 ½-inch (Travan version) or 5 ¼-inch cartridges Used: Usually used by smaller networks.

USB Ports on Removable Drives

Removable disk drives, other external storage devices, and many other types of computer peripherals use Universal Serial Bus (USB) connections. The USB hardware interface standard is popular because it enables you to connect multiple peripherals to a single port with high performance and little device configuration. For example, you can plug a USB drive into your computer's USB port and the device will be automatically detected and installed and available for backups within a few minutes.

The flat type A USB connector on a cable connects to the computer; the squared-off type B connector connects to the device. PCs typically come with one to four USB ports installed, and you can add and daisy-chain USB hubs to add more ports. In all, you can connect up to 127 USB devices, including the hubs, to a single USB port. Many USB devices receive power through the USB connection, rather than requiring an external power transformer or power cord.

Rotation Methods

Definition:

A backup *rotation method* is the schedule that determines how many backup tapes or other media sets are needed, and the sequence in which they are used and reused. The rotation method also specifies the standards for labeling and storing the media. It might also specify the schedule for permanently archiving backup sets, the offsite and onsite tape storage locations, and if any extra tape sets are required when tapes are in transit between onsite and offsite storage.

Example: The Grandfather-Father-Son (GFS) Rotation Method

A common, secure backup rotation method is the grandfather-father-son (GFS) method. For daily backups, use four backup sets: One backup set is designated for Mondays, one for Tuesdays, one for Wednesdays, and one for Thursdays. These backup sets are reused on the same day the following week. A new weekly backup set is created on each of the first four Fridays of the month. The next month, these Friday backup sets are reused in the same order. A new month-end backup set is created on the last business day of the month. (If a month has five Fridays, the last Friday of the month will also be the last business day of the month.) Depending on your needs, these monthly backup sets can be reused the following year, or archived and replaced with new backup sets. Label each of the daily "son" backup sets with the name of the day of the week; label the weekly "father" tapes with number 1 through 4 for each Friday; and label the monthly "grandfather" tapes with the name of the month. If you always have one tape in transit to your offsite storage location, you will also need one extra daily, weekly, and monthly tape.

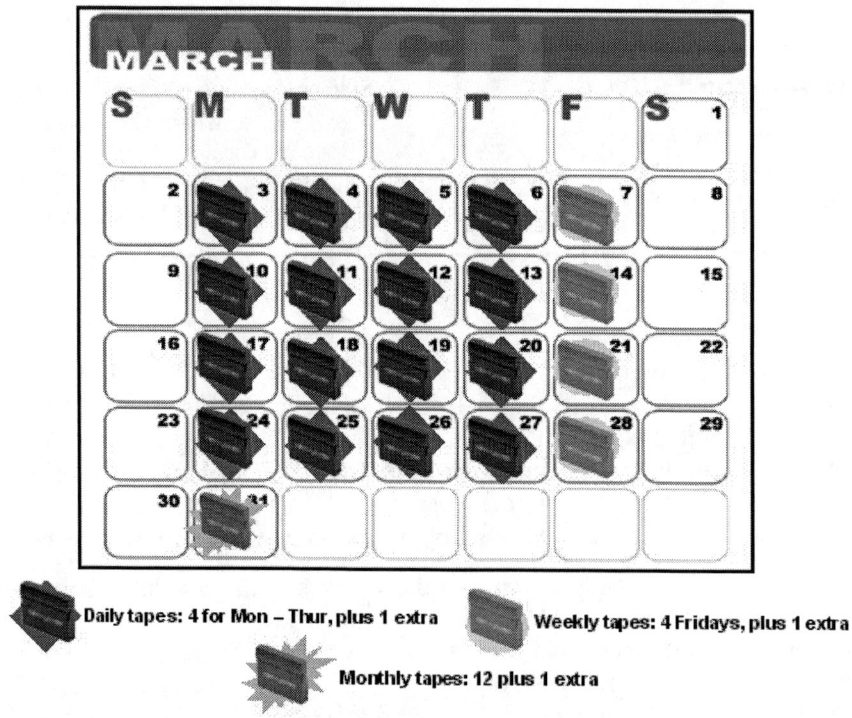

Figure 13-4: *The GFS rotation method.*

Example: The Tower of Hanoi Rotation Method

The Tower of Hanoi rotation method typically requires five media sets. Media set A is used every other day. Media set B is used every fourth day. Media set C is used every eighth day. Media set D is used every sixteenth day. Media set E alternates with media set D. This doubles the backup history with each media set used (2, 4, 8, or 16 days until the media set is overwritten). This enables you to have media sets with the most recent versions of files (those media sets used most frequently, such as sets A and B). Label each of the media sets with a letter or number (media set 1 or A). You can apply this rotation method to a daily or weekly rotation schedule. You will need five media sets for a daily rotation, and eight media sets for a weekly rotation.

The Tower of Hanoi rotation method is named for a Chinese board game in which you move a stack of disks from peg to peg. A smaller disk can only be placed on a larger disk.

Day	1	2	3	4	5	6	7	8	9	10	11	12	13	14	15	16
Media Set	A		A		A		A		A		A		A		A	
		B				B				B				B		
				C								C				
								D								
																E

Media Set	Used Every
A	2 days
B	4 days
C	8 days
D & E	16 days alternating between set D and E

Figure 13-5: *The Tower of Hanoi rotation method.*

Backup Types

Backup types determine which files on a volume are backed up in a given backup operation, and also affect the requirements for restoring the data.

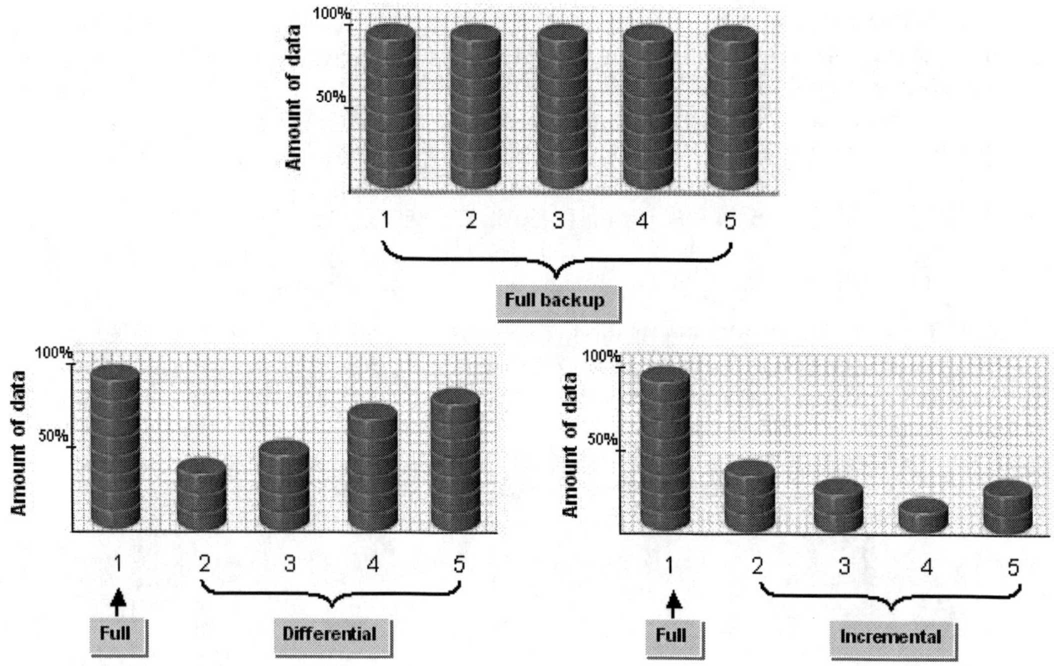

Figure 13-6: *Backup types.*

Backup Type	Description and Purpose
Full or normal	A full or normal backup backs up all selected files. It clears the archive file bit to mark files as backed up. The full backup marks the starting point of a backup rotation cycle. This backup type takes the most time but permits the fastest full restores.
Incremental	An incremental backup backs up files that were created or modified since the last full or incremental backup. It marks files as backed up. This backup type takes the least time to back up, but can take the longest to restore because a full restore requires the last full backup plus all subsequent incremental backup sets.
Differential	A differential backup backs up files that were created or modified since the last full backup. It does not mark files as backed up. This backup type requires the last full backup plus the last differential backup to perform a full restore. The amount of time required to back up or restore depends on the size of the current differential backup.

Custom Backup Types

Some backup systems permit custom backup types that you can use to back up files by selection or by date without marking them as backed up. These are useful for backing up files on an ad hoc basis without interfering with a normal backup rotation.

Data Backup System Maintenance

To ensure that your data is secure and that you can restore it properly, you must follow regular backup system maintenance procedures.

Maintenance Procedure	Description
Verify backups	Tape backup software has a verification utility that you should regularly use to test your backups to ensure that they completed as scheduled.
Test restoration	Even if a tape verifies, it still might not correctly restore. It's also possible that the backup job was not set up correctly and the data you need wasn't actually put on the tape. You should always do a full restore and then test the data captured on the tape after any changes are made to the backup jobs.
Review logs	In between full test restores, you can compare the backup logs against the list of files that should be on the tape and restore a sample of files from the tape. In particular, test any tapes that will be removed from the rotation for long-term storage to ensure that their contents are correct.
Replace tapes on schedule	All magnetic media decays over time. It decays faster when it's used regularly, but even tapes sitting on a shelf decay and need to be replaced regularly. Most tape manufacturers recommend refreshing your long-term storage every year. That means restoring the data on the tape to a drive, reformatting the tape, and backing up the tape again. Many administrators swap the tape for a brand new one and then place the one from storage into the normal backup rotation. When a tape is used in a rotation, most manufacturers recommend no more than 60 backups per tape. Others simply list a 12-month life cycle. Whatever your replacement policy, consider tapes as a consumable and replace them now and then.
Maintain tapes and tape drives	Some tapes and tape drives require a lot of maintenance. Follow the procedures your manufacturer recommends. In particular, every DLT tape should be inspected every time it's going to be inserted. DLT drives suffer from a condition known as swallowing the tongue. There is a tab on the end of the tape that connects to a pickup leader on the tape drive. The pickup leader pulls the tape into the drive. If the leader misses its pickup, the tab is pulled back into the drive and must be manually pulled back out. Unfortunately, this means returning the drive to a service center.
Clean tape drives	Tape drives require regular cleaning. Cleaning a tape drive is simple. Place a cleaning tape into the drive. The tape drive detects the cleaning tape, runs a cleaning routine, and then ejects the tape. Some manufacturers actually recommend running a cleaning tape between each tape change; others recommend running cleaning tapes weekly.
Replace damaged tapes	When a tape drive fails and the drive is swapped out, all of the tapes that were used in that drive should also be replaced. Many times the tape drive damages the tapes or the tapes themselves become contaminated and could very well cause failure in the new tape drive.

Specialized Data Backups

Certain data types may require specialized procedures or additional software components to perform a successful backup.

Backup Type	Description
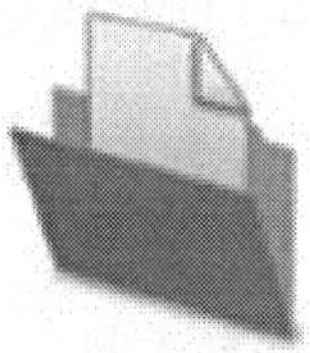 Open files	Files that are opened by an application are locked to ensure that only one client makes changes at a time. It's a nice feature, but also one that causes a few problems for network backup software. Specifically, the backup software has to deal with a client making changes during the backup, which can create errors in the backup (remember that backups are relatively slow). It also has to deal with the locked files. To help, you can deploy an open files agent with the backup software. When the backup software encounters a locked file, it uses the open files agent to take a snapshot of the file. The snapshot temporarily disables the file's ability to be edited and copies the file to a temporary location on the drive. The backup software then backs up the snapshot. This happens very quickly and doesn't disrupt the client using the file.
 Database	Databases are essentially big, open files. Some backup software handles simple databases with nothing more than an open files agent. However, larger databases have special considerations. In a database, the actual data on the drive might not be current because of write-behind caching, a technique that temporarily stores database changes in server memory while the server is busy. Sometimes, database logs need to be reset when a database is backed up. Log files are often stored on a different drive than the database itself. These databases may require either a manual backup procedure to close open files and clear logs, or the use of a database agent, which can back up the database and reset the logs while the database is online.
 Email	Email servers are essentially modified database servers that store users' mailboxes. Data is still in a database data store, which means that the email server can be backed up just like a database server. In fact, a standard backup and restore of a mail server contains all the same elements that backing up a database does. When a mail server is backed up, like a database, one restore option is to restore all the data and then extract the damaged mailbox. There is another type of mail server backup called the brick-level backup, which uses a special agent that is aware of the database's data structure. Brick-level backups enable a database to be backed up mailbox by mailbox, which takes longer, and then restored one mailbox at a time. Some agents even enable the mail to be restored message by message.
 Power user workstations	Some power users on your network might have sensitive data on their personal workstations that you would choose to include in a backup plan. Workstations are easy to back up when they have an agent installed that enables backup software to access them. However, they have to be powered on to be backed up. This used to be a problem, but today most network cards and PCs support a technology called Wake on LAN (WOL), in which backup software sends a signal to the workstation (awakens it), waits for it to boot up, backs it up, and then turns it off again.

Backup Type	Description
 Mobile users	When remote users are on the network, they are backed up the same way that workstations are. However, when they are primarily offline, backups require a different solution. Many backup software manufacturers use a remote agent to back up remote users when the users connect to the network. The agent copies changed data from the laptop to a network drive. This is always a partial backup, so it's faster than copying all the data off the laptop. But how do you back up remote users if they're not connected to the network? Some backup software uses over-the-web backups. The process is the same as already described except that the user attaches to a secure website and uploads data.
 Enterprise backups	Many companies have moved to an enterprise-wide solution for data backups. A high-performance backup solution is deployed from a central location and all backup data is stored in the central location. Many of these solutions cross manufacturers' boundaries, enabling one setup to get backups from PC servers, UNIX mainframes, mid-range servers, and workstations, regardless of manufacturer and operating system.

Snapshot Backups

Snapshots can be used to take complete backups of drives and databases, as well as to copy open files. There are a number of different snapshot technologies that are implemented in software, in hardware, or in combinations of the two. Depending on the technology in use, snapshots might clone an entire copy of a volume to another physical drive, or they might record only file changes or only pointers to file locations. See your storage or backup vendors for specifics on the snapshot backup implementation they offer.

Offline Files

Windows XP Professional, Windows Server 2003, and various other operating systems support offline files, which can serve as another backup method for remote users. The offline files process synchronizes a copy of a file on the network with a copy of the same file on a remote computer. This enables other users to access and use the network copy of the file at the same time that the remote user edits the remote copy. Any changes to the file are synchronized with the remote user's copy whenever the remote user connects to the network.

ACTIVITY 13-3

Backing Up Data

There is a simulated version of this activity available on the CD-ROM that shipped with this course. You can run this simulation on any Windows computer to review the activity after class, or as an alternative to performing the activity as a group in class. The activity simulation can be launched either directly from the CD-ROM by clicking the Interactives link and navigating to the appropriate one, or from the installed data file location by opening the C:\Data\Simulations\Lesson#\Activity# folder and double-clicking the executable (.exe) file.

Data Files:

- C:\Data\Sales Data\Proposal.rtf
- C:\Data\Sales Data\Specifications.rtf

Setup:

Before you begin this activity, insert a blank, formatted floppy disk into your floppy-disk drive.

Scenario:

You support a user who has asked for help in creating a backup copy of some client information files he keeps on his workstation. The files are in a folder called Sales Data on the user's Windows Server 2003 computer.

What You Do	How You Do It
1. **Back up the Sales Data folder.**	a. **Choose Start→All Programs→Accessories→System Tools→Backup** to run the Windows Server 2003 Backup Or Restore Wizard.
	b. In the Backup Or Restore Wizard, **click Next.**
	c. **Verify that Back Up Files And Settings is selected and click Next.**
	d. **Select Let Me Choose What To Back Up and click Next.**
	e. In the Items To Back Up list, **expand My Computer, Local Disk (C), and Data.**

f. **Check the Sales Data folder and click Next.**

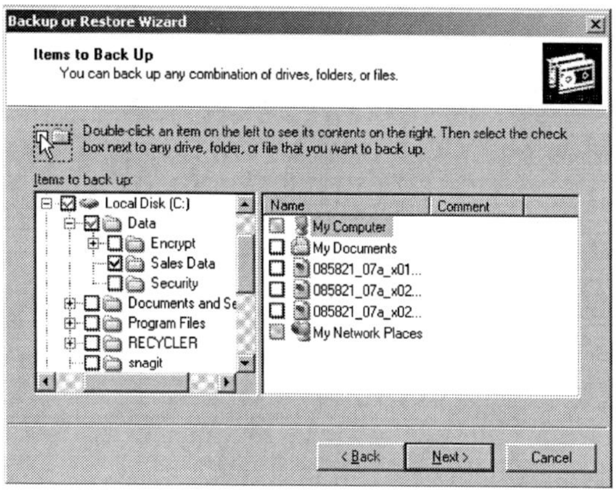

g. Next to the Choose A Place To Save Your Backup drop-down list, **click Browse.**

h. In the File Name text box, **type *a:\Sales Data.bkf* and click Save.**

i. **Verify the backup location and name and click Next.**

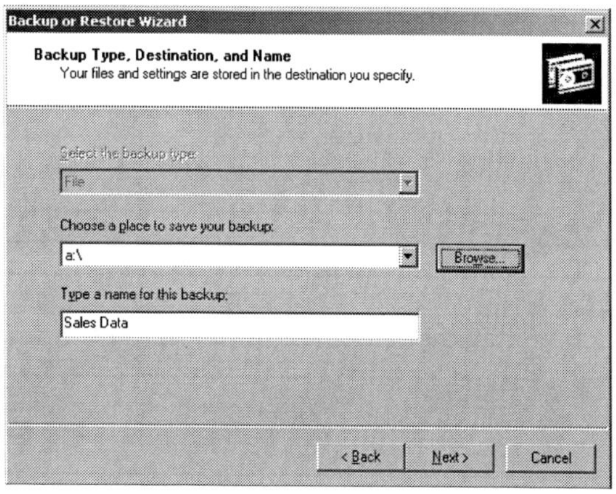

j. **Verify the backup settings and click Finish.**

k. During the backup operation, the Backup Progress window appears. **Verify that the backup is progressing.**

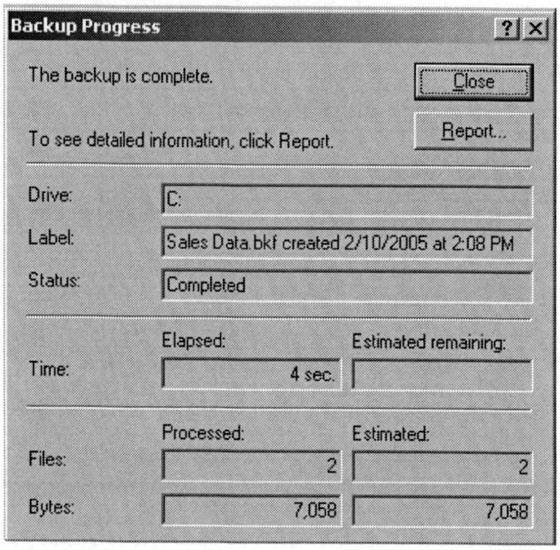

---

2. **Review the log to verify the backup operation.**

   a. When the backup is complete, in the Backup Progress window, **click Report.**

   b. The backup log file opens in Notepad. **Verify that the backup type is Normal, that two files were backed up, and that there are no errors.**

   c. **Close Notepad.**

   d. In the Backup Progress window, **click Close.**

---

3. **Verify that the backup file exists.**

   a. **Choose Start→My Computer.**

   b. **Double-click the A drive.**

   c. **Verify that the Sales Data.bkf file appears on the A drive and close the drive window.**

---

4. **What other steps should you take to complete the backup?**

   a) Restart the system.

   b) Label the backup media.

   c) Store the backup media in a safe place.

   d) Back up the operating system files.

---

5. **In a production backup system, what types of media might you use for a small data backup such as this?**

    a) External removable drives

    b) Writeable CDs or DVDs

    c) A RAID array

    d) A separate partition on the same hard disk

ACTIVITY 13-4

Restoring Data

There is a simulated version of this activity available on the CD-ROM that shipped with this course. You can run this simulation on any Windows computer to review the activity after class, or as an alternative to performing the activity as a group in class. The activity simulation can be launched either directly from the CD-ROM by clicking the Interactives link and navigating to the appropriate one, or from the installed data file location by opening the C:\Data\Simulations\Lesson#\Activity# folder and double-clicking the executable (.exe) file.

Setup:

There is a floppy disk containing the Sales Data.bkf backup set in the floppy-disk drive. Before you begin this activity, delete the C:\Data\Sales Data folder from the hard disk to simulate a data loss.

Scenario:

A user's laptop has crashed and he lost some critical client files. Fortunately, you have a backup copy of the files, so you can restore the data to the user's new laptop.

What You Do	How You Do It
1. **Restore the missing data from the backup.**	a. **Choose Start→Backup** to run the Windows Server 2003 Backup Or Restore Wizard.
	b. In the Backup Or Restore Wizard, **click Next.**
	c. **Select Restore Files And Settings and click Next.**
	d. In the Items To Restore list, **expand File.**
	e. **Expand the Sales Data.bkf backup set.**
	f. **Double-click the C drive.**

g. **Expand the Data folder and check the Sales Data folder.**

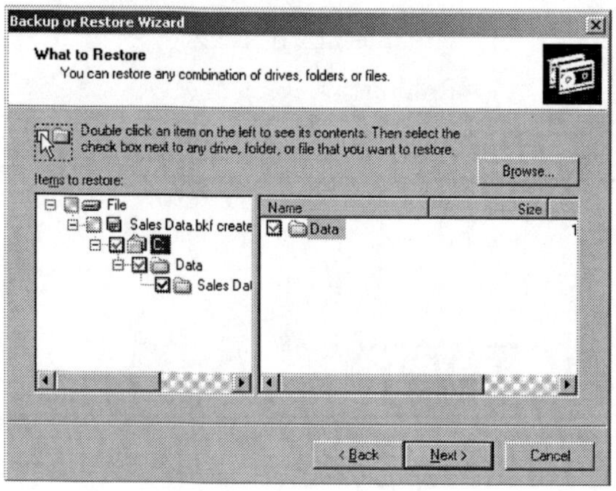

h. **Click Next.**

i. **Click Finish.**

j. The Restore Progress window appears during the restoration. **Verify that the restoration is progressing.**

---

2. **Verify that the data has been restored.**

a. When the restoration is complete, in the Restore Progress window, **click Close.**

b. **Choose Start→Run.**

c. **Type *C:\Data* and click OK.**

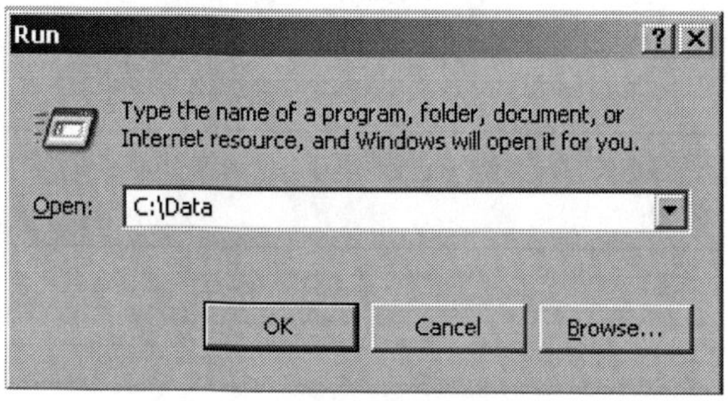

d. **Double-click the Sales Data folder.**

e. **Verify that the Proposal.rtf and Specifications.rtf files appear in the folder.**

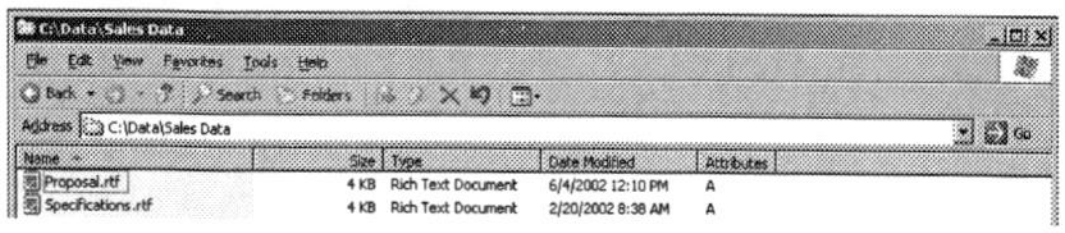

f. **Close the folder window.**

g. **Remove the floppy disk from the drive.**

PRACTICE ACTIVITY 13-5

Designing a Backup and Restore Plan

Scenario:

You've been asked to develop a tape rotation plan for an insurance office with data and files stored on a single server. They require a monthly archive on the first Monday of every month, to be retained for one year. They want reports run on the data every Monday and stored for two months. Lastly, they would like the security of at least one week's worth of tapes stored offsite. This office has production hours from 8:00 A.M. to 7:00 P.M., Monday through Friday. They generate many changes daily and you want to minimize the amount of time required for each backup operation.

1. **What backup schedule will you implement?**

2. **How many tapes would be required for a year's worth of backups, assuming that you do not need extra tapes for the transit to offsite?**

3. **What would be a good time during the week to transfer the tapes to offsite storage?**

4. **It's Monday afternoon and your office manager is looking at a file that she swears she edited on Friday, but the file appears to be the old one from the previous Thursday. With your plan, how do you restore the file?**

5. **The company experiences a complete disk failure at 10 A.M. on Thursday. How do you restore the data?**

TOPIC C

Fault Tolerance Methods

In the previous topic, you saw how effective data backup policies and procedures contributed to smooth disaster recovery. Effective fault tolerance methods can also lessen the impact of a disaster. In this topic, you will identify tools and technologies used to implement fault tolerance.

Disaster recovery planning provides contingency procedures in the event of catastrophic events that you cannot reasonably foresee or prevent. In contrast, fault tolerance planning is intended to prevent the negative impact of mishaps that you can reasonably foresee, such as a temporary power outage or the inevitable failure of a hard disk. With proper fault tolerance measures in place, you will keep these minor occurrences from turning into disasters for your organization.

Fault Tolerance

Definition:

Fault tolerance is the ability of a network or system to withstand a foreseeable component failure and continue to provide an acceptable level of service. There are several categories of fault tolerance measures, including those that protect power sources, disks and data storage, and network components.

Example:

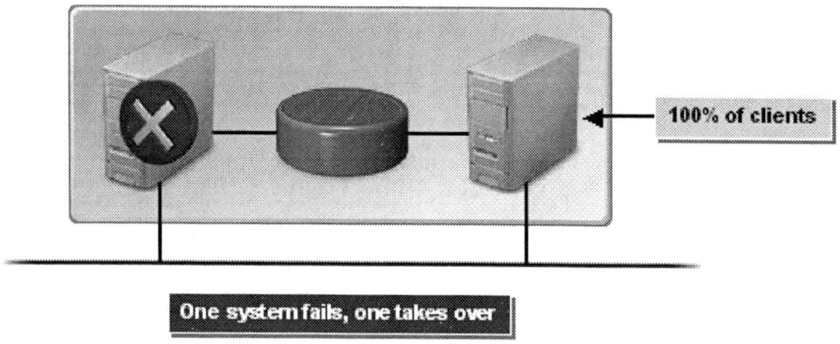

Figure 13-7: *Fault tolerance.*

Uninterruptible Power Supplies (UPSs)

Definition:

An *uninterruptible power supply (UPS)* is a device that provides backup power when the electrical power fails or drops to an unacceptable voltage level. This helps reduce or eliminate server data loss and limit or prevent server damage during power surges or brownouts. UPSs can be online or offline models.

Usually only servers and server-related devices, such as routers, are connected to UPSs. Workstations are not routinely connected to UPSs; therefore, users are likely to still lose data in workstation RAM during a power outage.

Example:

Figure 13-8: *A UPS.*

Comparing Online and Offline UPSs

With an online UPS, power always flows through the UPS to the devices connected to it. Because it is always actively monitoring power, it provides an added benefit by functioning as a line conditioner, reducing or eliminating surges and brownouts to the attached equipment. Online UPS systems tend to be more expensive than offline systems.

With an offline UPS, the UPS monitors power and activates only when there is a drop, so there is a very slight delay before the UPS becomes active. However, system power is not usually lost because the delay is so short. Some operating systems provide UPS monitoring so that users can be alerted to log off and the operating system can be shut down properly if there is a power outage.

Partitions

Definition:

A *partition* is a logical area of disk space that you can format and treat as a single storage unit. Most operating systems support two types of partitions: one type to boot the system and one type for general storage purposes. On DOS and Windows systems, *primary partitions* are the partitions that you can use to boot the computer, whereas *extended partitions* are storage partitions that you can further subdivide into logical drives. An area of a disk that isn't included in a partition is called free space.

Example:

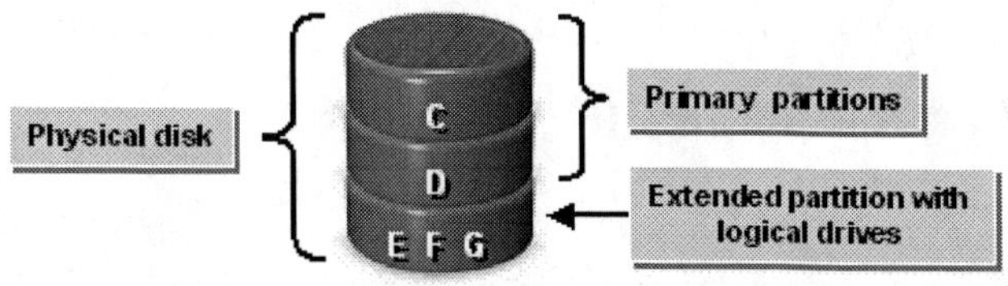

Figure 13-9: *Partitions.*

Partition Limits in Windows Systems

On master boot record (MBR) basic disks in Windows Server 2003 and many older versions of Windows, any one physical disk can contain a maximum of four partitions. Of the four, one can be an extended partition.

For more information on partition configuration in Windows, see "Basic Disks and Volumes" on the Microsoft website at **www.microsoft.com/resources/documentation/WindowsServ/2003/standard/proddocs/en-us/dm_basicvol_overview.asp**

Redundant Array of Independent Disks (RAID) Standards

Definition:

The *Redundant Array of Independent Disks (RAID)* standards are a set of vendor-independent specifications for fault-tolerant configurations on multiple-disk systems. If one or more of the disks fails, data can be recovered from the remaining disks.

RAID can be implemented through operating system software, but hardware-based RAID implementations are more efficient and are more widely deployed. There are several RAID levels, each of which provides a different combination of features and efficiencies. RAID levels are identified by number; RAID 0, RAID 1, and RAID 5 are the most common.

The original RAID specifications were titled Redundant Array of Inexpensive Disks. As the disk cost of RAID implementations has become less of a factor, the term "Independent" disks has been widely adopted instead.

Example:

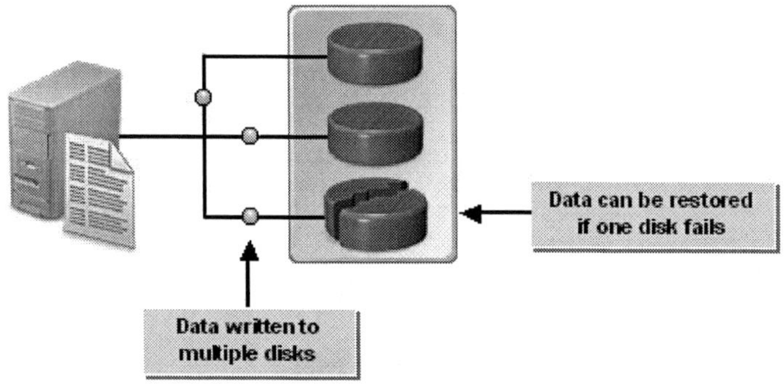

Figure 13-10: *RAID.*

The Original RAID Levels

The original RAID standards were developed in 1987, but the specification has grown to include additional RAID types that are variations on or combinations of the original standards. The following table summarizes the original RAID types.

RAID Level	Name
RAID 0	Striping
RAID 1	Mirroring or duplexing
RAID 2	Striping with error correction code (ECC)
RAID 3	Striping with parity on a single drive
RAID 4	Striping by block with parity on a single drive
RAID 5	Striping with parity information spread across drives.

Striping (RAID Level 0)

RAID level 0 implements *striping*, which is the process of spreading data across multiple drives. Striping can dramatically improve read and write performance. Striping provides no fault tolerance, however; because the data is spread across multiple drives, if any one of the drives fails, you will lose all of your data. You must have at least two physical disk drives to implement striping.

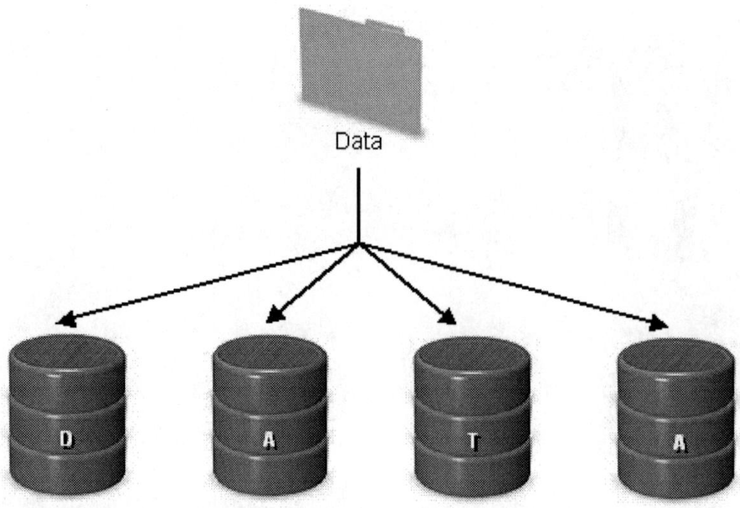

Figure 13-11: *Striping.*

Windows and NetWare Support

Windows Servers provide built-in support for RAID level 0. NetWare 6.5 also provides software support for this RAID level.

Mirroring or Duplexing (RAID Level 1)

In RAID level 1, data from an entire partition is duplicated on two identical drives by either mirroring or duplexing. In *mirroring*, the two disks share a drive controller. In *duplexing*, each disk has its own drive controller, so the controller card is not a single point of failure. Data is written to both halves of the mirror simultaneously.

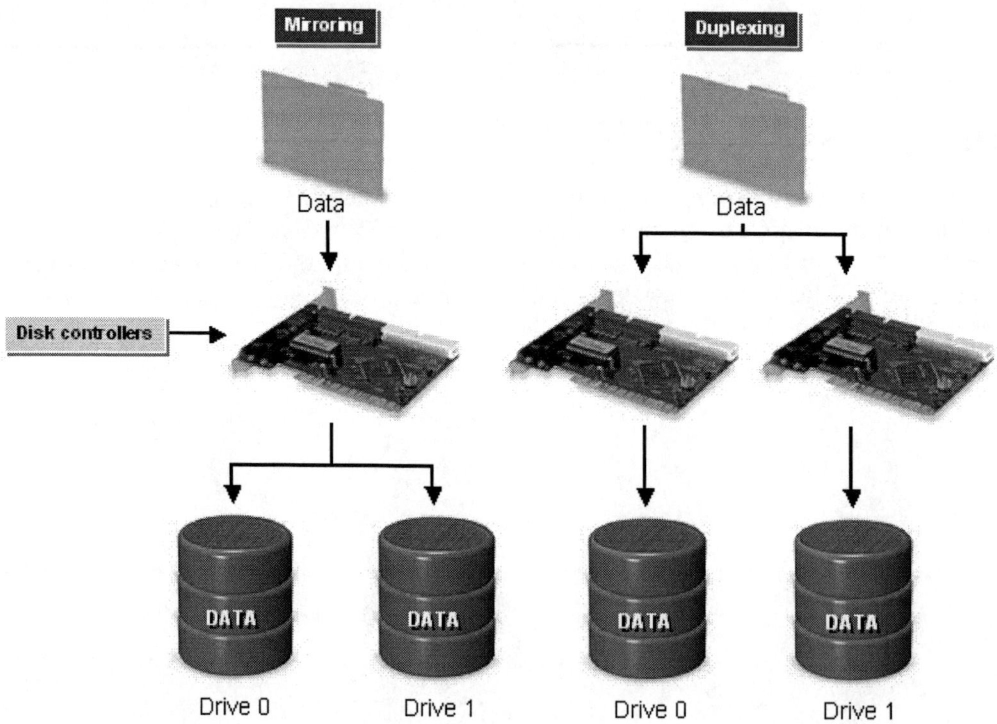

Figure 13-12: *Mirroring or duplexing.*

Benefits and Drawbacks of RAID 1

Mirroring and duplexing are easy to set up and configure. However, they are expensive; you need twice as much disk space as you have data, which means a 50-percent storage space overhead requirement. Plus, duplexing requires a second disk controller.

Windows and NetWare Support

Windows Servers support both mirroring and duplexing across SCSI, ESDI, and IDE disk drives. You can use mirroring or duplexing on Windows systems to protect the contents of the system or boot partitions. NetWare 6.5 also provides software support for this RAID level.

RAID 10 and Other Nested RAID Levels

RAID implementations that combine the technology of multiple RAID systems are sometimes referred to as "nested" RAID. For example, RAID 10 combines the features of RAID 0 and RAID 1 systems by both striping and mirroring the data. RAID 10 solutions require at least four disks—two for the striping and two to mirror the striped set. This provides some performance enhancements along with fault tolerance, without the parity-calculation overhead of other RAID systems. The mirroring component still requires a 50-percent storage space overhead.

Striping with Parity Spread Across Multiple Drives (RAID Level 5)

RAID level 5 systems spread data byte by byte across multiple drives, with parity information also spread across multiple drives. You need at least three physical disk drives. If one drive fails, the parity information on the remaining drives can be used to reconstruct the data. With RAID 5, disk performance is enhanced because more than one read and write can occur simultaneously. However, the parity calculations create some write-performance overhead.

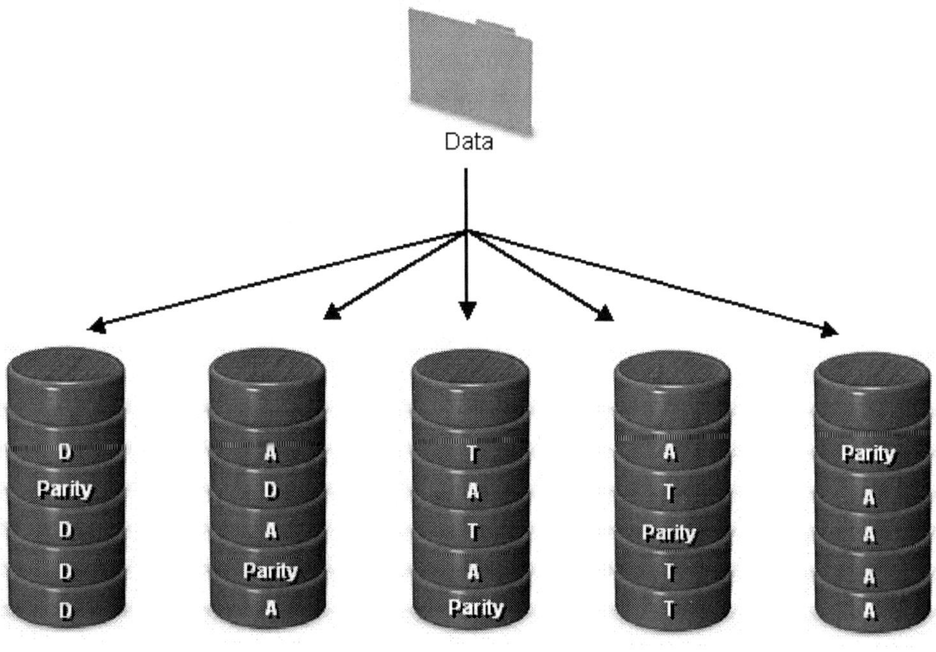

Figure 13-13: *Striping with parity.*

Hardware-Based RAID 5

Hardware-based RAID level 5 systems offer advanced features, such as continuous operation, the ability to schedule failed-drive replacement, and even the ability to hot-swap failed drives.

Windows and NetWare Support

Windows Servers support RAID 5 through software. The Windows system and boot partitions cannot be part of a software-based RAID 5 volume, but must be stored on a separate partition. NetWare 6.5 also provides software support for this RAID level.

RAID 6

RAID 6 is the term applied to extensions of RAID 5 in which two different levels of parity calculations are spread across the disks along with the data. This is also called double-parity RAID.

Other RAID Levels

RAID levels 2, 3, and 4 are generally considered to be obsolete. The following table describes the obsolete RAID levels.

Obsolete RAID Level	Description
Striping with error correction code (RAID level 2)	Striping with error correction code spreads data, bit by bit, across multiple drives. Error correction code information is built from the bits and stored on a separate drive.
Striping with parity on a single drive (RAID level 3)	In a RAID level 3 system, data is spread byte by byte across multiple drives. Parity information is stored on a separate drive. A RAID level 3 system requires at least three, and usually no more than five, drives. RAID level 3 systems provide both performance and fault tolerance enhancements. In multi-drive systems, files can be written (or read) faster than in a single drive system. If a drive fails in a RAID level 3 system, the information that was on that drive can be rebuilt from the remaining drives and the parity drive. In fact, many hardware-based RAID level 3 systems simply log the event of a drive failure and continue operating. Then, at your convenience, you replace the failed hard drive. Some RAID level 3 systems even allow you to install a new drive while the system is up and running (sometimes called hot swapping).

Obsolete RAID Level	Description
Striping by block with parity on a single drive (RAID level 4)	A RAID level 4 system spreads data block by block across multiple drives. A block refers to whatever the block size is on the disks. Usually, blocks are groups of 1 to 16 disk sectors. Parity information is stored on a separate drive. A RAID level 4 system uses at least two, and usually no more than five, drives. RAID level 4 systems provide both read-performance and fault tolerance enhancements. Potentially, the system can read as many single-block-sized files as there are drives at one given time. However, because a single parity drive is used and every write must be accompanied by an associated parity write, only one file at a time can be written. As with RAID level 3, if a single drive in a RAID level 4 system fails, the data can be rebuilt from the remaining drives and the parity drive.

Other Disk Fault Tolerance Features

RAID systems are the primary means of providing disk fault tolerance. Some operating systems and versions support other types of fault tolerance systems. The following table lists some of the other fault tolerance methods that you might encounter.

Fault Tolerance Feature	Description
Sector sparing	A system in which every time the operating system reads or writes data to the disk, it checks the integrity of the sectors to which the data is being written. If a problem is detected, the data is moved to another sector and the problem sector is marked as bad. Bad sectors won't be reused. Windows servers automatically use sector sparing in systems that use SCSI disks. Sector sparing isn't available on ESDI or IDE disk drives.
Read-after-write verification	NetWare supports read-after-write verification with the Hot Fix technology. After a block of data is written to a hard disk, it is read back from the hard disk and compared to the original data in memory. If, after several attempts, data read from the hard disk does not match the data in memory, NetWare stores the data in a block in the Hot Fix Redirection Area and marks the bad block so that it will not be used again.
Duplicate FATs and DETs	NetWare stores disk and file configuration information in File Allocation Table (FAT) and Directory Entry Table (DET) indexes on each volume. If a portion of a FAT or DET becomes damaged, files might be damaged or lost. To reduce the possibility of losing data this way, NetWare maintains duplicate copies of FATs and DETs. If one copy of a table is damaged, data can be retrieved by using the remaining table. If the table were damaged because of a bad block, the table would be remapped by the Hot Fix feature, and the repaired table would be updated from the good copy.

Fault Tolerance Feature	Description
Transaction tracking systems	The Novell Transaction Tracking System (TTS) provides the ability to back out transactions, such as changes in a database file, that have been interrupted by the failure of a network component. For example, in a banking system, if power is interrupted after funds are deducted from a customer's savings account but before they are credited to the customer's checking account, the system will roll back the transaction to the original savings account balance.

Link Redundancy

Definition:

Link redundancy is a network fault-tolerance method that provides alternative network connections that can function if a critical primary connection is interrupted. The duplicate link can be fully redundant and provide the same level of performance, service, and bandwidth as the primary link. Alternatively, the redundant link can be a simple dial-up connection to provide basic connectivity until the main link is restored.

Example: Link Redundancy in a Small Office

For a small office, a fully fault-tolerant network might be too expensive, but a backup dial-in connection might be a reasonable and cost-effective precaution. Some broadband routers include a serial port where you can attach an external modem so that you can create a dial-up connection when a DSL or cable connection fails.

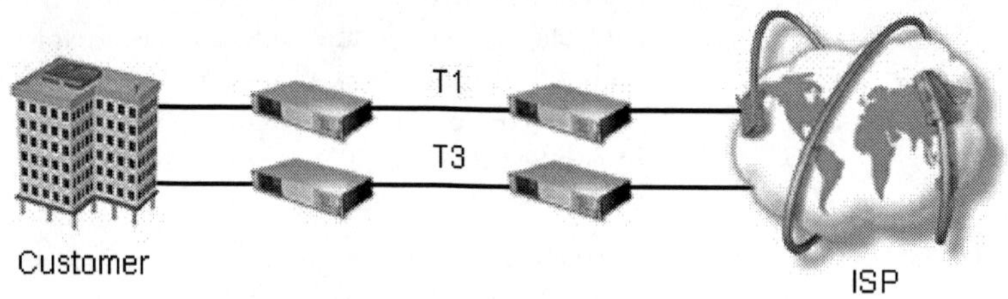

Figure 13-14: *Link redundancy.*

Planning for Link Redundancy

Not all network links must be made redundant. Each company must evaluate how critical each of its LAN and WAN links is to ongoing operations, and weigh the impact of losing connectivity for a given period of time against the cost of maintaining a redundant link.

Enterprise Fault Tolerance

A well-defined enterprise-wide fault tolerance plan adequately balances the need for service continuity against the cost of implementing fault tolerance measures to meet critical business requirements.

Guidelines

To implement enterprise fault tolerance, follow these guidelines:

- Identify network devices and servers that need to be protected from power surges and outages, and implement UPS power protection.
- Identify critical data sources and implement appropriate disk fault tolerance measures.
- Design and implement a backup plan.
- Identify critical network services and implement redundant servers to provide DHCP, name resolution, and authentication service continuity.
- Analyze your need for redundant network links. Implement redundant WAN links where needed and justified by cost. For internal routers, consider implementing dynamic routing over a mesh topology that provides multiple paths through the internal network.
- Identify the need for redundant hot spare and cold spare devices, and purchase and configure the required devices.

Example:

ABC Company is developing a fault tolerance plan. They assess their needs to protect against power failures, data loss, and network downtime and decide to implement several fault tolerance measures:

- All critical servers, routers, and other infrastructure equipment will be protected with UPS devices. User workstations will not have individual power protection.
- Any disks containing large databases, sensitive company data, or mission-critical files should be deployed in RAID configurations.
- All this data must be backed up using a standard backup rotation method; the backup tapes must be stored offsite and rotated back to the office as needed for reuse.
- A supply of spare parts for routers, disks, and other major hardware elements is kept on hand so that critical infrastructure devices can be swapped in as needed. However, some user downtime is acceptable, so there is no need to maintain a redundant inventory of laptop and desktop systems for user-level tasks.
- ABC Company maintains two directory servers and two DHCP servers onsite for logon and address assignment redundancy. Their Internet service provider is contracted to maintain redundant DNS name resolution services.
- There are four internal routers; ABC company adds enough links to create a redundant mesh topology.
- The company leases a single T3 WAN link. To maintain minimal network connectivity if this line goes down, they negotiate with their service provider to make a dial-up connection available as needed.

ACTIVITY 13-6

Discussing Fault Tolerance

Scenario:

In this activity, you will examine various fault tolerance technologies.

1. **What is the best description of fault tolerance?**

   a) To protect personnel and resources and restore system functioning in the event of unforeseeable catastrophic failure.

   b) To ensure continuous access to resources and network services in the event of a routine mishap or predictable failure.

   c) To provide archive copies of important data.

   d) To document current system configurations.

2. **Match the fault tolerance feature with the description.**

___	Protects against power loss or power surges.	a.	RAID
___	Specifications for fault tolerance configurations on multiple-disk systems.	b.	Link redundancy
___	Provides a separate network connection for use if the main connection goes down.	c.	UPS

3. **Match the RAID level with its description.**

___	RAID 0	a.	Disk mirroring or disk duplexing.
___	RAID 1	b.	Striping with parity spread across drives.
___	RAID 5	c.	Disk striping without parity. Provides no fault tolerance.
___	RAID 3	d.	An obsolete RAID level.

4. **Match the RAID level with the minimum hardware required.**

___	RAID 0	a.	2 disks
___	RAID 1	b.	2 disks and possibly 2 controllers
___	RAID 5	c.	3 disks
___	RAID 10	d.	4 disks

5. **Which of the following networks have implemented link redundancy?**
   a) A small office network with a broadband Internet connection and a separate dial-up one.
   b) A large company with two leased T1 lines from the same WAN provider.
   c) A large company with an internal routed network and a leased T3 WAN connection.
   d) A home-based worker with a cable modem and standard home phone service.

Lesson 13 Follow-up

In this lesson, you identified issues and technologies related to disaster recovery. As a network professional, one of your most important responsibilities will be to protect the network and its data, and ensure that the network can resume functioning as quickly as possible if it is damaged.

1. **Describe a disaster recovery operation you have been involved with, or that you have heard or read about. What were the issues and challenges? How successful was the recovery?**

2. **Explain why good data backups and effective fault tolerance measures reduce the need for disaster recovery.**

Notes

LESSON 14
Network Data Storage

Lesson Time
1 hour(s), 15 minutes

Lesson Objectives:

In this lesson, you will identify major data storage technologies and implementations.

You will:

- Identify requirements and technologies that are part of enterprise data storage implementations.
- Identify the tools and technologies used in implementing clustering.
- Identify the tools and technologies required for a NAS implementation.
- Identify the tools and technologies required for a SAN implementation.

LESSON 14

Introduction

In the previous lesson, you examined the tools and techniques involved in the general network support function of disaster recovery. Another important general network function is supporting the network data storage needs of your organization. In this lesson, you will identify major network data storage technologies and implementations.

Network storage always seems to be in short supply. Until recently, storage methods used in PC networking lagged behind those used in other forms of networks. Today, with new developments by major vendors, the business of network storage is exploding. As a network professional, you need to understand the technologies that are used in high-capacity, enterprise-wide data storage systems so that you can support them in your organization.

This lesson covers the following CompTIA Network+ (2005) certification objectives:

- Topic A:
  - Objective 3.11: Identify the purpose and characteristics of fault tolerance in storage.
- Topic B:
  - Objective 3.11: Identify the purpose and characteristics of fault tolerance in storage and services.
- Topic C:
  - Objective 3.11: Identify the purpose and characteristics of fault tolerance in storage.
- Topic D:
  - Objective 3.11: Identify the purpose and characteristics of fault tolerance in storage.

TOPIC A

Enterprise Data Storage Techniques

In this lesson, you will identify major network data storage technologies and implementations. Before looking at the specific data storage technology implementations, it's helpful to examine some general concepts and issues that come into play when planning or evaluating enterprise data storage solutions. In this topic, you will identify general requirements and technologies that are part of enterprise data storage implementations.

Whatever kind of storage system you evaluate or implement, you'll find that you'll always be concerned with some of the same issues. You'll be asking questions like "Does it scale well?" or "How can we get an uptime rating of five nines?" Understanding general issues like these will help you support your network's data storage system effectively.

High Availability

Definition:

High availability is a rating that expresses how closely systems approach the goal of providing data availability 100 percent of the time while maintaining a high level of system performance. The system should also be available to different platforms, such as UNIX and Microsoft servers. High-availability systems are usually rated as a percentage that shows the proportion of uptime to total time.

An uptime rating of 99.999%, or "five nines," is considered to be the ultimate achievable level of availability. Five nines translates into approximately five minutes of total downtime for a system over the course of a year.

CompTIA Network+ Exam Objectives

An Appendix is available to assist you in mapping CompTIA Network+ exam objectives to the course content. You can download the Appendix at the end of this lesson.

Example:

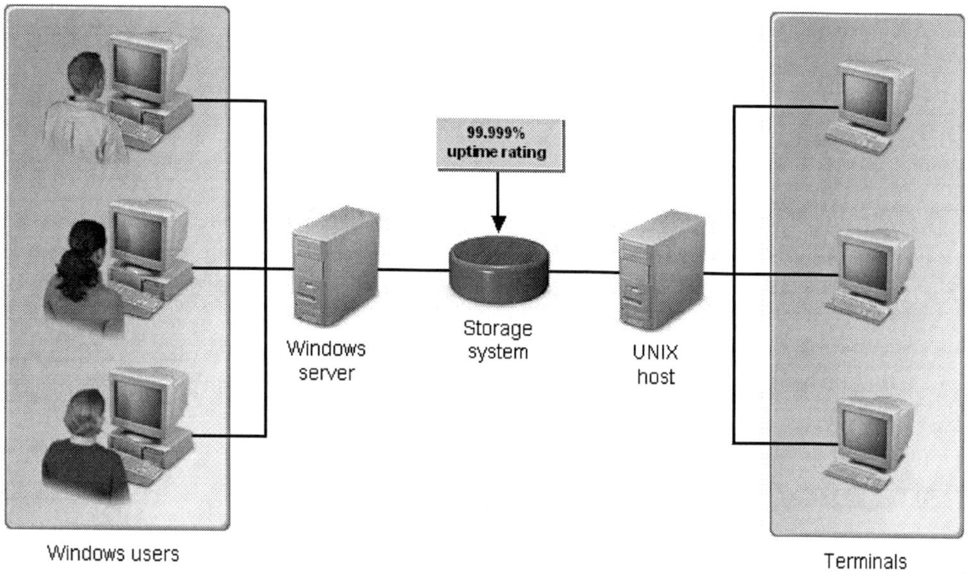

Figure 14-1: *High availability.*

Availability Ratings

"Five nines" and other availability rating figures are determined through a series of industry-standard calculations that take into account a variety of factors, such as the amount of time between failures and the time required to restore the system. For a discussion of availability ratings, translations of the ratings, and sample formulas, see **www.bcr.com/bcrmag/2002/05/p22.php** and other web resources.

Scalability

Definition:

Scalability is the ability of a system to grow smoothly to meet increasing demand without having to be replaced, reconfigured, or redesigned. When an enterprise data-storage facility supports high-storage and high-growth business functions, it must be able to scale while continuing to provide a high level of access as it grows.

Two examples of business functions that require high-growth and high-capacity storage systems are data warehousing and e-business.

Example:

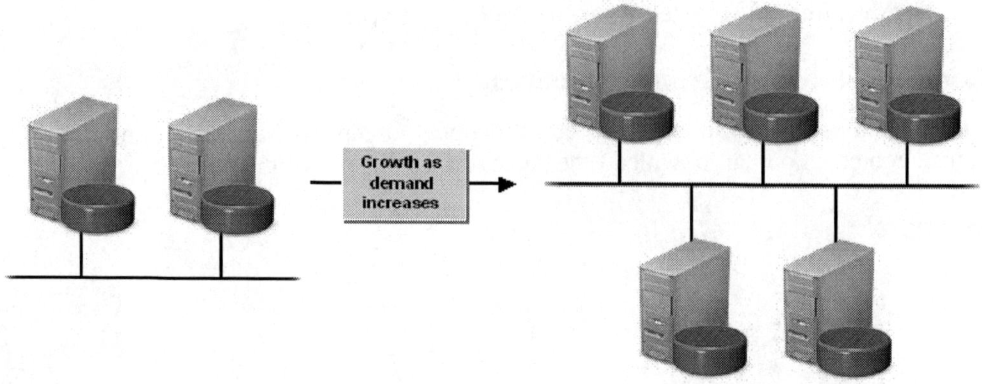

Figure 14-2: *Scalability.*

Types of Scalability

Systems can scale in two directions. When systems "scale out," or "scale horizontally," it means that more resources are added to the existing infrastructure. You might scale out your website hosting capability by adding more servers. When systems "scale up," or "scale vertically," it means that existing components are replaced with components that have more capacity. You could scale up an individual server by adding more memory or a larger or faster hard disk.

Distributed Storage Systems

Definition:

A *distributed storage* system makes data stored in different physical locations appear to the user as a contiguous storage structure. The data can be managed as a single entity. This centralization increases the administrative manageability of storage systems. An administrator can reconfigure the physical storage system without any effect on the users or on data availability.

Example:

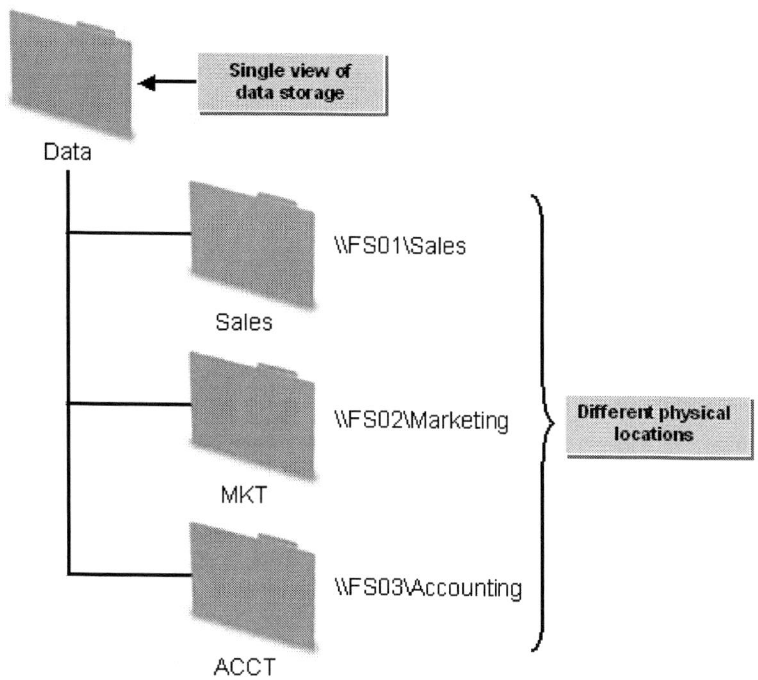

Figure 14-3: *A distributed storage system.*

Types of Distributed Storage Systems

Many systems include built-in support for distributed storage, and there are also third-party implementations in both software and hardware that you can purchase if you need additional performance.

For example, Microsoft's Distributed File System (DFS) is a software-based distributed hierarchical storage implementation that is built into Windows Server 2003 and other Windows server software. It provides users with a simple and convenient way to access shared folders that are distributed throughout the network. With DFS, administration can make files that are distributed across multiple servers appear to users as if they all reside in a single location on the network. DFS is comprised of three main components. The first is the DFS root, which is a share containing folders and files that is visible on the network. The DFS link resides below the root and it redirects the user to a share that exists somewhere on the network. The DFS target (or replica) allows you to group two identical shares, usually stored on different servers, as DFS targets under the same link.

High Performance Drive Arrays

Definition:

A high-performance *drive array* is any group of separate disks that are configured to work as a unit to improve performance, availability, and fault tolerance. Performance improves over a single disk because data on multiple disks can be accessed at the same time to serve multiple requests. Availability is high because the array can function even if one drive is down. The array can be configured to use different RAID levels to provide fault tolerance.

Example:

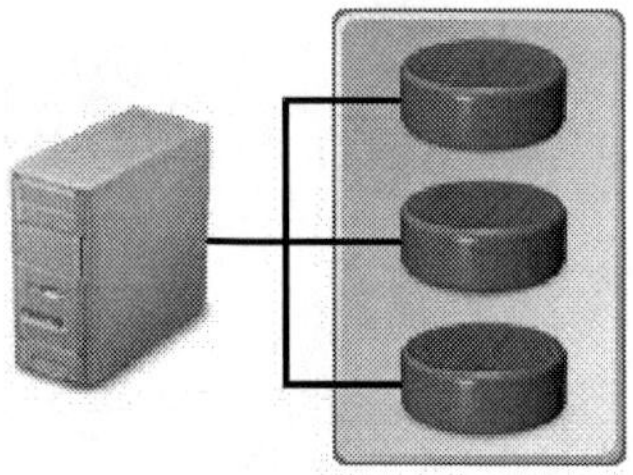

Figure 14-4: *A high-performance drive array.*

ACTIVITY 14-1

Discussing Enterprise Data Storage

Scenario:

In this activity, you will examine various enterprise data storage requirements and technologies.

1. **What is the highest realistic reliability goal for a high-availability system?**
   a) 100% uptime
   b) Five nines uptime
   c) Four nines uptime
   d) Three nines uptime

2. **What is the best description of scalability?**
   a) The ability to access data a high percentage of the time.
   b) The ability of one system to take over when another fails.
   c) The ability of a system to grow smoothly to meet increasing demand.
   d) The ability to share workload between systems.

3. **What are characteristics of distributed storage systems?**
   a) Data can be managed as a single entity.
   b) Data in different physical locations appears as a unified structure.
   c) Users access data by locating different physical servers.
   d) Administrators can reconfigure storage on the fly.

4. **What is the best description of a drive array?**
   a) A group of separate disks that are configured to work as a unit.
   b) A specialized file server that is designed and dedicated to support data storage needs.
   c) A group of servers working together to provide fault tolerance and load balancing.
   d) A private network dedicated to data storage.

TOPIC B

Clustering

In the previous topic, you identified general ideas and elements that come into play in a number of data storage solutions. Next, you can examine some specific data storage technologies. One common data storage technology is clustering. In this topic, you will identify the tools and technologies used in implementing clustering.

Clustering is a very common data storage implementation. It's implemented to support many different kinds of network applications, so it's very likely that you will be using or supporting some kind of clustering technology in your network career. A solid understanding of basic clustering concepts will be useful no matter what type of cluster your organization implements.

Clusters

Definition:

A *cluster* is two or more servers that appear to the network as a single system. Clustering is one of the most common techniques used to ensure high availability on an enterprise network. Almost any type of network server can be clustered. Servers in the cluster are referred to as nodes. The nodes use cluster-aware software to communicate with each other to report their condition, track client status, and send updates called heartbeats between the cluster members.

The clustering software can also manage the cluster's *failover* features so that each node can provide the full services of the cluster should the others fail or become busy.

Usually, nodes in the cluster have at least two network connections; one private to the other cluster nodes, and one to the public LAN. The cluster can store data on local hard disks on the cluster members, or on external storage devices.

There are three general cluster configurations that support service failover: active/active, active/passive (also known as active/standby), and fault-tolerant (also known as high-availability). Nodes in all of these clusters need to have access to at least one common storage device.

Clustering is not needed for servers that already have built-in fault tolerance, such as domain controllers and DNS servers.

Example:

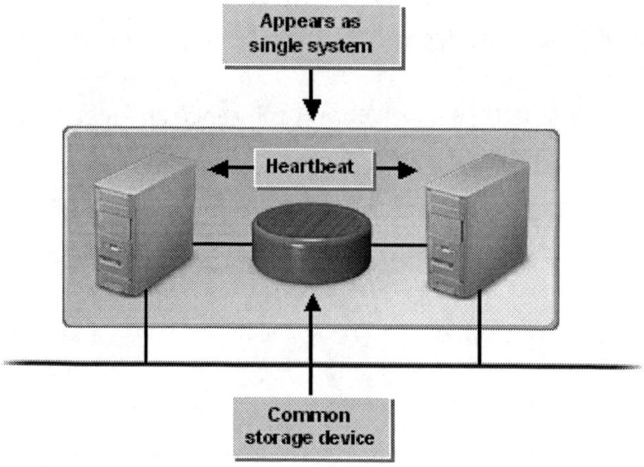

Figure 14-5: *Clusters.*

Cluster Implementations

There are various products that enable you to implement clustering. Many software manufacturers include built-in clustering support. Microsoft includes Cluster Server with Windows Server 2003; Novell supports clustering with Novell Cluster Services for NetWare. There are various third party solutions from companies such as EMC. You should be aware that most clustered servers have special hardware requirements, meaning that you might need special hardware in order to create server clusters.

Single-Node Clusters

Besides the main cluster configurations, it is also possible to install a single system as a single-node cluster. This might be done to provide a platform to develop and test cluster-aware applications, or to take advantage of some of the features of the cluster software, such as creating separate virtual storage areas for separate departments on a single storage server, or for temporary server consolidation.

Network Load Balancing

Clusters can also be implemented to provide network *load balancing,* which optimizes network traffic between redundant systems. One simple way to accomplish load balancing is to use the round-robin capabilities of DNS to route successive network requests to different servers within a group. Another method is to use clustering technology that is specifically designed to provide load balancing, by grouping several nodes so that they appear to share a single MAC address. There are load-balancing products available from Citrix and other vendors.

Windows servers also include a Network Load Balancing (NLB) feature that explicitly distributes incoming IP traffic across multiple nodes, such as multiple web servers. Hosts that are grouped together by NLB are referred to as NLB clusters to distinguish them from Cluster Server clusters.

Active/Active Clustering

Definition:

Active/active clusters have all nodes online, constantly providing services. This cluster type has the greatest resource efficiency because all nodes service clients. If a node fails, the cluster resources fail over to one of the remaining nodes. That node will lose some performance as it takes on the resources and workload of the failed node. Latency in failover can range from seconds to minutes, depending on cluster configuration and the services on each cluster.

Example:

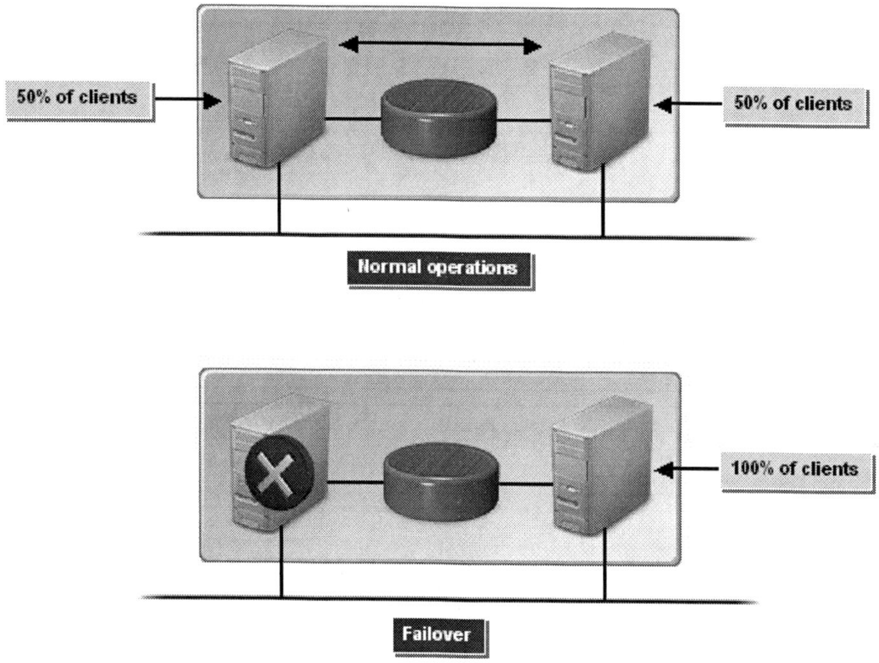

Figure 14-6: *An active/active cluster.*

Active/Passive Clustering

Definition:

An *active/passive cluster* includes at least two nodes, at least one of which is in active mode and handles the full workload, while one node is a backup and does not own any resources in the cluster. If an active server fails, the passive node will take over the resources from the failed active node. Performance during failover is relatively unaffected as long as the two servers have similar capacity. Latency in failover can range from seconds to minutes, depending on cluster configuration and services.

An active/passive cluster is also known as an *active/standby cluster.*

Example:

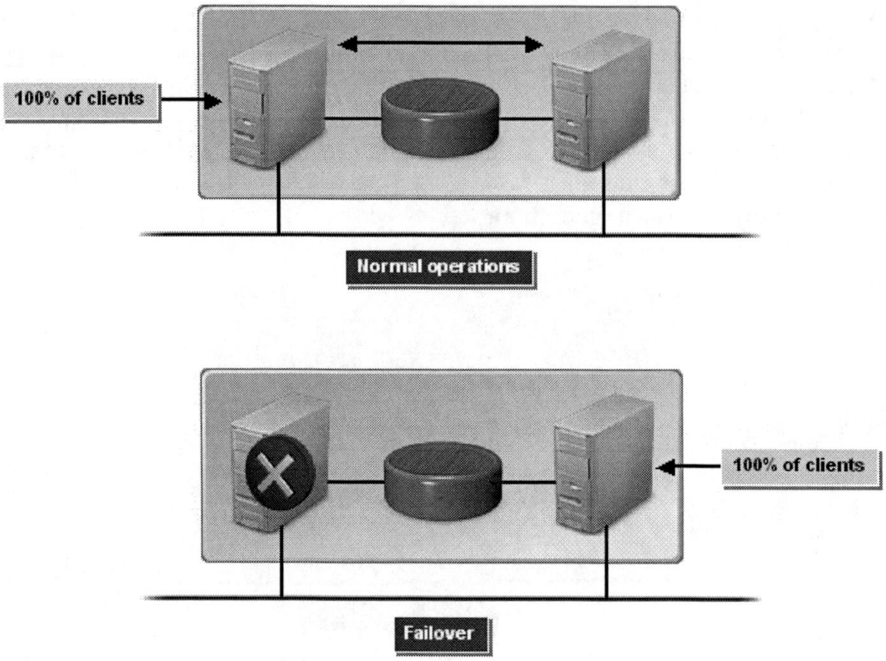

Figure 14-7: *An active/passive cluster.*

Fault-Tolerant Clustering

Definition:

A *fault-tolerant cluster,* or *high-availability cluster,* is a general term for implementations that use clustering, RAID, redundant hardware, and other technologies to achieve five nines of uptime. In "shared everything" clusters, nodes share common hardware resources such as processors, memory, and disks, and can execute commands simultaneously so that a node can take over immediately if one fails. Failover times are in milliseconds, and there is often no performance degradation at all.

Example:

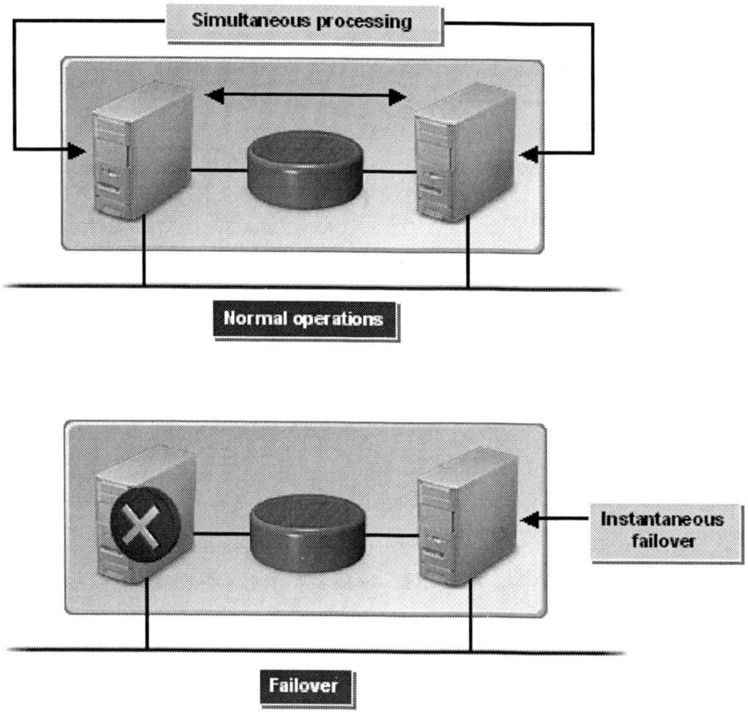

Figure 14-8: *A fault-tolerant cluster.*

High-Availability Cluster Implementations

High-availability clustering solutions are complicated to set up, configure, and maintain, and can cost hundreds of thousands of dollars to implement. However, they offer the highest level of failover performance, and are the best choice for organizations, such as banks, brokerage firms, and airlines, that require "five nines" of uptime for financial or other reasons. Even just a few minutes of downtime in these organizations can cost millions and millions of dollars.

ACTIVITY 14-2

Discussing Clustering

Scenario:

In this activity, you will examine various aspects of cluster technology.

1. **What is the best description of a cluster?**

   a) A specialized file server that is designed and dedicated to support data storage needs.

   b) A group of separate disks that are configured to work as a unit.

   c) A private network dedicated to data storage.

   d) A group of servers working together to provide fault tolerance and load balancing.

2. **Which are hardware requirements of multiple nodes in a cluster?**

   a) Cluster-aware software.

   b) Two network connections.

   c) Access to a common storage device.

   d) External tape drives.

3. **Match the cluster type with the description.**

___	Active/active	a.	A cluster that includes nodes that handle the full workload during normal operations, and other nodes in standby mode.
___	Active/passive	b.	A cluster in which servers can provide almost instantaneous failover.
___	Fault-tolerant or high-availability	c.	A cluster that has all nodes online, constantly providing services.

4. **Which cluster type has the best failover response time?**

   a) Active/active

   b) Active/passive

   c) Fault-tolerant

5. **Which cluster type has the best resource efficiency?**

   a) Active/active

   b) Active/passive

   c) Fault-tolerant

6. **In an active/passive configuration, how does the passive server know that the active server has failed?**

    a) The active server sends an ABEND message.

    b) The administrator brings the standby server online.

    c) The heartbeat stops.

    d) The passive server reboots.

TOPIC C

Network-Attached Storage (NAS)

In the previous topic, you learned that clustering is one technology that can support enterprise data storage needs. Another technology used in enterprise data storage is network-attached storage. In this topic, you will identify tools and technologies required for a NAS implementation.

Network-attached storage is a versatile and efficient system that is an attractive data storage solution for many organizations. So, there is a good chance that you will work with or evaluate a NAS system at some point in your networking career. NAS systems have specific software, hardware, and configuration requirements that you should understand if you find yourself evaluating, implementing, or supporting NAS in your environment.

NAS Systems

Definition:

A *network-attached storage (NAS)* system is a specialized file server designed and dedicated to support only data storage needs. The NAS server typically has no mouse, keyboard, or monitor. It runs a streamlined operating system, and can contain a variety of storage devices. The NAS system has an IP address and is commonly attached to a high-performance network such as FDDI or ATM. The NAS can be accessed by clients and servers running different operating systems.

Example:

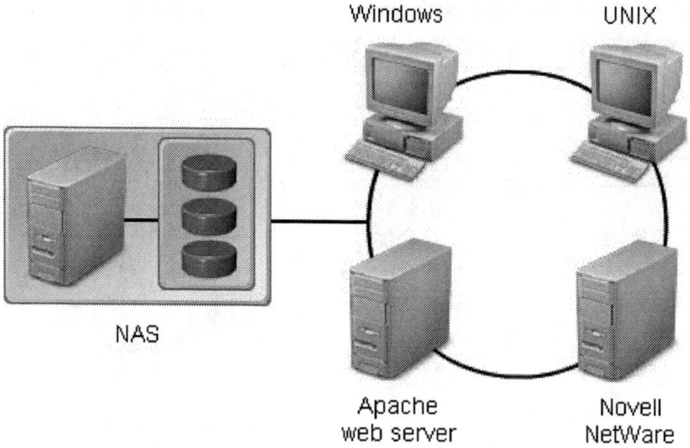

Figure 14-9: *Network-attached storage.*

NAS Storage Devices

A NAS system can use high-performance storage devices such as large hard disk arrays or tape drives. Or, the NAS system itself can simply be a hard drive that has an Ethernet port.

Advantages of NAS

It can be expensive to implement a specially designed and dedicated NAS server to replace or supplement existing general-purpose file servers. However, there are several advantages to implementing NAS:

- The NAS system is often more reliable and less prone to downtime than a traditional file server, which improves data availability.
- The NAS system can scale efficiently because it is relatively inexpensive to add additional storage devices once the NAS is implemented.
- Because the NAS system is dedicated to storage management, data storage and retrieval performance is very high.
- NAS systems are easier to secure than traditional file systems because there are fewer points of access to the device. For example, without a keyboard and monitor, no one can log on directly to the system console.
- NAS facilitates data backups because the data can be backed up over a local bus system inside the NAS while it continues to serve client requests. Or, a separate high-performance network link can be created between the NAS and a backup server.
- NAS improves administrative efficiencies because it turns an entire company's storage into a single management entity. Data can be managed and reconfigured without affecting clients or their ability to access the data.

NAS Systems

Various storage vendors offer NAS system products. Some examples include the IBM TotalStorage NAS Gateway, the Iomega NAS 200m and Iomega NAS 300m storage servers, and the HP ProLiant storage server line.

NAS Operating Systems and Protocols

All NAS systems have a specially modified operating system. Some NAS appliances use a custom microkernel written specifically to control the storage hardware; others use modified network operating systems such as Windows Server 2003 or Linux. By stripping out unnecessary functions, the NAS operating system becomes very efficient, providing much higher performance than a traditional file server.

Clients use a file access application protocol such as Network File System (NFS) or Server Message Block (SMB) to access the NAS over the network.

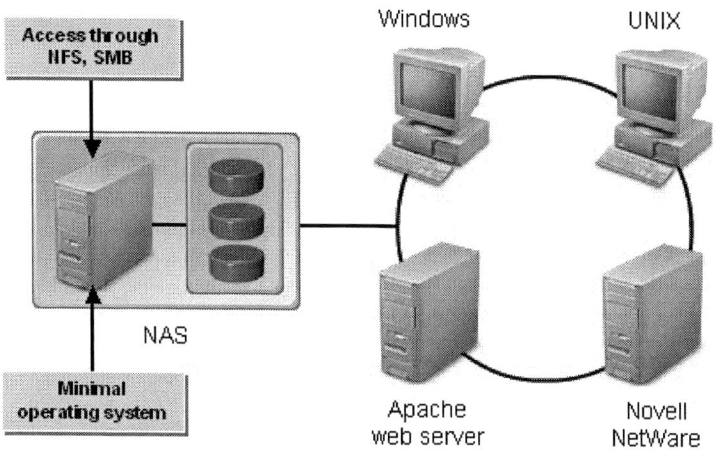

Figure 14-10: *NAS operating systems and protocols.*

NAS Connection Options

Clients can access the NAS either directly or through a server that provides connectivity to the NAS. When users connect directly, it is like connecting to any other server or share.

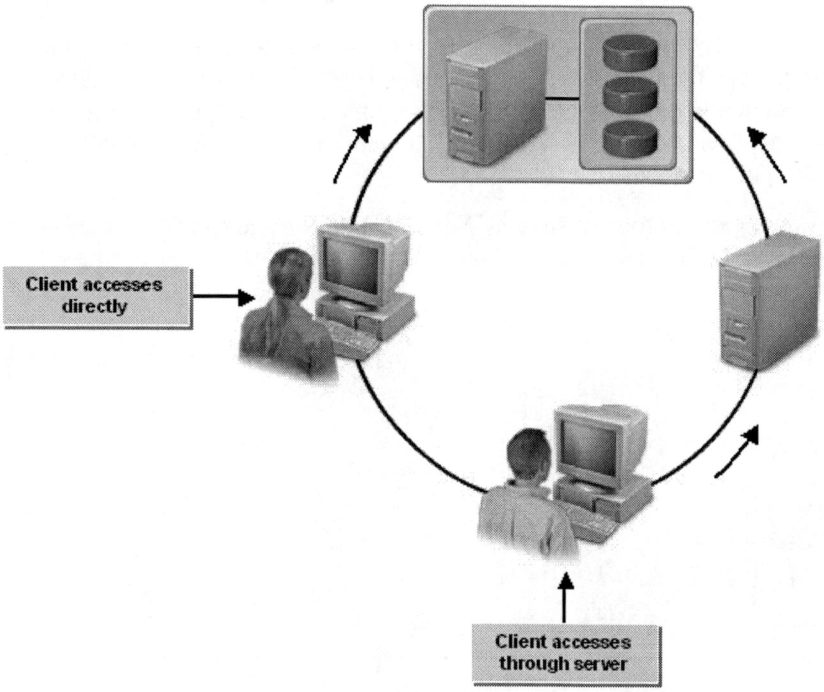

Figure 14-11: *Connecting to a NAS.*

When a server provides connectivity, it either acts as a gateway to the NAS, or hosts a distributed file system through which the client can access the data on the NAS. In either case, the client is unaware of the NAS as a separate device, and the client does not need to be reconfigured if the data structure on the NAS changes.

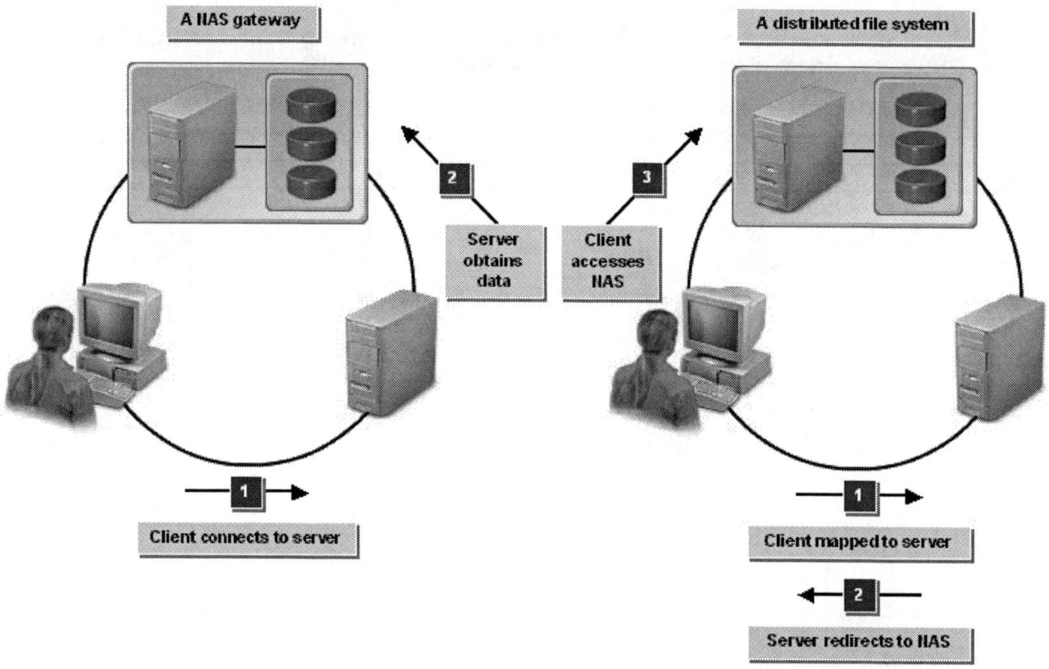

Figure 14-12: *Connecting to a NAS through a server.*

Server Connectivity Options

The two NAS server connectivity options have different advantages and disadvantages.

When a server acts as a gateway for the NAS appliance, it connects to the NAS on behalf of the client and retrieves the data for a client. The client might not even know that the NAS is on the network. However, many times a server must run special client or gateway software to make the connection to the NAS data. This software isn't available to clients, but even if a client discovered where the NAS is on the network, it can't attach to it without proper configuration. One big advantage to using a gateway to connect to a NAS is that the network media containing the NAS doesn't have to be compatible with the client. As long as the server has a connection on both networks, the NAS can be on almost any type of high-performance network media.

When a server distributes a share on a NAS, it provides a point to which the client can map, but the drives the client connects to are actually aliases for drives on the NAS or other machines. When the client connects to the share, the server redirects it to the NAS for the actual data. In this case, the distributing server can possibly provide added security and functionality features not available on the NAS. Also, because the server does not handle the data directly, its equipment requirements might be less.

ACTIVITY 14-3

Discussing Network-Attached Storage

Scenario:

In this activity, you will examine various aspects of NAS technology.

What You Do	How You Do It

1. **Which is the most appropriate description of a NAS system?**
   - a) A specialized file server that is designed and dedicated to support data storage needs.
   - b) A group of servers working together to provide fault tolerance and load balancing.
   - c) A group of separate disks that are configured to work as a unit.
   - d) A private network dedicated to data storage.

2. **How do NAS systems differ from standard file server configurations?**
   - a) They run a special operating system.
   - b) They are not connected to the network.
   - c) They have no hard disk.
   - d) They have no monitor, keyboard, or mouse.

3. **Which are file access protocols commonly used with NAS systems?**
   - a) SMB
   - b) NFS
   - c) NSS
   - d) NTFS

4. **What are the options for connecting clients to a NAS?**

   a) Clients connect directly.

   b) Clients install special access software.

   c) Clients connect through a server gateway.

   d) Clients connect using a distributed file system.

TOPIC D

Storage Area Network (SAN) Implementations

In the previous topic, you identified how to use NAS as part of an enterprise data storage solution. Storage area networks are another type of enterprise data storage technology. In this topic, you will identify tools and technologies required for a SAN implementation.

Implementing a SAN is an intriguing possibility for organizations that need extremely-high-performance storage solutions. But what about the cost? The complexity? What are the tradeoffs of selecting this type of solution over a NAS, a traditional server cluster, or even basic file servers? You'll need to understand these and other technical issues if you ever support an organization that considers a SAN implementation.

Storage Area Networks

Definition:

A *storage area network (SAN)* is a special-purpose high-speed network that is dedicated to data storage. The SAN contains servers that share access to data storage devices such as disk arrays or tape drives. The servers and devices within the SAN interconnect using a high-speed networking technology such as Fibre Channel, FDDI, ATM, or high-speed Ethernet.

Data can be stored and accessed quickly, and because the servers and storage devices all have redundant connections, data remains available during a server failure. The direct data traffic between servers and storage appliances on the SAN is separated from traffic on the production network. However, SANs can be complex to implement and the required redundancies mean they are quite expensive.

Example:

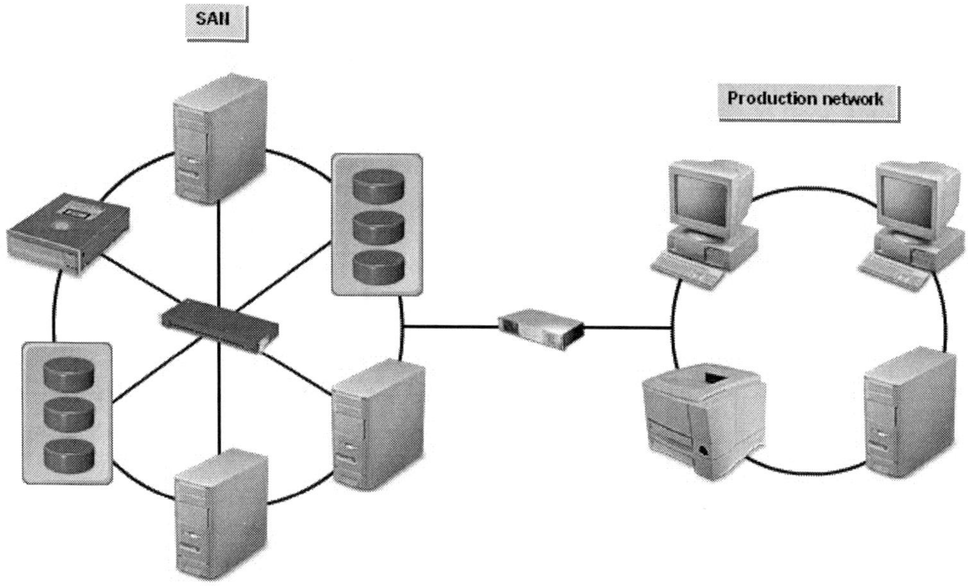

Figure 14-13: *Storage area networks.*

SANs vs. Network-Attached Storage with SCSI

SANs overcome some of the technical limitations of network-attached storage. Typically, the NAS servers attach to drive arrays using parallel SCSI buses. This can create system bottlenecks as the high-speed data rate of multiple SCSI controllers has to interface with the slower data rate of the server's internal PCI bus. Also, SCSI limits the number of drives per channel. Finally, network-attached SCSI drives must be in close proximity to NAS servers. SANs enable the arrays to be distributed throughout the network.

The SAN uses a high-speed network connection to replace the SCSI communications channel between the drive controller in the server and the data controller on the disk array. This removes the drive limit, data rate limits, and separation distance limits of NAS and SCSI.

SAN Implementations

SANs can be used when it is important to have flexibility in the placement of storage devices. Data centers can be set up with servers on one side and storage on the other, or custom laser-powered, single-mode fiber optic links can be used for separation distances of up to 100 kilometers. This greater distance enables companies to separate their data mirrors and provide security from local disasters.

SANs have become an integral part of clustering and other high-availability solutions. Because a SAN can support multiple servers accessing the same data and because the data is separate from any server, it makes sense to use a SAN as the shared data storage solution in a cluster. The drives appear local to the individual nodes in the cluster. If the active server fails, the passive server can access the same data that the active server was accessing on the SAN.

SAN Systems

Various storage vendors offer SAN system products. Some examples include the IBM TotalStorage brand SAN switches, Network Appliance (NetApp) Fibre Channel SAN Storage Solutions, and the HP StorageWorks SAN.

Fibre Channel

Fibre Channel was the first technology to be widely used for connectivity in SAN environments and is now the de facto standard. Fibre Channel is a hardware-focused data transport method designed and developed specifically for high-speed communication among servers and mass storage devices. The channels are switched, point-to-point, or loop connections that move data at transfer rates of up to 1 or 2 Gbps because of the very low overhead.

Fibre Channel has its own protocol for moving and switching data that is compatible with existing upper-level networking protocols. It can be implemented over fiber optic cable, as well as coax and twisted pair. Over fiber optic, devices can be as far as 10 kilometers apart.

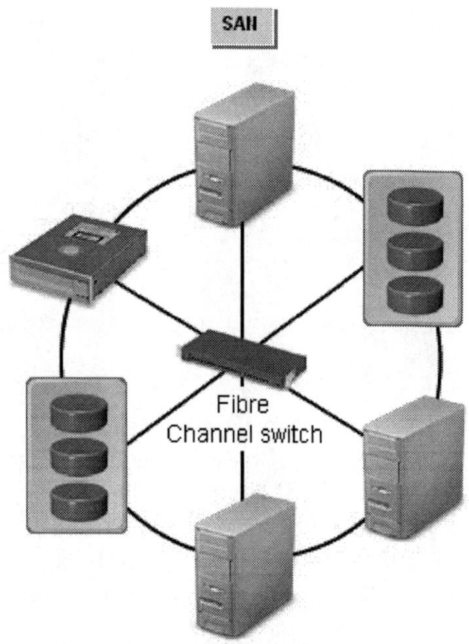

Figure 14-14: *Fibre Channel.*

Fibre Channel Topologies

Fibre Channel can be implemented in three different topologies.

Fibre Channel Topology	Description
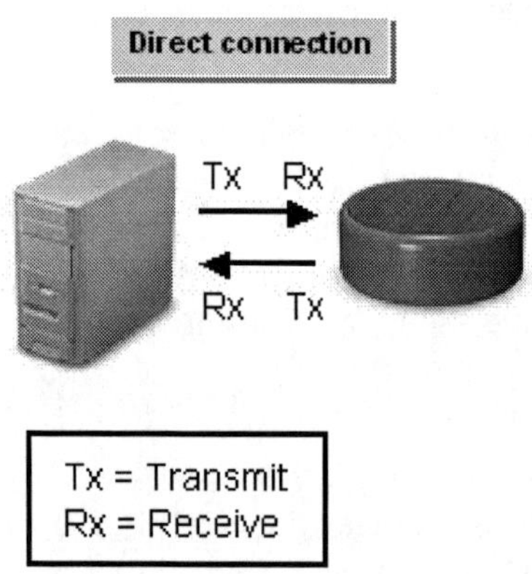	Direct connection is made up of two end nodes connected directly together. The connection is full duplex, enabling both to transmit and receive at the same time. Direct connections aren't scalable and are limited to two nodes.

Fibre Channel Topology	Description
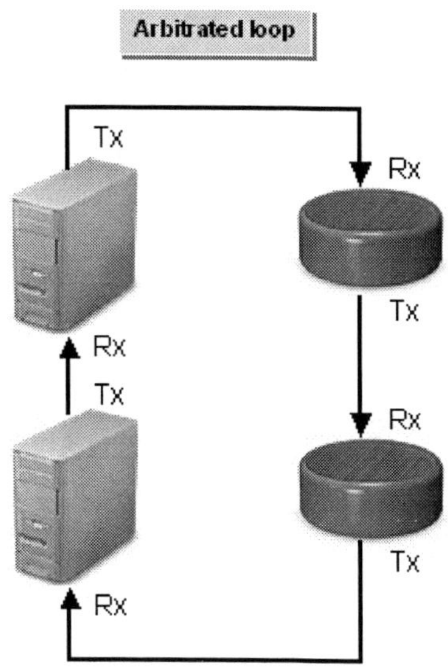	Arbitrated loops can support up to 127 nodes arranged in a ring topology with only one device sending data at a time. Hardware can be implemented in both a logical ring and a physical ring. Many SANs implement the topology as a physical ring because it requires less hardware and is a lower-cost implementation. The physical ring topology has the same disadvantages as any other physical ring but many are countered by the fact that a SAN is a tightly controlled network and doesn't have the variables of a production network.
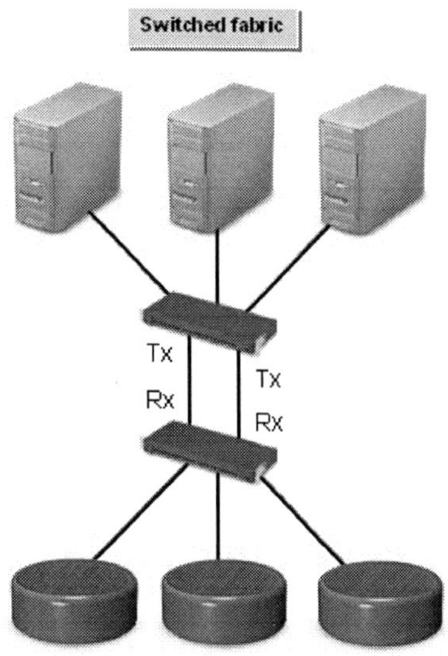	Switched fabric is the highest performance and most expensive method of connecting devices to a Fibre Channel network. Switched fabric networks use a Fibre Channel switch that acts very much like a network switch, segregating the traffic to only the involved ports. Switches can be linked together to form the network fabric. In a switched fabric Fibre Channel network, more than one node can exchange data at once because switches usually have large data buffers. The two biggest advantages of a switched fabric Fibre Channel network are scalability and performance.

SANs over TCP/IP

SANs can be implemented over TCP/IP using other network transport technologies such as ATM or high-speed Ethernet. This provides a viable lower-cost solution for small- and medium-sized networks when the extremely high data-transfer speeds of Fibre Channel are not a requirement.

Other Benefits of SANs over TCP/IP

Cost is not the only advantage of implementing SANs over TCP/IP. In an organization with a fully-routed network, the TCP/IP infrastructure already exists, so a network storage device can easily be placed at a remote site for a hot backup. Also, separate servers can be placed in remote offices and still share a common data storage location, which helps to keep distributed data synchronized.

ACTIVITY 14-4

Discussing SANs

Scenario:

In this activity, you will examine various aspects of SAN implementations.

What You Do	How You Do It

1. **Which is the best description of a SAN?**
    a) A drive that has an Ethernet port and TCP/IP address and is used mainly as a file server.
    b) A server designed for and dedicated to file storage.
    c) A group of servers sharing the same network function.
    d) A private network dedicated to data storage.

2. **What are hardware requirements for a SAN?**
    a) A private network topology over Fibre Channel, FDDI, ATM, or high-speed Ethernet.
    b) Shared access to data storage devices.
    c) SCSI-attached drive controllers.
    d) TCP/IP.

3. **What are valid reasons for employing Fibre Channel within a SAN?**
    a) Low cost.
    b) High data-transfer rate.
    c) Choice of lower-layer protocols.
    d) Choice of physical media.
    e) Choice of upper-layer protocols.

4. **Match the Fibre Channel topology with the description.**

___	Direct connection	a.	Two end nodes in a full-duplex connection.
___	Arbitrated loop	b.	Interconnected nodes that can have multiple senders.
___	Switched fabric	c.	Nodes arranged in a ring with one sender at a time.

5. **What are potential advantages to implementing SANs over TCP/IP?**
    a) High data-transfer rate.
    b) Low cost.
    c) Use of existing infrastructure.
    d) Higher storage capacity than Fibre Channel SANs.

Lesson 14 Follow-up

In this lesson, you identified major data storage technologies and implementations. As a network professional, you need to understand the technologies that are used in high-capacity, enterprise-wide data storage systems so that you can support these kinds of systems in your organization.

1. **What factors will be most important in the data storage solutions you implement for your organization, or for an organization you are familiar with? For example, will you consider response time more important than cost? Will scalability be a factor? What percentage of uptime will be required?**

2. **From your own point of view, what are the advantages and disadvantages of the data storage implementations discussed in this lesson? Which might you choose to implement in your organization?**

Notes

LESSON 15

Network Operating Systems

Lesson Time
2 hour(s), 45 minutes

Lesson Objectives:

In this lesson, you will identify the primary network operating systems.

You will:

- Identify major Microsoft network operating system software.
- Identify the features of various Novell NetWare versions.
- Identify the major functions and releases of UNIX and Linux.
- Identify the network support features of Macintosh operating systems.

LESSON 15

Introduction

In this course, you have been examining the various components of computer networks. One necessary network component is a network operating system. In this lesson, you will identify the primary network operating systems.

The operating system in use on your network not only enables basic communication between systems, but also provides you with your primary network administrative tools. Because the network operating system has such a great impact on day-to-day network functions and tasks, a basic understanding of the features and capabilities of each of the major operating systems will help prepare you to support a variety of network environments.

This lesson covers the following CompTIA Network+ (2005) certification objectives:

- Topic A:
  - Objective 3.1: Identify the basic capabilities (for example, client support, interoperability, authentication, file and print services, application support, and security) of the Windows server operating system to access network resources.
  - Objective 3.4: Given a remote connectivity scenario comprising a protocol, an authentication scheme, and physical connectivity, configure the connection. Include a connection to a Windows server.
  - Objective 4.5: Given a troubleshooting scenario between a client and the Windows server environment, identify the cause of a stated problem.
- Topic B:
  - Objective 3.1: Identify the basic capabilities (for example, client support, interoperability, authentication, file and print services, application support, and security) of the NetWare server operating system to access network resources.
  - Objective 3.4: Given a remote connectivity scenario comprising a protocol, an authentication scheme, and physical connectivity, configure the connection. Include a connection to a NetWare server.
  - Objective 4.5: Given a troubleshooting scenario between a client and the NetWare server environment, identify the cause of a stated problem.
- Topic C:
  - Objective 3.1: Identify the basic capabilities (for example, client support, interoperability, authentication, file and print services, application support, and security) of the UNIX/Linux server operating systems to access network resources.
  - Objective 3.4: Given a remote connectivity scenario comprising a protocol, an authentication scheme, and physical connectivity, configure the connection. Include connections to UNIX/Linux servers.
  - Objective 4.5: Given a troubleshooting scenario between a client and the UNIX/Linux server environments, identify the cause of a stated problem.
- Topic D:
  - Objective 3.1: Identify the basic capabilities (for example, client support, interoperability, authentication, file and print services, application support, and security) of the Mac OS X Server operating system to access network resources.
  - Objective 3.4: Given a remote connectivity scenario comprising a protocol, an authentication scheme, and physical connectivity, configure the connection. Include a connection to Mac OS X Server.
  - Objective 4.5: Given a troubleshooting scenario between a client and the Mac OS X Server environment, identify the cause of a stated problem.

TOPIC A

Microsoft Operating Systems

In this lesson, you will identify the characteristics of various network operating systems. Microsoft produces several of the most widely used network operating system products. In this topic, you will identify major Microsoft network operating system software.

With Microsoft operating system products dominating the marketplace for both server and desktop software, it's a virtual guarantee that you will be working with or supporting some combination of Microsoft systems at some point in your networking career. A solid understanding of the capabilities of Windows networking software is a fundamental requirement for any network administrator today.

Windows Server 2003

Windows Server 2003 is the current version of Microsoft's server-oriented Windows operating system. Windows Server 2003 provides:

- The Active Directory directory service.
- Integrated network services such as DNS and DHCP.
- Advanced services such as clustering, public-key infrastructure, routing, and web services.
- User and group security on the file and object level.
- And advanced security features such as a built-in firewall, file encryption, and IPSec.

Windows Server Versions

Windows Server 2003 is available in different versions, each optimized for different network roles.

Windows Server Version	Description
Windows Server 2003, Standard Edition	Designed for file and print servers, web servers, and workgroups. Provides improved network access for branch offices. Suitable for small businesses and departments.
Windows Server 2003, Enterprise Edition	Designed for networking, messaging, inventory and customer service management, database, and e-commerce applications. Suitable for businesses of all sizes.
Windows Server 2003, Datacenter Edition	Designed for business-critical and mission-critical applications, such as large data warehouses, online transaction processing (OLTP), large-scale simulations, and server consolidation projects.
Windows Server 2003, Web Edition	Designed for building and hosting web applications, web pages, and XML web services sites.

Windows XP

Microsoft Windows XP is the recommended desktop operating system both for single-user or small-office peer-to-peer networks, or as a client of an Active Directory network using Windows Server 2003. Windows XP provides secure user logons, file- and folder-level security and encryption, and peer-to-peer resource sharing capabilities. Windows XP comes in Home and Professional editions.

Windows 9x Client Systems

There are other Windows client systems you might encounter, including Windows 95, Windows 98, and Windows Me. Collectively, these systems are known as Windows 9x. They are similar to each other in technical functions because they are built on a common code base, which is separate from the code base used in Windows XP. For example, you cannot create separate user account objects on Windows 9x systems. Windows 9x systems have no file-level security, and directory security is share-level rather than user-level. Microsoft is no longer pursuing development of systems built on the Windows 9x code base or its predecessor, Windows 3.x.

Active Directory

Active Directory is Microsoft's LDAP-compatible enterprise directory service. In an Active Directory-based network, all user accounts, resources, and services are centralized in the directory database, which is stored on Windows Server computers that run the Active Directory service. Active Directory performs authentication, manages security, enforces policies, and publishes resources such as files, printers, and applications.

The directory structure as well as the types and properties of objects allowed in the directory database are controlled by the directory *schema,* which can be modified to suit the needs of a particular organization. Active Directory naming conventions follow DNS naming rules, and a DNS server is required to store the DNS records necessary for clients to locate Active Directory services.

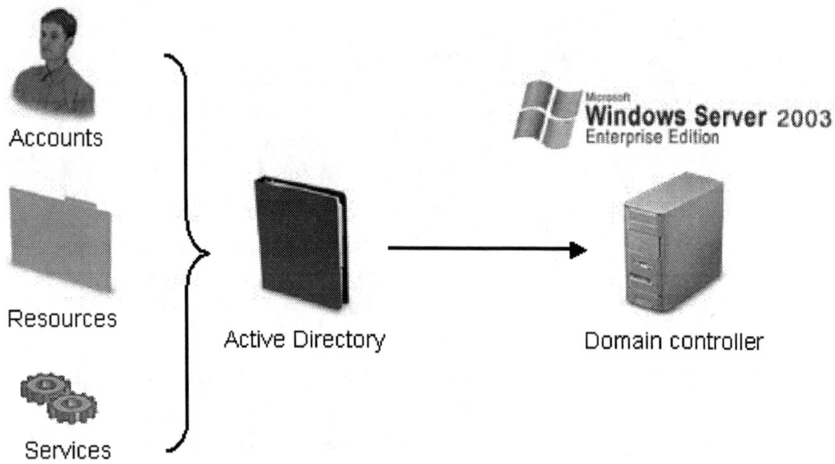

Figure 15-1: *Active Directory.*

The Security Accounts Manager (SAM) Database

User accounts can be created on local Windows computers as well as in Active Directory. Windows computers store all local user account information in a database local to each computer called the *Security Accounts Manager (SAM).* A SAM user who wishes to log on to a different computer must have the local user account information duplicated in the SAM on the other computer, by manually re-creating the user account on the other system. In Active Directory environments, the SAM typically stores only the Administrator account object that is local to a specific computer; all other user logons are managed centrally by the directory.

The Active Directory Structure

There are several components to the Active Directory structure.

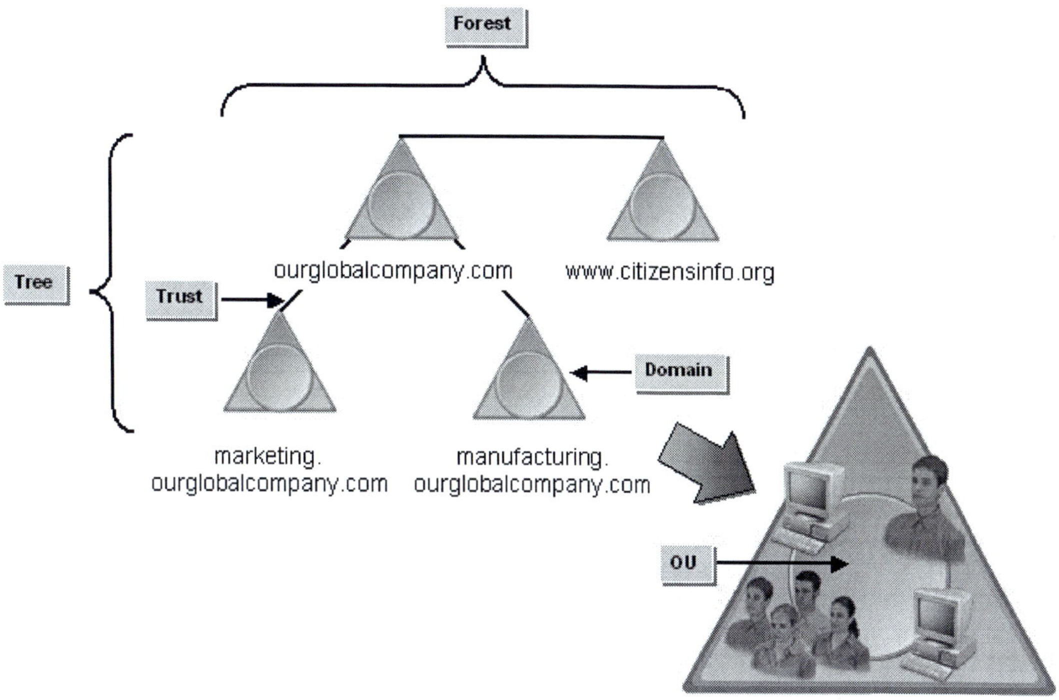

Figure 15-2: *The Active Directory structure.*

Active Directory Component	Description
Domain	The domain is the fundamental security component of Active Directory. You must install at least one domain when you install Active Directory. A domain is a security boundary. Each domain has a unique name that corresponds to a DNS name. Permissions and rights set at the domain level are inherited by objects within the domain.
Tree	A tree is a group of one or more domains that have a hierarchical relationship. The first domain created is the root of the tree. Domains within the tree automatically trust each other transitively, and administrative authority can be delegated between domains.

Active Directory Component	Description
Forest	A forest is a group of one or more trees that can have disjunct naming structures but share a common directory schema. The first tree created is the root of the forest and the administrator of the root domain of this tree has enterprise-wide administrative authority.
Organizational unit (OU)	An organizational unit (OU) is an administrative container within a domain. Directory objects can be grouped inside the OU for ease of administration, and administrative authority to the OU can be delegated to desired user accounts. OUs can be nested. Permissions and rights set at the OU level are inherited by objects within the OU.
Domain controller (DC)	A domain controller (DC) is a Windows Server computer that runs the Active Directory service. Directory information is automatically replicated between the DCs in a given forest.
Other directory objects	Directory objects such as users, groups, printers, servers, and shared folders are created at the appropriate location in the directory hierarchy to enable user authentication and resource access to the desired sections of the directory.

Workgroup Membership

On a Windows network, every computer is either a member of a domain or of a *workgroup.* Windows workgroups are arbitrary peer-to-peer groupings of computers under a common naming scheme to simplify the network view and facilitate resource location. Workgroups have no centralized security and each computer is administered independently. User accounts are stored separately on each computer. Any user with administrative authority can create or join a workgroup simply by entering the workgroup name in the computer's system properties.

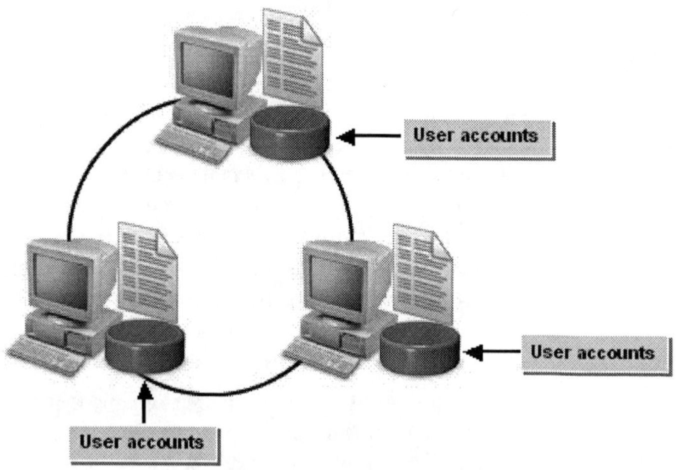

Figure 15-3: *Workgroup membership.*

OPTIONAL ACTIVITY 15-1

Configuring Workgroup Membership

There is a simulated version of this activity available on the CD-ROM that shipped with this course. You can run this simulation on any Windows computer to review the activity after class, or as an alternative to performing the activity as a group in class. The activity simulation can be launched either directly from the CD-ROM by clicking the Interactives link and navigating to the appropriate one, or from the installed data file location by opening the C:\Data\Simulations\Lesson#\Activity# folder and double-clicking the executable (.exe) file.

Setup:

Your computer is currently a member of the Classnet domain. You have a user account, User##, that has administrative authority on your local workstation and on the Classnet domain. The password for that account and for the local Administrator account on your computer is !Pass1234.

Before starting this activity, you must remove Certificate Services. In Control Panel, open Add Or Remove Programs and click Add/Remove Windows Components. Uncheck Certificate Services, click Next, and then click Finish. Close Add Or Remove Programs.

Scenario:

You will be using Microsoft Windows computers in your home-based business. Because you have few users and simple security requirements, you plan to implement workgroup-based computing. You want to configure your new Windows Server computer as a member of your business workgroup.

What You Do	How You Do It
1. Configure workgroup membership.	a. **Choose Start→Control Panel→System.**
	b. **Select the Computer Name tab.**
	c. **Click Change.**
	d. **Select the Workgroup radio button.**
	e. In the Workgroup text box, **type a workgroup name of your choice and click OK.** The name must be 15 characters or fewer. 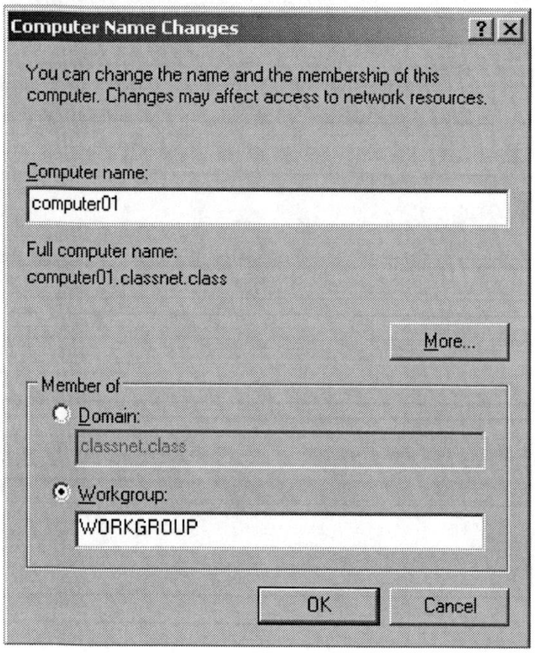
	f. In the User Name text box, **type *User##***
	g. In the Password text box, **type *!Pass1234* and click OK.**
	h. In the message box, **click OK.**
	i. In the message box, **click OK.**
	j. In the System Properties dialog box, **click OK.**
	k. To restart the computer, **click Yes.**

2. **Log on as the local Administrator.**

a. In the Welcome To Windows dialog box, **press Ctrl+Alt+Del.**

b. In the User Name text box, **type *Administrator***

c. In the Password text box, **type *!Pass1234***

d. **Click Options twice.** You no longer have the option to log on to the domain.

e. **Click OK.**

f. **Close the Manage Your Server window.**

---

3. **Verify workgroup membership.**

a. **Choose Start→My Computer.**

b. **Click the Address drop-down arrow and select My Network Places.**

c. **Double-click Entire Network.**

d. **Double-click Microsoft Windows Network.**

e. **Verify that multiple workgroups appear on the network.**

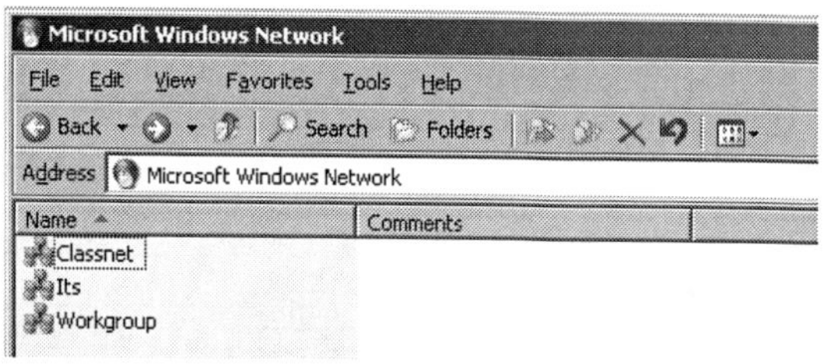

f. **Double-click your workgroup.**

g. **Verify that your computer appears in the workgroup.**

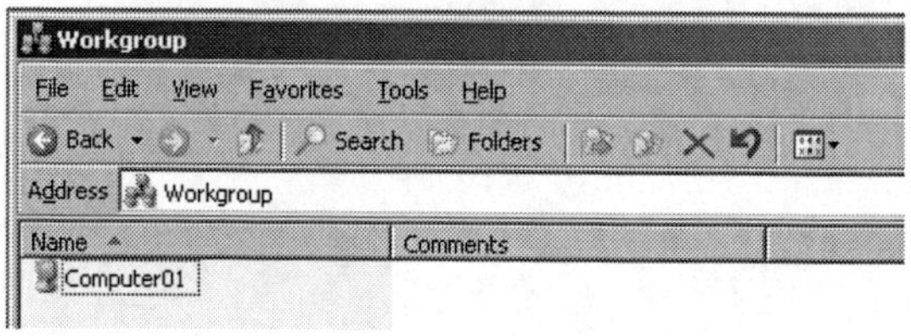

h. **View the computers in other workgroups.**

i. **Close the workgroup window.**

Domain Membership

Windows Server and Windows XP computers can join Active Directory domains and function as domain members. Domain membership means:

- The computer has a computer account object within the directory database.
- Computer users can log on to the domain with domain user accounts.
- The computer and its users are subject to centralized domain security, configuration, and policy settings.
- Certain domain accounts automatically become members of local groups on the computer.

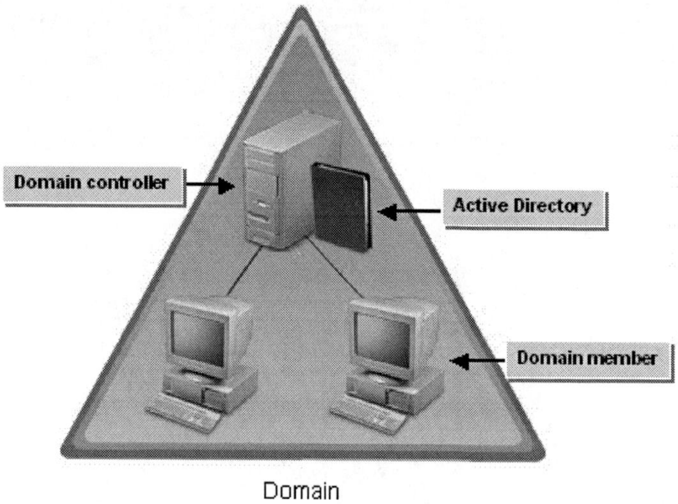

Figure 15-4: *Domain membership.*

Windows 9x Clients and Domains

Windows 9x clients can authenticate user logons against user account objects in the centralized Active Directory database. However, Windows 9x cannot become full members of the domain. That is, Windows 9x computers cannot have computer objects in the domain and cannot participate in centralized domain policy or security management. Windows 9x computers must install Directory Services Client software in order to access and use Active Directory services and resources.

Windows Me systems are intended for home use, not for deployment in a domain, and do not support the Directory Services Client.

OPTIONAL ACTIVITY 15-2

Joining a Domain

There is a simulated version of this activity available on the CD-ROM that shipped with this course. You can run this simulation on any Windows computer to review the activity after class, or as an alternative to performing the activity as a group in class. The activity simulation can be launched either directly from the CD-ROM by clicking the Interactives link and navigating to the appropriate one, or from the installed data file location by opening the C:\Data\Simulations\Lesson#\Activity# folder and double-clicking the executable (.exe) file.

Setup:

The domain name on your network is Classnet.class. You have a domain user account called User## that has administrative privileges in the domain. The password for this account is !Pass1234.

Scenario:

Your company has implemented an Active Directory domain structure on your network. You have a domain administrative account, and you need to use it to join your new Windows Server computer to the domain.

What You Do	How You Do It
1. Join the domain.	a. **Choose Start→Control Panel→System.**
	b. **Select the Computer Name tab.**
	c. **Click Change.**
	d. **Select the Domain radio button.**

e. In the Domain text box, **type *classnet* and click OK.**

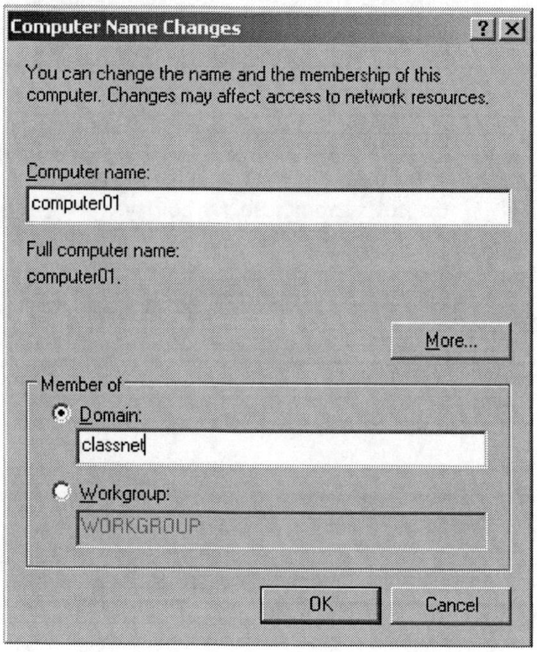

f. In the User Name text box, **type *User##***

g. In the Password text box, **type *!Pass1234* and click OK.**

h. In the message box, **click OK.**

i. In the message box, **click OK.**

j. In the System Properties dialog box, **click OK.**

k. To restart the computer, **click Yes.**

2. **Log on as a domain administrator.**

   a. In the Welcome To Windows dialog box, **press Ctrl+Alt+Del.**

   b. In the User Name text box, **type *User##***

   c. In the Password text box, **type *!Pass1234***

   d. If the Log On To text box is not visible, **click Options.**

   e. From the Log On To drop-down list, **select Classnet.**

   f. **Click OK.**

---

3. **Verify domain membership.**

   a. **Choose Start→My Computer.**

   b. **Click the Address drop-down arrow and select My Network Places.**

   c. **Double-click Entire Network.**

   d. **Double-click Microsoft Windows Network.**

   e. **Double-click the Classnet domain.**

   f. **Verify that your computer appears in the domain.**

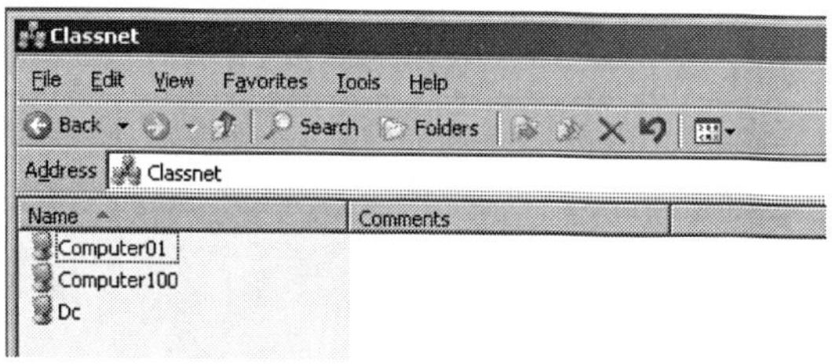

   g. **Close the domain window.**

---

4. **Examine the domain groups that have been added to the local groups.**

a. **Choose Start→Administrative Tools→ Computer Management.**

b. **Expand Local Users And Groups.**

c. In the left pane, **select Groups.**

d. **Double-click the Administrators group.**

e. **Verify that the Domain Admins group is a member and click Cancel.**

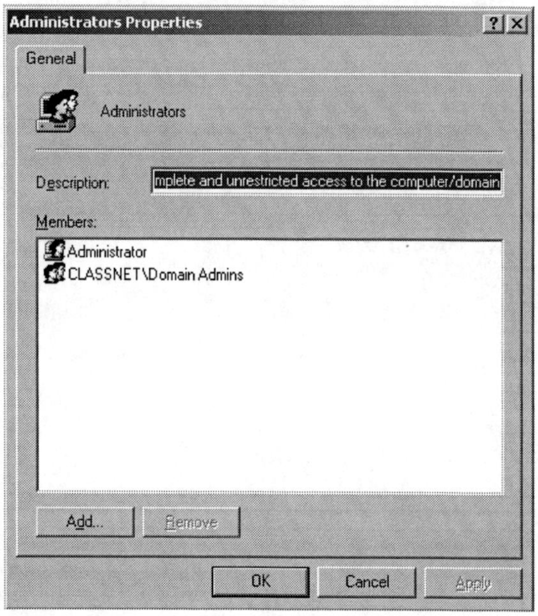

f. **Double-click the Users group.**

g. **Verify that the Domain Users group is a member and click Cancel.**

h. **Close Computer Management.**

Windows File Systems

Windows Server and Windows XP computers support two types of file systems.

File System	Characteristics
NTFS	The primary file system for Windows computers, providing file- and folder-level permissions, encryption, and compression. NTFS also supports advanced file-system features, such as journaling, disk quotas, large file and volume sizes, and small cluster sizes for efficient space usage.
File Allocation Table (FAT) and FAT32	The FAT and FAT32 file systems are legacy file systems included primarily to format floppy disks, and to provide compatibility for computers installed to multiple-boot between Windows Server or Windows XP and down-level operating systems. FAT functions best on small drives; FAT32 is an enhanced version of FAT that scales better to larger drives. FAT and FAT32 provide no security, encryption, or compression features, and are not recommended for implementation on most single-boot Windows systems.

Other Windows Servers

Microsoft produces several specialized server products that can be installed on computers running Windows Server 2003. Some of the most common of these include:

- Exchange Server, for email.
- ISA Server, a combination firewall, NAT, and proxy system.
- SharePoint Portal Server, a web-based team collaboration tool.
- SQL Server, an enterprise-level database system.
- And Systems Management Server, a comprehensive network-management system.

Windows Server System Products

Collectively, the additional server-based products from Microsoft are known as the Windows Server System. The following table lists the components of the Windows Server System. You can get more information about these products from Microsoft **www.microsoft.com/windowsserversystem/default.mspx**.

Windows Server System Product	Description
Application Center	Microsoft's solution to deploy and manage web applications.
BizTalk Server	A suite of tools and services to allow businesses to integrate applications independent of the operating systems or programming languages.
Commerce Server	A framework for rapid development and deployment of e-commerce solutions.
Content Management Server	Enables companies to build, deploy, and maintain shared websites quickly and efficiently.

Windows Server System Product	Description
Exchange Server	An enterprise-level email and messaging server.
Host Integration Server	An application server that bridges data and applications for legacy systems.
Identity Integration Server	A centralized service that stores and integrates identity information for organizations with multiple directories.
Internet Security and Acceleration (ISA) Server	An integrated web proxy, address translation, and firewall server.
Live Communications Server	An enterprise-level real-time communications server for Microsoft Office applications.
Operations Manager	Operations-management software designed to improve efficiency and manageability of IT operations.
SharePoint Portal Server	A collaboration and information-sharing system for business teams and enterprises.
Speech Server	Provides speech recognition and speech synthesis for applications that can be accessed by telephones and other voice-dependent devices.
SQL Server	An enterprise-level database system.
System Center	An integrated server-management interface tool.
Systems Management Server (SMS)	A comprehensive tool for deploying, monitoring, managing, and maintaining operating system and application software throughout an enterprise.
Virtual Server	Creates separate virtual environments on a single physical system for software testing, server consolidation, and application hosting.
Windows Small Business Server 2003	An integrated server system for small businesses, providing most key server functions in a single package.
Windows Storage Server	Dedicated file-storage server software.

Older Windows Server Versions

Windows Server 2003 is the latest implementation of a common Microsoft server code base.

Windows Server Version	Description
Windows 2000 Server	The first version of Windows to implement Active Directory. Also featured an updated user interface and the Microsoft Management Console (MMC) tool for common access to management software. Also released in a workstation version, Windows 2000 Professional.

Windows Server Version	Description
Windows NT 4.0	The first Windows Server version to use TCP/IP as the preferred protocol. Used the same fundamental directory structure as Windows NT 3.1, but performance enhancements made it more scalable. Also released in a workstation version, Windows NT Workstation 4.0.
Windows NT 3.5x	The first robust, enterprise-ready version of the Windows Server software. Version 3.5 used the NetBEUI protocol; version 3.51 used NWLink. Both versions used the Windows 3.x user interface and implemented domains based on the proprietary SAM model. In this model, a single Primary Domain Controller (PDC) stored the only editable copy of the domain database, which was replicated to Backup Domain Controllers (BDCs) that could process logons. Trusts and replication between domains had to be manually configured and maintained by administrators, and the directory did not scale well to large enterprises.
Windows NT 3.1 Advanced Server	The first 32-bit version of Windows and the first to use the microkernel architecture. Microsoft released Windows NT 3.1 Advanced Server and the client version, Windows NT 3.1, in July 1993.

ACTIVITY 15-3

Installing and Using Windows Administrative Tools

There is a simulated version of this activity available on the CD-ROM that shipped with this course. You can run this simulation on any Windows computer to review the activity after class, or as an alternative to performing the activity as a group in class. The activity simulation can be launched either directly from the CD-ROM by clicking the Interactives link and navigating to the appropriate one, or from the installed data file location by opening the C:\Data\Simulations\Lesson#\Activity# folder and double-clicking the executable (.exe) file.

Setup:

The Adminpak.msi installation file for the administrative tools is available on the network at \\dc\2003install. All network services are running on the computer dc.classnet.class. You are logged on as a domain user with administrative privileges.

Scenario:

You are an administrator for your company's Active Directory network. The domain controllers and DNS and DHCP servers are located in a secure server room. You need to install administrative tools on your workstation so that you can administer the network without having to access the network servers physically.

What You Do	How You Do It
1. **Install the administrative tools.**	a. **Choose Start→Run.**
	b. **Enter** ***\\dc\2003install\adminpak.msi*** **and click OK.**
	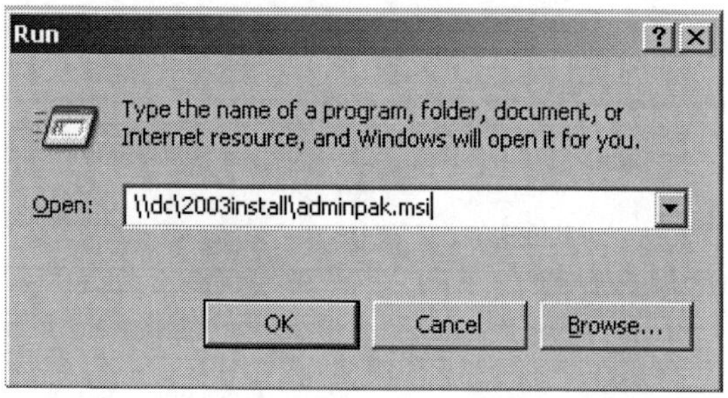
	c. **Click Open** to launch the installation process.
	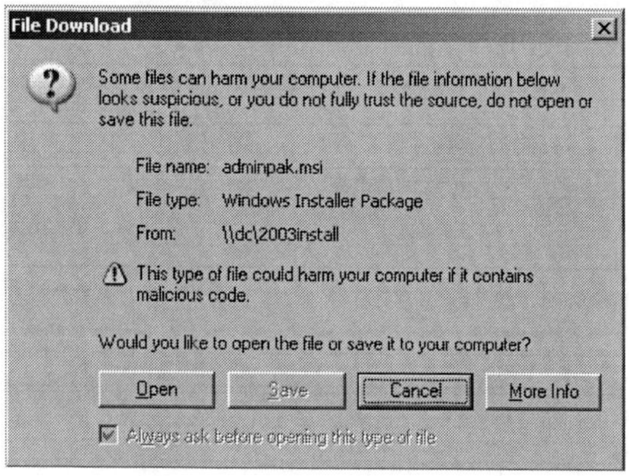
	d. **Click Next.**
	e. When the installation is complete, **click Finish.**

2. **View the Active Directory.**

a. **Choose Start→Administrative Tools→ Active Directory Users And Computers.**

b. **Expand the Classnet.class domain.**

c. **Select the Users container.**

d. **Double-click the Administrator user account.**

e. **Select the Member Of tab.**

f. The Administrator user is a member of several domain groups. **Click Cancel.**

g. **Double-click the Domain Users group.**

h. **Select the Members tab.**

i. All user accounts in the domain are members of this group. **Click Cancel.**

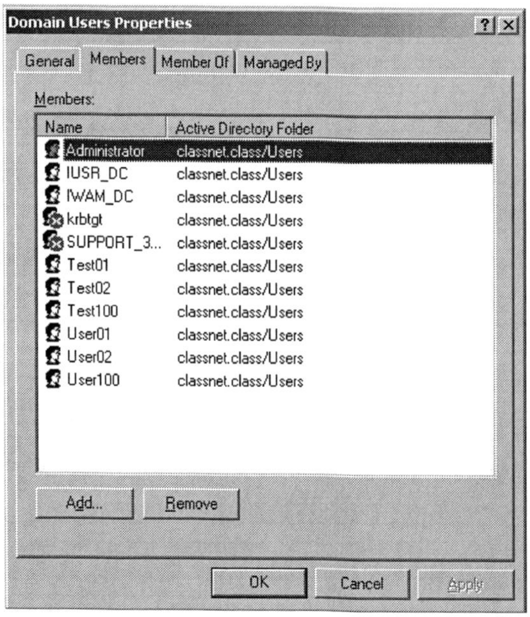

j. **Explore other objects in the directory.**

k. **Close Active Directory Users And Computers.**

3. **View the DNS server.**

a. **Choose Start→Administrative Tools→DNS.**

b. **Select The Following Computer.**

c. In the The Following Computer text box, **type *dc* and click OK.**

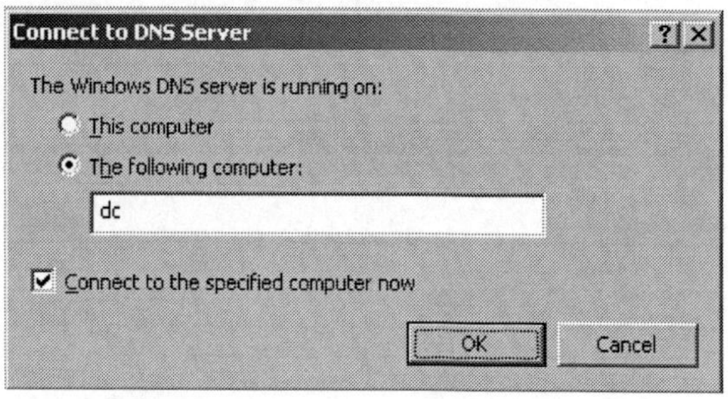

d. In the Dnsmgmt window, **expand dc and expand the Forward Lookup Zones folder.**

e. **Select Classnet.class.**

f. The Classnet.class DNS domain contains the DNS folders and records for your Active Directory network. **Choose Action→Properties.**

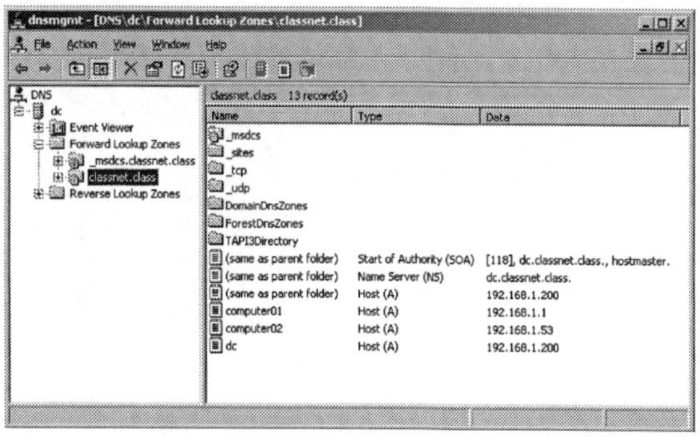

g. The DNS information is integrated into the Active Directory database. **Click Cancel.**

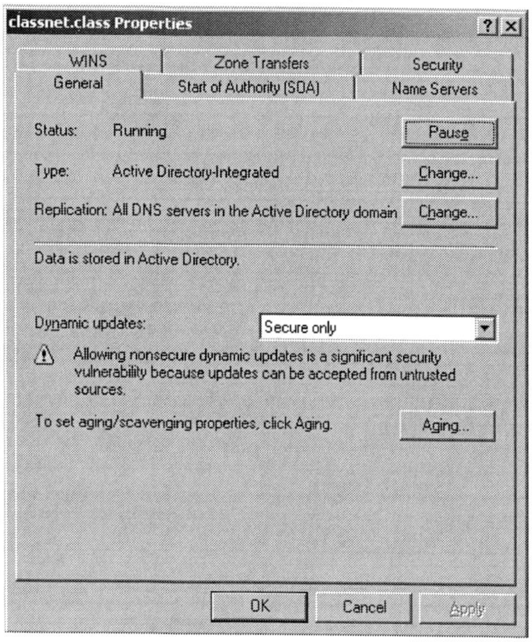

h. **Explore other DNS objects.**

i. **Close the Dnsmgmt window.**

---

4. **View the DHCP server.**

a. **Choose Start→Administrative Tools→ DHCP.**

b. **Choose Action→Add Server.**

c. **Select This Authorized DHCP Server.**

d. **Verify that dc.classnet.class is selected and click OK.**

e. **Expand dc.classnet.class.**

f. **Expand the scope object.**

g. **Select Address Pool.**

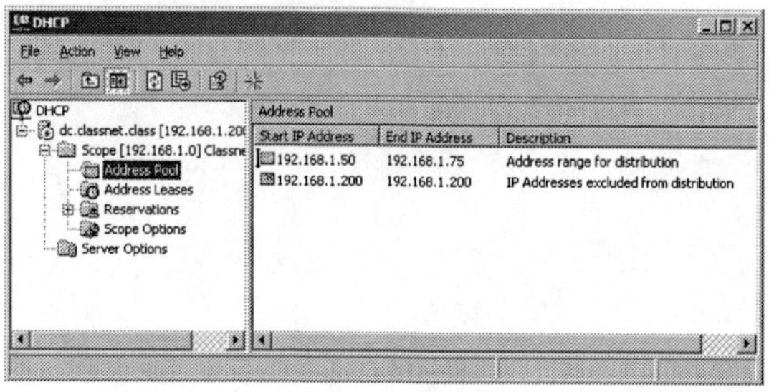

h. **Select Scope Options.**

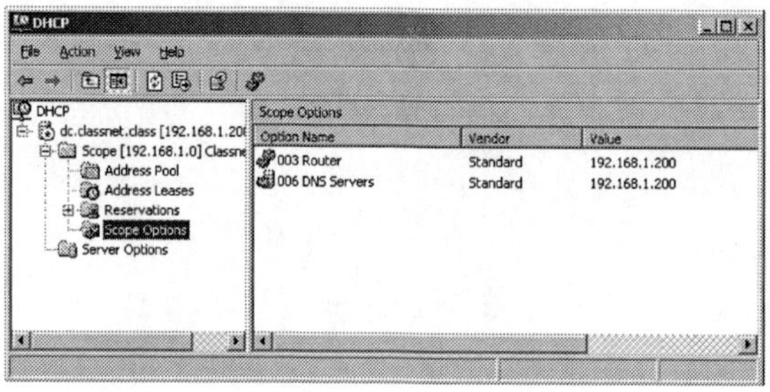

i. **Explore other objects in the DHCP console.**

j. **Close the DHCP window.**

ACTIVITY 15-4

Discussing Windows Operating Systems

Scenario:

In this activity, you will identify features of Windows operating systems and discuss Windows troubleshooting scenarios.

1. **Which services are included with Windows Server 2003?**

   a) An LDAP-compliant directory service

   b) A mail server

   c) DNS and DHCP network services

   d) Public-key infrastructure

   e) Network-management services

2. **Match the Active Directory component to its description.**

___	Domain controller	a.	A container for Active Directory objects that provides for delegation of administration.
___	Organizational Unit	b.	A unit of the Active Directory that has a unique DNS name and provides a security boundary.
___	Domain	c.	A group of domains that share a contiguous namespace.
___	Tree	d.	A Windows Server computer that runs the Active Directory service.
___	Forest	e.	A group of domains that share a directory schema but have disjunct names.

3. **Select the characteristics of workgroup membership.**

   a) The computer is represented by a computer account object in the directory database.

   b) User accounts are stored separately on each individual computer.

   c) Groups computers under a common naming scheme.

   d) Provides centralized security.

4. **Match the Windows Server System product with its description.**

___	Exchange Server	a.	Email services.
___	SQL Server	b.	Firewall services.
___	SMS Server	c.	Website deployment and management services.
___	ISA Server	d.	Network management services.
___	Content Management Server	e.	Team collaboration services.
___	SharePoint Portal Server	f.	Database services.

5. You have just implemented an Active Directory domain on your network. Formerly, all computers were configured as workgroup members. One of the Windows XP Professional users calls to say he can't log on to the domain. What are some of the things you could check to try to resolve the problem?

6. A Windows XP user's computer has just been joined to the domain. She is complaining that her desktop appearance and some of her menus have changed. What could be the issue?

7. A Windows Me user is trying to access a shared folder on another Windows Me computer in her workgroup. Access is denied. What could be the problem?

8. You have some legacy Windows 98 computers that you would like to access domain services while you schedule upgrades to Windows XP. What can you do to enable these clients to access domain services?

TOPIC B

Novell NetWare

In the previous topic, you discussed the features of Microsoft network operating systems. Another important PC-based network operating system is Novell NetWare. In this topic, you will identify the features of various Novell NetWare versions.

Novell NetWare was one of the first LAN-based, PC-based network operating systems to be widely deployed, and it has a long and highly respected history. Although Microsoft operating systems might dominate the current industry playing field, Novell is still present in many corporate environments. As a networking professional, you might be called upon to support NetWare implementations in both pure and mixed environments, so you'll need to have a working understanding of this product's major features and functions.

NetWare 6.x

NetWare is the proprietary network operating system from Novell, Inc. NetWare version 6.5 includes:

- The eDirectory LDAP-compliant directory service.
- Native TCP/IP networking.
- The iManager browser-based administrative tool.
- iPrint web-enabled printing.
- iFolder web-enabled file access.
- Mixed-environment management with Nsure Identity Manager.
- Clustering and SAN support.
- And branch-office support with Nterprise Branch Office.

Nsure Identity Manager was previously known as DirXML.

NetWare Loadable Modules (NLMs)

Definition:

NetWare Loadable Modules (NLMs) are software modules that run on NetWare servers and extend the core network and application functionality of the operating system. NLMs can be loaded and unloaded at any time during server operation.

There are four categories of NLMs.

NLM Category	Description
Disk drivers	Disk drivers communicate with storage devices. They have a .DSK extension.
LAN drivers	LAN drivers communicate with network interface cards. They have a .LAN extension.
Name space modules	Name space modules enable NetWare to store non-DOS file names. They have a .NAM extension.
NLM utilities	NLM utilities extend the server functionality in a variety of ways. They have a .NLM extension.

NLMs are similar in functionality to UNIX daemons and Microsoft services.

Example:

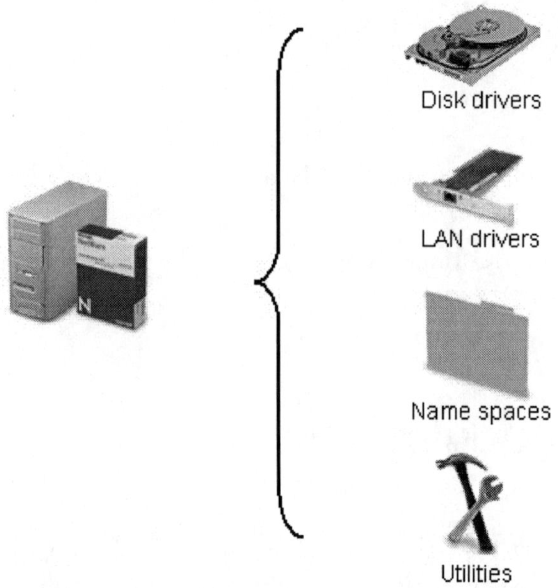

Figure 15-5: *NLMs.*

Novell eDirectory

Novell *eDirectory* is Novell's standards-based, enterprise-level directory service. It is an object-oriented database organized as a hierarchical tree. The eDirectory is LDAP-compliant and supports HTTP and SSL. It is portable to Windows, Linux, and UNIX platforms, and supports the grafting and moving of directory trees.

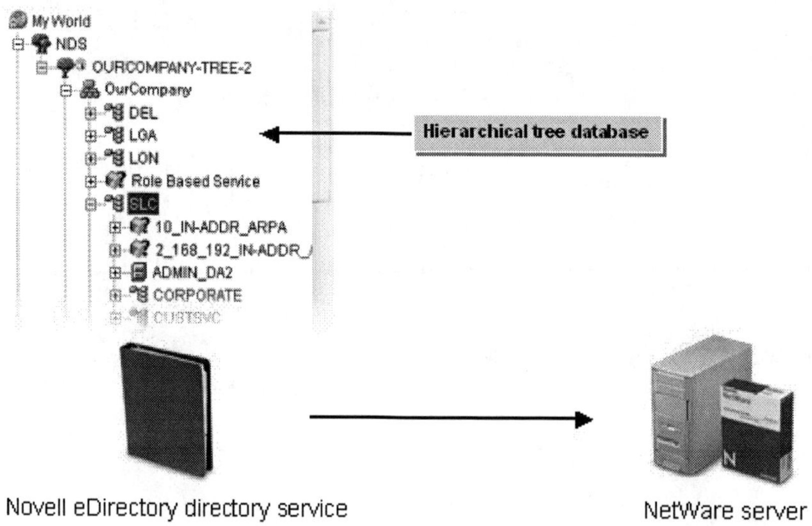

Figure 15-6: *The Novell eDirectory.*

Novell Directory Services (NDS)

The eDirectory is an evolution of earlier versions of Novell's directory service, which was called *Novell Directory Services (NDS)*. NDS was one of the first standards-based directory services, and predated Microsoft's Active Directory. NDS directories comply with X.500, an International Telecommunication Union (ITU) standard for hierarchical object-based enterprise-wide directories, and are LDAP compliant.

The Bindery

Prior to NDS and eDirectory, Novell servers stored network database information in a flat-file structure known as the *bindery.* The bindery was specific to a particular server and required users to log on and authenticate to a particular machine rather than to the network in general. If users needed to access multiple servers, the user accounts had to be duplicated on each server.

The eDirectory Tree Structure

The top of the eDirectory is the directory tree, which is installed automatically when you install the first NetWare server and represents an administrative boundary. The tree includes container objects and leaf objects. Leaf objects are security principals, such as users, groups, and printers. Container objects can contain leaf objects or other containers. Rights and permissions assigned at upper levels of the tree hierarchy are inherited by child objects.

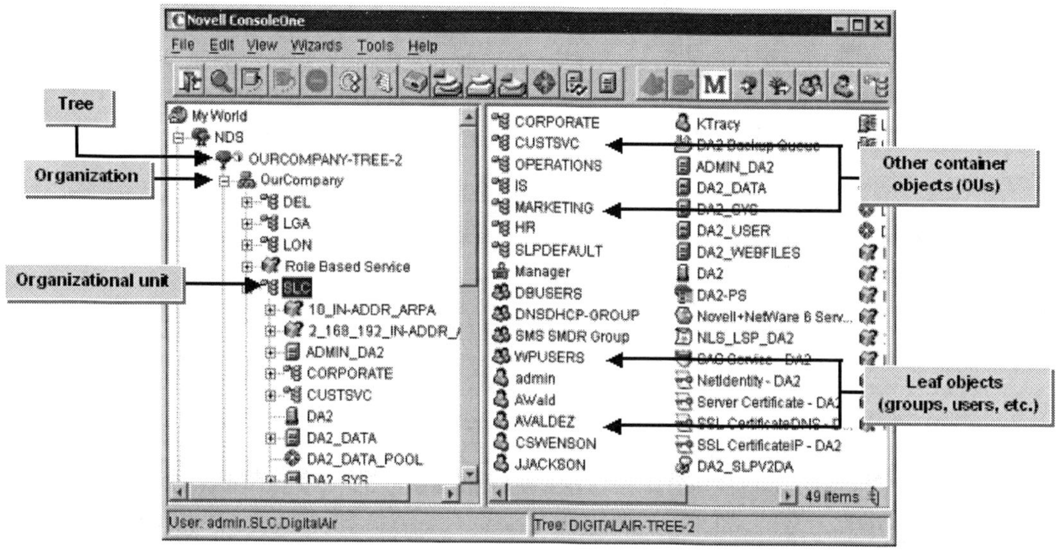

Figure 15-7: *The eDirectory tree structure.*

The eDirectory Hierarchy

The eDirectory container hierarchy includes Country, Locality, Licensed Product, Organization, and Organizational Unit objects. At least one Organization object is required.

Directory Context

The location of an object within the directory tree is known as the object's *context.* You need to know the context of your user account object in order to log on; you also need to know the context of a directory resource in order to access it. The directory context is like a path to a file within a file system. When you are browsing the directory tree, the container object that you have open is known as your *current context.* Within the current context, you can locate resources by their resource name alone; you do not need to provide the context. Recent versions of NetWare support contextless login, so that the user does not need to specify a context in order to log in. However, the administrator must configure this feature on the eDirectory tree. The administrator can also configure the correct context in the user's login script. Incorrect context can be a cause of login failure on NetWare networks.

Novell Client Software

To authenticate to and access resources on NetWare networks, a user must have a valid NetWare user account object and password, and the user's workstation must have Novell client software installed. The Novell Client enables users to access all eDirectory resources and services.

Figure 15-8: *Novell client software.*

Obtaining Novell Client Versions

Currently, Novell Client version 4.91 is compatible with Windows NT, Windows 2000, and Windows XP; Novell Client 3.4 is compatible with Windows 95 and Windows 98. The Novell Client ships on CD-ROM or can be downloaded from **download.novell.com.**

Other NetWare Clients

Earlier versions of NetWare had specific corresponding versions of client software, sometimes called the DOS requester or the workstation shell. Earlier NetWare clients included the Virtual Loadable Module (VLM) client and the NETX client.

Microsoft also provides NetWare client software, known as either the Microsoft Client for Novell Networks or the Client Service for NetWare (CSNW), as part of its Windows products. CSNW will only bind to NWLink, not to TCP/IP, so the NWLink protocol is automatically installed when you install CSNW on a Windows computer. You can only have one NetWare client installed, so you cannot run both the Novell Client and the Microsoft NetWare client software at the same time.

Native File Access Protocols

An alternative method for accessing Novell resources is through native file access protocols. With this method, the client uses file systems already present on the workstation to access NetWare file resource. With native file access protocols, the user does not log in to NetWare. Instead, the user first logs in to his or her local system, and then browses the network to locate NetWare resources using the file system native to the local operating system. The user must have a NetWare user account and supply a special password called a simple password.

Workstation Type	Native File System
Windows	Common Internet File System (CIFS)
Macintosh	Apple Filing Protocol (AFP)
UNIX/Linux	Network File System (NFS)

Novell Storage Services (NSS)

Novell Storage Services (NSS) is Novell's 64-bit, high-performance, high-capacity, journaled file storage system for volumes on NetWare servers. NSS volumes can be of an unlimited size and store up to 8 trillion files. NSS supports file sizes up to 8 terabytes, and each server can mount up to 255 NSS volumes. The iFolder feature provides web-based access to NSS storage.

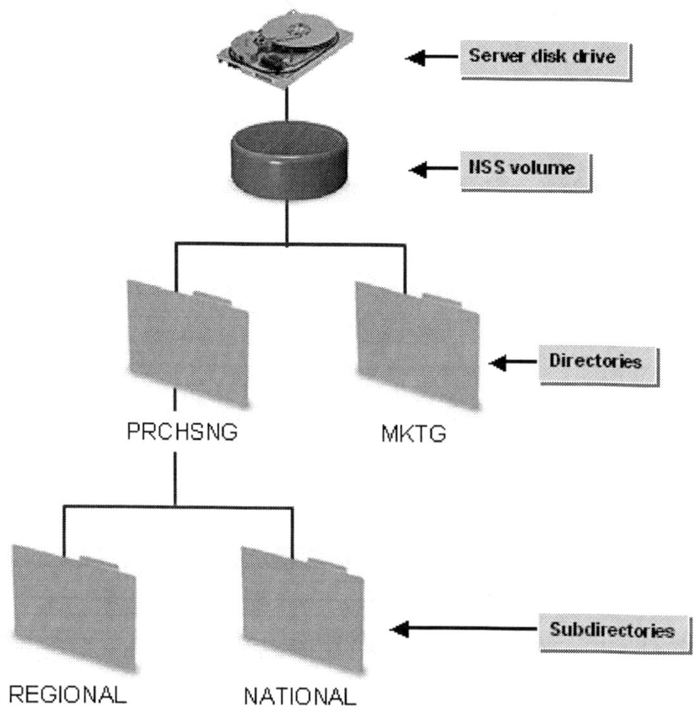

Figure 15-9: *NSS.*

Traditional NetWare Volumes

NetWare 6.x also supports another volume type called a *traditional NetWare volume.* Traditional NetWare volumes have size and speed limitations that NSS has eliminated, so Novell is moving away from traditional volumes to standardization on NSS.

Novell Distributed Print Services (NDPS)

Novell Distributed Print Services (NDPS) combines the functions of print server, print queue, and printer object into a single eDirectory object called a printer agent. The printer agent facilitates printer setup by automatically downloading drivers when users connect to network printers. It also enables the administrator to centrally manage all network printing. iPrint provides web-based access to NDPS.

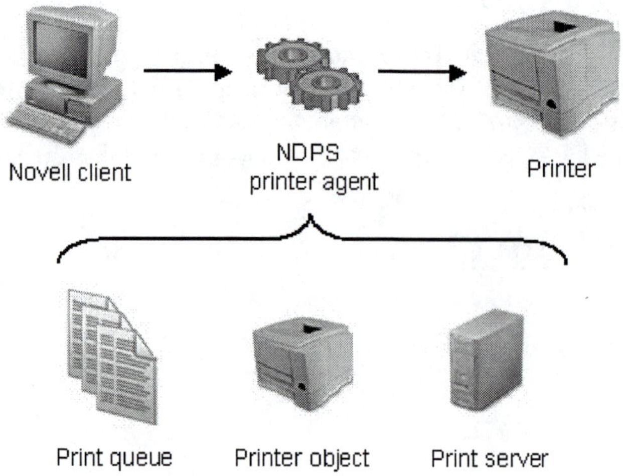

Figure 15-10: *NDPS.*

NDPS and Print Queues

Previously, NetWare administrators had to create, configure, and link print queue, print server, and printer objects separately. NDPS is backward-compatible with these earlier queue-based printing implementations.

Early NetWare Versions

Prior versions of NetWare each had specific capabilities and features.

NetWare Version	Key Features
NetWare 5.x	First version of NetWare to support TCP/IP as the native transport protocol. Integrated DHCP and DNS services. Introduced the NSS and NDPS services, ZENWorks network management software, and the Console One graphical management tool.
NetWare 4.x	First version of NetWare to incorporate NDS. First release of the Novell Client32 client software for Windows desktop systems. Provided improved printing capabilities and printing management. Provided a graphical network-management tool, NetWare Administrator.
NetWare 3.x	Used bindery-based authentication and NLMs. Supported IEEE 802.x standards. Allowed binding to multiple network cards.
NetWare 2.x	Implemented the proprietary NetWare kernel, NetWare Core Protocol (NCP), and provided APIs for developing server applications and drivers to interface with NCP. Different NetWare versions were released for compatibility with Intel 80286 and 80386 processors.
NetWare	The earliest form of NetWare, released in 1983, ran only on proprietary IBM server hardware and network interface cards.

Remote Connectivity in NetWare

Prior versions of NetWare included a remote-access service called NetWare Connect. In NetWare 5, NetWare Connect was bundled with MultiProtocol Router as the Novell Internet Access Server (NIAS). However, the NIAS functionality was removed from NetWare 6, because Novell believes that the majority of Novell NetWare installations rely on dedicated third-party remote access solutions, such as the remote access and VPN appliances available from vendors such as Shiva, Symantic, Citrix, and Nortel.

A remote client running Windows who needs to connect to a NetWare network will need either dial-in or Internet physical connectivity to the remote access device. The client will also need to create and configure a dial-up or VPN connection object and use it to establish the remote connection. The client will then use the Novell Client software to authenticate to the NetWare network in order to access network resources.

ACTIVITY 15-5

Discussing Novell NetWare

Scenario:

In this activity, you will examine various features of Novell NetWare.

---

1. **Select the features of NetWare 6.x.**

   a) Bindery-based authentication

   b) Native TCP/IP networking

   c) Web-based file and printer access

   d) The eDirectory directory service

---

2. **Match the eDirectory tree object to its description.**

___	Tree	a.	The lowest level of the organizational hierarchy.
___	Organization	b.	The top level of the eDirectory hierarchy.
___	User account	c.	An optional container object.
___	Country	d.	A leaf object.
___	Organizational Unit	e.	A required container object.

---

3. **Select the benefits of NSS.**

   a) Up to 64 volumes per server

   b) High-capacity volumes

   c) Journaled file system

   d) Slow mount time

4. **What printing features are incorporated into an NDPS printer agent?**
   a) Print driver and print queue
   b) Print server and print driver
   c) Print server, print queue, and bindery
   d) Print server, print queue, and printer object

5. **Match the version of NetWare to its description.**

___	First version to support TCP/IP as the native protocol.	a.	NetWare 2.x
___	First version to include a graphical management tool.	b.	NetWare 4.x
___	First version to be compatible with standard Intel processors.	c.	NetWare 3.x
___	Last version to support only bindery-based authentication.	d.	NetWare 5.x

6. **Your Novell NetWare network uses a dedicated Symantec VPN gateway appliance to provide secure remote access. Connections are created using L2TP. The gateway appliance is accessed using the public IP address 207.175.43.150. Each user who needs remote access has remote account information they can use to access the gateway. What do you need to configure on the NetWare network to enable remote users to access resources?**

7. **A remote user needs to access the NetWare network. The user has Internet access through a broadband connection to an ISP. What instructions would you provide to a remote user to connect securely to the VPN gateway device?**

8. **How would you instruct the user to access resources on the NetWare network?**

9. **What resources will the remote user be able to access on the NetWare network?**

10. You provide network consulting services on a volunteer basis to a small non-profit agency. The agency relies on legacy networking hardware and software because of the expense of upgrading to current technologies. Their network uses a mix of Novell server versions that all use the IPX/SPX protocol. Clients have intermittent problems connecting to different NetWare servers and have asked you for help resolving the problem. What do you suspect is the cause?

---

11. How can you correct the problem?

---

12. You manage a mixed network that includes both Windows Server 2003 and NetWare 6 servers. Most clients only need access to the Windows servers, but there are a few departments who need to use specialized databases on the NetWare systems. A new user joins the department and needs to connect to a NetWare server from her Windows XP Professional workstation. She configures the properties of her Local Area Connection object to add the CSNW client. She still cannot connect to the NetWare servers. What could be the problem?

---

13. A user from the Sales department is attempting to log on to NetWare and is encountering difficulty. You check his login screen and find the following:

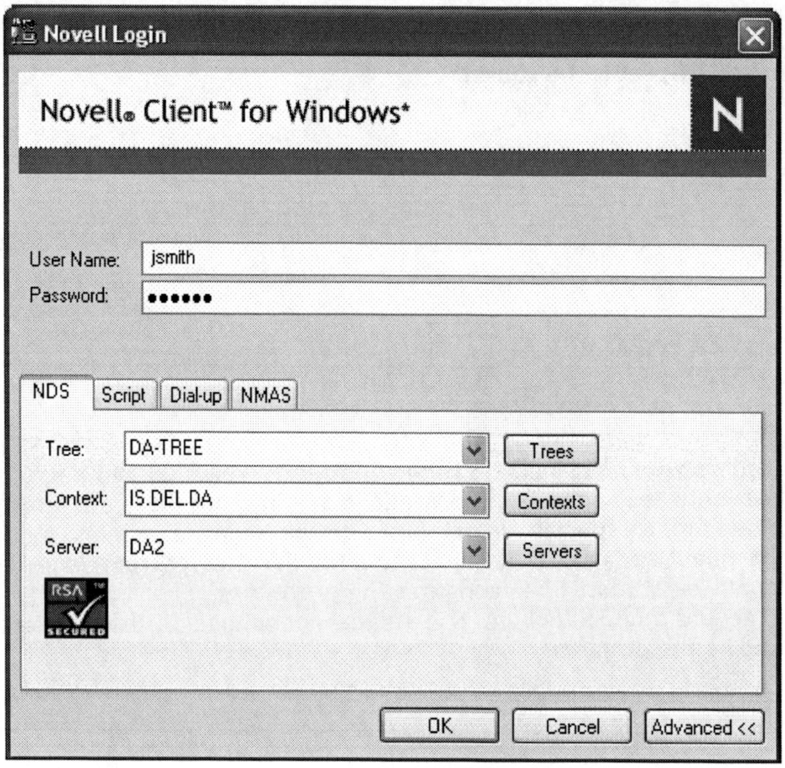

What is the likely problem and how can you correct it?

TOPIC C

UNIX and Linux Operating Systems

UNIX and Linux are two similar, popular categories of operating system software. In this topic you will identify the major functions and releases of UNIX and Linux.

Although Microsoft Windows might be the most commonly deployed operating system and network software in most organizations, there are many situations in which the UNIX operating system and its cousin, Linux, are the platforms of choice. As a networking professional, you can potentially encounter UNIX and Linux systems anywhere in an enterprise, from desktop systems for high-end users and programmers, to high-powered back-end servers that keep the network infrastructure running.

UNIX

UNIX is a trademark for a family of operating systems originally developed at Bell Laboratories (which was part of AT&T) beginning in the late 1960s. At the time, a few programmers wanted to work in an interactive programming environment in which they could take a more modular approach to designing, building, and testing programs. Ken Thompson and Dennis Ritchie, two employees at Bell Labs, designed a new programming environment from the bottom up, that is, a new operating system, which evolved into the UNIX operating system.

AT&T could not sell both computing hardware and software without breaching antitrust laws during the 1970s. Anyone could license the UNIX source code and enthusiastic adopters included large companies, governmental systems, and educational institutions. Researchers at the University of California at Berkeley made extensive contributions to the UNIX operating system as well as to the development of the TCP/IP protocol on UNIX. Berkeley Software Distribution (BSD) is the Berkeley version of UNIX.

Two other groups are key players in the evolution of the UNIX operating system: the SCO Group and the Open Group. The SCO group now owns the UNIX source code and organizations can license the code and make modifications to suit their specific needs. The Open Group owns the UNIX trademark and the group verifies and tests modifications made to the source code. Manufacturers who develop a proprietary version of UNIX must pay a licensing fee to the SCO Group for the source code and pay testing and trademark use fees to the Open Group.

UNIX

Figure 15-11: *UNIX.*

The predecessor to UNIX was an experimental mainframe operating system called Multics, for Multiplexed Information and Computing System. When Bell Labs engineers reconceived this operating system to run on smaller platforms, they renamed it Uniplexed Information and Computing System, and shortened the name to UNICS and eventually UNIX.

Since AT&T developed UNIX, both the trademark and the rights to the software code itself have been sold, first to Novell, Inc., and later to The Open Group and The SCO Group. There is currently a dispute between SCO and Novell as to the ultimate right to license UNIX software.

UNIX and the C Programming Language

Development of the UNIX operating system and the C programming language were intertwined. The UNIX system was originally written in low-level computer assembly language, but was redeveloped in C, a highly portable, high-level programming language. The C language itself was extended and refined to meet the requirements of the UNIX platform. UNIX now consists primarily of C-language instructions, which is a major reason why UNIX is highly favored among software developers.

UNIX Versions

Many different companies and organizations have licensed the UNIX name and technology and marketed their own UNIX versions, leading to a proliferation of different UNIX families, system names, and interfaces. Different hardware manufacturers tend to favor particular versions, or "flavors," of UNIX. The following table lists some of the most important UNIX categories you will encounter.

UNIX Version	Description
Berkeley Software Distribution (BSD) UNIX	Any of a group of UNIX versions that followed the innovations incorporated into UNIX at the University of California at Berkeley. Darwin is the newer version of BSD.
System V Release 4 (SVR4) UNIX	The standard for UNIX systems that follow the AT&T development architecture. It was issued to unify standards and features in competing versions of UNIX, including BSD UNIX, and it is the foundation for current UNIX-based systems.

UNIX Version	Description
Portable Operating System for Computer Environments (POSIX)	A set of IEEE standards for portability of applications from one UNIX environment to another. An application should run identically on any POSIX-compliant platform.
Single UNIX Specification (SUS)	A set of specifications issued by The Open Group (**www.opengroup.org**), setting software standards for operating systems that qualify for the name UNIX.
Advanced Interactive eXecutive (AIX)	Launched by IBM and used on their mainframe computers.
Sun Solaris	Developed by Sun Microsystems.
HP-UX	A flavor of UNIX developed by Hewlett-Packard.

Features of UNIX

Although there are many "flavors" of UNIX, all versions of the UNIX operating system offer a common set of features:

- Source code portability. Code from one system can be used, or "ported," to another UNIX system.
- A Graphical User Interface (GUI) that allows the user to configure the operating system easily. The most popular GUI is the X Window System.
- The ability to use the command-line interface exclusively. In Windows, some configurations must be done via the GUI.
- File and directory permissions to increase security and privacy.
- Ability to run multiple programs (tasks) simultaneously.
- Full multi-tasking capabilities with protected memory. Multiple users can run several programs at the same time without overloading and crashing the system. The UNIX C and Korn shells allow you to manage background processes and to suspend running programs.
- The ability to create scripts using shell commands. Users can string together commands and utilities to accomplish complicated tasks and simplify administrative tasks.
- The ability to use a visual editor such as vi.
- The ability to send a print job to several different printers attached to one machine.
- The ability to assign aliases (abbreviations) for commands used repeatedly.
- Support for a wide range of programming languages.
- Use of the TCP/IP protocol suite and support for all applications used in networking infrastructures (UNIX often is used in back-end server and mainframe systems to support enterprise networks).
- Support for non TCP/IP protocols such as Novell's IPX/SPX.
- Support for many network topologies such as Ethernet, FDDI, Token Ring, and Wireless.

It may seem like a daunting task to master UNIX. There are many different varieties, each supported by a different vendor or group. The power of UNIX lies with the shell, and its extensive command listing and programming options can be intimidating. However, if you master one variety of UNIX, you will be able to learn others fairly quickly.

The UNIX System Architecture

All UNIX systems share a kernel/shell architecture.

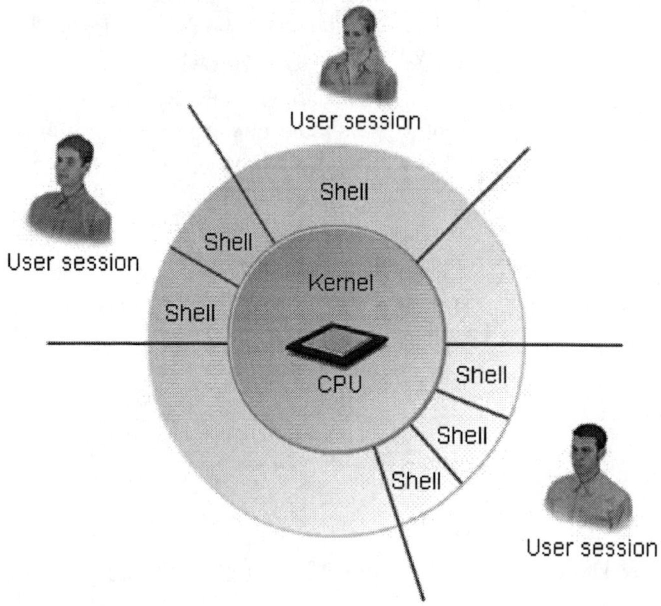

Figure 15-12: *UNIX architecture.*

The UNIX operating system is organized into three layers. The first, or innermost, layer is the kernel, which is the core, or actual operating system. When you turn on your computer, the kernel loads into and resides in memory. It controls functions such as process scheduling, memory management, and file systems. The next layer of the UNIX system is composed of utilities, programs, and commands. Basic commands such as making directories, copying, and removing files are part of a program and not part of the kernel. All UNIX commands and utilities are implemented as programs that have become standardized across most versions of the operating system. The third and outermost layer is the shell, which is the command interpreter that translates typed commands into machine instructions that the system understands and executes.

The UNIX File and Directory Structure

UNIX systems were the first to use a hierarchical file system. This is a highly efficient organizational system in which directories contain files and other directories. Most operating systems, including Windows, now implement a similar hierarchical structure.

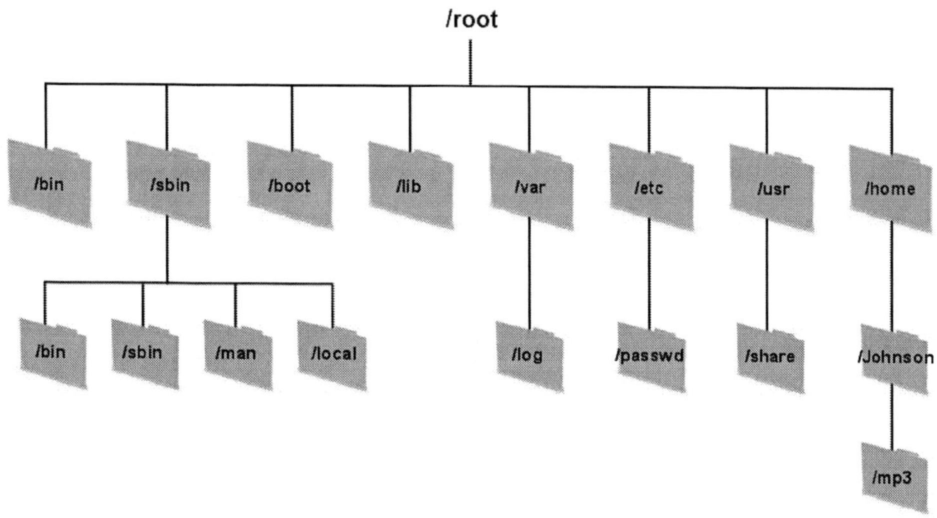

Figure 15-13: *The UNIX directory and file hierarchy.*

On UNIX and UNIX-type systems, the /boot directory contains the kernel and initialization files necessary for booting the system. The /bin directory contains essential system commands and programs (in machine-readable, or "bin"ary format). The directory /sbin contain commands used by the superuser ("root," which is the same as the Administrator in Windows) for system administration. The /lib directory contains system libraries, and these libraries are files that contain program code common to several applications. The /var directory contains administrative files such as system logs and data such as incoming mail. The /etc directory contains essential system-wide configuration files. As a UNIX administrator, you would often edit files in this directory to modify system services and settings. The /usr directory contains many sub-directories. For example, usr/bin contains many of the programs on your UNIX system. The /home directory contains the home directories of all users. This directory functions much the same way as it does in Windows. It is the storage area where a user generally keeps personal files.

UNIX Interfaces

This table lists some of the common UNIX command-line shells and GUIs.

Shell	Description
Bourne shell	One of the first UNIX shells, developed by Steve Bourne at Bell Laboratories. It is available in almost every UNIX system. The default command prompt is the $ character.
C shell	Developed to support C language development environments at Berkeley, and implemented in most BSD UNIX versions. The default command prompt is the % character.
Korn shell	A superset of the Bourne shell that incorporates C shell features. The default command prompt is the $ character.

Shell	Description
X Window system	A popular GUI interface to UNIX systems, originated at MIT in the 1980s. It has since been ported to most modern operating systems.

UNIX Commands

The command line is the main method for interacting with a UNIX or UNIX-type system such as Linux. Although you can use a GUI, the real power and flexibility of the system lies with the command line. This table lists some basic command used in UNIX systems. Note that in UNIX systems, commands, command options, and filenames are all case sensitive.

Command	Description
cat *test*	Displays the contents of the file *test*.
cp	Copies files.
ls	Lists files in a directory and their attributes.
mv	Changes file name or directory location.
rm	Removes files.
In	Creates another link (name) to a file.
chmod	Sets file permissions.
crypt	Encodes or decodes a file with a private key.
gzip, gunzip	Compresses/decompresses a file.
find	Finds files that match certain criteria.
more	Shows text with paging option.
head	Shows the first few lines of a file.
tail	Shows the last few lines of a file.
pico	Screen editor used for modifying text files.
grep	Displays lines that match a pattern (for example, looking for a particular word).
lpr	Sends a file to line printer.
diff	Compares two files and shows the differences.
cd	Changes directory.
mkdir	Creates a new directory.
remdir	Removes an empty directory.
pwd	Shows a full pathway for the current directory.
exit	Logs the user off the machine.
date	Displays the current date and time.
passwd	Changes a user's password.
env	Lists environment variables.
chmod *rights*	Changes user permissions.
startx	Starts the X Window system.

Windows Services for UNIX

Administrators who work in heterogeneous networks need solutions that help them seamlessly share information between UNIX and Windows systems. Microsoft's latest incarnation of Windows Services for UNIX, v 3.5, offers impressive integrative support for UNIX systems. Microsoft's design goals are as follows:

- Seamless sharing of data between Windows and UNIX network protocols.
- Remote control line access to both Windows-based computers and Unix-based computers using existing UNIX practices and policies.
- Heterogeneous network administration, including common directory management and user password synchronization.
- Full UNIX scripting support on Windows, including shells, utilities, hard and soft (symbolic) links, and a single rooted file system.
- High-performance application development and execution environment to permit easy retargeting of key business applications.
- A single, integrated installation process.
- Simplicity of administration and management of SFU components.

Open Standards

Definition:

Open standards are any type of software-development standards that are arrived at cooperatively and are not owned, copyrighted, or maintained by any particular organization or commercial enterprise. Open-standards software can be customized to suit a particular implementation, and tends to be less expensive than proprietary software because it does not need to be licensed from the software owner. However, open-standards software can also change rapidly, and might not have single sources for documentation, utilities, and support.

Example: Open and Proprietary Standards

Standards for Internet technologies such as the TCP/IP network protocol are open because they are established through the cooperative Request for Comments (RFC) system. By contrast, the IPX/SPX network protocol was a proprietary system developed, owned, and licensed by Novell, Inc.

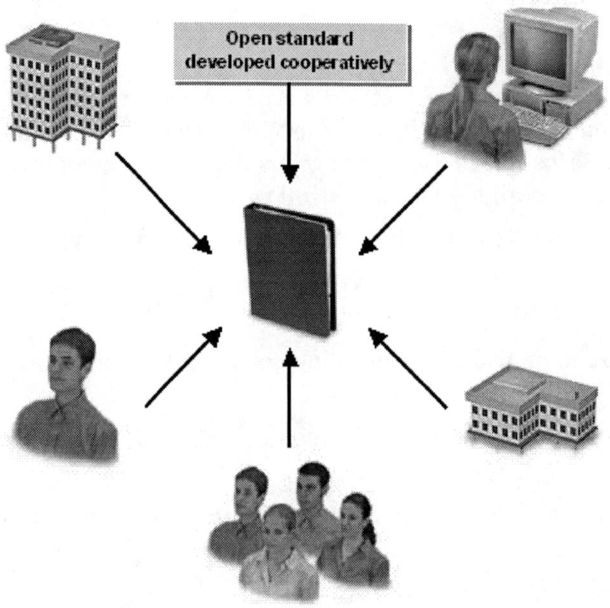

Figure 15-14: *Open standards.*

Proprietary UNIX

Any implementation of the UNIX operating system for which an organization pays a licensing fee to the SCO Group is proprietary UNIX. There are several proprietary versions of UNIX, but the main three are IBM's AIX, which runs on its Power PC computers; Apple MAC OS X, which runs on Intel processors (Apple used to use Power PCs); and Sun Microsystems's Sun Solaris, which runs on their SPARC computer systems. There are several advantages to deploying a proprietary UNIX system, which include:

- Vendor support. If something goes awry with your systems, you have support from a team of professionals who have in-depth knowledge of the operating system.
- Reliability and scalability. Many manufacturers produce both the UNIX software and the hardware on which it runs. This tight integration ensures that the OS and hardware function together seamlessly. Vendors also can customize the operating system so it scales well with an organization.
- Stability. Vendors must assure customers that their proprietary system will be stable. That means that new releases of the OS and patches usually undergo extensive testing by the vendor before they are released to organizations that, in turn, perform their own tests before installation.

Despite the advantages of working with a specific vendor, there are disadvantages to choosing a proprietary UNIX system. Perhaps the greatest disadvantage is that you have no access to the source code so you cannot make modifications to the OS as needs dictate. Open source UNIX offers an alternative to proprietary UNIX.

Open Source UNIX

Open source UNIX is an open standard developed cooperatively by individuals and is not owned, copyrighted, or maintained by any particular organization or commercial enterprise. Open source software may be customized to suit a particular implementation, and tends to be significantly less expensive than proprietary software because there are no licensing fees. Also, you can find freely available UNIX distributions that will run on different hardware platforms: Intel, PowerPC, and Sparc. Furthermore, since you have full access to the source code, you can modify the code. There are, however, some disadvantages to deploying open source software. New releases may not undergo extensive testing to ensure reliability and compatibility and there may not be single sources for documentation, utilities, and support.

Many open source UNIX distributions are freely available for download from the web or you may choose to purchase distributions. If you choose to purchase a distribution, often it will come bundled with an array of utilities and freeware programs. Open source UNIX and UNIX-based software includes GNU (GNU's Not UNIX), BSD, and Linux.

Linux

Linux is an open-standards UNIX derivative originally developed and released by a Finnish computer science student named Linus Torvalds. The Linux source code was posted publicly on a computing newsgroup, and the code was developed and tested cooperatively all over the world. Because the source code is open, it can be downloaded, modified, and re-posted freely, and undergoes continual revisions, upgrades, and improvements. Linux is typically available in a stable release and a development release.

Linux is usually pronounced "LIN-ux." It is a combination of Linus Torvalds's first name (pronounced LEEN-us TOUR-valds) and UNIX.

The official symbol of the Linux operating system is the penguin, which serves as a mascot for the Linux community and as a Linux logo. For information about the Linux penguin, see **www.linux.org/info/logos.html.**

Linux Release Versions

The first version of the Linux kernel that was publicly released was version .02, released in 1991. Since then, the Linux version numbering has been standardized. Linux version numbering consists of three numbers: the major number, the minor number, and the patch level. The major number is incremented when there is a significant change in version. If the minor version number is even, it indicates the stable release; if it is odd, it indicates the development release. The stable release has been tested and verified, while the development release incorporates all current experimental features. The patch level represents a kernel patch, or revision, and is also even if it is stable and odd if it is in development. Linux version 2.6.12 was available as of April 2005, while the 2.7 development release had not yet been initiated. For more information about Linux and its versions, see the Linux home page at **www.linux.org**.

GNU

The original open-source UNIX movement began with a project launched by Richard Stallman in 1983. Stallman wanted to create a complete, free operating system using open-source strategies. The name GNU (which is sometimes pronounced guh-NOO) is a whimsical reverse acronym that stands for "GNU's Not UNIX." The GNU movement inspired Linux development, and GNU utilities and software are often incorporated into Linux. However, the two initiatives are separate. The GNU initiative continues under the auspices of the Free Software Foundation (**www.fsf.org**).

Linux Distributions

Definition:

A *Linux distribution* is a complete Linux implementation, including kernel, shell, applications, utilities, and installation media, that is packaged, distributed, and supported by a software vendor. Some distributions are available free of charge, while others are sold or licensed for a fee. While the Linux source code itself can be freely obtained and modified, many organizations prefer to purchase and implement a complete distribution to ensure consistency, reliability, and the availability of technical support.

Example:

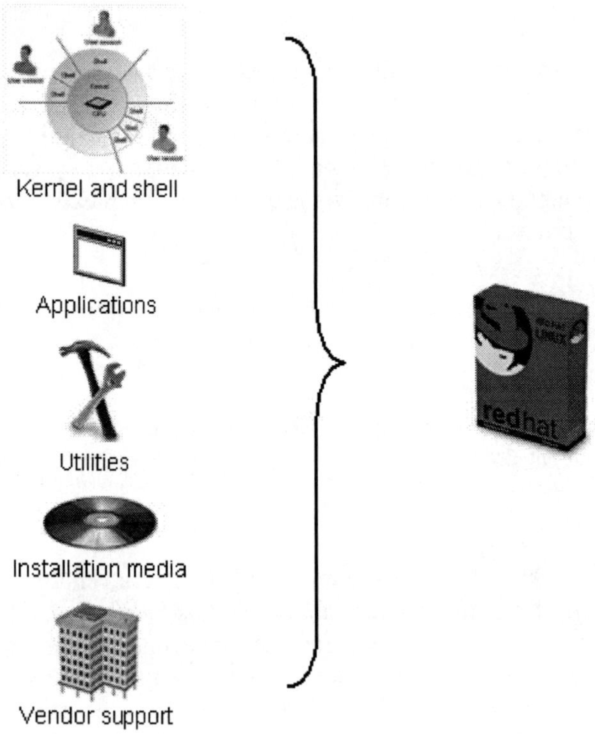

Figure 15-15: *Linux distributions.*

Popular Linux Distributions

The following table lists some popular Linux distributions.

Vendor	Description
Red Hat Linux	A popular USA distribution designed to be easy for new users to install and use.
SuSE	A popular European distribution, now owned by Novell.
Mandrake Linux	A free Red Hat variant optimized for Pentium processors.
Debian	A free distribution assembled by volunteers that contains many utilities and supports many hardware platforms.

Vendor	Description
Gentoo	A source-code distribution designed for professional developers and computer hobbyists.

SuSE is properly pronounced ZOO-zuh, but is often pronounced to rhyme with Suzie.

Linux Server Applications

Linux is a popular server platform for a number of server-based applications.

Server Application	Description
Web servers	Many of the web servers on the Internet today run on Linux platforms. Apache, the world's most popular web server, is an open-source system that runs on Linux and other platforms. Apache supports popular web features such as PERL programming scripts, CGI scripts, and SSL.
Name resolution servers	Linux is a commonly deployed operating system platform for Internet DNS servers. Linux incorporates a popular DNS implementation called Berkeley Internet Name Domain (BIND), which is the de facto DNS standard on the Internet.
File servers	Linux's high performance provides powerful file-server and file-management capabilities. It supports Samba and the Network File System (NFS) for interoperability with other platforms, including Microsoft systems. It provides native support for disk quotas, user-level file security, and support for journaled file systems, which use logging to preserve data in the event of a system crash.
Mail servers	Linux provides support for powerful email server implementations, such as the Sendmail email package.
Database servers	Linux's high performance, reliability, and manageability make it a good choice for a database server platform. There are many Linux-based implementations of the popular Oracle database package.

File Systems in Linux

Linux currently supports several file systems.

File System	Description
Ext2 (second extended file system)	The long-standing standard file system on most Linux implementations. It is not a journaled file system, but is fast and otherwise reliable.
Ext3 (third extended file system)	A alternative to ext2 that incorporates a journaled file system. It is becoming the standard in the latest Linux releases. Without the addition of the journaling component, it functions as an ext2 system.
JFS	An open-source, journaled file system created by IBM.
ReiserFS	A journaled file system created by Hans Reiser. It was the first journaled file system to be included in the kernel (version 2.4.1) and is the default in many distributions. Now sometimes referred to as Reiser3 to distinguish it from Reiser4.
Reiser4	A new version of ReiserFS that incorporates various advanced features and enhancements.
XFS	An open-source, journaled file system developed by SGI (Silicon Graphics, Inc.).

NTFS is a journaled file system that is supported on current versions of Microsoft Windows.

SAMBA

Samba is the Linux implementation of the Server Message Block (SMB) protocol and its successor, the Common Internet File System (CIFS) protocol. As an open source suite, SAMBA allows for interoperability between Linux/UNIX servers and Windows-based clients. Binary packages of SAMBA are included in most Linux and UNIX distributions. Using SAMBA enables the following:

- Mount Microsoft Windows folders onto Linux machines.
- Mount Linux file system segments onto Windows machines as well as other machines running SMB such as MACS and Unix.
- Send print jobs to a printer attached to a Windows machine from a Linux machine.
- Send print jobs to a Linux machine attached to a Windows machine.

Samba consists of two primary programs, smbd and nmbd. These programs are used to implement four CIFS services: file and print services, authentication and authorization services, name resolution services, and service announcements (browsing). A primary reason to implement SAMBA is for file and print services. The SMB daemon, smbd, handles all TCP/IP-based connection services for file and print-based operations. It also controls share and user mode authentication and authorization. Share mode is a simple authentication schema in which an administrator assigns a password to a shared directory or printer and the password is given to everyone who is allowed to use the share. With user authentication, each user has his or her own user name and password and the administrator grants or denies access to network resources on an individual basis.

The nmbd daemon handles all name registration and resolution requests and its main function is network browsing such as Network Basic Input/Output System (NetBIOS) name resolution. NetBIOS enables applications to communicate with machines by a NetBIOS name. NetBIOS requests are sent as Network Control Blocks (NCBs), which include the NetBIOS name of the transmitting machine and the NetBIOS name of the receiving machine. The NCB hands off control to TCP.

The configuration file used to configure SAMBA under Linux usually resides in /etc/smb.conf or /user/local/samba/lib/smb.conf.

Remote Connectivity on UNIX and Linux

SSH is the most common command used to connect to remote UNIX or Linux systems. SSH is client-server software; both machines must have SSH installed and running for it to work. It uses TCP port 22.

To initiate an SSH connection, use the command "ssh". The syntax for this command is `ssh -l [username] [IP address of remote host]` You can also use the verbose mode switch `-v` to display complete ssh command information.

You will need to have a username on each remote server that you log in to. The first time you log in to a remote server, public key information is exchanged, and you are prompted to accept the key so that you can continue. After you enter yes, you are prompted for the user's password to finish logging in. Once your password is accepted, you have access to the remote system. You will be able to enter commands at the same security level your username would have if you were logged in to it locally.

ACTIVITY 15-6

Discussing UNIX and Linux

Scenario:

In this activity, you will discuss various aspects of UNIX and Linux operating systems.

1. **What are the architectural components of a UNIX operating system?**
   - a) The C programming language
   - b) The kernel
   - c) The shell
   - d) The CPU

2. **Which statements about UNIX are true?**
   - a) There are many versions of UNIX from different developers and distributors.
   - b) All versions of UNIX use the same shell, or user interface.
   - c) UNIX versions are proprietary.
   - d) UNIX is a multiuser, multitasking system.

3. **Which statements about Linux are true?**

   a) It was developed as open-source software.

   b) Developers must obtain permission to access and modify the source code.

   c) Development was initiated and managed by Linus Torvalds.

   d) Releases of Linux are unstable.

---

4. **A complete Linux implementation is called:**

   a) The Linux source code.

   b) A stable Linux release.

   c) A Linux version.

   d) A Linux distribution.

---

5. **Match the server software category with the Linux server application.**

___	Database server	a.	Apache
___	File server	b.	Samba and NFS
___	Name resolution server	c.	Oracle for Linux
___	Web server	d.	BIND

---

6. **You have a server running a UNIX operating system connected to a T1 line using TCP/IP as a communication protocol. The server has a public IP address and is accessible from any computer with Internet access. The server is running SSH. You have a home user running a Linux operating system. This user has a connection to the Internet with a local ISP. How will you instruct this user to connect to the remote UNIX server?**

---

7. **After connecting, what access will the user have to the remote system?**

---

8. **You have a server running a UNIX operating system connected to a T1 line using TCP/IP as a communication protocol. The server has a public IP address and is accessible over IP from any computer with Internet access. However, the server's name is not registered under your company's public DNS domain. The server is running SSH. You have a home user running a Linux operating system. This user has a connection to the Internet with a local ISP. The user typed in the following command:"ssh -l jsmith testserver"to connect to the remote UNIX server. The user received the following message: "ssh: testserver: Name or service not known." What is the most likely cause of this problem?**

---

9. You have a server running a Linux operating system connected to a corporate network using TCP/IP as a communication protocol. You have a user running a Linux operating system connected to the same network. The user typed in the following command, "ssh -l jsmith 192.168.1.1", to connect to the UNIX server. The user did not receive any error message, but was not prompted to log in. What is the first step you should take in determining the problem?

---

10. You have a newly installed Linux file sharing server connected to a corporate network. You have a user running a Windows operating system connected to the network that cannot connect and share files. Other Linux systems on the network don't have any problems connecting to the server and sharing files. What is the most likely cause of this problem? How can you correct it?

TOPIC D

Macintosh Networking

In the previous topic, you identified the features and functionality of UNIX and Linux operating systems. Current Macintosh operating systems are based on UNIX and Linux. In this topic, you will identify the network support features of Macintosh operating systems.

For many years, Macintosh computers have been very popular in schools and for graphic design firms, but have never achieved the universal implementation of Windows desktop and server systems. However, the current versions of the Macintosh operating system might be poised to change that, with their acceptance and integration of current networking and operating system standards. Whether you support a small specialized Macintosh implementation, or whether Mac computers are integrated throughout your entire enterprise, it will pay for you to understand the basic features that the current Mac systems have to offer.

The Macintosh Operating System (Mac OS X)

The current version of the Macintosh operating system is Mac OS X. It is a UNIX derivative with a Macintosh GUI called Exposé. It features:

- Fast user switching.
- Integrated Mac, Windows, and UNIX server, file, and printer browsing in the Finder.
- The Safari Web browser.

Mac OS X also includes:

- Native TCP/IP networking.
- Wireless networking using Apple AirPort technology.

- Security features such as file-level encryption, Kerberos authentication, and digital signature support.
- The HFS+ journaled file system.
- Support for a wide variety of hardware devices including USB, FireWire, and Bluetooth interfaces.
- And legacy support for AppleTalk networking, AppleShare IP, and the Apple Filing Protocol.

For more information on Mac OS X, see **www.apple.com/macosx/**

Darwin

The Mac OS X operating system is built on an open-source UNIX implementation called Darwin. It incorporates all standard UNIX commands and utilities, as well as a number of open-source utilities.

Older Macintosh Versions

Older versions of the Macintosh operating system were based on a proprietary system architecture and utilized the proprietary AppleTalk file and print services and LocalTalk network topology. Security was based on user roles, including administrative user accounts, normal user accounts, limited user accounts, and panel user accounts.

Mac OS X Server

The Mac OS X Server product offers:

- Integrated support for Macintosh, Windows, and UNIX clients in workgroups and domains.
- OpenDirectory, Apple Computing's LDAP-based directory service.
- Integrated web server features, including Apache software.
- Integrated email services.
- DNS, DHCP, NAT, and firewall services.
- And the Server Admin centralized administrative interface.

Macintosh Network Security

The Mac OS supports multiple users on a single computer. Mac OS X follows the UNIX security model, in which the root account has total control of the system. For security reasons, this account is disabled by default on Mac OS X, and the default account is set up in the Administrator role. The Administrator can create other accounts and secure them by assigning the UNIX-based read, write, and execute permissions to files and directories.

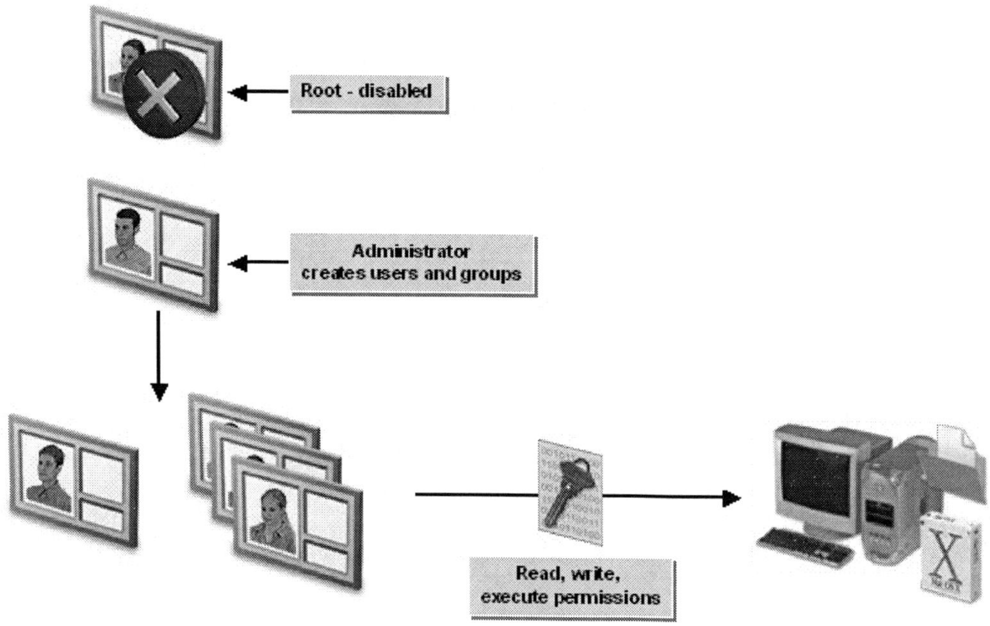

Figure 15-16: *Macintosh network security.*

Mac Account Types

There are two types of accounts on Mac OS X: Administrator and Standard User. The only difference between the two types is that Administrators can install applications, add and remove users, and set system preferences.

Remote Connectivity on Mac OS X Server

As with UNIX and Linux, Mac OS X Server uses SSH for remote connectivity. You must not only have SSH installed on both client and server, but you should also verify that Remote Login is turned on under the server's Sharing Preferences. Because Mac OS X Server is a UNIX-based operating system, the command syntax is exactly the same.

To initiate a remote SSH connection, open the terminal window and enter the command `ssh -l [username] [IP address ]`, where `[username]` is your username on the remote system and `[IP address]` is the IP address of the remote host. You can also use the verbose mode switch `-v` to display complete ssh command information.

After accepting the public key information, you will be prompted for your password. Upon a successful log in, you will have the same access to the remote system that you would have if you were logged in locally.

ACTIVITY 15-7

Discussing Macintosh Networking

Scenario:

In this activity, you will discuss various aspects of Macintosh networking.

1. **The current Macintosh operating system, Mac OS X, is a:**
   a) Windows derivative.
   b) UNIX derivative.
   c) NetWare derivative.
   d) Proprietary implementation.

2. **Which are features of Mac OS X Server?**
   a) An LDAP-based directory service.
   b) A proprietary networking architecture.
   c) An integrated web server.
   d) DNS, DHCP, and firewall services.

3. **Macintosh security is permission-based and provides:**
   a) Read, write, and execute permissions.
   b) Read, write, change, modify, and full control permissions.
   c) Read, write, create, erase, modify, file scan, and access control permissions.

4. **You have a system running Mac OS X Server that is connected to a T1 line using TCP/IP as a communication protocol. The server has a public IP address and is accessible from any computer with Internet access. You intend to use this system to provide network access to remote users. What should you instruct the server administrator to verify before remote users attempt to connect to the server?**

5. **You have a home user running a Mac OS X operating system. This user has a connection to the Internet with a local ISP. How will you instruct this user to connect to the remote Mac OS X Server?**

6. **Once connected, what access will the user have to the remote Mac OS X Server system?**

7. You have a server running Mac OS X Server as the operating system connected to a T1 line using TCP/IP as a communication protocol. The server has a public IP address and is accessible from any computer with Internet access. You have a home user running a Mac OS X operating system. This user has a connection to the Internet with a local ISP. He is typing in the following command: "ssh -l jsmith macserver.myglobalcompany.com:23" and receiving the error message: "Connection Refused: port 23". What is the most likely cause of this problem?

8. You have a newly installed Mac OS X Server connected to a corporate network. It has one LaserJet printer attached to it. All but one department is able to connect to the printer and print files. Unlike the rest of the company, that department has not yet upgraded from Mac OS 8 to Mac OS X. What is the most likely cause of this problem?

9. What are two ways that you can solve the problem?

Lesson 15 Follow-up

In this lesson, you identified the primary network operating systems. Because the network operating system affects basic network functionality as well as administrative procedures, a working understanding of the features and functions of each of the major operating systems will help prepare you for your role as a network professional in a variety of network environments.

1. Describe any experiences you have had with any of the operating systems discussed in this lesson.

2. Based on the information in this lesson and on your own background and experience, which of the operating systems do you think you might prefer to implement and use? Why?

Notes

LESSON 16
Network Troubleshooting

Lesson Time
2 hour(s), 30 minutes

Lesson Objectives:

In this lesson, you will identify major issues, models, tools, and techniques in network troubleshooting.

You will:

- List the components of a troubleshooting model.
- List TCP/IP troubleshooting utilities.
- List major hardware troubleshooting tools.
- List major system monitoring tools.
- Identify the tools and technologies required to perform network baselining.

Lesson 16

Introduction

So far in this course, you have learned about all the different components, theories, technologies, and tasks that a certified network administrator will draw upon to perform job functions. One of the most important of those functions, which requires knowledge about all aspects of the network, is network troubleshooting. In this lesson, you will identify major issues, models, tools, and techniques in network troubleshooting.

Network problems can arise from a variety of sources outside your control. As a network professional, your users, your managers, and your colleagues will all look to you to identify and resolve those problems efficiently. To do that, you'll need a strong fundamental understanding of the tools and processes involved in network troubleshooting.

This lesson covers the following CompTIA Network+ (2005) certification objectives:

- Topic A:
  - Objective 4.5: Given a troubleshooting scenario between a client and the following server environments, identify the cause of a stated problem: UNIX/Linux/Mac OS X Server, NetWare, Windows, and AppleShare IP (Internet Protocol).
  - Objective 4.7: Given a troubleshooting scenario involving a network with a particular physical topology (for example, bus, star, mesh, or ring) and including a network diagram, identify the network area affected and the cause of the stated failure.
  - Objective 4.8: Given a network troubleshooting scenario involving a wired or wireless infrastructure problem, identify the cause of the stated problem (for example, bad media, interference, network hardware, or environment).
  - Objective 4.9: Given a network problem scenario, select an appropriate course of action based on a logical troubleshooting strategy. This strategy can include the following steps: 1. Identify the symptoms and potential causes; 2. Identify the affected area; 3. Establish what has changed; 4. Select the most probable cause; 5. Implement an action plan and solution, including potential effects; 6. Test the result; 7. Identify the results and effects of the solution; and 8. Document the solution and process.
- Topic B:
  - Objective 4.1: Given a troubleshooting scenario, select the appropriate network utility from the following: Tracert (Traceroute), Ping, Arp, Netstat, Nbtstat, Ipconfig/Ifconfig, Winipcfg, and Nslookup/Dig.
  - Objective 4.2: Given output from a network diagnostic utility (for example, those utilities listed in objective 4.1), identify the utility and interpret the output.
  - Objective 4.6: Given a scenario, determine the impact of modifying, adding, or removing network services, such as DHCP (Dynamic Host Configuration Protocol), DNS (Domain Name Service), and WINS (Windows Internet Name Service), for network resources and users.
  - Objective 4.7: Given a troubleshooting scenario involving a network with a particular physical topology (for example, bus, star, mesh, or ring) and including a network diagram, identify the network area affected and the cause of the stated failure.
  - Objective 4.8: Given a network troubleshooting scenario involving a wired or wireless infrastructure problem, identify the cause of the stated problem (for example, bad media, interference, network hardware, or environment).
- Topic C:
  - Objective 3.3: Identify the appropriate tool for a given wiring task (for example, wire crimper, media tester/certifier, punch down tool, or tone generator).

— Objective 4.3: Given a network scenario, interpret visual indicators, such as link LEDs (Light Emitting Diodes) and collision LEDs (Light Emitting Diodes), to determine the nature of a stated problem.

TOPIC A

Troubleshooting Models

In this lesson, you will troubleshoot network problems. The first step in learning to troubleshoot is to select a troubleshooting model. In this topic, you will list the components of a troubleshooting model.

Because troubleshooting network problems is such a big part of a network administrator's or network engineer's job, you should always use some sort of systematic approach to problem-solving. Troubleshooting models provide you with processes on which to base your troubleshooting techniques. Learning and using an effective troubleshooting model can help you resolve problems efficiently and painlessly.

Troubleshooting

Troubleshooting is the recognition, diagnosis, and resolution of problems. Troubleshooting begins with the identification of a problem, and does not end until services have been restored and the problem no longer adversely affects users. Troubleshooting can take many forms, but all approaches have the same goal: solving a problem efficiently with a minimal interruption of service.

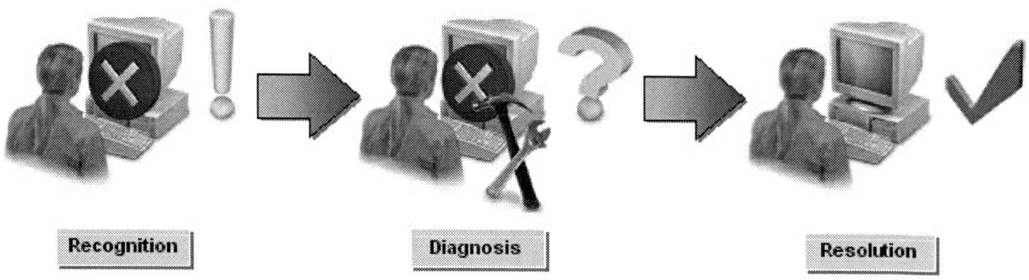

Figure 16-1: *Troubleshooting.*

CompTIA Network+ Exam Objectives

An Appendix is available to assist you in mapping CompTIA Network+ exam objectives to the course content. You can download the Appendix at the end of this lesson.

Troubleshooting Models

Definition:

A *troubleshooting model* is any standardized step-by-step approach to the troubleshooting process. The model serves as a framework for correcting a problem efficiently without introducing further problems or making unnecessary modifications to the system. Models can vary in the sequence, number, and name of the steps, but all models have the same goal: to move in a methodical and repeatable manner through the troubleshooting process.

Example:

Figure 16-2: *Troubleshooting models.*

The CompTIA Network+ Troubleshooting Model

The CompTIA Network+ troubleshooting model has eight steps:

1. Establishing the symptoms and potential causes.
2. Identifying the affected area.
3. Establishing what has changed.
4. Selecting the most probable cause.
5. Implementing an action plan and solution, including recognizing potential effects.
6. Testing the result.
7. Identifying the results and effects of the solution.
8. Documenting the solution and process.

Establishing the Symptoms and Potential Causes

To establish the symptoms and potential causes, start by gathering as much information as you can.

- Look for error messages on screens or in log files.
- Ask the user to describe what happened. Ask open-ended questions instead of yes/no questions to get as much information as you can.

Re-create the problem. A repeatable problem is easier to solve than an intermittent one.

- Have the user try the procedure again, recording all actions taken and all results received. Verify that the procedure is correct.
- Try to perform the task yourself at the user's workstation and at your workstation.
- Have another user try the task at the user's workstation and on an equivalent workstation.

As you gather information, make a list of causes that could produce the same symptoms.

Example: Establishing Symptoms for a Logon Problem

For instance, if a user can't log on to the network, have him try again—but don't just ask if the logon fails, ask him to describe exactly what happens and what he sees. Think about possible causes: A user who suddenly can't log on could indicate a problem with a network cable or adapter, a local DHCP server, the local network connection, or the authentication server.

Identifying the Affected Area

Determine if the problem is limited to one workstation, several workstations, one server, one segment, or the entire network. If only one person is experiencing a certain problem, the problem is most likely at the workstation. If groups of users are affected, the problem might lie at a part of the network that the users all have in common, such as a particular software application or database, a server, the network segment, or the network configuration.

Example: Identifying the Affected Area for a Logon Problem

For instance, a logon problem can affect one user or many users.

- When one user can't log on to the network, try logging on as that user from another workstation in the same group of users. If logon is successful, start by checking the workstation's NIC and cabling, and then move on to more detailed workstation troubleshooting.
- When several users can't log on, find out what they have in common. If all the affected users use the same server, verify that the server is up and running smoothly, and check the user connections and security levels. If several network segments appear to be affected, check for network address conflicts. If all users are having problems, check any components (such as servers, routers, and hubs) that all users access. Also remember to check any WAN connections by verifying that stations on both sides of the WAN link can communicate; if they can't, you'll need to check the WAN hardware along with other devices between the sending and receiving stations.

Establishing What Has Changed

To establish what has changed, ask diagnostic questions such as:

- Could you do this task before? If this is a new task, perhaps the user needs different system permissions, or additional hardware or software.
- If you could do it before, when did you first notice that you couldn't do it anymore? Try to discover what happened immediately before the problem arose, or at least pinpoint the time, since the source of the problem might be related to other changes elsewhere on the network.
- What's changed since the last time you were able to do this task? Users can give you information about events that might affect their local systems. You can help them with leading questions such as, "Did someone add something to the computer?" or, "Did you do something differently this time?" Be sure not to be judgmental or imply that the user is to blame; it will be harder for the user to report their conditions accurately if you do so.

Example: Establishing What Has Changed for a Logon Problem

For example, if a user can't log on, ask if she is aware of anything that has changed since the last time she could log on, even if it is as simple as restarting the computer for that morning's work.

Selecting the Most Probable Cause

To select the most probable cause, use a systematic approach. Eliminate possible causes, starting with the most obvious and simplest one and working back through other causes. Don't overlook straightforward and simple corrections that can fix a range of problems and don't cost much time or effort to try. You might find that you can resolve the issue on the spot.

Example: Selecting the Most Probable Cause for a Connectivity Problem

If a user has lost Internet connectivity, check to make sure the network cable is plugged in and that the user's IP configuration is correct before you check the connection to your ISP.

Implementing an Action Plan and Solution

Once you have determined the cause, if you find that you cannot correct it immediately, you should create an action plan before you start making changes. You should also make sure that you can put the system back to the condition it was in before the problem occurred. Users will not be happy if you leave the system in a worse state than it was in before you started troubleshooting. You need to think about how the action plan will affect the user or other aspects of the network. If you think ahead, you can help ensure that productivity doesn't suffer and that downtime is minimized. Implement the action plan step by step to fix the problem. If you make multiple changes at once, you will be unable to verify exactly which adjustment was correct.

Example: Implementing an Action Plan for a Workstation Problem

For example, if you are taking a user's workstation to be rebuilt, think about how this might affect their productivity in the interim. You might need to provide a loaner workstation to a user whose machine needs to be rebuilt, and you might need to transfer user data to a safe location while you work on the old system.

Testing the Result

Test the solution. Make sure that the solution that you've implemented actually solved the problem and didn't cause any new ones. Use several options and situations to conduct your tests. For instance, try the task yourself, and then have the user try the task while you observe the process, or test the workstation both before and after it's connected to the network. Sometimes, you'll need to test over time to ensure that your solution is the correct one. Remember to verify that the user agrees that the problem is solved before you proceed.

Identifying the Results and Effects

Even if the problem is solved from the user's perspective, the solution you implemented might have effects elsewhere on the local system or on the network. Think about those potential effects and test for them before you close out the issue.

Example: Identifying the Results for a Software Problem

If you reinstall a software application, you might find that the newly installed application makes changes that affect other applications, such as changing file associations on the system. You should have identified this potential effect before reinstalling; afterward, make sure the associations for those other applications are functioning the way the user desires.

Documenting the Solution and Process

Document the problem and process you used to arrive at the solution. Maintain the records as part of your overall network documentation plan. Not only will this provide you with an ever-growing database of information specific to your network, but it will also be valuable reference material for use in future troubleshooting instances—especially if the problem is specific to the organization. You might even want to create a troubleshooting template so that you can be sure that necessary information is included in all trouble reports, and that all reports are consistent, no matter which support person completes them.

Troubleshooting Documentation

Some of the things you might want to include in a troubleshooting documentation template are:

- A description of the initial trouble call, including date, time, who's experiencing the problem, and who's reporting the problem.
- A description of the conditions surrounding the problem, including the type of computer, the type of NIC, any peripherals, the desktop operating system and version, the network operating system and version, the version of any applications mentioned in the problem report, and whether or not the user was logged on when the problem occurred.
- Whether or not you could reproduce the problem consistently.
- The possible cause or causes you isolated.
- The exact issue you identified.
- The correction or corrections you formulated.
- The results of implementing each correction you tried.
- The results of testing the solution.
- Any external resources you used, such as vendor documentation, addresses for vendor and other support websites, names and phone numbers for support personnel, and names and phone numbers for third-party service providers.

ACTIVITY 16-1

Discussing Troubleshooting Models

Scenario:

In this activity, you will discuss elements of the Network+ troubleshooting model.

1. **Put the first four steps of the Network+ troubleshooting model in the correct order.**

   Identifying the affected area.

   Establishing the symptoms and potential causes.

   Selecting the most probable cause.

   Establishing what has changed.

2. **Put the last four steps of the Network+ troubleshooting model in the correct order.**

   Implementing an action plan and solution, including recognizing potential effects.

   Testing the result.

   Identifying the results and effects of the solution.

   Documenting the solution and process.

3. **Users on the third floor can't connect to the Internet, but they can log on to the local NetWare network. What should you check first?**

   a) Router configuration tables.

   b) If viruses exist.

   c) If the power cable to the hub is connected.

   d) If users on other floors are having similar problems.

4. **You reinstall the operating system for a user who is having problems. Later, the user complains that she cannot find her familiar desktop shortcuts. What step of the troubleshooting model did you omit?**

   a) Documenting the solution and the process.

   b) Identifying the results and effects of the solution.

   c) Establishing what has changed.

   d) Establishing the symptoms and potential causes.

5. **Which techniques will help you identify the affected area?**

   a) Ask the user open-ended questions about the problem.

   b) Try to replicate the problem on another workstation nearby.

   c) Make a list of problems that can all cause the same symptoms.

   d) Find out if users in other parts of the building are having the same problem.

6. A user calls to say that his computer won't boot. He mentions that everything was fine until a brief power outage on his floor. What stage of the troubleshooting model can this information help you with most directly?

   a) Selecting the most probable cause.

   b) Implementing an action plan and solution, including recognizing potential effects.

   c) Documenting the solution and process.

   d) Establishing what has changed.

---

7. A user calls the help desk and says he can't open a file. You are not able to visit the user's workstation because he is located in a different building. What are the first steps you need to take to be able to diagnose the problem?

---

8. What are some of the questions you should ask?

---

9. Through your diagnostic questions, you establish that the file is a word-processing document stored on a network file server. The user last accessed the file three months ago; he has since been out of the office on an executive loan program to a local charity. By reviewing the activity logs on the file server, you find that there is a bi-monthly cleanup routine that automatically backs up and removes user data files that have not been accessed since the last cleanup date. The backups are stored in an offsite facility for one year. Given this information, what is your action plan, how will you implement it, and what potential side effects of the plan do you need to consider?

---

10. What steps should you take to test, verify, and document the solution?

TOPIC B

TCP/IP Troubleshooting Utilities

In the previous topic, you learned how to apply a structured troubleshooting model. To implement your model, you will utilize various troubleshooting tools. In this topic, you will identify the functions of TCP/IP troubleshooting utilities.

It doesn't pay to try to drive in a nail with a screwdriver, or loosen a bolt with a hammer. Knowing the right tool for the right job is an important part of correcting any problem. As a networking professional, you'll need to be familiar with the uses of several categories of tools. With TCP/IP being the most commonly implemented network protocol today, the TCP/IP utility suite will often be the first place you'll turn to start figuring out a problem and fixing it.

Troubleshooting with IP Configuration Utilities

With TCP/IP networking problems, a common first step is to verify that the host's IP addressing information is correct. Use the appropriate utility for your system (Ipconfig, Ifconfig, or Winipcfg) to determine if the host is configured for static or dynamic IP addressing and if it has a valid address. If the host is getting an incorrect dynamic IP address and you believe there is a valid DHCP server, you can use the utility to release and renew the address.

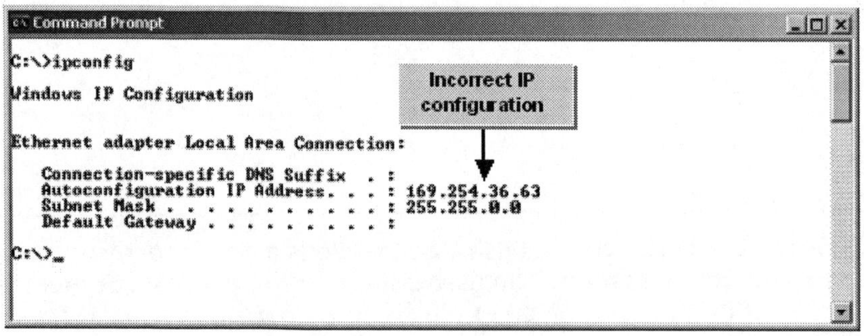

Figure 16-3: *Troubleshooting IP configuration.*

Troubleshooting with Ping

Use the Ping utility as an initial step in diagnosing general connectivity problems.

- Ping a specific system to verify that it is running and on the network.
- Ping by IP address instead of host name to determine if a problem is related to name resolution.
- Localize the problem:
    1. Ping the local loopback address.
    2. Ping the system's own IP address.
    3. Ping the address of the default gateway.
    4. Ping the address of a remote host.

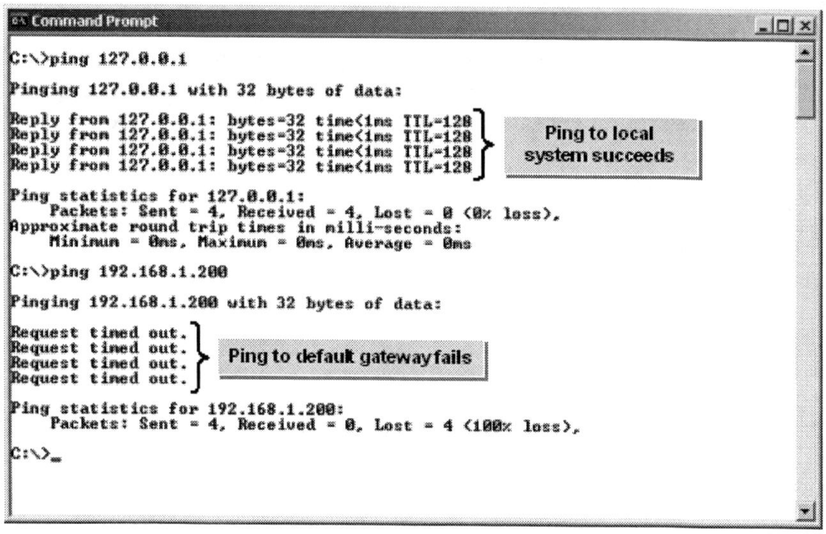

Figure 16-4: *Troubleshooting with Ping.*

Troubleshooting with Tracert

If you cannot connect to a particular remote host, you can use Tracert to determine where the communication fails. Issue a tracert command to the server to see how far the trace gets before receiving an error message. Using the IP address of the last successful connection, you'll know where to begin troubleshooting the problem, and potentially even pinpoint a specific failed device.

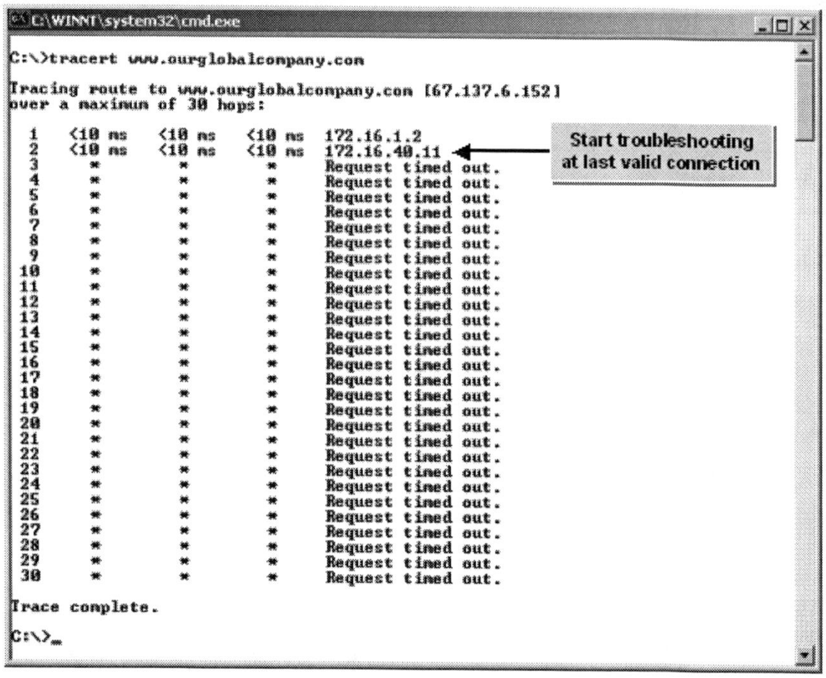

Figure 16-5: *Troubleshooting with Tracert.*

Troubleshooting with Arp

Arp can be used both to help troubleshoot duplicate IP address problems and to diagnose why a workstation can't connect to a specific host. If a host is reachable from one workstation but not from another, you can use the arp command on both workstations to display the current entries in the ARP table. If the MAC address on the problem workstation does not match the correct MAC address, you can use Arp to delete the incorrect entry.

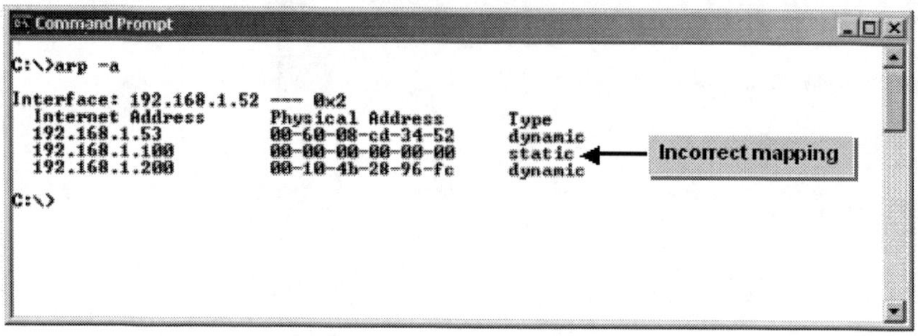

Figure 16-6: *Troubleshooting with Arp.*

Troubleshooting with Telnet

Telnet is usually used to issue commands in a terminal session to a remote host. However, you can also use this utility to help you troubleshoot problems. If upper-level OSI protocols or applications aren't working, you can sometimes telnet into a system and send commands directly to a server process.

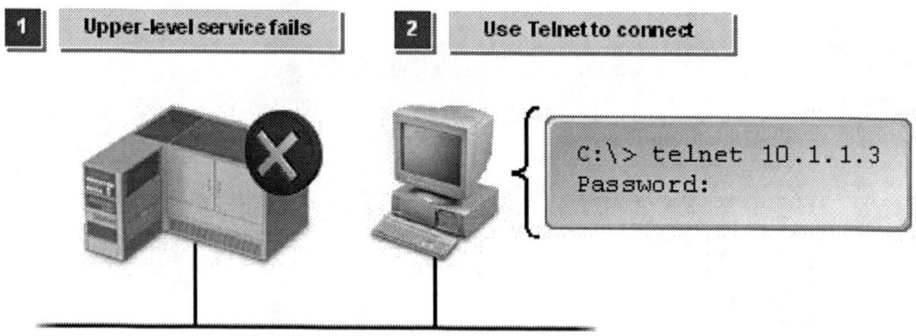

Figure 16-7: *Troubleshooting with Telnet.*

Troubleshooting with Nbtstat

Nbtstat can be very helpful in identifying problems that are specific to Windows computers that use NetBIOS naming. Nbtstat was developed specifically as a NetBIOS diagnostic tool, and it displays NetBIOS information that isn't available with other TCP/IP utilities. In particular, by examining the hidden 16th byte in registered NetBIOS names, you can verify that the correct services are running on a given system.

For a complete list of the 16th-byte NetBIOS service codes, see **support.microsoft.com/default.aspx?scid=kb;en-us;163409**

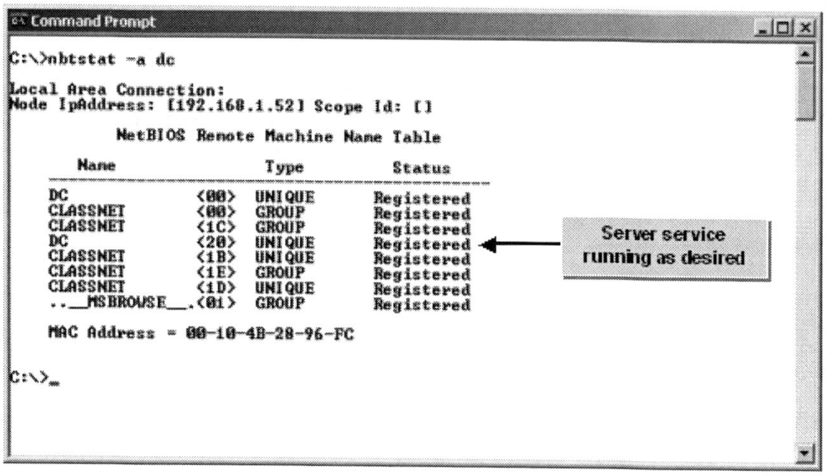

Figure 16-8: *Troubleshooting with Nbtstat.*

Troubleshooting with Netstat

Netstat is a versatile troubleshooting tool that can serve several functions:

- You can use Netstat to find out if a TCP/IP-based program, such as SMTP or FTP, is listening on the expected port. If not, the system might need to be restarted.
- You can check statistics to see if the connection is good. If there is a bad connection, this usually means there are no bytes in the send or receive queues.
- You can use statistics to check network adapter error counts. If the error count is high, it could be a problem with the card, or could indicate generally high network traffic.
- You can also use Netstat to display routing tables and check for network routing problems.

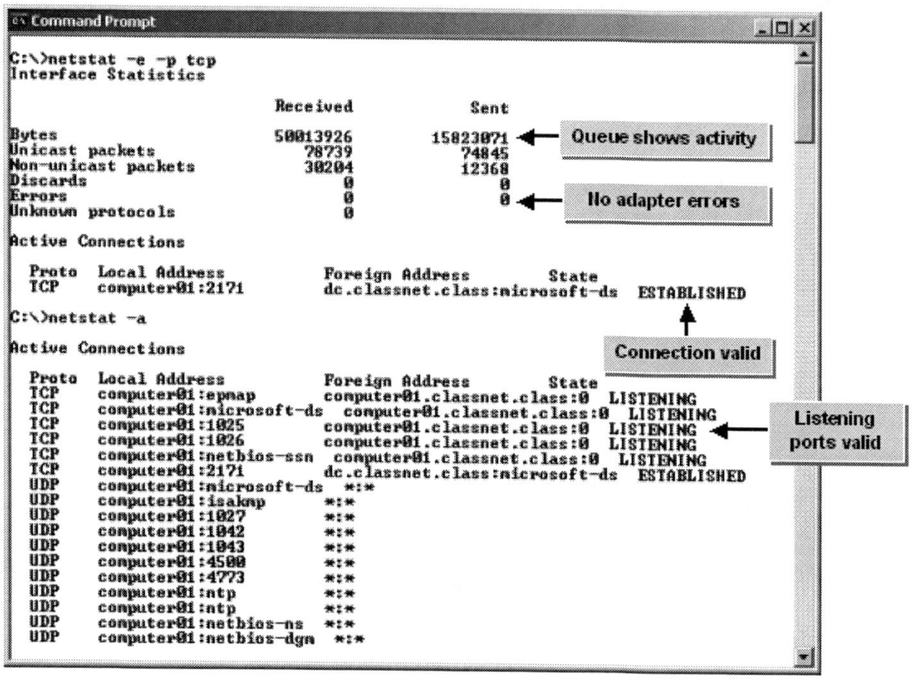

Figure 16-9: *Troubleshooting with Netstat.*

Troubleshooting with FTP

FTP can assist you in troubleshooting because it is a common way to access vendor resource sites from which you can download patches and other support information. You can connect to FTP sites from most browsers or by using the command-line FTP tool. However, if you use FTP frequently to manage large downloads, it might be most efficient to install a dedicated graphical FTP software package.

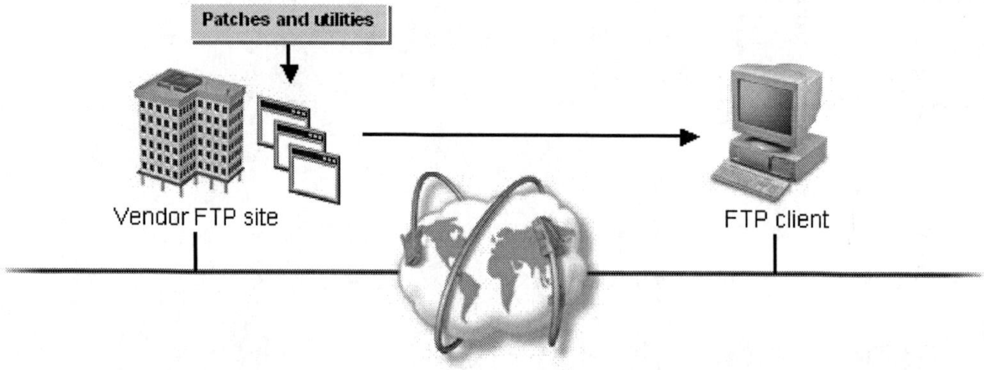

Figure 16-10: *Troubleshooting with FTP.*

Tip: Automating FTP

You can help automate the FTP download process by creating a text file containing the FTP commands to be issued, and then calling this on a Windows system with the `ftp -s` option. For example, if you want to connect to the ftp.novell.com site, and download the current patch for NetWare to a directory on your workstation, you could create the file NWDL.TXT with the appropriate FTP commands. When you want to download the file, enter `ftp -s NWDL.TXT` and it will use those FTP commands.

Troubleshooting with Nslookup

You can use Nslookup to display information about DNS servers. You can verify that:

- The system is configured with the correct DNS server.
- The server is responding to requests.
- The entries on the server are correct.
- The DNS server can communicate with other servers in the DNS hierarchy to resolve names.

Figure 16-11: *Troubleshooting with Nslookup.*

Troubleshooting with the Dig Utility

Domain Internet Groper (Dig) is a UNIX/Linux command-line tool that can be used to display name server information. Some experts consider it to be generally easier to use than Nslookup, and that it supports more flexible queries and is easier to include in command scripts. It is included with the BIND version of DNS, and can be downloaded from many UNIX and Linux resource sites on the Internet.

ACTIVITY 16-2

Troubleshooting with TCP/IP Utilities

There is a simulated version of this activity available on the CD-ROM that shipped with this course. You can run this simulation on any Windows computer to review the activity after class, or as an alternative to performing the activity as a group in class. The activity simulation can be launched either directly from the CD-ROM by clicking the Interactives link and navigating to the appropriate one, or from the installed data file location by opening the C:\Data\Simulations\Lesson#\Activity# folder and double-clicking the executable (.exe) file.

Data Files:

- C:\Data\Problem.bat
- C:\Data\Problem2.bat

Setup:

Your instructor might need to introduce network problems before each diagnostic step in the exercise. Check with your instructor before proceeding with each diagnostic step.

Scenario:

You are working at the help desk for your company's TCP/IP network. Various users report problems that you must diagnose and solve.

What You Do	How You Do It
1. **A user reports that he cannot connect to the dc.classnet.class server from his workstation. Diagnose the problem.**	a. **Open a command prompt window.** b. To reproduce the problem, **enter *ping dc.classnet.class*** c. **Enter *ipconfig***

2. **What is the problem?**

a) The computer is configured with an incorrect static address.

b) The computer has not initialized TCP/IP.

c) The system has an APIPA address.

d) The computer's DNS server information is incorrect.

3. **Correct the problem.**	a. At the command prompt, **enter** ***ipconfig /renew*** b. To verify the address assignment, **enter** ***ipconfig*** c. To verify connectivity, **enter** ***ping dc.classnet.class*** d. **Close the command prompt window.**
4. **Run the problem.bat file to introduce another problem.**	a. **Choose Start→Run.** b. In the Run text box, **type** ***c:\data\problem.bat*** **and click OK.**
5. **A user reports that she cannot connect to the dc.classnet.class server. Diagnose the problem.**	a. **Open a command prompt window.** b. To reproduce the problem, **enter** ***ping dc.classnet.class*** c. **Enter** ***ipconfig*** d. The IP configuration is correct. **Enter** ***arp -a***

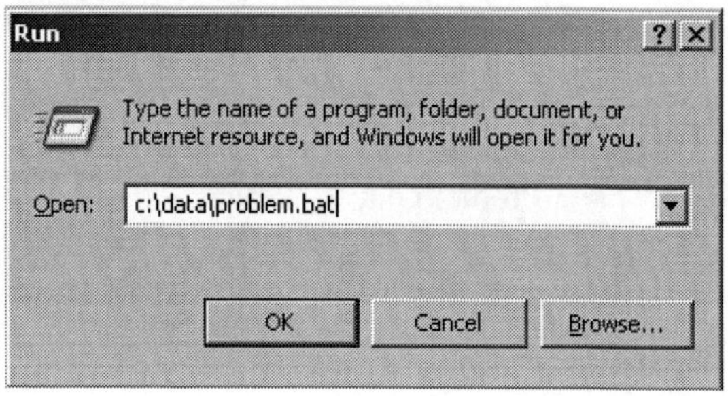

6. **What is the problem?**

   a) The ARP cache has an incorrect static entry.

   b) The computer has an incorrect static IP address.

   c) The computer has an APIPA address.

   d) The computer has incorrect DNS server information.

	Task		Steps
7.	Correct the problem.	a.	In the command prompt window, **enter** ***arp -d 192.168.1.200***
		b.	To verify connectivity, **enter** ***ping dc.classnet.class***
		c.	To verify the ARP cache, **enter** ***arp -a***
		d.	**Close the command prompt window.**
8.	Run the problem2.bat file to introduce another problem.	a.	**Choose Start→Run.**
		b.	In the Run text box, **type** ***c:\data\problem2.bat*** **and click OK.**
9.	A user reports that she cannot connect to computers or websites by FQDN. Diagnose the problem.	a.	**Open a command prompt window.**
		b.	To reproduce the problem, **enter** ***ping dc.classnet.class***
		c.	**Enter** ***ipconfig***
		d.	The IP address is correct. **Enter** ***arp -a***
		e.	The ARP cache is correct. **Enter** ***nslookup***
		f.	The connection to the DNS server fails. **Enter** ***exit*** to exit Nslookup.
		g.	**Enter** ***ipconfig /all***

10. **What is the problem?**

a) The computer is configured with an incorrect static IP address.

b) The computer has an incorrect DNS server address.

c) The computer has an APIPA IP address.

d) There is an incorrect static entry in the ARP cache.

11. **Correct the problem.**
    a. At the command prompt, **enter *ipconfig /release***
    b. **Enter *ipconfig /renew***
    c. To verify the address assignment, **enter *ipconfig /all***
    d. To verify that you can contact the DNS server, **enter *nslookup***
    e. **Enter *exit*** to exit Nslookup.
    f. To verify connectivity to the host, **enter *ping dc.classnet.class***
    g. **Close the command prompt window.**

ACTIVITY 16-3

Discussing TCP/IP Troubleshooting Utilities

Scenario:

In this activity, you will discuss which TCP/IP troubleshooting utilities you might use in a number of network problem scenarios.

1. **1) You have installed a Linux system in your test lab so that application developers can test new software. Because the lab is isolated from the main network, there is no DHCP service running. A software engineer has loaded a network application on the system, but cannot connect to it from a client. She has already tried to ping the Linux system by name and IP address. What should you check next and why?**

2. **In the same lab, you are testing a shared Windows application that is installed on a Windows Server 2003 computer. You want to verify that it will run on a number of Windows clients. You connect to the server successfully from a Windows XP system, but when you try to connect from a Windows 98 client, the connection fails. What should you check first and why?**

3. A user is having trouble connecting to your company's intranet site (internal.everythingforcoffee.com), which is on your company's private network inside your firewall. She is not having general Internet connectivity problems. What is the best first step to take to try to narrow down the possible problem?

---

4. You can connect to the intranet site with no difficulty. You check your IP configuration against the user's and find that you are configured with different DNS server addresses. You do not have DNS administrative utilities installed on your workstation. What can you do to diagnose the DNS problem?

---

5. You had to reboot a DHCP server earlier in the day. A Windows 98 user calls to say that she has no network connectivity at all. What can you do to correct the problem?

---

6. You provide consulting services for a small non-profit agency that is using legacy Windows 98 systems configured in a workgroup. To optimize performance on the older systems, you have disabled unnecessary services on some of the machines. A user has just installed a printer and wants to share it so that his system can function as a print server for the rest of the workgroup. He is unable to share the printer. What can you do to help?

---

7. You are the IT operations manager for an Internet service provider (ISP). Your IT operations center includes numerous clustered web servers as well as clustered Linux systems running DNS BIND to provide your clients with Internet name resolutions. You would like to automate some of your diagnostic and management tasks by running scripts on the DNS BIND servers. What can you do?

---

8. Your test environment includes a number of different clients, including Windows systems, Linux systems, and Mac OS X clients. You would like to be able to examine the network performance of each system while you run a batch file to generate network load. What utility can you use?

---

9. You are experiencing a number of dropped packets and slow response time on your routed private network. You suspect there may be a routing loop and you would like to look more closely at packet transmissions through the network. How can you examine the path of the transmissions?

10. Servers on your internal network are manually configured with IP addresses in the range 192.168.20.200 through 192.168.20.225. You are trying to open an ftp session with the ftp server that is located on your internal network at 192.168.20.218. Although you can ping the system by IP address, sometimes you can connect over FTP and sometimes you cannot. You suspect there may be two hosts configured with duplicate addresses. How can you verify which physical host system is using the FTP server's address?

TOPIC C

Hardware Troubleshooting Tools

In the previous topic, you identified the functions of TCP/IP troubleshooting utilities. Another common category of troubleshooting utilities is hardware troubleshooting tools. In this topic, you will identify the functions of various hardware troubleshooting tools.

As a network technician, you might not pick up a screwdriver or a pair of pliers as often as a cable installer or an electrician does, but there are still cases where hardware and hand tools come in handy. You should know which hardware tools you will need to use in your job, and when and how to use them.

Network Technician's Hand Tools

In the computer industry, a good toolbox includes these basic hand tools:

- A variety of screwdrivers and spare screws.
- Long-nose pliers.
- Small diagonal cutting pliers.
- A small adjustable wrench.
- A variety of wrenches or nut drivers.
- A small AA or AAA flashlight.

- And an anti-static wrist strap with clip.

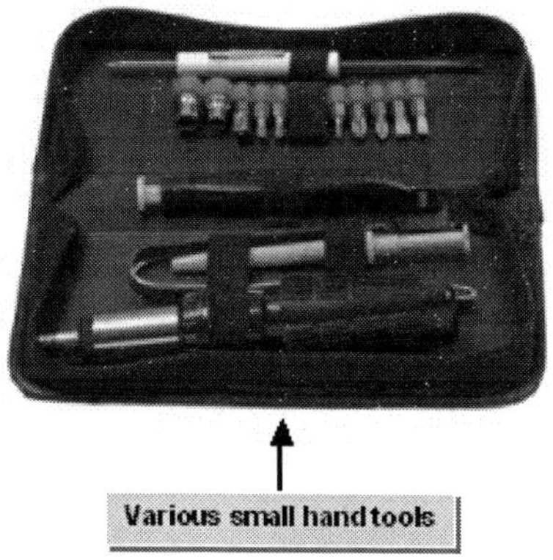

Figure 16-12: *Network technician's hand tools.*

Wrench and Screwdriver Types

Depending on the equipment in your organization, your toolbox should have a variety of wrenches and screwdrivers. You should include #1, #2, and #3 Philips screwdrivers; 1/4″ and 3/16″ flat blade screwdrivers; and T-15 and T-20 Torx screwdrivers, as well as any specialty security screwdrivers you need for your equipment. You should also include 3/16″, 1/4″, and 5/16″ wrenches or nut drivers.

Security Screwdriver Sets

Many companies prefer to assemble their computers with security screws, which commonly require a specialty screwdriver not available at every hardware store. You can find this type of screwdriver at specialty tool stores and electronics suppliers. There are a few different types of security screws on the market—some have a slip collar on the outside to prevent unscrewing with anything like a wrench or pliers, and others simply have a post in the middle of a Torx or Allen socket-head screw that prevents a standard tool from being used.

Many technicians like to buy a complete screwdriver set with multiple bits, including those for the security screws. Some manufacturers even have tool sets that include all of the bits and tools for their equipment.

Electrical Safety Rules

Only a professional electrician should test and maintain electric power equipment. Network technicians can safely test low-power communication circuits in network cabling. When you work with electrical power, follow these basic safety rules:

- Always disconnect or unplug electrical equipment before opening or servicing it.
- Work with a partner.
- Never bypass fuses or circuit breakers.
- Use anti-static mats and wristbands to protect yourself and equipment from static discharge.

Wire Crimpers

Definition:

A *wire crimper* is a tool that attaches media connectors to the ends of cables. You can use it if you need to make your own network cables or trim the end of a cable. There are different crimpers for different types of connectors, so select the one that is appropriate for the type of network media you are working with.

Example:

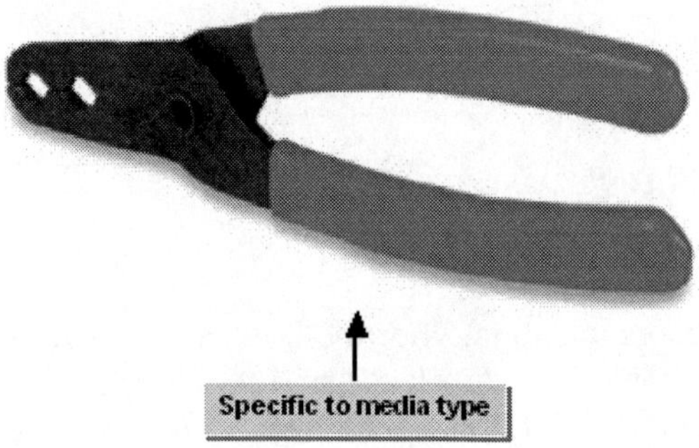

Figure 16-13: *Wire crimpers.*

Punch Down Tools

Definition:

A *punch down tool* is used in a wiring closet to connect cable wires directly to a patch panel. The tool strips the insulation from the end of the wire and embeds the wire into the connection at the back of the panel.

The technical name for a punch down tool is an Insulation Displacement Connector (IDC).

Example:

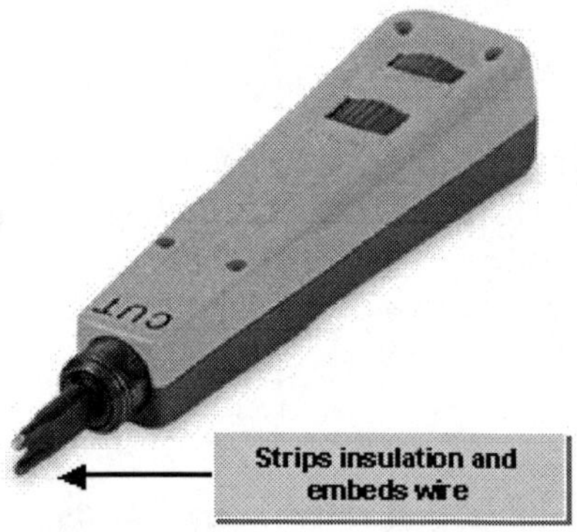

Figure 16-14: *A punch down tool.*

Wiring without a Punch Down Tool

The punch down tool makes connecting wires to a patch panel easier than it would be to connect them by hand. Without the punch down tool, you would have to strip the wire manually and connect it by twisting it or tightening it around a connection pole or screw.

Circuit Testers

Definition:

A *circuit tester* is an electrical instrument that displays whether an electrical outlet is wired correctly and tests the polarity and safety of the grounds. Plug the circuit tester into the socket and it will display a pattern of lights depicting how the circuit is wired.

A simple circuit tester is very easy to use. Nevertheless, you should always read the instructions that come with a particular piece of equipment.

Example:

Figure 16-15: *A circuit tester.*

Voltmeters

Definition:

A *voltmeter* measures voltage and resistance between two points in a circuit. Voltmeters come in both digital and analog forms. A digital voltmeter (DVM) provides scales for reading voltage in both AC and DC, resistance, and current. It can be used to test resistances between cable endpoints or voltages inside a low-power system. It shouldn't be used to service high-power or high-frequency equipment.

While not a required tool, a voltmeter can provide a lot of information about the systems in a network.

Example:

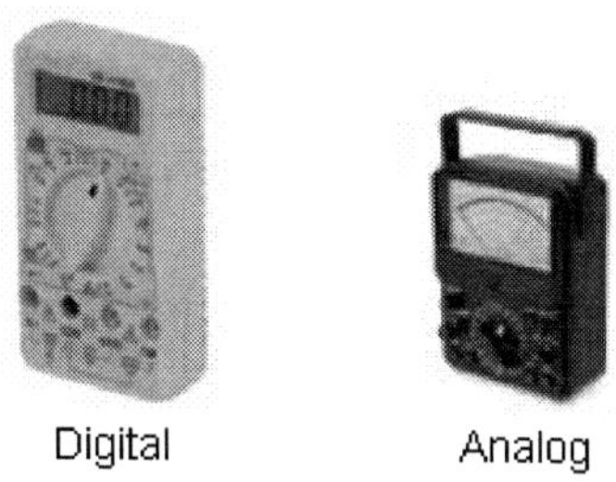

Figure 16-16: *Voltmeters.*

Cable Testers

Definition:

A *cable tester,* also called a *media tester,* is an electrical instrument that verifies if a signal is present on a cable. A simple cable tester will determine whether a cable has an end-to-end connection and can detect shorts or opens, but can't certify the cable for transmission quality—that is the cable installer's responsibility.

Example:

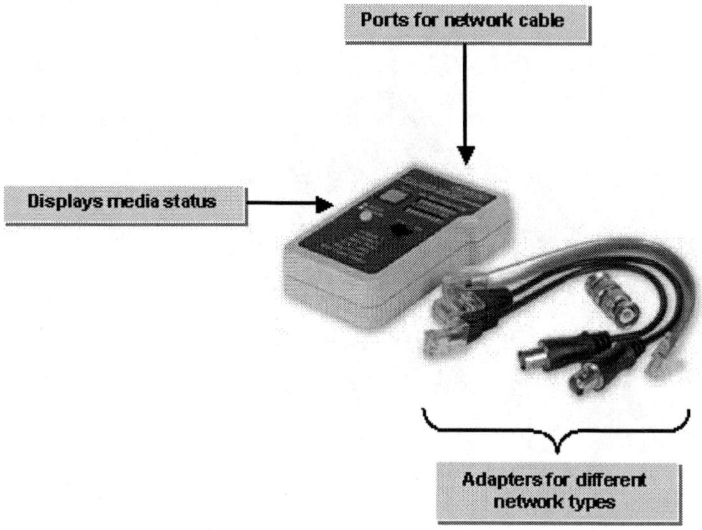

Figure 16-17: *A cable tester.*

Types of Cable Testers

A simple cable tester consists of a signal input at one end and a set of lights at the other. (Other testers include more features.) It's a good idea to get a tester with a remote detector so it can be used on long or installed cables.

Several other pieces of equipment fall into the general category of cable testers.

- Multimeters are used to test for breaks in copper cabling.
- Optical cable testers are used to test for breaks in fiber optic cable.
- Optical Time-Domain Reflectometers (OTDRs) are used to locate a break in a fiber optic cable.

Crossover Cables

Definition:

A *crossover cable* is a special network cable used in Ethernet UTP installations that enables you to connect two hubs, or to connect two stations without using a hub. In a crossover cable, the transmit and receive lines are crossed—a function that is normally taken care of by the hub or the switch. In troubleshooting, crossover cables let you connect two stations' network adapters directly so that you can test communications between them.

Example:

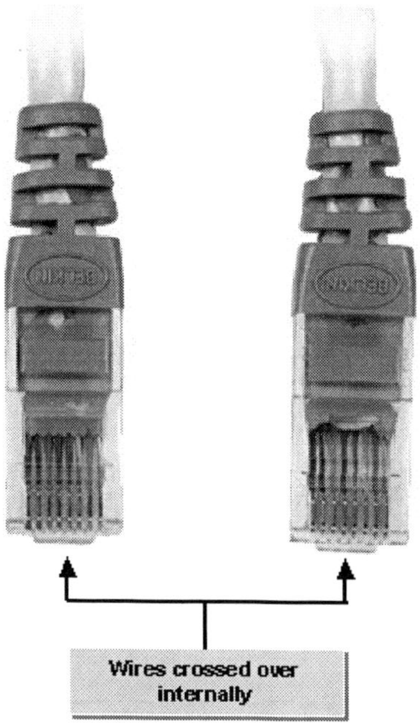

Figure 16-18: *Crossover cables.*

Crossover Cable Wiring

In a regular Ethernet UTP patch cable, four wires are used. Pins 1 and 2 transmit and Pins 3 and 6 receive. All lines are straight-wired (Pin 1 is wired to Pin 1, Pin 2 to Pin 2, and so forth). In a crossover cable, Pins 1 and 2 connect to Pins 3 and 6, and Pins 3 and 6 connect to Pins 1 and 2.

Cascading Hubs with a Crossover Cable

If you connect hubs via a crossover cable, you can cascade the hubs to provide more ports for a workgroup area, rather than buying and installing a larger hub.

Example: Troubleshooting with a Crossover Cable

If you suspect that a server's NIC might be bad, you can use a crossover cable to attach a laptop's NIC directly to the server's NIC. Provided that both NICs are configured correctly, you should be able to log on to the server if the server's NIC is good.

Hardware Loopback Plugs

Definition:

A *hardware loopback plug* is a special connector used for diagnosing transmission problems that redirects electrical signals back to the transmitting system. It plugs into a port and crosses over the transmit line to the receive line. Hardware loopback plugs are commonly used to test Ethernet NICs. The plug directly connects Pin 1 to Pin 3 and Pin 2 to Pin 6.

Example:

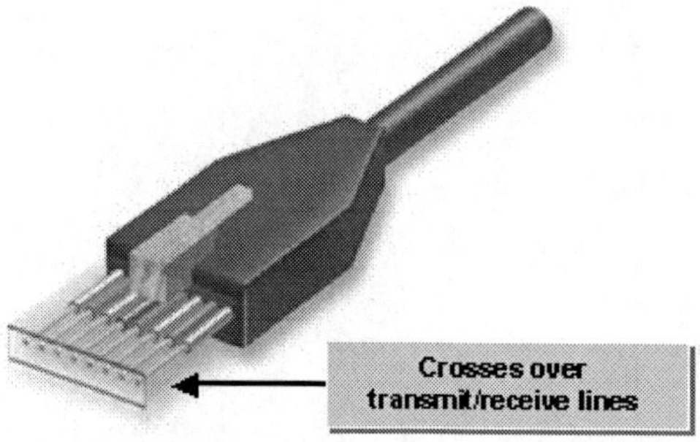

Figure 16-19: *A hardware loopback plug.*

Using a Loopback Plug

If a NIC comes with hardware diagnostic capabilities, the loopback plug will be included with the NIC. Connect the loopback plug to the installed NIC's network port, and run the diagnostic software to verify that the NIC can send and receive data.

LED Indicator Lights

The state of the *Light Emitting Diode (LED)* lights on network adapters, hubs, switches, routers, and cable and DSL modems can give you information about the status of the network connection.

There are several types of LED lights.

LED Type	Description
Link light	Most adapters have a link light that indicates if there is a signal from the network. If the link light is not lit, there is generally a problem with the cable or the physical connection.
Activity light	Most adapters also have an activity light that flickers when packets are received or sent. If the light flickers constantly, the network might be overused or there might be a system generating network noise.
Speed light	Some dual-mode adapters have a speed light to show whether the adapter is operating at 10 Mbps or at 100 Mbps.
Dual-color LED	Some types of equipment combine the functions of more than one light into dual-color LEDs. For example, a green flickering light might indicate normal activity, while an orange flickering light indicates collisions.

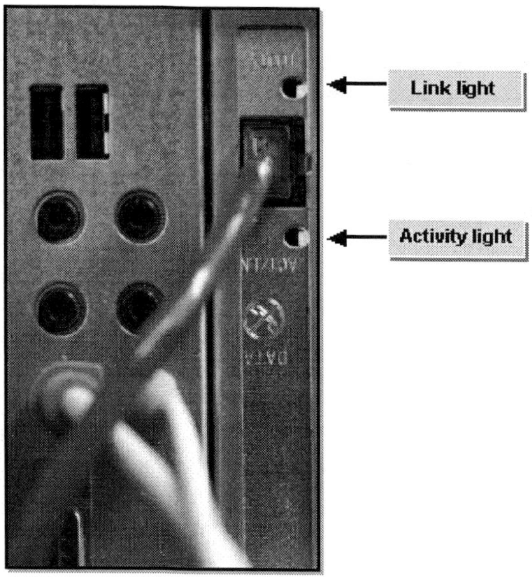

Figure 16-20: *LED indicator lights.*

Tone Generators and Tone Locators

Definition:

A *tone generator* is an electronic device that sends an electrical signal through one set of UTP wires. A *tone locator* is an electronic device that emits an audible tone when it detects a signal in a set of wires. Tone generators and tone locators are most commonly used on telephone systems to trace wire pairs.

The combination of tone generator and tone locator is frequently referred to as the "fox and hound."

Do not confuse tone generators and tone locators with cable testers. Tone generators and tone locators can only help you determine which UTP cable is which.

Example:

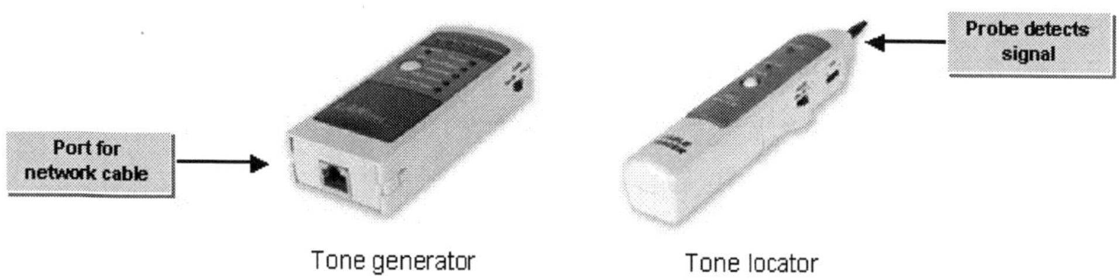

Figure 16-21: *Tone generators and tone locators.*

Using the Tone Generator and Tone Locator

To trace one cable in a group of cables, connect the tone generator to the copper ends of the wire pair you want to find; then move the tone locator over the group of cables. A soft beeping tone indicates that you are close to the correct wire set; when the beeping is loudest, you've found the cable. Don't ever connect a tone generator to a cable that's connected to a NIC or a hub. The signal sent by the tone generator can destroy network equipment.

ACTIVITY 16-4

Identifying Hardware Troubleshooting Tools

Scenario:

In this activity, you will identify the functions of various hardware troubleshooting tools.

What You Do	How You Do It

1. **You have a cable with a frayed end. You want to trim the cable and reattach the connector. You need a:**
   a) Punch down tool
   b) Wire crimper
   c) Cable tester
   d) Voltmeter

2. **You need to trace a UTP cable in a large bundle of cables. You need a:**
   a) Voltmeter
   b) Circuit tester
   c) Cable tester
   d) Tone generator and tone locator

3. **A workstation and server on your small office network can't communicate. To see if one of the network adapters is bad, you can connect them directly by using a:**
   a) Crossover cable
   b) Hardware loopback plug
   c) Tone generator and tone locator
   d) Punch down tool

4. **A user tells you he can't log on. You ask him to check the back of his network adapter and he says there is one steady light and one flashing light. What does this tell you?**
   a) That he has a network connection but is not receiving data.
   b) That he has no network connection.
   c) That he has a network connection and is receiving data.
   d) That the network adapter has a defect.

5. **Your instructor will show examples of various types of hardware tools. Identify each tool and its function, and give an example of how you would use it in network troubleshooting.**

6. **What does the amber light on a network interface card (NIC) indicate?**

   a) A frame error

   b) A dysfunctional transceiver on the NIC

   c) Successful network connectivity

   d) Transmission collisions

   e) A break in the cable

7. **You are a network administrator and you recently replaced the NIC card in a user's machine. You receive a call from the user, who complains that there is no network connectivity. Which LED on the NIC should you check first?**

   a) Activity light

   b) Collision light

   c) Link light

   d) Cable light

OPTIONAL ACTIVITY 16-5

Assembling a Patch Cable

Scenario:

You need an extra length of patch cable to attach a client computer to the network. You do not have a cable assembled, but you do have some cable wire and loose connectors.

1. **Strip the cable jacket back about 3/4 of an inch.** Don't cut or nick the inner pairs of wire.

2. **Place the pairs in color order so they lay flat and slip into the connector.**

3. **Slip the wires into the connector and be sure they're properly seated and in correct order.** Make sure the outer jacket is far enough into the connector that it will be captured by the strain relief tab.

   A 5x magnification eye loupe will help you examine the wires.

4. **Insert the cable/connector assembly into the crimping tool and crimp it.**

5. **Use the cable tester to test your cable.**

TOPIC D

System Monitoring Tools

So far in this lesson, you have identified many different software- and hardware-based troubleshooting utilities. There is another common category of system tools that support troubleshooting by enabling you to monitor your networks and systems. In this topic, you will identify the functions of major system monitoring tools.

The specific TCP/IP utilities and hardware-based troubleshooting tools you have used can help you identify and resolve specific problems on your network. But there are several major types of monitoring tools that you can use both to assess the overall functioning of your network, and to diagnose the cause of general complaints such as "the network is too slow" or "I'm having problems on and off getting to this server." Use these tools to keep tabs on your network's performance, in order to recognize and correct problems as well as to anticipate and eliminate problems before they start.

Performance Monitors

Definition:

A *performance monitor* is a software tool that monitors the state of services, processes, and resources on a system. Performance monitors track one or more *counters,* which are individual statistics about the operation of different objects on the system, such as software processes or hardware components. Some objects can have more than one instance; for example, a system can have multiple CPUs.

When a counter value reaches a given *threshold,* it indicates that the component may be functioning outside acceptable limits. Many operating systems include basic performance monitor tools, or you can obtain more complex third-party tools that are based on the SNMP protocol.

Example: The Performance Tool in Windows Server 2003

Many Windows systems include a basic performance monitor tool. In Windows Server 2003, the tool is called Performance. It is located in the Administrative Tools group. Performance incorporates two functions: System Monitor, to track system functions in real time, and Performance Logs and Alerts, to log system functions and to notify the administrator if they exceed desired levels.

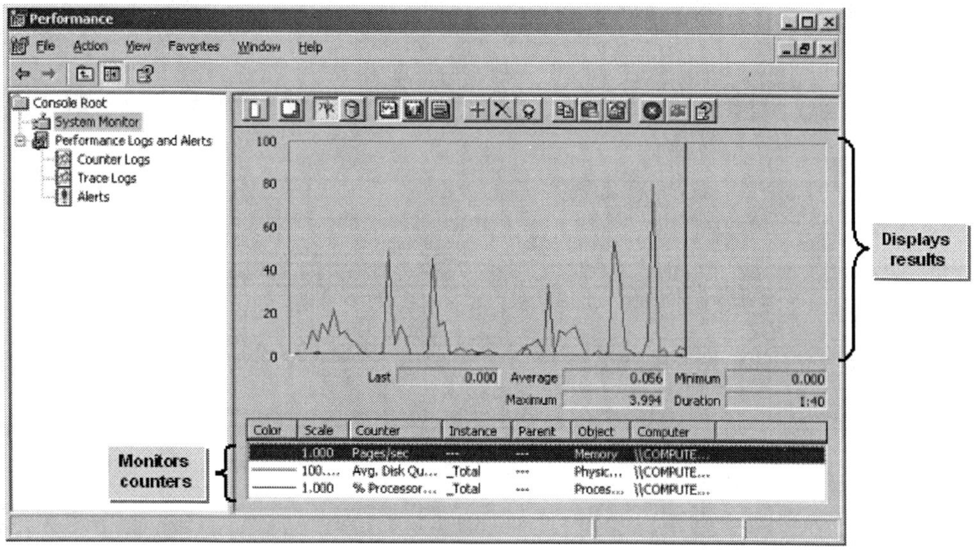

Figure 16-22: *A performance monitor.*

Counter Threshold Values

System administrators generally take action when counter values they are monitoring reach a certain threshold value. Threshold values can be set in different ways. This list gives examples of thresholds for common counters in the Performance tool.

- Some counters have generally accepted threshold values. For example, the Processor/% Processor Time counter should generally not exceed 85%.
- Some counters will have thresholds that depend upon the particular piece of equipment. You will need to consult the documentation from your equipment's manufacturer. For example, the Physical Disk/Average Disk Queue Length value should be no more than the number of disk spindles plus 2.
- Some counters have values that administrators set subjectively based on actual network performance. For example, if network performance is acceptable at a given value for the Memory/Pages/Sec counter, then the counter is not yet at its threshold. An administrator would monitor for sudden or gradual increases in this value, and correlate those to performance problems occurring on the network, to determine the threshold of unacceptable performance.

ACTIVITY 16-6

Using the Performance Tool in Windows Server 2003

There is a simulated version of this activity available on the CD-ROM that shipped with this course. You can run this simulation on any Windows computer to review the activity after class, or as an alternative to performing the activity as a group in class. The activity simulation can be launched either directly from the CD-ROM by clicking the Interactives link and navigating to the appropriate one, or from the installed data file location by opening the C:\Data\Simulations\Lesson#\Activity# folder and double-clicking the executable (.exe) file.

Scenario:

You administer several Windows Server 2003 systems. Part of your job duties will be to monitor these systems' general performance. Rather than purchase a third-party monitoring tool, you plan to use the built-in Performance tool to view performance information, and you need to familiarize yourself with its functions and user interface.

What You Do	How You Do It
1. **View the current performance statistics.**	a. **Choose Start→Administrative Tools→Performance.**
	b. **Verify that the graph contains three default counters.**
	c. To see the measurements in text format, **click the View Report button.**

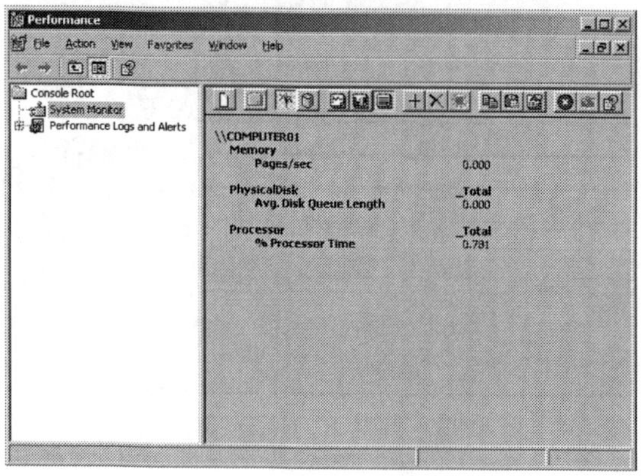

d. **Click the View Graph button.**

2. **Examine the available counters.**

a. **Click the Add icon** [+].

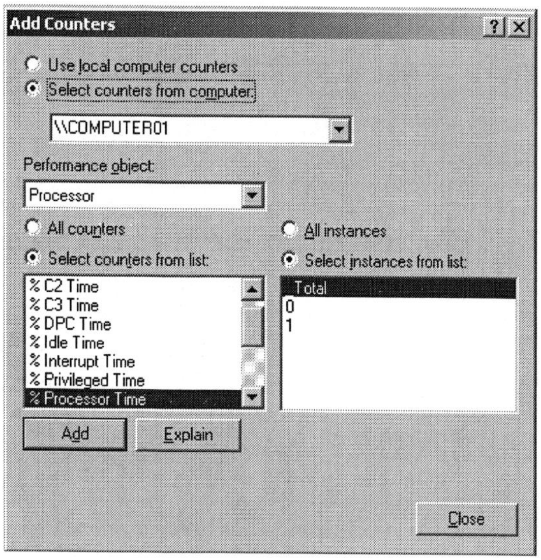

b. To identify the available performance objects, **click the Performance Object drop-down arrow.**

c. From the Performance Object drop-down list, **select Memory.**

d. With the Pages/Sec counter selected, **click Explain.**

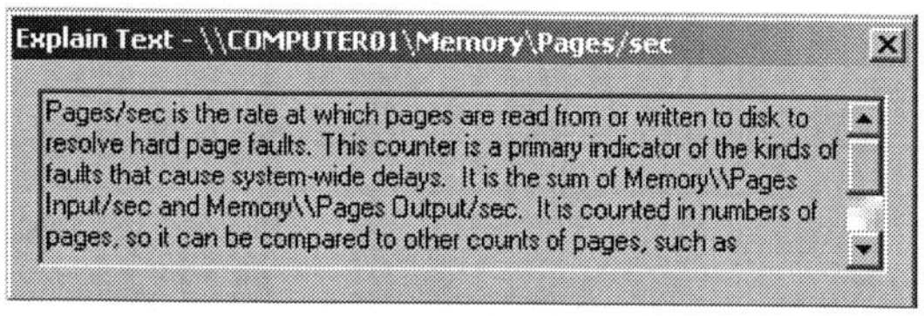

e. **Scroll to view the remaining text in the Explain Text window.**

f. **Close the Explain Text window.**

g. **View the explanations for other performance counters.**

h. **Click Close.**

i. **Close Performance.**

Protocol Analyzers

Definition:

A *protocol analyzer*, or *network analyzer*, is a type of diagnostic software that can examine and display data packets that are being transmitted over a network. It can examine packets from protocols that operate in the Physical, Data-link, Network, and Transport layers of the OSI model.

Example: The Windows Network Monitor Tool

Most Windows systems include a basic protocol analyzer tool called Network Monitor. There are two versions of Network Monitor; one ships with Windows but is not installed by default. You must add it using Add/Remove Windows Components. This version of Network Monitor can only capture packets that travel to or from the computer on which it is installed. There is also a full version of Network Monitor that is included with Systems Management Server, and can be installed separately from the full Systems Management Server product. This version can capture packets sent to or from any computer on the network.

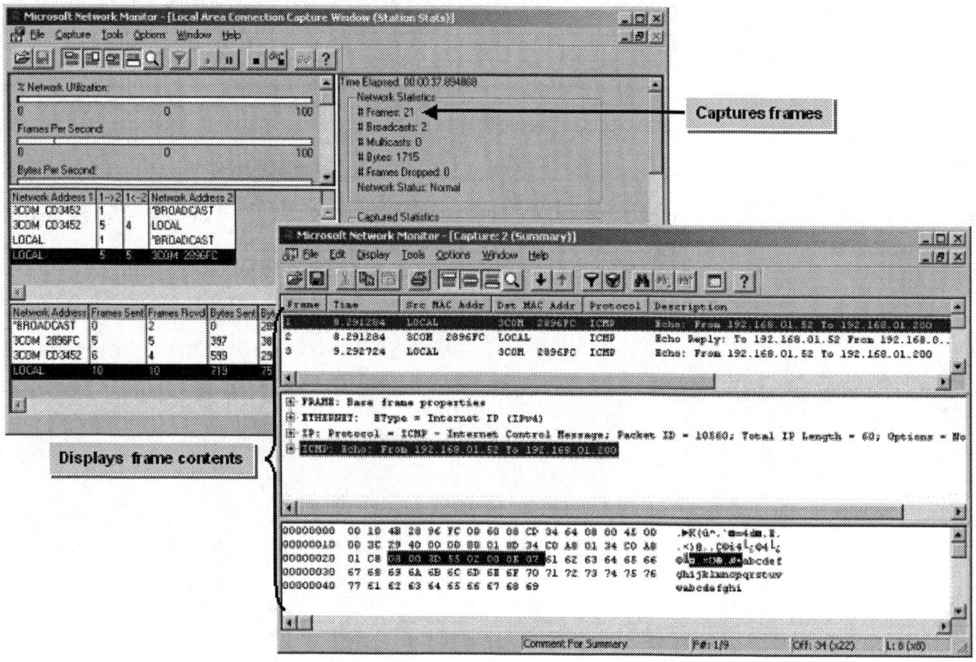

Figure 16-23: *A protocol analyzer.*

Protocol Analyzer Functionality

Different protocol analyzers have different levels of functionality. Some have only software components; others use a combination of hardware and software to gather and analyze network information. Higher-end solutions usually provide support for more protocols, the ability to send test traffic, higher speeds, and more analytical information. The product that you should use depends on your specific environment and the needs of your company.

Commercial Protocol Analyzers

You can purchase a commercial protocol analyzer from a number of third-party vendors. Some popular products include Sniffer, Mentor, NetLens, LANdecoder, Observer, Network Advisor, NetSight/LANDesk Analysis, and Ethereal.

Promiscuous Mode Adapter Operation

To capture all packets sent on a network, protocol analyzers require a special type of network adapter and driver that support promiscuous mode operation. Promiscuous mode enables the station running the analyzer to recognize all packets being sent over the network, no matter what the source or destination is. In promiscuous mode, a network card passes all network events to the operating system and running applications. In normal modes of operation, some network events are filtered out and not available to applications, including the error conditions that the protocol analyzer is designed to detect. Promiscuous mode drivers are available for most network interface cards; contact the manufacturer of your cards for the most recent drivers.

The Protocol Analysis Process

Protocol analyzers capture and then decode packets. First, the protocol analyzer places copies of a series of packets into memory, where the packets can be analyzed without disrupting network traffic. Then, the protocol analyzer decodes the packet contents and displays the source, destination, protocol, and data inside the packet. You can then analyze this information to determine the nature of the traffic on the network.

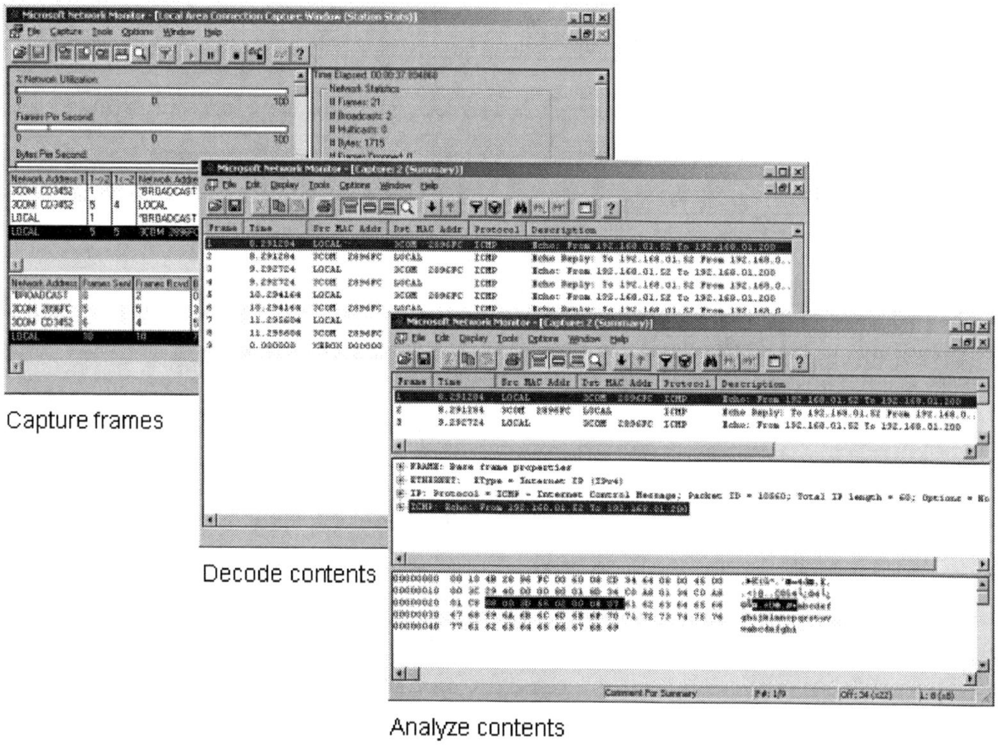

Figure 16-24: *The protocol analysis process.*

Protocol Analysis

A set of captured network packets is often called a *trace*. Analyzing a network trace provides a lot of information about the nature of the traffic on a particular network. For example, you can determine the protocols that are used most often, the types of websites users are accessing, and which NICs are sending out corrupted or unnecessary packets ("jabbering").

ACTIVITY 16-7

Capturing Network Data with Windows Network Monitor

There is a simulated version of this activity available on the CD-ROM that shipped with this course. You can run this simulation on any Windows computer to review the activity after class, or as an alternative to performing the activity as a group in class. The activity simulation can be launched either directly from the CD-ROM by clicking the Interactives link and navigating to the appropriate one, or from the installed data file location by opening the C:\Data\Simulations\Lesson#\Activity# folder and double-clicking the executable (.exe) file.

Setup:

The Windows Server 2003 installation files are available on the network at \\dc\2003Install. Your system has multiple network interfaces installed.

Scenario:

You want to use Network Monitor to capture data about your system's network performance. You do not need to capture data sent to and from other stations on the network. Network Monitor has not yet been installed on the system.

What You Do	How You Do It
1. **Install Network Monitor.**	a. **Choose Start→Control Panel→Add Or Remove Programs.**
	b. **Click Add/Remove Windows Components.**
	c. In the Components list, **select Management And Monitoring Tools** but do not check the check box.

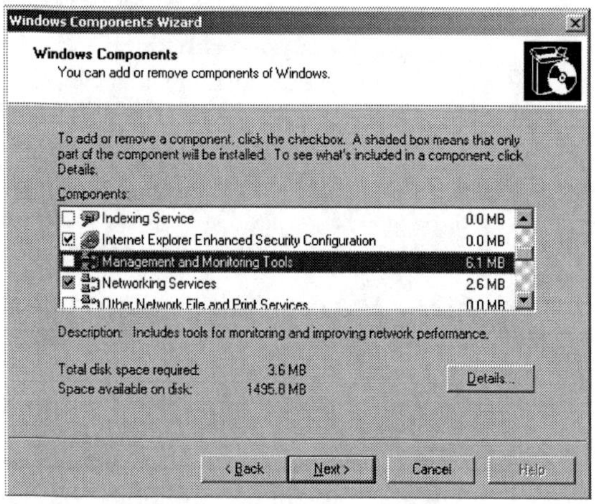

d. **Click Details.**

e. **Check Network Monitor Tools and click OK.**

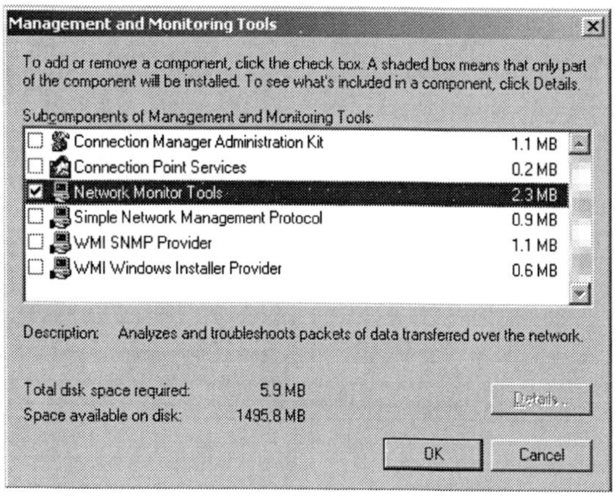

f. **Click Next.**

g. When prompted for the Windows Server 2003 installation CD-ROM, **click OK.**

h. In the Copy Files From text box, **type *\\dc\2003install* and click OK.**

i. When the installation is complete, **click Finish.**

j. **Close Add Or Remove Programs.**

---

2. **Select a network interface to monitor.**

a. **Choose Start→Administrative Tools→Network Monitor.**

b. When prompted to choose a network, **click OK.**

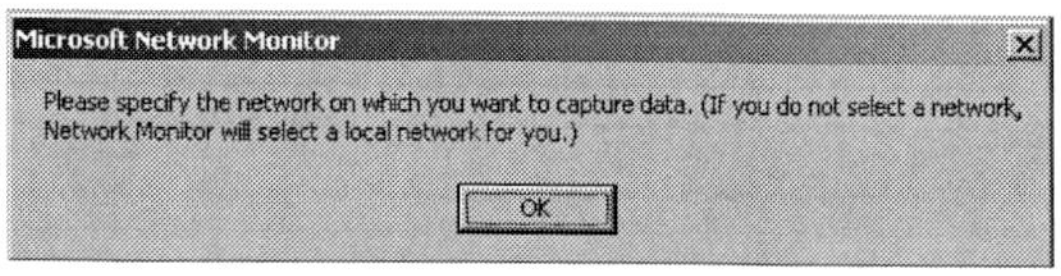

c. **Expand Local Computer.**

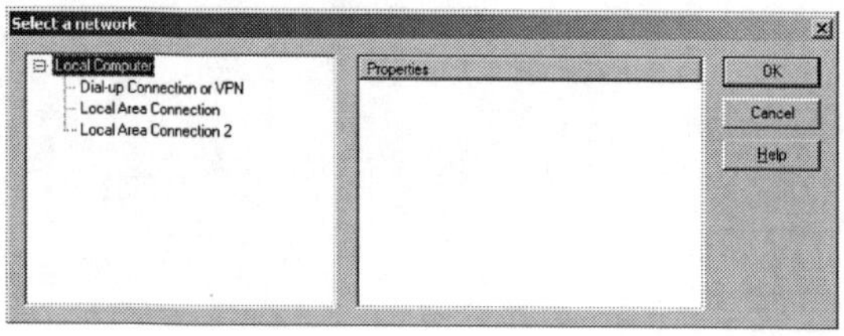

d. **Select Local Area Connection.**

e. **Verify that the connection supports promiscuous mode and click OK.**

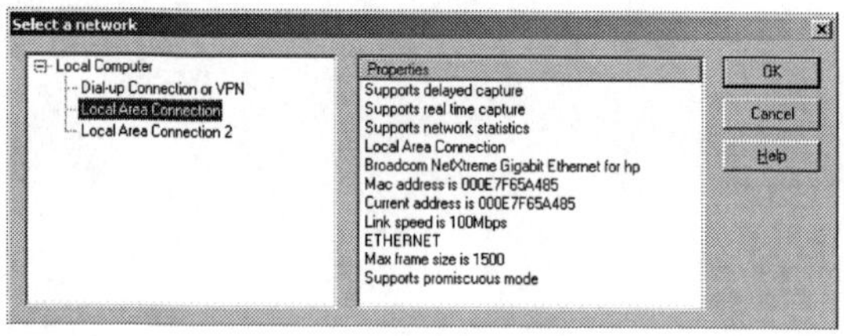

---

3. **Capture network data.**

a. **Maximize the Microsoft Network Monitor window.**

b. **Maximize the Local Area Connection Capture window.**

c. **Click the Start Capture button** .

d. To generate network traffic, **choose Start→Run.**

e. **Type *ping dc* and click OK.**

f. A command prompt window will open and close when the ping operation is complete. In Network Monitor, **click the Stop And View Capture button** .

---

4. **Examine the captured data.**

a. The Capture Summary window displays the captured network data. In the Capture Summary window, **double-click the first frame.**

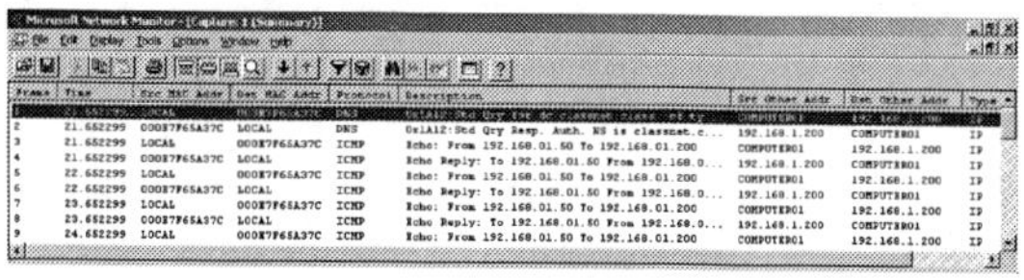

b. The window splits to show the contents of the frame. **Click the second frame.**

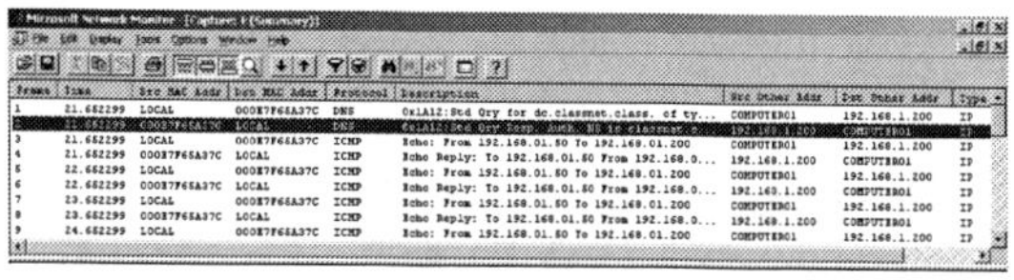

c. The window shows the contents of this frame. **Double-click the first frame** to display the frame list again.

d. **Examine the contents of other captured frames.** See how much information you can gather about the network transmission.

e. **Choose File→Close** to close the Capture Summary window.

f. **Choose File→Exit.**

g. When prompted to save the capture data to a file, **click No.**

h. If prompted to save entries to the address database, **click No.**

TOPIC E

Network Baselining

In the previous topic, you identified the functions of software troubleshooting tools. A common way to apply these tools is to use them to develop a network baseline. In this topic, you will identify the components and processes required to develop a network baseline.

Network baselining might not seem to fit in well with network troubleshooting, because the very word "baseline" tells you that everything is working normally. But taking and updating baseline measurements on a regular basis is a crucial part of the overall troubleshooting function. A good understanding of your network's baseline performance is necessary for you to be able to recognize when performance falters, and also for you to demonstrate that parts of the network might need modification or upgrades.

Network Baselines

Definition:

A *baseline* is a record of a system's performance statistics under normal operating conditions. A network baseline documents the network's current performance level and provides a quantitative basis for identifying abnormal or unacceptable performance. It can also reveal where bottlenecks are impeding system performance, and provide evidence for upgrading systems to improve performance.

Taking a baseline is like taking your temperature once in a while when you are healthy. If you know what your normal temperature range is, then you can recognize an abnormal reading if you take your temperature when you are unwell. Because there is no single "normal" reading for different networks, you need to establish what the normal values are for your network so that you can recognize an abnormal state.

Example: Baselining Network Bandwidth

For example, if a company is expanding a remote office that is connected to the corporate office with a Fractional T1, the baseline can help determine if there is enough reserve bandwidth to handle the extra user load, or if the Fractional T needs to be upgraded to a full T.

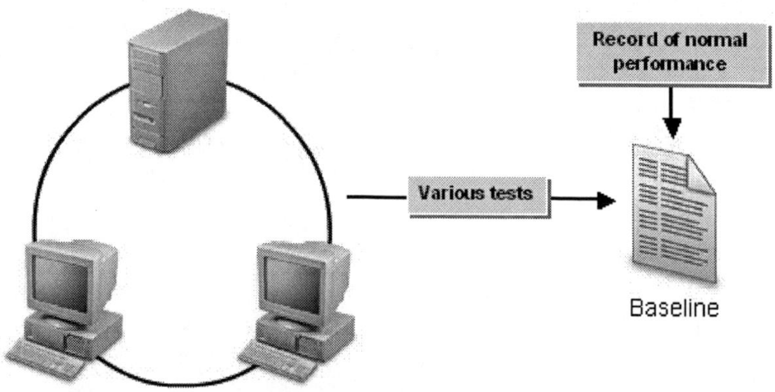

Figure 16-25: *A baseline.*

Customizing the Baseline

The number, type, and frequency of tests performed and recorded in the baseline will vary depending upon the systems and the needs of the organization. The organization must also decide how often to establish a new baseline to reflect current performance.

The Baseline Process

Creating and applying a baseline is a cycle that organizations should continually repeat.

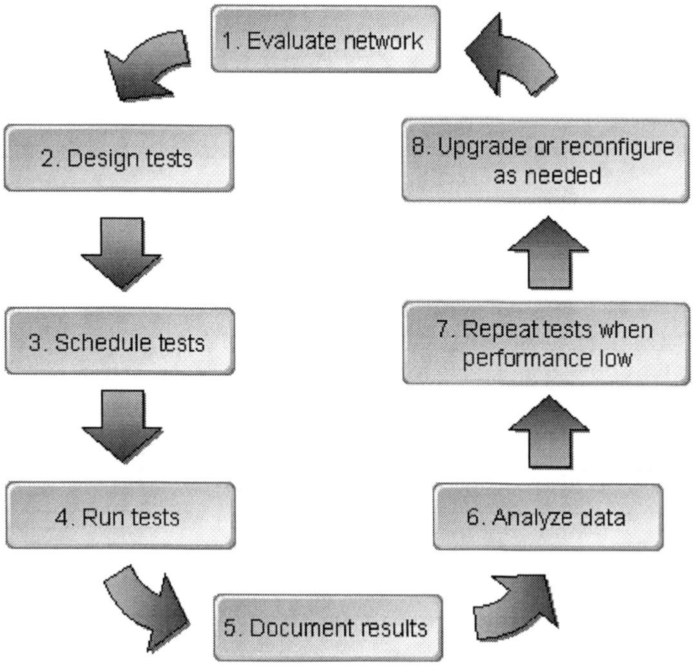

Figure 16-26: *The baseline process.*

Step	Description
Evaluate network	To decide what statistics to measure, evaluate the network's purpose. You will monitor differently on a network that primarily provides file access than you would on one that hosts web servers.
Design tests	Develop a suite of tests that reveals the network's performance level. Make the tests consistent and yield scalable results, speed times, percentages, and other ratings. Avoid tests that don't show improvement or degradation.
Schedule tests	Determine when to run the tests. The tests should include a sampling of different network usage levels, including peak and off-peak usages, and should be run over a period of time to present a realistic profile.
Run tests	Run the tests.
Document results	Document the test results. Record the data in a way that can be saved and compared with future tests.

Step	Description
Analyze data	Analyze the data to identify *bottlenecks,* which are parts of the system that perform poorly as compared to other components and reduce overall system performance.
Repeat tests	Repeat the tests at regular intervals or when network performance seems low. If the performance data compares unfavorably to the baseline, try to identify the cause and troubleshoot the problem.
Upgrade as needed	On an ongoing basis, upgrade or reconfigure components to remove bottlenecks, and then repeat the tests to establish new baseline values.

Baseline Logging

Typically, you will record baseline measurements to a log file that you can review later, rather than examining the measurements in real time. Most performance or network monitoring systems enable you to save log data. For example, Network Monitor enables you to save each capture to a log, and Performance gives you the option to record data directly to log format. When you log data in Performance, you can select all counters for a selected object, or specific counters. You can examine the counter values by selecting the counters to add when you open the log file in Chart view.

ACTIVITY 16-8

Discussing Network Baselines

Scenario:

In this activity, you will discuss various aspects of network baselines.

1. **What are the benefits of a network baseline?**

   a) To establish a record of problems and solutions to assist you in troubleshooting similar problems.

   b) To document user complaints.

   c) To enable you to recognize an abnormal performance state.

   d) To establish patterns that can help you recognize and eliminate ongoing bottlenecks.

2. **Which would be an appropriate testing interval for a baseline?**

   a) A 10-minute reading at noon every day for a week.

   b) An hour-long sample starting at 8:00 one Monday morning.

   c) Five-minute readings once per hour during a 24-hour period midweek.

   d) A 24-hour-long reading from Saturday at 1 A.M. until Sunday at 1 A.M.

3. **Which performance criteria should you use the baseline to analyze?**
   a) Server response and performance.
   b) Network infrastructure response and performance.
   c) Network media response and performance.
   d) User performance and error frequency.

4. **Put the steps of creating a baseline in the correct order.**
   Decide when to run the tests.
   Run the tests.
   Document the test results.
   Evaluate the network's purpose.
   Design a suite of tests.

ACTIVITY 16-9

Using Performance to Establish a Baseline

There is a simulated version of this activity available on the CD-ROM that shipped with this course. You can run this simulation on any Windows computer to review the activity after class, or as an alternative to performing the activity as a group in class. The activity simulation can be launched either directly from the CD-ROM by clicking the Interactives link and navigating to the appropriate one, or from the installed data file location by opening the C:\Data\Simulations\Lesson#\Activity# folder and double-clicking the executable (.exe) file.

Scenario:

Part of your regular duties on your company's network support team is to take and record baseline performance measurements for key systems on your network. The next system you are scheduled to baseline is a corporate file server. Because this system doesn't run any special services, you will baseline the default performance measurements for Windows Server 2003.

What You Do	How You Do It
1. Set up the performance log.	a. **Choose Start→Administrative Tools→Performance.**
	b. **Expand Performance Logs And Alerts.**
	c. **Select Counter Logs.**
	d. **Double-click the System Overview log object.**

e. **Verify that there are three default counters, and that the sampling interval is every 15 seconds.**

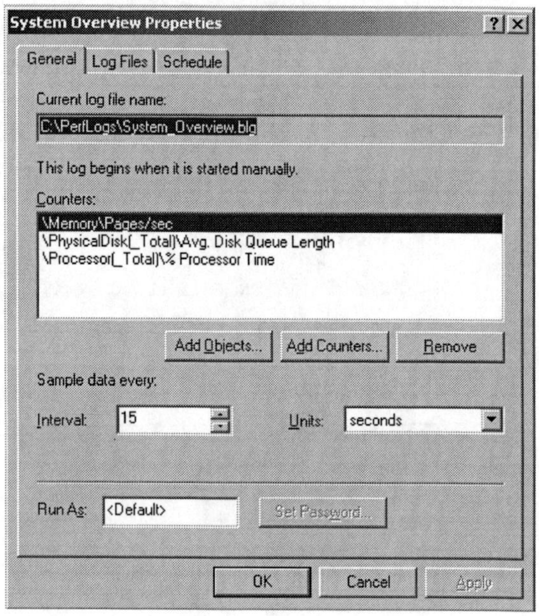

f. **Select the Log Files tab.**

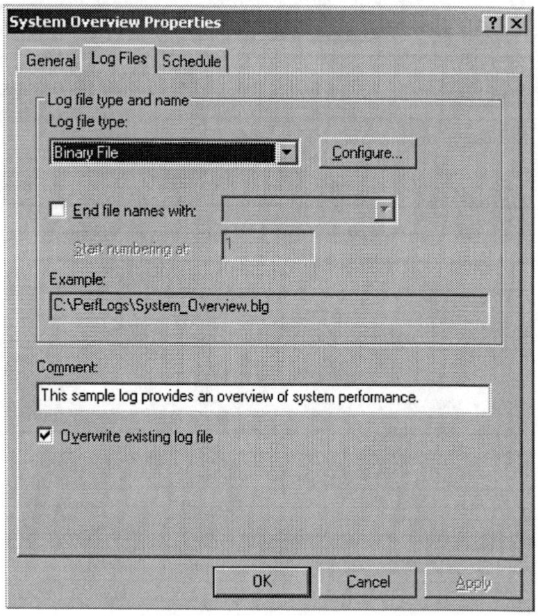

g. The file will be saved in a binary format that you can open later to view. **Select the Schedule tab.**

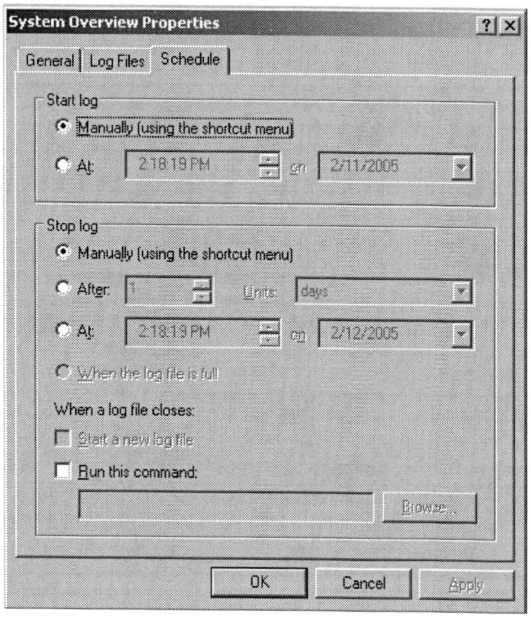

h. You will start this log manually. **Click Cancel.**

---

2. **Measure network activity with the log.**

a. **Choose Action→Start** to start the log.

b. **Run the log for 5 or 10 minutes, while you generate system activity by opening and closing programs, opening and closing documents, and connecting to other systems on the network.**

c. After 5 or 10 minutes have passed, **select the System Overview log object in Performance.**

d. **Choose Action→Stop.**

---

3. **Examine the log data.**

a. In Performance, **select System Monitor.**

b. **Click the View Log Data button** .

c. **Select Log Files and click Add.**

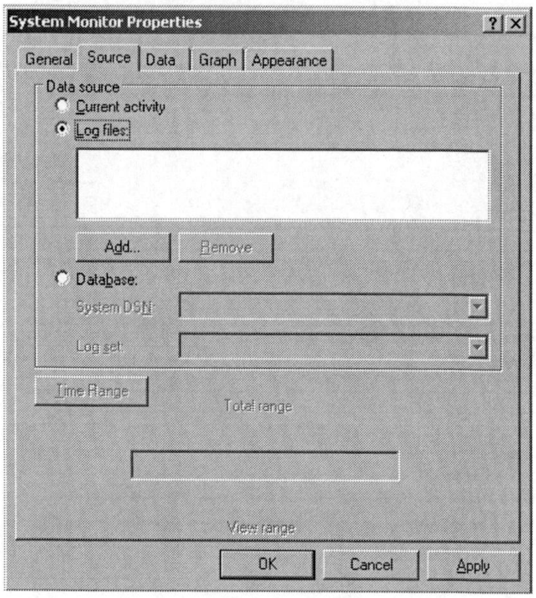

d. **Select System_Overview.blg and click Open.**

e. **Click OK.**

f. By default, the data appears in Graph view. **Click the View Report button.**

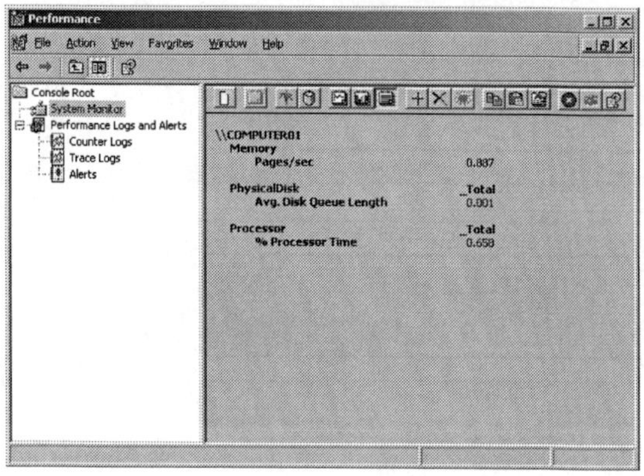

g. **Close Performance.**

Lesson 16 Follow-up

In this lesson, you identified major issues, models, tools, and techniques in network troubleshooting. While it's always best to avoid trouble when possible, network problems can arise from a variety of sources outside your control. Because troubleshooting is a crucial function of any network professional, a good grasp of troubleshooting principles, tools, and processes will be important no matter what your professional role.

1. **Describe a troubleshooting situation you were involved in, or that you read or heard about. Was it resolved through a structured methodology?**

2. **Which of the troubleshooting tools and processes presented in this lesson do you think you will find most useful or use most frequently? Why?**

FOLLOW-UP

Follow-up

In this course, you identified and described all the major networking technologies, systems, skills, and tools in use in modern PC-based computer networks. You also learned information and skills that will be helpful as you prepare for the CompTIA Network+ certification examination, 2005 objectives (exam number N10-003).

What's Next?

The material in *CompTIA Network+ Certification* provides foundational information and skills required in any network-related career. It also assists you in preparing for the CompTIA Network+ certification exam. Once you have completed *CompTIA Network+ Certification*, you might wish to continue your certification path by taking the Element K course *Security+®: A CompTIA Certification*, which can help you prepare for the CompTIA Security+ certification exam. Or, you can take any one of a number of vendor-specific networking technology or administration courses from Element K, including courses leading to professional-level certifications from Microsoft and Novell.

APPENDIX A

Mapping Network+ Course Content to the CompTIA Network+ Exam Objectives

The following tables will assist you in mapping the Network+ course content to the CompTIA Network+ certification exam objectives.

Exam Objective Domain 1.0 — Media and Topologies	Network+ Lesson and Topic Reference
1.1: Recognize the following logical or physical network topologies given a diagram, schematic, or description: • Star • Bus • Mesh • Ring	Lesson 1, Topic D
1.2: Specify the main features of 802.2 (Logical Link Control), 802.3 (Ethernet), 802.5 (Token Ring), 802.11 (wireless), and FDDI (Fiber Distributed Data Interface) networking technologies, including: • Speed • Access method—CSMA/CA (Carrier Sense Multiple Access/Collision Avoidance) and CSMA/CD (Carrier Sense Multiple Access/ Collision Detection) • Topology • Media	Lesson 2, Topic B Lesson 5, Topic C, D, E, and F

APPENDIX A

Exam Objective Domain 1.0 — Media and Topologies	Network+ Lesson and Topic Reference
1.3: Specify the characteristics (for example, speed, length, topology, and cable type) of the following cable standards: • 10BASE-T and 10BASE-FL • 100BASE-TX and 100BASE-FX • 1000BASE-T, 1000BASE-CX, 1000BASE-SX and 1000BASE-LX • 10 GBASE-SR, 10 GBASE-LR and 10 GBASE-ER	Lesson 5, Topic C
1.4: Recognize the following media connectors and describe their uses: • RJ-11 (Registered Jack) • RJ-45 (Registered Jack) • F-Type • ST (Straight Tip) • SC (Subscriber Connector or Standard Connector) • IEEE 1394 (FireWire) • Fiber LC (Local Connector) • MT-RJ (Mechanical Transfer Registered Jack) • USB (Universal Serial Bus)	Lesson 4, Topic A Lesson 10, Topic B Lesson 13, Topic B
1.5: Recognize the following media types and describe their uses: • Category 3, 5, 5e, and 6 • UTP (unshielded twisted pair) • STP (shielded twisted pair) • Coaxial cable • SMF (single-mode fiber) optic cable • MMF (multimode fiber) optic cable	Lesson 4, Topic A

Appendix A

Exam Objective Domain 1.0 — Media and Topologies	Network+ Lesson and Topic Reference
1.6: Identify the purposes, features, and functions of the following network components: • Hubs • Switches • Bridges • Routers • Gateways • CSU/DSU (Channel Service Unit/Data Service Unit) • NICs (network interface cards) • ISDN (Integrated Services Digital Network) adapters • WAPs (wireless access points) • Modems • Transceivers (media converters) • Firewalls	Lesson 2, Topic C Lesson 4, Topic D Lesson 5, Topic F Lesson 9 Lesson 10, Topic B, C Lesson 11, Topic F
1.7: Specify the general characteristics (for example, carrier speed, frequency, transmission type, and topology) of the following wireless technologies: • 802.11 (frequency hopping spread spectrum) • 802.11x (direct sequence spread spectrum) • Infrared • Bluetooth	Lesson 4, Topic B Lesson 5, Topic F
1.8: Identify factors that affect the range and speed of wireless service (for example, interference, antenna type, and environmental factors).	Lesson 5, Topic F

Exam Objective Domain 2.0 — Protocols and Standards	Network+ Lesson and Topic Reference
2.1: Identify a MAC (Media Access Control) address and its parts.	Lesson 3, Topic A
2.2: Identify the seven layers of the OSI (Open Systems Interconnection) model and their functions.	Lesson 5, Topic A

APPENDIX A

Exam Objective Domain 2.0 — Protocols and Standards	Network+ Lesson and Topic Reference
2.3: Identify the OSI (Open Systems Interconnection) layers at which the following network components operate: • Hubs • Switches • Bridges • Routers • NICs (network interface cards) • WAPs (wireless access points)	Lesson 5, Topic A Lesson 9, Topic E
2.4: Differentiate between the following network protocols in terms of routing, addressing schemes, interoperability, and naming conventions: • IPX/SPX (Internetwork Packet Exchange/ Sequence Packet Exchange) • NetBEUI (Network Basic Input/Output System Extended User Interface) • AppleTalk/AppleTalk over IP (Internet Protocol) • TCP/IP (Transmission Control Protocol/Internet Protocol)	Lesson 6 Lesson 7 Lesson 8, Topic A, B, C
2.5: Identify the components and structure of IP (Internet Protocol) addresses (IPv4, IPv6) and the required setting for connections across the Internet.	Lesson 6, Topic B Lesson 8, Topic D
2.6: Identify classful IP (Internet Protocol) ranges and their subnet masks (for example, Class A, B, and C).	Lesson 6, Topic C
2.7: Identify the purpose of subnetting.	Lesson 1, Topic B Lesson 6, Topic D
2.8: Identify the differences between private and public network addressing schemes.	Lesson 6, Topic C
2.9: Identify and differentiate between the following IP (Internet Protocol) addressing methods: • Static • Dynamic • Self-assigned—APIPA (Automatic Private Internet Protocol Addressing)	Lesson 7, Topic A

Exam Objective Domain 2.0 — Protocols and Standards	Network+ Lesson and Topic Reference
2.10: Define the purpose, function, and use of the following protocols used in the TCP/IP (Transmission Control Protocol/Internet Protocol) suite: • TCP (Transmission Control Protocol) • UDP (User Datagram Protocol) • FTP (File Transfer Protocol) • SFTP (Secure File Transfer Protocol) • TFTP (Trivial File Transfer Protocol) • SMTP (Simple Mail Transfer Protocol) • HTTP (Hypertext Transfer Protocol) • HTTPS (Hypertext Transfer Protocol Secure) • (POP3/IMAP 4 (Post Office Protocol version 3/Internet Message Access Protocol version 4) • Telnet • SSH (Secure Shell) • ICMP (Internet Control Message Protocol) • ARP/RARP (Address Resolution Protocol/ Reverse Address Resolution Protocol) • NTP (Network Time Protocol) • NNTP (Network News Transport Protocol) • SCP (Secure Copy Protocol) • LDAP (Lightweight Directory Access Protocol) • IGMP (Internet Group Multicast Protocol) • LPR (Line Printer Remote)	Lesson 6, Topic E Lesson 7, Topic E, F
2.11: Define the function of TCP/UDP (Transmission Control Protocol/User Datagram Protocol) ports.	Lesson 6, Topic E

Exam Objective Domain 2.0 — Protocols and Standards	Network+ Lesson and Topic Reference
2.12: Identify the well-known ports associated with the following commonly used services and protocols: • 20 FTP (File Transfer Protocol) • 21 FTP (File Transfer Protocol) • 22 SSH (Secure Shell) • 23 Telnet • 25 SMTP (Simple Mail Transfer Protocol) • 53 DNS (Domain Name Service) • 69 TFTP (Trivial File Transfer Protocol) • 80 HTTP (Hypertext Transfer Protocol) • 110 POP3 (Post Office Protocol version 3) • 119 NNTP (Network News Transport Protocol) • 123 NTP (Network Time Protocol) • 143 IMAP4 (Internet Message Access Protocol version 4) • 443 HTTPS (Hypertext Transfer Protocol Secure)	Lesson 6, Topic E
2.13: Identify the purpose of the following network services and protocols: • DNS (Domain Name Service) • NAT (Network Address Translation) • ICS (Internet Connection Sharing) • WINS (Windows Internet Name Service) • SNMP (Simple Network Management Protocol) • NFS (Network File System) • Zeroconf (Zero configuration) • SMB (Server Message Block) • AFP (Apple File Protocol) • LPD (Line Printer Daemon) • Samba	Lesson 7, Topic B, C, F Lesson 8, Topic C Lesson 10, Topic C Lesson 11, Topic F
2.14: Identify the basic characteristics (for example, speed, capacity, and media) of the following WAN (wide area network) technologies: • Packet switching • Circuit switching • ISDN (Integrated Services Digital Network) • FDDI (Fiber Distributed Data Interface) • T1 (T-Carrier level 1)/E1/J1 • T3 (T-Carrier level 3)/E3/J3 • OCx (Optical Carrier) • X.25	Lesson 5, Topic E Lesson 10, Topic A, B

Exam Objective Domain 2.0 — Protocols and Standards	Network+ Lesson and Topic Reference
2.15: Identify the basic characteristics of the following Internet access technologies: • xDSL (Digital Subscriber Line) • Broadband cable (cable modem) • POTS/PSTN (Plain Old Telephone Service/ Public Switched Telephone Network) • Satellite • Wireless	Lesson 5, Topic F Lesson 10, Topic B
2.16: Define the function of the following remote access protocols and services: • RAS (Remote Access Service) • PPP (Point-to-Point Protocol) • SLIP (Serial Line Internet Protocol) • PPPoE (Point-to-Point Protocol over Ethernet) • PPTP (Point-to-Point Tunneling Protocol) • VPN (Virtual Private Network) • RDP (Remote Desktop Protocol)	Lesson 12
2.17: Identify the following security protocols and describe their purpose and function: • IPSec (Internet Protocol Security) • L2TP (Layer 2 Tunneling Protocol) • SSL (Secure Sockets Layer) • WEP (Wired Equivalent Privacy) • WPA (Wi-Fi Protected Access) • 802.1x	Lesson 5, Topic F Lesson 11, Topic D, E Lesson 12, Topic D
2.18: Identify the following authentication protocols: • CHAP (Challenge Handshake Authentication Protocol) • MS-CHAP (Microsoft Challenge Handshake Authentication Protocol) • PAP (Password Authentication Protocol) • RADIUS (Remote Authentication Dial-In User Service) • Kerberos • EAP (Extensible Authentication Protocol)	Lesson 11, Topic D Lesson 12, Topic C

APPENDIX A

Exam Objective Domain 3.0 — Network Implementation	Network+ Lesson and Topic Reference
3.1: Identify the basic capabilities (for example, client support, interoperability, authentication, file and print services, application support, and security) of the following server operating systems to access network resources: • UNIX/Linux/Mac OS X Server • NetWare • Windows • AppleShare IP (Internet Protocol)	Lesson 15 Lesson 8, Topic C
3.2: Identify the basic capabilities needed for client workstations to connect to and use network resources (for example, media, network protocols, and peer and server services).	Lesson 1, Topic A Lesson 6, Topic A
3.3: Identify the appropriate tool for a given wiring task (for example, wire crimper, media tester/certifier, punch down tool, or tone generator).	Lesson 16, Topic C
3.4: Given a remote connectivity scenario comprising a protocol, an authentication scheme, and physical connectivity, configure the connection. Include connectionsto the following servers: • UNIX/Linux/Mac OS X Server • NetWare • Windows • AppleShare IP (Internet Protocol)	Lesson 8, Topic C Lesson 10, Topic B Lesson 12 Lesson 15
3.5: Identify the purpose, benefits, and characteristics of a firewall.	Lesson 11, Topic F
3.6: Identify the purpose, benefits, and characteristics of a proxy service.	Lesson 11, Topic F
3.7: Given a connectivity scenario, determine the impact on network functionality of a particular security implementation (for example, port blocking/filtering, authentication, and encryption).	Lesson 1, Topic A Lesson 9, Topic E Lesson 11, Topic D, E
3.8: Identify the main characteristics of VLANs (virtual local area networks).	Lesson 9, Topic E
3.9: Identify the main characteristics and purpose of extranets and intranets.	Lesson 1, Topic E
3.10: Identify the purpose, benefits, and characteristics of antivirus software.	Lesson 11, Topic B
3.11: Identify the purpose and characteristics of fault tolerance in the following categories: • Power • Link redundancy • Storage • Services	Lesson 13, Topic C Lesson 14

Exam Objective Domain 3.0 — Network Implementation	Network+ Lesson and Topic Reference
3.12: Identify the purpose and characteristics of disaster recovery in the following categories: • Backup/restore • Offsite storage • Hot and cold spares • Hot, warm, and cold sites	Lesson 13, Topic A, B

Exam Objective Domain 4.0 — Network Support	Network+ Lesson and Topic Reference
4.1: Given a troubleshooting scenario, select the appropriate network utility from the following: • Tracert/Traceroute • Ping • Arp • Netstat • Nbtstat • Ipconfig/Ifconfig • Winipcfg • Nslookup/Dig	Lesson 16, Topic B
4.2: Given output from a network diagnostic utility (for example, those utilities listed in objective 4.1), identify the utility and interpret the output.	Lesson 7, Topic A, D Lesson 16, Topic B
4.3: Given a network scenario, interpret visual indicators (for example, link LEDs and collision LEDs (Light Emitting Diodes) to determine the nature of a stated problem.	Lesson 16, Topic C
4.4: Given a troubleshooting scenario involving a client accessing remote network services, identify the cause of the problem (for example, file services, print services, authentication failure, protocol configuration, physical connectivity, or SOHO (Small Office / Home Office) router).	Lesson 10, Topic B Lesson 12
4.5: Given a troubleshooting scenario between a client and the following server environments, identify the cause of a stated problem: • UNIX/Linux/Mac OS X Server • NetWare • Windows • AppleShare IP (Internet Protocol)	Lesson 8, Topic B, C Lesson 15 Lesson 16

Exam Objective Domain 4.0 — Network Support	Network+ Lesson and Topic Reference
4.6: Given a scenario, determine the impact of modifying, adding, or removing network services such as DHCP (Dynamic Host Configuration Protocol), DNS (Domain Name Service), and WINS (Windows Internet Name Service) for network resources and users.	Lesson 7, Topic A, B, C Lesson 16, Topic B
4.7: Given a troubleshooting scenario involving a network with a particular physical topology (for example, bus, star, mesh, or ring) and including a network diagram, identify the network area affected and the cause of the stated failure.	Lesson 1, Topic D Lesson 4, Topic D Lesson 5, Topic D, E Lesson 16
4.8: Given a network troubleshooting scenario involving a wired or wireless infrastructure problem, identify the cause of the stated problem (for example, bad media, interference, network hardware, or environment).	Lesson 4 Lesson 5, Topic F Lesson 16
4.9: Given a network problem scenario, select an appropriate course of action based on a logical troubleshooting strategy. This strategy can include the following steps: 1. Identify the symptoms and potential causes. 2. Identify the affected area. 3. Establish what has changed. 4. Select the most probable cause. 5. Implement an action plan and solution, including potential effects. 6. Test the result. 7. Identify the results and effects of the solution. 8. Document the solution and process.	Lesson 16, Topic A

Appendix B

OSPF Route Discovery and Maintenance

OSPF Route Discovery

Adjacencies, or neighbor relationships, between routers that are connected to the same segment are established and maintained by the OSPF *Hello packet* (RFC 2178). The Hello packet is a means of gathering routing information. It is used to create a connection between two consecutive network routers, announce its address and subnet mask, discover neighboring routers, establish the time interval between subsequent Hello packets, and discover the *designated routers (DRs)* and *backup designated routers (BDRs)*.

All network routers must have a common Hello interval, or they cannot recognize each other.

DRs and BDRs are elected according to their priorities. The network router with the highest priority becomes the DR, and that with the next highest priority becomes the BDR. A DR or BDR is not replaced until and unless it goes offline. For example, if a router with a higher priority than the DR is introduced to the network, it does not become the DR until the current DR becomes inactive. At that time, the current BDR becomes the DR and the new, high-priority router becomes the BDR. You can manually configure router priority, but be careful when assigning a priority of zero, since that prevents a router from becoming DR or BDR.

The OSPF protocol uses a two-step process to learn internetwork routes. First, it establishes communication by using the Hello packet. Then, it creates a database of internetwork routes.

The OSPF Route Database

Once Hello packets are exchanged and the DR and BDR are established, each router must create a database in which to store routing information and synchronize it with those of the DR and BDR.

Prior to synchronization, routers exchange data description packets (DDPs) with the DR and the BDR. The packets contain a summary of routers' databases. At this stage, the routers are in a two-way state. Once synchronization takes place, each router is described as having an adjacency to one another and the relationship changes to a full-neighbor state.

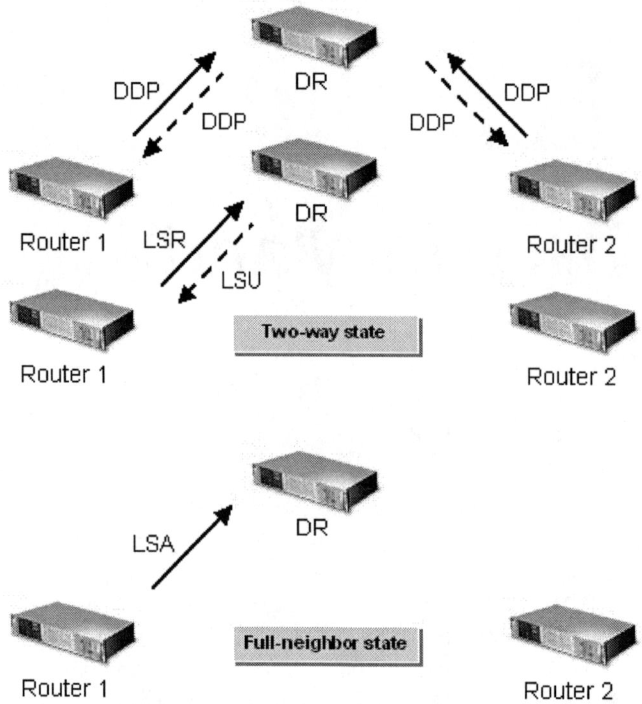

Figure B-1: *OSPF routers synchronize their databases.*

Routers 1 and 2 send their summary packets (DDPs) to the designated router. In return, the DR sends its DDP to R1 and R2. The routers are in a two-way state. R1 and R2 compare the information in the DDP sent by the DR with their current database entries. R1 sees that it has an outdated entry so it sends a Link State Request (LSR) to the DR, requesting the updated entry information. The DR returns a Link State Update (LSU) to R1 containing the requested information. Finally, R1 incorporates the new information into its database and sends a Link State Acknowledgement (LSA) to the DR. Having synchronized their databases, the routers are now in a full-neighbor state. The DR and BDR should have a full-neighbor relationship with each network router. However, each network router should have a full-neighbor relationship with only the DR and the BDR.

OSPF Route Selection and Maintenance

An OSPF router uses its database to see the entire internetwork. When creating a route table, a router uses the OSPF algorithm to figure out how many hops it takes to get to a particular network. Then, it adds the number of hops to get the total cost of the route. For multiple routes to the same network, the route with the lowest cost is added to the route table. The table information remains until a change is reflected in a link state advertisement. OSPF waits until a group of changes has occurred, and then performs the algorithm again and rebuilds the route table. By making several changes at once, OSPF does not run the algorithm unnecessarily.

OSPF will work properly only if all routers agree on the autonomous system's link state (the routers are synchronized).

If an OSPF router detects a change in the network, it issues LSU packets at a default interval of every 30 minutes. If no network change is detected, the router intermittently floods the internetwork with LSUs for every entry in its route table. Each receiving router compares the LSUs with its database and returns an LSA to the sending router. Each router deletes entries for which the aging timer has reached a value four times the Router Dead interval.

An OSPF router resynchronizes using DDPs only when its full state changes. DDPs are also used when routers and the DR and BDR are out of sync. In this case, adjacencies must be re-established.

Notes

Notes

APPENDIX C

Additional IP Addressing and Subnetting Practice

Lesson Time
1 hour(s)

Objectives:

In this lesson, you will practice working with IP addressing and subnetting.

You will:

- Practice working with IP addresses and subnet masks.

APPENDIX C

Introduction

If your job requires you to design custom IP subnets or analyze IP network addressing schemes, you might require some supplemental information and skills beyond the TCP/IP addressing information required for the basic Network+ curriculum and exam objectives. This appendix provides you with supplemental IP information and gives you additional opportunities to practice IP addressing and subnet design tasks.

TOPIC A

Additional Practice for IP Addressing and Subnetting

This topic contains additional content and activities to support the IP addressing and subnetting content in the main part of the course.

Network Addresses

You should use the following guidelines when assigning the network portion of an IP address:

- Each network address must be unique for each network segment. If your network connects to the Internet, you must request an address from the InterNIC.
- The first byte in a network address cannot be 0 (binary value of 00000000). A network address of 0 indicates that a packet belongs on the local network and will not be routed.
- The first byte in a network address cannot be 255 (binary value of 11111111); 255 is reserved for broadcasting messages to all hosts.
- The network address cannot be 127.0.0.0 because this address is reserved for troubleshooting purposes.

The following table summarizes the valid network address ranges for Class A, Class B, and Class C networks.

Network Class	Starting Network Address	Ending Network Address
A	1.host.host.host	126.host.host.host
B	128.0.host.host	191.255.host.host
C	192.0.0.host	223.255.255.host

The extra byte(s) of network addresses in Class B and C networks can be any value from 0 to 255. For example, 187.255.0.0 is a valid Class B network address. The addresses of 0 or 255 are permitted for the second and third bytes because they do not indicate a network address of all 0s or 255s.

Determining Address Validity

You might want to develop the habit of splitting an IP address into its network and host portions. It is very helpful to develop an "eye" for network and host addresses because it is much easier to determine if the addresses are valid when you look at only the relevant portions of the address. At first glance, an address of 131.255.255.1 might appear invalid, when, in fact, it is a good address. The network address is 131.255 and the host address is 255.1, both of which conform to the addressing guidelines.

Host Addresses

You should use the following guidelines when assigning the host portion of an IP address:

- Each host address must be unique to the local network.
- The host address bits cannot all be 0. If all host bits are 0, then the resulting IP address is the network address. For example, if the network address is 100 (Class A), and the host bits are all 0, then the resulting IP address is 100.0.0.0. This IP address is invalid because it is reserved to determine the network address for routing purposes.
- The host address bits cannot be all 1s (a decimal value of 255 for each byte). If all host address bytes are set to 255, the transmission is thought to be a broadcast.

Although the host address portion of the IP address must be unique, the network address portion must be the same for all hosts on the same segment of the network.

The following table outlines the range of valid host addresses.

Network Class	Starting Host Address	Ending Host Address
A	net.0.0.1	net.255.255.254
B	net.net.0.1	net.net.255.254
C	net.net.net.1	net.net.net.254

The first byte(s) of host addresses in Class A and B networks can be any value from 0 to 255. For example, 255.1 is a valid Class B host address.

Guidelines for Assigning Host Addresses

While there are no rules for assigning specific addresses to different types of computers, you can make assigning host addresses much easier if you establish some guidelines. For example, you may find it easier to remember the function of a specific machine if you group the host addresses by type. If you use one of the bytes from the host address in a Class A or Class B network, you could assign a specific number to servers or UNIX hosts. The following table provides some examples.

Network Class	IP Address	Example
A	net.host.host.host	Use net.101.host.host to identify servers. Use net.201.host.host to identify UNIX hosts or printers with network cards.

Network Class	IP Address	Example
B	net.net.host.host	Use net.net.101.host to identify servers. Use net.net.201.host to identify UNIX hosts or printers with network cards.

You could even assign specific ranges of numbers for the second or third byte of the address based on the type of operating system a computer runs. For example, you could assign 51 to Windows 2000 Professional machines, 52 to Windows XP Professional machines, 101 to Windows 2000 Servers, 102 to Windows Server 2003 servers, 110 to NetWare servers, and 201 to UNIX hosts.

You might also choose to assign values for the second or third byte of an IP address based on a machine's geographic location. For example, an address could be used to identify hosts on different floors in your building. Use the rest of the host address bytes to identify workstations and routers. For example, you could use host addresses from 1 to 224 for workstations, and 225 to 254 for routers.

By using guidelines to assign your IP addresses, you can get more information from an IP address than just the network segment a computer is located on. For example, if your network address is 154.131 and the host address is 52.1, then the above guidelines would tell you that this computer is located on segment 154.131, and runs Windows XP Professional. In contrast, an address of 154.131.101.254 would tell you that this computer is located on segment 154.131, runs Windows 2000 Server, and functions as an IP router.

ACTIVITY C-1

Determining the Validity of IP Addresses

Scenario:

In this activity, you will examine several IP addresses and determine if they are valid or invalid.

1. **True or False? The IP address 100.100.100.1 is invalid because the first and second bytes of a network address cannot be the same.**

   __ True

   __ False

2. **Is 157.35.205.0 a valid network address?**

   __ Yes

   __ No

3. **Is 187.255.1.1 a valid host address?**

   __ Yes

   __ No

4. **True or False? The IP address 131.0.5.29 is invalid because of the zero in the second octet.**

   __ True

   __ False

---

5. **Is 221.100.155.0 a valid host address?**

   __ Yes

   __ No

---

6. **Is 187.131.255.5 a valid host address?**

   __ Yes

   __ No

---

7. **Is 121.0.0.1 a valid host address?**

   __ Yes

   __ No

---

8. **Match the following invalid IP addresses with the reason that they are not valid.**

___	157.100.257.1	a.	This network address is reserved for multicasts.
___	127.1.254.254	b.	The decimal value of any byte cannot exceed 255.
___	224.254.254.254	c.	This host address is reserved for broadcasts on the local network.
___	198.254.254.255	d.	This network address is reserved for testing purposes.
___	255.255.255.255	e.	The value of the first byte of any network address cannot be 0.
___	0.153.98.32	f.	This address is reserved for broadcasts on the entire network.

ACTIVITY C-2

Assigning Network and Host Addresses

Scenario:

You have been assigned the task of assigning IP addresses to a large network that contains 210 Windows 2000 Professional workstations, 25 NetWare servers, 54 network printers, 150 Windows XP Professional workstations, 1 Linux server, and 100 Windows Server 2003 servers. The corporate policy is to assign host addresses based on the machine function and operating system, where:

- Workstations are identified by numbers in the 50s; for instance, 50 identifies Windows 2000 Professional machines, 51 identifies Windows XP Professional machines, 52 identifies Macintosh workstations, and 55 identifies Linux workstations.
- Servers are identified by numbers in the 100s; for instance, 100 identifies Windows 2000 Servers, 105 identifies Windows Server 2003 machines, 110 identifies Linux servers, and 115 identifies NetWare servers.
- Printers and other network peripherals are identified by numbers in the 70s; for instance, 71 identifies network scanners and 75 identifies network printers.

1. **What address class(es) would be valid to use on this network?**

   a) A

   b) B

   c) C

   d) D

   e) E

2. **What network address(es) would be valid for this network?**

   a) 198.5.33.0

   b) 100.0.0.0

   c) 231.5.254.0

   d) 128.1.0.0

3. **You've decided to use the network address 128.1.0.0. According to the corporate host addressing policy, which address(es) would be valid for any of the Windows 2003 Server machines?**

   a) 128.1.0.105

   b) 128.1.100.10

   c) 128.105.1.55

   d) 128.1.105.98

   e) 128.1.105.0

ACTIVITY C-3

Assigning Network and Host Addresses on Multisegment Networks

Scenario:

You have been assigned the task of assigning network and host addresses to a network that has several segments. Network 1 contains 150 Windows Server 2003 machines and 250 Windows XP Professional workstations, and Network 2 contains 300 Windows 2000 Professional workstations and 25 Linux hosts. A router connects Networks 1 and 2, and another router connects Network 2 with a WAN.

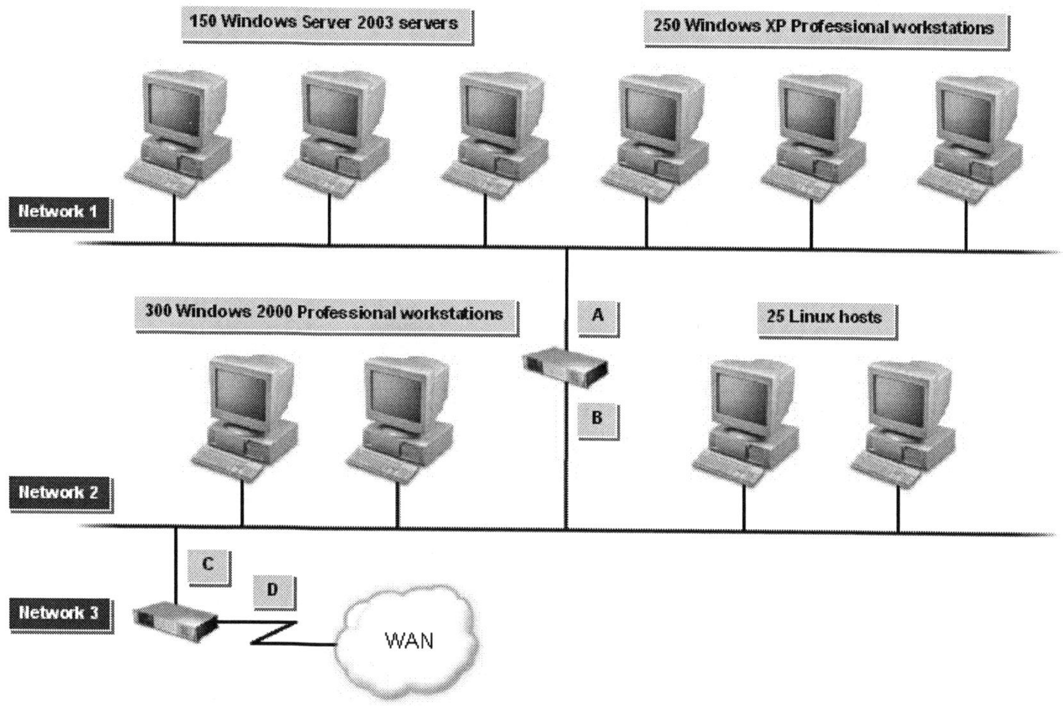

Figure C-1: *A multisegment network.*

1. **How many network addresses will be needed?**
   - a) 1
   - b) 2
   - c) 3
   - d) 4

2. **How many host addresses are needed for Network 1?**
    a) 150
    b) 250
    c) 400
    d) 401

---

3. **How many host addresses are needed for Network 2?**
    a) 300
    b) 325
    c) 326
    d) 327
    e) 397

---

4. **What class(es) of network address can be used for these network segments?**
    a) A
    b) B
    c) C
    d) D
    e) E

---

5. **Which router network card's address would you assign as the default gateway for the Windows 2000 Professional computers to access the Windows Server 2003 servers?**
    a) Router interface A
    b) Router interface B
    c) Router interface C
    d) Router interface D

ACTIVITY C-4

Identifying IP Addressing Problems

Scenario:

A colleague has asked you to help identify problems with IP addressing.

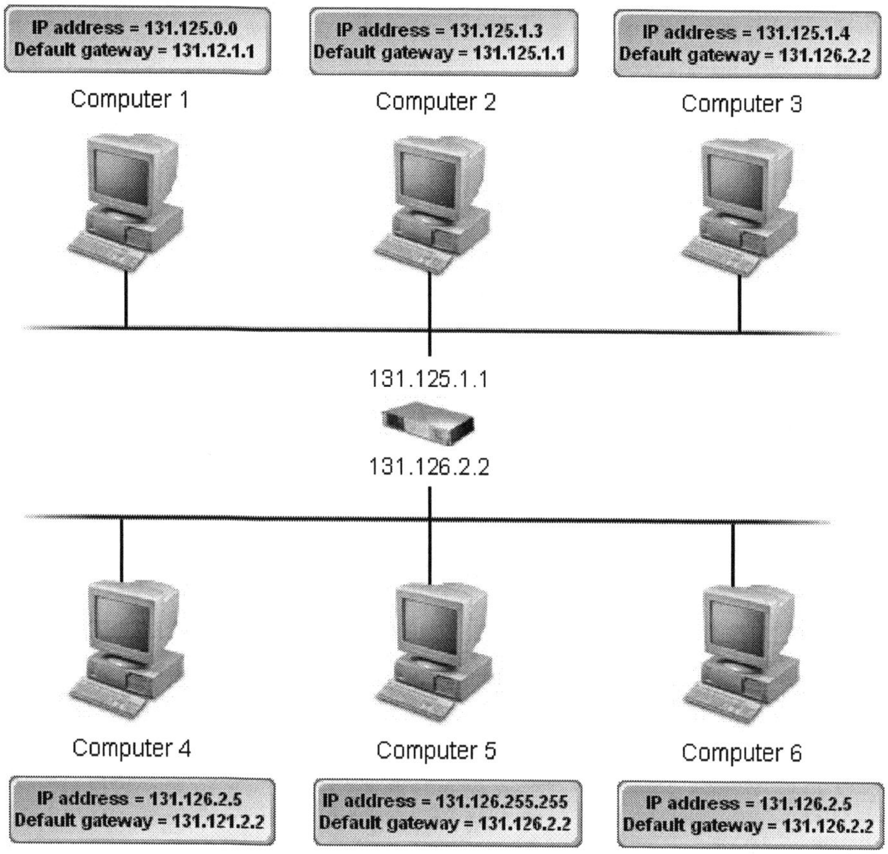

Figure C-2: *A network with incorrect IP addresses.*

1. **Match the computer name with the appropriate description.**

___	Computer 1	a.	You can't use a broadcast address for a host address.
___	Computer 2	b.	This address is duplicated on the network, and the default gateway is incorrect.
___	Computer 3	c.	You can't use a network address for a host address, and the default gateway is incorrect.
___	Computer 4	d.	This address is duplicated on the network.
___	Computer 5	e.	No changes are needed.
___	Computer 6	f.	The default gateway is incorrect.

Appendix C

Subnetting and Segmenting

Each network segment requires its own unique network address, just as each street in your town requires its own unique street name. In the TCP/IP environment, network segments are called subnets if each network segment's address must be derived from a single IP network address. This situation often occurs if your company's network IP address is assigned by the InterNIC; if your network has multiple physical segments, you must create multiple network addresses from the single Internet IP address.

The process of subdividing a single network address to allow for unique network addresses on each subnet is called *subnetting*. To subnet, use a custom subnet mask to "borrow" bits from the host portion of the network address. (A subnet mask distinguishes the host portion of the IP address from the network portion.) Use the borrowed bits to create subnetwork addresses.

If your network does not connect to the Internet, then you may assign any unique network address to each network segment and use the default subnet mask. Although you will commonly hear this procedure described as subnetting, it is more properly called *segmenting*, because there is no need to subdivide a single network address.

Reasons for Subnetting or Segmenting

Reasons for subnetting or segmenting your network include:

- To divide a large network into smaller segments to reduce traffic.
- To connect networks across geographical areas.
- To connect different topologies, such as Ethernet, Token Ring, and FDDI, together via routers.
- To avoid physical limitations such as maximum cable lengths or exceeding the maximum number of computers on a segment.

Subnetting a Segmented Network

If your network is connected to the Internet, you must subnet your assigned IP address if your network has multiple segments. In order to implement subnet addresses on your network, you must first ask yourself some questions:

- How many network addresses will I need? You will need one address per subnet, including one for each connection to a WAN.
- How many host addresses will I need? This number determines the class of IP network address you can use for your network. You will need one host address per computer, including one for each network card in a router or printer.

The answers to these questions will help you to define the subnet mask, network addresses, and host addresses for your network.

ACTIVITY C-5

Reviewing Subnetting Concepts

Scenario:

You are preparing to subnet a large network, and want to review your knowledge of subnetting before taking any other action.

1. **True or False? One reason to subnet a network is because you have been given only one network address to work with.**

    __ True

    __ False

2. **Why might you segment a network?**

    a) To reduce the number of machines on a single segment in order to reduce network traffic.

    b) To reduce the number of network addresses needed.

    c) To overcome physical limitations such as exceeding the maximum number of machines on a given segment.

    d) To increase the number of host addresses available.

    e) To connect different topologies, such as Ethernet and Token Ring.

3. **If a network consists of three segments connected by two routers, how many subnets will you need?**

    a) 2

    b) 3

    c) 4

    d) 5

4. **True or False? If a network consists of 2 segments, each containing 30 machines, connected by 2 routers, you will need 62 host addresses.**

    __ True

    __ False

Subnet Masks

Every host on a TCP/IP network must have a subnet mask, even if the network consists of only one segment or does not connect to the Internet. A subnet mask is 32 bits long, the same length as an IP address. The subnet mask's primary purpose is to mask the host portion of the IP address in order to identify whether a transmitted packet's destination is to a local or a remote host. However, you can also customize the subnet mask and use it to subdivide a single assigned IP address.

- A default subnet mask distinguishes between local and remote transmissions. It masks the host portion of the IP address for the sender and receiver of a packet, leaving the network portion visible. TCP/IP compares the network address of the sender and receiver to determine if the packet belongs on the local or remote network.
- A custom subnet mask also distinguishes between local and remote transmissions by masking the host portion of the IP address. In addition, it subdivides a single assigned network address by borrowing bits from the host portion of the IP address to create additional network addresses from a single assigned address.

Using Subnet Masks to Identify Local and Remote Transmissions

The subnet mask also enables TCP/IP to identify whether a packet that is being transmitted belongs on the local network or on a remote network. The subnet mask identifies the network portion of the IP address by masking the host address for both the sender and the receiver of the packet. Once TCP/IP has determined the network addresses for the sender and receiver, it compares the two addresses. If the network addresses are the same, the packet belongs on the local network; if the two addresses are different, the packet belongs on a remote network. If a packet belongs on a remote network, then TCP/IP sends the packet to the address of the default gateway, which routes the packet to the appropriate destination or to another router.

You must look at the subnet mask to determine if a packet belongs on the local network or on a remote network. If you look only at the network addresses, you might not identify local and remote hosts correctly. Consider the following examples, where Node 1's address is 100.100.4.10, and Node 2's address is 100.100.8.17:

- If the subnet mask is 255.0.0.0, the transmission is local.
- If the subnet mask is 255.255.0.0, the transmission is local.
- If the subnet mask is 255.255.255.0, the transmission is remote.

ACTIVITY C-6

Determining Local and Remote Transmissions

Scenario:

In this activity, you will examine subnet masks to determine if a packet belongs on the local network or on a remote network.

---

1. **If the sender's IP address is 145.107.3.10 and the destination IP address is 145.107.5.10, you can determine if the packet's destination is local or remote by examining the ______ _____ .**

---

2. **If the sender's IP address is 129.100.12.10, the receiver's IP address is 129.100.0.18, and the subnet mask is 255.255.0.0, will this transmission be local or remote?**

   __ Local

   __ Remote

---

3. If the sender's IP address is 142.100.17.50, the receiver's IP address is 142.100.21.5, and the subnet mask is 255.255.255.0, will this transmission be local or remote?

   __ Local

   __ Remote

---

4. If you AND the IP address 145.10.50.5 and the subnet mask 255.255.0.0, what is the resulting network address?

   a) 145.10.50.0

   b) 145.10.0.0

   c) 145.0.0.0

   d) 145.50.0.0

---

5. If you AND the IP address 145.49.50.5 and the subnet mask 255.255.252.0, what is the resulting network address?

   a) 145.49.0.0

   b) 145.49.50.0

   c) 145.49.48.0

   d) 145.47.0.0

---

6. If the sender's IP address is 145.10.50.5, with a subnet mask of 255.255.0.0, and the receiver's IP address is 145.49.50.5, with a subnet mask of 255.255.252.0, is the transmission local or remote?

   __ Local

   __ Remote

Using Custom Subnet Masks to Subdivide Network Addresses

The subnet mask is customized when it "borrows" some of the bits from the host address to identify the different subnet segments. The number of subnets required for your physical network determines the number of bits that must be borrowed from the host portion of the IP address. The subnet mask requires that the equivalent number of borrowed bits be set to a value of 1. The 1s in the subnet portion of the mask enable subnet addresses to "pass through." This is because the subnet mask is ANDed to the IP address, and 1 AND any number results in the same number. The custom subnet mask determines if the destination of a packet transmitted on the network is local or remote. Packets transmitted to the Internet appear as if they come from the single assigned network address regardless of the subnet address, because the Internet applies only the default subnet mask.

Remember that all computers within the same network must use the same subnet mask.

To calculate the number of available subnet addresses, use the formula $2^x - 2$, where x is the number of borrowed bits for subnetting. Two of the available addresses are subtracted because a value of all 1s or 0s in the subnet address is not permitted in networks that comply with RFC 950. (RFC 1812 does permit the use of all 1s or all 0s in CIDR-compliant environments; in this case, you would not have to subtract two subnets. The discussions and activities in this appendix assume a standard RFC 950 subnetting environment.)

See **www.microsoft.com/resources/documentation/Windows/2000/server/reskit/en-us/cnet/cnbb_tcp_rlgr.asp** for more information on subnetting.

For example, consider a situation where a custom subnet mask for a Class B address uses the entire third byte for subnet addressing. Because there are 8 bits in a byte, the formula is 2^8-2, yielding 254 possible subnet addresses. This leaves 8 bits for host addresses, so (using the same formula) there could be up to 254 hosts on each subnet.

	Decimal	Binary
Address	145.98.20.5	10010001.01100010.00010100.00000101
Subnet Mask	255.255.255.0	11111111.11111111.11111111.00000000
Network Address	145.98.20.0	10010001.01100010.00010100.00000000
Host Address	0.0.0.5	00000000.00000000.00000000.00000101

But what if you have a situation where you need more than 254 host addresses per subnet? If you borrow all eight bits from the third byte, you will not have enough host addresses. You will need to borrow only enough bits from the third byte to identify all subnets, and leave the remaining bits for host addresses. Let's see what happens when we borrow only four bits from the third byte. Using the formula 2^4-2, we can have 14 possible subnet addresses. With 12 bits for host addressing, the formula 2^{12}-2 yields 4,094 possible host addresses per subnet.

	Decimal	Binary
Address	145.98.20.5	10010001.01100010.00010100.00000101
Subnet Mask	255.255.240.0	11111111.11111111.11110000.00000000
Network Address	145.98.16.0	10010001.01100010.00010000.00000000
Host Address	0.0.4.5	00000000.00000000.00000100.00000101

Guidelines for Creating Custom Subnet Masks

You can use the following guidelines to define a subnet mask for your network:

- Determine the number of subnets you need now and plan for future growth.
- Convert the number of subnets necessary to its binary value; for example, if you need six subnets, the binary equivalent is 00000110.
- Use the number of bits required to show the binary value of the number of subnets as the high-order bits in the subnet mask. In the previous example, it takes three bits to represent six, thus the binary value of the mask will be 11100000.

You can also use the following conversion tables to identify which subnet mask you need for Class A or Class B network addresses.

Number of Class A Subnets Needed	Number of Hosts	Number of Bits Used in Subnet Mask	Subnet Mask
2	4,194,302	2	255.192.0.0
6	2,097,150	3	255.224.0.0
14	1,048,574	4	255.240.0.0
30	524,286	5	255.248.0.0
62	262,142	6	255.252.0.0
126	131,070	7	255.254.0.0
254	65,534	8	255.255.0.0

Number of Class B Subnets Needed	Number of Hosts	Number of Bits Used in Subnet Mask	Subnet Mask
2	16,382	2	255.255.192.0
6	8,190	3	255.255.224.0
14	4,094	4	255.255.240.0
30	2,046	5	255.255.248.0
62	1,022	6	255.255.252.0
126	510	7	255.255.254.0
254	254	8	255.255.255.0

ACTIVITY C-7

Using and Calculating Custom Subnet Masks

Scenario:

In this activity, you will use and develop custom subnet masks.

1. **If you borrow three bits from the host portion of a Class B address, how many subnets will you be able to assign unique addresses to?**
   - a) 2
   - b) 3
   - c) 6
   - d) 8

2. **If you borrow three bits from the host portion of a Class B address, how many host addresses will be available per subnet?**
   - a) 30
   - b) 8,190
   - c) 8,192
   - d) 65,534

3. **If your IP address is 145.8.17.96 and the subnet mask is 255.255.255.0, what is the subnet address?**
   - a) 0.0.12.0
   - b) 145.8.17.0
   - c) 145.8.0.0
   - d) 0.0.17.0

4. **If you have the network address 145.100.0.0 and you need 12 subnets, what custom subnet mask should you use?**
   - a) 255.255.0.0
   - b) 255.255.248.0
   - c) 255.255.240.0
   - d) 255.255.255.0

5. **If you have the network address 145.100.0.0 and you need 12 subnets, how many hosts can be on each subnet?**
   - a) 8,190
   - b) 4,094
   - c) 2,046
   - d) 510

6. **If you have the network address 145.100.0.0 and you need 12 subnets, how many subnet addresses will be left over?**
   a) 0
   b) 2
   c) 6
   d) 18

Assigning Network Addresses with a Custom Subnet Mask

Subnet addresses are calculated by varying the number of bits borrowed from the host portion of the address. The following table lists the possible bit combinations for the subnet address if you borrow three bits from the host address.

Subnet Address	Decimal Value
000 00000	0 (Invalid in standard subnetting—cannot have 0 for subnet address)
001 00000	32
010 00000	64
011 00000	96
100 00000	128
101 00000	160
110 00000	192
111 00000	224 (Invalid in standard subnetting—cannot have all 1s for subnet address)

The 0 and 224 subnet mask values would be valid in a CIDR environment, in accordance with RFC 1812. The CIDR subnet mask is expressed as a prefix giving the number of 1 bits in the mask, not as dotted-decimal octets as in standard subnetting.

The maximum number of subnet addresses is 2^3-2, or 6. If this were a subnet mask for a Class B network address, then you would borrow the three bits from the third byte of the IP address. The combination of the assigned network address and the subnet address creates a unique network address for each subnet.

To enable TCP/IP to identify the subnet addresses, the subnet mask would be 255.255.224.0, or 11111111.11111111.11100000.0. If your assigned network address is 145.10, then the available subnet addresses with a subnet mask of 255.255.224.0 are as follows: 145.10.32.0, 145.10.64.0, 145.10.96.0, 145.10.128.0, 145.10.160.0, and 145.10.192.0.

The maximum number of available hosts on each subnet would be 2^{13}-2 or 8,190 (13 being the number of remaining bits for the host address; five from the third byte plus eight from the fourth byte).

Although you can calculate the available subnet addresses in binary, a simpler method is to use a decimal increment. In the aforementioned three-bit subnet mask example, the decimal value of the lowest bit in the subnet mask is 32; thus, the subnet address increment is also 32. Use the following guidelines for determining the subnet increment:

- Identify the binary value of the subnet mask.
- Convert the lowest-order bit to its equivalent decimal value.
- The resulting number is the subnet address increment.

ACTIVITY C-8

Calculating Subnet Addresses with Custom Subnet Masks

Scenario:

In this activity, you will determine the number of available subnet addresses for custom subnet masks. Your Class A network (117.0.0.0) address requires 50 subnets. Assume that your network complies with the RFC 950 standards for subnetting.

---

1. **How many bits must be borrowed from the host portion of the IP address to enable the creation of 50 subnets?**

   a) 4

   b) 5

   c) 6

   d) 8

---

2. **To have 50 subnets, what would the subnet mask need to be?**

   a) 255.240.0.0

   b) 255.248.0.0

   c) 255.252.0.0

   d) 255.254.0.0

---

3. **How many host addresses are available for each subnet?**

   a) 1,048,574

   b) 524,280

   c) 262,142

   d) 131,070

---

4. **What is the maximum number of subnets allowed?**

   a) 36

   b) 62

   c) 126

   d) 254

---

5. **What is the network address increment?**

   a) 2

   b) 4

   c) 6

   d) 7

---

6. **True or False? One of the available network addresses is 117.64.0.0.**

   __ True

   __ False

Calculating Host Addresses with a Custom Subnet Mask

The available host addresses are calculated based on the network addresses by varying the remaining bits of the host portion byte(s). The number of bits that can be varied is determined by how many bits are borrowed for subnetting. In the three-bit subnet mask example for the Class B address of 145.10, the available host addresses for each of the six subnets are calculated as follows (note that it is easier to see the subnet and host addresses in binary than it is in decimal).

Start Value (binary)	End Value (binary)	Start Value (decimal)	End Value (decimal)
145.10.00100000.00000001	145.10.00111111.11111110	145.10.32.1	145.10.63.254
145.10.01000000.00000001	145.10.01011111.11111110	145.10.64.1	145.10.95.254
145.10.01100000.00000001	145.10.01111111.11111110	145.10.96.1	145.10.127.254
145.10.10000000.00000001	145.10.10011111.11111110	145.10.128.1	145.10.159.254
145.10.10100000.00000001	145.10.10111111.11111110	145.10.160.1	145.10.191.254
145.10.11000000.00000001	145.10.11011111.11111110	145.10.192.1	145.10.223.254

Rather than calculating the host addresses in binary, you can use the following shortcut method to calculate the host addresses in decimal:

- Identify the starting value for a subnet with a host address of 1. For example, the starting value for the host addresses for a given subnet will always be network.network.subnet.1, where the network portion is the assigned address from the InterNIC, the subnet portion is the valid subnet address, and the starting host address is always 1.

- The ending value for host addresses for that subnet will be the decimal value of the next available subnet address minus 1. For example, if the subnet increment is 32, then the next available subnet address is 64. Thus, the ending host address for subnet 32 is network.network.(64-1).254, or network.network.63.254.

ACTIVITY C-9

Assigning Host Addresses for Custom Subnets

Scenario:

In this activity, you will calculate the available host addresses for a given subnet address. Your Class B network address is 155.8.0.0, with a subnet mask of 255.255.240.0.

---

1. **How many bits are you borrowing from the third byte to create subnet addresses?**

    a) 3

    b) 4

    c) 6

    d) 7

---

2. **How many subnets will this subnet mask support?**

    a) 6

    b) 8

    c) 14

    d) 62

---

3. **What is the network address increment?**

    a) 4

    b) 8

    c) 12

    d) 16

---

4. **What are the available network addresses?**

    a) 155.8.0.0, 155.8.24.0, 155.8.48.0, 155.8.72.0, 155.8.96.0, and so forth.

    b) 155.8.8.0, 155.8.16.0, 155.8.24.0, 155.8.32.0, 155.8.40.0, and so forth.

    c) 155.8.12.0, 155.8.24.0, 155.8.36.0, 155.8.48.0, 155.8.60.0, and so forth.

    d) 155.8.16.0, 155.8.32.0, 155.8.48.0, 155.8.64.0, 155.8.80.0, and so forth.

---

5. What are the available host addresses for the first subnet?
   a) 155.8.24.1 through 155.8.47.254
   b) 155.8.16.1 through 155.8.31.254
   c) 155.8.12.1 through 155.8.23.254
   d) 155.8.4.1 through 155.8.7.254

ACTIVITY C-10

Identifying Subnet Masks

Scenario:

In this activity, you will identify subnet masks for the given situations.

1. You have been assigned a Class C network address for your local, single-segment network. What subnet mask should you use?
   a) 255.255.0.0
   b) 255.255.240.0
   c) 255.255.255.0
   d) 255.255.255.192

2. True or False? The maximum number of hosts on a Class C network is 255.
   __ True
   __ False

3. You received an address assignment of 167.5.0.0. What class of address is this?
   a) Class A
   b) Class B
   c) Class C
   d) Class D

4. If your network address is 167.5.0.0 and you need to create five subnets, what subnet mask should you use?
   a) 255.255.0.0
   b) 255.255.240.0
   c) 255.255.224.0
   d) 255.255.192.0

5. True or False? If your network address is 167.5.0.0 and you need to create five subnets, the subnet mask you use will leave one unused subnet available for future use.

   __ True

   __ False

---

6. You are using a Class A network address on a single-segment network. What subnet mask should you use?

   a) 255.0.0.0

   b) 255.240.0.0

   c) 255.255.0.0

   d) 255.255.240.0

   e) 255.255.255.0

---

7. Why do you need a subnet mask if the network has only one segment?

---

8. You have a Class B network with 65 subnets. What subnet mask is required to support the subnets?

   a) 255.240.0.0

   b) 255.255.0.0

   c) 255.255.254.0

   d) 255.255.240.0

---

9. True or False? On a Class B network with 65 subnets, the maximum number of hosts per subnet is 1,022.

   __ True

   __ False

---

10. You are using a Class B network address with 13 subnets. Your company is merging with another company, and your network will increase to 25 subnets. What subnet mask should you use?

    a) 255.255.0.0

    b) 255.255.248.0

    c) 255.255.196.0

    d) 255.255.255.0

---

11. True or False? After you change the subnet mask to support 25 subnets, you will have 5 extra subnets after the merger.

    __ True

    __ False

---

12. **On a Class B network with 25 subnets, how many hosts can each subnet contain?**

    a) 4,094

    b) 2,046

    c) 1,022

    d) 510

ACTIVITY C-11

Troubleshooting Addressing Errors

Scenario:

In this activity, you will troubleshoot addressing errors and explain the consequences of those errors. Use these figures to help you answer the questions.

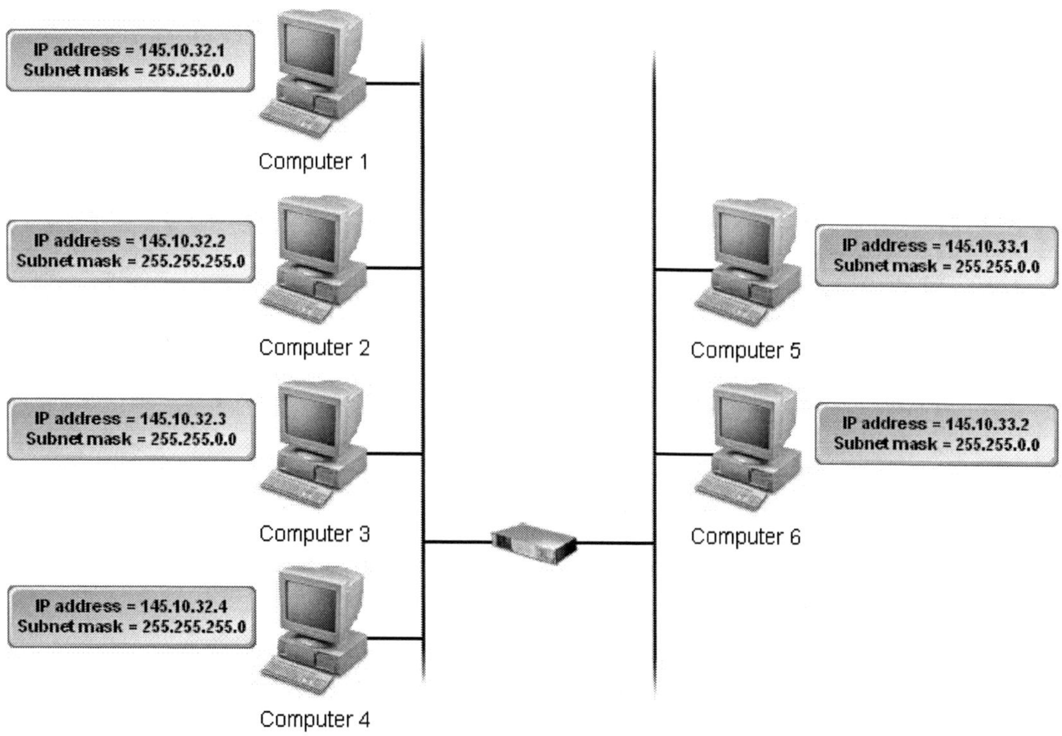

Figure C-3: *Addressing problems on multiple subnets.*

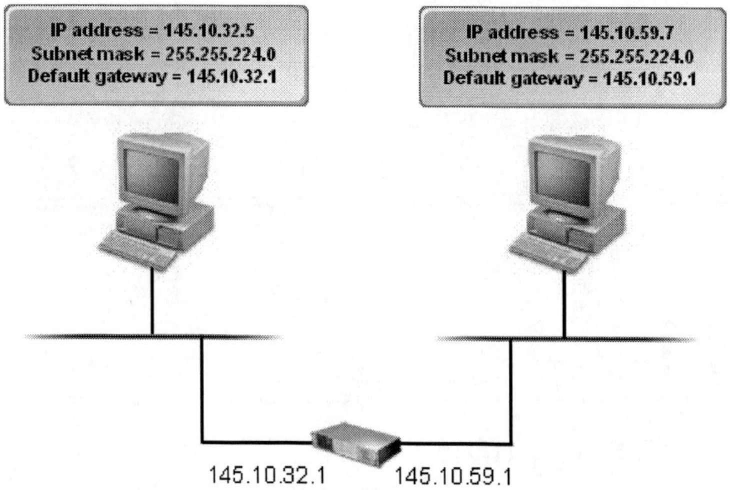

Figure C-4: *Addressing problems on two subnets.*

---

1. **In Figure C-3, which hosts are using the wrong subnet mask?**
   a) 1
   b) 2
   c) 3
   d) 4
   e) 5

---

2. **True or False? Using the wrong subnet mask will prevent the hosts from communicating with other local hosts.**
   __ True
   __ False

---

3. **For this scenario, what is the correct subnet mask?**
   a) 255.0.0.0
   b) 255.255.0.0
   c) 255.255.255.0

---

4. **What is wrong with the subnet mask assignments in Figure C-4?**

---

5. **True or False? The hosts will be able to communicate through the router because the default gateway settings are accurate.**
   __ True
   __ False

---

6. What subnet mask could you use for this network?
   a) 255.255.255.0
   b) 255.255.254.0
   c) 255.0.0.0
   d) 255.252.0.0
   e) 255.255.248.0

ACTIVITY C-12

Assigning Subnet and Host Addresses

Scenario:

Your network has been assigned a Class B address of 165.125.0.0. You need 12 subnets, so the subnet mask is 255.255.240.0. The number of bits used for the subnet mask is four.

1. How many subnets are possible?
   a) 16
   b) 14
   c) 8
   d) 6

2. The binary and decimal values for the first subnet are ________ ___ __.

3. The binary and decimal values for the second subnet are ________ ___ __.

4. The binary and decimal values for the third subnet are ________ ___ __.

5. The binary and decimal values for the fourth subnet are ________ ___ __.

6. The binary and decimal values for the fifth subnet are ________ ___ __.

7. The binary and decimal values for the sixth subnet are ________ ___ __.

8. The binary and decimal values for the seventh subnet are ________ ___ ___.

9. The binary and decimal values for the eighth subnet are ________ ___ ___.

10. The binary and decimal values for the ninth subnet are ________ ___ ___.

11. The binary and decimal values for the 10th subnet are ________ ___ ___.

12. The binary and decimal values for the 11th subnet are ________ ___ ___ .

13. The binary and decimal values for the 12th subnet are ________ ___ ___ .

14. The binary and decimal values for the 13th subnet are ________ ___ ___ .

15. The binary and decimal values for the 14th subnet are ________ ___ ___ .

16. List the range of available host addresses for the first subnet.

17. List the range of available host addresses for the second subnet.

18. List the range of available host addresses for the third subnet.

19. List the range of available host addresses for the fourth subnet.

20. List the range of available host addresses for the fifth subnet.

21. List the range of available host addresses for the sixth subnet.

22. List the range of available host addresses for the seventh subnet.

23. List the range of available host addresses for the eighth subnet.

24. List the range of available host addresses for the ninth subnet.

25. List the range of available host addresses for the 10th subnet.

26. List the range of available host addresses for the 11th subnet.

27. List the range of available host addresses for the 12th subnet.

28. List the range of available host addresses for the 13th subnet.

29. List the range of available host addresses for the 14th subnet.

ACTIVITY C-13

Addressing a Class C Network

Scenario:

You have been assigned a Class C network address of 221.100.55.0. Your network consists of two segments connected by a router.

1. How many subnets do you need?
   a) 0
   b) 1
   c) 2
   d) 3
   e) 4

2. How many bits will be used for the subnet mask?
   a) 0
   b) 1
   c) 2
   d) 3
   e) 4

3. True or False? You can have up to 126 hosts on each subnet.
   __ True
   __ False

4. The correct subnet mask is ______________ .

5. What are the binary and decimal values for the first subnet address?

6. What are the binary and decimal values for the second subnet?

7. For the first subnet, what is the range of available host addresses?

8. For the second subnet, what is the range of available host addresses?

Lesson Labs

Due to classroom setup constraints, some labs cannot be keyed in sequence immediately following their associated lesson. Your instructor will tell you whether your labs can be practiced immediately following the lesson or whether they require separate setup from the main lesson content.

Lesson 1 Lab 1

Applying Network Theory

Activity Time:

15 minutes

Scenario:

In this activity, you will identify the components of and apply your understanding of networking theory.

1. **Mom-N-Pop Realty has four employees who need to share information and hardware such as the scanner and printer. They also need Internet access. None of the users have advanced computing skills. Which type of network (network category) would best suit their needs?**
   a) Client/server network
   b) Peer-to-peer network
   c) UNIX-based centralized network

2. **Match the network term to its definition.**

___	Server	a.	A computer that uses the resources of other networked computers.
___	Client	b.	The process of identifying who or what is trying to gain access to a network resource.
___	Host	c.	A computer that shares its resources with other networked computers.
___	Authentication	d.	A powerful centralized computer that performs storage and processing tasks for other network devices.
___	Encryption	e.	Encoding information so that it cannot be read by anyone other than its intended recipient.

3. **True or False? A segment is a physical subdivision of a larger network, whereas a subnet is a logical subdivision.**

   __ True

   __ False

4. **When two or more devices share resources across a network without using the services of a server or host, these computers are participating in a:**

   a) Client/server network

   b) Mixed-mode network

   c) Peer-to-peer network

   d) Host-based network

LESSON 2 LAB 1

Selecting Communications Methods

Activity Time:

15 minutes

Scenario:

You are given the task of choosing the transmission, media access, and signaling methods that will be used on your company's new network. You have been asked by your management team to submit responses to the following questions as a means of justifying your network design choices.

---

1. **Your network will include servers, workstations, printers, and network-accessible fax servers. Select the type of transmission method that these devices will most commonly use.**

   a) Unicast

   b) Broadcast

   c) Multicast

---

2. **Match the media access method with its description.**

___	Polling	a.	Transmitting devices check to see if the media is available. If so, they transmit, checking to see if a collision has occurred. If so, they wait and then re-transmit.
___	Multiplexing	b.	Devices that possess a special packet are permitted to transmit. All other devices must listen.
___	Carrier Sense Multiple Access with Collision Detection (CSMA/CD)	c.	Transmitting devices check to see if the media is available. If so, they transmit a blocking signal before transmitting their data.
___	Carrier Sense Multiple Access with Collision Avoidance (CSMA/CA)	d.	A central device asks each device, in turn, if it has data to transmit.
___	Token-based	e.	Data from multiple devices is combined into a single signal through a time-sharing method or the use of multiple frequencies.

---

3. **True or False? To communicate, devices must use the same media access method.**

   __ True

   __ False

---

4. **True or False? Network communications use digital signals exclusively.**

   __ True

   __ False

5. **Select the characteristics that describe parallel data transmission.**

   a) Data bits are transmitted one after the other across the medium.

   b) Multiple bits are transferred per clock cycle.

   c) Uses multiple wires to carry signals.

   d) Clocking signals must be modulated with data signals.

LESSON 3 LAB 1

Exploring Network Data Delivery

Activity Time:

15 minutes

Scenario:

In this activity, you will identify the characteristics of network data delivery methods.

1. **True or False? A datagram is another name for a packet.**

   __ True

   __ False

2. **Select the components of a packet.**

   a) Header

   b) Data

   c) Footer

   d) Frame

3. **Match the error detection technique with the amount of data that it protects.**

___	Parity	a.	Byte
___	CRC	b.	Block
___	EDAC	c.	Packet

4. True or False? Sliding windows typically offer better performance than fixed length windows.

    __ True

    __ False

Lesson 4 Lab 1

Investigating Network Media and Hardware

Activity Time:

15 minutes

Scenario:

In this activity, you will list and describe network media and hardware components.

1. Which unbounded media uses multiple radio frequencies to reduce interference and the likelihood of eavesdropping?

    a) Infrared

    b) Microwave

    c) Spread spectrum

    d) Broadcast

2. Match the network media with the connector typically used with it.

___	Coaxial cable	a.	RJ-45 connector
___	Twisted pair cable	b.	MTRJ connector
___	Fiber optic cable	c.	BNC connector

3. True or False? You can unwind as much of a twisted pair cable's conductors as you need without affecting its performance characteristics.

    __ True

    __ False

4. You need to connect twisted pair drops to form a logical bus network. You need maximum speed between nodes and expect considerable simultaneous traffic. Select the appropriate network device.

    a) Router

    b) Bridge

    c) Switch

    d) Repeater

    e) Hub

5. **Match the source of noise with the means by which you can lessen or eliminate its impact.**

___	Fluorescent lights	a.	Don't install PCs or network devices on the same electrical circuit or in close proximity.
___	Motor noise	b.	Avoid running drops alongside electric service cables; don't unwind conductor pairs.
___	Solar interference	c.	Use shielded cabling, with proper termination and grounding.
___	Crosstalk	d.	Don't run cables within 20 inches; run perpendicular if a drop must cross.

6. **Match the network connectivity device to its description.**

___	Gateway	a.	Any device, software, or system that converts data between incompatible systems.
___	Wireless access point	b.	A networking device used to connect the drops in a physical star topology network into a logical bus topology.
___	Router	c.	A device that provides connection between wireless devices and can connect to wired networks.
___	Bridge	d.	A network device that divides a logical bus network into subnets.Examines the MAC address of each packet and forwards packets only as necessary.
___	Switch	e.	A networking device used to connect the drops in a physical star topology network into a logical bus topology, forwarding packets to only the correct port based on MAC addresses.
___	Hub	f.	A networking device that connects multiple networks that use the same protocol.

LESSON 5 LAB 1

Examining Network Implementations

Activity Time:

15 minutes

Scenario:

In this activity, you will check your understanding of the major types of networks.

---

1. **The OSI model is a ________________________.**
    a) Specification for the interoperability of Ethernet networks
    b) Framework for how computers exchange data packets
    c) Type of error correction method used in Token Ring networks
    d) Specification for Token Ring-to-Ethernet connectivity

---

2. **True or False? Only folders can be shared.**
    __ True
    __ False

---

3. **In Windows, a shared folder can be hidden by ____________________.**
    a) Setting certain permission levels
    b) Adding a % symbol to the beginning of the share name
    c) Adding a $ to the end of the share name
    d) Adding a % to the beginning and a $ to the end of the share name

---

4. **True or False? Ethernet technology utilizes CSMA/CD technology.**
    __ True
    __ False

---

5. **Token Ring networks are ____________________.**
    a) Deterministic networks
    b) Priority networks
    c) Shared networks
    d) Captured networks

---

6. **The dual rings of a FDDI network provide ____________________.**
   a) Easier maintenance
   b) Fault tolerance
   c) Reduced costs for large networks
   d) Easier manageability

7. **True or False? Infrared wireless networks are ideal for large areas with obstacles.**
   __ True
   __ False

LESSON 6 LAB 1

Networking with TCP/IP

Activity Time:

15 minutes

Scenario:

In this activity, you will identify how to network with TCP/IP.

1. **Define the function of the routing family of protocols.**

2. **Define the function of the file access family of protocols.**

3. **In Windows Server 2003, where would an administrator determine which protocols were bound to a NIC?**

4. Convert the following IP addresses from decimal values to their equivalent binary numbers:

   255

   8

   198.131.205.5

   224.254.100.8

5. Is the IP address of 172.16.5.255 with a subnet mask of 255.255.0.0 a valid IP address?

6. Determine if the following addresses are on local or remote networks. Both addresses share the same subnet mask.

   Node 1 = 227.16.90.30; Node 2 = 227.16.87.26; Subnet Mask = 255.255.0.0

7. How do you calculate the available number of host addresses for a Class B address?

8. You've been asked to implement TCP/IP on a divided network. There are two subnets separated by a Layer 3 network device. There is no Internet connection. Subnet one has 235 nodes and subnet two has 1,500 nodes. Using the default address classes, how would you assign IP addresses?

9. **You're the administrator of a quickly growing company. Your corporate headquarters is concerned with address depletion of its internal addresses and has asked you to convert a Class B IP network to a CIDR scheme. Your present default gateway address is 172.16.255.254 and can't be changed. You have 2,400 nodes on your network. Determine the CIDR network ID.**

---

10. **Match the TCP/IP network layer with its description.**

___	Application	a.	Provides connection and communication services.
___	Transport	b.	Provides addressing and routing services.
___	Internet	c.	Contains utilities such as socket services and NetBIOS over TCP/IP.
___	Network	d.	Contains services that send frames to and receive frames from the network.

---

11. **What is the purpose of port numbers?**

LESSON 7 LAB 1

Identifying TCP/IP Services

Activity Time:

15 minutes

Scenario:

In this activity, you will identify the major services deployed on TCP/IP networks.

1. **A Windows Me user logs on and gets a message that her IP address is already in use. This user gets her IP address through a DHCP server. What tool can you use to release and renew her IP address from the DHCP server?**

   a) At a command prompt, type ipconfig /release and then ipconfig /renew.

   b) At a command prompt, type winipcfg. Click More Info. Click the Release button. Restart the computer to lease a new address.

   c) At a command prompt, type ifconfig /release and then ifconfig /renew.

2. **Match the TCP/IP service with its description.**

___	Dynamic Host Configuration Protocol (DHCP)	a.	Used to map NetBIOS names to IP addresses to reduce the number of NetBIOS name resolution broadcasts.
___	Domain Name System (DNS)	b.	Used to automate the TCP/IP configuration settings of network devices.
___	Windows Internet Name Service (WINS)	c.	Used to translate fully qualified domain names into IP addresses and vice versa.
___	IP configuration utilities	d.	Used to gather TCP/IP configuration information about network devices and traffic.

3. **Match the TCP/IP upper-layer service with its description.**

___	File Transfer Protocol (FTP)	a.	Enables a user at one site to simulate a session on a remote host.
___	Telnet	b.	Retrieves email messages from a mail server.
___	Network Time Protocol (NTP)	c.	Enables the transfer of files between a user's workstation and a remote host.
___	Simple Mail Transfer Protocol (SMTP)	d.	Synchronizes the clock times of computers in a network to the millisecond against the U.S. Naval Observatory master clocks in Washington, D.C., and Colorado Springs, CO.
___	Internet Mail Access Protocol (IMAP4)	e.	Sends email from a client to a server or between servers.
___	Hypertext Transfer Protocol (HTTP)	f.	Defines the interaction between a web server and a browser.

4. **Match the TCP/IP interoperability service with its description.**

___	Line Printer Remote (LPR) and Line Printer Daemon (LPD)	a.	Collects information from network devices for diagnostic and maintenance purposes.
___	Network File System (NFS)	b.	Enables users to access shared files stored on different types of computers and work with those files as if they were stored locally on their own computers.
___	Secure Shell (SSH)	c.	Enables sharing resources, such as files, printers, and serial ports, between computers.
___	Server Message Block (SMB)	d.	Establishes connections between client workstations and network printers.
___	Lightweight Directory Access Protocol (LDAP)	e.	Enables a user or application to log on to another computer over a network, execute commands on a remote machine, and move files from one machine to another. Used with Secure Copy Protocol (SCP) to securely transfer computer files between a local and a remote host, or between two remote hosts.
___	Simple Network Management Protocol (SNMP)	f.	Defines how a client can access information, perform operations, and share directory data on a directory server.

LESSON 8 LAB 1

Discussing Alternate Network Protocols

Activity Time:

15 minutes

Scenario:

In this activity, you will identify characteristics of various network protocols.

1. **What are some advantages and disadvantages of NetBEUI?**

2. What is a common connectivity problem on IPX/SPX networks, and how would you solve it?

---

3. Describe the functions of the IPX and SPX protocols.

---

4. What are the three components of an AppleTalk address?

---

5. List the steps in the AppleTalk addressing process.

---

6. What is the role of AFP in the AppleTalk protocol suite?

---

7. What major networking trend is driving the development and adoption of IPv6?

---

8. What are some of the potential advantages of IPv6?

LESSON 9 LAB 1

Discussing LAN Infrastructure

Activity Time:

15 minutes

Scenario:

In this activity, you will examine various aspects of the LAN infrastructure.

---

1. **What type of bridge connects different networks across media such as a leased phone line, fiber optic link, or wireless media?**
   a) Remote bridge
   b) Translational bridge
   c) Transparent bridge

---

2. **What advantage does a router have over a switch?**
   a) Routers translate data between different operating systems.
   b) Routers translate data between different types of networks.
   c) Routers can block unwanted traffic.

---

3. **An ___________ ______ is a group of routers managed or administered by the same entity.**

---

4. **True or False? The first decision made by a sending node about the route of a packet is whether the data is bound for a local or remote subnet.**
   __ True
   __ False

---

5. **If a router doesn't have a default gateway specified, and a data packet doesn't meet the requirements of any of the router's programming, what does the router do with the data packet?**
   a) It drops the data packet.
   b) It forwards the data packet to the nearest border router.
   c) It returns the packet to the sender.
   d) It saves the packet and reports an error to the network administrator.

---

6. **A _______ _____ is a database created by a route discovery protocol that contains network locations as perceived by a specific router.**

---

7. **Which of the following are advantages of a static routing table?**

   a) They don't require maintenance.

   b) They don't cause extra network traffic because the routers don't need to communicate with each other.

   c) They're totally controlled by an administrator.

   d) They do not require specialized routing protocols.

---

8. **Which of the following are components of a routing table?**

   a) Destination

   b) Network mask

   c) Subnet number

   d) Metric

   e) Default TTL

---

9. **True or False? A default route in a routing table is the route to a specific network address.**

   ___ True

   ___ False

---

10. **Which of the following describes how routers exchange information such as the address of the next router in the path and the number of hops to the destination?**

    a) Count-to-Infinity

    b) Link-state routing

    c) Distance-vector routing

    d) Split horizon

---

11. **Which of the following describes how routers exchange information about a route and its quality, bandwidth, and availability?**

    a) Link-state routing

    b) Distance-vector routing

    c) Split horizon

    d) Poison reverse

---

12. **Which solution to the Count-to-Infinity problem takes less time and produces larger updates?**

    a) Poison reverse

    b) Split horizon

    c) Convergence

    d) Routing loops

---

13. **The primary disadvantage of ___ is it exchanges the entire route table with periodic broadcasts that might use up too much bandwidth on large networks.**

---

14. True or False? RIP supports multicasting, password protection for routers, and multiple subnet masks.

    __ True

    __ False

---

15. Which of the following is best used in small- to medium-sized networks that don't change very much?

    a) RIP

    b) RIP II

    c) OSPF

    d) IGRP

---

16. ____ improves the distance-vector method by enabling an administrator to configure six extra metrics that are combined into a composite metric.

---

17. A ____________ is a map of network routers that contains information about the condition of the links and multiple routes to destinations.

---

18. True or False? OSPF differs from RIP in that it sends only updates in router advertisements instead of the entire route table.

    __ True

    __ False

---

19. What is the result of output filtering on a router?

    a) Data is blocked from being sent out through the router.

    b) Data is not accepted at the router on specific interfaces.

    c) Data is accepted at the router but is returned to the sender and an error is generated.

    d) Data is blocked from being sent out through a specific interface on a router. The data can still be sent through other interfaces on the router.

---

20. What is required to implement a VLAN environment?

    a) A bridge that's VLAN-configurable.

    b) A switch that's VLAN-configurable.

    c) A router that's VLAN-configurable.

    d) A hub that's VLAN-configurable.

---

21. True or False? VLANs are implemented in the software configuration of a VLAN switch.

    __ True

    __ False

---

22. True or False? VLANs are less expensive than a regular switched environment.

    __ True

    __ False

LESSON 10 LAB 1

Discussing WAN Infrastructure

Activity Time:

15 minutes

Scenario:

In this activity, you will examine various aspects of WAN infrastructure.

1. **Describe circuit switching, packet switching, and cell switching.**

2. **What are the benefits and drawbacks of dial-up connectivity?**

3. **Both DSL and cable are popular home and small-office broadband connectivity services. What is the technical difference between DSL and cable?**

4. **What are the benefits and drawbacks of ATM?**

5. **What is the primary physical media type for SONET?**

6. **What are some of the physical equipment types used to connect LAN implementations to WAN transmission media?**

7. What are the benefits and drawbacks of VoIP?

Lesson 11 Lab 1

Discussing Network Security

Activity Time:

15 minutes

Scenario:

In this activity, you will discuss various aspects of network security.

1. Describe Trojan horses and explain why they are dangerous.

2. What are some ways that you can guard against network data theft?

3. Are there any disadvantages to strong virus protection plans?

4. Describe strong passwords.

5. What are the security advantages of a drive-level security system such as NTFS?

6. Summarize the Kerberos authentication process.

7. How can digital certificates support network security?

8. Describe some of the security benefits of IPSec.

9. Distinguish between NAT servers, firewalls, and proxy servers.

LESSON 11 LAB 2

Designing a Network Security Plan

Activity Time:

15 minutes

Scenario:

You have been asked to design a security proposal for a network with five remote offices, and to provide web services to its users.

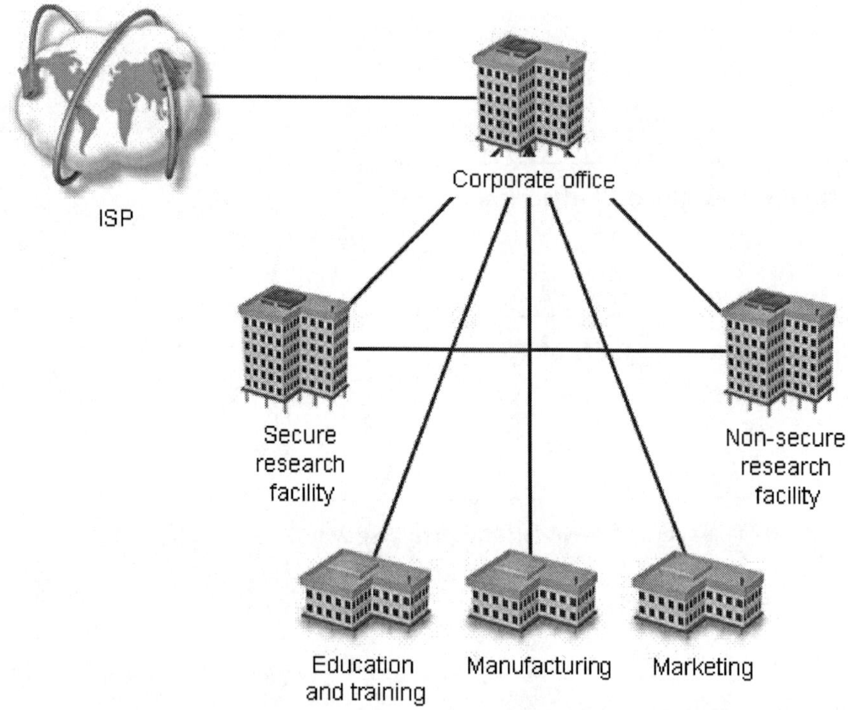

Figure 11-A: *The network security diagram.*

You have the following information and requirements:

- The customer wants you to address all aspects of security and virus protection applicable to the company.
- The corporate office houses all HR, payroll, and corporate-wide servers except for the research facility servers. A single web server in the corporate office hosts both internal and external websites.
- The non-secure research facility houses an imaging server that contains a directory with scanned images from the company's electron microscope. These scans are needed by the secure research facility.
- The secure research facility requires Internet access and access to the scanned images server, but no data can leave the facility or be uploaded to any Internet server.
- The manufacturing facility and marketing office need access to corporate servers and the Internet.
- The education facility hosts both internal and external users, creating the risk of exposure of corporate or secure data. This risk needs to be eliminated, and the education facility staff needs access to corporate servers and the Internet. The classrooms also need access to the Internet.

1. **How would you recommend implementing a virus protection program?**

2. Where would you need firewalls and NATs?

---

3. What is the best way to ensure that users at the secure research facility can gain access to scans on the image server?

---

4. How can the web server be configured to allow access both inside and outside the company?

---

5. **Sketch your network design.**

LESSON 12 LAB 1

Discussing Remote Networking

Activity Time:

15 minutes

Scenario:

In this activity, you will investigate remote networking issues.

1. **Match each job role with the most appropriate remote networking architecture.**

___	Data entry associate	a.	Remote access
___	Telecommuter	b.	Terminal services
___	Network administrator	c.	Remote control

2. **Which types of remote networking are associated with the RDP protocol?**
   a) Remote access
   b) Remote control
   c) Terminal services

3. **What are the necessary components for a dedicated thin client?**
   a) Input devices
   b) Output device
   c) Network connection
   d) Client software
   e) Boot ROM

4. **How is web-based remote access accomplished in Windows Server 2003?**
   a) Remote Desktop Connection
   b) Remote Assistance
   c) RRAS
   d) Remote Desktop Web Connection
   e) IIS

5. **True or False? The main difference between PAP and CHAP is how they handle user passwords.**
   __ True
   __ False

6. **Which remote access protocol is used with cable modem connections?**

   a) SLIP

   b) PPP

   c) PPPoE

   d) EAP

---

7. **In an environment that has several RAS servers, the main benefit of implementing ______ is central administration of remote access policies.**

---

8. **True or False? Tunneling enables nonroutable data to be sent over the Internet.**

   __ True

   __ False

---

9. **Which is a VPN protocol?**

   a) SLIP

   b) PPP

   c) PPTP

   d) PPPoE

   e) EAP

LESSON 13 LAB 1

Discussing Disaster Recovery

Activity Time:

15 minutes

Scenario:

In this activity, you will analyze various aspects of the disaster recovery process.

---

1. **Distinguish between disaster recovery planning and fault tolerance planning.**

---

2. What are some of the different personnel who are involved in designing and implementing a disaster recovery plan, and what are their roles?

3. What do you feel is the most important aspect of a disaster recovery plan? Why?

4. Why is it important to update a disaster recovery plan regularly?

5. How many tape sets are required when using the grandfather-father-son rotation method?

6. List and describe the three major backup types.

7. What is a brick-level backup of a mail server?

8. What are some special issues involved in backing up databases?

9. Which RAID level provides high fault tolerance but also high disk-space overhead?

10. What is the benefit of implementing RAID level 0?

11. How could you make a network with a single external WAN link and an internal routed topology fault-tolerant?

12. What factors should you consider when planning enterprise fault tolerance for your organization?

LESSON 14 LAB 1

Discussing Network Data Storage

Activity Time:

15 minutes

Scenario:

In this activity, you will examine various network data storage concepts and technologies.

1. What are some of the characteristics of a network that will affect its data storage requirements?

2. What are some of the factors you should evaluate when considering a data storage solution?

3. From a performance-to-cost standpoint, what is the most effective cluster implementation type?

4. How do nodes in a cluster monitor each other?

5. What two types of software are always required on a NAS system?

6. What hardware components are included in a NAS system, and which are omitted?

7. What improvements does a SAN have over a NAS?

8. What network technologies can be used for connectivity in a SAN?

LESSON 15 LAB 1

Discussing Network Operating Systems

Activity Time:

15 minutes

Scenario:

In this activity, you will examine various aspects of network operating systems.

---

1. **List some of the advanced network services supported natively on Windows Server 2003.**

---

2. **List some of the additional server products supported on the Windows Server 2003 platform.**

---

3. **Describe an important distinction between the Windows NT 4.0 server family, and prior versions of Windows Server.**

---

4. **Compare the NetWare terms eDirectory, NDS, and bindery.**

---

5. **What are some similarities between Active Directory and eDirectory?**

---

6. **How do the terms service, NLM, and daemon relate?**

---

7. Define the term open source as it relates to the Linux operating system.

8. What were some reasons for the popularity of UNIX for those who implemented it?

9. What are some of Linux's primary server functions?

10. How does loading a different shell affect a UNIX or Linux environment?

11. What are some of the advanced server features included with Mac OS X?

LESSON 16 LAB 1

Analyzing Network Troubleshooting Procedures

Activity Time:

15 minutes

Scenario:

In this activity, you will discuss the appropriate network troubleshooting procedures to follow in various situations.

1. What are some ways that you can determine the scope of a networking problem?

2. What are some things that all troubleshooting models have in common?

3. **What are some of the benefits of clearly documenting the results of troubleshooting problems?**

4. **Users on the third floor report that they can't connect to the Internet, but they can connect to the NetWare server. What would you check first?**
   a) Router configuration tables.
   b) If viruses exist on the network.
   c) Power cable to the hub.
   d) If users on other floors have similar problems.

5. **You're working the help desk and get a call that a user can't access the UNIX host at 150.150.32.157. You are on the same subnet as the user and the UNIX host and you can successfully ping both the UNIX host and the user's workstation. When you ask the user to enter ping 150.150.32.157, all he gets is a series of Destination Unreachable messages. What might you do?**

6. **You're a network administrator and have been receiving complaints that users aren't able to post files to or download files from the FTP server. What might you do to determine the status of the server?**

7. **A Windows XP user logs on and gets a message that the system's IP address is already in use. This user receives an IP address through a DHCP server. How can the user get a valid IP address?**

8. **A client calls from the California office saying that she isn't able to connect to the server ICANY in New York. This server is on a routed IP network. This is the second client from California who has called with this problem. No users from other sites have called. What should you do?**

9. Which troubleshooting tool can help you if you need to download a large software patch file from a vendor site?
   a) Telnet
   b) Ipconfig
   c) FTP
   d) Tracert

10. What indicator shows if a computer is connected to the network?

11. What can a simple cable tester show?

12. Explain the function of a network adapter's promiscuous mode.

13. Explain some cases in which a network's baseline performance might change.

14. Your assistant has deployed a new hub in a peer-to-peer network in order to add 10 new user workstations. The hub was cascaded off an empty port on the existing hub. The new users can browse to each other but can't browse to the older workstations. Where would you begin to look for the solution?

15. Users are complaining that the network seems to be slow, but you haven't changed anything or added any new users. What can you do to determine where the slowdown is and what might be causing it?

LESSON 16 LAB 2

Discussing Network Troubleshooting Scenarios

Activity Time:

15 minutes

Scenario:

In this activity, you will discuss the proper procedures to follow in a number of network troubleshooting scenarios.

---

1. **A user calls to say that she has lost her Internet connection and can't bring up a web page she needs to do her job. What is some of the other information you might need in order to diagnose and solve her problem?**

---

2. **What questions will you ask her to help determine where her problem is?**

---

3. **What utilities can you instruct her to use to help find the area of the problem?**

---

4. **How will you test for functional name resolution to the website she wants?**

---

5. **You're the administrator of a small office. One of your users keeps complaining that he is losing his connection to the network. He can reboot and log on again each time, but loses the connection again shortly afterward. What items would you check?**

   a) The logon server's network connection.

   b) The network cable to the user.

   c) User rights and permissions.

   d) The network card driver.

   e) Ports on the hub.

---

6. If you wanted to test the user's network card driver, how would you do it?

---

7. If you wanted to test the user's network cable, how would you do it?

---

8. You're a network consultant working for an integrator/solutions provider. You've been called out to a financial office that says its network went down suddenly. They report that all servers seem to be functioning but users can't log on. The network has approximately 200 workstations and servers distributed across six hubs. You place a network analyzer online, and observe that all traffic seems to be coming from one MAC address. The data isn't legible. What do you conclude is the most likely problem?

---

9. How can you bring most of the network back online while you troubleshoot this problem?

---

10. How will you identify the individual machine causing the problem?

---

11. You have just moved a workstation from one office to another. It worked fine in the old office but won't connect to the network in the new office. You suspect that the wall plate in the new office may not be "hot"—that is, not patched into the hub in the data center. How can you quickly test to see if there is a connection?

---

12. If the user has no network connection, what is the next step toward finding the problem?

---

13. A user calls and complains that he can't connect to the Internet but can connect to servers inside the company. You ask him to open a command prompt window and ping the company website. He does so but gets no reply. You ping the website and get a reply from your workstation. You ask him to ping the IP address of the website. He does so and gets the correct reply. What is keeping the user from connecting to the website?

---

14. What is the next step in resolving the problem?

15. You're presently working as a network engineer for a computer services company. One of your customers calls and complains that the network's main server keeps rebooting itself. When you arrive, the system seems to be running properly and then all of a sudden turns itself off. A few seconds later, it turns itself back on and starts a normal boot procedure. Where can you look to get more information on what was happening right before the server went down?

16. Is this most likely a software problem or a hardware problem?

17. Your company is planning changes to its deployment of web-based services. Currently, all services are being hosted by an outside vendor. The goal is to bring all the web servers inside the company to better control them. What is the first step in predicting the impact that the new incoming web traffic will have on the network?

18. What component in the current network will be affected most?

19. How will your baseline information help you decide where to place the new servers?

SOLUTIONS

Lesson 1

Activity 1-2

1. A network computer that shares resources with and responds to requests from other computers is known as a:

   a) Client

   ✓ b) Server

   c) Terminal

   d) Key

2. A network computer that utilizes the resources of other network computers is known as a:

   a) Server

   b) Host computer

   ✓ c) Client

   d) Media

3. A group of computers connected together to communicate and share resources is known as:

   ✓ a) A computer network

   b) A server

   c) A client

   d) Authentication

4. A self-sufficient computer that acts as both a server and a client is known as a:

   a) Host computer

   b) Client

   c) Server

   ✓ d) Peer

5. True or False? A host computer transmits data to another computer for processing and displaying the result to the user.

   __ True

   ✓ False

6. **A powerful, centralized computer system that performs data storage and processing tasks on behalf of clients and other network devices is known as a:**

   a) Client

   ✓ b) Host computer

   c) Terminal

   d) Network

7. **Match the term with the definition.**

b	Authentication	a.	A network security measure in which information is encoded or scrambled prior to transmission so that it cannot be read unless the recipient knows the decoding mechanism.
a	Encryption	b.	A network security measure in which a computer user or some other network component proves its identity in order to gain access to network resources.
c	Key	c.	In an encryption scheme, the piece of information required to encode or decode the encrypted data.

8. **Match the standards organization to its description.**

c	ISO	a.	An organization dedicated to advancing theory and technology in the electrical sciences.
a	IEEE	b.	A United States standards institute that facilitates the formation of a variety of national standards, as well as promoting those standards internationally.
b	ANSI	c.	A nongovernmental organization issuing voluntary standards in fields ranging from agriculture to textiles.
e	TIA/EIA	d.	An organization that develops and maintains Internet standards and contributes to the evolution and smooth operation of the Internet.
d	IEFT	e.	An organization that develops and issues standards for telecommunications and electronics.

9. **True or False? A network directory is a centralized database of user names and passwords that the network server uses as a reference to authenticate network clients.**

   ✓ True

   __ False

Activity 1-3

1. **Any network device that can connect to the network and can generate, process, or transfer network data is:**

   a) An endpoint

   b) A segment

   ✓ c) A node

   d) A redistribution point

2. **Match the term with the definition.**

	Term		Definition
d	Backbone	a.	Any portion of a network that has been assigned a unique logical address within the addressing scheme of the larger network.
b	Segment	b.	A discrete physical subdivision of a network.
a	Subnet	c.	A network node that is the source or destination of network data.
c	Endpoint	d.	The highest-speed transmission path that carries the majority of the network data.

3. **True or False? A network node that is used to transfer data is a redistribution point.**

   ✓ True

   __ False

Activity 1-4

1. **Which of the following terms describes how the nodes on a network interact and share control of the network communications?**

   a) Network directory

   ✓ b) Network model

   c) Network theory

   d) Network structure

2. **On your network, users share files stored on their Windows XP computers between themselves directly. Additionally, they access shared storage, and printing and fax resources, which are connected to a department-wide server. Your network uses which network model?**

   a) Peer-to-peer

   b) Client/server

   c) Centralized

   ✓ d) Mixed mode

3. **Match the network model with its description.**

c	Centralized network	a.	A network in which some nodes act as servers to provide special services on behalf of other nodes.
a	Client/server network	b.	A network in which resource sharing, processing, and communications control are completely decentralized.
b	Peer-to-peer network	c.	A network in which a central host computer controls all network communication and performs the data processing and storage on behalf of network clients.
d	Mixed mode network	d.	A network that displays characteristics of more than one of the three standard network models.

Activity 1-5

1. **True or False? Physical topology is the topology that describes data flow patterns in the network.**

   __ True

   ✓ False

2. **Match the physical topology with its description.**

c	Physical bus	a.	Exhibits the characteristics of more than one standard topology.
e	Physical star	b.	Network nodes are connected in a continuous circle.
b	Physical ring	c.	Network nodes are arranged in linear format.
d	Physical mesh	d.	Network nodes all have a direct connection to every other node.
a	Hybrid	e.	Network nodes are connected by a central connectivity device that provides separate connections to each device.

3. **The network topology in which all nodes see the network signal at the same time, regardless of the physical wiring of the network, is a:**

   ✓ a) Logical bus topology

   b) Physical bus topology

   c) Logical ring topology

   d) Physical ring topology

Activity 1-6

1. State University maintains a network that connects all residences, academic buildings, and administrative facilities. All the locations share a common data center in the Computing Services building. This network fits the category of a:

   a) WAN

   b) LAN

   ✓ c) CAN

2. The company Chester Unlimited has a remote office that must have access to its corporate office with relatively high bandwidth. This network fits the category of a:

   a) LAN

   ✓ b) WAN

   c) CAN

   Williams Ltd. occupies four floors in the East building of the River View Business Complex. Their network would fit the category of a:

   ✓ a) LAN

   b) WAN

   c) CAN

3. Select the portions of the network in the figure that are LANs.

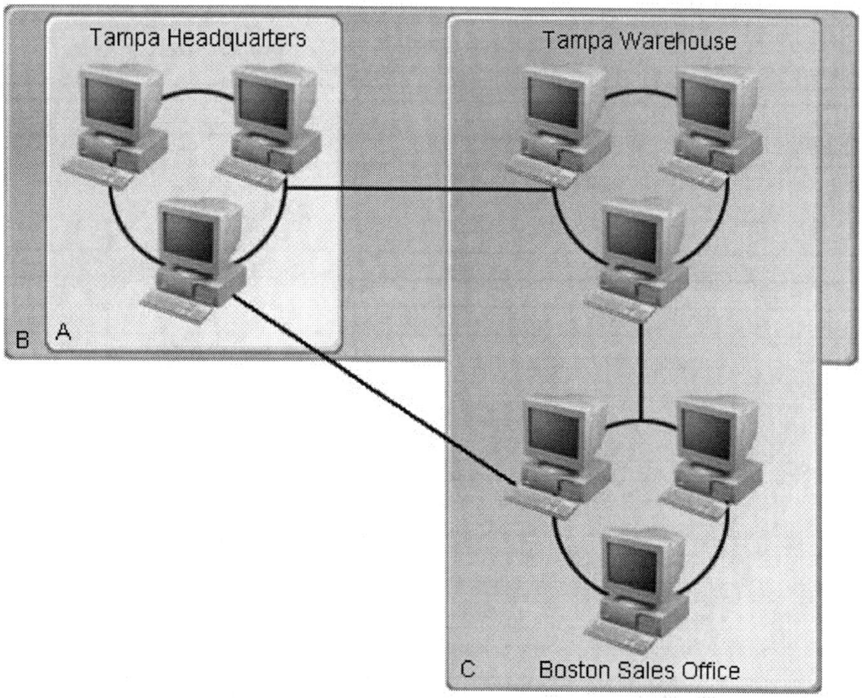

   ✓ a) Section A—Tampa Headquarters

   ✓ b) Section B—Tampa Headquarters and Tampa Warehouse

   c) Section C—Tampa Warehouse and Boston Sales Office

4. Select the portion of the network in the figure that is a WAN.

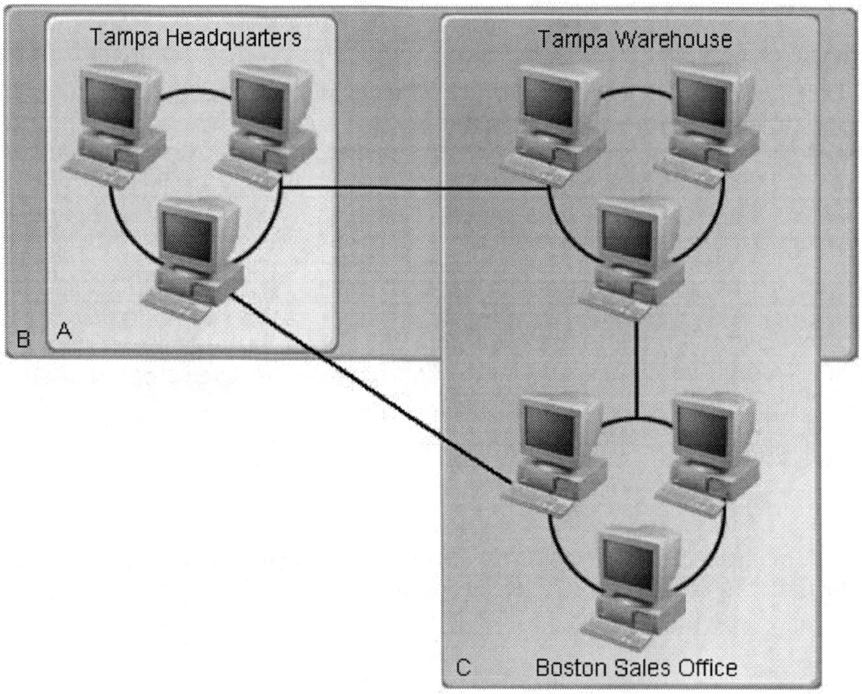

a) Section A—Tampa Headquarters

b) Section B—Tampa Headquarters and Tampa Warehouse

✓ c) Section C—Tampa Warehouse and Boston Sales Office

5. **Match the type of network with its corresponding section in the figure.**

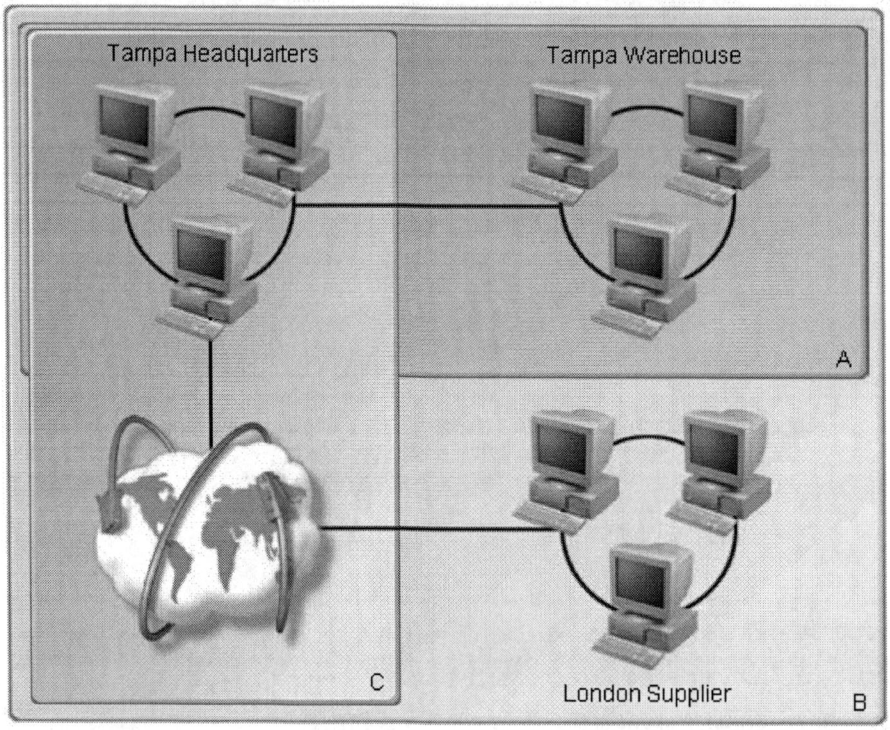

b	Section A—Tampa Headquarters and Tampa Warehouse	a.	Internet
c	Section B—Tampa Headquarters, Tampa Warehouse, London Supplier, and Internet	b.	Intranet
a	Section C—Tampa Headquarters and Internet	c.	Extranet

Lesson 1 Follow-up

Lesson 1 Lab 1

1. **Mom-N-Pop Realty has four employees who need to share information and hardware such as the scanner and printer. They also need Internet access. None of the users have advanced computing skills. Which type of network (network category) would best suit their needs?**

   a) Client/server network

   ✓ b) Peer-to-peer network

   c) UNIX-based centralized network

2. **Match the network term to its definition.**

c	Server	a.	A computer that uses the resources of other networked computers.
a	Client	b.	The process of identifying who or what is trying to gain access to a network resource.
d	Host	c.	A computer that shares its resources with other networked computers.
b	Authentication	d.	A powerful centralized computer that performs storage and processing tasks for other network devices.
e	Encryption	e.	Encoding information so that it cannot be read by anyone other than its intended recipient.

3. **True or False? A segment is a physical subdivision of a larger network, whereas a subnet is a logical subdivision.**

   ✓ True

   __ False

4. **When two or more devices share resources across a network without using the services of a server or host, these computers are participating in a:**

   a) Client/server network

   b) Mixed-mode network

   ✓ c) Peer-to-peer network

   d) Host-based network

Lesson 2

Activity 2-1

1. **Identify the transmission method depicted in the graphic.**

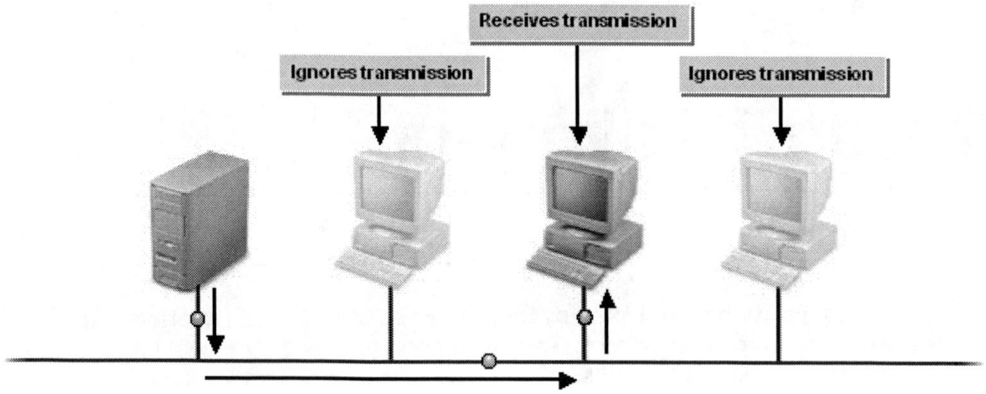

✓ a) Unicast
b) Broadcast
c) Multicast

2. **True or False? Multicasting can be a more efficient use of the network media than unicast transmissions when many clients need to receive a communication from the server.**

✓ True
__ False

3. **Match the transmission method to its description.**

b	Unicast	a.	Transmission of data to all nodes.
a	Broadcast	b.	Transmission of data directly to the intended receiving device.
c	Multicast	c.	Transmission of data to a subset of nodes.

Activity 2-2

1. **From the following choices, select the statements that describe deterministic media access.**

✓ a) Controls when the node can place data on the network.
b) Competes for network access.
c) Is the most popular method and easiest to implement.
✓ d) Is used when the node must access the network in a predictable manner.

2. **From the following choices, select the statements that describe contention-based media access.**

    a) Controls when the node can place data on the network.

    ✓ b) Competes for network access.

    ✓ c) Is the most popular method and easiest to implement.

    d) Is used when the node must access the network in a predictable manner.

3. **True or False? Polling uses the bandwidth of the network medium more efficiently than CSMA/CD.**

    __ True

    ✓ False

4. **Which statement describes the purpose of a contention domain?**

    a) Defines the group of computers that will be polled by the hub.

    b) Logically groups CSMA/CD devices so that they can be more easily managed.

    ✓ c) Improves network performance by reducing the number of devices that contend for media access.

Activity 2-3

1. **Match the signal characteristic with its description.**

b	Frequency	a.	The distance a wave varies from the starting value.
a	Amplitude	b.	The period of the wave, measured in hertz.
c	Wavelength	c.	The distance between peaks or crests in a wave.

2. **Constantly varying electrical signals that change in a smooth, rounded pattern are:**

    ✓ a) Analog

    b) Digital

    c) Discrete

    d) Demodulated

3. **True or False? Binary bits are used to create digital signals.**

    ✓ True

    __ False

4. **Place these units of binary data in order from smallest to largest.**

    2 Crumb

    5 Word

    4 Byte

    1 Bit

    3 Nibble

5. **The modulation/demodulation process:**

   ✓ a) Enables transmission of data signals over long distances.

   b) Occurs only on the sending end of the transmission.

   ✓ c) Places the data signal on top of and removes it from a high frequency analog carrier.

   d) Sends the data as a digital signal.

6. **Digital signals are built around the _____ number system.**

   a) Hexadecimal

   ✓ b) Binary

   c) Decimal

   d) Alphanumeric

7. **Serial digital data:**

   ✓ a) Is synchronized by a clock signal.

   b) Uses multiple lines to send data a byte at a time.

   c) Is the data signaling method typically used within a computer system.

   ✓ d) Can be synchronous or asynchronous.

8. **The transmission method that allows multiple signals to be carried separately on the same media at the same time is:**

   a) Baseband.

   ✓ b) Broadband.

   c) Modulated.

   d) Multicast.

Lesson 2 Follow-up

Lesson 2 Lab 1

1. **Your network will include servers, workstations, printers, and network-accessible fax servers. Select the type of transmission method that these devices will most commonly use.**

   a) Unicast

   b) Broadcast

   ✓ c) Multicast

2. **Match the media access method with its description.**

d	Polling	a.	Transmitting devices check to see if the media is available. If so, they transmit, checking to see if a collision has occurred. If so, they wait and then re-transmit.
e	Multiplexing	b.	Devices that possess a special packet are permitted to transmit. All other devices must listen.
a	Carrier Sense Multiple Access with Collision Detection (CSMA/CD)	c.	Transmitting devices check to see if the media is available. If so, they transmit a blocking signal before transmitting their data.
c	Carrier Sense Multiple Access with Collision Avoidance (CSMA/CA)	d.	A central device asks each device, in turn, if it has data to transmit.
b	Token-based	e.	Data from multiple devices is combined into a single signal through a time-sharing method or the use of multiple frequencies.

3. True or False? To communicate, devices must use the same media access method.

✓ True

__ False

4. True or False? Network communications use digital signals exclusively.

__ True

✓ False

5. Select the characteristics that describe parallel data transmission.

a) Data bits are transmitted one after the other across the medium.

✓ b) Multiple bits are transferred per clock cycle.

✓ c) Uses multiple wires to carry signals.

d) Clocking signals must be modulated with data signals.

Lesson 3

Activity 3-4

1. Select the example of a MAC address.

a) webserver1

b) 201.183.100.2

✓ c) 00-08-02-D4-F6-4C

d) M123-X7-FG-128

2. **Select the example of a network address.**

   a) webserver1

   ✓ b) 201.183.100.2

   c) 00-08-02-D4-F6-4C

   d) M123-X7-FG-128

3. **Select the example of a network name.**

   ✓ a) webserver1

   b) 201.183.100.2

   c) 00-08-02-D4-F6-4C

   d) M123-X7-FG-128

4. **Match the packet component with its definition.**

b	Header	a.	Includes an error checking code.
c	Data	b.	Includes the destination address and source address.
a	Footer	c.	Includes the data to be transmitted.

Activity 3-5

1. **Match the form of transmission with its description.**

b	Simplex	a.	Two-way transmission of data, but only in one direction at a time.
a	Half duplex	b.	One-way transmission of data.
c	Full duplex	c.	Two-way transmission of data, in both directions simultaneously.

2. **Which transmission methods enable the sender to use the full bandwidth of the medium?**

   ✓ a) Simplex

   ✓ b) Half duplex

   c) Full duplex

   d) Full simplex

3. **Match the connection service with its description**

b	Unacknowledged connectionless	a.	With this connection service, nodes acknowledge the successful receipt of packets. However, they do not establish a virtual connection.
a	Acknowledged connectionless	b.	With this connection service, applications provide their own reliability checks. No acknowledgement of successfully transmitted data is provided by the service.
c	Connection-oriented	c.	With this connection service, nodes negotiate communication parameters and share security information to establish a virtual connection for the duration of the session. Additionally, this connection service provides the means for flow control, packet sequencing, and error recovery functions.

Activity 3-6

1. **Which are examples of error detection?**

   a) Sliding windows

   ✓ b) Parity checking

   ✓ c) CRC

   ✓ d) EDAC

   e) Buffering

2. **True or False? Parity checking adds overhead to network transmissions while ensuring that data is error free.**

   ✓ True

   __ False

3. **Which statement best distinguishes sliding windows from fixed length windows?**

   a) Sliding windows are groups of packets selected at random from transmitted data, whereas fixed length windows always include the same sequence of packets.

   b) Fixed length windows always contain the same number of packets, while sliding windows contain either 8, 16, or 32 packets.

   ✓ c) Sliding windows contain a variable number of packets in a block, while fixed length windows always contain the same number.

   d) Fixed length windows contain a variable number of packets in a block, while sliding windows always contain the same number.

4. **Buffer flooding is:**

   a) Overfilling the buffers in the sender.

   b) Corrupting the buffers in the receiver.

   c) Filling the buffer of the receiver with padding (empty) packets.

   ✓ d) Overfilling the buffers in the receiver.

Lesson 3 Follow-up

Lesson 3 Lab 1

1. **True or False? A datagram is another name for a packet.**

   ✓ True

   __ False

2. **Select the components of a packet.**

   ✓ a) Header

   ✓ b) Data

   ✓ c) Footer

   d) Frame

3. **Match the error detection technique with the amount of data that it protects.**

a	Parity	a.	Byte
c	CRC	b.	Block
b	EDAC	c.	Packet

4. **True or False? Sliding windows typically offer better performance than fixed length windows.**

   ✓ True

   __ False

Lesson 4

Activity 4-1

1. **Match the media type with its definition.**

b	IEEE 1394	a.	Multiple insulated conductors clad in a protective and insulating outer jacket carry the signal. Wires are grouped in colored pairs.
c	Fiber optic	b.	A shielded cable similar to STP with either four or six conductors that can be used to connect up to 63 devices to form a small local network.
a	Twisted pair	c.	The least sensitive of any cable type, light pulses from a laser or high-intensity LED carry the signal through the core.
d	Coaxial	d.	A central copper conductor carries the signal. It is surrounded by braided or foil shielding designed to reduce electromagnetic interference. A dialectic insulator separates the conductor from the shield.

2. Identify the type of network cabling shown in the illustration.

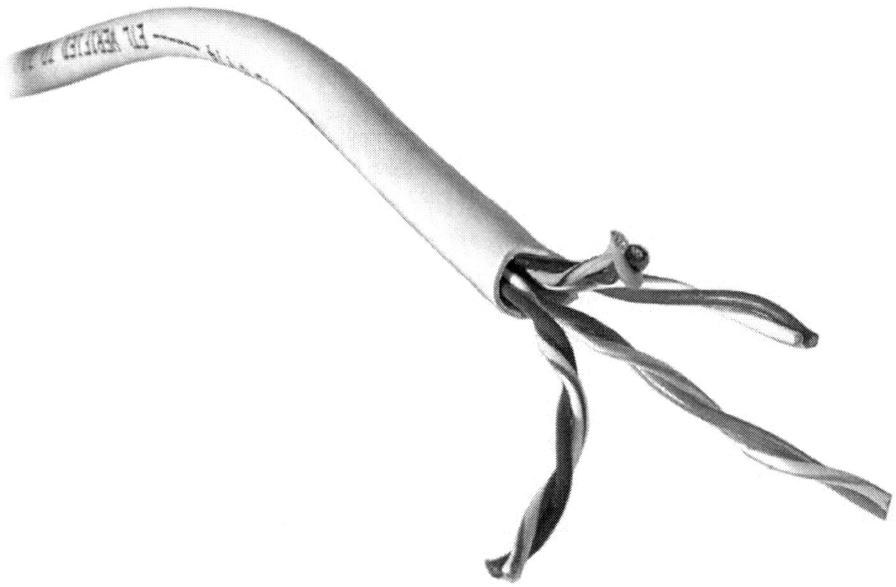

✓ a) Twisted pair
b) Coax
c) Fiber optic

3. Identify the type of network cabling shown in the illustration.

a) Unshielded twisted pair

b) Shielded twisted pair

✓ c) Coax

d) Fiber optic

4. **Select the reason or reasons that plenum cable is permitted in air handling spaces and can be run through firebreaks.**

✓ a) It does not give off noxious or poisonous gases when burned.

b) It gives off noxious or poisonous gases when burned.

✓ c) Fire cannot travel through the cable because the jacket is closely formed to the conductors.

d) Fire can travel through the cable because the jacket loosely surrounds the conductors.

e) It is stiffer than PVC cable.

Activity 4-2

1. **Identify the cable type used to connect your computer to the classroom network.**

   The most common type of bounded media is twisted pair. Other possible cable types are coax and fiber optic.

2. **Identify the types of connectors used in the classroom network.**

   The network should use the connectors appropriate to the cable type. For example, if the cable type is twisted pair, the connectors will be the RJ-45 type.

3. **Your instructor will provide samples of a variety of media and connector types. Identify each of the media and connectors.**

   Answers will vary depending upon the media samples provided.

Activity 4-3

1. **Select the characteristic(s) of unbounded media.**

a) Uses a physical conductor.

✓ b) Installs easily in hazardous areas.

c) Physical shielding protects against noise.

✓ d) Uses electromagnetic energy.

✓ e) Some media require line of sight.

2. **Which form of unbounded media uses nondirectional RF signals to transmit signals?**

✓ a) radio

b) Infrared

c) Microwave

3. **In frequency hopping spread spectrum (FHSS), a data signal is:**

a) Divided into multiple chips; each chip is transmitted across a different frequency.

b) Sent over a single high-frequency RF transmission band.

✓ c) Transmitted across a single frequency for a set period, after which the signal is sent over a new, randomly selected frequency.

✓ d) Less likely to be intercepted but not significantly less susceptible to noise.

4. **True or False? Infrared transmissions require that the receiver and the sender have an unobstructed view of each other.**

✓ True

__ False

Activity 4-4

1. **Choose the statement that defines electrical noise.**

a) Solar radiation or man-made sources of data signals.

✓ b) Unwanted signals introduced onto network media.

c) The reception of transmitted signals from man-made sources.

d) Unwanted signals that impede the proper reception of interference.

2. **Select the items that are sources of electrical noise.**

✓ a) Fluorescent lights

✓ b) Solar storms

c) Wind storms

✓ d) HVAC equipment

e) Water current

3. **True or False? Differential signaling is an electrical noise reduction technique for distinguishing between the signal on two conductors.**

✓ True

__ False

4. **Installing a resistor or other device on the end of a cable to prevent signal reflections and noise is called:**

a) Impedance

b) Grounding

✓ c) Terminating

d) Ohms

Activity 4-6

1. **You need to connect multiple networks. You want data to be sent between networks, only as needed. All your networks use the same protocol. Which networking device would best meet your needs?**

   ✓ a) Router

   b) Bridge

   c) Gateway

   d) Switch

2. **A device that connects drops, turning a physical star into a logical bus network, while connecting only those ports required for a particular transmission is called a:**

   a) Hub

   b) Router

   c) Gateway

   ✓ d) Switch

3. **True or False? A gateway subdivides a LAN into subnets.**

   __ True

   ✓ False

4. **Which of the following are components of premise wiring?**

   ✓ a) Drop cables

   b) Routers

   ✓ c) Patch cables

   ✓ d) Patch panels

5. **You work for a small tech company that supports small, local businesses. You receive a call from an insurance sales office in which users have complained that file sharing on their peer-to-peer network is slow. The manager recently replaced a 10-Mbps hub with an auto-sending 10/100 Mbps hub, but users still complain that the network is too slow. You have been asked to evaluate the situation and make recommendations The network consists of one 10/100-Mbps auto-sensing, six-port hub, but you discover that transmission speeds are limited to 10 Mbps. What upgrades will you suggest to increase transmission speeds to 100 Mbps?**

   At least one if not all of the computers have NIC cards installed that operate at a maximum speed of 10 Mbps. You need to install 10/100 NIC cards. You may also have to change the cable.

Activity 4-7

1. **Some of your network users are complaining that they cannot access a network printer. You perform a physical network inspection and discover the situation shown in the graphic.**

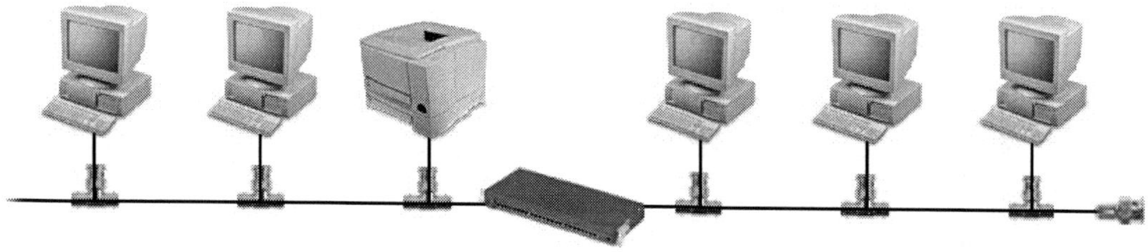

What type of network topology is this? What component of the network has failed?

It is a bus topology. The terminator on one end of a cable segment has become detached.

2. Which network device(s) will be affected? Why?

   All the devices on that segment will be affected as the network signals will be reflected back from the end of the wire. The bridge will keep the problem traffic confined to the local network so that it does not affect other segments.

3. You receive a call from a network user who has lost all network connectivity. You examine the network components on the user's station and segment and discover the situation shown in the graphic.

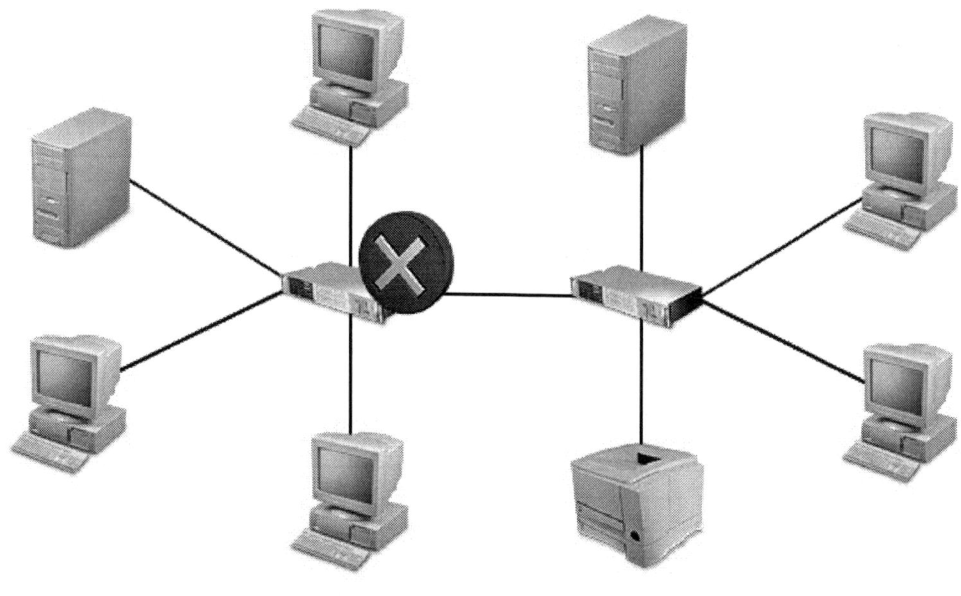

What type of network topology is this? Which network component has failed?

It is a star topology. One of the network hubs has failed.

4. Which network device(s) will be affected? Why?

   All devices on that segment because they all rely on the hub for connectivity with each other and with the rest of the network.

5. Another network user calls complaining that he can't connect to a server. You try to connect to various network devices and examine the network components and discover the situation shown in the graphic.

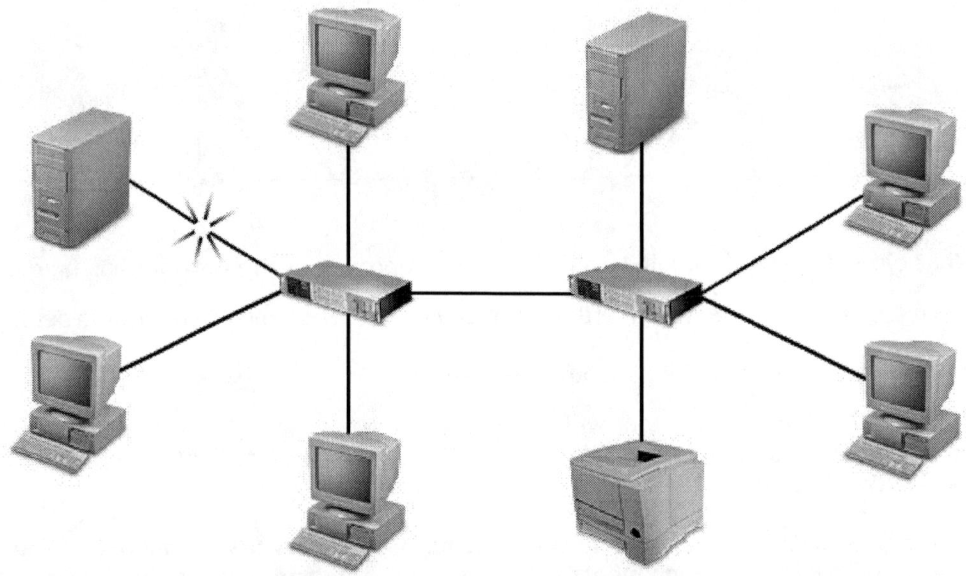

What type of network topology is this? What is the cause of the connectivity failure?

It is a star topology. A cable drop has failed or broken.

6. **Which network device(s) will be affected? Why?**

   Only connectivity to and from the server will be affected because it is the only system to use that cable drop.

7. **Your company's network is spread across several locations within the city. One of your network operations centers has experienced a power surge and you are concerned about the effect on network connectivity. You try to connect to various network devices and discover the situation shown in the graphic.**

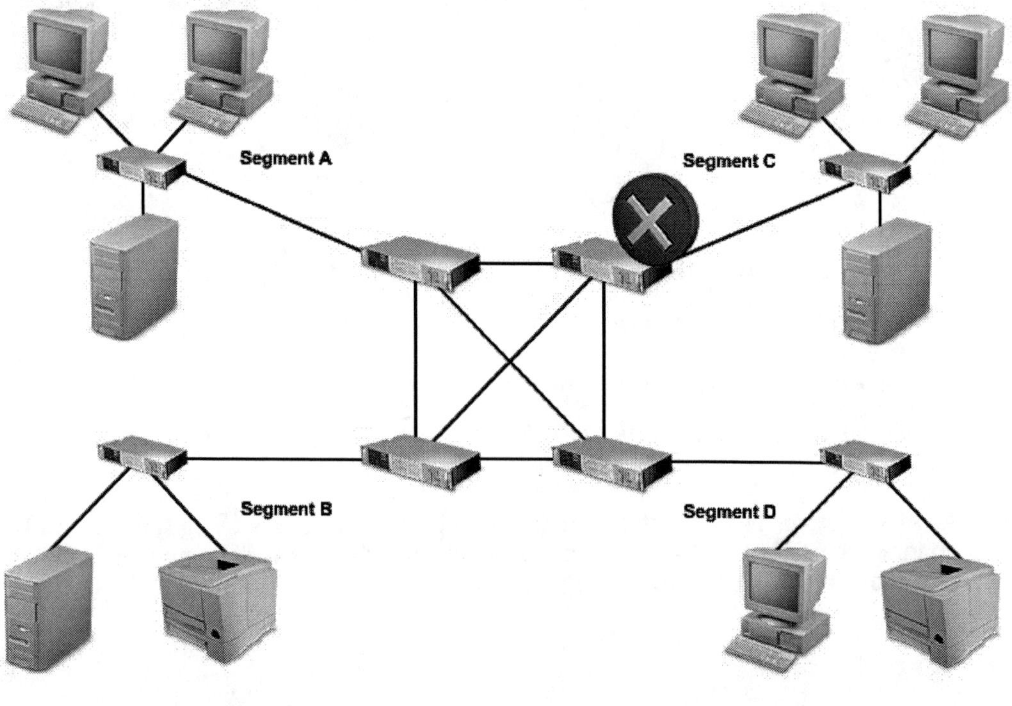

What type of network is this? Which network device has failed?

It is a hybrid network. There is a mesh topology between the four routers, and then a star topology on each individual LAN segment. One of the routers has failed.

8. **What area of the network will be affected?**

   Only the nodes on Segment C will be affected. The mesh topology between the routers will enable the network to bypass the fault.

9. **Your company occupies part of a floor in a large office building. The office suite adjacent to your location has recently been vacated and you are going to expand into the empty space. You have hired a contractor to run new cable for both your telephone and network infrastructure into the new space. After users have moved into the new space, they begin complaining that network performance is not comparable to the existing network. You examine the cable installation and notice that "CAT 1" is printed on all the cable. What is the most likely cause of the network connectivity problems?**

   The contractor has attempted to save money by using CAT 1 cable for both the telephone and the network installation. CAT 1 is not rated for network use and should not be used in network installations.

10. **How can you correct the situation?**

    Replace the CAT 1 phone cable with CAT 5 network cable.

11. **Your network uses UTP CAT 5 cable throughout the building. There are a few users who complain of intermittent network connectivity problems. You cannot determine a pattern for these problems that relates to network usage. You visit the users' workstations and find that they are all located close to an elevator shaft. What is a likely cause of the intermittent connectivity problems?**

    The UTP cable might be run too close to the elevator equipment. When the elevator motor activates, it produces interference on the network wire.

12. **How might you correct the problem?**

    Replace the UTP cable with STP.

13. **You have been called in as a network consultant for a small company. The company's network uses a star-wired bus with individual nodes connected to a series of hubs, which are then connected together. Network performance seems slow and unreliable. You run network diagnostics and discover that the network media on all segments is saturated with traffic and that there is a high number of collisions. The company does not have the budget to completely re-wire the network or replace a large number of network interface cards. What are options you can recommend to improve performance on this network?**

    You can replace the hubs with another network connectivity device, such as bridges, switches, or routers.

14. **What are the factors you should consider when making your decision?**

    If the extra traffic is largely due to unicast transmissions, you can replace the hubs with bridges or switches to contain the unicast traffic to a single network segment. If the extra traffic is largely due to broadcasts, you may need to replace the hubs with routers, in which case you will need to make sure you implement and configure a routable protocol.

Lesson 4 Follow-up

Lesson 4 Lab 1

1. **Which unbounded media uses multiple radio frequencies to reduce interference and the likelihood of eavesdropping?**

   a) Infrared

   b) Microwave

   ✓ c) Spread spectrum

   d) Broadcast

2. **Match the network media with the connector typically used with it.**

c	Coaxial cable	a.	RJ-45 connector
a	Twisted pair cable	b.	MTRJ connector
b	Fiber optic cable	c.	BNC connector

3. **True or False? You can unwind as much of a twisted pair cable's conductors as you need without affecting its performance characteristics.**

   __ True

   ✓ False

4. **You need to connect twisted pair drops to form a logical bus network. You need maximum speed between nodes and expect considerable simultaneous traffic. Select the appropriate network device.**

   a) Router

   b) Bridge

   ✓ c) Switch

   d) Repeater

   e) Hub

5. **Match the source of noise with the means by which you can lessen or eliminate its impact.**

d	Fluorescent lights	a.	Don't install PCs or network devices on the same electrical circuit or in close proximity.
a	Motor noise	b.	Avoid running drops alongside electric service cables; don't unwind conductor pairs.
c	Solar interference	c.	Use shielded cabling, with proper termination and grounding.
b	Crosstalk	d.	Don't run cables within 20 inches; run perpendicular if a drop must cross.

6. **Match the network connectivity device to its description.**

a	Gateway	a.	Any device, software, or system that converts data between incompatible systems.
c	Wireless access point	b.	A networking device used to connect the drops in a physical star topology network into a logical bus topology.
f	Router	c.	A device that provides connection between wireless devices and can connect to wired networks.
d	Bridge	d.	A network device that divides a logical bus network into subnets.Examines the MAC address of each packet and forwards packets only as necessary.
e	Switch	e.	A networking device used to connect the drops in a physical star topology network into a logical bus topology, forwarding packets to only the correct port based on MAC addresses.
b	Hub	f.	A networking device that connects multiple networks that use the same protocol.

Lesson 5

Activity 5-1

1. **Match each layer of the OSI model with a description of its function.**

f	Application	a.	Establishes a connection between network devices, maintains that connection, and then terminates it when appropriate.
e	Presentation	b.	Ensures that individual frames get from one device to another without error. After sending frames, waits for acknowledgements from receiving devices.
a	Session	c.	Addresses and delivers packets across a network.
g	Transport	d.	Moves bits of data on and off the physical cabling media.
c	Network	e.	Translates data so that it can be moved on the network.
b	Data-link	f.	Provides services and utilities that enable application programs to access a network and its resources.
d	Physical	g.	Ensures reliable data transmission by breaking up big data blocks into smaller packets that can be sent more efficiently on the network.

2. **At which OSI layer is the MAC address applied to a data packet?**
   - a) Layer 1 - Physical layer
   - b) Layer 3 - Network layer
   - c) Layer 4 - Transport layer
   - ✓ d) Layer 2 - Data-link layer

3. **Which layer determines how fast data can be sent?**
   - a) Layer 6 - Presentation layer
   - b) Layer 7 - Application layer
   - ✓ c) Layer 1 - Physical layer
   - d) Layer 4 - Transport layer

4. **What is the highest level of the OSI model at which Telnet operates?**
   - a) Data Link
   - b) Physical
   - ✓ c) Application
   - d) Presentation
   - e) Session

5. **At which layer does a WAP operate?**
   - a) Session
   - b) Application
   - ✓ c) Data Link
   - d) Network
   - e) Presentation

6. **Which OSI layer is responsible for establishing connections between two devices?**
   - ✓ a) Session
   - b) Presentation
   - c) Application
   - d) Physical
   - e) Data Link

7. **What is the main purpose of Layer 5?**

   Layer 5 is the Session layer and it controls the conversation between two endpoints.

8. **What is the main purpose of Layer 7?**

   Layer 7 is the Application layer and it provides standardized services to applications.

9. **What is the purpose of Layer 1?**

   Layer 1 is the Physical layer and it is responsible for encoding energy signals onto the medium (the cable wire, for example) and for receiving energy signals.

10. **At which layer is the MAC address defined?**
   a) Layer 3
   ✓ b) Layer 2
   c) Layer 5
   d) Layer 6
   e) Layer 1

11. **Which OSI layer usually encapsulates using both a header and a trailer?**
   a) Session
   b) Application
   c) Network
   ✓ d) Data Link
   e) Presentation

Activity 5-2

1. **Shares are ______________________________.**
   a) Network resources that are unavailable
   b) Network resources that are available
   ✓ c) Disks, folders, or printers that are available to other users on the network.
   d) Ethernet resources

2. **To hide a share, you must add a ____________________ to the share name.**
   a) % character
   ✓ b) $ character
   c) @ character
   d) # character

3. **My Network Places allows you to ____________________________.**
   a) Attach drives to your computer
   b) Control the network
   c) Find other users
   ✓ d) Browse the network

4. **True or False? A mapped network drive is a directory shared by a network server that appears to be a drive on your local machine.**
   _✓_ True
   ___ False

5. **Network searching allows you to _______________________.**
   ✓ a) Search for specific items by name or by location
   b) Search for specific items by name only
   c) Search for specific items by location only
   d) Search for online users only

Solutions

Activity 5-3

1. **Ethernet is a:**

   a) Cost-effective network topology

   ✓ b) Segmented LAN topology

   c) Token-passing network topology

   d) Topology that uses FDDI NIC cards

2. **The four data speeds accommodated by Ethernet are:**

   a) 10 Mbps, 100 Mbps, 500 Mbps, and 1000 Mbps

   b) 1 Mbps, 10 Mbps, 100 Mbps, and 10 Gbps

   ✓ c) 10 Mbps, 100 Mbps, 1 Gbps, and 10 Gbps

   d) 100 Mbps, 10 Gbps, 100 Gbps, and 500 Mbps

3. **The maximum amount of data an Ethernet frame can transmit is:**

   a) 1518 bytes

   b) 64 bytes

   c) 100 bytes

   ✓ d) 1500 bytes

4. **True or False? The 802.2 standard determines where frames of data start and end.**

   _✓_ True

   __ False

5. **Which IEEE standard describes Gigabit Ethernet?**

   a) 802.3u

   ✓ b) 802.3z

   c) 802.3

   d) 802.ae

   e) 802.5

6. **Which of the following do not use copper cabling?**

   a) 100BaseTX

   b) 100BaseCX

   ✓ c) 100BaseFX

   ✓ d) 100BaseLR

7. **Which fiber optic cable types use single mode?**

   ✓ a) 10GBaseER

   b) 10GBaseSR

   ✓ c) 10GBaseLR

   d) 10GBaseCX

8. **What is the maximum segment length for 1000BaseSX?**
   - a) 25 meters
   - b) 100 meters
   - ✓ c) 550 meters
   - d) 3,000 meters

9. **What is the maximum segment length for 100BaseFX?**
   - ✓ a) 2 kilometers
   - b) 5 kilometers
   - c) 200 meters
   - d) 20 kilometers

10. **What is the maximum segment length for 1000BaseCX?**
    - a) 100 meters
    - b) 550 meters
    - c) 40,000 meters
    - ✓ d) 25 meters

Activity 5-4

1. **True or False? IBM Token Ring specifications and IEEE 802.5 specifications both require a Token Ring network to be implemented using a star topology.**

   __ True

   ✓ False

2. **Match the token state with its description.**

d	Captured	a.	A priority system used by both IBM and 802.5 Token Ring.
c	Acknowledgement	b.	There is no data in the payload.
a	Reserved	c.	Positive or negative notification.
b	Available	d.	There is a valid data payload.

3. **Which device connects Token Ring clients into a physical star configuration?**
   - a) Edge router
   - ✓ b) Multi Station Access Units
   - c) Media Access Units
   - d) Hubs

4. **You manage a Token Ring network. A user calls and says that she suddenly can't access any network resources. You examine and test various network devices and discover the situation shown in the graphic.**

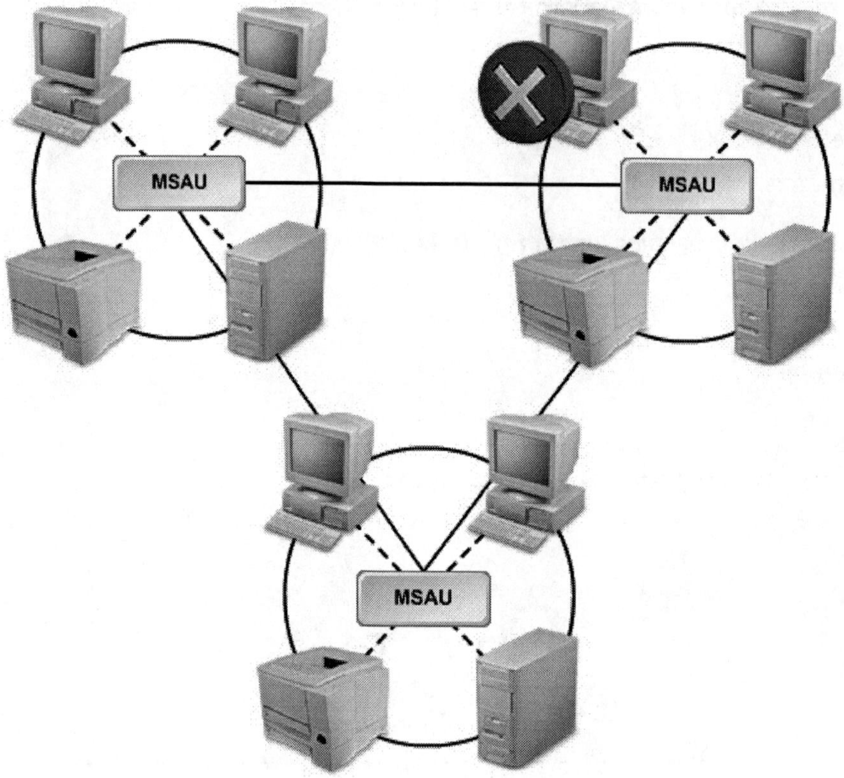

What is the most likely cause of the problem?

The user's network card has failed.

5. **Which network device(s) will be affected? Why?**

   Only the user's computer. The MSAU will break the ring when it detects the unresponsive device, and the remaining stations will take on a star configuration.

Activity 5-5

1. **FDDI networks operate at ____________________.**

   a) 10 Mbps

   b) 1000 Mbps

   c) 500 Mbps

   ✓ d) 100 Mbps

2. **True or False? The second ring of a FDDI network can be utilized in some circumstances to increase total throughput.**

   ✓ True

   __ False

3. Dual Attached Stations (DASs) are connected ____________________.

a) To a concentrator

b) To an edge router

✓ c) To both primary and secondary rings

d) To a backbone router

4. Auto-reconfiguration occurs when ____________________.

a) There is excessive traffic on the network

b) There is no traffic on the network

c) There is a new node added to the network

✓ d) There is a loss of connectivity to the next station

5. You manage a FDDI network for a financial institution. A municipal construction project is taking place adjacent to one of your network operations centers. You are concerned about the effect on your equipment so you are monitoring your network infrastructure closely. During a periodic test of the network media, you discover the situation shown in the graphic.

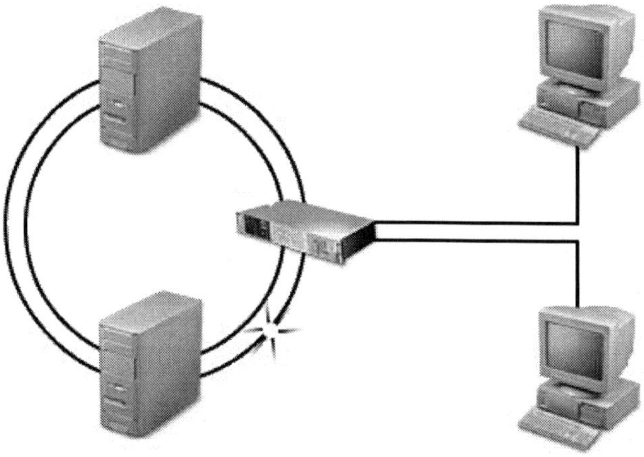

What appears to be the cause of the problem?

The primary ring has broken.

6. Which network device(s) will be affected?

None; the network loops the signal around the fault. However, you should repair the broken segment promptly so the network is not vulnerable to other failures.

Activity 5-6

1. True or False? Radio networks are ideal for large area coverage with obstacles.

✓ True

__ False

2. Which condition affects the operation of infrared wireless networks?

a) Atmospheric conditions

b) The presence of other electrical equipment

✓ c) Bright sunlight

d) Data rate

3. True or False? Infrastructure mode wireless networks use either Basic Service Set or Extended Service Set protocols.

✓ True

__ False

4. True or False? Bluetooth is a long-range radio technology designed to simplify communications among Internet devices.

__ True

✓ False

5. A user on your network uses a Personal Digital Assistant (PDA) to keep track of her calendar and contact list. She synchronizes the PDA data frequently with her laptop computer via the systems' infrared ports. She complains that she intermittently loses the infrared connection between the two devices. You visit her workstation and find that she is seated in close proximity to a large window. What problem do you suspect?

Bright sunlight from the window can occasionally interfere with the infrared transmission.

6. What can you advise the user?

Use blinds or shades, or arrange her work area so that the two devices are further from the window.

7. Your company's network has a downtown location and a suburban location. You are using a dish-style microwave antenna for wireless connectivity between the two locations. A luxury hotel is being constructed in the block adjacent to your downtown location. The hotel structure is planned to be lower than your existing microwave installation; nevertheless, you have started to experience connectivity problems with the suburban site. There is a great deal of construction equipment on the site. What is the likely cause of the connectivity issues?

Construction equipment, such as tall construction cranes, might be temporarily interfering with the direct line-of-sight connectivity required for the directional microwave transmission.

8. Your company has installed a wireless network. There are ceiling dome transmitters at various locations in your building, and you have upgraded users' laptop systems with wireless NICs. There is one wireless antenna to serve the warehouse area. The coverage area is adequate; however, users in the warehouse report intermittent connectivity problems as they move in and out of the tall metal storage shelving. What problem do you suspect?

The metal in the shelves is interfering with the omni-directional radio signals from the transmitter. If you need complete coverage in the warehouse area, you might need to install additional antenna stations in the areas between shelving units.

9. 5) Your CEO is concerned with security on the new wireless network. Clients, guests, and contractors often enter the building bringing their own laptops equipped with wireless adapters. How can you ensure that only authorized systems connect to your wireless network?

   The best available option at the present time is to implement WPA for secure data encryption and user authentication on the wireless network.

10. What is the maximum transmission speed that IrDA 1.1 can support?

    a) 3 Mbps

    b) 10 Mpbs

    c) 11 Mpbs

    ✓ d) 4 Mbps

    e) 54 Mbps

11. At what radio frequency does Bluetooth operate?

    a) 5 GHz

    ✓ b) 2.4 GHz

    c) 54 Mbps

    d) 11 Mbps

12. At which radio frequency does IEEE 802.11a operate?

    a) 2.5 GHz

    b) 10 GHz

    ✓ c) 5.0 GHz

    d) 2.4 GHz

Lesson 5 Follow-up

Lesson 5 Lab 1

1. The OSI model is a ________________________.

   a) Specification for the interoperability of Ethernet networks

   ✓ b) Framework for how computers exchange data packets

   c) Type of error correction method used in Token Ring networks

   d) Specification for Token Ring-to-Ethernet connectivity

2. True or False? Only folders can be shared.

   __ True

   ✓ False

3. **In Windows, a shared folder can be hidden by ________________________.**

   a) Setting certain permission levels

   b) Adding a % symbol to the beginning of the share name

   ✓ c) Adding a $ to the end of the share name

   d) Adding a % to the beginning and a $ to the end of the share name

4. **True or False? Ethernet technology utilizes CSMA/CD technology.**

   ✓ True

   __ False

5. **Token Ring networks are ______________________.**

   ✓ a) Deterministic networks

   b) Priority networks

   c) Shared networks

   d) Captured networks

6. **The dual rings of a FDDI network provide ____________________________.**

   a) Easier maintenance

   ✓ b) Fault tolerance

   c) Reduced costs for large networks

   d) Easier manageability

7. **True or False? Infrared wireless networks are ideal for large areas with obstacles.**

   __ True

   ✓ False

Lesson 6

Activity 6-1

2. **Match the Network- and Transport-layer protocol families with their functions.**

b	Reliability protocols	a.	Responsible for transmitting data to its correct destination in the most efficient manner.
c	Connection protocols	b.	Ensure that data transfer is successful.
a	Routing protocols	c.	Ensure that the communication is established and maintained during data transfer.

3. **Match the Application-, Presentation-, and Session-layer protocol families with their functions.**

d	Terminal-emulation protocols	a.	Enables network communication of various software processes.
b	Remote-action protocols	b.	Responsible for determining whether the process will be performed by the client or server node.
e	Multiple-session protocols	c.	Translate data between coding schemes for different nodes.
a	Task-to-task protocols	d.	Allow access to a host and translate keyboard and video-display information.
c	Codeset-and-data-structure protocols	e.	Establishes multiple network links.

4. **True or False? If you need to run more than one protocol on your computer, each protocol must be bound to its own NIC.**

   __ True

   ✓ False

Activity 6-2

2. **Identify the required components of TCP/IP addressing.**

   ✓ a) Node address

   ✓ b) Subnet mask

   c) Gateway address

   d) Name resolution service

3. **Match the binary value with its decimal equivalent.**

a	01100100	a.	100
e	11100000	b.	100.100.2.1
c	11111111.11111111.11110000.00000000	c.	255.255.240.0
b	01100100.01100100.00000010.00000001	d.	127.0.0.1
d	01111111.00000000.00000000.00000001	e.	224

4. **Local or Remote? Determine if Node 2 is local or remote to Node 1.**

   Node 1=192.225.16.8

   Node 2=192.225.14.8

   Subnet Mask=255.255.255.0

   __ Local

   ✓ Remote

5. **Is the subnet mask 11111111.11111111.10101111.00000000 valid or invalid?**

   __ Valid

   ✓ Invalid

SOLUTIONS

Activity 6-3

1. **Match the IP address range with its class.**

e	Class A	a.	224.0.0.0 to 239.255.255.255
c	Class B	b.	240.0.0.0 to 255.255.255.255
d	Class C	c.	128.0.0.0 to 191.255.255.255
a	Class D	d.	192.0.0.0 to 223.255.255.255
b	Class E	e.	1.0.0.0 to 127.255.255.255

2. **Select the IP address classes that can be assigned to hosts.**

   ✓ a) Class A

   ✓ b) Class B

   ✓ c) Class C

   d) Class D

   e) Class E

3. **True or False? To implement TCP/IP on your network, you must lease a block of IP addresses from ICANN.**

   __ True

   ✓ False

4. **True or False? To route traffic to Internet destinations, you must lease a block of IP addresses from ICANN if you do not receive them from an ISP.**

   ✓ True

   __ False

5. **How many bits comprise an IP address?**

   a) 16

   ✓ b) 32

   c) 10

   d) 8

6. **True or False? The two parts of an IP address are the network and host.**

   ✓ True

   __ False

7. **True or False? The IP address 127.0.0.0 is a valid address to use on a network.**

   __ True

   ✓ False

Activity 6-4

1. **How many individual network IDs do you need?**

   a) One

   b) Two

   ✓ c) Three

   d) Four

2. **If you were going to use default subnet masks for the networks, which default subnet would be applied to each network?**

   a) Subnets 1, 2, and 3 would all use 255.255.0.0.

   b) Subnets 1, 2, and 3 would all use 255.255.255.0.

   c) Subnets 1 and 2 would use 255.255.0.0 and Subnet 3 would use 255.255.255.0.

   ✓ d) Subnets 1 and 3 would use 255.255.255.0 and Subnet 2 would use 255.255.0.0

   e) Subnets 2 and 3 would use 255.255.0.0 and Subnet 1 would use 255.255.255.0.

3. **Which is a valid example of an appropriate network address and subnet mask for Subnet 1?**

   ✓ a) IP address: 192.168.10.0; Subnet mask: 255.255.255.0

   b) IP address: 172.16.0.0; Subnet mask: 255.255.0.0

   c) IP address: 192.168.10.0; Subnet mask: 255.255.0.0

   d) IP address: 172.16.0.0; Subnet mask: 255.255.255.0

Activity 6-5

1. **Select the correct base network ID for 203.121.45.6 /22.**

   a) 203.121.45.0

   b) 203.224.45.0

   ✓ c) 203.121.44.0

   d) 203.121.45.6

2. **Select the correct base network ID for 10.10.123.164 /27.**

   a) 10.10.123.0

   b) 10.10.123.164

   ✓ c) 10.10.123.160

   d) 10.10.120.0

Activity 6-6

1. **Match the OSI layers with the TCP/IP layers.**

c	Application, Presentation, Session	a.	Network
b	Transport	b.	Transport
d	Network	c.	Application
a	Data-link, Physical	d.	Internet

2. **True or False? UDP is a connectionless, best-effort-delivery protocol.**

   ✓ True

   __ False

3. **True or False? ARP uses a multicast session to resolve any IP address to MAC address it does not have in its cache.**

   __ True

   ✓ False

4. **Which is a function of the ICMP protocol?**

   a) Use to control multicast sessions.

   ✓ b) Can request that a sender speed up or slow down data traffic based on network conditions.

   c) Resolves IP addresses to MAC addresses.

   d) Provides best-effort data delivery.

5. **Match the port number ranges with their reserved block.**

a	Well-known ports	a.	1 to 1023
c	Registered ports	b.	49,152 to 65,535
b	Dynamic or private ports	c.	1024 to 49,151

6. **For the socket address example {tcp, 110.105.25.5, 23}, identify the components.**

c	tcp	a.	The port number of the local service.
b	110.105.25.5	b.	The IP address of the local computer.
a	23	c.	The protocol.

Lesson 6 Follow-up

Lesson 6 Lab 1

1. **Define the function of the routing family of protocols.**

   Ensures that data is transferred to the correct destination; determines strategies used to transmit data through the network.

2. **Define the function of the file access family of protocols.**

   Enables nodes to use network files; provides a common means to access network files.

3. **In Windows Server 2003, where would an administrator determine which protocols were bound to a NIC?**

   In the This Connection Uses The Following Items list box of each network connection's Properties dialog box.

4. **Convert the following IP addresses from decimal values to their equivalent binary numbers:**

   255

   8

   198.131.205.5

   224.254.100.8

   255 = 11111111

   8 = 00001000

   198.131.205.5 = 11000110.100000011.11001101.00000101

   224.254.100.8 = 11100000.11111110.01100100.00001000

5. **Is the IP address of 172.16.5.255 with a subnet mask of 255.255.0.0 a valid IP address?**

   Yes. Although the last octet is all 1s, the host portion of the address is made up of the final two octets.

   In binary: 00000101.11111111

   Although the final octet is all ones, it is a valid host address because the second-to-last octet is not all ones.

   A host address of 172.16.255.255 with a subnet mask of 255.255.0.0 would be invalid, because the host portion of the address would be all ones in binary: 11111111.11111111

6. **Determine if the following addresses are on local or remote networks. Both addresses share the same subnet mask.**

   Node 1 = 227.16.90.30; Node 2 = 227.16.87.26; Subnet Mask = 255.255.0.0

   Local.

7. **How do you calculate the available number of host addresses for a Class B address?**

   Two raised to the number of bits available by class. Because Class B addresses have 2 bytes, or 16 bits, available for the host address, the formula is 2^16-2 = 65,534.

8. **You've been asked to implement TCP/IP on a divided network. There are two subnets separated by a Layer 3 network device. There is no Internet connection. Subnet one has 235 nodes and subnet two has 1,500 nodes. Using the default address classes, how would you assign IP addresses?**

   You need a Class C addresses on subnet one and a Class B address on subnet two.

   One possible address scheme:

   Subnet 1: Base network ID of 192.168.10.0; Subnet Mask of 255.255.255.0; IP Address Range of 192.168.10.1 to 192.168.10.235; Default Gateway of 192.168.10.254

   Subnet 2: Base network ID of 172.16.0.0; Subnet Mask of 255.255.0.0; IP Address Range of 172.16.0.1 to 172.16.5.225; Default Gateway of 172.16.5.254

9. **You're the administrator of a quickly growing company. Your corporate headquarters is concerned with address depletion of its internal addresses and has asked you to convert a Class B IP network to a CIDR scheme. Your present default gateway address is 172.16.255.254 and can't be changed. You have 2,400 nodes on your network. Determine the CIDR network ID.**

   172.16.240.0 /20

   12 node bits and 20 network bits will support 2,400 nodes.

   Gateway ID: 10101100.00010000.11111111.11111110

   Subnet Mask: 11111111.11111111.11110000.00000000

   Network ID: 10101100.00010000.11110000.00000000

10. **Match the TCP/IP network layer with its description.**

c	Application	a.	Provides connection and communication services.
a	Transport	b.	Provides addressing and routing services.
b	Internet	c.	Contains utilities such as socket services and NetBIOS over TCP/IP.
d	Network	d.	Contains services that send frames to and receive frames from the network.

11. **What is the purpose of port numbers?**

    To track the Application-layer service that the data is intended for. This allows nodes to exchange data with multiple services at the same time.

Lesson 7

Activity 7-5

2. **What is the only active entry in the HOSTS file?**

   The only active entry in the file is the entry that maps the 127.0.0.1 loopback address to the localhost host name.

3. **What are the three components of this entry?**

   The three components of the entry are the IP address, a series of spaces, and the host name itself.

4. **Why are the other entries not active?**

   Because they are preceded by the # sign, the entries on the other lines are interpreted as comments.

Activity 7-6

1. **Which are fully qualified domain names?**

   ✓ a) www.everythingforcoffee.com

   b) \\fs001\data\new\accounts.mdb

   c) data1.electrocon.dom.\users\home

   ✓ d) citizensinfo.org

2. **What is the name of the top of the DNS hierarchy?**

   a) Host record

   b) Zone

   ✓ c) Root

   d) First-level domain

3. **True or False? If a preferred DNS server can't resolve a client's name request, it contacts the DNS server immediately above it in the hierarchy.**

   __ True

   ✓ False

4. **True or False? An advantage of using a HOSTS file for DNS name resolution services is that updates to the file are automatic.**

   __ True

   ✓ False

Activity 7-7

2. **Are there any active entries in the sample file?**

   No. All the entries in the file are preceded by the # sign and are interpreted as comments.

3. **Identify the components of one of the sample entries.**

   The components of the sample entry are the IP address, a series of spaces, the NetBIOS name, a series of spaces, and comments specific to the entry, preceded by the # sign.

Activity 7-8

1. **How many standard characters are allowed in a NetBIOS name?**

   a) Twelve. An additional byte is reserved for the service identifier.

   ✓ b) Fifteen. An additional byte is reserved for the service identifier.

   c) Sixteen. An additional byte is reserved for the service identifier.

   d) Eight. An additional byte is reserved for the service identifier.

2. **True or False? Systems that cannot automatically register NetBIOS names with a WINS server, such as those running UNIX, can use a WINS proxy agent.**

   ✓ True

   __ False

3. **Put the steps of the NetBIOS name resolution process in the correct order.**

   4 Check LMHOSTS file

   3 Broadcast for name

   1 Check NetBIOS name cache

   2 Query WINS server

Activity 7-10

1. **Match the TCP/IP utility with its function.**

b	Tracert	a.	Used to manage the cache of MAC addresses.
d	Netstat	b.	Used to determine the route that data takes to get to a specific destination.
e	Nbtstat	c.	Used to test and troubleshoot DNS servers.
c	Nslookup	d.	Used to display information about a computer's active TCP and UDP connections.
a	Arp	e.	Used to view and manage NetBIOS name cache information.

2. **You're working the help desk and get a call that a user can't access the UNIX host at 150.150.32.157. You are on the same subnet as the user and the UNIX host, and try to ping the UNIX host. You can successfully do so. You can also ping the user's workstation. When you ask the user to enter ping 150.150.32.157, all they get is a series of Destination Unreachable messages. What should you do?**

   a) Log in to the UNIX host and enter netstat -a to see if it is listening on the correct port.

   b) Use the ipconfig /release and /renew commands to update the workstation's IP address lease.

   ✓ c) From the problem workstation, enter arp -a to list the ARP cache.

   d) Use nslookup to query the DNS server for the UNIX host.

3. **You're a network administrator and have been receiving complaints that users aren't able to post files to or download files from an FTP server. What might you do to determine the status of the server?**

   a) Ping the server's IP address.

   ✓ b) Log on to the FTP server and enter netstat -a to see if its listening on the correct port.

   c) At a workstation, enter arp -d to delete the entry to the FTP server. Then, manually add the corrected entry.

   d) Use the nbtstat command to list statistics about the FTP server's NetBT connections.

4. **You are a networking administrator. Two Microsoft XP workstations have the same IP address, which results in an IP address conflict. Which command will you use to determine which two computers have the same IP address?**

   a) ipconfig /all

   b) ifconfig /all

   c) Netstat -e

   ✓ d) Arp -a

   e) Arp -d

5. **You want to add a static IP address to MAC address mapping to the local ARP table. Which command will you use?**

   a) arp -d

   b) arp -a

   c) arp -g

   d) arp inet_addr

   ✓ e) arp -s

6. You want to view active connections on your system. Which command will you use?

   a) tracert

   b) Nbtstat

   c) arp -a

   ✓ d) Netstat -a

   e) Ping -t

7. You want to view the IP information on a Linux workstation. Which command will you use?

   a) Ipconfig /all

   b) winipcfg

   c) Ping

   ✓ d) Ifconfig

8. You are a network administrator and several users call you complain that they cannot reach the company's website. They can, however, reach other websites. Which command will you use first to identify the problem?

   a) arp -a

   b) Nbtstat

   ✓ c) Tracert

   d) Ipconfig /all

   e) ping

Activity 7-14

1. Your sales department wants to sell supplies over the Internet and wants to make sure that the transactions are secure. Which protocol should be configured on the web server?

   a) FTP

   ✓ b) HTTPS

   c) NNTP

   d) SMTP

2. Your company has a production floor with several shared computers. The production staff needs to be able to check their email from whichever computer is free. Which email protocol should you use?

   a) UUCP

   b) NTP

   ✓ c) IMAP4

   d) NNTP

3. True or False? Telnet is a terminal emulation program that allows users to connect to the USENET system and read newsgroup messages.

   __ True

   ✓ False

4. **Your sales force needs to retrieve sales prospective documents and upload completed sales order forms to corporate headquarters while they are on the road. What service should you use?**

   a) Telnet

   b) NNTP

   c) NTP

   ✓ d) FTP

Activity 7-15

1. **If you desire to monitor network devices on your TCP/IP network for diagnostic purposes, which upper-layer TCP/IP service would you implement?**

   a) Zeroconf

   ✓ b) SNMP

   c) SMB

   d) NFS

   e) LPR/LPD

2. **Which two services work together to securely transfer computer files between a local and a remote host, or between two remote hosts?**

   a) LPR and LPD

   b) SMB and NFS

   ✓ c) SCP and SSH

   d) NFS and LDAP

   e) NFS and SSH

3. **True or False? To establish connections between client workstations and network printers in TCP/IP networks, LPR is installed on the client and LPD is installed on the print server.**

   ✓ True

   __ False

4. **Samba, which enables UNIX and Windows machines to share printers and files, is what type of a service?**

   a) NFS

   b) SCP

   c) LDAP

   ✓ d) SMB

5. **Zeroconf networks provide which automatic configuration services?**

   ✓ a) Multicast address assignment

   b) User account creation

   c) Printer sharing

   ✓ d) Name resolution

Lesson 7 Follow-up

Lesson 7 Lab 1

1. **A Windows Me user logs on and gets a message that her IP address is already in use. This user gets her IP address through a DHCP server. What tool can you use to release and renew her IP address from the DHCP server?**

   a) At a command prompt, type ipconfig /release and then ipconfig /renew.

   ✓ b) At a command prompt, type winipcfg. Click More Info. Click the Release button. Restart the computer to lease a new address.

   c) At a command prompt, type ifconfig /release and then ifconfig /renew.

2. **Match the TCP/IP service with its description.**

Answer	Service		Description
b	Dynamic Host Configuration Protocol (DHCP)	a.	Used to map NetBIOS names to IP addresses to reduce the number of NetBIOS name resolution broadcasts.
c	Domain Name System (DNS)	b.	Used to automate the TCP/IP configuration settings of network devices.
a	Windows Internet Name Service (WINS)	c.	Used to translate fully qualified domain names into IP addresses and vice versa.
d	IP configuration utilities	d.	Used to gather TCP/IP configuration information about network devices and traffic.

3. **Match the TCP/IP upper-layer service with its description.**

Answer	Service		Description
c	File Transfer Protocol (FTP)	a.	Enables a user at one site to simulate a session on a remote host.
a	Telnet	b.	Retrieves email messages from a mail server.
d	Network Time Protocol (NTP)	c.	Enables the transfer of files between a user's workstation and a remote host.
e	Simple Mail Transfer Protocol (SMTP)	d.	Synchronizes the clock times of computers in a network to the millisecond against the U.S. Naval Observatory master clocks in Washington, D.C., and Colorado Springs, CO.
b	Internet Mail Access Protocol (IMAP4)	e.	Sends email from a client to a server or between servers.
f	Hypertext Transfer Protocol (HTTP)	f.	Defines the interaction between a web server and a browser.

4. **Match the TCP/IP interoperability service with its description.**

d	Line Printer Remote (LPR) and Line Printer Daemon (LPD)	a.	Collects information from network devices for diagnostic and maintenance purposes.
b	Network File System (NFS)	b.	Enables users to access shared files stored on different types of computers and work with those files as if they were stored locally on their own computers.
e	Secure Shell (SSH)	c.	Enables sharing resources, such as files, printers, and serial ports, between computers.
c	Server Message Block (SMB)	d.	Establishes connections between client workstations and network printers.
f	Lightweight Directory Access Protocol (LDAP)	e.	Enables a user or application to log on to another computer over a network, execute commands on a remote machine, and move files from one machine to another. Used with Secure Copy Protocol (SCP) to securely transfer computer files between a local and a remote host, or between two remote hosts.
a	Simple Network Management Protocol (SNMP)	f.	Defines how a client can access information, perform operations, and share directory data on a directory server.

Lesson 8

Activity 8-1

1. **On what type of network are you most likely to find the NetBEUI protocol?**
    a) On networks running the Windows Server 2003 operating system.
    ✓ b) On networks running the Windows NT 4.0 operating system.
    c) On networks running Linux or UNIX.
    d) On home networks running Windows XP Professional.

2. **NetBEUI's reliance on broadcast traffic makes it:**
    a) Complex to install and administer.
    ✓ b) Simple to install and administer.
    c) Efficient in comparison to other protocols.
    ✓ d) Inefficient in comparison to other protocols.

3. **Because NetBEUI is implemented at the Data-link layer, it:**

   a) Is suitable for large internetworks.

   b) Requires administrative configuration.

   c) Requires no name resolution.

   ✓ d) Is not routable.

Activity 8-4

3. **You administer an older mixed AppleTalk/Windows network. Windows users are complaining that they cannot locate the AppleShare IP server. You can see the server in the Chooser on your Macintosh client. How can you help the Windows clients connect?**

   Because Windows clients need to use the TCP/IP protocol to connect to the AppleShare IP server, you should first verify basic TCP/IP connectivity by pinging the AppleShare IP server from the Windows clients. Once TCP/IP connectivity is established, it may take some time for the server to appear in the browse list; in the meantime, users can connect directly by using the Start, Run command or mapping a network drive to the server.

4. **A Windows 98 user is complaining that he cannot log on to the AppleShare IP server. No other Windows clients are having difficulty. What should you check?**

   Verify that the user is logging on to his Windows system with the same user name and password that you have configured for him on the AppleShare IP server.

Lesson 8 Follow-up

Lesson 8 Lab 1

1. **What are some advantages and disadvantages of NetBEUI?**

   NetBEUI is simple to implement because it requires no configuration or special network services. However, its reliance on broadcasts for name resolution and network discovery makes it inefficient, and it is not routable so it is only suitable for single-segment networks.

2. **What is a common connectivity problem on IPX/SPX networks, and how would you solve it?**

   Nodes using different frame types cannot communicate. If there is only one frame type on the network, make sure the nodes are set to autodetect the frame type. If there are multiple types, make sure that the nodes are manually assigned the correct type, or that there is a server configured to route between frame types.

3. **Describe the functions of the IPX and SPX protocols.**

   IPX is a connectionless Network-layer protocol that provides best-effort data delivery. SPX is a connection-oriented Transport-layer protocol that provides guaranteed data delivery.

4. **What are the three components of an AppleTalk address?**

   Network number, node number, and socket address.

5. **List the steps in the AppleTalk addressing process.**

   The node discovers its assigned network address when it comes online. The node then randomly generates a node address for itself, and sends a broadcast request to see if the address is in use.

6. **What is the role of AFP in the AppleTalk protocol suite?**

   AFP (AppleTalk Filing Protocol) provides access to file and print resources on AppleTalk networks.

7. **What major networking trend is driving the development and adoption of IPv6?**

   The depletion of the 32-bit classful IPv4 address space.

8. **What are some of the potential advantages of IPv6?**

   A practically unlimited address space; hierarchical addressing; time-sensitive data delivery; simplified message headers; and logical unicast addressing.

Lesson 9

Activity 9-1

1. **In the sample bridged network, which of the following MAC addresses would a bridge add to its routing table for its Interface 1?**

   ✓ a) 00-80-AD-09-0C-41
   b) 63-47-19-B1-70-20
   ✓ c) 00-80-A1-18-01-90
   d) 00-81-AD-17-0A-42
   e) 19-72-12-28-90-56

2. **In the sample bridged network, which of the following MAC addresses would a bridge add to its routing table for its Interface 3?**

   a) 00-81-AD-17-0A-42
   b) 00-80-A1-18-01-90
   ✓ c) 00-80-AC-09-0A-12
   ✓ d) 63-47-19-B1-70-20
   e) 00-80-0A-09-0C-41

3. **Match the bridge type with the description.**

c	Remote bridge	a.	Used to connect an Ethernet and a Token Ring network.
a	Translational bridge	b.	Used to divide a network without modifying data.
b	Transparent bridge	c.	Used across a CAN, MAN, or WAN connection.
d	Source-route	d.	Used in Token Ring networks.

4. **True or False? A switch improves network performance by isolating traffic between two ports.**

 ✓ True

 __ False

5. **True or False? Unlike bridges, switches do not flood broadcasts.**

 __ True

 ✓ False

Activity 9-4

2. **Which route determines the destination for packets to the 172.16.0.0 network? What adapter will they be delivered to?**

 The route with a network destination of 172.16.0.0. These packets will be delivered to the 172.16.0.## network adapter.

3. **Which interfaces will receive internetwork broadcasts? How can you tell?**

 Both interfaces will receive internetwork broadcasts. This is because there are two routes to the 255.255.255.255 destination—one to each network interface.

4. **Why is there no route to the 0.0.0.0 network destination on the 172.16.0.## interface?**

 Because there is no default gateway configured in the TCP/IP properties for this interface.

5. **If you wanted packets to a specific network to be routed to the 172.16.0.## network interface instead of to the default gateway, what would you do?**

 Use the route add command to create a static route to that specific network.

Lesson 9 Follow-up

Lesson 9 Lab 1

1. **What type of bridge connects different networks across media such as a leased phone line, fiber optic link, or wireless media?**

 ✓ a) Remote bridge

 b) Translational bridge

 c) Transparent bridge

2. **What advantage does a router have over a switch?**

 a) Routers translate data between different operating systems.

 b) Routers translate data between different types of networks.

 ✓ c) Routers can block unwanted traffic.

3. An *autonomous system* is a group of routers managed or administered by the same entity.

4. True or False? The first decision made by a sending node about the route of a packet is whether the data is bound for a local or remote subnet.

   ✓ True

   __ False

5. If a router doesn't have a default gateway specified, and a data packet doesn't meet the requirements of any of the router's programming, what does the router do with the data packet?

   ✓ a) It drops the data packet.

   b) It forwards the data packet to the nearest border router.

   c) It returns the packet to the sender.

   d) It saves the packet and reports an error to the network administrator.

6. A *routing table* is a database created by a route discovery protocol that contains network locations as perceived by a specific router.

7. Which of the following are advantages of a static routing table?

   a) They don't require maintenance.

   ✓ b) They don't cause extra network traffic because the routers don't need to communicate with each other.

   ✓ c) They're totally controlled by an administrator.

   ✓ d) They do not require specialized routing protocols.

8. Which of the following are components of a routing table?

   ✓ a) Destination

   ✓ b) Network mask

   c) Subnet number

   ✓ d) Metric

   e) Default TTL

9. True or False? A default route in a routing table is the route to a specific network address.

   __ True

   ✓ False

10. Which of the following describes how routers exchange information such as the address of the next router in the path and the number of hops to the destination?

   a) Count-to-Infinity

   b) Link-state routing

   ✓ c) Distance-vector routing

   d) Split horizon

11. **Which of the following describes how routers exchange information about a route and its quality, bandwidth, and availability?**

✓ a) Link-state routing

b) Distance-vector routing

c) Split horizon

d) Poison reverse

12. **Which solution to the Count-to-Infinity problem takes less time and produces larger updates?**

✓ a) Poison reverse

b) Split horizon

c) Convergence

d) Routing loops

13. **The primary disadvantage of *RIP* is it exchanges the entire route table with periodic broadcasts that might use up too much bandwidth on large networks.**

14. **True or False? RIP supports multicasting, password protection for routers, and multiple subnet masks.**

__ True

✓ False

15. **Which of the following is best used in small- to medium-sized networks that don't change very much?**

✓ a) RIP

b) RIP II

c) OSPF

d) IGRP

16. ***IGRP* improves the distance-vector method by enabling an administrator to configure six extra metrics that are combined into a composite metric.**

17. **A *link-state database* is a map of network routers that contains information about the condition of the links and multiple routes to destinations.**

18. **True or False? OSPF differs from RIP in that it sends only updates in router advertisements instead of the entire route table.**

✓ True

__ False

19. **What is the result of output filtering on a router?**

a) Data is blocked from being sent out through the router.

b) Data is not accepted at the router on specific interfaces.

c) Data is accepted at the router but is returned to the sender and an error is generated.

✓ d) Data is blocked from being sent out through a specific interface on a router. The data can still be sent through other interfaces on the router.

20. **What is required to implement a VLAN environment?**

   a) A bridge that's VLAN-configurable.

   ✓ b) A switch that's VLAN-configurable.

   ✓ c) A router that's VLAN-configurable.

   d) A hub that's VLAN-configurable.

21. **True or False? VLANs are implemented in the software configuration of a VLAN switch.**

   _✓_ True

   __ False

22. **True or False? VLANs are less expensive than a regular switched environment.**

   __ True

   _✓_ False

Lesson 10

Activity 10-1

1. **Which methods use the same path for all data traffic between two endpoints in a single session?**

   a) Packet switching

   ✓ b) Circuit switching

   ✓ c) Virtual circuits

   d) Cell switching

2. **Which method uses a fixed-length packet?**

   a) Packet switching

   b) Virtual circuits

   ✓ c) Cell switching

   d) Switched virtual circuits

3. **True or False? Virtual circuits are always switched.**

   __ True

   _✓_ False

4. **Which switching technology is used on the Internet?**

   a) Cell switching

   b) Circuit switching

   ✓ c) Packet switching

Activity 10-4

2. **If you enabled ICS on this host, what would be the effect on the network configuration?**

   The internal network connection on the ICS host would get a new private static IP address, and the ICS host would begin acting as a DHCP server and DNS server for internal clients.

3. **What are some of the other configuration requirements for ICS?**

   There must not be any DHCP or DNS servers on the network, and the ICS clients must be configured for dynamic IP addressing.

Activity 10-5

1. **What are advantages of Voice over Data systems as compared to traditional telephone systems?**

   ✓ a) Reduced long-distance costs

   ✓ b) Increased bandwidth

   ✓ c) Increased quality of service

   d) Dedicated circuit switching

2. **What component of a VoIP system translates between phone numbers and IP addresses?**

   a) The voice agent

   ✓ b) The dial plan map

   c) The PBX

   d) The router

   e) The DNS server

3. **Which component of a VoIP system converts the voice data to a digital signal?**

   a) The telephone instrument

   b) The dial plan map

   ✓ c) The voice agent

   d) The router

   e) The PBX

Lesson 10 Follow-up

Lesson 10 Lab 1

1. **Describe circuit switching, packet switching, and cell switching.**

   Circuit switching creates a fixed path between the two endpoints of the communication that lasts for the duration of the connection. Packet switching divides the communication into separate sections, each one of which can be routed on its own path. Cell switching is similar to packet switching, but the cells are of a fixed size.

2. **What are the benefits and drawbacks of dial-up connectivity?**

   The benefit of dial-up connectivity is that it is available wherever telephone service is available. It is also relatively inexpensive. However, the major drawback of dial-up connectivity is that it is much slower and provides less bandwidth than most other WAN technologies.

3. **Both DSL and cable are popular home and small-office broadband connectivity services. What is the technical difference between DSL and cable?**

   DSL uses existing copper-cable phone lines to transmit the digital signal in a separate channel from the analog voice signal. Cable Internet uses cable television transmission lines, with a splitter to separate the two signals.

4. **What are the benefits and drawbacks of ATM?**

   ATM is versatile and provides high bandwidth. However, it is relatively expensive to implement.

5. **What is the primary physical media type for SONET?**

   Fiber optic cable.

6. **What are some of the physical equipment types used to connect LAN implementations to WAN transmission media?**

   Multiplexers, CSU/DSU units, and standard modems.

7. **What are the benefits and drawbacks of VoIP?**

   VoIP can use the existing IP infrastructure and Internet connectivity that is in place in virtually every organization to transmit voice data without incurring additional overhead costs due to telephone charges. However, when voice data is broken into packets on the IP network, it becomes subject to delay and signal degradation in high-traffic environments if there is no Quality of Service provision.

Lesson 11

Activity 11-1

1. **Response time on the website that hosts the online version of your product catalog is getting slower and slower. Customers are complaining that they cannot browse the catalog items or search for products. What type of attack do you suspect?**

   a) A Trojan horse attack

   b) A spoofing attack

   c) A social engineering attack

   ✓ d) A Denial of Service (DoS) attack

2. **Jason arrives at work in the morning and finds that he can't log on to the network. The network administrator says his account was locked at 3 A.M. due to too many unsuccessful logon attempts. What type of attack do you suspect?**

   a) A man-in-the-middle attack

   ✓ b) A password attack

   c) A virus attack

   d) A hijacking attack

3. **Which of these examples can be classified as social engineering attacks?**

   ✓ a) A customer contacts your help desk asking for her user name and password because she cannot log on to your e-commerce website.

   ✓ b) A user gets a call from a person who states he is a help desk technician. The caller asks the user to go to an external website and download a file so that the technician can monitor the user's system.

   c) The CEO of your company calls you personally on the phone to ask you to fax salary data to her personal fax number. The fax number she gives you is listed in the company directory, and you recognize her voice.

   ✓ d) A user receives an email that appears to be from a bank; the bank says they need the user's name, date of birth, and social security number to verify account information.

4. **Which are considered legitimate network security measures?**

   ✓ a) Requiring complex passwords.

   ✓ b) Installing antivirus software.

   c) Denying users the ability to log on.

   d) Preventing users from storing data on network servers.

   ✓ e) Restricting physical access to the network.

Activity 11-2

1. **What is a macro virus?**

   a) A virus that is transmitted via email.

   ✓ b) A virus that uses a specific program's command language.

   c) A virus that attacks the boot sector.

   d) A virus that runs in the Windows scripting host.

2. **Why is a hoax dangerous?**

   a) The hoax is an actual virus that has the potential to cause damage.

   ✓ b) Propagation of the hoax can create DoS conditions.

   c) Users are annoyed by the hoax.

   ✓ d) The hoax can include elements of a social engineering attack.

3. **When should a virus administrator manually check for virus updates?**

   ✓ a) When an known threat is active.

   b) After each automatic update.

   c) Never.

   d) On a daily basis.

4. **You manage a small office network with a single gateway to an Internet service provider. The ISP maintains your corporate email on its own email server. There is an internal server for file and print services. As the administrator for this network, where should you deploy antivirus software?**

   ✓ a) On the desktop systems.

   ✓ b) On the gateway system.

   c) On the email server.

   ✓ d) On the file and print server.

Lesson 11 Follow-up

Lesson 11 Lab 1

1. **Describe Trojan horses and explain why they are dangerous.**

   Trojan horses are programs that masquerade as legitimate software. They are often distributed through email. One way that they are dangerous is that they can steal passwords and transmit them to another party.

2. **What are some ways that you can guard against network data theft?**

   Implement strong security policies for data storage and user account management, and enforce the policies.

3. **Are there any disadvantages to strong virus protection plans?**

   Yes. For example, scanning too many files too often can slow down response times on servers or user workstations. Network security is always a balance between protection and usability.

4. **Describe strong passwords.**

   Strong passwords are structured to conform to an administrator's password policy. Typically, strong passwords require a minimum password length, and must contain a mixture of uppercase and lowercase letters, numbers, and other non-alphanumeric characters.

5. **What are the security advantages of a drive-level security system such as NTFS?**

   A secure file system such as NTFS provides file- and folder-specific permissions on a user or group basis. This means that users must be authenticated by the system to gain access, rather than simply obtaining a resource password. (NTFS also provides user-level file encryption.)

6. **Summarize the Kerberos authentication process.**

   In Kerberos, clients are authenticated by a central authority called a key distribution center, and receive an encrypted session key. When they wish to access resources, they use the session key to obtain resource tickets from the central authority. The resources grant access on the basis of the tickets because they trust the key distribution center.

7. **How can digital certificates support network security?**

   They can be used to establish identity, by generating digital signatures that prevent spoofing. They can also be used for encryption to protect data.

8. **Describe some of the security benefits of IPSec.**

   IPSec is an independent protocol that can be implemented on any IP network. IPSec can provide end-to-end encryption and security for an entire network communication. It can also prevent insecure communications on a node-by-node basis.

9. **Distinguish between NAT servers, firewalls, and proxy servers.**

   NAT servers translate between a private and a public IP address scheme. Firewalls filter packets based on administrative criteria, but do not make addressing changes. Proxy servers re-generate packets as well as readdressing them, and can also provide address translation. All three types of services work together to create a secure solution.

Lesson 11 Lab 2

1. **How would you recommend implementing a virus protection program?**

   Establish an enterprise virus server and install the virus protection agent on all workstations and servers. Configure the enterprise server to check for updates and pass them to the agents. Set up virus protection to scan all emails and downloaded files from the Internet.

2. **Where would you need firewalls and NATs?**

   There should be a firewall and a NAT on the connection to the Internet. There should also be a firewall in education between the classrooms and the production network and two firewalls in the secure research facility.

3. **What is the best way to ensure that users at the secure research facility can gain access to scans on the image server?**

   By using permissions. Place the shared files in a shared folder on an NTFS volume. Create a user group for the secure researchers and grant that group read access only to the scans folder.

4. **How can the web server be configured to allow access both inside and outside the company?**

   You can create a DMZ through the firewall on the Internet connection, or place the web server outside the firewall.

5. **Sketch your network design.**

There is more than one possible solution.

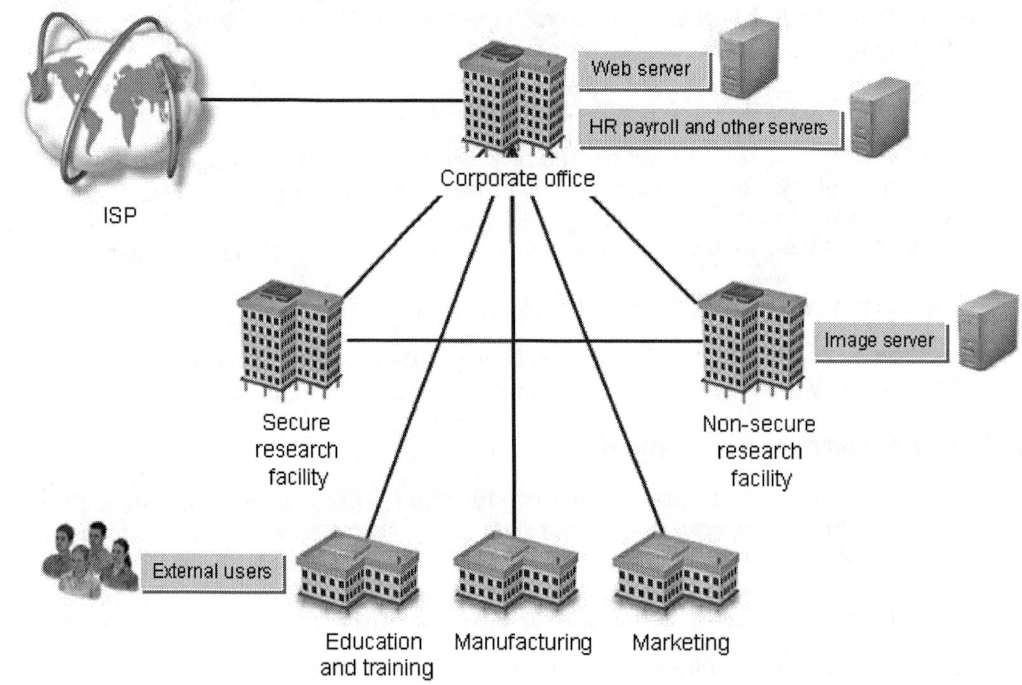

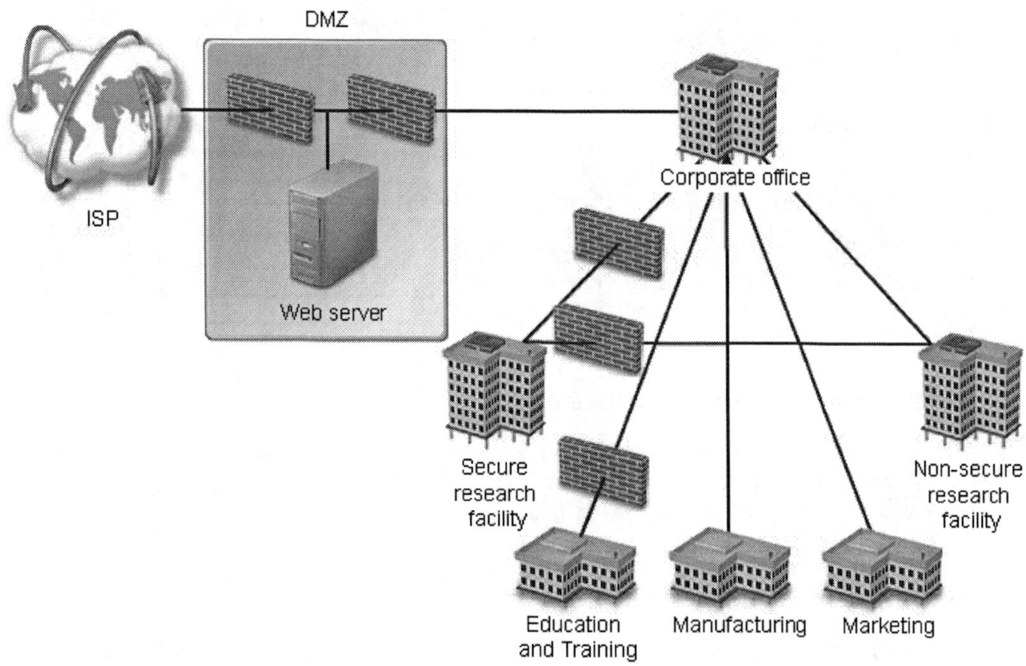

Lesson 12

Activity 12-3

1. **Match the remote networking technology with its description.**

c	Remote access	a.	Is often used as a troubleshooting or help desk tool.
a	Remote control	b.	Enables several computers to connect simultaneously.
b	Terminal services	c.	Lets traveling users work as if they are in the office.

2. **Which remote access method is best for accessing applications?**

   a) Remote access

   b) Remote control

   ✓ c) Terminal services

Activity 12-6

2. **True or False? VPNs can only be implemented over the Internet.**

   __ True

   ✓ False

3. **What provides the security for most VPNs?**

   ✓ a) Encapsulation

   b) Remote authentication

   ✓ c) Encryption

   d) Firewalls

4. **Which VPN protocol provides both encapsulation and encryption?**

   a) PPTP

   b) SSL

   ✓ c) IPSec

   d) MPPE

   e) L2TP

5. **Which VPN type is most likely to be used by satellite offices?**

   a) Access VPN

   ✓ b) Intranet VPN

   c) Extranet VPN

SOLUTIONS

Activity 12-7

1. **Your company hosts a VPN server using the L2TP protocol with IPSec encryption. A user trying to connect from his home PC consistently fails, although he can connect when he brings his laptop home from the office. What do you suspect is the cause of the failure?**

   The home system might not be configured with the correct IPSec policy, or the two systems might not have a common IPSec authentication method configured within their two policies.

2. **What should you do to correct the situation?**

   Because this type of VPN is intended to provide secure access from authorized hosts only, the user should connect using his company laptop only. This system has been appropriately configured for a secure remote connection.

3. **A user attempts to establish a dial-up connection with your company's RRAS server. The connection consistently fails with an authentication error. You ask the user to examine the properties of his dial-up connection object. Under Logon Security, in the Allow These Protocols section, only PAP is checked. What is the most likely cause of the failure?**

   PAP sends unencrypted passwords across the network and is not a secure authentication protocol. The RRAS server is most likely configured to require encrypted authentication via CHAP or MS-CHAP. Because the client cannot support encrypted authentication, the connection is dropped.

4. **What should you do to correct the situation?**

   Instruct the user to allow the dial-up connection object to use all versions of the CHAP authentication protocol, and remove the PAP authentication protocol.

5. **You provide help desk support for an ISP. A home user has called to say that he is trying to dial in but the system reports that there is no dial tone. His home phone is on the same line, and he obviously has a dial tone on the phone instrument. He could connect yesterday. What could be the problem?**

   The modem might have become disconnected because a cable was dislodged. If it is an external modem, tell the user to verify that it is connected, plugged in, and turned on. If it is an internal modem, verify that the phone line is connected. It is also possible, but less likely, that the modem or modem card has simply failed.

6. **You work for a large ISP that provides a number of PoP phone numbers for each metropolitan area where you provide service. A Chicago-based user is trying to connect using the first local dial-up number listed in your service guide, but receives an error that the remote system is busy or not responding. There is a high amount of traffic on your network, but all systems are functioning. What should you suggest to the user?**

   Configure the dial-up connection with one of the alternate PoP phone numbers and try again.

7. **You maintain a Microsoft RRAS server with several incoming phone lines to support network access for remote dial-up clients, and VPN service for Internet users. A home user running Linux can connect to the Internet through his local ISP, but cannot connect to your RRAS server. What should you check on the RRAS server?**

   Check to see what type of incoming VPN ports the RRAS server supports. It might only be configured to accept PPTP connections, which are generally only used by Microsoft clients.

8. **How might you enable the user to connect?**

   Open L2TP VPN ports on the RRAS server. This is desirable in any case, because L2TP is the Internet standard VPN protocol.

Lesson 12 Follow-up

Lesson 12 Lab 1

1. **Match each job role with the most appropriate remote networking architecture.**

b	Data entry associate	a.	Remote access
a	Telecommuter	b.	Terminal services
c	Network administrator	c.	Remote control

2. **Which types of remote networking are associated with the RDP protocol?**

   a) Remote access

   ✓ b) Remote control

   ✓ c) Terminal services

3. **What are the necessary components for a dedicated thin client?**

   ✓ a) Input devices

   ✓ b) Output device

   ✓ c) Network connection

   d) Client software

   ✓ e) Boot ROM

4. **How is web-based remote access accomplished in Windows Server 2003?**

   a) Remote Desktop Connection

   b) Remote Assistance

   c) RRAS

   ✓ d) Remote Desktop Web Connection

   e) IIS

5. **True or False? The main difference between PAP and CHAP is how they handle user passwords.**

   ✓ True

   __ False

6. **Which remote access protocol is used with cable modem connections?**

   a) SLIP

   b) PPP

   ✓ c) PPPoE

   d) EAP

7. In an environment that has several RAS servers, the main benefit of implementing <u>*RADIUS*</u> is central administration of remote access policies.

8. True or False? Tunneling enables nonroutable data to be sent over the Internet.

   ✓ True

   __ False

9. Which is a VPN protocol?

   a) SLIP

   b) PPP

   ✓ c) PPTP

   d) PPPoE

   e) EAP

Lesson 13

Activity 13-1

1. Which are common components of a disaster recovery plan?

   a) A list of employees' personal items

   ✓ b) Contact information for key individuals

   ✓ c) An inventory

   ✓ d) Plans to reconstruct the network

2. Which of these groups should you include in your disaster recovery contact list?

   ✓ a) Security officials

   ✓ b) Vendors, contractors, and manufacturers

   ✓ c) Network administrators and corporate managers

   d) All current employees

3. Company X pays a small monthly rental fee for a warehouse with phone and power hookups that they can use as a:

   a) Hot site

   ✓ b) Cold site

   c) Warm site

   d) Hot spare

   e) Cold spare

4. Which are components of a critical hardware inventory?

   ✓ a) Servers and workstations

   ✓ b) Connectivity devices

   c) Hand tools

   d) Operating system software

5. **Match the component of the network reconstruction plan with its description.**

a	Network diagram	a.	Information about the layout, configuration, and security credentials for the network.
b	Fall-back plan	b.	An alternate network design to implement temporarily.
c	Data restoration plan	c.	Details how you will retrieve and restore backups.

Activity 13-2

1. **What are the critical components of your kitchen?**

   A typical kitchen includes a refrigerator, stove, sink, disposal, dishwasher, oven, and microwave.

2. **Build a simple inventory and vendor list.**

   This should include a description of the item, the vendor and model number, and the place purchased. For example, an inventory entry for the refrigerator might read "GE model GER25SSWH; 25 cu. ft. side-by-side; ice/water on the door; purchased at Sears."

3. **Where will you store the manufacturers' documentation for your appliances?**

   The location should be safe but accessible. You might compile all the documents in a binder and store it in a closet or on a shelf.

4. **Is there an alternate source for manuals and documentation?**

   Most can be obtained from the manufacturers' websites. Make a note of the URLs and keep it separate from the hard copies of the documentation.

5. **Do you have a fall-back plan if water does damage your kitchen?**

   A contingency plan might include purchasing a camp stove and fuel, an ice chest, a generator, extra gasoline, and bottled water, and storing them in the garage.

6. **Draw a floor plan of your kitchen.**

   Results will vary.

7. **Reflect on the process of developing this plan. What were the difficulties? What aspects do you think would be most useful for you?**

   One difficult step might be the fact that you will need to research details about information that you normally take for granted. If you did not keep notes about the appliance models and manufacturers when you purchased them, it might be difficult to determine now. However, in the event of a total loss of the kitchen, it would indeed be very useful to have fall-back equipment as well as to have the configuration of the kitchen well documented.

Activity 13-3

4. **What other steps should you take to complete the backup?**
   a) Restart the system.
   ✓ b) Label the backup media.
   ✓ c) Store the backup media in a safe place.
   d) Back up the operating system files.

5. **In a production backup system, what types of media might you use for a small data backup such as this?**
   ✓ a) External removable drives
   ✓ b) Writeable CDs or DVDs
   c) A RAID array
   d) A separate partition on the same hard disk

Activity 13-5

1. **What backup schedule will you implement?**

   One possible schedule would be a full backup every Monday at 8:00 P.M., plus incremental backups Tuesday through Friday at the same time.

2. **How many tapes would be required for a year's worth of backups, assuming that you do not need extra tapes for the transit to offsite?**

   A total of 29 tapes: 12 tapes for the monthly Monday archives; 9 tapes for the weekly Monday reports (in case one of the two months in the reporting period contains five Mondays); and 8 tapes for the Tuesday-Friday backups (4 stored onsite, 4 offsite).

3. **What would be a good time during the week to transfer the tapes to offsite storage?**

   Tuesday afternoon or Wednesday morning, to allow time to test the Monday backups before archiving them but to avoid retaining them onsite any longer than necessary.

4. **It's Monday afternoon and your office manager is looking at a file that she swears she edited on Friday, but the file appears to be the old one from the previous Thursday. With your plan, how do you restore the file?**

   The tape from last Friday should be offsite, so it will have to be retrieved. The tape needs to be cataloged, and the file found and marked for restore. The restore job should be run, and the file stored in an alternate location and checked to verify that it is the correct file. If it is the correct file, it can be moved into the correct directory.

5. **The company experiences a complete disk failure at 10 A.M. on Thursday. How do you restore the data?**

   Replace the hard disk and then restore the full backup tape from Monday, the incremental backup from Tuesday, and the incremental backup from Wednesday. To the extent possible, users will have to manually repost any changes and transactions that occurred between the Wednesday incremental backup and the Thursday morning disk failure.

Activity 13-6

1. **What is the best description of fault tolerance?**

   a) To protect personnel and resources and restore system functioning in the event of unforeseeable catastrophic failure.

   ✓ b) To ensure continuous access to resources and network services in the event of a routine mishap or predictable failure.

   c) To provide archive copies of important data.

   d) To document current system configurations.

2. **Match the fault tolerance feature with the description.**

c	Protects against power loss or power surges.	a.	RAID
a	Specifications for fault tolerance configurations on multiple-disk systems.	b.	Link redundancy
b	Provides a separate network connection for use if the main connection goes down.	c.	UPS

3. **Match the RAID level with its description.**

c	RAID 0	a.	Disk mirroring or disk duplexing.
a	RAID 1	b.	Striping with parity spread across drives.
b	RAID 5	c.	Disk striping without parity. Provides no fault tolerance.
d	RAID 3	d.	An obsolete RAID level.

4. **Match the RAID level with the minimum hardware required.**

a	RAID 0	a.	2 disks
b	RAID 1	b.	2 disks and possibly 2 controllers
c	RAID 5	c.	3 disks
d	RAID 10	d.	4 disks

5. **Which of the following networks have implemented link redundancy?**

   ✓ a) A small office network with a broadband Internet connection and a separate dial-up one.

   ✓ b) A large company with two leased T1 lines from the same WAN provider.

   c) A large company with an internal routed network and a leased T3 WAN connection.

   d) A home-based worker with a cable modem and standard home phone service.

Lesson 13 Follow-up

Lesson 13 Lab 1

1. **Distinguish between disaster recovery planning and fault tolerance planning.**

   Disaster recovery planning enables you to restore network services in the event of catastrophic damage that is either not foreseeable or preventable. Fault tolerance measures enable systems to keep functioning in the event of a mishap that can reasonably be predicted. Without fault tolerance measures in place, those events could actually trigger disastrous system loss.

2. **What are some of the different personnel who are involved in designing and implementing a disaster recovery plan, and what are their roles?**

   Network administration personnel are primarily responsible for designing, testing, and documenting the plan. Corporate managers and administrators must provide input to the plan and understand their responsibilities if the plan is implemented. Key vendors and contractors should be aware of the role they will be expected to play in the plan, and the level of service they will be expected to provide.

3. **What do you feel is the most important aspect of a disaster recovery plan? Why?**

   Answers might vary, but documenting the plan adequately is probably the most important aspect. The people who composed the plan might not be those who implement it, so detailed documentation is critical to implementing it successfully.

4. **Why is it important to update a disaster recovery plan regularly?**

   Primarily to make sure that records of passwords, responsible parties, and recovery agents are current. The plan can fail if the security information is incorrect.

5. **How many tape sets are required when using the grandfather-father-son rotation method?**

   One set each for Monday through Thursday (four), one set for each Friday of the month (four; if there are five Fridays, the fifth Friday will be the month-end tape), and 12 month-end sets (one for the last business day of each month), for a total of 20. If you use an extra daily, weekly, and monthly tape, the total is 23.

6. **List and describe the three major backup types.**

   In a Full backup, all information is backed up.

   In an Incremental backup, new files and files created or modified since the last full or incremental backup are backed up and the archive bit is cleared.

   In a Differential backup, all files created or modified since the last full backup are backed up and the archive bit is not cleared.

7. **What is a brick-level backup of a mail server?**

   A brick-level backup is a backup at the mailbox level, enabling you to restore individual mailboxes.

8. **What are some special issues involved in backing up databases?**

   The database must be closed, or there must be an agent software that can back it up while open. The transaction logs may need to be cleared when the backup is complete. These logs may need to be replayed if there is a restore, so that the database can be brought to the most current state possible.

9. **Which RAID level provides high fault tolerance but also high disk-space overhead?**

   RAID 1 (mirroring and duplexing). Because all data is duplicated to a second drive, you can only use 50% of the available disk space for unique data storage.

10. **What is the benefit of implementing RAID level 0?**

    Purely to enhance read/write performance by accessing multiple drives simultaneously. Because there is no parity, RAID 0 provides no fault tolerance.

11. **How could you make a network with a single external WAN link and an internal routed topology fault-tolerant?**

    Add a fall-back WAN link for use if the primary link goes down. Depending on the size of the network and the connectivity needs, this could be a simple dial-up connection or a redundant leased line. Internally, primary routers can be configured in a mesh topology, providing redundant routes through the network. Routing tables either need to be configured with the backup routes manually, or you can employ a dynamic routing protocol for more efficiency.

12. **What factors should you consider when planning enterprise fault tolerance for your organization?**

    For a true enterprise solution, you will need to consider and implement all elements of fault tolerance planning, including power protection for key systems; disk fault tolerance; a backup plan; server redundancy for DNS, DHCP, directory, and other key services; network link redundancy; and the availability of spares for critical devices.

Lesson 14

Activity 14-1

1. **What is the highest realistic reliability goal for a high-availability system?**

   a) 100% uptime

   ✓ b) Five nines uptime

   c) Four nines uptime

   d) Three nines uptime

2. **What is the best description of scalability?**

   a) The ability to access data a high percentage of the time.

   b) The ability of one system to take over when another fails.

   ✓ c) The ability of a system to grow smoothly to meet increasing demand.

   d) The ability to share workload between systems.

3. **What are characteristics of distributed storage systems?**

   ✓ a) Data can be managed as a single entity.

   ✓ b) Data in different physical locations appears as a unified structure.

   c) Users access data by locating different physical servers.

   ✓ d) Administrators can reconfigure storage on the fly.

4. **What is the best description of a drive array?**

   ✓ a) A group of separate disks that are configured to work as a unit.

   b) A specialized file server that is designed and dedicated to support data storage needs.

   c) A group of servers working together to provide fault tolerance and load balancing.

   d) A private network dedicated to data storage.

Activity 14-2

1. **What is the best description of a cluster?**

   a) A specialized file server that is designed and dedicated to support data storage needs.

   b) A group of separate disks that are configured to work as a unit.

   c) A private network dedicated to data storage.

   ✓ d) A group of servers working together to provide fault tolerance and load balancing.

2. **Which are hardware requirements of multiple nodes in a cluster?**

   a) Cluster-aware software.

   ✓ b) Two network connections.

   ✓ c) Access to a common storage device.

   d) External tape drives.

3. **Match the cluster type with the description.**

c	Active/active	a.	A cluster that includes nodes that handle the full workload during normal operations, and other nodes in standby mode.
a	Active/passive	b.	A cluster in which servers can provide almost instantaneous failover.
b	Fault-tolerant or high-availability	c.	A cluster that has all nodes online, constantly providing services.

4. **Which cluster type has the best failover response time?**

   a) Active/active

   b) Active/passive

   ✓ c) Fault-tolerant

5. **Which cluster type has the best resource efficiency?**

   ✓ a) Active/active

   b) Active/passive

   c) Fault-tolerant

6. **In an active/passive configuration, how does the passive server know that the active server has failed?**

   a) The active server sends an ABEND message.

   b) The administrator brings the standby server online.

   ✓ c) The heartbeat stops.

   d) The passive server reboots.

Activity 14-3

1. **Which is the most appropriate description of a NAS system?**

   ✓ a) A specialized file server that is designed and dedicated to support data storage needs.

   b) A group of servers working together to provide fault tolerance and load balancing.

   c) A group of separate disks that are configured to work as a unit.

   d) A private network dedicated to data storage.

2. **How do NAS systems differ from standard file server configurations?**

   ✓ a) They run a special operating system.

   b) They are not connected to the network.

   c) They have no hard disk.

   ✓ d) They have no monitor, keyboard, or mouse.

3. **Which are file access protocols commonly used with NAS systems?**

   ✓ a) SMB

   ✓ b) NFS

   c) NSS

   d) NTFS

4. **What are the options for connecting clients to a NAS?**

   ✓ a) Clients connect directly.

   b) Clients install special access software.

   ✓ c) Clients connect through a server gateway.

   ✓ d) Clients connect using a distributed file system.

Activity 14-4

1. **Which is the best description of a SAN?**

   a) A drive that has an Ethernet port and TCP/IP address and is used mainly as a file server.

   b) A server designed for and dedicated to file storage.

   c) A group of servers sharing the same network function.

   ✓ d) A private network dedicated to data storage.

2. **What are hardware requirements for a SAN?**

   ✓ a) A private network topology over Fibre Channel, FDDI, ATM, or high-speed Ethernet.

   ✓ b) Shared access to data storage devices.

   c) SCSI-attached drive controllers.

   d) TCP/IP.

3. **What are valid reasons for employing Fibre Channel within a SAN?**

   a) Low cost.

   ✓ b) High data-transfer rate.

   c) Choice of lower-layer protocols.

   ✓ d) Choice of physical media.

   ✓ e) Choice of upper-layer protocols.

4. **Match the Fibre Channel topology with the description.**

a	Direct connection	a.	Two end nodes in a full-duplex connection.
c	Arbitrated loop	b.	Interconnected nodes that can have multiple senders.
b	Switched fabric	c.	Nodes arranged in a ring with one sender at a time.

5. **What are potential advantages to implementing SANs over TCP/IP?**

   a) High data-transfer rate.

   ✓ b) Low cost.

   ✓ c) Use of existing infrastructure.

   d) Higher storage capacity than Fibre Channel SANs.

Lesson 14 Follow-up

Lesson 14 Lab 1

1. **What are some of the characteristics of a network that will affect its data storage requirements?**

   The applications run; the number of users; the size, number, and type of enterprise databases; and the size, number, and type of data files.

2. **What are some of the factors you should evaluate when considering a data storage solution?**

   Whether the level of availability will meet your needs; whether it will scale to meet your future needs; cost; and ease of implementation and support.

3. **From a performance-to-cost standpoint, what is the most effective cluster implementation type?**

   Active/active. In this design, all nodes in the cluster serve customer requests.

4. **How do nodes in a cluster monitor each other?**

   By sending regular signals called heartbeats between servers on the internal cluster network.

5. **What two types of software are always required on a NAS system?**

   A streamlined NAS operating system, and file-access protocols so that clients can access the data.

6. **What hardware components are included in a NAS system, and which are omitted?**

   The NAS includes a dedicated server with direct high-speed links to large-capacity storage systems such as drive arrays or tape drives. The NAS usually does not include input/output devices such as monitor, keyboard, and mouse.

7. **What improvements does a SAN have over a NAS?**

   The SAN replaces the SCSI connection in a NAS implementation with a high-performance network channel. This keeps data off the main network and removes many of the hardware limitations of a SCSI connection.

8. **What network technologies can be used for connectivity in a SAN?**

   Fibre Channel is the de facto standard and is the fastest medium. SANs can also use existing high-performance TCP/IP implementations over media such as ATM or fast Ethernet. The cost advantages of this might be beneficial to small- or medium-sized networks that do not need the extremely high performance of Fibre Channel.

Lesson 15

Activity 15-4

1. **Which services are included with Windows Server 2003?**

   ✓ a) An LDAP-compliant directory service

   b) A mail server

   ✓ c) DNS and DHCP network services

   ✓ d) Public-key infrastructure

   e) Network-management services

2. **Match the Active Directory component to its description.**

d	Domain controller	a.	A container for Active Directory objects that provides for delegation of administration.
a	Organizational Unit	b.	A unit of the Active Directory that has a unique DNS name and provides a security boundary.
b	Domain	c.	A group of domains that share a contiguous namespace.
c	Tree	d.	A Windows Server computer that runs the Active Directory service.
e	Forest	e.	A group of domains that share a directory schema but have disjunct names.

3. **Select the characteristics of workgroup membership.**

   a) The computer is represented by a computer account object in the directory database.

   ✓ b) User accounts are stored separately on each individual computer.

   ✓ c) Groups computers under a common naming scheme.

   d) Provides centralized security.

4. **Match the Windows Server System product with its description.**

a	Exchange Server	a.	Email services.
f	SQL Server	b.	Firewall services.
d	SMS Server	c.	Website deployment and management services.
b	ISA Server	d.	Network management services.
c	Content Management Server	e.	Team collaboration services.
e	SharePoint Portal Server	f.	Database services.

5. **You have just implemented an Active Directory domain on your network. Formerly, all computers were configured as workgroup members. One of the Windows XP Professional users calls to say he can't log on to the domain. What are some of the things you could check to try to resolve the problem?**

   First, verify that the user's system was actually joined to the domain; see if there is a Log On To drop-down list available and that the domain name appears there. If so, make sure that he selects the domain from the list. Finally, verify that there is a domain user account created and that he is logging on using the domain user name and password.

6. **A Windows XP user's computer has just been joined to the domain. She is complaining that her desktop appearance and some of her menus have changed. What could be the issue?**

   Centralized policies on the domain may be creating a new default desktop appearance. Depending on the security settings, the user may be able to reconfigure some of her preferences.

7. **A Windows Me user is trying to access a shared folder on another Windows Me computer in her workgroup. Access is denied. What could be the problem?**

   The share permissions on the folder could be set incorrectly. Or, the user's account might not exist in the SAM on the other Windows Me computer.

8. **You have some legacy Windows 98 computers that you would like to access domain services while you schedule upgrades to Windows XP. What can you do to enable these clients to access domain services?**

   Install the Directory Services Client software.

Activity 15-5

1. **Select the features of NetWare 6.x.**

   a) Bindery-based authentication

   ✓ b) Native TCP/IP networking

   ✓ c) Web-based file and printer access

   ✓ d) The eDirectory directory service

2. **Match the eDirectory tree object to its description.**

b	Tree	a.	The lowest level of the organizational hierarchy.
e	Organization	b.	The top level of the eDirectory hierarchy.
d	User account	c.	An optional container object.
c	Country	d.	A leaf object.
a	Organizational Unit	e.	A required container object.

3. **Select the benefits of NSS.**

   a) Up to 64 volumes per server

   ✓ b) High-capacity volumes

   ✓ c) Journaled file system

   d) Slow mount time

4. **What printing features are incorporated into an NDPS printer agent?**

   a) Print driver and print queue

   b) Print server and print driver

   c) Print server, print queue, and bindery

   ✓ d) Print server, print queue, and printer object

5. **Match the version of NetWare to its description.**

d	First version to support TCP/IP as the native protocol.	a.	NetWare 2.x
b	First version to include a graphical management tool.	b.	NetWare 4.x
a	First version to be compatible with standard Intel processors.	c.	NetWare 3.x
c	Last version to support only bindery-based authentication.	d.	NetWare 5.x

6. **Your Novell NetWare network uses a dedicated Symantec VPN gateway appliance to provide secure remote access. Connections are created using L2TP. The gateway appliance is accessed using the public IP address 207.175.43.150. Each user who needs remote access has remote account information they can use to access the gateway. What do you need to configure on the NetWare network to enable remote users to access resources?**

   You would need to configure the same items you would for local network users: a valid user account object and password within the directory tree, and the appropriate access rights to resources.

7. **A remote user needs to access the NetWare network. The user has Internet access through a broadband connection to an ISP. What instructions would you provide to a remote user to connect securely to the VPN gateway device?**

   First, log on locally to the Windows client computer. Then, create a VPN connection object to connect to the 207.175.43.150 IP address over the L2TP VPN protocol. Configure the VPN connection with the username and password needed to access the gateway device. Next, use the existing network connection object to connect to the ISP and access the Internet. Use the VPN object to establish the VPN connection to the gateway device.

8. **How would you instruct the user to access resources on the NetWare network?**

   The user needs to verify that the Novell Client software is installed and configured with the appropriate user credentials for the directory tree. Once the VPN connection is established, the user can use the Novell Client to authenticate to the NetWare network.

9. **What resources will the remote user be able to access on the NetWare network?**

   The user should be able to access the same resources as if she were logged on to the local network.

10. **You provide network consulting services on a volunteer basis to a small non-profit agency. The agency relies on legacy networking hardware and software because of the expense of upgrading to current technologies. Their network uses a mix of Novell server versions that all use the IPX/SPX protocol. Clients have intermittent problems connecting to different NetWare servers and have asked you for help resolving the problem. What do you suspect is the cause?**

    Frame type mismatch is the most common cause of connectivity problems on IPX/SPX networks, and occurs most frequently when there is a mix of server versions. Novell 3.11 servers ran the 802.3 frame type; later servers used 802.2. Clients will default to whichever frame they detect when they first connect to the network, so each time a client boots it could configure a different frame type and have connectivity only to specific servers.

11. **How can you correct the problem?**

    Configure one of the servers to route between frame types.

12. **You manage a mixed network that includes both Windows Server 2003 and NetWare 6 servers. Most clients only need access to the Windows servers, but there are a few departments who need to use specialized databases on the NetWare systems. A new user joins the department and needs to connect to a NetWare server from her Windows XP Professional workstation. She configures the properties of her Local Area Connection object to add the CSNW client. She still cannot connect to the NetWare servers. What could be the problem?**

    The Microsoft CSNW client only binds to NWLink. Because NetWare 6 uses TCP/IP natively, it is better to install the Novell Client software and use it to connect to both NetWare and Windows networks over TCP/IP.

13. A user from the Sales department is attempting to log on to NetWare and is encountering difficulty. You check his login screen and find the following:

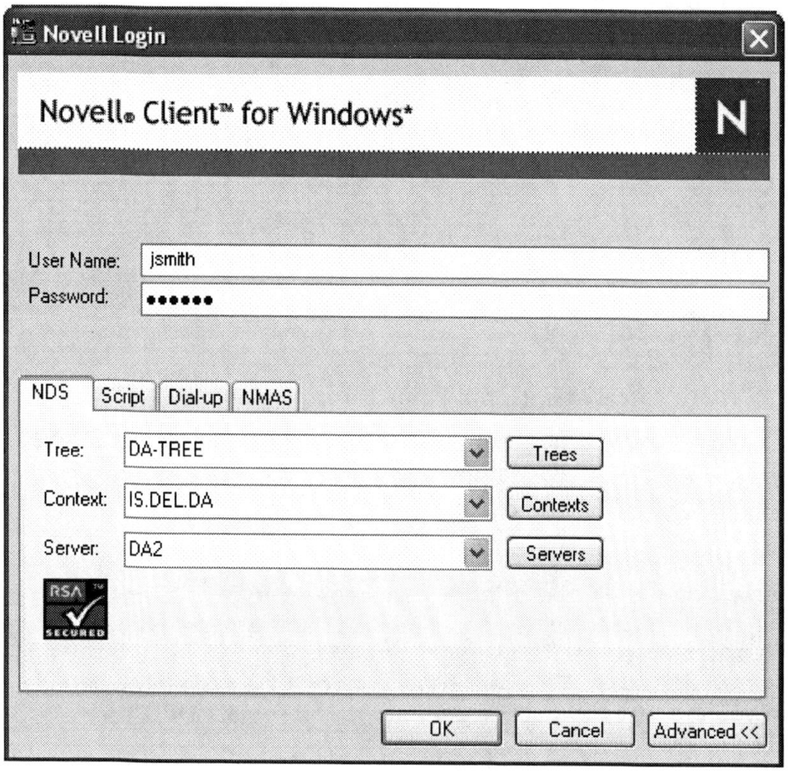

What is the likely problem and how can you correct it?

The user may be attempting to log on to the wrong context. Information Systems users are probably in the IS context; the user may need to log on to a context called Sales.

Activity 15-6

1. **What are the architectural components of a UNIX operating system?**

   a) The C programming language

   ✓ b) The kernel

   ✓ c) The shell

   d) The CPU

2. **Which statements about UNIX are true?**

   ✓ a) There are many versions of UNIX from different developers and distributors.

   b) All versions of UNIX use the same shell, or user interface.

   ✓ c) UNIX versions are proprietary.

   ✓ d) UNIX is a multiuser, multitasking system.

3. **Which statements about Linux are true?**

   ✓ a) It was developed as open-source software.

   b) Developers must obtain permission to access and modify the source code.

   ✓ c) Development was initiated and managed by Linus Torvalds.

   d) Releases of Linux are unstable.

4. **A complete Linux implementation is called:**

   a) The Linux source code.

   b) A stable Linux release.

   c) A Linux version.

   ✓ d) A Linux distribution.

5. **Match the server software category with the Linux server application.**

c	Database server	a.	Apache
b	File server	b.	Samba and NFS
d	Name resolution server	c.	Oracle for Linux
a	Web server	d.	BIND

6. **You have a server running a UNIX operating system connected to a T1 line using TCP/IP as a communication protocol. The server has a public IP address and is accessible from any computer with Internet access. The server is running SSH. You have a home user running a Linux operating system. This user has a connection to the Internet with a local ISP. How will you instruct this user to connect to the remote UNIX server?**

   Have the user make sure they are logged into their system. Verify that they have an SSH client installed on their system. Then, at the command line, type ssh -l [insert username] [insert IP address of remote server] and press Enter. The user will need to accept the remote server's public key and type in a password for the remote system.

7. **After connecting, what access will the user have to the remote system?**

   The user will have the same access he or she would have when logged on locally with the same username and password.

8. **You have a server running a UNIX operating system connected to a T1 line using TCP/IP as a communication protocol. The server has a public IP address and is accessible over IP from any computer with Internet access. However, the server's name is not registered under your company's public DNS domain. The server is running SSH. You have a home user running a Linux operating system. This user has a connection to the Internet with a local ISP. The user typed in the following command:"ssh -l jsmith testserver"to connect to the remote UNIX server. The user received the following message: "ssh: testserver: Name or service not known." What is the most likely cause of this problem?**

   The host name is either mistyped, or there isn't an entry in the user's HOSTS file that points to the testserver IP address.

9. **You have a server running a Linux operating system connected to a corporate network using TCP/IP as a communication protocol. You have a user running a Linux operating system connected to the same network. The user typed in the following command, "ssh -l jsmith 192.168.1.1", to connect to the UNIX server. The user did not receive any error message, but was not prompted to log in. What is the first step you should take in determining the problem?**

   Tell the user to run the ssh command with the -v option. This will display the verbose mode of ssh, printing each successful or unsuccessful step to the screen.

10. **You have a newly installed Linux file sharing server connected to a corporate network. You have a user running a Windows operating system connected to the network that cannot connect and share files. Other Linux systems on the network don't have any problems connecting to the server and sharing files. What is the most likely cause of this problem? How can you correct it?**

    The most likely problem is that the server does not have Samba installed. Samba allows a Windows system to connect to a Linux system and share files. Once Samba is installed and operational, the Windows user will be able to connect and share files.

Activity 15-7

1. **The current Macintosh operating system, Mac OS X, is a:**
   - a) Windows derivative.
   - ✓ b) UNIX derivative.
   - c) NetWare derivative.
   - d) Proprietary implementation.
2. **Which are features of Mac OS X Server?**
   - ✓ a) An LDAP-based directory service.
   - b) A proprietary networking architecture.
   - ✓ c) An integrated web server.
   - ✓ d) DNS, DHCP, and firewall services.
3. **Macintosh security is permission-based and provides:**
   - ✓ a) Read, write, and execute permissions.
   - b) Read, write, change, modify, and full control permissions.
   - c) Read, write, create, erase, modify, file scan, and access control permissions.
4. **You have a system running Mac OS X Server that is connected to a T1 line using TCP/IP as a communication protocol. The server has a public IP address and is accessible from any computer with Internet access. You intend to use this system to provide network access to remote users. What should you instruct the server administrator to verify before remote users attempt to connect to the server?**

   You will want to have the server administrator verify that the server is running SSH, and that Remote Login is turned on under the server's Sharing Preferences.
5. **You have a home user running a Mac OS X operating system. This user has a connection to the Internet with a local ISP. How will you instruct this user to connect to the remote Mac OS X Server?**

   Have her log into her local system. Verify that she has a SSH client installed. Open a terminal window and type ssh -l [insert username] [insert IP address of remote server] and press Enter. The user will need to accept the remote server's public key and then type the password for the remote system.
6. **Once connected, what access will the user have to the remote Mac OS X Server system?**

   The user will have the same access he or she would have when logged on locally with the same username and password.

7. **You have a server running Mac OS X Server as the operating system connected to a T1 line using TCP/IP as a communication protocol. The server has a public IP address and is accessible from any computer with Internet access. You have a home user running a Mac OS X operating system. This user has a connection to the Internet with a local ISP. He is typing in the following command: "ssh -l jsmith macserver.myglobalcompany.com:23" and receiving the error message: "Connection Refused: port 23". What is the most likely cause of this problem?**

   Port 23 is not the default port for SSH; port 22 is. It is most likely the case that the user mistyped the port number.

8. **You have a newly installed Mac OS X Server connected to a corporate network. It has one LaserJet printer attached to it. All but one department is able to connect to the printer and print files. Unlike the rest of the company, that department has not yet upgraded from Mac OS 8 to Mac OS X. What is the most likely cause of this problem?**

   In older versions of Mac OS, AppleTalk was used to connect to network printers. Mac OS X Server uses TCP/IP natively and AppleTalk is disabled by default.

9. **What are two ways that you can solve the problem?**

   You can enable AppleTalk on the Mac OS X Server, or you can upgrade the users immediately to Mac OS X.

Lesson 15 Follow-up

Lesson 15 Lab 1

1. **List some of the advanced network services supported natively on Windows Server 2003.**

   DHCP, DNS, routing, remote access, certificates, Terminal Services, clustering, and IPSec, among others.

2. **List some of the additional server products supported on the Windows Server 2003 platform.**

   Exchange Server, SQL Server, Systems Management Server, SharePoint Portal Server, Commerce Server, Content Management Server, ISA Server, and Windows Small Business Server 2003, among others.

3. **Describe an important distinction between the Windows NT 4.0 server family, and prior versions of Windows Server.**

   Windows NT 4.0 was the first version of Windows to support Active Directory. Prior to that, directories were stored in a flat-file SAM database that could only be modified on a single server on the network.

4. **Compare the NetWare terms eDirectory, NDS, and bindery.**

   They are all directory database systems used on NetWare servers. The bindery was a flat-file database that was specific to particular NetWare servers. NDS was the first enterprise-wide, standards-based directory system. The eDirectory system is the current implementation of NDS.

5. **What are some similarities between Active Directory and eDirectory?**

   Both are enterprise-wide, standards-based directories that are LDAP compatible. Both are built on a tree-like structure, and offer the option to organize objects into containers to simplify the directory structure and delegate administration. Both support inheritance of rights and permissions from the upper levels to lower levels of the hierarchy.

6. **How do the terms service, NLM, and daemon relate?**

   All are ways to load and unload functionality in a modular way onto network servers. Windows uses services, NetWare uses NLMs, and UNIX and Linux (and compatible systems) use daemons.

7. **Define the term open source as it relates to the Linux operating system.**

   Open source is one term used to contrast with proprietary. It means the software has no single owner, and is developed in a cooperative way, with many developers freely accessing the source code. Linux was conceived of and implemented as an open source project, and the Linux code base continues to evolve based on the modifications made by many independent programmers.

8. **What were some reasons for the popularity of UNIX for those who implemented it?**

   It was portable to almost any hardware platform, and it provided excellent support for application development.

9. **What are some of Linux's primary server functions?**

   Linux is used for web servers, DNS/BIND servers, and file, mail, and database servers.

10. **How does loading a different shell affect a UNIX or Linux environment?**

    It changes the user interface and the supported commands and syntax. It does not change the underlying system structure (the kernel).

11. **What are some of the advanced server features included with Mac OS X?**

    DNS, DHCP, and firewall services; Open Directory; integrated support for Mac, Windows, and UNIX/Linux clients; an integrated web server; and integrated email, among others.

Lesson 16

Activity 16-1

1. **Put the first four steps of the Network+ troubleshooting model in the correct order.**

   _*2*_ Identifying the affected area.

   _*1*_ Establishing the symptoms and potential causes.

   _*4*_ Selecting the most probable cause.

   _*3*_ Establishing what has changed.

2. **Put the last four steps of the Network+ troubleshooting model in the correct order.**

   1 Implementing an action plan and solution, including recognizing potential effects.

   2 Testing the result.

   3 Identifying the results and effects of the solution.

   4 Documenting the solution and process.

3. **Users on the third floor can't connect to the Internet, but they can log on to the local NetWare network. What should you check first?**

   a) Router configuration tables.

   b) If viruses exist.

   c) If the power cable to the hub is connected.

   ✓ d) If users on other floors are having similar problems.

4. **You reinstall the operating system for a user who is having problems. Later, the user complains that she cannot find her familiar desktop shortcuts. What step of the troubleshooting model did you omit?**

   a) Documenting the solution and the process.

   ✓ b) Identifying the results and effects of the solution.

   c) Establishing what has changed.

   d) Establishing the symptoms and potential causes.

5. **Which techniques will help you identify the affected area?**

   a) Ask the user open-ended questions about the problem.

   ✓ b) Try to replicate the problem on another workstation nearby.

   c) Make a list of problems that can all cause the same symptoms.

   ✓ d) Find out if users in other parts of the building are having the same problem.

6. **A user calls to say that his computer won't boot. He mentions that everything was fine until a brief power outage on his floor. What stage of the troubleshooting model can this information help you with most directly?**

   a) Selecting the most probable cause.

   b) Implementing an action plan and solution, including recognizing potential effects.

   c) Documenting the solution and process.

   ✓ d) Establishing what has changed.

7. **A user calls the help desk and says he can't open a file. You are not able to visit the user's workstation because he is located in a different building. What are the first steps you need to take to be able to diagnose the problem?**

   You need to define the specific symptoms of the problem so that you can begin to consider potential causes; you need to find out if other users are affected and, if so, who; and you need to find out if anything has changed on the user's system or the network since he could last access the file.

8. **What are some of the questions you should ask?**

   Ask the user to describe his system and his physical location. What application is he using to open the file? Can he open other files with that application? If so, the problem is with the file and not the software. Ask him to describe the specific problem he is having; can he find the file but receives an error when he opens it? Or does the file open but looks corrupted? To localize the problem, ask where the file is saved; is it on a local disk or on a network drive? Can he open other files from that location? If not, it may be a problem with the storage media itself. Or is it in an email attachment? Find out when he could last open the file, if ever. If he could open the file previously, find out anything that might have occurred since that time to change the situation. If the file is in a network location, review network activity logs to see if there have been any issues or changes to that server.

9. **Through your diagnostic questions, you establish that the file is a word-processing document stored on a network file server. The user last accessed the file three months ago; he has since been out of the office on an executive loan program to a local charity. By reviewing the activity logs on the file server, you find that there is a bi-monthly cleanup routine that automatically backs up and removes user data files that have not been accessed since the last cleanup date. The backups are stored in an offsite facility for one year. Given this information, what is your action plan, how will you implement it, and what potential side effects of the plan do you need to consider?**

   You need to locate the tape containing the archived copy of the document and restore it to the network location. You might need to work with your company's backup administrator to identify the tape and retrieve it from the offsite storage location. You need to ensure that you identify the correct file and restore only that file so that you do not overwrite later data.

10. **What steps should you take to test, verify, and document the solution?**

    Make sure the user can open the restored file and that its contents are correct. Check the modification dates of other files in the restore location to ensure that you have not inadvertently overwritten an existing file with an archived copy. Enter the information from the service call in your service form and file it as prescribed by your company's Help Desk policies.

Activity 16-2

2. **What is the problem?**

   a) The computer is configured with an incorrect static address.

   b) The computer has not initialized TCP/IP.

   ✓ c) The system has an APIPA address.

   d) The computer's DNS server information is incorrect.

6. **What is the problem?**

   ✓ a) The ARP cache has an incorrect static entry.

   b) The computer has an incorrect static IP address.

   c) The computer has an APIPA address.

   d) The computer has incorrect DNS server information.

10. **What is the problem?**

    a) The computer is configured with an incorrect static IP address.

    ✓ b) The computer has an incorrect DNS server address.

    c) The computer has an APIPA IP address.

    d) There is an incorrect static entry in the ARP cache.

Activity 16-3

1. **1) You have installed a Linux system in your test lab so that application developers can test new software. Because the lab is isolated from the main network, there is no DHCP service running. A software engineer has loaded a network application on the system, but cannot connect to it from a client. She has already tried to ping the Linux system by name and IP address. What should you check next and why?**

   Use the ifconfig utility to verify that you have configured the test system with an appropriate static IP address.

2. **In the same lab, you are testing a shared Windows application that is installed on a Windows Server 2003 computer. You want to verify that it will run on a number of Windows clients. You connect to the server successfully from a Windows XP system, but when you try to connect from a Windows 98 client, the connection fails. What should you check first and why?**

   Use the winipcfg utility to verify that you have configured the Windows 98 system with an appropriate static IP address. You do not need to ping the Windows 98 system to verify IP connectivity because you are working directly at the Windows 98 computer.

3. **A user is having trouble connecting to your company's intranet site (internal.everythingforcoffee.com), which is on your company's private network inside your firewall. She is not having general Internet connectivity problems. What is the best first step to take to try to narrow down the possible problem?**

   Because the user does not seem to be having general TCP/IP problems, the problem may be with the web server that hosts the intranet site. You can ping internal.everythingforcoffee.com by name from different systems to verify that the name is being resolved. If there is no response, ping the system by IP address to see if you can connect to it at all.

4. **You can connect to the intranet site with no difficulty. You check your IP configuration against the user's and find that you are configured with different DNS server addresses. You do not have DNS administrative utilities installed on your workstation. What can you do to diagnose the DNS problem?**

   Use the nslookup command to see if the user's server can resolve the internal.everythingforcoffee.com address and to examine the entries on both DNS servers.

5. **You had to reboot a DHCP server earlier in the day. A Windows 98 user calls to say that she has no network connectivity at all. What can you do to correct the problem?**

   Use winipcfg to see if the user is receiving a dynamic address. If not, use the utility to renew the DHCP address configuration.

6. You provide consulting services for a small non-profit agency that is using legacy Windows 98 systems configured in a workgroup. To optimize performance on the older systems, you have disabled unnecessary services on some of the machines. A user has just installed a printer and wants to share it so that his system can function as a print server for the rest of the workgroup. He is unable to share the printer. What can you do to help?

   Tell the user to use the nbtstat -n command to see if the system has registered a name with a service code entry of 20. If not, the Server service has been turned off on this workstation, and you can step the user through the procedure to re-enable it.

7. You are the IT operations manager for an Internet service provider (ISP). Your IT operations center includes numerous clustered web servers as well as clustered Linux systems running DNS BIND to provide your clients with Internet name resolutions. You would like to automate some of your diagnostic and management tasks by running scripts on the DNS BIND servers. What can you do?

   The dig utility is a good choice for performing command-line DNS management tasks through administrative scripts.

8. Your test environment includes a number of different clients, including Windows systems, Linux systems, and Mac OS X clients. You would like to be able to examine the network performance of each system while you run a batch file to generate network load. What utility can you use?

   The netstat utility is a versatile tool for examining general network status and performance on a variety of systems.

9. You are experiencing a number of dropped packets and slow response time on your routed private network. You suspect there may be a routing loop and you would like to look more closely at packet transmissions through the network. How can you examine the path of the transmissions?

   Use the tracert command to trace the routes of packets between various source and destination hosts. This can help you locate a packet looping between routers, or the point at which a route fails.

10. Servers on your internal network are manually configured with IP addresses in the range 192.168.20.200 through 192.168.20.225. You are trying to open an ftp session with the ftp server that is located on your internal network at 192.168.20.218. Although you can ping the system by IP address, sometimes you can connect over FTP and sometimes you cannot. You suspect there may be two hosts configured with duplicate addresses. How can you verify which physical host system is using the FTP server's address?

    First ping the system, and then use the arp command to view your arp cache. The cache will display the MAC address of the system that first responded to the ping request. You can then try to open an FTP session and arp again; if the session succeeded, you know which physical system is the FTP server; if it failed, you know which physical system is incorrectly configured.

SOLUTIONS

Activity 16-4

1. **You have a cable with a frayed end. You want to trim the cable and reattach the connector. You need a:**

   a) Punch down tool

   ✓ b) Wire crimper

   c) Cable tester

   d) Voltmeter

2. **You need to trace a UTP cable in a large bundle of cables. You need a:**

   a) Voltmeter

   b) Circuit tester

   c) Cable tester

   ✓ d) Tone generator and tone locator

3. **A workstation and server on your small office network can't communicate. To see if one of the network adapters is bad, you can connect them directly by using a:**

   ✓ a) Crossover cable

   b) Hardware loopback plug

   c) Tone generator and tone locator

   d) Punch down tool

4. **A user tells you he can't log on. You ask him to check the back of his network adapter and he says there is one steady light and one flashing light. What does this tell you?**

   a) That he has a network connection but is not receiving data.

   b) That he has no network connection.

   ✓ c) That he has a network connection and is receiving data.

   d) That the network adapter has a defect.

5. **Your instructor will show examples of various types of hardware tools. Identify each tool and its function, and give an example of how you would use it in network troubleshooting.**

   Answers will vary depending on the tools available.

6. **What does the amber light on a network interface card (NIC) indicate?**

   a) A frame error

   b) A dysfunctional transceiver on the NIC

   c) Successful network connectivity

   ✓ d) Transmission collisions

   e) A break in the cable

7. **You are a network administrator and you recently replaced the NIC card in a user's machine. You receive a call from the user, who complains that there is no network connectivity. Which LED on the NIC should you check first?**

   a) Activity light

   b) Collision light

   ✓ c) Link light

   d) Cable light

Activity 16-8

1. **What are the benefits of a network baseline?**

   a) To establish a record of problems and solutions to assist you in troubleshooting similar problems.

   b) To document user complaints.

   ✓ c) To enable you to recognize an abnormal performance state.

   ✓ d) To establish patterns that can help you recognize and eliminate ongoing bottlenecks.

2. **Which would be an appropriate testing interval for a baseline?**

   a) A 10-minute reading at noon every day for a week.

   b) An hour-long sample starting at 8:00 one Monday morning.

   ✓ c) Five-minute readings once per hour during a 24-hour period midweek.

   d) A 24-hour-long reading from Saturday at 1 A.M. until Sunday at 1 A.M.

3. **Which performance criteria should you use the baseline to analyze?**

   ✓ a) Server response and performance.

   ✓ b) Network infrastructure response and performance.

   ✓ c) Network media response and performance.

   d) User performance and error frequency.

4. **Put the steps of creating a baseline in the correct order.**

   _3_ Decide when to run the tests.

   _4_ Run the tests.

   _5_ Document the test results.

   _1_ Evaluate the network's purpose.

   _2_ Design a suite of tests.

Lesson 16 Follow-up

Lesson 16 Lab 1

1. **What are some ways that you can determine the scope of a networking problem?**

   Try to replicate the problem on a different system. Check with users in other areas to see if the problem is occurring there. Find out if other similar problems have been reported.

2. **What are some things that all troubleshooting models have in common?**

   Verifying that the client software is loaded on the workstation, that the user is using the correct logon name and password, and that the workstation is physically connected to the network.

3. **What are some of the benefits of clearly documenting the results of troubleshooting problems?**

   It provides a database of problems that you can refer to, so you can save time when similar problems arise. It can also serve as a record of problems so that you can look for patterns that might indicate underlying problems you can anticipate and correct proactively.

4. **Users on the third floor report that they can't connect to the Internet, but they can connect to the NetWare server. What would you check first?**

   a) Router configuration tables.

   b) If viruses exist on the network.

   c) Power cable to the hub.

   ✓ d) If users on other floors have similar problems.

5. **You're working the help desk and get a call that a user can't access the UNIX host at 150.150.32.157. You are on the same subnet as the user and the UNIX host and you can successfully ping both the UNIX host and the user's workstation. When you ask the user to enter ping 150.150.32.157, all he gets is a series of Destination Unreachable messages. What might you do?**

   From the problem workstation, enter arp -a to list the ARP cache to see if there is a bad MAC address entry in the cache. If so, you can delete the entry.

6. **You're a network administrator and have been receiving complaints that users aren't able to post files to or download files from the FTP server. What might you do to determine the status of the server?**

   You could log on to the FTP server and enter netstat -a to see if it is listening on port 21. You might also try to telnet into the system to see if you get a ready message.

7. **A Windows XP user logs on and gets a message that the system's IP address is already in use. This user receives an IP address through a DHCP server. How can the user get a valid IP address?**

   Ping the DHCP server to make sure it is up, and then use the ipconfig /release and ipconfig /renew commands at a command prompt to obtain a new valid address from the DHCP server.

8. **A client calls from the California office saying that she isn't able to connect to the server ICANY in New York. This server is on a routed IP network. This is the second client from California who has called with this problem. No users from other sites have called. What should you do?**

   Try pinging the server from your workstation. If you are able to reach the server, ask the client to do the same and see if the client gets a response that the server is available. (She'll most likely get a Destination Host Unreachable message.) If she can't connect, have the client enter tracert icany to see how far the trace can reach before timing out. You'll then be able to figure out which device is causing the problem, because the next device that would be encountered on the route between the client and ICANY is the problem device.

9. **Which troubleshooting tool can help you if you need to download a large software patch file from a vendor site?**

   a) Telnet

   b) Ipconfig

   ✓ c) FTP

   d) Tracert

10. **What indicator shows if a computer is connected to the network?**

    The link light on the network adapter will be lit.

11. **What can a simple cable tester show?**

    A simple tester can tell if a cable run is connected end to end, and it can detect basic electrical connections or errors in the connections, such as opens or shorts and misrouted wires.

12. **Explain the function of a network adapter's promiscuous mode.**

    When a network analyzer operates in promiscuous mode, it captures all the data traffic that moves on its subnet regardless of the source or destination.

13. **Explain some cases in which a network's baseline performance might change.**

    Many factors change the demands or performance of the network: when a large number of users are added to or removed from the network; when servers are added to or removed from the network; and when the network is opened up for remote access. The network should be re-baselined periodically to account for these changes.

14. **Your assistant has deployed a new hub in a peer-to-peer network in order to add 10 new user workstations. The hub was cascaded off an empty port on the existing hub. The new users can browse to each other but can't browse to the older workstations. Where would you begin to look for the solution?**

    The most likely solution would be the connection between the two hubs. You should check to ensure that the connection is properly crossed over between the two hubs.

15. **Users are complaining that the network seems to be slow, but you haven't changed anything or added any new users. What can you do to determine where the slowdown is and what might be causing it?**

    Redo the network baseline and compare your results to those from the last baseline. This should point to any changes that may have caused a bottleneck. It should also indicate if this is just a temporary increase of activity that is within normal limits, or a genuine problem condition.

SOLUTIONS

Lesson 16 Lab 2

1. **A user calls to say that she has lost her Internet connection and can't bring up a web page she needs to do her job. What is some of the other information you might need in order to diagnose and solve her problem?**

   You must determine if she has connectivity to the local network, and then determine if she has lost connectivity to a DNS name server, or if she has lost all connectivity to the Internet.

2. **What questions will you ask her to help determine where her problem is?**

   Can she connect to anything on the local network? Can she log on? Can she get to her home directory on the network? Ask her what might have changed on her workstation. Has something changed in her TCP/IP settings? Can she ping any remote hosts by name or by IP address? Can she get to any of the major websites, such as Yahoo or MSN? What web address is she trying to connect to? Test that website from your own PC to verify that it's up.

3. **What utilities can you instruct her to use to help find the area of the problem?**

   In addition to normal GUI elements, she might need to use an IP configuration utility, and Ping or Tracert.

4. **How will you test for functional name resolution to the website she wants?**

   You can ask her to ping the desired website by name. If it returns an IP address but doesn't get a reply from the site, you'll know whether name resolution works, but not whether the website is online. Nslookup could also be used but tends to be a bit more confusing to users over the phone.

5. **You're the administrator of a small office. One of your users keeps complaining that he is losing his connection to the network. He can reboot and log on again each time, but loses the connection again shortly afterward. What items would you check?**

   a) The logon server's network connection.

   ✓ b) The network cable to the user.

   c) User rights and permissions.

   ✓ d) The network card driver.

   ✓ e) Ports on the hub.

6. **If you wanted to test the user's network card driver, how would you do it?**

   Either reinstall the same driver or update the driver, and check the manufacturer's website to see if it is a known problem that has a fix.

7. **If you wanted to test the user's network cable, how would you do it?**

   Swap out the patch cord, use a cable tester to check for shorts or opens, or call a technician to certify the cable to the correct category specifications.

8. **You're a network consultant working for an integrator/solutions provider. You've been called out to a financial office that says its network went down suddenly. They report that all servers seem to be functioning but users can't log on. The network has approximately 200 workstations and servers distributed across six hubs. You place a network analyzer online, and observe that all traffic seems to be coming from one MAC address. The data isn't legible. What do you conclude is the most likely problem?**

   You have a machine that is causing a broadcast storm. The problem is most likely due to a faulty network card.

9. **How can you bring most of the network back online while you troubleshoot this problem?**

   By isolating the hub connected to the faulty machine. Disconnect each hub until the storm stops on the remainder of the network.

10. **How will you identify the individual machine causing the problem?**

    You could record the source MAC address in the bad packets, and then use Ipconfig to search for that machine one by one, or you could move a network analyzer to the isolated hub and remove the patch cables connected to the hub one by one, testing after each to see if the storm goes away. Once you find the connection causing the storm, you can bring the rest of the hub back onto the network.

11. **You have just moved a workstation from one office to another. It worked fine in the old office but won't connect to the network in the new office. You suspect that the wall plate in the new office may not be "hot"—that is, not patched into the hub in the data center. How can you quickly test to see if there is a connection?**

    Check the link light on the network card.

12. **If the user has no network connection, what is the next step toward finding the problem?**

    If there is no link, check to be sure the cable run to the office is patched in, and then test the cable with a simple point-to-point cable tester.

13. **A user calls and complains that he can't connect to the Internet but can connect to servers inside the company. You ask him to open a command prompt window and ping the company website. He does so but gets no reply. You ping the website and get a reply from your workstation. You ask him to ping the IP address of the website. He does so and gets the correct reply. What is keeping the user from connecting to the website?**

    The user isn't getting DNS resolution.

14. **What is the next step in resolving the problem?**

    Check to see if he has the correct settings in the TCP/IP properties on his workstation.

15. **You're presently working as a network engineer for a computer services company. One of your customers calls and complains that the network's main server keeps rebooting itself. When you arrive, the system seems to be running properly and then all of a sudden turns itself off. A few seconds later, it turns itself back on and starts a normal boot procedure. Where can you look to get more information on what was happening right before the server went down?**

    The server's event logs might tell what was going on at the time of failure.

16. **Is this most likely a software problem or a hardware problem?**

    The problem is most likely related to hardware judging from the fact that the server seemed to turn itself off.

17. **Your company is planning changes to its deployment of web-based services. Currently, all services are being hosted by an outside vendor. The goal is to bring all the web servers inside the company to better control them. What is the first step in predicting the impact that the new incoming web traffic will have on the network?**

    Get records from the current Internet service provider to predict how much extra traffic will be added to the network.

18. **What component in the current network will be affected most?**

    The Internet connection will have to handle the extra traffic.

19. **How will your baseline information help you decide where to place the new servers?**

    The baseline will show you where you have the most available bandwidth to accommodate the new servers.

Appendix C

Activity C-1

1. **True or False? The IP address 100.100.100.1 is invalid because the first and second bytes of a network address cannot be the same.**

    __ True

    ✓ False

2. **Is 157.35.205.0 a valid network address?**

    ✓ Yes

    __ No

3. **Is 187.255.1.1 a valid host address?**

    ✓ Yes

    __ No

4. **True or False? The IP address 131.0.5.29 is invalid because of the zero in the second octet.**

    __ True

    ✓ False

5. **Is 221.100.155.0 a valid host address?**

    __ Yes

    ✓ No

6. **Is 187.131.255.5 a valid host address?**

   ✓ Yes

   __ No

7. **Is 121.0.0.1 a valid host address?**

   ✓ Yes

   __ No

8. **Match the following invalid IP addresses with the reason that they are not valid.**

b	157.100.257.1	a.	This network address is reserved for multicasts.
d	127.1.254.254	b.	The decimal value of any byte cannot exceed 255.
a	224.254.254.254	c.	This host address is reserved for broadcasts on the local network.
c	198.254.254.255	d.	This network address is reserved for testing purposes.
f	255.255.255.255	e.	The value of the first byte of any network address cannot be 0.
e	0.153.98.32	f.	This address is reserved for broadcasts on the entire network.

Activity C-2

1. **What address class(es) would be valid to use on this network?**

   ✓ a) A

   ✓ b) B

   c) C

   d) D

   e) E

2. **What network address(es) would be valid for this network?**

   a) 198.5.33.0

   ✓ b) 100.0.0.0

   c) 231.5.254.0

   ✓ d) 128.1.0.0

3. **You've decided to use the network address 128.1.0.0. According to the corporate host addressing policy, which address(es) would be valid for any of the Windows 2003 Server machines?**

   a) 128.1.0.105

   b) 128.1.100.10

   c) 128.105.1.55

   ✓ d) 128.1.105.98

   ✓ e) 128.1.105.0

Activity C-3

1. How many network addresses will be needed?
   - a) 1
   - b) 2
   - ✓ c) 3
   - d) 4
2. How many host addresses are needed for Network 1?
   - a) 150
   - b) 250
   - c) 400
   - ✓ d) 401
3. How many host addresses are needed for Network 2?
   - a) 300
   - b) 325
   - c) 326
   - ✓ d) 327
   - e) 397
4. What class(es) of network address can be used for these network segments?
   - ✓ a) A
   - ✓ b) B
   - c) C
   - d) D
   - e) E
5. Which router network card's address would you assign as the default gateway for the Windows 2000 Professional computers to access the Windows Server 2003 servers?
   - a) Router interface A
   - ✓ b) Router interface B
   - c) Router interface C
   - d) Router interface D

Activity C-4

1. Match the computer name with the appropriate description.

c	Computer 1	a.	You can't use a broadcast address for a host address.
e	Computer 2	b.	This address is duplicated on the network, and the default gateway is incorrect.
f	Computer 3	c.	You can't use a network address for a host address, and the default gateway is incorrect.
b	Computer 4	d.	This address is duplicated on the network.
a	Computer 5	e.	No changes are needed.
d	Computer 6	f.	The default gateway is incorrect.

Activity C-5

1. True or False? One reason to subnet a network is because you have been given only one network address to work with.

✓ True

__ False

2. Why might you segment a network?

✓ a) To reduce the number of machines on a single segment in order to reduce network traffic.

b) To reduce the number of network addresses needed.

✓ c) To overcome physical limitations such as exceeding the maximum number of machines on a given segment.

d) To increase the number of host addresses available.

✓ e) To connect different topologies, such as Ethernet and Token Ring.

3. If a network consists of three segments connected by two routers, how many subnets will you need?

a) 2

✓ b) 3

c) 4

d) 5

4. True or False? If a network consists of 2 segments, each containing 30 machines, connected by 2 routers, you will need 62 host addresses.

✓ True

__ False

Activity C-6

1. If the sender's IP address is 145.107.3.10 and the destination IP address is 145.107.5.10, you can determine if the packet's destination is local or remote by examining the *subnet mask* .

2. If the sender's IP address is 129.100.12.10, the receiver's IP address is 129.100.0.18, and the subnet mask is 255.255.0.0, will this transmission be local or remote?

   ✓ Local

   __ Remote

3. If the sender's IP address is 142.100.17.50, the receiver's IP address is 142.100.21.5, and the subnet mask is 255.255.255.0, will this transmission be local or remote?

   __ Local

   ✓ Remote

4. If you AND the IP address 145.10.50.5 and the subnet mask 255.255.0.0, what is the resulting network address?

   a) 145.10.50.0

   ✓ b) 145.10.0.0

   c) 145.0.0.0

   d) 145.50.0.0

5. If you AND the IP address 145.49.50.5 and the subnet mask 255.255.252.0, what is the resulting network address?

   a) 145.49.0.0

   b) 145.49.50.0

   ✓ c) 145.49.48.0

   d) 145.47.0.0

6. If the sender's IP address is 145.10.50.5, with a subnet mask of 255.255.0.0, and the receiver's IP address is 145.49.50.5, with a subnet mask of 255.255.252.0, is the transmission local or remote?

   __ Local

   ✓ Remote

Activity C-7

1. If you borrow three bits from the host portion of a Class B address, how many subnets will you be able to assign unique addresses to?

   a) 2

   b) 3

   ✓ c) 6

   d) 8

2. If you borrow three bits from the host portion of a Class B address, how many host addresses will be available per subnet?

   a) 30

   ✓ b) 8,190

   c) 8,192

   d) 65,534

3. If your IP address is 145.8.17.96 and the subnet mask is 255.255.255.0, what is the subnet address?

   a) 0.0.12.0

   b) 145.8.17.0

   c) 145.8.0.0

   ✓ d) 0.0.17.0

4. If you have the network address 145.100.0.0 and you need 12 subnets, what custom subnet mask should you use?

   a) 255.255.0.0

   b) 255.255.248.0

   ✓ c) 255.255.240.0

   d) 255.255.255.0

5. If you have the network address 145.100.0.0 and you need 12 subnets, how many hosts can be on each subnet?

   a) 8,190

   ✓ b) 4,094

   c) 2,046

   d) 510

6. If you have the network address 145.100.0.0 and you need 12 subnets, how many subnet addresses will be left over?

   a) 0

   ✓ b) 2

   c) 6

   d) 18

Activity C-8

1. How many bits must be borrowed from the host portion of the IP address to enable the creation of 50 subnets?

   a) 4

   b) 5

   ✓ c) 6

   d) 8

2. To have 50 subnets, what would the subnet mask need to be?

   a) 255.240.0.0

   b) 255.248.0.0

   ✓ c) 255.252.0.0

   d) 255.254.0.0

3. How many host addresses are available for each subnet?

   a) 1,048,574

   b) 524,280

   ✓ c) 262,142

   d) 131,070

4. What is the maximum number of subnets allowed?

   a) 36

   ✓ b) 62

   c) 126

   d) 254

5. What is the network address increment?

   a) 2

   ✓ b) 4

   c) 6

   d) 7

6. True or False? One of the available network addresses is 117.64.0.0.

   _✓_ True

   __ False

Activity C-9

1. How many bits are you borrowing from the third byte to create subnet addresses?

   a) 3

   ✓ b) 4

   c) 6

   d) 7

2. How many subnets will this subnet mask support?

   a) 6

   b) 8

   ✓ c) 14

   d) 62

3. What is the network address increment?

   a) 4

   b) 8

   c) 12

   ✓ d) 16

4. What are the available network addresses?

   a) 155.8.0.0, 155.8.24.0, 155.8.48.0, 155.8.72.0, 155.8.96.0, and so forth.

   b) 155.8.8.0, 155.8.16.0, 155.8.24.0, 155.8.32.0, 155.8.40.0, and so forth.

   c) 155.8.12.0, 155.8.24.0, 155.8.36.0, 155.8.48.0, 155.8.60.0, and so forth.

   ✓ d) 155.8.16.0, 155.8.32.0, 155.8.48.0, 155.8.64.0, 155.8.80.0, and so forth.

5. What are the available host addresses for the first subnet?

   a) 155.8.24.1 through 155.8.47.254

   ✓ b) 155.8.16.1 through 155.8.31.254

   c) 155.8.12.1 through 155.8.23.254

   d) 155.8.4.1 through 155.8.7.254

Activity C-10

1. You have been assigned a Class C network address for your local, single-segment network. What subnet mask should you use?

   a) 255.255.0.0

   b) 255.255.240.0

   ✓ c) 255.255.255.0

   d) 255.255.255.192

2. True or False? The maximum number of hosts on a Class C network is 255.

   __ True

   ✓ False

3. You received an address assignment of 167.5.0.0. What class of address is this?

   a) Class A

   ✓ b) Class B

   c) Class C

   d) Class D

4. If your network address is 167.5.0.0 and you need to create five subnets, what subnet mask should you use?

   a) 255.255.0.0

   b) 255.255.240.0

   ✓ c) 255.255.224.0

   d) 255.255.192.0

5. True or False? If your network address is 167.5.0.0 and you need to create five subnets, the subnet mask you use will leave one unused subnet available for future use.

   ✓ True

   __ False

6. **You are using a Class A network address on a single-segment network. What subnet mask should you use?**

   ✓ a) 255.0.0.0
   b) 255.240.0.0
   c) 255.255.0.0
   d) 255.255.240.0
   e) 255.255.255.0

7. **Why do you need a subnet mask if the network has only one segment?**

   The TCP/IP protocol requires that you assign a subnet mask even when a network is strictly local, with no routers.

8. **You have a Class B network with 65 subnets. What subnet mask is required to support the subnets?**

   a) 255.240.0.0
   b) 255.255.0.0
   ✓ c) 255.255.254.0
   d) 255.255.240.0

9. **True or False? On a Class B network with 65 subnets, the maximum number of hosts per subnet is 1,022.**

   __ True
   ✓ False

10. **You are using a Class B network address with 13 subnets. Your company is merging with another company, and your network will increase to 25 subnets. What subnet mask should you use?**

   a) 255.255.0.0
   ✓ b) 255.255.248.0
   c) 255.255.196.0
   d) 255.255.255.0

11. **True or False? After you change the subnet mask to support 25 subnets, you will have 5 extra subnets after the merger.**

   ✓ True
   __ False

12. **On a Class B network with 25 subnets, how many hosts can each subnet contain?**

   a) 4,094
   ✓ b) 2,046
   c) 1,022
   d) 510

Activity C-11

1. In Figure C-3, which hosts are using the wrong subnet mask?

   a) 1

   ✓ b) 2

   c) 3

   ✓ d) 4

   e) 5

2. True or False? Using the wrong subnet mask will prevent the hosts from communicating with other local hosts.

   ✓ True

   __ False

3. For this scenario, what is the correct subnet mask?

   a) 255.0.0.0

   ✓ b) 255.255.0.0

   c) 255.255.255.0

4. What is wrong with the subnet mask assignments in Figure C-4?

   Once you AND the IP address with the subnet masks, you can see that both hosts appear to each other as if they were local. They both appear to be on subnet 145.10.32.0.

5. True or False? The hosts will be able to communicate through the router because the default gateway settings are accurate.

   __ True

   ✓ False

6. What subnet mask could you use for this network?

   ✓ a) 255.255.255.0

   ✓ b) 255.255.254.0

   c) 255.0.0.0

   d) 255.252.0.0

   ✓ e) 255.255.248.0

Activity C-12

1. How many subnets are possible?

   a) 16

   ✓ b) 14

   c) 8

   d) 6

2. The binary and decimal values for the first subnet are *00010000 and 16*.

3. The binary and decimal values for the second subnet are *00100000 and 32*.

4. The binary and decimal values for the third subnet are *00110000 and 48* .
5. The binary and decimal values for the fourth subnet are *01000000 and 64* .
6. The binary and decimal values for the fifth subnet are *01010000 and 80* .
7. The binary and decimal values for the sixth subnet are *01100000 and 96* .
8. The binary and decimal values for the seventh subnet are *01110000 and 112* .
9. The binary and decimal values for the eighth subnet are *10000000 and 128* .
10. The binary and decimal values for the ninth subnet are *10010000 and 144* .
11. The binary and decimal values for the 10th subnet are *10100000 and 160* .
12. The binary and decimal values for the 11th subnet are *10110000 and 176* .
13. The binary and decimal values for the 12th subnet are *11000000 and 192* .
14. The binary and decimal values for the 13th subnet are *11010000 and 208* .
15. The binary and decimal values for the 14th subnet are *11100000 and 224* .
16. List the range of available host addresses for the first subnet.

    165.125.16.1 through 165.125.31.254

17. List the range of available host addresses for the second subnet.

    165.125.32.1 through 165.125.47.254

18. List the range of available host addresses for the third subnet.

    165.125.48.1 through 165.125.63.254

19. List the range of available host addresses for the fourth subnet.

    165.125.64.1 through 165.125.79.254

20. List the range of available host addresses for the fifth subnet.

    165.125.80.1 through 165.125.95.254

21. List the range of available host addresses for the sixth subnet.

    165.125.96.1 through 165.125.111.254

22. List the range of available host addresses for the seventh subnet.

    165.125.112.1 through 165.125.127.254

23. List the range of available host addresses for the eighth subnet.

    165.125.128.1 through 165.125.143.254

24. List the range of available host addresses for the ninth subnet.

    165.125.144.1 through 165.125.159.254

25. List the range of available host addresses for the 10th subnet.

165.125.160.1 through 165.125.175.254

26. List the range of available host addresses for the 11th subnet.

165.125.176.1 through 165.125.191.254

27. List the range of available host addresses for the 12th subnet.

165.125.192.1 through 165.125.207.254

28. List the range of available host addresses for the 13th subnet.

165.125.208.1 through 165.125.223.254

29. List the range of available host addresses for the 14th subnet.

165.125.224.1 through 165.125.239.254

Activity C-13

1. How many subnets do you need?

a) 0
b) 1
✓ c) 2
d) 3
e) 4

2. How many bits will be used for the subnet mask?

a) 0
b) 1
✓ c) 2
d) 3
e) 4

3. True or False? You can have up to 126 hosts on each subnet.

___ True
_✓_ False

4. The correct subnet mask is *255.255.255.192* .

5. What are the binary and decimal values for the first subnet address?

01000000 and 64

6. What are the binary and decimal values for the second subnet?

10000000 and 128

7. For the first subnet, what is the range of available host addresses?

221.100.55.65 through 221.100.55.126

8. **For the second subnet, what is the range of available host addresses?**

   221.100.55.129 through 221.100.55.190

GLOSSARY

3DES
See "Triple DES."

802.11
An IEEE standard that specifies an over-the-air interface between a wireless client and a base station or between two wireless clients.

Active Directory
Microsoft's LDAP-compatible enterprise directory service, available on Windows Server systems.

active hub
A hub that regenerates the signal similar to a repeater.

active/active cluster
A cluster that has all nodes online, constantly providing services.

active/passive cluster
A cluster that includes at least two nodes, at least one of which is in active mode and handles the full workload, while one node is in passive or standby mode to act as a backup server. Also called an active/standby cluster.

active/standby cluster
See "active/passive cluster."

Ad-hoc mode
A peer-to-peer wireless configuration where each wireless workstation talks directly to other workstations.

algorithm
A set of rules for solving a problem.

analog signal
A signal that oscillates over time between minimum and maximum values and can take on any value between those limits.

antivirus software
An application that scans files for executable code that matches patterns known to be common to viruses, and monitors systems for activity associated with viruses.

APIPA
(Automatic Private IP Addressing) A service that configures a DHCP client computer with an IP address on the 169.254.0.0 network if no DHCP servers respond to the client's DHCP discover broadcast.

AppleTalk
A proprietary routable protocol used on legacy Macintosh networks.

Application layer
Layer of the OSI model that provides services and utilities that enable application programs to access a network and its resources.

arp command
A command that enables an administrator to view and manipulate the ARP cache, including deleting it or adding an entry.

ARP
(Address Resolution Protocol) A communications protocol that resolves IP addresses to MAC addresses.

AS
(Autonomous system) A self-contained network on the Internet that deploys a single protocol and has a single administration.

asymmetric encryption
See "key-pair encryption."

Glossary

ATM
(Asynchronous Transfer mode) A versatile, cell switching network designed for universal deployment in LANs, WANs, and telephone networks.

attenuation
The fading or degradation of a signal as it travels across a network medium.

AUI connector
A 15-pin D-shaped connector. Also known as a DIX connector, named for the three companies that invented it: Digital Electronics Corporation (DEC), Intel, and Xerox.

authentication by assertion
Authentication based entirely on a user name/password combination.

authentication
A network security measure in which a computer user or some other network component proves its identity in order to gain access to network resources.

backbone
The highest-speed transmission path that carries the majority of the network data.

backoff
The random amount of time a node in a CSMA/CD network waits after a collision has occurred before attempting to again send its data. A typical backoff period is a few milliseconds long.

baseband
A transmission technique in which digital signaling is used to send data over a single transmission medium using the entire bandwidth of that medium. Communication is bidirectional over the single medium.

baseline
A record of a system's performance statistics under normal operating conditions.

BDR
(Backup designated router) An OSPF router with the second highest priority value.

bindery
The flat-file, per-server network database system used in Novell NetWare prior to version 4.0.

binding
The assignment of a protocol to a particular network interface card.

border router
A router situated on the edge of an AS that connects the AS to one or more remote networks.

bottleneck
A component of the system that performs poorly when compared to other components and reduces overall system performance.

bounded media
A networking medium that uses a physical conductor, typically made of metal or glass.

bridge routing table
A table built by a bridge containing all the MAC addresses on each of its interfaces.

bridge
A network device that divides a logical bus network into subnets. Bridges examine the MAC address of each packet and forward packets only as necessary.

broadband
A transmission technique in which analog signaling is used to send data over a transmission medium using a portion of the bandwidth of that medium. Communication can be bidirectional over a single transmission medium by using frequency-division multiplexing.

broadcast radio
A form of RF networking that is nondirectional, uses a single frequency for transmissions, and comes in low- and high-power versions.

broadcast transmission
A transmission method in which data goes from a source node to all other nodes on a network.

brute force password attack
A method of guessing passwords by using software that systematically generates password combinations until a valid one is found.

BSS
(Basic Service Set) A group of wireless workstations and an access point.

buffer
A high speed memory location that holds data temporarily until the CPU is ready to work with it.

CA
(Certificate Authority) A server that can issue digital certificates and the associated public/private key pairs.

cable Internet access
A WAN connectivity technology that uses a cable television connection and a specialized interface device known as a cable modem to provide high-speed Internet access to homes and small businesses.

cable tester
An electrical instrument that verifies if signal is present on a cable. Also called a media tester.

cache
A buffer.

CAN
(Campus area network) A network that covers an area equivalent to an academic campus or business park.

cell switching network
A type of network, similar to a packet switching network, in which the data is transmitted in fixed-length cells.

centralized network
A network in which a central host computer controls all network communication and performs the data processing and storage on behalf of network clients.

CHAP
(Challenge Handshake Authentication Protocol) An encrypted remote-access authentication method that enables connections from any authentication method requested by the server, except for PAP and SPAP unencrypted authentication.

CIDR
(Classless Inter Domain Routing) A subnetting method that selects a subnet mask that meets an individual network's network and node requirements and then treats the mask like a 32-bit binary word.

circuit switching network
A network where a connection is created when it's needed and dropped when it's not. There is no guarantee that the connection will always follow the same path through the network.

circuit tester
An electrical instrument that displays whether an electrical outlet is wired correctly.

Class A addresses
A block of IP addresses from 1.0.0.0 to 127.255.255.255 that provides the largest number of nodes (16,777,214) and the smallest number of networks (126).

Class B addresses
A block of IP addresses from 128.0.0.0 to 191.255.255.255 that provides a good balance between the number of networks and the number of nodes per network—16,382 networks of 65,534 nodes each.

Class C addresses
A block of IP addresses from 192.0.0.0 to 223.255.255.255 that provides the largest number of networks (2,097,150) and the smallest number of nodes per network (254).

Class D addresses
A block of IP addresses from 224.0.0.0 to 239.255.255.255 used to support multicast sessions.

Class E addresses
A block of IP addresses from 240.0.0.0 to 255.255.255.255 used for research and experimentation purposes.

GLOSSARY

client
A network computer that utilizes the resources of other network computers.

client/server network
A network in which some nodes act as servers to provide special services on behalf of other client nodes.

cluster
Two or more servers that appear to the network as a single system.

coax
Pronounced "CO-ax," this term is a common abbreviation for coaxial cable.

coaxial cable
A type of copper cable that features a central conductor surrounded by braided or foil shielding. A dialectric insulator separates the conductor and shield and the entire package is wrapped in an insulating layer called a jacket. The data signal is transmitted over the central conductor. The outer shielding serves to reduce electromagnetic interference.

codec
Software or hardware that codes and decodes data to and from analog format. A modem is a type of codec.

cold site
A predetermined alternate location where a network can be rebuilt after a disaster.

cold spare
A duplicate piece of backup equipment that can be configured to use as an alternate if needed.

collision domain
A contention domain.

computer network
A group of computers that are connected together to communicate and share resources.

connection
A virtual link between two nodes established for the duration of a communication session. Connections provide flow control, packet sequencing, and error recovery functions to ensure reliable communications between nodes.

contention domain
A group of nodes on a contention-based network that compete with each other for access to the media. Also called a collision domain.

contention-based media access
A media access method in which the nodes compete or cooperate among themselves for media access time. Also called competitive media access.

context
In a NetWare directory, the location of an object within the directory tree.

controlled media access
A media access method in which some centralized device or system controls when and for how long each node can transmit. Also called deterministic media access.

cost
The number of hops along a route between two networks.

counter
An individual statistic about the operation of system objects such as software processes or hardware components, monitored by a performance monitor.

CRC
(Cyclic Redundancy Check) An error detection method that can be applied to blocks of data, rather than individual words. Both sender and receiver calculate error detection code; if they match, the data is assumed to be valid.

crossover cable
A special network cable used in Ethernet UTP installations, in which the transmit and receive lines are crossed, that enables you to connect two hubs, or to connect two stations without using a hub.

CSMA/CA
(Carrier Sense Multiple Access/Collision Avoidance) A contention-based media access method in which nodes can transmit whenever they have data to send. However, they take steps before they transmit to ensure that the media is unused.

CSMA/CD
(Carrier Sense Multiple Access/Collision Detection) A contention-based media access method in which nodes can transmit whenever they have data to send. However, they must detect and manage the inevitable collisions that occur when multiple nodes transmit at once.

CSU/DSU
(Channel Service Unit/Data Service Unit) A combination of two WAN connectivity devices that work together to connect a digital WAN line with a customer's LAN.

current context
When browsing a NetWare directory tree, the container that is currently open.

DAS
(Dual attached station) A FDDI network connection in which nodes are connected directly to both the primary and secondary rings.

data theft
A type of attack in which unauthorized access is used to obtain protected network information.

data window
A flow control technique in which multiple packets are sent as a unit. The recipient acknowledges each window rather than each packet, resulting in higher throughput.

Data-link layer
Layer of the OSI model that ensures that individual frames get from one device to another without error. After sending frames, the Data-link layer waits for acknowledgements from receiving devices.

datagram
A packet.

DDoS (Distributed Denial of Service) attack
A type of DoS attack that uses multiple computers on disparate networks to launch the attack from many simultaneous sources.

dedicated lines
See "leased lines."

default gateway
The IP address of the router that will route remote traffic from the computer's local subnet to remote subnets.

default gateway
The IP address of the router that will route remote traffic from the computer's local subnet to remote subnets.

definition
A code pattern that identifies a virus. Also called a signature.

demand priority
A polling technique in which nodes signal their state—either ready to transmit or idle—to a hub. The hub polls the state of each node and grants permission to transmit in turn.

demodulation
The process of decoding or removing a low frequency data signal from a high frequency carrier waveform. See modulation.

DES
(Data Encryption Standard) A shared-key encryption algorithm that uses a 56-bit encryption key to encode data in 64-bit blocks.

DHCP relay agent
A server service that captures a BootP broadcast and forwards it through the router as a unicast transmission to a DHCP server on a remote subnet.

DHCP
(Dynamic Host Configuration Protocol) A network service that provides automatic assignment of IP addresses and other TCP/IP configuration information.

dial-up lines
Local-loop phone connections that use modems and standard telephone technology.

dialectric
An insulator—a material that does not conduct electricity—that permits electrostatic attraction and repulsion to take place across it.

differential signaling
A noise reduction technique in which the signals from two inputs are compared; signals that are identical on the two inputs are ignored, while those that are different on the inputs are accepted.

digital certificate
An electronic document that associates credentials with a public key.

digital signal
An electrical signal that holds only two values: ones and zeros.

digital signature
A piece of data, encrypted with a sender's private key, which is attached to a message and decrypted with the sender's public key to prove the sender's identity and that the data has not been altered in transit.

directory
A centralized database that includes objects such as servers, clients, computers, user names, and passwords. Also called directory service.

disaster recovery plan
A policy and set of procedures that documents how people and resources will be protected in case of disaster, and how the organization will recover from the disaster and restore normal functioning.

disaster recovery
The administrative function of protecting people and resources while bringing a failed network or system back online as quickly as possible.

disaster
A catastrophic loss of system functioning due to a cause that cannot reasonably be foreseen or avoided.

distributed storage
A storage system that makes data stored in different physical locations appear to the user as a contiguous storage structure.

DMZ
(Demilitarized zone) A small section of a private network that is located between two firewalls and made available for public access.

DNS
(Domain Name System) A TCP/IP name resolution service that translates FQDNs into IP addresses.

DoS (Denial of Service) attack
An attack that is mounted for the purpose of disabling systems that provide network services, rather than to steal data or inflict damage.

DR
(Designated router) An OSPF router with the highest priority value.

drain
The connection point between a shield and ground.

drive array
Any group of separate disks that are configured to work as a unit to improve performance, availability, and fault tolerance.

drone
Unauthorized software introduced on multiple computers to manipulate the computers into mounting a DDos attack. Also called a zombie.

DSL
(Digital Subscriber Line) A broadband Internet connection method that transmits digital signal over existing phone lines.

DSSS
(Direct sequence spread spectrum) A type of radio transmission in which a single data signal is converted into multiple digital data signals called chips. The set of chips is sent across a wide band of adjacent channels. Upon receiving the data, the receiver combines and converts the signals back into the original.

duplexing
Disk mirroring in which the two drives in the mirror each have a dedicated disk controller.

EAP
(Extensible Authentication Protocol) An authentication protocol that enables systems to use hardware-based identifiers, such as fingerprint scanners or smart card readers, for authentication.

EDAC
(Error detection and correction) The process of determining if transmitted data has been received correctly and completely, and if not, rebuilding the data to its correct form.

eDirectory
Novell's standards-based, enterprise-level directory service; an evolution of the earlier NDS directory.

EIGRP
(Enhanced Interior Gateway Routing Protocol) An improvement over IGRP that includes features that support VLSM and classful and classless subnet masks.

electrical noise
Unwanted signals that are introduced into network media. Noise interferes with the proper reception of transmitted signals.

encryption
A network security measure in which information is encoded or scrambled prior to transmission so that it cannot be read unless the recipient knows the decoding mechanism, or key.

endpoint
A network node that is the source or destination of network data.

enterprise network
A network that encompasses all the separate network components employed by a particular organization.

error detection
The process of determining if transmitted data has been received correctly and completely.

ESS
(Extended Service Set) A configuration of multiple BSSs used to handle roaming on a wireless network.

Ethernet frame
A complete package of data containing all the information required to move data between its source and destination.

Ethernet
A LAN technology used for connecting computers and servers in the same building or campus.

extended partition
On DOS and Windows systems, a partition that can be subdivided into separate logical drives.

exterior router
Any router entirely outside an AS.

extranet
A private network that uses Internet protocols and network connectivity to provide access to company web pages via a web browser.

failover
The ability of one system to take over the functions of a failed system without interruption in service.

fall-back plan
An alternate network reconstruction design that can be implemented temporarily to enable critical network elements to function.

fault tolerance
The ability of a network or system to withstand a foreseeable component failure and continue to provide an acceptable level of service.

fault-tolerant cluster
A general term for implementations that use clustering, RAID, redundant hardware, and other technologies to achieve 99.999 percent uptime. In "shared everything" cluster implementations, servers in the cluster share common hardware resources such as processors, memory, and disks, and can execute the same commands simultaneously for almost instantaneous failover. Also called a high-availability cluster.

FDDI
(Fiber Distributed Data Interface) A dual-ring, fault-tolerant, token-passing fiber network that operates at 100 Mbps.

FHSS
(Frequency hopping spread spectrum) A type of radio transmission in which a signal is sent on one channel at a time. At predetermined fixed intervals, the channel changes.

fiber optic cable
A type of cable in which one or more glass or plastic strands, plus additional fiber strands or wraps, are surrounded by a protective outer jacket. Light pulses carry the signal through fiber optic cable.

firewall
A software program or hardware device that protects networks from unauthorized data by blocking unsolicited traffic.

fixed length window
A type of data window in which each block of packets is the same size. Typically, fixed length windows are small to avoid flooding the buffers of less-powerful receivers.

flooding
A network transmission state in which data arrives at a receiving node too quickly to be processed.

flow control
A class of techniques for optimizing the exchange of data between systems.

FQDN
(Fully qualified domain name) The host name combined with the host's domain name.

frame relay
A packet switching implementation first offered in 1992 by AT&T and Sprint as a more efficient alternative to X.25.

FTP
(File Transfer Protocol) A communications protocol that enables the transfer of files between a user's workstation and a remote host.

full duplex
A mode of communication that permits simultaneous two-way communications.

GAN
(Global area network) Any worldwide network.

gateway
Any device, software, or system that converts data between incompatible systems.

half duplex
A mode of communication that permits two-way transmission, but in only one direction at a time.

hardware loopback plug
A special connector used for diagnosing transmission problems that redirects electrical signals back to the transmitting system.

Hello packet
A means of gathering router information when using OSPF.

hertz
A measure of the number of cycles per second in an analog signal. One cycle per second equals one hertz.

high availability
A rating that expresses how closely systems approach the goal of providing data availability 100 percent of the time while maintaining a high level of system performance.

high-availability cluster
See "fault-tolerant cluster."

highly directional antenaa
An antenna with a concentrated narrow beam width that is used to provide long-distance, highly focused transmission from one point to another.

hoax
Any type of incorrect or misleading information that is disseminated to multiple users through unofficial channels.

hop
The action of forwarding a packet from one router to the next.

host computer
A powerful, centralized computer system that performs data storage and processing tasks on behalf of clients and other network devices.

host name
The unique name given to a network node on a TCP/IP network.

HOSTS file
A plain text file configured on a client machine containing a list of IP addresses and their associated host names, which can be used for host name resolution as an alternative to DNS.

hot site
A fully configured alternate network that can be online quickly after a disaster.

hot spare
A fully configured and operational piece of backup equipment that can be swapped into a system with little to no interruption in functionality.

HTML
(Hypertext Markup Language) The standard language that defines how web pages are formatted and displayed.

HTTP
(Hypertext Transfer Protocol) A protocol that defines the interaction between a web server and a browser.

HTTPS
(Hypertext Transfer Protocol Secure) A secure version of HTTP that supports e-commerce by providing a secure connection between web browser and server.

hub
A networking device used to connect the drops in a physical star topology network into a logical bus topology.

hybrid topology
Any topology that exhibits characteristics of more than one standard topology.

IBSS
(Independent Basic Service Set) A peer-to-peer network where each wireless station or client acts as both a client and a wireless AP.

ICA
(Independent Computing Architecture) A remote terminal protocol used by Citrix MetaFrame and MetaFrame XP software as add-ons to Microsoft Terminal Services.

ICANN
(Internet Corporation for Assigned Names and Numbers) The international organization that is responsible for leasing IP addresses worldwide.

ICMP
(Internet Control Message Protocol) A service added to the IP protocol that attempts to report on the condition of a connection between two nodes.

ICS
(Internet Connection Sharing) A WAN connectivity method that connects multiple computers to the Internet by using a single Internet connection.

IGMP
(Internet Group Management Protocol) A protocol in the TCP/IP suite that supports multicasting in a routed environment.

IGRP
(Interior Gateway Routing Protocol) A distance-vector routing protocol developed by Cisco as an improvement over RIP and RIP II.

IMAP4
(Internet Mail Access Protocol) A protocol used to retrieve email messages and folders from a mail server.

impedance
A force that opposes the flow of electricity in an alternating current (AC) circuit. Impedance is measured in Ohms (Ω).

infrared transmission
A form of wireless transmission over unbounded media in which signals are sent via pulses of infrared light.

Infrastructure mode
A wireless configuration that uses one or more WAPs to connect wireless workstations to the cable backbone.

interior router
A router arranged inside an AS and completely controlled by the AS administrator.

Internet proxy
A system that isolates internal networks from the Internet by downloading and storing Internet files on behalf of internal clients.

intranet
A private network that uses Internet protocols and services to share a company's information with its employees.

IP address
A 32-bit binary number assigned to a computer on a TCP/IP network.

IP
(Internet Protocol) A communications protocol that primarily serves to assign the correct destination address to a data packet.

IPSec
(IP Security) A versatile, nonproprietary suite of security standards that provides end-to-end authentication and encryption for secure communications sessions on IP networks.

IPX/SPX
(Internetwork Packet Exchange/Sequenced Packet Exchange) A proprietary routable network protocol developed by Novell for use in versions 3 and 4 of the Novell NetWare network operating system.

ISDN
(Integrated Services Digital Network) A digital circuit switching technology that carries both voice and data.

Kerberos
A nonproprietary Internet standard authentication protocol that links a user name and password to a certifying authority, called a Kerberos Authentication Server (KAS).

kernel
The core of most operating systems, which controls hardware, performs low-level functions, and manages task and user scheduling.

key-pair encryption
An encryption system in which an individual has two encryption keys: the public key that anyone can use to encode the message, and the user's private key, which is used to decode messages.

key
In an encryption scheme, the piece of information required to encode or decode the encrypted data.

L2TP
(Layer Two Tunneling Protocol) The de facto standard VPN protocol for tunneling PPP sessions across a variety of network protocols such as IP, Frame Relay, or ATM.

LAN
(Local area network) A self-contained network that spans a small area, such as a single building, floor, or room.

LDAP
(Lightweight Directory Access Protocol) A communications protocol that defines how a client can access information, perform operations, and share directory data on a directory server.

leased lines
Dedicated high-quality connection lines that are leased from telephony companies to provide a company with a permanent connection between two locations. Also called dedicated lines.

LED
(Light Emitting Diode) An indicator light on network adapters and on some other types of network equipment.

link redundancy
A network fault-tolerance method that provides alternative network connections that can function if a critical primary connection is interrupted.

Linux distribution
A complete Linux implementation, including kernel, shell, applications, and utilities, that is packaged, distributed, and supported by a software vendor.

Linux
An open-standards UNIX derivative originally developed and released by a Finnish computer science student named Linus Torvalds.

LLC layer
(Logical Link Control layer) The upper sublayer of the Data-link layer in the OSI model.

LMHOSTS
A text file that contains NetBIOS name–to–IP address mappings.

load balancing
The ability of systems within a group, such as a cluster, to share workload to optimize system response time.

logical bus topology
A network topology in which all nodes see the network signal at the same time, regardless of the physical wiring layout of the network.

logical ring topology
A network topology in which each node receives data only from its upstream neighbor and retransmits it only to its downstream neighbor, regardless of the physical layout of the network.

logical star topology
A network topology in which a central device controls network access for nodes that are wired as a physical bus.

logical topology
The topology that describes data flow patterns in the network.

LPD
(Line Printer Daemon) A TCP/IP print protocol used on the print server to establish a connection between the client and a network printer.

LPR
(Line Printer Remote) A TCP/IP print protocol used on the client to establish a connection between the client and a network printer.

MAC address
A unique, hardware level address assigned to every networking device by its manufacturer. MAC addresses are six bytes long. Also known as a physical address.

MAC layer
(Media Access Control layer) The lower sublayer of the Data-link layer in the OSI model.

man-in-the-middle attack
A data-theft technique in which the attacker interposes a device between two legitimate hosts to gain access to their data transmissions. The intruder device responds actively to the two legitimate hosts as if it were the intended source or destination.

MAN
(Metropolitan area network) A network that covers an area equivalent to a city or other municipality.

media access method
The network communications mechanism that determines whether or not a particular node can place data on the network wire at a given time.

media tester
See "cable tester."

microwave transmission
A form of wireless transmission over unbounded media in which signals are sent via pulses of electromagnetic energy in the microwave region of the spectrum.

millisecond
One thousandth of a second.

mirroring
A disk fault-tolerance method in which data from an entire partition is copied onto a second drive.

mixed mode network
A network that displays characteristics of more than one of the three standard network models.

modem
A device that modulates and demodulates data over an analog signal sent via a common telephone line.

modulation
The process of superimposing a low frequency data signal over a high frequency carrier waveform. See demodulation.

MSAU
(Multi Station Access Unit) Connects Token Ring networks into physical star models while keeping the logical ring characteristics required for Token Ring.

multicast transmission
A transmission method in which data is sent from a server to specific nodes that are defined as members of a multicast group.

multimode fiber
A type of fiber optic cable that carries multiple light signals on a single strand.

multiplexing
A controlled media access method in which a central device combines the signals from multiple nodes and transmits the combined signal across the medium.

mux
A multiplexer; a device that manages muliplexed access to a data transmission medium.

My Network Places
A Windows operating system feature enabling a user to look for resources on the network.

NAS
(Network-attached storage) A specialized file server that is designed and dedicated to support data storage needs.

NAT
(Network address translation) A simple form of Internet security that conceals internal addressing schemes from the public Internet by translating between a single public address on the external side of a router and private nonroutable addresses internally.

Nbtstat
A Windows utility that is used to view and manage NetBIOS name cache information.

NDPS
(Novell Distributed Print Services) Novell's enterprise printing implementation that combines the functions of print server, print queue, and printer object into a single eDirectory object called a printer agent.

NDS
(Novell Directory Services) Novell's original X.500-based directory service.

NetBEUI
(NetBIOS Extended User Interface) A fast, simple protocol developed by Microsoft and IBM for implementation on small networks.

NetBIOS name
A 16-byte common name developed by IBM and Microsoft to identify network devices.

Netstat
A TCP/IP utility that shows the status of each active connection.

NetWare
The proprietary network operating system developed and marketed by Novell, Inc.

network address
A protocol-specific identifier assigned to a node. Typically, a network address includes a portion that identifies a particular node and another portion that identifies the network to which the node is connected.

network analyzer
See "protocol analyzer."

network browsing
The process of looking for resources on the network.

network drive mapping
When a directory from another computer can be seen on someone's else's computer.

Network layer
Layer of the OSI model that addresses and ensures delivery of packets across a network.

network model
A network design specification for how the nodes on a network interact and share control of the network communication.

network name
A word or phrase assigned to a node to help users and technicians more easily recognize the device. Network names are mapped to network addresses by a naming service.

network protocol
Rules by which network operations are conducted.

network resource
Anything that is available to be used on a network.

network searching
Seeking and locating resources on the network.

networking standard
A set of specifications, guidelines, or characteristics applied to network components to ensure interoperability and consistency between them.

NFS
(Network File System) A client/server application that enables users to access shared files stored on different types of computers and work with those files as if they were stored locally on their own computers.

NIC
(Network interface card) A device that serves as an intermediary between the computer's data bus and the network.

NLM
(NetWare Loadable Module) Software modules that run on NetWare servers and extend the core network and application functionality of the operating system.

NNTP
(Network News Transfer Protocol) A protocol used to post and retrieve messages from newsgroups, usually from the worldwide bulletin board system called USENET.

node
Any network device that can connect to the network and can generate, process, or transfer network data. In clustering solutions, nodes are individual members of a cluster.

noise
Electromagnetic interference that disrupts the signal.

Nslookup
A utility that is used to test and troubleshoot domain name servers.

NSS
(Novell Storage Services) Novell's high-performance, high-capacity, journaled file storage system for volumes on NetWare servers.

NTP
(Network Time Protocol) An Internet standard protocol that enables synchronization of computer clock times in a network of computers.

ohm
A unit of electrical resistance.

omni-directional antenna
An antenna that radiates the signal beam out in all directions over a horizontal plane.

open standards
Any type of software-development standards that are arrived at cooperatively and are not owned or maintained by any particular organization or commercial enterprise.

OSI model
(Open Systems Interconnection model) A seven-layer framework for defining how a network handles data packets The ISO began development of the OSI model in the early 1980s.

OSPF
(Open Shortest Path First) A link-state routing protocol used on IP networks.

packet switching network
A network in which data is broken up into separate packets and each packet is separately routed, without a dedicated connection between the endpoints.

packet
A unit of data sent across the network. Packets vary by protocol, but in general contain a header, the data itself, and a footer.

PAP
(Password Authentication Protocol) A remote-access authentication method that sends client IDs and passwords as cleartext.

parity
An error detection method in which the number of ones within a data word transmitted is compared with those received. If the count matches, the data is assumed to be valid.

partition
A logical area of disk space that you can format and treat as a single storage unit.

passive hub
A hub that receives data transmitted from a device to one port and broadcasts it out to the devices connected on all other ports.

password attack
Any type of unauthorized effort to discover a user's valid password.

PBX
(Private Branch Exchange) A private telephone network used inside a company or organization. The PBX includes a number of outside lines for communicating with the PSTN.

peer-to-peer network
A network in which resource sharing, processing, and communications control are completely decentralized.

peer
A self-sufficient computer that acts as both a server and a client.

performance monitor
A software tool that monitors the state of services, processes, and resources on a system.

permission
A security setting that determines the level of access a user or group account has to a particular resource.

physical bus topology
A physical topology in which network nodes are arranged in a linear format.

Physical layer
Layer of the OSI model that moves bits of data on and off the physical cabling media.

physical mesh topology
A network topology in which each node has a direct, point-to-point connection to every other node.

physical ring topology
A network topology in which all network nodes are connected in a continuous circle.

physical star topology
A network topology that uses a central connectivity device with separate point-to-point connections to each node.

physical topology
The topology that describes the network's physical layout and shape.

Ping
A TCP/IP utility used to verify the network connectivity of a computer.

PKI
(Public key infrastructure) A hierarchical system that is composed of Certificate Authorities (CAs), certificates, software, services, and other cryptographic components, for the purpose of enabling authenticity and validation of data and/or entities—for example, to secure transactions over the Internet.

plenum cable
A grade of cable that does not give off noxious or poisonous gases when burned. Unlike PVC cable, plenum cable can be run through the plenum and firebreak walls.

plenum
An air handling space, including ducts and other parts of the HVAC system in a building.

poison reverse
An algorithm that prevents count-to-infinity loops by ensuring that a router broadcasts a route cost of 16 for all transmissions on its network.

polling
A controlled media access method in which a central device contacts each node in turn to see whether it has data to transmit.

POP3
(Post Office Protocol version 3) A protocol used to retrieve email from a mailbox on the mail server.

port
The endpoint of a logical connection that client computers use to connect to specific server programs.

POTS
(Plain Old Telephone Service) Another name for traditional local and long distance telephone networks.

PPP
(Point-to-Point Protocol) The VPN protocol that is the current Internet standard for sending IP datagram packets over serial point-to-point links.

PPPoE
(Point-to-Point Protocol over Ethernet) A remote-access standard that provides the features and functionality of PPP to DSL or cable modem connections that use Ethernet to transfer signals from the carrier to the client.

PPTP
(Point-to-Point Tunneling Protocol) A VPN protocol that is an extension of the PPP remote-access protocol.

premise wiring
The collection of drop cables, patch panels, and patch cables that together make a functional network.

Presentation layer
Layer of the OSI model that translates data so that it can be moved on the network.

primary partition
On DOS and Windows systems, a partition that can be used to boot the computer.

private key
In key-pair encryption, the key that is known only to an individual and is used to decode data.

protocol analyzer
A type of diagnostic software that can examine and display data packets that are being transmitted over a network. Also called a network analyzer.

PSTN
(Public Switched Telephone Network) A term for traditional local and long distance telephone networks.

public key
In key-pair encryption, the key that is available to all and is used to encode data.

punch down tool
A tool used in a wiring closet to connect cable wires directly to a patch panel.

PVC
(Polyvinyl chloride) A flexible rubber-like plastic used to surround some twisted pair cabling. It is flexible and inexpensive, but gives off noxious or poisonous gases when burned.

radio networking
A form of wireless communications in which signals are sent via RF waves. Also called RF networking.

RADIUS
(Remote Authentication Dial-In User Service) A protocol that enables one server to provide standardized, centralized authentication of remote users.

RAID
(Redundant Array of Independent or Inexpensive Disks) A set of vendor-independent specifications for fault-tolerant configurations on multiple-disk systems.

RARP
(Reverse Address Resolution Protocol) A protocol that allows a node on a local area network to discover its IP address from a router's Address Resolution Protocol (ARP) table or cache.

RDP
(Remote Desktop Protocol) The protocol that provides the remote input and output capabilities that are the basis for the functionality of both Terminal Server and Remote Desktop.

redistribution point
A network node that is used to transfer data.

remote access protocol
A type of protocol that enables users to log on to a computer or network within an organization from an external location.

remote networking
A type of network communication that enables users to access resources that are not at their physical locations.

repeater
A device that regenerates a signal to improve transmission distance. Repeaters are used with coax media, and thus are not commonly used in modern networks.

RF
This abbreviation for radio frequency usually refers to network or other communications that take place via radio waves in the 10 KHz and 1 GHz range.

right
A security setting that controls whether or not a user can perform a system-wide function.

RIP
(Routing Information Protocol) A routing protocol that configures routers to periodically broadcast their entire routing tables. RIP routers broadcast their tables regardless of whether or not any changes have occurred on the network.

rotation method
The schedule that determines how many backup tapes or other media sets are needed, and the sequence in which they are used and reused.

routable protocol
A network protocol in which network and node addresses are separate. Network traffic sent using routable protocols, such as TCP/IP and IPX/SPX, can be sent between networks by using routers.

router
A networking device that connects multiple networks that use the same protocol.

routing loops
A situation that occurs when two routers discover different routes to the same location that include each other but never reach the endpoint.

routing table
A database created manually or by a route discovery protocol that contains network locations as perceived by a specific router. A router uses its route table to forward packets to another network or router.

SA
(Security Association) A connection between endpoints in an IPSec session that contains the security parameters for that session.

SAM
(Security Accounts Manager) A local database on each Windows computer that stores local user account information.

SAN
(Storage area network) A special-purpose high-speed network that is dedicated to data storage.

SAS
(Single attached station) A FDDI network connection in which nodes are connected to a concentrator, which is connected to both rings.

scalability
The ability of a system to grow smoothly to meet increasing demand without having to be replaced, reconfigured, or redesigned.

schema
Companion information to the Active Directory database that controls the directory structure as well as the types and properties of objects allowed in the directory.

SCP
(Secure Copy Protocol) A protocol that is used to securely transfer computer files between a local and a remote host, or between two remote hosts, using Secure Shell (SSH).

segment
A discrete physical subdivision of a network.

segmenting
Assigning a unique network address to each network segment and using the default subnet mask.

semi-directional antenna
An antenna that concentrates the signal beam in a cone shape.

server
A network computer that shares resources with and responds to requests from other network computers.

session hijacking
A type of spoofing in which the attacker takes over an existing network communication between two devices after the session has already been authenticated.

Session layer
Layer of the OSI model that establishes a connection between network devices, maintains that connection, and then terminates it when appropriate.

share
Disks, folders, or printers that are available to other users on the network.

shared-key encryption
An encryption system in which a single key is shared between parties in a communication and used to both encode and decode the message.

shielding
Any grounded conductive material placed around the data media to block the introduction of noise into the media.

signal
The electromagnetic communications you want to be transmitted across a network medium.

signature
A code pattern that identifies a virus. Also called a definition.

simplex
A one-way mode of communication. Radio and television broadcasts are simplex mode transmissions.

single-mode fiber
A type of fiber optic cable that carries a single optical signal.

sliding window
A type of data window in which block sizes are variable. Window size is continually re-evaluated during transmission, with the sender always attempting to send the largest window it can to speed throughput.

SLIP
(Serial Line Internet Protocol) An older VPN protocol used for sending IP bytestreams over serial lines such as modem/phone connections.

SMB
(Server Message Block) A protocol used for sharing files, printers, serial ports, and communications devices, such as named pipes and mail slots, between computers.

SMTP
(Simple Mail Transfer Protocol) A communications protocol used to send email from a client to a server or between servers.

sniffer
A device or program that monitors network communications and captures data.

SNMP
(Simple Network Management Protocol) An Application-layer service used to exchange information between network devices.

social engineering attack
A non-technical attack in which the attacker attempts to obtain data or access directly from network users by employing deception and trickery.

socket
A piece of software within an operating system that connects an application with a network protocol.

SONET
(Synchronous Optical Network) A standard for synchronous data transport over fiber optic cable.

split horizon
An algorithm that prevents count-to-infinity loops by preventing a router from broadcasting internal network information.

spoofing
A type of attack in which a device outside the network uses an internal network address to masquerade as a device inside the network.

spread spectrum
A form of radio transmission in which the signal is sent over more than one frequency to improve signal-to-noise ratios and discourage eavesdropping.

SSH
(Secure Shell) A program that enables a user or application to log on to another computer over a network, execute commands in a remote machine, and move files from one machine to another.

store and forward
Can send data to a server or a router where the data is stored until the next hop becomes available.

STP
(Shielded twisted pair) A type of twisted pair cabling that includes shielding around its conductors to improve the cable's resistance to interference and noise.

striping
A disk-performance-enhancement feature in which data is spread across multiple drives to improve read and write access speeds.

strong password
A password that meets complexity requirements that are set by a system administrator and documented in a password policy.

subnet mask
A 32-bit number that is assigned to each host to divide the 32-bit binary IP address into network and node portions.

subnet
A segment of a larger network.

subnetting
Subdividing a single network address to allow for unique network addresses on each subnet

switch
A networking device used to connect the drops in a physical star topology network into a logical bus topology. Unlike a hub, switches forward packets to only the correct port based on MAC addresses.

switched Ethernet
A LAN technology that connects host computers and network segments by using switches, enabling the devices on each switched connection to utilize the full bandwidth of the medium.

symmetric encryption
See "shared-key encryption."

TCP
(Transmission Control Protocol) A connection-oriented, guaranteed-delivery protocol that sends data, waits for an ACK, and fixes erroneous data.

TCP/IP subnet
A class of leased addresses that has been divided up into smaller groups to serve the networks needs.

TCP/IP
(Transmission Control Protocol/Internet Protocol) A nonproprietary, routable network protocol suite that enables computers to communicate over a network, including the Internet.

Telnet
A terminal emulation protocol that enables a user at one site to simulate a session on a remote host.

terminal emulator
Software that enables a standard client computer to appear to a host computer as a dedicated terminal.

terminal
An end user's network device on a host-based network, dedicated to transmitting data to the host for processing and displaying the result to the user.

termination
Adding a resistor to the end of a coax network segment to prevent reflections that would interfere with the proper reception of network signals.

terminator
A resistor or other device added to the end of a cable to ensure that the end of the cable is not a source of signal reflections and noise.

thin client
Any machine that uses a thin client protocol to connect to a server in order to access and run applications.

threshold
When monitoring performance, the value that signals that an object or component is functioning outside acceptable performance limits.

Token Ring
A LAN protocol that resides at the Data-link layer of the OSI model.

token-based media access
A controlled media access method in which computers pass a special sequence of bits between them; only the node holding this token can transmit on the network. After transmitting its data, or if it has no data to transmit, a node passes the token to the next computer on the network.

token
A special sequence of bits used in a token-based media access method network. The computer possessing the token is permitted to transmit on the network; all others must not transmit.

tone generator
An electronic device that sends an electrical signal through one set of UTP wires.

tone locator
An electronic device that emits an audible tone when it detects a signal in a set of wires.

topology
A network specification that determines the network's overall layout and the network's signaling and data flow patterns.

trace
A set of captured network packets.

Tracert
A utility used to determine the route data takes to get to a particular destination.

traditional NetWare volume
A nonjournaled volume type used on prior versions of NetWare; it has lower performance and lower capacity than current NSS volumes.

transceiver
A device that both sends and receives data. In networking, transceivers are used to connect a computer's network interface card and the network media.

Transport layer
Layer of the OSI model that ensures reliable data transmission by breaking up big data blocks into smaller packets that can be sent more efficiently on the network.

trap
A situation in which an SNMP agent sends data to the management system without first being queried.

Triple DES
(3DES) A more-secure variant of DES that repeatedly encodes the message using three separate DES keys.

Trojan horse attack
An attempt to gain unauthorized access through the use of a Trojan horse program, which masquerades as valid software.

Trojan horse
Unauthorized software that masquerades as legitimate software.

troubleshooting model
Any standardized step-by-step approach to the troubleshooting process.

troubleshooting
The recognition, diagnosis, and resolution of problems.

TTL
(Time to live) A value that determines how many hops an IP packet can travel before being discarded.

tunneling
A data-transport technique in which a data packet is transferred inside the frame or packet of another protocol, enabling the infrastructure of one network to be used to travel to another network.

twisted pair
A type of cable in which multiple insulated conductors are twisted around each other and clad in a protective and insulating outer jacket.

UDP
(User Datagram Protocol) A connectionless, best-effort-delivery protocol that sends data the best way it can, but doesn't take responsibility for the data's integrity. UDP is a store and forward protocol.

unauthorized access
Any type of network or data access that is not explicitly approved by the organization.

unbounded media
A networking medium that does not use a physical conductor. Instead, electromagnetic signals are transmitted through the air with radio, microwave, or infrared radiation.

UNC
(Universal Naming Convention) A standard for identifying and locating resources on remote computers.

unicast transmission
A transmission method in which data is transferred between individual nodes.

UNIX
A family of operating systems originally developed at Bell Laboratories and characterized by portability, multiuser support, and built-in multitasking and networking functions.

UPS
(Uninterruptible power supply) A device that provides backup power when the electrical power fails or drops to an unacceptable voltage level.

UTP
(Unshielded twisted pair) A type of twisted pair cabling that does not include shielding around its conductors.

vampire tap
A clamshell-like device that clamps over an RG8 cable, making contact with its conductors, permitting a networking device to connect to the ThickNet segment.

virtual circuit
A routing technique that connects endpoints logically through a provider's network.

virus
A self-propagating unauthorized software program.

VLAN switch
A device that creates a logical network structure.

VLAN
(Virtual LAN) A point-to-point physical network with no real physical characteristics.

VLSM
(Variable length subnet mask) A classless subnet mask that can be customized to a different length for each subnet based on the number of nodes on that subnet.

VoATM
(Voice over ATM) An alternative to VoIP in which voice traffic is routed over an ATM network.

VoFR
(Voice over Frame Relay) An alternative to VoIP in which voice traffic is routed over a frame relay WAN.

Voice over Data
Communications systems that replace traditional telephone links by transmitting analog voice communications over digital WAN networking technologies.

VoIP
(Voice over IP) A Voice over Data implementation in which voice signals are transmitted over IP networks.

voltmeter
An electrical instrument that measures voltage and resistance between two points in a circuit.

VPN protocols
Protocols that provide VPN functionality.

VPN
(Virtual private network) A private network that is configured within a public network such as the Internet.

WAN
(Wide area network) A network that spans multiple geographic locations, connecting multiple LANs using long-range transmission media.

WAP
(Wireless access point) A device that provides connection between wireless devices and can connect to wired networks.

warm site
An business site that performs noncritical functions under normal conditions, but which can be rapidly converted to a key operations site if needed.

waveform
The shape of an analog signal when plotted on an oscilloscope or graph.

WINS
(Windows Internet Name Service) Microsoft's NetBIOS name resolution server that uses a name resolution table to map NetBIOS names to protocol addresses.

wire crimper
A tool that attaches media connectors to the ends of cables.

wireless communication
A type of communication that is transmitted without using bounded media of any sort. Signals are transmitted as electromagnetic energy, such as radio, microwave, or light pulses.

wireless LAN
A LAN implementation in which nodes use a wireless network card to connect to other stations.

workgroup
On a Windows network, an arbitrary peer-to-peer grouping of computers under a common naming scheme to simplify the network view and facilitate resource location.

worm
A self-contained program similar to a virus that spreads and can exist without a carrier file.

WPA
(Wi-Fi Protected Access) A security standard that provides additional encryption capabilities for wireless transmissions.

WPAN
(wireless personal area network) A network that connects devices in very close proximity but not through a wireless access point.

X.25
A legacy packet switching network technology developed in the 1970s to move data across less than reliable public carriers.

Zeroconf
(Zero Configuration Networking) A proposed set of standards that provides for automatic configuration and IP address allocation on both Ethernet and wireless networks.

zombie
Unauthorized software introduced on multiple computers to manipulate the computers into mounting a DDoS attack. Also called a drone.

NOTES

INDEX

INDEX

INDEX

E

INDEX

S

INDEX

X

Z

NOTES

New Horizons Classroom Learning

Technical Post-Event Survey

New Horizons® Computer Learning Centers
CHOOSE. LEARN. SUCCEED.

Instructor Name: ______________________ Course: ____________________ End Date: ______________

Student Name: __________________________ Student E-mail Address: ____________________________

Company ___________________________________ Job Role: ________________________________

The quality of your experience is very important to us and your comments are an integral part of our quality control. Please take a moment to provide us with your observations. Thank you.

1. What was your main objective for completing this training?
   - ☐ Solve a particular problem
   - ☐ Prepare for a new product deployment or software upgrade
   - ☐ Build new skills and knowledge (not related to a new software deployment)
   - ☐ Prepare for a certification exam
   - ☐ Better understand products before purchasing new software
   - ☐ Prepare for a career change
   - ☐ Other (please specify) _______________________

2. **How would you rate this training on the following dimensions?**

Classroom	Extraordinary/Outstanding					Unacceptable/Poor			
Quality of the classroom environment	9	8	7	6	5	4	3	2	1
Performance of the technology used in the classroom(hardware/software)	9	8	7	6	5	4	3	2	1

Classroom Comments (if any) ____

Instructor	Extraordinary/Outstanding					Unacceptable/Poor			
Instructor's knowledge of the subject matter	9	8	7	6	5	4	3	2	1
Instructor's response to questions	9	8	7	6	5	4	3	2	1
Instructor's ability to provide real world experiences and examples	9	8	7	6	5	4	3	2	1
Instructor's presentation skills	9	8	7	6	5	4	3	2	1
Instructor's overall performance	9	8	7	6	5	4	3	2	1

Instructor Comments (if any) ____

Training Content	Extraordinary/Outstanding					Unacceptable/Poor			
Clarity of the training content	9	8	7	6	5	4	3	2	1
Flow of the training content	9	8	7	6	5	4	3	2	1
Technical depth of the training content	9	8	7	6	5	4	3	2	1
Effectiveness of the labs in reinforcing the knowledge/skills learned in the modules	9	8	7	6	5	4	3	2	1
Relevance of the labs to real world job situations	9	8	7	6	5	4	3	2	1
Effectiveness of the practices within in each lesson to reinforce the knowledge and skills learned in the lesson	9	8	7	6	5	4	3	2	1
Time dedicated to activities such as discussions, practices, and labs (as opposed to lecture)	9	8	7	6	5	4	3	2	1
Language quality of the courseware (grammar, terminology, style)	9	8	7	6	5	4	3	2	1

How would you change the training content to improve your learning experience?

____

Other training content comments (if any)

____

3. **How would you rate this training on the following dimensions?**

Learning Effectiveness	Extraordinary/Outstanding					Unacceptable/Poor			
Knowledge and skills gained from this training	9	8	7	6	5	4	3	2	1
Impact of this training on your job effectiveness	9	8	7	6	5	4	3	2	1
Impact of this training on your career potential	9	8	7	6	5	4	3	2	1

	Exceeded Expectations					Did not meet expectations at all			
4. **How well did this training meet your expectations?**	9	8	7	6	5	4	3	2	1

5. **Overall, how satisfied are you with this training?**
   O Very Satisfied O Somewhat Satisfied O Somewhat Dissatisfied O Very Dissatisfied

6. What percent of your total work time requires the knowledge/skills presented in this training? Check only one.

☐0% ☐10% ☐20% ☐30% ☐40% ☐50% ☐60% ☐70% ☐80% ☐90% ☐100%

7. If you think this training will have a positive impact on your job performance, what areas will be impacted most? Check all that apply.
   - ☐ increasing quality
   - ☐ increasing productivity
   - ☐ increasing sales
   - ☐ increasing ability to innovate
   - ☐ decreasing time to complete task(s)
   - ☐ decreasing costs
   - ☐ increasing customer satisfaction
   - ☐ increasing employee satisfaction

8. Please indicate how much you expect your job performance related to the course subject matter to improve as a result of this training and other business improvements in your organization.
   ☐0% ☐10% ☐20% ☐30% ☐40% ☐50% ☐60% ☐70% ☐80% ☐90% ☐100%

9. How much of the improvement in your job performance will be a direct result of this training? (For example if you feel that half of your improvement is a direct result of the training, enter 50% here.)
   ☐0% ☐10% ☐20% ☐30% ☐40% ☐50% ☐60% ☐70% ☐80% ☐90% ☐100%

10. **Would you like to be notified about advanced or complementary courses?** ☐ Yes ☐ No

Additional Questions

Strongly Agree **Strongly Disagree**

- My Account Executive/Educational Consultant is: ____________
- My Account Executive/Ed. Consultant has serviced my account satisfactorily 9 8 7 6 5 4 3 2 1
- Is this your first time at New Horizons? ❍ Yes ❍ No
- Would you recommend New Horizons to others? ❍ Yes ❍ No
- Other classes you are interested in but not included in your learning plan: ____________
- Comments Suggestions to improve your experience? ____________

Thank you for completing the survey.

To make your own nameplate:

1. Remove this page from the book.
2. Print your name on the lines provided.
3. Fold as illustrated.

—FOLD HERE—

Print Your Name Here

New Horizons
Computer Learning Centers, Inc.

—FOLD HERE—

New Horizons
Computer Learning Centers, Inc.

Print Your Name Here

NH85821SPB rev 2.0

0 99751 08945 7

E0312090023